# THE NEXT GENERATION *of* IMPACT ASSESSMENT

A Critical Review of the Canadian *Impact Assessment Act*

# The Next Generation *of* Impact Assessment

## A Critical Review of the Canadian *Impact Assessment Act*

EDITED BY

*Meinhard Doelle & A. John Sinclair*

The Next Generation of Impact Assessment: A Critical Review of the Canadian
*Impact Assessment Act*
© Irwin Law Inc, 2021



Published in 2021 by

Irwin Law Inc
Suite 206, 14 Duncan Street
Toronto, Ontario    M5H 3G8
www.irwinlaw.com

ISBN: 978-1-55221-573-9 | e-book ISBN: 978-1-55221-574-6


**Library and Archives Canada Cataloguing in Publication**

Title: The next generation of impact assessment : a critical review of the Canadian
    Impact Assessment Act / edited by Meinhard Doelle & A. John Sinclair.
Names: Doelle, Meinhard, 1964– editor. | Sinclair, A. John, editor.
Description: Includes bibliographical references and index.
Identifiers: Canadiana (print) 20210229411 | Canadiana (ebook) 20210229608 |
    ISBN 9781552215739 (softcover) | ISBN 9781552215746 (PDF)
Subjects: LCSH: Canada. Impact Assessment Act. | LCSH: Environmental impact
    analysis—Law and legislation—Canada.
Classification: LCC KE5110 .N49 2021 | LCC KF5505 .N49 2021 kfmod |
    DDC 344.7104/6—dc23

Cover photo of the Peace River Valley: Adobe Stock

Printed and bound in Canada.

1  2  3  4  5    25  24  23  22  21

# Summary Table of Contents

# Detailed Table of Contents

*chapter 3*

## An Overview of the *Impact Assessment Act*   53

MEINHARD DOELLE AND A JOHN SINCLAIR

## PART II: REFLECTIONS ON THE *IMPACT ASSESSMENT ACT*  71

*chapter 4*
### The Process of Reform: Real Change?  73
HUGH BENEVIDES

*chapter 8*

**Putting Multi-jurisdictional Impact Assessment into Action Under the *Impact Assessment Act***  165

PATRICIA FITZPATRICK, ARLENE KWASNIAK, AND A JOHN SINCLAIR

*chapter 9*

**Introducing the *Impact Assessment Act*'s Sustainability-Based Agenda**  194
ROBERT B GIBSON

*chapter 20*

## Human Rights and the *Impact Assessment Act*: Proponents and Consultants as Duty Bearers  443

ADEBAYO MAJEKOLAGBE, SARA L SECK, AND PENELOPE SIMONS



*chapter 21*

## Science and Indigenous Knowledge as the Evidentiary Basis for Impact Assessment  466

MARTIN OLSZYNSKI AND JUSTINA RAY

chapter 24
## The Path Forward   527
MEINHARD DOELLE AND A JOHN SINCLAIR

# PART I

# Introduction and Context

# Introduction

*A John Sinclair and Meinhard Doelle*

## A.  SETTING THE CONTEXT

Impact assessment is now practised in over 150 countries worldwide, and as knowledge and understanding of it evolve, so do the laws guiding it. Federally, Canada entered a new chapter in 2015 by fundamentally reconsidering how best to undertake environmental assessment. This is a task that no other country has embarked on in the last decade or more. Many people and organizations from a wide range of sectors, both within and outside Canada, participated in and keenly watched the process of review and reform unfold. The process started with mandate letters that Prime Minister Justin Trudeau provided to his new Cabinet. The 12 November 2015 letter to Minister of Environment and Climate Change Catherine McKenna asked her to "immediately review Canada's environmental assessment processes to regain public trust and help get resources to market and introduce new, fair processes."[1]

By 2016, the minister had struck the Multi-Interest Advisory Committee, representing Indigenous, industry, and environmental non-governmental organizations to advise her and the Canadian Environmental Assessment Agency on the development of a new Act. The

---

1    Prime Minister Justin Trudeau to Catherine McKenna, Minister of Environment and Climate Change, "Minister of Environment and Climate Change Mandate Letter" (12 November 2015), online: *Office of the Prime Minister* https://pm.gc.ca/en/mandate-letters/2015/11/12/archived-minister-environment-and-climate-change-mandate-letter.

minister then established the four-person Expert Panel for the Review of Environmental Assessment Processes (Expert Panel) to consult the public, report on how to restore public trust in impact assessment, and otherwise meet the stated goals of the reform effort. The government followed the Expert Panel's consultation and report with the "Environmental and Regulatory Reviews: Discussion Paper" in June 2017.[2]

Public expectations regarding the outcomes of the process of revision and review were high and arose from several sources, which we briefly highlight here. The first was the federal government's own expectations as expressed in the prime minister's mandate letter to Minister McKenna, as well as other official documents released by the federal government during the course of the reform process.[3] The key expectations, as indicated in the mandate letter to the minister, included the following:

- restore oversight and thorough environmental assessments in areas under federal jurisdiction while working with provinces and territories to avoid duplication
- ensure that decisions are based on science, facts, and evidence and serve the public's interest
- provide ways for Canadians to express their views and opportunities for experts to participate meaningfully
- require project advocates to choose the best technologies available to reduce environmental impacts

The second source was the report of the Expert Panel and its recommendations for reform. The Panel was given terms of reference that directed it to engage broadly with Canadians, Indigenous peoples, provinces and territories, and key stakeholders. It travelled across Canada for seven months and received input from thousands of Canadians through presentations to the Panel, written submissions, and responses to an online "choicebook." The Expert Panel heard from the public, project proponents, intervenors, practitioners, and academics and in the process received perspectives on the federal assessment process from

---

2   Environment and Climate Change Canada, "Environmental and Regulatory Reviews: Discussion Paper" (Ottawa: June 2017), online: *Government of Canada* www.canada.ca/en/services/environment/conservation/assessments/environmental-reviews/share-your-views/proposed-approach/discussion-paper.html.

3   *Ibid.*

industry; Indigenous communities; environmental organizations; and provincial, territorial, municipal, and Indigenous governments. In the end, the Panel offered sweeping recommendations for moving forward, which were captured in its report issued in April of 2017.[4] The results of the Expert Panel's work are referred to throughout this book; the key elements of their proposed reforms included the following:

1) An expanded project list combined with a formal petition process for projects not listed
2) An assessment process to be run by an independent agency with a mandate to focus on cooperation and consensus
3) Cooperative assessments with the active engagement of all affected jurisdictions as the primary tool for harmonization and jurisdictional cooperation, with substitution only under strict conditions
4) A tiered approach to regional, strategic, and project assessments, where project assessments are informed by higher-tier assessments
5) A broad scope of assessment that includes all impacts and benefits of proposed projects
6) Meaningful public participation through early and ongoing opportunities to engage and full access to all relevant information, including an open and searchable database for all data collected from current and past assessments
7) A focus on learning throughout the assessment process
8) An approach to the engagement of Indigenous peoples in the assessment process and project decisions that is consistent with Canada's constitutional obligations and its commitment to the *United Nations Declaration on the Rights of Indigenous Peoples (UNDRIP)*[5]
9) An improved follow-up process, including improved transparency, coordination, and accountability

The federal government also released various communications about the review of assessment processes that established high expectations, outlining, for example, the following goals:

---

4　Expert Panel for the Review of Environmental Assessment Processes, *Building Common Ground: A New Vision for Impact Assessment in Canada* (Ottawa: Canada Environmental Assessment Agency, 2017), online (pdf): *Government of Canada* www.canada.ca/content/dam/themes/environment/conservation/environmental-reviews/building-common-ground/building-common-ground.pdf.
5　GA Res 61/295, UNGAOR, 61st Sess, UN Doc A/RES/61/295 (13 September 2007).

- more and earlier opportunities for meaningful participation
- more Indigenous leadership of and partnership in the process
- better coordination with provinces
- consideration of all of a project's impacts to foster sustainability, including environmental, health, social, and economic impacts
- more transparency and certainty that decisions are based on robust science, evidence, and Indigenous traditional knowledge
- more predictable and consistent timelines[6]

## B. OUR INTENT

The review and revision process ended with the introduction into the House of Commons and eventual passage of the *Impact Assessment Act* (*IAA*) in 2019.[7] Our intent with this book is to present and assess the *IAA*, testing it against a number of benchmarks, including standards for good assessment in the academic literature, the stated goals of the reform initiative as articulated by the government itself, the recommendations of the Expert Panel, and the long history of federal assessment processes in Canada.

In setting out to achieve this, we invited a host of scholars with expertise in the essential elements of impact assessment to participate in the process of revision and review of the assessment process. Like us, all of the contributors have dedicated years to impact assessment research and/or practice. We asked all of them to consider the provisions of the *IAA* in relation to their area of expertise and to assess these provisions against their own understanding of proven practice, as well as what has been established in the literature and during the review process itself. Based on this assessment, each author was also asked to outline any action they felt was needed to ensure effective implementation of the *IAA* through regulations, policy, guidance, or further reform.

---

6    "Bill Amendments" (31 July 2018), online: *Government of Canada* www.canada.ca/en/ services/environment/conservation/assessments/environmental-reviews/bill-c-69.html.

7    SC 2019, c 28, s 1.

## C. ORGANIZATION

We have organized the book into three parts. In Part I, we set the stage for understanding impact assessment in Canada. This involves providing an overview of the evolution of the Canadian assessment process in Chapter 1, starting from a federal guidelines order to the predecessor of the *IAA*, the *Canadian Environmental Assessment Act, 2012*.[8] In Chapter 2, we consider essential components that the next generation of assessment process and law should contain as established in the literature and through proven practice. This helps us to establish some of the benchmarks that are considered in relation to the *IAA* in the chapters that follow, as well as establishing key aspects for the analysis of the *IAA* that is undertaken. In the third and final chapter of Part I, we describe the basic components of the *IAA*, providing a high-level overview and outlining its key provisions.

In Part II, the authors apply their expertise to expand the basic framework of the *IAA* set out in Part I by providing a comprehensive and detailed analysis of various sections and provisions of the Act. We start Part II with a more detailed assessment of the reform process. We then delve into some of the foundational considerations, such as how the Constitution affects the role and reach of the federal government in the context of assessment. This is followed by consideration of the various essential elements of assessment as established in Part I of the book, covering a wide range of assessment issues over the course of nineteen chapters. Each chapter provides an in-depth analysis of the *IAA* in regard to the contents of the Act; regulations and guidance; an assessment of these provisions based on the literature; best practices related to the essential elements of impact assessment and federal government commitments made; and establishing any action needed to ensure effective implementation of the *IAA*.

In Part III, we bring the analysis of the various authors together along with our own reflections in drawing conclusions about the overall achievements of the *IAA*, areas of concern for implementation, and needed areas of reform. In addition to drawing on the chapters themselves, we considered chapter highlights or lessons learned by contributors to help bring their voices to the conclusion of the book.

---

8    SC 2012, c 19, s 52.

## D.   A NOTE ON TERMINOLOGY

An issue that has long vexed the authors of assessment literature and supporting documents, in government and otherwise, is the usage of terms such as *environmental assessment, environmental impact assessment,* and *impact assessment.* In fact, various books and journals use a mix of these terms to capture assessment processes. As Gibson et al noted,

> The terms "environmental assessment" and "impact assessment" have been used variously over the past 50 years. Impact assessment is nominally more broadly scoped—able to cover socio-economic and cultural as well as biophysical considerations and even a more comprehensive and integrated sustainability agenda. In practice, however, many narrowly focused biophysical studies have been labelled impact assessments. Similarly, though in the reverse direction, environmental assessment is often taken to centre on biophysical effects, but the first legislated assessment process (under the US National Environmental Policy Act) and many since have defined "environment" broadly to include social, economic, cultural and other human factors.[9]

Until the *IAA,* federal assessment processes in Canada were referred to as "environmental assessment." In this book, the term *environmental assessment* is used to refer to the federal assessment process prior to the *IAA,* as well as when the term is used in the literature or documents being referenced. We reserve the use of the term *impact assessment* to refer to the process under the Act and when the term is used in the literature or documents being referenced. It is worth keeping in mind the ambiguity outlined in the quotation above because even federal environmental assessment in Canada prior to the *IAA* considered impacts beyond biophysical ones.

---

9   Robert B Gibson et al, *Synthesis at the Nexus of Sustainability Assessment, Regional/Strategic Assessment and Indigenous Partnerships* (2020), Report prepared with support from the Knowledge Synthesis Grant Program: Informing Best Practices in Environmental and Impact Assessments, Social Sciences and Humanities Council of Canada and the Impact Assessment Agency of Canada.

## E. CLOSING THOUGHTS

Given the widespread interest in the *IAA* from both within and outside Canada, our goal was to produce this book soon after the passage of the Act. Work began before the Act was passed, and we were able to gain some time as the bill leading to the *IAA* was held up while making its way through the legislative process. We want to acknowledge Irwin Law for recognizing the importance of this book and for guiding us through the production process so efficiently. We also want to thank our contributors for producing such high-quality chapters and responding to reviews in a timely way. Each chapter was peer-reviewed, and we owe a debt of gratitude to all of our colleagues who agreed to help out with the peer-review process. Their timely and constructive feedback significantly strengthened the end product. We could not have completed this project without the financial support from SSHRC and without the assistance of our student researchers, particularly Grace O'Brien, Kristina Manas-Chmielowski, and Kelsey Margraf. Lastly, we all appreciated the editorial expertise Gary Schneider brought to the volume. It is a testament to Gary's editing skills that his suggestions were almost always accepted by the authors. Gary can now return to owl hooting and tree whispering.

The reader should keep in mind that impact assessment laws and processes are highly contested. They have been the subject of numerous court cases here in Canada, as outlined in part in the chapters that follow, and elsewhere around the world. For some, assessment is viewed as a hurdle, a regulatory process that limits the amount, cost, and speed of development. Others view assessment as essential to what Beanlands and Duinker termed "minimum regret planning" as it should ensure that externalities are identified, evaluated, and incorporated into decision-making processes.[10] Interpretations of assessment law and policy often become contested when they are viewed as an impediment to development, such as the rhetoric (particularly from the Government of Alberta and the pipeline industry) around the *IAA* being an anti-pipeline bill. In the pages that follow, the analysis of the Act is based on proven practice, the literature, and the voices of Canadians as reflected

---

10    Gordon E Beanlands & Peter N Duinker, *An Ecological Framework for Environmental Impact Assessment in Canada* (Halifax: Institute for Resource and Environmental Studies, Dalhousie University & Federal Environmental Assessment Review Office, 1983).

in part through the work of the Expert Panel. There will, of course, be other analyses of the *IAA* that the reader can consider in light of the conclusions drawn in this volume. But we hope that our work here will help all interested parties to become better informed about this important legislation and the implications it has for all Canadians.

# CHAPTER 1

# The Evolution of Canadian Environmental Assessment Practice and Literature

*Meinhard Doelle and A John Sinclair*

## A. INTRODUCTION

Environmental assessment (EA) processes have been an important tool in the governance toolbox in Canada for over forty years. EAs are intended to inform decisions about whether and under what conditions to permit proposed new endeavours.[1] At the federal level in Canada, the assessment process has gone through a number of transitions, from voluntary to binding, and then through several legislative efforts, in the form of the *Canadian Environmental Assessment Act (CEAA 1995)*,[2] the *Canadian Environmental Assessment Act, 2012 (CEAA 2012)*,[3] and the *Impact Assessment Act (IAA)* of 2019.[4]

Although the focus of this book is on the *IAA*, it is important to note that in Canada, practitioners, decision makers, and academics have been very active since the late 1970s in the field of federal EAs. They have greatly contributed to our understanding of the uncertainties inherent in achieving a more sustainable society and the role of assessment in that shift. The early work of institutions such as the

1  Barry Sadler, *International Study of the Effectiveness of Environmental Assessment* (Ottawa: Canadian Environmental Assessment Agency, 1996); see also Christopher Wood, *Environmental Impact Assessment: A Comparative Perspective* (Essex, UK: Longman, 1995).

2  SC 1992, c 37. The entry into force of the Act was delayed until 1995 to allow for key regulations to be developed and passed.

3  SC 2012, c 19, s 52.

4  SC 2019, c 28, s 1.

Canadian Environmental Assessment Research Council set the stage for Canadians to contribute to virtually every aspect of assessment design. We capture some of this history below, showing how it underpins the evolution of assessment at the federal level up to today. This journey of EA in Canada is referenced in the chapters that follow. For a more complete history of the federal assessment process, the reader is directed to other volumes, such as Hazell (1999) and Doelle (2008).[5]

## B. A BRIEF HISTORY OF FEDERAL ENVIRONMENTAL ASSESSMENT IN CANADA

In tracing the history of the federal EA process in Canada, it is useful to consider some of the milestones in the evolution of the process, as well as how the focus and purpose of EA have shifted over time. Four stages in the evolution, as identified by Gibson and Hanna, provide a useful road map to the evolution of the federal EA process. They include the following:

- *Stage 1.* This stage involves assessments that focused on pollution control solutions to locally significant adverse environmental impacts, generally in the form of releases of pollutants into air, water, or soil.
- *Stage 2.* In this stage, the focus shifts to more proactive efforts to identify and mitigate possible environmental impacts of proposed activities. It remains a technical process, with little public participation and no consideration of socio-economic factors.
- *Stage 3.* In the third stage, EA processes seek to integrate environmental considerations into broader planning decisions but still in the context of individual activities proposed. This involves consideration of a full range of factors that affect whether a proposed activity should proceed, including environmental, cultural, historical, and economic impacts. This stage involves consideration of the need for the proposed activity and alternatives and requires active public engagement to be effective.

---

5   Stephen Hazell, *Canada v. the Environment: Federal Environmental Assessment 1984–1998* (Toronto: Canadian Environmental Defence Fund, 1999); Meinhard Doelle, *The Federal Environmental Assessment Process: A Guide and Critique* (Markham, ON: LexisNexis Canada, 2008).

- *Stage 4.* The final stage identified by Gibson and Hanna involves integrated planning and decision making for sustainability. This stage involves full integration of EA processes with planning processes and requires the inclusion of policies, plans, and programs in the assessment process.[6]

When the federal Cabinet decided in 1972 to establish the Federal Environmental Assessment Review Office to oversee the newly established non-legislative EA process, it clearly fell within the first stage of EA process design. The focus was on a screening process to identify proposed federal projects that had the potential to cause unacceptable pollution. Proposed projects identified through the screening process were expected to go through a more thorough EA process.

The initial Cabinet decision in 1972 was followed with a broader Cabinet policy directive in 1973 to carry out an EA of significant new proposals. The main implication of the 1973 directive was to broaden the application of EA from federal projects to private projects, with federal involvement in the form of federal financial support, land, or regulatory oversight. Federal EAs continued to be non-legislative and remained comfortably positioned in the first stage of evolution. The determination of whether a full assessment was needed and the design and implementation of the EA process were left in the hands of those responsible for the ultimate project decision.

The period from 1974 to 1980 brought about the first evolution of federal EA in Canada. A catalyst for this evolution was the Berger Inquiry into the proposed Mackenzie Valley Pipeline, which took place between 1974 and 1977.[7] The inquiry and resulting report have greatly influenced, and continue to influence, impact assessment in Canada, especially in regard to its groundbreaking aspects, such as early public involvement and scope of assessment (see Box 1.1).

In parallel with the Berger Inquiry from 1974 to 1977, the federal EA process was gradually strengthened and formalized as the

---

6    Robert B Gibson & Kevin S Hanna, "Progress and Uncertainty: The Evolution of Federal Environmental Assessment in Canada" in Kevin S Hanna, ed, *Environmental Impact Assessment: Practice and Participation* (Oxford: Oxford University Press, 2005) 16 at 16, 17.

7    Thomas R Berger, *Northern Frontier, Northern Homeland: The Report of the Mackenzie Valley Pipeline Inquiry*, vols 1, 2 (Ottawa: Ministry of Supply and Services Canada, 1977), online: *Prince of Wales Northern Heritage Centre* www.pwnhc.ca/exhibitions/berger/documentation.

Environmental Assessment and Review Process (EARP). Some of the early changes included encouraging earlier public consultations and not including federal decision makers on review panels if they were involved in proposing the activity to be assessed. Nevertheless, it was still common for major projects to be approved before the EA was completed or even without any assessment.[8]

In the early 1980s, further events influenced the evolution of federal EA. First among these was a proposed new approach to environmental impact assessment published by Beanlands and Duinker in 1983.[9] It has been among the most cited, if not always followed, methodologies for EAs in Canada ever since. Around the same time, Charles Caccia became the federal environment minister, and he convinced his Cabinet to formalize the EARP as a guidelines order issued by Cabinet. The order was drafted in mandatory language. However, federal departments did not consider themselves bound until a series of court cases confirmed the binding nature of the EARP guidelines order.[10]

The order was passed in 1984 following both an internal and an external review.[11] It applied to proposals that were "initiatives, undertakings, and activities" for which the federal government had a "decision making responsibility." During the implementation of the EARP, it became clear that proposals included not only physical projects and activities but also policies, plans, and programs. At the same time, the requirement that there had to be a "decision-making responsibility" for something to be considered a proposal was interpreted narrowly to mean a legal duty. For EARP purposes, this duty can relate to the federal government as proponent, financial contributor, landowner, or regulator.

---

8   Robert B Gibson & Kevin S Hanna, "Progress and Uncertainty: The Evolution of Federal Environmental Assessment in Canada" in Hanna, ed, *Environmental Impact Assessment: Practice and Participation* (Oxford: Oxford University Press, 2005) 16 at 20.

9   Gordon E Beanlands & Peter N Duinker, *An Ecological Framework for Environmental Impact Assessment in Canada* (Halifax: Institute for Resource and Environmental Studies, Dalhousie University & Federal Environmental Assessment Review Office, 1983).

10  *Attorney General of Canada v Saskatchewan Water Corporation et al*, [1991] 2 WWR 614 (Sask CA). See also *Friends of the Oldman River Society v Canada (Minister of Transport and Minister of Fisheries and Oceans)*, [1992] 1 SCR 3.

11  For a more detailed description of EARP, see Rodney Northey, *The 1995 Annotated Canadian Environmental Assessment Act* (Toronto: Carswell, 1994) at 21.

**BOX 1.1 THE BERGER INQUIRY**

The Berger Inquiry was established in 1974 through an order of the Privy Council.[12] The terms of reference as set out in the order include "the social, environmental and economic impact regionally, of the construction, operation and subsequent abandonment of the proposed pipeline in the Yukon and the Northwest Territories."[13] In the order, Justice Berger is authorized to hold hearings at his discretion, to summon witnesses, to establish practices and procedures for the inquiry, and to engage the services of a range of experts as he deems necessary. The order does not impose a time limit for the inquiry but directs Justice Berger to report to the minister of Indian affairs and northern development with "all reasonable dispatch."

Justice Berger held a round of preliminary hearings to make contact with affected communities and individuals and to seek input into the process. There was no formal scoping decision. However, in a set of preliminary rulings, Justice Berger made it clear that he interpreted the terms of reference for the inquiry broadly. He noted, "[T]his inquiry is not just about a gas pipeline; it relates to the whole future of the North."[14] It is clear from other preliminary rulings as well as the final report that Justice Berger took this conclusion to heart. In addition to the project itself and the full range of issues dealing with the biophysical environment, topics covered included health, education, social services, energy supply, employment, economic growth, impact on the renewable resource base, transportation, and communications.[15]

The inquiry process has a number of other features of interest to EA processes. For example, Justice Berger established a Pipeline Application Assessment Board, composed of experts within the public service who were seconded to the inquiry to review material submitted by proponents and to prepare a technical report in which the submissions of the proponents were evaluated. In addition, Justice Berger had access to the Environmental Protection Board, composed of independent experts with relevant science and engineering backgrounds who were retained at the expense of proponents but provided advice and expertise to the inquiry unimpeded by the proponents.[16]

---

12   See Berger, above note 7, vol 2 at App II, Inquiry Documents, PC Order: PC 1974-641, 21 March 1974.

13   *Ibid* at 2. The original Privy Council order refers to a single pipeline. This was later supplemented by the referral of additional pipeline proposals made by other proponents after the establishment of the inquiry.

14   *Ibid* at App II, Inquiry Documents, Preliminary Rulings (I).

15   *Ibid*.

16   *Ibid* at App I, The Inquiry Process, at 2. The Environmental Protection Board was funded by the proponents, Arctic Gas and Foothills, in the amount of $3.5 million.

In many other respects, the Berger Inquiry process looks very familiar to anyone who has followed federal EA panel reviews over the past two decades. Following the preliminary hearings designed to seek input into the process and scope of the inquiry, several studies and reports were commissioned by Justice Berger. Some were prepared by the proponents, similar to environmental impact statements now commonly prepared at the start of EA processes. Others were commissioned by the inquiry, which rarely happens today due to funding constraints. Still others were funded through an intervenor funding program, which is still an important part of the federal EA process.

The study and reporting stage was followed by the hearing stage. Justice Berger made a point of ensuring that the process was inviting to anyone interested in or concerned about the proposed pipelines, not just to lawyers and experts.[17] The stated goal was for the process to be effective and inviting to the range of experts and to community members. Furthermore, proponents were successfully encouraged to make presentations to correct factual errors rather than rely on cross-examination.

With respect to the assessment of impacts and the final outcome of the inquiry, Justice Berger pointed to a few key features of the inquiry in his summary of the process. He made the point that his inquiry was unique at the time in giving full consideration to cumulative effects rather than to considering the impacts of the proposed activity in isolation. The inquiry's recommendations are conclusions that did not have to be implemented. However, given the nature and extent of the consultation and the thorough consideration and reporting on the range of potential impacts of the proposed pipelines, government decision makers in the end were not prepared to ignore the recommendations in the final report.

The concept of an exclusion list of projects known to cause insignificant adverse environmental effects was introduced in the EARP, as were the concepts of substitution (of other assessment processes for the federal) and joint assessments (with other jurisdictions). The responsibility to carry out the EA process under EARP rested with the initiating federal department (e.g., the Department of Fisheries and Oceans, Parks Canada) or any department of the federal government with a decision-making responsibility for a given proposal. The EA contemplated under EARP essentially consisted of an initial assessment of the project to determine whether a full panel review was warranted. This assessment was to be carried out as early as possible, before irrevocable

---

17    See Chapter 15.

decisions were made.[18] If a public review was warranted, it was to be carried out by a review panel independent of the initiating department.

In response to ongoing criticism of the federal EA process under the EARP and the growing number of successful court challenges involving the federal EA process,[19] in 1995 the government enacted the *Canadian Environmental Assessment Act* (*CEAA 1995*).[20] *CEAA 1995* differed from EARP in a number of ways.[21] The most obvious difference was that the *CEAA* was statutory, making it less susceptible to interference by government without the approval of Parliament. Another key difference was that *CEAA 1995* was limited in its application to undertakings and physical activities. The assessment of policies, plans, and programs was excluded from the legislation and left to a separate process under a Cabinet directive. A regulation that lists all regulatory decisions that trigger an EA under *CEAA 1995* was another key feature of the new process, as was the comprehensive study process, which was designed to be a hybrid between the self-assessment approach (assessments done by approval authorities such as Parks Canada and the Department of Fisheries and Oceans) in the form of a screening and the independent public review in the form of a review panel. The independence and impartiality of panel members, mediation, more direction on the scope of the project and the scope of the assessment, and provision for the assessment of projects with transboundary impacts were among the other features of *CEAA 1995*.

The evolution of federal EA from the original EARP in 1972 to *CEAA 1995* moved the process from Gibson and Hanna's stage 1 to stage 2 and possibly beyond. The formal legal test for the application of the EA process and the scoping requirements moved it toward a more proactive

---

18  Northey, above note 11 at 28.

19  For a discussion of some of these developments, including cases involving EARP, see Jamie Benidickson, "Environmental Law Survey (1980-92), Part I" (1992) 24 *Ottawa Law Review* 733 at 785–811. See also Northey, above note 11, at 255 for a summary of key EARP decisions.

20  For a detailed account of the evolution of the federal EA process from the EARP guidelines order to the *CEAA*, see Hazell, above note 5.

21  For a more detailed comparison of the EARP guidelines order and the *CEAA*, see Joseph de Pencier, "The Federal Environmental Assessment Process: A Practical Comparison of the EARP Guidelines Order and the Canadian Environmental Assessment Act" (1994) 4 *Journal of Environmental Law & Practice* 329. See also Meinhard Doelle, "CEAA, New Uncertainties, but a Step in the Right Direction" (1994) 4 *Journal of Environmental Law & Practice* 59.

assessment of impacts and mitigation options. The focus was still on biophysical impacts; however, the legislation did include some socio-economic effects in the assessment and provided for the consideration of some impacts of a cultural, historical, and Aboriginal nature if these could be associated with the biophysical effects. The role of the public in the EA process still largely depended on the exercise of discretion by government decision makers. In the case of panel reviews, active public engagement was guaranteed; otherwise, it remained the exception rather than the rule.

Some modest adjustments were made to *CEAA 1995* in 2003 and 2010. Shortly after the 2010 amendments were passed, a complete overhaul of the federal EA process was initiated, which resulted in a new Act, *CEAA 2012*. The new process applied to only about a dozen projects a year, was limited in scope to some areas of federal legislative responsibility (such as fishing, some endangered and migratory species, and Indigenous peoples), reduced opportunities for public participation, imposed strict timelines, and shifted responsibility for most assessments from regulators to the Canadian Environmental Assessment Agency.[22] Dissatisfaction with *CEAA 2012* led to an election promise by the Trudeau Liberals to reform the process. After the election, a three-year law reform process was initiated (explored in some detail in Chapter 4), which eventually led to the passage of the *IAA* in 2019.

As indicated above, the evolution from EARP to EA legislation in the form of *CEAA 1995* resulted in the separation of project assessments from the assessment of proposed policies, plans, and programs. Rather than include the assessment of policies, plans, and programs under *CEAA 1995*, a separate, non-legislated process for the assessment of policies and program proposals was announced in 1993.[23] The process was described in a Cabinet directive as informal and discretionary. The directive was revised in 1999 and 2004 to include plans and to require

---

22  See Meinhard Doelle, "CEAA 2012: The End of Federal EA as We Know It?" (2012) 24 *Journal of Environmental Law & Practice* 1; Robert B Gibson, "In Full Retreat: The Canadian Government's New Environmental Assessment Law Undoes Decades of Progress" (2012) 30:3 *Impact Assessment and Project Appraisal* 179. See also A John Sinclair & Meinhard Doelle, "Environmental Assessment in Canada: Encouraging Decisions for Sustainability" in Bruce Mitchell, ed, *Resource and Environmental Management in Canada: Addressing Conflict and Uncertainty*, 5th ed (Toronto: Oxford University Press, 2015) 11.

23  The substance of the initial policy and program review process is summarized in Northey, above note 11 at 585.

a public statement on the environmental effects identified during any detailed strategic EA.[24]

According to the Cabinet directive, a strategic EA of a proposed policy, plan, or program is to be carried out if a proposal that may result in important environmental effects is submitted to a minister or Cabinet for approval. Strategic EAs are expected to consider issues such as scope, likely environmental effects, mitigation measures, and the importance of any residual environmental effects. Environmental, economic, and social considerations are to be considered on equal footing in the decision-making process. Public participation is encouraged but not required. The general approach is very similar to a screening under *CEAA 1995*; however, the directive is careful to use different terminology.[25]

The various iterations of formalized impact assessment in Canada, as outlined above, are referred to throughout this volume as they provide important benchmarks for consideration of the new Act. The authors refer to EARP, *CEAA 1995*, *CEAA 2012*, and *IAA*.

## C. CANADIAN PERSPECTIVES ON ENVIRONMENTAL ASSESSMENT METHODS

Many Canadians have contributed to the development of EA in Canada and abroad. A much-referenced overview of EA methods that was meant to direct the EA process in Canada is provided by Beanlands, one of the Canadian delegates who presented a paper at a 1983 symposium on environmental impact assessment.[26] Beanlands defined an EA method as any "specified, orderly approach to the assembly, analysis and interpretation of information for the stated purpose of environmental impact assessment."[27] He traced the origins of EA methods back to the

---

24  The 1999 Cabinet directive and the 2004 amendments are conveniently reproduced in ch 4 of the *Report of the Commissioner of the Environment and Sustainable Development to the House of Commons* (Ottawa: Minister of Public Works and Government Services, 2004) at 5.

25  Such as the use of "important" in the place of "significant."

26  Gordon E Beanlands, "Do EIA Methods Have a Future?" (Paper presented to the Symposium on Environmental Impact Assessment: Current Status and Future Projects, Hania, Crete, 10–17 April 1983) [unpublished]. For a conference summary, see Robert GH Turnbull, "International Symposium on Environmental Impact Assessment (EIA): Current Status and Future Prospects" (1983) 10:4 *Environmental Conservation* 363 at 364.

27  *Ibid* at 1.

*National Environmental Policy Act* (*NEPA*) in the United States[28] and from this starting point identified three stages in their evolution. First, there was an initial stage of "inventing" simplistic methods to implement the legal requirements of the *NEPA*, but without much consideration to the effectiveness of the end product. The second phase, from 1975 to 1979, was referred to as the introspective years. Beanlands termed the third phase, which started in 1980, the realistic years as it was only then that realistic, science-based EA methods emerged.

At the core of Beanlands' paper is the proposition that EA methods, to be effective, have to follow the four key steps in any EA process. Step one is to understand the receiving environment. Step two involves making predictions about the interaction of the proposed activity with the receiving environment. Step three involves proceeding with the proposed activity. Step four involves a monitoring program to determine whether the impact predictions were accurate. What is interesting about this paper is that it sought to counter the prevailing view at the time that EA is simply about identifying, with a high degree of certainty, the impacts of a proposed activity and the mitigation of any found to be unacceptable. Beanlands thereby reminded us that our ability to make accurate predictions is limited and that we often lack good baseline data.

His paradigm of EA also pointed out that project implementation in accordance with the environmental impact statement is critical and that monitoring and follow-up are preconditions for improving our predictive capability and ability to manage impacts that the statement failed to predict accurately or at all. The issues raised by Beanlands are ones that EA processes (as well as proponents and practitioners) continue to struggle with today. Our understanding of the receiving environment often continues to be too limited to make accurate predictions about its interaction with proposed activities, and we have made precious little use of monitoring programs as tools to improve our predictive skills over time, as outlined in the chapters that follow.

Whitney and Maclaren, from the University of Toronto, focused on assessment "methodology."[29] The term was used to convey a consideration of all of the components of an overall EA process rather than a

---

28    42 USC § 4321 et seq.

29    JBR Whitney & VW Maclaren, "A Framework for the Assessment of EIA Methodologies" in JBR Whitney & VW Maclaren, eds, *Environmental Impact Assessment: The Canadian Experience* (Toronto: Institute for Environmental Studies, 1985) 1 at 1.

specific method to achieve a specific purpose that may only be part of the overall process. The authors pointed to a number of common shortcomings of EA methodologies, including the following:

- Some assessment methodologies do not distinguish between the predictive and the evaluative aspects of EA. The predictive aspect deals with the prediction of what effects are expected to result from the proposed activity, and the evaluative aspect deals with the relative importance of various effects identified.
- Where the distinction is made, methodologies often do not adequately incorporate both but rather tend to focus on either the predictive or the evaluative aspects of EA.
- Many methodologies wrongly designate predictive aspects as objective and evaluative aspects as subjective, when both have subjective elements and both can be applied in an objective, scientific manner.

Having concluded that the key to an effective EA methodology is that it applies an objective and scientific approach to predicting and evaluating expected effects of a proposed activity, the authors proposed scoping, prediction, significance assessment, evaluation, monitoring, and mitigation as the basic steps of an effective process. How these steps are used to ensure an appropriate integration of the predictive and evaluative aspects of EA is considered next.

According to Whitney and Maclaren, appropriate integration of the predictive and evaluative aspects of EA is achieved through the use of scientific and public input at the various stages of the EA process. The basic premise in much of the early literature is that EA is about informing decision makers. To achieve this objective, EA has to predict future consequences of alternative scenarios that are within the power of decision makers to realize. Accurate predictions, in turn, require rigorous science. The public's role is to inform value judgments about the range of factors to be tracked and the relative desirability of the various predicted outcomes.[30]

At the heart of the debate over methods and methodologies is the dual role of EA processes: the predictive and the evaluative. An analysis of the practice of EA over the past four decades clearly shows that on the

---

30    See Beanlands & Duinker, above note 9.

whole we lack the ability to apply a purely scientific approach and accurately predict the consequences of alternative courses of actions. The limits of our predictive ability highlight the need for value judgments, the need for public engagement, and the importance of monitoring and follow-up to ensure opportunities to learn and adjust over time.

## D. SELECTED CANADIAN PERSPECTIVES ON GOOD ENVIRONMENTAL ASSESSMENT

The ultimate test for the effectiveness of any EA is its impact on the participants and the choices they make as a result of the process. Understandably, the focus has been on the proponents and government decision makers, but the impact of an effective EA process will extend to all participants. From the early days of Canadian EA in the 1970s, observers such as Andrews have been concerned that the process is at risk of achieving the opposite, of being little more than a paper exercise to justify decisions already made.[31] According to Andrews, the overriding purpose of EA processes should be to strike a more appropriate balance in decision making among "environmental, social, economic, technical and other considerations."[32] This requires decision makers to be influenced by the social and environmental consequences of a proposed activity, not just by the expected economic or other benefits that motivated the proposed action.

To achieve this, Andrews pointed out that it is critical for EA processes to go beyond benefit–cost analysis to forecasting the range of consequences of alternative actions. The public has a key role to play in deciding which set of consequences associated with the various alternatives considered is the most desirable. Active engagement of the decision maker in the EA process itself is also seen as key to ensuring that the process meets its goal of improved decision making. In light of our limited ability to accurately forecast future consequences and our constantly evolving valuation of the consequences of various alternatives, EA processes cannot end when the project is approved.[33] Academics and

---

31   See, for example, RNL Andrews, "A Philosophy of Environmental Impact Assessment" (1973) 28 *Journal of Soil and Water Conservation* 197 at 198.

32   *Ibid.*

33   See Meinhard Doelle, *The Federal Environmental Assessment Process: A Guide and Critique* (Markham, ON: LexisNexis Butterworths, 2008) at 31, 334.

practitioners alike have struggled with these challenges of EA processes in Canada.

An important contribution to the literature on the evolution of EA process in Canada is a 1985 collection of papers edited by Whitney and Maclaren.[34] In it, a range of leading Canadian academics and practitioners pick up on the key challenges for EA—identified through practice and research—that need to be addressed through EA law, regulation, policy, and guidance. Many of the challenges discussed in this volume (examples of which follow) are those already identified and familiar to those who have been engaged in the practice of EA. Interestingly, many of the solutions have been proposed for more than two decades, yet relatively few have been effectively implemented.

Beanlands' chapter in Whitney and Maclaren emphasizes a scientific approach to environmental impact assessment. Interestingly, the starting point for Beanlands is the identification of valued environmental components, something that has become a common term in environmental impact statements. It seems clear that Beanlands envisaged that the process of identifying which environmental components were sufficiently valuable to be included in the rigorous scientific process of predicting impacts of the proposed activity and its alternatives would be left to society at large. This suggests a combination of public and government engagement as the starting point of an effective EA process, something that still happens all too rarely in practice in the context of project assessment in Canada.[35] In practice, the important role for the public in this value judgment has largely given way to professional or governmental judgment, particularly for projects of small and medium size.

In their chapter, Jones and Greig picked up on a point made repeatedly in the literature: that our ability to predict future consequences of a range of choices faced by decision makers is limited and ill-understood.[36] They suggested that our overall approach to EA in Canada should recognize that our predictions are likely to be inaccurate. The key point is that EA processes need to address the consequences of

---

34  Virginia White Maclaren & Joseph B Whitney, eds, *New Directions in Environmental Impact Assessment in Canada* (Toronto: Methuen, 1985).

35  Gordon E Beanlands, "Ecology and Impact Assessment in Canada" in Maclaren & Whitney, above note 34 at 1.

36  Michael L Jones & Lorne A Greig, "Adaptive Environmental Assessment and Management: A New Approach to Environmental Impact Assessment" in Maclaren & Whitney, above note 34 at 21.

predictions being wrong, or to expect the unexpected. The solution offered is to explicitly recognize uncertainty during the EA process and to make design decisions for the developments under assessment that allow them to adapt to unexpected consequences. The basic proposal has surfaced again in the context of adaptive management. An issue not addressed by Jones and Greig that has been raised more recently in the context of adaptive management is the concern that the commitment to adaptive management replaces the need for rigour in the prediction of consequences. Another issue not raised here is the link between uncertainty and the precautionary approach, specifically when our inability to predict the consequences of an action leads to the conclusion that the action should not be permitted.[37]

Duinker also picked up on our limited ability to make accurate predictions and our limited understanding of the accuracy of our predictions.[38] However, he took a somewhat different approach to the problem than Jones and Greig, focusing on the opportunity to test our ability to predict future consequences. Duinker made the point that the greatest obstacle to improving our ability to predict is the failure to implement proper monitoring programs that include the analysis necessary to determine the accuracy of the various predictions. Duinker defined monitoring as quantitative in nature and distinguished between compliance monitoring and effects monitoring. Duinker was particularly interested in effects monitoring compared to the predictions made during the course of the EA. He pointed out that the problem with EA processes in Canada is not that they do not refer to monitoring and follow-up programs; rather, the problems relate to the actual design and implementation of follow-up and monitoring programs. Most notably, the EA process is generally considered to be concluded at the project approval stage, and no one takes responsibility for ensuring that the results of monitoring programs are available and are used to improve the accuracy of predicting future consequences, issues that EA statutes need to address.

---

37    For a recent look at the issue of adaptive management, see Peter N Duinker & Lisa M Trevisan, "Adaptive Management: Progress and Prospects for Canadian Forests" in Philip J Burton et al, eds, *Towards Sustainable Management of the Boreal Forest* (Ottawa: NRC Research Press, 2003) 857.

38    Peter N Duinker, "Effects Monitoring in Environmental Impact Assessment" in Maclaren & Whitney, above note 34 at 117.

Whitney pointed to the ability to track interactions between the environmental, social, and economic effects of a proposed activity as a key aspect of an effective EA methodology.[39] He argued that unless EA is able to make predictions about the interaction between the environmental, economic, and social effects of a proposed activity over the long term, it cannot hope to become a useful decision-making tool. Whitney did not contend that all interactions have to be tracked. Instead, he advocated for the identification of relevant interactions. He did not resolve how relevance is to be determined but suggested that such interactions are more relevant in certain circumstances, such as large projects, projects with large impacts, and specific impacts with known interactions between society, the environment, and the economy.

A decade later, the issues were taken up again by, among others, Wood and Sadler in two separate publications.[40] Both publications sought to compare the experience with and current state of EA processes in a range of developed countries to evaluate their respective effectiveness and thereby impact the evolution of the assessment process in Canada. Looking at these studies today, what is more relevant than the conclusions reached about the various EA processes in place at the time are the views expressed by Wood and Sadler on what EA methods contribute to an effective process.

Wood began his evaluation with some general comments on what an effective EA process should accomplish. He stated that EA processes should lead to the "abandonment of environmentally unacceptable actions and to the mitigation to the point of acceptability of the environmental effects of proposals which are approved."[41] Although this statement is arguably still some distance from the concept that proposals should be approved only if they make a net positive contribution to sustainable development, Wood was among the first to explicitly recognize that the option of rejecting a proposal should be on par with allowing a project to proceed with mitigation. Much of the literature of the 1970s and 1980s appears to assume that the project would be

---

39 Joseph B Whitney, "Integrated Economic-Environmental Models in Environmental Impact Assessment" in Maclaren & Whitney, above note 34 at 53.

40  Sadler, above note 1; and Wood, above note 1.

41  *Ibid* at 1.

approved and that the purpose of the EA process was to identify mitigation measures to limit the damage.[42]

Effectiveness, efficiency, and fairness are proposed as the overall evaluation criteria for EA processes. A process is considered effective if the information gathered contributes to decision making, predictions made were accurate, and proposed mitigation measures achieved their expected objective. An EA process is considered efficient if decisions are timely and the cost of the process is reasonable. The process is considered fair if all interested parties have equal opportunities to influence the decision and those directly affected have equal access to compensation.[43]

Wood then proposed fourteen evaluation criteria as the basis for his review of EA processes in the United States, the European Union, the United Kingdom, the Netherlands, Canada, Australia, and New Zealand. Criteria included the legal basis for the EA process, coverage, consideration of alternatives, process decisions, scoping decisions, the EA report preparation and review, decision making, monitoring, mitigation, consultation, the costs and benefits of the process, and the incorporation of strategic EAs in the EA process.

Sadler's evaluation of EA processes looked at the same jurisdictions, but through a different lens. Sadler focused on specific issues he considered to be critical based on the state of development of the EA process. In the place of Wood's more general categories of effectiveness, efficiency, and fairness, Sadler focused on ten key issues categorized by theme. Under the theme of the adequacy of the EA system, he considered the guiding values and underlying principles of the EA process. Under the theme of the scope of the EA process, Sadler considered the incorporation of sustainability concepts into the EA process itself and the project decision it is intended to inform. The role of strategic EAs was also considered here, as were cumulative and large-scale effects of proposed activities. Under the elements of the approach, the relationship between the process and decision making was considered. Other issues under this theme included integration, public participation,

---

42   This has, in fact, been the experience under *CEAA 1995* and *CEAA 2012*.

43   Above note 39 at 10.

dispute settlement, post-project analysis (including follow-up), and total process management.[44]

An area of particular focus in recent years in Canada has been the role of the public in EA processes.[45] One of the most significant developments in this area has been an evolution from viewing the public as a source of information to be tapped into through the EA process to thinking of the engagement of the public as an interactive mutual learning process. Authors such as Sinclair, Fitzpatrick, and Diduck have applied transformative learning principles to focus on opportunities for mutual learning within the context of EA processes as a way to make EA a more effective tool for sustainability. Implicit in this approach is a perspective on how to make EA effective that goes beyond the formal process and beyond assessments for individual projects. The basic idea is that to maximize mutual learning opportunities in EA processes, they should be designed to provide the conditions under which individuals learn best. These conditions include the following:

- accurate and complete information
- freedom from coercion
- openness to alternative perspectives
- the ability to reflect critically on presuppositions
- equal opportunity to participate
- the ability to assess arguments in a systematic manner and accept a rational consensus as valid[46]

Two other related areas that have been the subject of much attention in the literature and in practice in Canada are the scope of assessments and the final outcome of an EA process. Under this category, the consideration of cumulative effects, the need to move beyond project-based

---

44    For a review of how the *CEAA* fits within the literature on EA at the time of its development, see Steven Penney, "Assessing CEAA: Environmental Assessment Theory and the CEAA" (1994) 4 *Journal of Environmental Law & Practice* 243.

45    See A John Sinclair & Alan P Diduck, "Public Involvement in EA in Canada: A Transformative Learning Perspective" (2001) 21 *Environmental Impact Assessment Review* 113; Alan P Diduck & A John Sinclair, "Public Involvement in Environmental Assessment: The Case of the Non-participant" (2002) 29:4 *Environmental Management* 578; Patricia Fitzpatrick & A John Sinclair, "Learning Through Public Involvement in Environmental Assessment Hearings" (2003) 67:2 *Journal of Environmental Management* 161.

46    Sinclair & Diduck, above note 45 at 115.

assessments, and the push for sustainability-based assessments have received considerable attention.

In terms of the consideration of cumulative effects, Duinker and Greig identified six major problems with cumulative effects assessment in the Canadian context: the application of cumulative effects assessment at a project level, an EA process focused on project approval rather than sustainability assessment, a general lack of understanding of ecological impact thresholds, separation of cumulative effects from project-specific impacts, weak interpretation of cumulative effects by practitioners, and the inappropriate handling of potential future development. The authors proposed some improvements to project EAs, dealing with issues such as impact thresholds, a shift in focus to sustainability assessment, and more appropriate treatment of possible future developments. In the view of the authors, the major difficulties with cumulative effects assessment can only be addressed through a shift toward regional EA frameworks or land use planning.[47]

Kennett proposed similar changes to cumulative effects assessments as implemented in the context of project EAs in Canada and advocated a shift of responsibility for cumulative effects away from proponents. Kennett suggested five features he considers essential for a new cumulative effects paradigm:

- a shift from reactive EA processes to proactive planning processes as the primary instrument for cumulative effects management
- governments, rather than proponents, bearing primary responsibility for cumulative effects management
- the establishment of specific thresholds and overall objectives for cumulative effects management
- a regional rather than a project-specific focus for cumulative effects assessment and management
- planning and EA processes operating within an integrated framework for land and resource management[48]

---

47 Peter N Duinker & Lorne A Greig, "The Impotence of Cumulative Effects Assessment in Canada: Ailments and Ideas for Redeployment" (2006) 37 *Environmental Management* 153.

48 Steven A Kennett, *Towards a New Paradigm for Cumulative Effects Management*, Occasional Paper No 8 (Calgary: Canadian Institute for Resources Law, 1999) at 50.

Many experiences with project-level EA processes in Canada have pointed to the need to look beyond project EAs for an effective overall approach to assessing proposed activities and their contribution to long-term sustainability. Noble and Dalal-Clayton and Sadler have written extensively on strategic EA and how it might be implemented, while acknowledging that the work of developing and implementing effective methodologies has been slow.[49] There seems to be less disagreement on principles and steps in the strategic EA process than with respect to the methodologies. The steps in a strategic EA process proposed by Dalal-Clayton and Sadler, for example, include many of the steps familiar from project EAs. They include the screening stage to determine whether the strategic EA process applies, scoping, gathering of information, review, public participation, documentation of results, decision making, and follow-up.[50]

Another area of focus in the literature has been on the basis for the final EA and project decisions at the conclusion of the process. Gibson and others have written extensively on the concept of moving from EA processes with a focus on mitigating significant adverse environmental effects to sustainability assessments that consider whether the proposed activity will make a net positive contribution to sustainable development.[51] This marks a shift from considering information about the environmental consequences as the missing link in appropriate government decision making to an approach that considers the EA process itself to be the most effective and appropriate mechanism to facilitate the appropriate integration of social, economic, and environmental

---

49  See, for example, Bram F Noble, "Strategic Environmental Assessment" in Kevin S Hanna, ed, *Environmental Impact Assessment: Practice and Participation* (Oxford, UK: Oxford University Press, 2005) 93 at 93; and Barry Dalal-Clayton & Barry Sadler, *Strategic Environmental Assessment* (London, UK: Earthscan, 2005).

50  Dalal-Clayton & Sadler, above note 49 at 15.

51  See Robert B Gibson, "Favouring the Higher Test: Contribution to Sustainability as the Central Criterion for Reviews and Decisions Under the Canadian Environmental Assessment Act" (2000) 10 *Journal of Environmental Law & Practice* 39; Sara Bruhn-Tysk & Mats Eklund, "Environmental Impact Assessment—A Tool for Sustainable Development?: A Case Study of Biofuelled Energy Plants in Sweden" (2002) 22:2 *Environmental Impact Assessment Review* 129; David P Lawrence, "Integrating Sustainability and Environmental Impact Assessment" (1997) 21 *Environmental Management* 23; and Robert B Gibson, "Sustainability Assessment: Basic Components of a Practical Approach" (2006) 24:3 *Impact Assessment and Project Appraisal* 170.

considerations in making decisions about proposed activities and their alternatives.

## E.  CONCLUSIONS

Understanding of effective, efficient, and fair assessment and assessment processes has evolved both in practice and in the literature in Canada as it has in other jurisdictions, although not always in a linear manner or at the same pace. In the 1980s and 1990s, the focus of the literature and practice in Canada was largely on methodologies to predict and evaluate the biophysical consequences of proposed activities to issues. Over the past two decades in Canada, the literature and, more recently, the practice have increasingly tended to pay serious attention to the assessment of cumulative effects; participatory decision making; sustainability assessments; and the integration of social, economic, and environmental considerations beyond individual activities.

In terms of the more recent Canadian literature, much is now pointing to the need for EA processes and the statutes that underpin them to get to the fourth stage of evolution if EA is to meet its promise of being an effective tool on the path to sustainability. Not surprisingly, there is still a divergence of views on how to get there, to some extent in the literature and certainly among those involved in implementing EA processes. Recently, the issues discussed here have been the subject of an effort to consider a package of reforms needed to move EA from its current state to a truly effective decision-making tool in the pursuit of sustainability. The term introduced to discuss this package of elements is *next-generation environmental assessment*. In the next chapter, we offer an overview of the key components of next-generation EA as a consolidation of this recent literature and possible standard against which to measure the new federal assessment process in the form of the *IAA*.

In terms of practice at the federal level, *CEAA 1995* represented a step forward on at least some of the issues identified in the literature at the time, with the inclusion of cumulative effects, public participation, and some socio-economic considerations. Efforts at improved implementation of cumulative effects, participation, and limited efforts at improving strategic assessments marked this period after its passage. *CEAA 2012* represented a step backward in some key areas, with the narrowing of the scope and application of the assessment process and restrictions to public participation.

From time to time during this period of EA evolution, provinces have made efforts to fill the gaps left at the federal level, particularly with respect to the application of the assessment process and broadening the scope of assessments. In Part II of the book, many contributors return to the history of EA in Canada, in particular the experience with *CEAA 1995* because of the standard it set for federal EA. In Part III, we reflect on the contribution the *IAA* is making to the evolution of EA practice in Canada.

# CHAPTER 2

# A Next-Generation Assessment Framework for Examining the *Impact Assessment Act*

*Robert B Gibson, A John Sinclair, and Meinhard Doelle*

## A. INTRODUCTION

In this book, the new Canadian federal assessment law is considered in light of global and national expectations for advanced impact assessment regimes. Both global and national expectations are rooted in what we can learn from past failures, oversights, and evident best practice, as well as what is needed to address current and looming challenges. These considerations are well documented in academic and professional journals, reported case material, and the broader literature on the contexts in which assessment regimes should operate.[1] No single compilation prevails. Authorities differ on how the key components should be defined and organized into a conceptual framework, how their interactions should be recognized, and how they should be adjusted for application in different jurisdictions. Nonetheless, it is not difficult to identify the core components of next-generation impact assessment regimes or to specify these requirements as criteria for the

---

1   See, for example, David P Lawrence, *Environmental Impact Assessment: Practical Solutions to Recurrent Problems*, 2d ed (Hoboken, NJ: John Wiley and Sons, 2013); Richard K Morgan, "Environmental Impact Assessment: The State of the Art" (2012) 30:1 *Impact Assessment and Project Appraisal* 5; Alan Bond, Angus Morrison-Saunders & Richard Howitt, eds, *Sustainability Assessment: Pluralism, Practice and Progress*, 1st ed (London, UK: Taylor and Francis, 2012); Christopher Wood, *Environmental Impact Assessment: A Comparative Review*, 2d ed (Harlow, UK: Pearson Education, 2003).

design, implementation, and evaluation of assessment law and policy for Canada at the federal level.

This chapter outlines a next-generation assessment framework that incorporates international learning as well as key themes in the Canadian deliberations surrounding the assessment law and policy reform process that led to the *Impact Assessment Act (IAA)*.[2] Several authors of chapters in this book have contributed to developing the framework and its components, which influenced the structure and content of Part II of the book. Many of the chapters in Part II also deal specifically with key components of next-generation assessment; others touch on them. We also apply the framework at the end of the book in considering how far the *IAA* moves us to the next generation.

## B.  BACKGROUND TO THE NEXT-GENERATION ASSESSMENT FRAMEWORK

Legislated impact assessment requirements were introduced over fifty years ago with the *National Environmental Policy Act* in the United States[3] and have since spread to approximately 160 jurisdictions around the world. Forms have varied widely, reflecting the global diversity of socio-ecological and governance systems and associated issues, traditions, capacities, ambitions, and power structures. Over time, assessment laws, policies, and structures have also evolved, devolved, and shifted in many directions, in part due to changes well beyond the realm of assessment law, policy, and practice.

Among the key influences have been expansions in the scale of concerns and opportunities. Assessment issues in the 1970s were primarily local matters, often involving tensions between desires for expansion of economic activities and fears of adverse contamination, resource depletion, and community disturbance. Over the following decades, assessments increasingly faced regional and international issues as well. Especially since the beginning of the twenty-first century, assessment regimes have been immersed in a world that is increasingly complex, demanding, and, in some ways, uncertain. The current global context for assessments is enormously richer in financial and technological capacities but also burdened by deeper concerns about unsustainable

---

2    SC 2019, c 28, s 1.

3    42 USC § 4321 et seq.

socio-economic and ecological trajectories, inequities, climate change, pandemics, and other shared vulnerabilities.[4]

These and related shifts have encouraged greater attention to cumulative effects, uncertainty, and precaution. They have fuelled public insistence on process transparency and meaningful opportunities for engagement and have encouraged extension of assessment application from individual projects to strategic-level undertakings. More broadly, they have provided much of the impetus for moves such as those we are seeing in the assessment regimes of some Canadian jurisdictions to go beyond mitigation of adverse environmental effects to deliver net positive contributions to lasting well-being. Not surprisingly, these expansions of demands and ambitions for assessment regimes have also raised concerns about added costs, decision delays, and uncertainties.

The initial diversity and further redesigns of assessment regimes have tested many different broad approaches and specific innovations. In Canada alone, in addition to the federal government, every province and territory has at least one set of law-based assessment requirements, as do many Indigenous authorities operating under modern land claims agreements and municipal and regional governments. Most assessment regimes have undergone revision over the years, and at no time have any two of them been identical. The differences — whether in Canada or globally — have been problematic and not always justified by needs to serve differing contexts. A positive consequence, however, is a rich base of experiential evidence about successes and failures, apparent core requirements, best practices, commonly unmet needs, areas of deficiency, and promising innovations.[5]

---

4    See, for example, Kate Raworth, *Doughnut Economics: Seven Ways to Think Like a 21-st Century Economist* (White River Junction, VT: Chelsea Green, 2017); Will Steffen et al, "Trajectories of the Earth System in the Anthropocene" (2018) 115:33 *Proceedings of the National Academy of Sciences* 825; "The Sustainable Development Goals Report 2019" (2019) online (pdf): *United Nations* https://unstats.un.org/sdgs/report/2019/The-Sustainable-Development-Goals-Report-2019.pdf.

5    See, for example, Alberto Fonseca & Robert B Gibson, "Testing an Ex-ante Framework for the Evaluation of Impact Assessment Laws: Lessons from Canada and Brazil" (2020) 81 *Environmental Impact Assessment Review*; Robert B Gibson et al, *Synthesis at the Nexus of Sustainability Assessment, Regional/Strategic Assessment and Indigenous Partnerships* (2020), Report prepared with support from the Knowledge Synthesis Grant Program: Informing Best Practices in Environmental and Impact Assessments, Social Sciences and Humanities Council of Canada and the Impact Assessment Agency of Canada; Andrew John Sinclair, Meinhard Doelle & Robert B Gibson, "Implementing

The next-generation assessment concept and associated frameworks represent a consolidation of lessons from experience and appreciation of the surrounding imperatives, pressures, possibilities, and learning to which assessment regimes must respond and from which they can draw. Next-generation assessment components can be presented as a set of globally applicable generic components and a working framework of criteria to inform assessment improvement efforts anywhere.[6] The components, however, overlap and influence each other and are best viewed as a package rather than as individual ideas that can be cherry-picked. They also need continuous revision in light of experience and new circumstances.

Any generic framework will have limited practical utility unless it is adjusted and elaborated on for the context of application. As noted above, assessment regimes operate in places with wildly divergent characteristics and demands. All assessment laws, policies, and implementing structures, as well as all applications of those laws, policies, and structures, need to be sensitive to and suitable for the jurisdiction and the cases and places of application. The generic next-generation assessment components are mostly useful for identifying commonly important considerations. For particular applications—such as evaluation of the new Canadian federal assessment law—the components are likely to need some reorganization and rephrasing to reflect the most salient issues, opportunities, and capacities and to recognize and emphasize matters not faced in all assessment regimes. In Canada, such matters include imperatives to contribute to the reassertion of Indigenous rights, understandings, and governance; to facilitate interjurisdictional

---

Next Generation Assessment: A Case Example of a Global Challenge" (2018) 72:1 *Environmental Impact Assessment Review* 166; Robert B Gibson, Meinhard Doelle & Andrew John Sinclair, "Fulfilling the Promise: Basic Components of Next Generation Environmental Assessment" (2016) 29 *Journal of Environmental Law & Practice* 25; Alan James Bond & Jenny Pope, "The State of the Art of Impact Assessment in 2012" (2012) 30:1 *Impact Assessment and Project Appraisal* 1; Angus Morrison-Saunders, Rose Marshall & Jos Arts, *EIA Follow-up: International Best Practice Principles*, Special Publications No 6 (Fargo, ND: International Association for Impact Assessment, 2007).

6   Robert B Gibson et al, *Sustainability Assessment: Criteria and Processes* (London, UK: Earthscan, 2005) [Gibson et al, *Sustainability Assessment*]; Gibson, Doelle & Sinclair, above note 5; Fonseca & Gibson, above note 5; Angus Morrison-Saunders, Jenny Pope & Alan Bond, eds, *Handbook of Sustainability Assessment* (Camberley, UK: Edward Elgar, 2015); Barry Dalal-Clayton & Barry Sadler, *Sustainability Appraisal: A Sourcebook and Reference Guide to International Experience* (London, UK: Earthscan, 2014).

collaboration given the complex constitutional distribution of powers and responsibilities; and to serve well in a wide range of socio-economic, biophysical, and cultural contexts.

The framework, summarized below, recognizes both global learning and Canadian considerations. Various versions of these next-generation assessment components were presented and applied by participants in and observers of the assessment reform process that led to the *IAA* and that continues with the elaboration of regulatory and policy guidance and development of institutional practice.[7] Further adjustments are to be expected as new issues and understandings emerge.

## C. A FRAMEWORK OF NEXT-GENERATION ASSESSMENT COMPONENTS SPECIFIED FOR EVALUATION OF THE NEW FEDERAL IMPACT ASSESSMENT REGIME UNDER THE *IAA*

The following fourteen framework components are meant to represent the most important criteria to be met by an impact assessment regime

---

7    Environmental Planning and Assessment Caucus of the Canadian Environmental Network, *Achieving a Next Generation of Environmental Assessment: Submission to the Expert Review of Federal Environmental Assessment Processes* (14 December 2016), online (pdf): *Canadian Environmental Network* www.cqde.org/wp-content/uploads/2018/10/ Achieving-a-Next-Generation-of-Environmental-Assessment.pdf; Meinhard Doelle & Andrew John Sinclair, "The New IAA in Canada: From Revolutionary Thoughts to Reality" (2019) 79 *Environmental Impact Assessment Review*; Gibson, Doelle & Sinclair, above note 5; Robert B Gibson, "An Initial Evaluation of Canada's New Sustainability-Based Impact Assessment Act" (2020) 33:1 *Journal of Environmental Law and Practice* 1; Richard D Lindgren, *Ensuring Sustainability Through Statutory Reform: Essential Elements of Impact Assessment Law in Canada*, Submissions of the Canadian Environmental Law Association to the Government of Canada Regarding Environmental and Regulatory Reviews: Discussion Paper (June 2017) (Toronto: Canadian Environmental Law Association, 2017), online (pdf): *Canadian Environmental Law Association* https:// cela.ca/wp-content/uploads/2019/07/FederalEADiscPaper-CvrLtrandSubmission.pdf; *Next Generation Impact Assessment: Toward Sustainability, Submission to the Expert Panel on Environmental Assessment* (31 October 2016), online (pdf): *Nature Canada* https://naturecanada.ca/wp-content/uploads/2015/11/Submission-EA-Experts-Panel-october-31-2016_F.pdf; Anna Johnston, *Federal Environmental Assessment Reform Summit* (Vancouver, BC: West Coast Environmental Law, 2016), online (pdf): *West Coast Environmental Law* www.wcel.org/sites/default/files/publications/WCEL_ FedEnviroAssess_ExecSum%2Bapp_fnldigital.pdf [Johnston, *Federal Environmental Assessment Reform Summit*]; Anna Johnston, *Federal Environmental Assessment Reform Summit II* (Vancouver, BC: West Coast Environmental Law, 2017), online: *Envirolawsmatter* www.envirolawsmatter.ca/easummit2.

of law and associated policy and practice in Canada at the federal level. As noted above, the components overlap and interact. Also, they can be and have been organized in different ways without serious damage to their heuristic value. Although they can be used as a guide for evaluating the new legislation, they should be treated as a package of linked elements, each of which merits attention but should be designed to support the rest and can be used for post hoc and *ex ante* considerations.

## 1) Sustainability-Based Purpose, Scope, and Criteria for Evaluations and Decisions

The core purpose of the assessment regime should be to encourage government decisions that serve the lasting public interest through contributions to sustainability. That agenda widens the scope of relevant effects beyond the adverse and biophysical to the full range of sustainability considerations and their interactions.[8] It includes direct and indirect, individual and cumulative, positive and adverse effects on health; culture; gender and other identity factors; climate change;[9] and equity in the social, geographical, and intergenerational distribution of risks and benefits.[10] Effective implementation of this agenda entails application of explicit criteria that combine the basic requirements for progress toward sustainability with considerations specific to the case and context. The public interest goal is to deliver the best options for mutually reinforcing and fairly distributed contributions to lasting well-being while minimizing trade-offs and avoiding significant adverse effects.[11]

---

8   See chapters 9 and 14.

9   See Chapter 13.

10   See chapters 12–14.

11   See, for example, Gibson et al, *Sustainability Assessment*, above note 6; Robert B Gibson, ed, *Sustainability Assessment: Applications and Opportunities* (London, UK: Earthscan, 2017); Bond, Morrison-Saunders & Howitt, above note 1; Lawrence, above note 1; Dalal-Clayton & Sadler, above note 6; Morrison-Saunders, Pope & Bond, above note 6; Sinclair, Doelle & Gibson, above note 5.

### 2) Application in Integrated, Tiered Assessments Covering All Potentially Significant Undertakings with Federal Jurisdiction/ Involvement at the Regional, Strategic, and Project Levels

Within the reach of federal jurisdiction, the regime's assessment requirements should apply to regional and strategic undertakings (policies, plans, and programs) as well as projects large and small that may have important direct or indirect implications for long-term well-being. The application structure should feature linked regional/ strategic- and project-level tiers so that project assessments help identify needs for regional/strategic assessments and the latter provide credible and authoritative higher-level guidance for project planning and assessment.[12] To enable such a structure, the tiers must share the same sustainability-based purposes, scope, and generic criteria and equivalent provisions for process credibility. These include impartiality, rigour, transparency, meaningful engagement, explicit criteria, and comparison of alternatives.[13] Process credibility is also crucial for decision making on which projects and regional/strategic issues and undertakings will be assessed.[14]

---

12  Jos Arts et al, "Planning in Tiers: Tiering as a Way of Linking SEA and EIA" in Barry Sadler et al, eds, *Handbook of Strategic Environmental Assessment* (London, UK: Earthscan 2011) 415; Timothy O'Riordan, "Beyond Environmental Impact Assessment" in Timothy O'Riordan and Richard D Hey, eds, *Environmental Impact Assessment* (Westmead, UK: Saxon House, 1976) 202; Barry Sadler et al, eds, *Handbook of Strategic Environmental Assessment* (London, UK: Earthscan, 2011); EB Peterson et al, *Cumulative Effects Assessment in Canada: An Agenda for Action and Research* (Hull, QC: Canadian Environmental Assessment Research Council & Minister of Supply and Services, 1987); Harry Spaling & Barry Smit, "Cumulative Environmental Change: Conceptual Frameworks, Evaluation Approaches, and Institutional Perspectives" (1993) 17:5 *Environmental Management* 587; Maria Rosário Partidário, "Strategic Environmental Assessment: Key Issues Emerging from Recent Practice" (1996) 16:1 *Environmental Impact Assessment Review* 31; Lex Brown & Riki Thérivel, "Principles to Guide the Development of Strategic Environmental Assessment Methodology" (2000) 18:3 *Impact Assessment and Project Appraisal* 183; Thomas Fischer, *The Theory and Practice of Strategic Environmental Assessment: Towards a More Systematic Approach.* (London, UK: Earthscan, 2007); Jill AE Gunn & Bram F Noble, "Sustainability Considerations in Regional Environmental Assessment" in Angus Morrison-Saunders, Jenny Pope, & Alan Bond, eds, *Handbook of Sustainability Assessment* (Camberley, UK: Edward Elgar, 2015) 103; Gibson, Doelle & Sinclair, above note 5; Andrew John Sinclair, Meinhard Doelle & Peter N Duinker, "Looking Up, Down, and Sideways: Reconceiving Cumulative Effects Assessment as a Mindset (2017) 62 *Environmental Impact Assessment Review* 183.

13  See chapters 10, 15, and 19.

14  See chapters 11 and 17.

### 3)  Interjurisdictional Cooperation, Collaboration, and Upward Harmonization

The issues to be faced in assessments at the regional/strategic and project levels rarely respect political and administrative boundaries. Especially in a federal nation, overlapping jurisdictional authority and responsibility present predictable alignment challenges but also opportunities for mobilizing diverse contributing capacities. Each assessment regime should provide for diverse interjurisdictional or multi-jurisdictional assessment arrangements.[15] Options include collaborative joint assessments, separate-but-aligned assessments, and cooperative regional/strategic studies leading to joint or parallel development and assessment of regional/strategic options and undertakings.[16] To facilitate mutual learning and continuous improvement, regimes should also ensure that all collaborations adopt the highest standards. Over time, case-by-case collaborative practice should reduce assessment process incompatibilities and encourage upward harmonization of processes to next-generation levels.

15    Steven A Kennett, "Hard Law, Soft Law and Diplomacy: The Emerging Paradigm for Intergovernmental Cooperation in Environmental Assessment" (1993) 31:4 *Alberta Law Review* 644; Jan Jaap deBoer, "Bilateral Agreements for the Application of the UN–ECE Convention on EIA in a Transboundary Context" (1999) 19:1 *Environmental Impact Assessment Review* 85; Robert G Connelly, "The UN Convention on EIA in a Transboundary Context: A Historical Perspective" (1999) 19:1 *Environmental Impact Assessment Review* 37; Deborah Carver et al, "Inter-jurisdictional Coordination of EA: Challenges and Opportunities Arising from Differences Among Provincial and Territorial Assessment Requirements and Processes" (20 November 2010), online (pdf): *Canadian Environmental Network* http://rcen.ca/sites/default/files/uploads/epa_interjurisdictional_coord_ea_1110.pdf; Meinhard Doelle, *The Federal Environmental Assessment Process: A Guide and Critique* (Markham, ON: LexisNexis, 2008); Nataša Đereg, "Environmental Impact Assessment in a Trans-boundary Context in the SEE Countries" in Massimiliano Montini & Slavko Bogdanovic, eds, *Environmental Security in South-Eastern Europe: International Agreements and Their Implementation* (Dordrecht, The Netherlands: Springer, 2011) 183; Jason MacLean, Meinhard Doelle & Chris Tollefson, "Polyjural and Polycentric Sustainability Assessment: A Once-in-a-Generation Law Reform Opportunity" (2016) 30:1 *Environmental Law and Practice* 35; Patricia Fitzpatrick & Andrew John Sinclair, "Multi-Jurisdictional Environmental Assessments in Canada" in Kevin S Hanna, ed, *Environmental Impact Assessment: Practice and Participation*, 3d ed (Toronto: Oxford University Press, 2016) 182.

16    See chapters 8 and 17.

### 4) Respect for Indigenous Rights, Facilitation of Reconciliation, and Encouragement of Co-governance with Indigenous Governing Bodies

Indigenous resilience through a long history of colonial appropriation, denial of Indigenous rights, and efforts to extinguish Indigenous cultures has been gradually forcing a national as well as an international shift to recognition and reconciliation. In Canada, assessment proceedings have been high-profile venues for the conversations and conflicts involved. Today, they are expected to be venues for effective responses. For legal, moral, and practical reasons, assessment regimes must play roles in reasserting Indigenous rights, governance, and understanding.[17] The imperatives include clarifying and meeting constitutional obligations and international commitments, establishing mutually respectful Nation-to-Nation relationships, and accepting Indigenous rights to grant or withhold free, prior, and informed consent to activities that may affect their rights or territories.[18] Moreover, these elements are closely linked to respecting and providing space for Indigenous knowledge, perspectives, and ways of seeing and for Indigenous laws and process.[19] For assessment applications, the relevant opportunities

17    See Chapter 6.

18    MIAC, *Advice to the Expert Panel Reviewing Environmental Assessment Processes from the Multi-Interest Advisory Committee* (Ottawa: 2016) (on file with authors). See also *United Nations Declaration on the Rights of Indigenous Peoples*, GA Res 61/295, UNGAOR, 61st Sess, UN Doc A/RES/61/295 (13 September 2007); Timothy O'Riordan & WR Derrick Sewell, "From Project Appraisal to Policy Review" in Timothy O'Riordan & WR Derrick Sewell, eds, *Project Appraisal and Policy Review* (New York: John Wiley & Sons, 1981); Timothy O'Riordan & WR Derrick Sewell, "Some Concluding Observations" in Timothy O'Riordan & WR Derrick Sewell, eds, *Project Appraisal and Policy Review* (New York: John Wiley & Sons, 1981) 297; Shin Imai, "Consult, Consent, and Veto: International Norms and Canadian Treaties" in Michael Coyle & John Borrows, eds, *The Right Relationship* (Toronto: University of Toronto Press, 2017); Martin Papillon & Thierry Rodon, "Proponent-Indigenous Agreements and the Implementation of the Right to Free, Prior, and Informed Consent in Canada" (2017) 62 *Environmental Impact Assessment Review* 216.

19    Cheryl Bartlett, Murdena Marshall & Albert Marshall, "Two-Eyed Seeing and Other Lessons Learned Within a Co-learning Journey of Bringing Together Indigenous and Mainstream Knowledges and Ways of Knowing" (2012) 2:4 *Journal of Environmental Studies and Sciences* 331; John Borrows, "Indigenous Legal Traditions in Canada" (2005) 19:1 *Washington University Journal of Law & Policy* 16; John Borrows, *Law's Indigenous Ethics* (Toronto: University of Toronto Press, 2019); Oonagh Fitzgerald et al, *Braiding Legal Orders: Implementing the United Nations Declaration on the Rights of Indigenous Peoples* (Waterloo, ON: Centre for International Governance Innovation, 2019); Brenda L Gunn

go beyond adjusting approaches to consultation and other assessment processes to centre on sharing decision-making authority in co-governance collaborations with Indigenous governing bodies.[20]

## 5)  Assessment Streams for Assessments of Projects and Regional/ Strategic Undertakings of Different Character and Significance

Many quite different projects and regional/strategic undertakings merit assessment. For best use of all parties' resources, assessment regimes should predefine more and less demanding basic assessment streams for these diverse undertakings. Process pathways in streams for all undertakings would meet next-generation assessment standards for rigour and credibility but recognize different levels of sustainability concern (e.g., for matters such as climate change and inequity in the distribution of risks and opportunities), uncertainty, and potential controversy.[21] Regional and strategic assessment streams would also accommodate needs in some cases to provide timely working guidance for ongoing project assessments or other immediate applications and in other cases to facilitate new research and analysis, interjurisdictional collaboration, extensive public deliberation, and pursuit of innovative solutions. More demanding streams may involve more detailed proponent submissions, longer timelines, more extensive review by government agencies and independent experts, more openings for effective public engagement including public hearings, final decision making by a higher authority (e.g., Cabinet rather than a minister), and/or opportunities for appeal.[22] To ensure that proponents and other participants can anticipate and act upon the applicable requirements, regimes should pre-assign predictable types of undertakings to the appropriate streams. Also needed are provisions for streaming unanticipated undertakings and processes for shifting assigned undertakings to more or less demanding streams.[23]

---

et al, *UNDRIP Implementation: Braiding International, Domestic and Indigenous Laws*, Special Report (Waterloo, ON: Centre for International Governance Innovation, 2017).

20   See Chapter 6.

21   Alan Bond et al, "Impact Assessment: Eroding Benefits Through Streamlining?" (2014) 45:1 *Environmental Impact Assessment Review* 46; Lawrence, above note 1; Meinhard Doelle, "The Implications of the SCC Red Chris Decision for EA in Canada" (2010) 20 *Environmental Law and Practice* 161.

22   Gibson, Doelle & Sinclair, above note 5.

23   See chapters 3 and 17.

### 6) Meaningful Public Participation

For process quality and credibility, effective mobilization of understanding and expertise, and enhancement of learning opportunities and assessment capacities, assessment regimes must encourage and facilitate meaningful public participation.[24] Active involvement of the full range of interested and informed participants—members of the public, non-governmental organizations, stakeholders, and independent experts, as well as proponents, government bodies, and other relevant authorities—should be a core feature of assessment deliberations. Provisions to enable effective participation should apply not only throughout the process for assessment of undertakings but also in deliberations leading to other assessment decisions (e.g., on application of assessment requirements to particular undertakings, development of regulations and policy guidance, and establishment of interjurisdictional agreements). Particularly important are measures to initiate meaningful engagement at the earliest point in deliberations (e.g., starting at the conception of undertakings subject to assessments). Basic requirements for meaningful participation in assessment law include, at a minimum, public notice, timely and easy access to information, realistic opportunities for informed public comment, public hearings, deliberative fora, mandatory reporting on how public contributions were addressed, and participant financial assistance, impartially administered.[25]

---

24    See Chapter 15.

25    Ciaran O'Faircheallaigh, "Public Participation and Environmental Impact Assessment: Purposes, Implications and Lessons for Public Policy Making" (2010) 30:1 *Environmental Impact Assessment Review* 19; Morgan, above note 1; Andrew John Sinclair & Alan Diduck, "Public Participation in Canadian Environmental Assessment: Enduring Challenges and Future Directions" in Kevin S Hanna, ed, *Environmental Impact Assessment: Practice and Participation*, 3d ed (Toronto: Oxford University Press, 2016) 65 [Sinclair & Diduck, "Public Participation in Canadian Environmental Assessment"]; Andrew John Sinclair & Alan Diduck, "Reconceptualizing Public Participation in Environmental Assessment as EA Civics" (2017) 62 *Environmental Impact Assessment Review* 174 [Sinclair & Diduck, "Reconceptualizing Public Participation"]; Gibson, Doelle & Sinclair, above note 5; Expert Panel for the Review of Environmental Assessment Processes, *Building Common Ground: A New Vision for Impact Assessment in Canada* (Ottawa: Canadian Environmental Assessment Agency, 2017), online (pdf): *Government of Canada* www.canada.ca/content/dam/themes/environment/conservation/environmental-reviews/building-common-ground/building-common-ground.pdf [*Building Common Ground*].

## 7) Full-Process Learning

Engagement in assessments has long been recognized for its potential to improve assessment practice.[26] Assessment regimes designed to encourage individual and social learning can strengthen participative skills, foster deeper understanding, and improve the knowledge base needed for capable and credible assessments. More broadly, learning from assessments can contribute to informed democratic engagement and help enable the transition to sustainability.[27] To capture this potential, assessment regimes need to establish mutual learning as a fundamental process purpose and responsibility for all assessment participants and facilitate collaborative multi-interest learning opportunities in all assessment components, from initial identification of issues and options to preparation and implementation of follow-up plans.[28] Key vehicles for learning in both project and regional/strategic assessment processes include early engagement, opportunities for collaborative partnerships, open access to information and science through searchable data platforms, independent and impartial processes, full transparency and accountability, and participative engagement in specifying clear, sustainability-based decision-making criteria.[29] However, engaged mutual learning can also be encouraged in other

26    Andrew John Sinclair, Alan Diduck & Patricia Fitzpatrick, "Conceptualizing Learning for Sustainability Through Environmental Assessment: Critical Reflections on 15 Years of Research" (2008) 28:7 *Environmental Impact Assessment Review* 415.

27    See, for example, Thomas Webler, Hans Kastenholz & Ortwin Renn, "Public Participation in Impact Assessment: A Social Learning Perspective" (1995) 15:5 *Environmental Impact Assessment Review* 443; Juan R Palerm, "An Empirical–Theoretical Analysis Framework for Public Participation in Environmental Impact Assessment" (2000) 43:5 *Journal of Environmental Planning and Management* 581.

28    See Chapter 22.

29    Richard NL Andrews, "Agency Responses to NEPA: A Comparison and Implications" (1976) 16:2 *Natural Resources Journal* 301; Robert Bartlett, "Ecological Reason in Administration: Environmental Impact Assessment and Administrative Theory" in Robert Paehlke & Douglas Torgerson, eds, *Managing Leviathan: Environmental Politics and the Administrative State* (London, UK: Belhaven Press, 1990) 81; Robert Bartlett, "The Rationality and Logic of NEPA Revisited" in Ray Clark & Larry Canter, eds, *Environmental Policy and NEPA: Past, Present, and Future* (Boca Raton, FL: St Lucie Press, 1997) 51; Sinclair, Diduck, & Fitzpatrick, above note 26; Urmila Jha-Thakur et al, "Effectiveness of Strategic Environmental Assessment: The Significance of Learning" (2009) 27:2 *Impact Assessment and Project Appraisal* 133; William R Sheate & Maria R Partidario, "Strategic Approaches and Assessment Techniques: Potential for Knowledge Brokerage Towards Sustainability" (2010) 30 *Environmental Impact Assessment Review* 278; Sinclair

deliberations and decision making (e.g., in developing regulatory and policy guidance, determining when assessments should be required, and framing interjurisdictional agreements). In this way, learning among all participants has the potential to build individual and organizational capacity for effective engagement, increase the rationality of assessment outcomes, help inform future assessments of related projects and regional/strategic undertakings, serve as civic education for participants, and provide information and reasoned positions and perspectives to enrich sustainability discourse—all of which can feed into informing and improving future assessments and our collective prospects for sustainability.

## 8) Early Process Initiation

Legislated assessment requirements are meant to foster planning and decision making that take all key public interest considerations into account. The requirements are most effective if the public interest considerations are incorporated from the initial stages of thinking about a project or regional/strategic undertaking. Early initiation of an assessment process is essential to ensuring that potential proponents and other participants understand their requirements from the outset and together engage in deliberations and consultations when initial purposes, issues, and options are being identified, well before selecting among alternatives for the undertaking. Mechanisms for early initiation include pre-identification of undertakings subject to assessment, early public notice, and delineation of early process steps. Provisions should be in place for multi-interest consultation on matters such as key concerns and opportunities; desired future objectives; priorities for assessment attention; sustainability-based criteria for evaluations; selection of an appropriate process stream; and continuing means of ensuring meaningful engagement of the public, relevant jurisdictions and experts, and other key players.[30] Early initiation also provides the time needed to discuss arrangements for interjurisdictional cooperation and/or collaboration, aiming to establish a smoothly coordinated,

---

& Diduck, "Public Participation in Canadian Environmental Assessment," above note 25; Gibson, Doelle & Sinclair, above note 5.

30   See chapters 8, 14, & 15.

comprehensive assessment process incorporating next-generation assessment standards.[31]

## 9) Rigorous and Credible Impact Assessments Focused on Cumulative and Interactive Effects and Uncertainties

Although assessments need to identify and evaluate the particular effects of proposed projects and regional/strategic initiatives, the effects that matter in the end are cumulative results of multiple interacting individual effects. Assessment regimes need to place cumulative effects (the combined effects of past, present, and future activities on natural and human systems) at the centre of impact assessment at both the project and regional/strategic levels.[32] A focus on cumulative effects, however, must be combined with recognition that these are effects on and in complex systems characterized by dynamic interactions at multiple scales. These systems are typically not well understood. Consequently, assessment regimes must be careful to respect and report the implications of uncertainties affecting impact predictions and grounds for confidence in proposed mitigation measures and other responses. Recognition of uncertainties and demands for rigour provide additional reasons to draw on the best, most independent, and otherwise impartial expertise from multiple sources of knowledge (including approaches to and areas of focus in modern science and Indigenous knowledge) and to favour precautionary approaches. Explicit justifications for selection among best practice assessment methods are also important. Finally, assessment regimes gain from multiple levels of assessment application. For example, findings at the regional/strategic level about potential cumulative effects and their implications, and about appropriate means

---

31    Theo Hacking, "The SDGs and the Sustainability Assessment of Private-Sector Projects: Theoretical Conceptualisation and Comparison with Current Practice Using the Case Study of the Asian Development Bank" (2019) 37:1 *Impact Assessment and Project Appraisal* 2; Gibson, Doelle & Sinclair, above note 5; Johnston, *Federal Environmental Assessment Reform Summit*, above note 7; Geoffrey McDonald & Lex Brown, "Going Beyond Environmental Impact Assessment: Environmental Input to Planning and Design" (1995) 15:6 *Environmental Impact Assessment Review* 483.

32    Sinclair, Doelle & Duinker, above note 12. See also chapters 11 and 17.

of avoiding adverse cumulative effects and enhancing positive ones, should make project-level assessments more efficient and effective.[33]

## 10) Comparative Evaluation of Potentially Reasonable Alternatives, Including the Null Option

To encourage design and delivery of best options in the lasting public interest, assessment regimes must require identification and comparison of fundamentally different approaches (alternatives to) as well as different design options (alternative means) for serving the public interest.[34] In both project- and regional/strategic-level assessments, the comparative evaluation of potentially reasonable options should serve as the means of identifying the best option to propose. Accordingly, the comparative evaluation must apply carefully specified sustainability-based public interest criteria and include identification and avoidance or minimization of trade-offs.[35] The range of potentially reasonable alternatives may vary between public and private sector proponents at the project level. Assessments at the regional/strategic level are likely to be needed in cases where project-level assessments lack the capacity to consider broader options that may contribute more positively to the lasting public interest. In all cases, the alternatives considered must include the option of not proceeding with the proposed, or any alternative, initiative.

---

33 See, for example, Joe Ravetz, "Integrated Assessment for Sustainability Appraisal in Cities and Regions" (2000) 21:1 *Environmental Impact Assessment Review* 31; Peter N Duinker & Lorne A Greig, "Scenario Analysis in Environmental Impact Assessment: Improving Explorations of the Future" (2007) 27:3 *Environmental Impact Assessment Review* 206; Gibson, Doelle & Sinclair, above note 5; Sinclair & Diduck, "Reconceptualizing Public Participation," above note 25, Sinclair & Diduck, "Public Participation in Canadian Environmental Assessment," above note 25.

34 See, for example, Gibson et al, *Sustainability Assessment*, above note 6; Angus Morrison-Saunders & Jenny Pope, "Conceptualising and Managing Trade-offs in Sustainability Assessment (2013) 38:2 *Environmental Impact Assessment Review* 54; Samuel Hayes & Thomas B Fischer, "Setting and Measuring Objectives in Sustainability Assessment" in Angus Morrison-Saunders, Jenny Pope & Alan Bond, eds, *Handbook of Sustainability Assessment* (Camberley, UK: Edward Elgar, 2015) 265; Gibson, Doelle & Sinclair, above note 5; Gibson, above note 11.

35 See Section C(1). See also Chapter 14.

## 11) Credible, Accountable, and Authoritative Decision Making for Assessed Undertakings, Policy Making, and Other Core Initiatives Under the Act

To be enforceable and effective, assessment regime decisions must rest on law-based authority. No less crucial, however, are credibility and accountability. Assessment decisions have important consequences for many interests. Often, they are controversial. They are most likely to spur conflict when the decision-making process is not transparent and places few constraints on the discretion of decision makers.[36] Better and more broadly accepted decision making depends on common recognition that the assessment process and decisions are open, fair, well-informed, and clearly justified.[37] These qualities, in turn, depend on law that ensures access to information and participative deliberations and clarity on how the information is gathered, analyzed, and used by decision makers. As well, the law must establish arm's-length administration, mobilize impartial expertise, and require published analyses of options and justification of decisions in light of explicit sustainability-based criteria and trade-off rules. Parallel characteristics are needed for other assessment regime components, including development of regulations and policies, decision making on application of or exemption from assessment requirements, and negotiation of interjurisdictional agreements. Ultimate decision making should be assigned to an elected authority using the information base (assessment analyses, conclusions, and recommended decisions and conditions, etc.) prepared by an arm's-length assessment body. Finally, the law should provide recourse to challenge decisions when their justifiability is in doubt. This could be done through judicial review, but the opportunity to appeal to an administrative tribunal tasked with ensuring consistent and effective application of legislative provisions could be more desirable. These components are a critical package, especially for assessments serving the long-term public interest in face of a persistent

---

36   Andrew John Sinclair & Meinhard Doelle, "Environmental Assessment in Canada: Encouraging Decisions for Sustainability" in Bruce Mitchell, ed, *Resource and Environmental Management in Canada: Addressing Conflict and Uncertainty*, 5th ed (Toronto: Oxford University Press, 2015) 11.

37   See Chapter 19.

tradition of minimally transparent political discretion in assessment processes and decision making.[38]

## 12) Follow-Up of Compliance with Conditions, Effect Predictions, and Effective Response to Monitoring Findings

Assessment law must require and facilitate monitoring of effects and enforcement of compliance with decision conditions for approved undertakings.[39] Especially for sustainability purposes in conditions of complexity and uncertainty, the law must anticipate needs for timely response to unexpected emerging problems and opportunities, favour adaptable projects and regional/strategic undertakings, and establish arrangements for ongoing governance covering the implementation of decisions. For both effects monitoring and compliance enforcement, the law must enable clear assignment of powers and responsibilities. Follow-up effects monitoring must include comparison of actual and predicted effects and reporting on the effectiveness of mitigation and enhancement measures and facilitate an effective response to monitoring findings. Compliance follow-up must cover proponent commitments as well as the terms and conditions of approvals and must be supported with suitable sanctions and other tools for enforcement action.[40] Learning through attention to uncertainties, adaptive design, and follow-up monitoring is particularly important for supporting adaptive management, making better future predictions, and improving regime design. More broadly, the law should provide for regular independent review and revision of follow-up programs and associated methods, as well as ongoing monitoring of how the overall assessment

---

38  William R Sheate, "Purposes, Paradigms and Pressure Groups: Accountability and Sustainability in EU Environmental Assessment, 1985–2010" (2012) 33:1 *Environmental Impact Assessment Review* 9; Gibson, Doelle & Sinclair, above note 5; Johnston, *Federal Environmental Assessment Reform Summit*, above note 7.

39  See Chapter 16.

40  Carol A Hunsberger, Robert B Gibson & Susan K Wismer, "Citizen Involvement in Sustainability-Centred Environmental Assessment Follow-up" (2005) 25:3 *Environmental Impact Assessment Review* 609; Rose Marshall, Jos Arts & Angus Morrison-Saunders, "International Principles for Best Practice EIA Follow-up" (2005) 23:3 *Impact Assessment and Project Appraisal* 175; Angus Morrison-Saunders et al, "Towards Sustainability Assessment Follow-up" (2014) 45 *Environmental Impact Assessment Review* 38; Johnston, *Federal Environmental Assessment Reform Summit*, above note 7; Gibson, Doelle & Sinclair, above note 5.

regime performs, including the strengths and deficiencies of impact predictions, public engagement efforts, trade-off avoidance, compliance, and effects monitoring.[41]

## 13)  Independent and Impartial Implementation and Administration

To build integrity and trust in assessment processes, assessment law must ensure that assessments are administered by an impartial, arm's-length body.[42] This is especially important given the assessment tradition of leaving important elements of the process in the hands of proponents and the long record of political controversies surrounding assessment decision making. As a public agency in the governance system, the administrative body must be designed, located, and empowered to be an independent and impartial servant of the long-term public interest, insulated to the extent possible from political influence, which tends to favour immediate partisan priorities. Impartiality is also enhanced by consistent application of explicit sustainability-based criteria, published reasons for administrative and review process decisions, and the other credibility and accountability steps discussed above. The need for independent legitimacy is particularly obvious in deliberations on which projects and regional/strategic undertakings merit assessment and in key elements of individual assessments. These elements include ensuring well-informed critique and impartial review of proposals and supporting documentation from proponents, facilitating meaningful engagement of other participants, tapping into independent expertise, preparing analyses in light of key decision considerations, drafting recommendations for decision makers, and establishing effective monitoring of effects and compliance.[43] However, arm's length impartiality is no less important in cross-cutting work developing regulatory and policy guidance and criteria, supervising overall process review, encouraging full-process learning, and facilitating interjurisdictional collaboration.[44] The administrative body would also need to cooperate in regular independent reviews of assessment successes and limitations,

---

41    See chapters 10, 13, 14, & 15.

42    Gibson, Doelle & Sinclair, above note 5; Johnston, *Federal Environmental Assessment Reform Summit*, above note 7.

43    See chapters 15, 16, 19, and 21.

44    See chapters 8 and 22.

looking at the strengths and deficiencies of impact predictions, public engagement, trade-off avoidance, and compliance and effects monitoring.

### 14) Effective, Efficient, and Fair Process

Assessment regime design has often been presented as a matter of selecting between effectiveness and efficiencies — in other words, between processes that are thorough and participative and ones that feature timely and certain results. The reality, however, is that effectiveness and efficiency are interdependent. The basic test of efficiency is how few resources need to be expended to deliver the desired effective result. Also, lasting effectiveness depends on the credibility of processes that are evidently both efficient and fair, as well as strong in the handling of other substantive considerations. In assessment regimes, the best means of combining effectiveness, efficiency, and fairness are distributed throughout the components discussed above and the chapters that follow. Key elements include an emphasis on early initiation of assessment deliberations, clarity, and consistency in core process requirements while facilitating flexibility of application in different contexts (e.g., different process streams, generic but also context-specified sustainability-based criteria and trade-off rules, a range of approaches to ensuring meaningful public participation, and defined but adjustable timelines) and full-process learning to build and mobilize additional capacities while applying lessons from experience. Especially with Canada's constitutional complexities, careful facilitation of interjurisdictional collaboration[45] is crucial, as is coordination with planning and regulatory bodies beyond the assessment process.[46]

## D.  THE NEXT-GENERATION ASSESSMENT FRAMEWORK, THE FEDERAL ASSESSMENT REFORM PROCESS, AND THE *IAA*

The *IAA* is the product of a reform process spurred by long-standing concerns about federal assessment limitations and a set of high-profile conflicts centred on major project assessments under the previous

---

45  See Chapter 8.
46  *Building Common Ground*, above note 25.

federal law, the *Canadian Environmental Assessment Act, 2012*.[47] The earliest stages of the reform process featured recognition of several next-generation assessment considerations, including the need to gain credibility for the assessment process and resulting decisions.[48] Many core next-generation themes were also picked up by the Expert Panel for the Review of Environmental Assessment Processes in its 2017 report,[49] including:

- an expanded project list combined with a formal petition process for designation of projects not listed
- an assessment process to be run by an independent agency with a mandate to focus on cooperation and consensus
- cooperative assessments with the active engagement of all affected jurisdictions as the primary tool for harmonization and jurisdictional cooperation, with substitution only under strict conditions
- a tiered approach to regional, strategic, and project assessments, where project assessments are informed by higher-tier assessments
- a broad sustainability-based scope of assessment that includes all impacts and benefits of proposed projects
- meaningful public participation through early and ongoing opportunities to engage and full access to all relevant information, including an open and searchable database for all data collected from current and past assessments
- a focus on learning throughout the assessment process
- an approach to the engagement of Indigenous peoples in the assessment process and project decisions that is consistent with Canada's constitutional obligations and its commitment to the *United Nations Declaration on the Rights of Indigenous Peoples (UNDRIP)*[50]

---

47   SC 2012, c 19, s 52.

48   See Chapter 4. See also Prime Minister Justin Trudeau to Catherine McKenna, Minister of Environment and Climate Change, "Minister of Environment and Climate Change Mandate Letter" (12 November 2015), online: *Office of the Prime Minister* https://pm.gc.ca/en/mandate-letters/2015/11/12/archived-minister-environment-and-climate-change-mandate-letter; *Building Common Ground*, above note 25 at Annex 1.

49   *Building Common Ground*, above note 25.

50   GA Res 61/295, UNGAOR, 61st Sess, UN Doc A/RES/61/295 (13 September 2007).

- a strengthened follow-up process, including improved transparency, coordination, and accountability[51]

As noted in the introduction to this chapter, various versions of the next-generation assessment framework outlined here were presented and applied during the deliberations leading to the passage of the *IAA* and continue to inform discussions on aspects of implementation.[52]

The extent to which next-generation principles and components were incorporated in the law as passed and in the early regulatory direction and policy guidance under the Act will be revealed in the following chapters. Clearly, however, transition to next-generation assessment in Canada is still a work in progress. Also, much of the character and effectiveness of the Act and implementation depend on regulations, policies, and gradually established customary institutional practice, only some of which are now in place and all of which will be subject to revision in light of experience and evolving circumstances.

---

51  *Building Common Ground*, above note 25.
52  Johnston, *Federal Environmental Assessment Reform Summit*, above note 7; *Building Common Ground*, above note 25.

# CHAPTER 3

# An Overview of the *Impact Assessment Act*

*Meinhard Doelle and A John Sinclair*

## A.  INTRODUCTION

As discussed in the preceding chapters, the federal legislation that underpins impact assessment (IA) in Canada has continued to evolve and most recently has taken the form of the *Impact Assessment Act (IAA).*[1] The reform process that led to the enactment of the *IAA* is discussed in more detail in Chapter 4. The process started with mandate letters from Prime Minister Justin Trudeau to his new Cabinet in 2015.[2] In 2016, the minister of environment and climate change struck the Multi-Interest Advisory Committee, composed of representatives from Indigenous, industry, and environmental non-governmental organizations, to advise her and the Canadian Environmental Assessment Agency on the new Act. The minister then established the four-person Expert Panel for the Review of Environmental Assessment Processes (Expert Panel) to consult the public and report on how to restore public trust in IA and

---

1    SC 2019, c 28, s 1.

2    See, for example, Prime Minister Justin Trudeau to Catherine McKenna, Minister of Environment and Climate Change, "Minister of Environment and Climate Change Mandate Letter" (12 November 2015), online: *Office of the Prime Minister* https://pm.gc.ca/en/mandate-letters/2015/11/12/archived-minister-environment-and-climate-change-mandate-letter.

otherwise meet the stated goals of the reform effort. The government followed the Panel's 2017 report with a discussion paper in June 2017.[3]

The formal legislative process started in the fall of 2017 with a memorandum to Cabinet seeking approval to draft new legislation. Once the bill was introduced in February 2018, it was referred to public hearings held by the House of Commons Standing Committee on Environment and Sustainable Development, made up of members of Parliament from all parties. The bill passed third reading in June 2018 and was sent to the Senate for review and approval. The Senate Standing Committee on Energy, the Environment and Natural Resources held public hearings in early 2019 and proposed further amendments, many of which would have weakened the bill and were rejected by the House of Commons. The government passed the bill just before the end of the last Parliamentary session on June 21, before the fall 2019 federal election. The Act came into force in August 2019 along with regulations critical for its implementation.

The purpose of this chapter is to offer a high-level overview of the *IAA*. Many elements of the Act are considered in detail in Part II of this book. Here we offer an overview of the key components of the *IAA*, organized around five key elements of IA regime design: triggering the assessment process, scoping, process options and design, decision making, and post-decision follow-up.[4] It is important to note at the outset that although the focus in this chapter is on the assessment process for designated projects, the Act includes other important processes that are considered in some detail in Part II of the book. A separate part of the Act deals with projects on federal lands and outside Canada. In addition, there are separate provisions for regional and strategic assessments.[5]

---

3   Canada, Environment and Climate Change Canada, *Environmental and Regulatory Reviews: Discussion Paper*, (Ottawa: Environment and Climate Change Canada, June 2017), online: *Government of Canada* www.canada.ca/en/services/environment/conservation/assessments/environmental-reviews/share-your-views/proposed-approach/discussion-paper.html.

4   See Meinhard Doelle, *The Federal Environmental Assessment Process: A Guide and Critique* (Markham, ON: LexisNexis Canada, 2008); Kevin Hanna, ed, *Environmental Impact Assessment: Practice and Participation*, 3d ed (Don Mills, ON: Oxford University Press, 2016) at Part II; Bram Noble, *Environmental Impact Assessment: A Guide to Principles and Practice*, 3d ed (Don Mills, ON: Oxford University Press, 2015).

5   The requirements for projects on federal lands and projects outside Canada are discussed in detail in Chapter 18, and separate processes for regional and strategic assessments are considered in chapters 11 and 17.

Figure 3.1 highlights the key steps in the assessment process for designated projects under the *IAA*. This chapter reviews the requirements under the *IAA* for each of the major steps in the process: triggers for the assessment process; the planning process and scoping; process options and design; multi-jurisdictional coordination; project decision making; and post-approval monitoring, follow-up, and compliance.

**Figure 3.1  The IA Process for Designated Projects at a Glance**

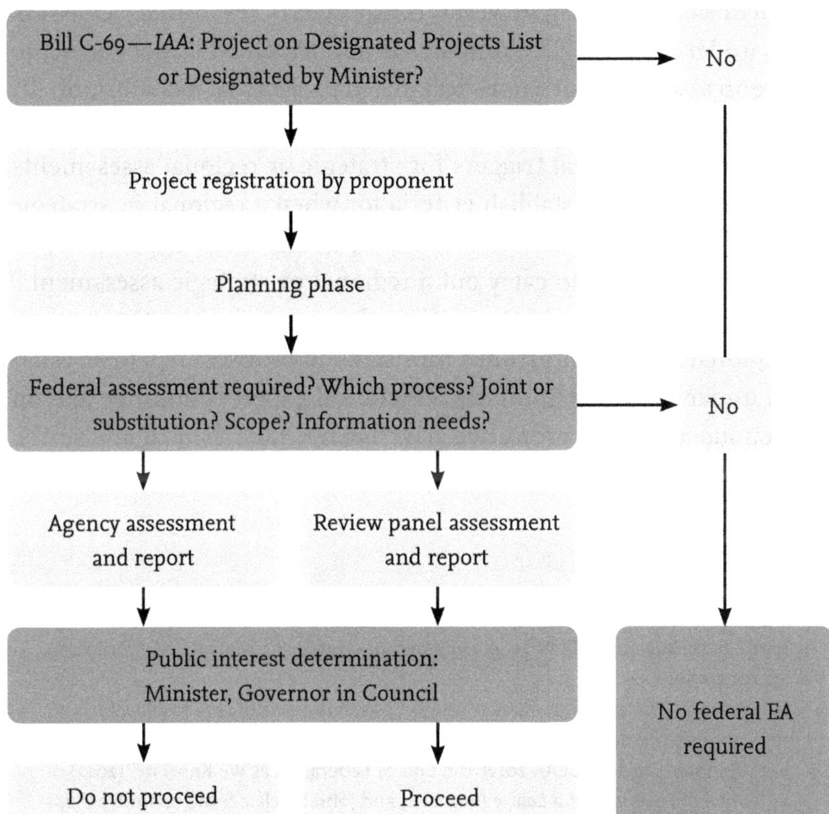


## B.  TRIGGERS AND THE APPLICATION OF THE ASSESSMENT PROCESS

At the core of the triggering process for project assessments is a designated projects list established in regulation.[6] The regulation was passed in time for the coming into force of the *IAA* in August 2019

---

6    The triggering process is considered in more detail in Chapter 7.

along with other key regulations needed to operationalize the Act.[7] The initial expectation had been that the designated projects list would be expanded from the *Canadian Environmental Assessment Act, 2012* (*CEAA 2012*)[8] to increase the number of assessments carried out under the *IAA*. This expectation resulted in part from criticisms of the drastic reduction in federal assessments from the *Canadian Environmental Assessment Act* (*CEAA 1995*)[9] to *CEAA 2012*, the Expert Panel recommendations, and the commitment to re-establish trust in the federal assessment process.[10] The finalized project list, however, is expected to result in fewer assessments under the *IAA*.[11] The minister is not permitted under the Act to require an assessment of a non-designated project that has substantially begun or a project that has already received federal approval.[12]

There are no formal triggers for strategic or regional assessments, and the Act does not establish criteria for when a regional or strategic assessment may be warranted. There is, however, an opportunity to petition the minister to carry out a regional or strategic assessment.[13] In addition, the minister is to receive advice on priorities for strategic and regional assessments from a minister's advisory council to be established under the *IAA*.[14] Similarly, a technical expert committee and an Indigenous advisory committee have been established to advise the Impact Assessment Agency of Canada (the Agency) on a range of matters,

---

7   *Designated Classes of Projects Order*, SOR/2019-323; *Information and Management of Time Limits Regulations*, SOR/2019-283; *Physical Activities Regulations*, SOR/2019-285.

8   SC 2012, c 19, s 52.

9   SC 1992, c 37. The entry into force of the Act was delayed until 1995 to allow for key regulations to be developed and passed.

10   See Meinhard Doelle, "CEAA 2012: The End of Federal EA as We Know It?" (2012) 24 *Journal of Environmental Law & Practice* 1, and John Sinclair & Meinhard Doelle, "Environmental Assessment in Canada: Encouraging Decisions for Sustainability" in Bruce Mitchell, ed, *Resource and Environmental Management in Canada: Addressing Conflict and Uncertainty*, 5th ed (Toronto: Oxford University Press, 2015) 11.

11   *IAA*, above note 1, s 9(1). For a more detailed discussion of the triggering provisions of the *IAA*, see Chapter 7. At the time of writing, Coalspur Mines Limited, a proponent of the Vista coal mine in Alberta, had indicated its intention to test this provision in court in relation to a decision by the minister to require an assessment of its proposed expansion of the Vista coal mine.

12   *Ibid*, s 9(7).

13   *Ibid*, s 97(1).

14   *Ibid*, s 117(1).

including strategic and regional assessments.[15] Ultimately, the initiation of regional or strategic assessments is at the discretion of the minister.[16]

For projects on federal lands or outside Canada that are not on the designated projects list, there is no formal triggering mechanism leading to an established assessment process. As explored in Chapter 18, the *IAA* instead establishes a general obligation on federal decision makers to consider whether proposed projects on federal lands and outside Canada are likely to cause significant adverse effects, and, if so, whether those effects are justified in the circumstances. This triggering process for federal projects is similar to *CEAA 1995*, which required an assessment of projects on federal lands, projects using federal funds, and projects proposed by federal authorities. The term *trigger* may be a bit misleading, however, because what is triggered is not a process but a decision.[17]

## C.  THE PLANNING PROCESS AND SCOPING

The planning phase for project assessments is among the *IAA*'s innovations.[18] The planning phase marks the beginning of the assessment process. It starts with an initial project description prepared by the proponent in accordance with requirements set out in regulations. The timing of the initiation is left to the discretion of the proponent. The goals of the planning phase are to decide whether an assessment is required; to coordinate with interested Indigenous communities, provinces, territories, and municipalities; to decide which process to use; and to determine the information needs of the assessment.

Under section 11, the public is to have an opportunity to participate "meaningfully" in the planning process, which will be led by the Agency established under the *IAA*. This responsibility to engage with the public is in addition to the Agency's obligation to reach out to Indigenous communities and other jurisdictions to invite them to participate in the planning stage.[19] The Act incorporates the principle of meaningful public participation throughout the process, including in the planning

---

15    *Ibid*, ss 157(1) and 158(1).

16    *Ibid*, ss 92 and 95(1).

17    See Chapter 18 for a detailed description and assessment of the provisions dealing with projects on federal lands and outside Canada.

18    *IAA*, above note 1, ss 10–20.

19    *Ibid*, s 12.

phase. The details on how to make public participation meaningful within the 180-day time limit are left to policy and guidance. In a departure from past practice, there is a requirement to include all key stages of the assessment in participant funding programs to be established for each project.[20]

The planning phase, including the decision whether to require an assessment, is to be completed within 180 days of commencement, a time limit that can be extended by up to 90 days.[21] Within this time frame, the Agency has to determine the information and reports required in preparation for the assessment. Decisions on whether to carry out a standard assessment under the supervision of the Agency or a review panel are required to be made within forty-five days of the commencement of the assessment.[22]

Determination of the scope of the assessment is to start during the planning process. During this initial stage, however, the focus is on the information to be collected and provided by the proponent, resulting in Tailored Impact Statement Guidelines (TIS Guidelines) to be issued on the basis of which the proponent can put together its IA report. It is less clear whether the scoping process will be concluded during the planning phase or whether it will continue after the guidelines are issued to the proponent. The scoping process is to start with the Agency proposing a list of issues, based on input from the public and any jurisdiction the Agency has consulted with. The proponent then responds with an indication of the information it intends to provide in response to the issues that have been identified. The scope of these factors is ultimately to be determined by the Agency.[23]

Importantly, the scope of the assessment under section 22 has been expanded from *CEAA* 2012 to include a much broader range of biophysical, social, cultural, health, and economic impacts. Among the notable elements are impacts on Indigenous communities and Indigenous rights, the need for and purpose of the project, alternative means and some alternatives to the project, the project's contribution to sustainability, the results of regional and strategic assessments, impacts on

---

20   *Ibid*, s 75. See Chapter 15.

21   *Ibid*, ss 18(1) and (3).

22   *Ibid*, s 36(1).

23   *Ibid*.

the intersection of sex and gender with other identity factors, and the impact of the project on Canada's environmental obligations and climate change commitments.[24] It is unclear whether there will be a formal scoping determination or determinations on information needs beyond the development of the TIS Guidelines to be issued to the proponent.

Important new requirements are imposed during the planning phase. A plan for undertaking meaningful public participation to guide the rest of the assessment process must be developed by the Agency. If other provincial or territorial jurisdictions are parties to the process, discussions and a decision on how to coordinate and conduct a collaborative assessment need to take place and an IA cooperation plan is to be developed. A plan for Indigenous involvement and co-governance and a permitting plan must also be developed.[25]

At the conclusion of the planning phase, the Agency determines whether to proceed with an assessment or whether the project can move through the regulatory process without an assessment. The existence and results of a regional or strategic assessment can be considered in making this determination, a rare instance of direction in the Act related to the use of the results of strategic and regional assessments.[26] The decision whether to refer the project to a review panel is a separate decision made by the minister after the Agency decides to proceed with an assessment. This decision has to be made within forty-five days of the notice of commencement.[27] The minister can also decide at the end of the planning stage to provide written notice to the proponent that the project will be rejected without an assessment where the minister determines that the project will cause unacceptable environmental effects within federal jurisdiction or that a federal authority has advised that it will not exercise a statutory power needed for the project to proceed.[28]

---

24 *Ibid*, s 22(1). For more guidance on taking into account each outlined factor, see also Impact Assessment Agency of Canada, "Tailored Impact Statement Guidelines Template for Designated Projects Subject to the Impact Assessment Act," online: https://perma.cc/LM5Q-UMWY ["TIS Guidelines"].

25 *IAA*, above note 1, ss 2, 11, & 12. See also ss 21, 22(n), (o), (q), & (r). Section 2 defines *jurisdiction*.

26 *Ibid*, s 16(2)(e).

27 *Ibid*, s 36(1).

28 *Ibid*, 17(1).

## D. PROCESS OPTIONS AND DESIGN

In this section, we briefly review the two main process options under the *IAA* for designated projects that have gone through the planning stage and are now ready to commence with the assessment phase. We start with what has been referred to as the standard assessment process, an assessment led by the Agency. This is followed by an overview of the main alternative, an assessment led by a review panel.

### 1) The Standard Assessment Process

The standard assessment process is carried out by the Agency. The key pieces of information gathered to start the assessment are the project description from the planning phase, information provided by the proponent as specified in the TIS Guidelines developed during the planning phase, and information provided by government expert departments and agencies. This will, of course, be supplemented by information provided by intervenors and others during the course of the assessment process.

The details of the process will have been worked out during the course of the planning phase, including the engagement of other jurisdictions, Indigenous communities and governments, and the general public. The main process requirements set out in the Act are public notice obligations and timelines for completing specific steps in the process.[29] The Agency is given 300 days to complete a standard environmental assessment. Time spent by the proponent to fulfill its obligations can be excluded from the 300 days through the suspension of time, although the use of this power can be restricted through regulations.[30] No timelines are imposed on proponents for their role in the process.

Given the broad range of factors to be considered under section 22, it is reasonable to expect that the Agency will play a central role in the assessment phase of the process, that the proponent will play a supporting role, and that government departments and agencies will play an increasingly important role as sources of information on the much broader scope of the assessments. The *IAA* does not use the term

---

29   *Ibid*, ss 24–30.
30   *Ibid*, s 28(2).

*impact statement.* From the guidance issued, however, it appears that the proponent will still be expected to prepare some version of an impact statement in line with the TIS Guidelines.[31]

Beyond identifying the proponent's responsibility to provide information under section 19 and a general responsibility for federal authorities with expertise to assist, the Act does not delineate the allocation of responsibility for the gathering of the information needed. This is particularly surprising in light of the much broader scope of the assessment.[32] Nor is the *IAA* clear about the impact of information gathering during the assessment phase on the time limits imposed other than to aim to have as much of the information as possible gathered before the start of the assessment phase.

Much of the new broader scope of a particular assessment may be outside the expertise of some proponents. There is an opportunity to shift responsibility for important elements of an assessment, such as the consideration of societal need for assessment, purpose and rationale of the project, alternatives, and cumulative effects, away from proponents toward appropriate expert departments and agencies. It will be up to the Agency, through general guidance and informed by the planning phase on a project-by-project basis, to provide appropriate direction on this allocation of responsibility.

Beyond the section 22 factors and notice requirements and timelines, the *IAA* provides limited direction on the process to be followed. In particular, there is considerable flexibility with respect to the forms and extent of public engagement in the standard assessment process. The details are not set out in the Act but rather are to be worked out in the planning phase. Similarly, there is limited direction in the *IAA* on the content of the assessment report other than that it needs to identify adverse effects within federal jurisdiction, report on the use of Indigenous knowledge, and summarize comments received from the public.[33]

---

31  *Ibid,* s 19, and "TIS Guidelines," above note 24; see also Impact Assessment Agency of Canada, "Practitioner's Guide to Federal Impact Assessments Under the Impact Assessment Act" (2019), online: *Government of Canada* www.canada.ca/en/impact-assessment-agency/services/policy-guidance/practitioners-guide-impact-assessment-act.html for more general guidelines on the process.

32  See Chapter 9. One avenue for addressing this might be memoranda of understanding being negotiated with key federal departments on their role in the assessment process.

33  *IAA,* above note 1, s 28(3).

### 2) The Panel Review Process

The *IAA* continues the recent trend toward strict timelines to decide whether to proceed with a panel review and for carrying out such a review. The decision whether to proceed to a panel is to be made within forty-five days of the notice of commencement.[34] The decision must be based on the potential for adverse effects on areas of federal jurisdiction, public concern, opportunities for collaboration with other jurisdictions, and any impact on the rights of Indigenous peoples. Subject to these parameters, the decision is discretionary and left in the hands of the minister.[35] Terms of reference are to be established within forty-five days of the decision to refer an assessment to a panel.

Similar to the TIS Guidelines issued by the Agency in the case of the standard assessment process, the minister identifies the information to be gathered by the proponent prior to the commencement of the assessment and before the formal establishment of the panel.[36] The *IAA* offers very limited guidance on the content of the terms of reference or the process to be followed. The Act does set out what has to be included in the review panel's final report. However, the requirements do not offer much clarity on the role of the panel report in informing the decision-making factors in section 63 or the public interest determination.[37]

The timeline for completing the panel review process has been shortened from two years to 600 days compared to *CEAA 2012*, although, under the *IAA*, the proponent has to complete its impact statement before the start of the review process.[38] The assessment can be as short as 300 days for projects involving certain life-cycle energy regulators under section 37.1(1). Such energy projects cannot proceed by way of a standard assessment but rather have to be carried out by a panel. Time taken up by the proponent in responding to information requests after the impact statement is filed will no longer automatically be subtracted from the panel's time, potentially further shortening the timelines for

---

34    *Ibid*, s 36(1).

35    *Ibid*, ss 36(1)–(2).

36    *Ibid*, s 38.

37    Section 51 provides a list of general duties of the panel, including obligations to ensure a transparent process, to conduct hearings, and to prepare a report.

38    *IAA*, above note 1, s 37(2).

panel reviews compared to *CEAA 2012*.[39] The discretion to suspend time rests with the Agency, and limited discretion rests with the minister to extend time limits.[40] Panels do not have the power to suspend or extend time.

There is no legislative clarity on what happens if a panel, in carrying out its work after the impact statement is completed, determines that additional information is required either from the proponent, a federal agency, or some other source. As noted above, there are only limited opportunities to suspend time. The Cabinet has broader powers to extend the timelines during the course of a panel review, but it remains to be seen whether this is a practical option in the case of a panel faced with delays in getting the information it needs.[41]

Section 56 allows the minister to seek additional information from the proponent at the conclusion of the panel review process to inform its conclusion on whether the project is in the public interest. Any information gathered at this stage in the process would not be available to the panel and would therefore not be subject to the same level of public and independent scrutiny.

## E.  MULTI-JURISDICTIONAL COORDINATION

As explored in detail in Chapter 8, jurisdictional coordination can take many forms, from joint assessments to delegation and substitution. Compared to *CEAA 2012*, there is a notable difference in tone and preference in favour of cooperation under the *IAA*, but the main substantive change is the elimination of equivalency, which allowed the full delegation of both process and decision to another authority.[42] Otherwise, the focus on cooperation, although reflected in the purposes of the Act, is dependent largely on the exercise of ministerial discretion.

The discretion to delegate is broad, whereas the discretion to substitute is subject to more specific limitations under section 33(1). The Agency's discretion in the planning stage of the process not to require an assessment can also be used to avoid any federal assessment in situations where other jurisdictions are carrying out their own assessment. In such

---

39    *Ibid*, s 37.1(1).
40    *Ibid*, ss 37.1(3) and 37(3).
41    *Ibid*, s 37(4).
42    See Chapter 8.

a case, there would not be a federal assessment decision, similar in terms of the ultimate effect to the equivalency provisions under *CEAA 2012*.

For panel reviews, the effort to coordinate with other affected jurisdictions is focused on joint assessments in the *IAA*. This includes the continuation of the long tradition of carrying out joint panel reviews with provinces. The *IAA* includes a new variation on the long-standing effort to identify an appropriate role for energy regulators in the assessment process. The focus is on the new Canadian Energy Regulator (the CER, replacing the National Energy Board [NEB]), as well as the Canada Nuclear Safety Commission (CNSC) and the Nova Scotia and Newfoundland offshore petroleum boards, all energy regulators.[43]

With respect to these four energy regulators, special rules apply to what are being termed integrated panel reviews in the case of projects they regulate.[44] The energy regulators are expected to support the IA process and will be directly involved in it. Most importantly, the Act calls for at least some, but not a majority, of the panel members to be appointed from these energy regulators when the project is one that they regulate. This is a significant change as energy regulators previously managed their own panel processes. The panels, at least in the case of some of the regulators, are authorized to exercise powers of the energy regulator, suggesting that the panels will have a dual regulatory and assessment function, similar to joint *CEAA*/NEB panels of the past. They can be chaired by energy regulator appointments to the panel.[45]

The Act calls for all projects on the designated projects list that are regulated by one of the four energy regulators to be assessed by way of a review panel (assuming that the projects are assessed at all). In other words, the standard Agency assessment option has been eliminated for these energy projects. It is unclear what effect these provisions have had on which regulated projects were listed on the designated projects list. It would be fair to expect that smaller energy projects that were considered not to warrant a panel review were taken off the list.[46]

The *IAA* treats the Nova Scotia and Newfoundland offshore petroleum boards in a manner similar to the CER and the CNSC. The main

---

43  *IAA*, above note 1, ss 13(2), 43–51, 58(3), 61, and 67.

44  See Chapter 8 for a more detailed discussion of the role of these energy regulators in the federal assessment process, including the role of these integrated panel reviews.

45  *IAA*, above note 1, ss 44(1) and 47(1).

46  *Ibid*, s 16(1).

difference is that in cases of panel reviews involving the offshore boards, the panels are to consist of five panel members, two of whom are to be appointed from a roster from the boards. The effect appears to be similar: to carry out a panel review that has a significant but not a majority presence from the regulator. The ultimate question is what effect these alterations to the panel review process involving energy regulators will have on the quality and focus of the process and its ability to consider alternatives and provide an appropriate impartial basis for conclusions on the section 63 factors and the "public interest" determination.[47]

## F.  PROJECT DECISION MAKING

For project assessments, the ultimate decision to be made is whether "a proposed project is in the public interest" in light of the project's effects on areas of federal jurisdiction.[48] The new decision-making process requires the identification of effects on areas of federal jurisdiction and then considers whether the project is in the public interest in light of the factors set out in section 63. The minister either makes this decision or makes a recommendation to Cabinet, with Cabinet then making the ultimate decision on whether a project is in the public interest. The public interest determination is to be based on the assessment report filed by the Agency or a review panel and is to consider the factors set out in section 63, which include the following:

- the extent to which adverse effects on areas of federal jurisdiction are significant
- the implementation of mitigation measures (defined to include compensation)
- impacts on Indigenous communities and Indigenous rights
- impacts on Canada's environmental obligations and climate commitments
- the extent to which the project contributes to sustainability

The step of identifying effects on areas of federal jurisdiction appears designed not to replace the significance finding under *CEAA 2012* but rather to clarify the basis for federal jurisdiction to make a project decision. There is no legislative direction on the scale of the impact

47    *Ibid*, ss 60–63.
48    *Ibid*, ss 60(1), 62, & 63.

on an area of federal jurisdiction that will enable decision makers to consider the public interest and the broader effects of the project. But it seems clear that if the determination is made that there is an absence of impacts on areas of federal jurisdiction, the broader impacts and benefits will not be relevant, and the proposed project will be given the green light under the *IAA* and can proceed to applicable regulatory processes. The term *significant* was reintroduced by the Senate, but it is unclear from the legislation exactly what role it will play in federal assessments going forward.[49]

The decision maker, whether it is the minister or Cabinet, has to give reasons for the decision in a manner that demonstrates that the decision is based on the assessment report by a panel or the Agency (which in turn has to consider the factors in section 22).[50] The reasons have to demonstrate that the factors in section 63 were considered in making the public interest determination. There is no direction on the level of detail to be provided in the reasons or the underlying analysis for determining, for example, whether a project makes a net contribution to sustainability or contributes to or hinders Canada's ability to meet its climate commitments. There is no legislative opportunity to appeal or otherwise review the project decision or its basis, leaving judicial review as the only avenue.[51]

The final project decision must be published in the form of a decision statement.[52] The *IAA* provides for the decision statement, but not the underlying decision, to be amended.[53] There is no explicit link to monitoring and follow-up, such as the ability or responsibility to adjust terms and conditions if mitigation measures turn out to be ineffective or predictions made during the course of the assessment turn out to be wrong. Although this connection is not made explicit in the *IAA*, it may very well be the intention to connect follow-up monitoring with the power to amend terms and conditions. If the project is approved, the decision has to include a time period within which the proponent has to commence with the project, after which the approval expires.[54]

---

49    *Ibid*, ss 60–63.
50    See, for example, *ibid*, s 65(2).
51    See Chapter 19.
52    IAA, above note 1, s 65(1).
53    *Ibid*, s 68(1).
54    *Ibid*, ss 70(1)–(3).

## G.  POST-APPROVAL MONITORING, FOLLOW-UP, AND COMPLIANCE

The final element of the assessment process under the *IAA* is the post-approval stage. Three key objectives of the post-approval stage are compliance with terms and conditions, verification of the accuracy of predictions made during the assessment, and assessment of the effectiveness of mitigation measures. Tools available for these three objectives include monitoring, reporting, enforcement, and adaptive management.[55] Another often neglected objective of the post-approval process of impact assessment is the importance of learning to improve the predictions and mitigation measures for future assessments.

Follow-up is defined in the *IAA* as including efforts to confirm the accuracy of the assessment and the effectiveness of mitigation, but not compliance. The requirements of the follow-up program have to be considered during the course of the assessment, as required under section 22 of the Act. Similarly, the final assessment report is required to include recommendations with respect to follow-up. The terms and conditions of approval are to include the requirements of the follow-up program and, as appropriate, an adaptive management plan. Participant funding is extended to the implementation of the follow-up program. The results of the follow-up program are to be made available on the public registry along with all relevant documents from the planning, information-gathering, assessment, and decision-making stages of the process.[56]

## H.  STRATEGIC AND REGIONAL ASSESSMENTS

The *IAA* allows the minister to initiate regional and strategic assessments under sections 92 and 95. As discussed in more detail in chapters 11 and 17, neither is defined, and neither is required to be conducted until the minister decides to initiate an assessment. Some regional assessment may be entirely on federal lands, but it can also be carried out in regions that are partly or completely outside federal lands. If the assessment includes areas outside federal lands, a cooperative approach is preferred under section 93, but a "federal only" regional assessment is an option. The assessments are to be carried out by the Agency or

---

55   *Ibid*, ss 64(4) and 156(2)(e); see Chapter 16.

56   *Ibid*, s 105(2)(e) contains the registry requirements for the follow-up program.

through a committee, with terms of reference to be established (or approved) by the minister.[57]

Strategic assessments can also be conducted either by the Agency or through a committee. The focus of strategic assessments is on federal policies, plans, and programs and their impact on project assessments and on classes of designated projects. Strategic assessments appear limited to the implication of policies, plans, and programs for project assessments rather than broader questions about the environmental or sustainability implications of policies, plans, or programs themselves.[58] There is no legislated link between project assessments and regional or strategic assessments in the *IAA*, although a regulation-making power suggests more detail to come, including circumstances under which a regional assessment may eliminate the requirement for project-level assessments.[59]

The future of the Cabinet directive on strategic environmental assessment is not addressed in the bill, but it is clear that it continues to apply.[60] Given that assessments under the directive are not covered under the *IAA*, the expectation is that it will continue as the main vehicle for strategic environmental assessments of proposed new federal policies, plans, and programs.

Consistent with other key steps in the process, the public is to have an opportunity to participate meaningfully in any regional or strategic assessment and to have access to relevant information.[61] No further details are provided in the *IAA* on the process or the outcome of a regional or strategic assessment. The final assessment report is to be filed with the minister, but there is no provision for decision making, and no legislated guidance on how the results of a regional or strategic

---

57    *Ibid*, ss 92 & 93.

58    *Ibid*, s 95.

59    *Ibid*, s 112(1)(a.3). See also chapters 11 and 17. For an early example of a regional assessment leading to project exemptions, see "Regional Assessment of Offshore Oil and Gas Exploratory Drilling East of Newfoundland and Labrador," online: *Impact Assessment Agency of Canada* https://iaac-aeic.gc.ca/050/evaluations/proj/80156.

60    Canada, Privy Council Office and Canadian Environmental Assessment Agency, *Strategic Environmental Assessment: The Cabinet Directive on the Environmental Assessment of Policy, Plan and Program Proposals: Guidelines for Implementing the Cabinet Directive* (Ottawa: Privy Council Office and Canadian Environmental Assessment Agency, 2010).

61    *IAA*, above note 1, s 99.

assessment are to be used in future project decisions other than the determination on the need for a project assessment under section 16(2).

## I.   PROJECTS ON FEDERAL LANDS AND OUTSIDE CANADA

Projects on federal lands or outside Canada are covered under separate *IAA* provisions unless a particular project is listed on the designated projects list, in which case the process for designated projects applies. As explored in Chapter 18, the Act does not establish a process for the assessment of such projects, but it does impose a general obligation to consider whether such projects are likely to cause significant adverse effects and, if so, whether those effects are justified in the circumstances. The Act provides for public notice and an opportunity to comment but otherwise leaves the scope and process to the discretion of the federal decision maker.

## J.   CONCLUSION

With the *IAA* now passed by Parliament and entered into force, we, of course, have yet to see how it will work in practice. Successful implementation will depend on the regulations, policy, and guidance that need to be developed, especially regarding key issues such as scope, process selection, the application of decision criteria, meaningful participation, and participant funding. The Agency itself lists fourteen policy and guidance products that are needed for implementation of the Act. For many stakeholders and members of the public involved in the development of the *IAA*, the process started with great ambition and the sense that significant steps forward would be made in how IA is practised in Canada—which would in turn provide leadership on IA internationally. In Part II of the book, subject matter experts consider in detail how the Act measures up in key areas. We then return in Part III to an overall assessment of the *IAA*.

# Reflections on the *Impact Assessment Act*

# CHAPTER 4

# The Process of Reform: Real Change?

*Hugh Benevides*

## A.  INTRODUCTION

The stage for the process of reform of Canada's federal environmental assessment (EA) regime was partly set when major energy projects (including the Energy East, Northern Gateway, and Trans Mountain Expansion pipeline proposals and the Site C hydroelectric power project) attracted significant public controversy. During the 2015 federal election campaign, several political parties made legislative proposals for improving relevant processes that might prevent such controversies in the future. When the Liberal Party won a majority of seats in that election, it followed through on its campaign commitment to replace the EA legislation put in place in 2012, when the Conservative Party controlled a majority of seats in the House of Commons.[1] This chapter traces the nearly four-year process that followed, leading to the enactment of the *Impact Assessment Act (IAA)* in 2019.[2]

Although my main purpose is to describe the processes leading to the enactment of the *IAA*, in this chapter I also trace the fate of three

---

1    See, for example, Mark Winfield, "A New Era of Environmental Governance in Canada: Better Decisions Regarding Infrastructure and Resource Development Projects" (May 2016) at 7–8, online (pdf): *Metcalf Foundation* https://metcalffoundation.com/site/uploads/2016/05/Metcalf_Green-Prosperity-Papers_Era-of-Governance_final_web.pdf.

2    SC 2019, c 28, s 1.

substantive areas of possible reform[3] through the legislative process. If these reforms had been adopted, they might have changed federal assessment law in a manner suggesting "real change," the theme of the Liberals' 2015 election campaign platform.[4] The chapter describes the major stages of the process that were transparent to the public: an Expert Panel process, a government discussion paper responding to the Panel's report, the tabling of a draft bill, and its consideration in both houses of Parliament.

The first possible reform considered here is the establishment of binding decision criteria that would give meaning to the notion of "sustainability." In previous federal EA laws, decisions turned on a ministerial or Cabinet judgment as to whether a project would result in significant adverse effects that were said to be justifiable by mitigative measures. In a reformed process, decisions would turn on "explicit grounds for decision making"[5] that would point development in the direction of sustainability in the sense of creating lasting well-being.

The second possible reform is the assignment of impact assessment (IA) decision making to an expert, quasi-judicial tribunal rather than the conventional Canadian approach, whereby elected officials (Cabinet ministers) make final assessment decisions. Although advocates and scholars did not uniformly recommend decision making by a tribunal, such a change would have marked a significant reform and would have responded to some critiques of decision making by elected officials. Some did suggest that approval decision making by an impartial

---

3   Focusing on just three areas of reform means neglecting other important considerations, such as linkages to Indigenous knowledge, rights, cooperation, and decision making (see Chapter 6) and science in IA (see Chapter 21 and Alana Westwood & Aerin Jacob, "Evaluating the Role of Science in the Proposed Impact Assessment Act" (May 2018), online (pdf): *Research Gate* www.researchgate.net/publication/324992499_Evaluating_the_role_of_science_in_the_proposed_Impact_Assessment_Act#fullTextFileContent.

4   Liberal Party of Canada, "Real Change: A New Plan for Canada's Environment and Economy" (2015), online (pdf): *Scribd* www.scribd.com/document/335878417/A-New-Plan-for-Canadas-Environment-and-Economy ["Real Change"]. This document was originally posted at www.liberal.ca/wp-content/uploads/2015/08/A-new-plan-for-Canadas-environment-and-economy.pdf, but is no longer available at that address.

5   Robert B Gibson, Meinhard Doelle & A John Sinclair, "Fulfilling the Promise: Basic Components of Next Generation Environmental Assessment" (2016) 29 *Journal of Environmental Law & Practice* 251 at 257. Chapter 14 of this book explores the role and importance of clear criteria (beyond merely identifying sustainability as a factor) in decision making.

government authority, at arm's length from departmental mandates and partisan pressures and with ministerial or Cabinet review, was the best option.[6]

The third area of reform relates to cumulative effects assessment. The new law could be said to represent "real change" if it were to set out rules to improve analysis of cumulative effects through the conduct of regional and strategic assessments and tiering with project assessment and decision making. Some practitioners suggested that the cumulative effects of development needed to be better addressed and that the new legislation should "compel or promote" the use of regional and strategic assessment.[7]

A fourth important matter, but not necessarily an area of reform, was which projects would trigger an IA. The government determined that a project list would be defined in a regulation rather than in the bill and delayed making its proposed "project list" regulation public until after Parliament had finished reviewing the bill. This fourth matter is discussed in Section B(5) of this chapter.

Rather than marking significant change, the *IAA* is strikingly similar to its predecessor laws. None of the three reforms described above was realized, and the new project list will result in fewer projects assessed than ever before. The chapter concludes by suggesting why the process occurred as it did. The hypothesis is that the central motivating factor for the enactment of an EA regime — in this case, an IA regime — in a liberal democracy, despite what is declared publicly, is the legitimacy that the regime is thought to lend to projects, proponents, and governments. In hindsight, the process of enacting the *IAA* can be seen as primarily motivated by a determination to reinforce legitimacy in favour of the same interests.

---

6    *Ibid* at 266–67.

7    See, for example, Cheryl Chetkiewicz et al, *Regional and Strategic Impact Assessment and the Case for Regional Impact Assessment in the Ring of Fire, Ontario: Submission of the Wildlife Conservation Society (WCS) Canada to the Standing Committee on Environment and Sustainable Development Regarding Part 1 of Bill C-69 (Impact Assessment Act)* (Toronto: WCS Canada, April 2018) at 7. The Multi-Interest Advisory Committee (MIAC) that provided advice to the Expert Panel also recognized the need to integrate regional and cumulative effects assessment into a project assessment–based regime geared toward sustainability: see MIAC, *Advice to the Expert Panel Reviewing Environmental Assessment Processes from the Multi-Interest Advisory Committee* (Ottawa: 2016) at 1–7 and throughout (on file with authors) .

## B.  WHAT HAPPENED

### 1)  New Government: Prospects for Real Change?

With the enactment of the *Canadian Environmental Assessment Act, 2012* (*CEAA 2012*),[8] the federal Conservative government ensured that EAs of resource development projects would be streamlined and hastened. *CEAA 2012* restricted public participation in assessments and greatly reduced the number of projects assessed. Meanwhile, the government stifled science related to the environment, attacked environmental groups, and abandoned Canada's international climate change commitments.[9] Canadians' attention was consequently focused on EA (albeit indirectly, in particular through the lens of controversial development proposals) in unprecedented fashion as the 2015 federal election approached.

The platform of the successful party in that election, Justin Trudeau's Liberals, committed the government to the "immediate public review of Canada's EA processes."[10] Foreshadowing favourite Liberal slogans for environmental and climate change policies during the forty-second Parliament,[11] the platform document declared that without public trust, not only was federal EA "not doing a good enough job at protecting our environment, but we are not getting our resources to market."[12]

In language nearly identical to that of the subsequent mandate letter from the new prime minister to his minister of the environment

---

8   SC 2012, c 199, s 52.

9   See, for example, Paul Wells, *The Longer I'm Prime Minister: Stephen Harper and Canada, 2006—* (Toronto: Vintage Canada, 2014) at 358–75.

10   "Real Change," above note 4.

11   See, for example, Government of Canada, News Release, "Government of Canada Takes Steps to Ensure a Clean Environment and Strong Economy" (8 February 2018), online: *Government of Canada* www.canada.ca/en/environment-climate-change/news/2018/02/government_of_canadatakesstepstoensureacleanenvironment-andstrong.html ("A clean environment and a strong economy go hand in hand—that's why the Government of Canada is bringing forward better rules for the review of major projects. Better rules will protect our environment, fish and waterways, rebuild public trust, and create new jobs and economic opportunities for the middle class and those working hard to join it." Connecting these themes was central to the Liberal brand as early as October 2012, when Trudeau launched his bid for leadership of the party); see Aaron Wherry, *Promise and Peril: Justin Trudeau in Power* (Toronto: HarperCollins, 2019) at 8–9.

12   "Real Change," above note 4 at 8–9.

and climate change,[13] the party pledged to launch a review and replace *CEAA 2012*

> with a new, comprehensive, timely, and fair process that:
> - Restores robust oversight and thorough environmental assessments … of areas under federal jurisdiction, while also working with provincial and territorial governments to ensure that processes are not duplicated;
> - Ensures decisions are based on science, facts, and evidence, and serve the public's interest;
> - Provides ways for interested Canadians to express their views and for experts to meaningfully participate in assessment processes; and
> - Requires project proponents to choose the best technologies available to reduce environmental impacts.[14]

Like the platform document, the mandate letter implied that the review would both "regain public trust and help get resources to market." The Liberals seemed confident that regardless of the substantive content of reforms that might result, trust and legitimacy would follow. The mandate letters of ministers with related portfolios asked them to play roles in support of the review,[15] suggesting that a "whole-of-government" approach driven by Cabinet was to be taken. If so, this would mark a departure from the prevailing practice whereby agenda and priorities

---

13 Prime Minister of Canada Justin Trudeau to Catherine McKenna, Minister of Environment and Climate Change, *Minister of Environment and Climate Change Mandate Letter* (Ottawa: Office of the Prime Minister, 12 November 2015), online: *Office of the Prime Minister* https://pm.gc.ca/en/mandate-letters/2015/11/12/archived-minister-environment-and-climate-change-mandate-letter. Unlike the platform document, the mandate letter did not stipulate that the new process should be "comprehensive."

14 "Real Change," above note 4 at 9.

15 See, for example, Prime Minister Justin Trudeau to Kirsty Duncan, Minister of Science, *Minister of Science Mandate Letter* (12 November 2015), online: *Office of the Prime Minister* https://pm.gc.ca/en/mandate-letters/2015/11/12/archived-minister-science-mandate-letter, and Chapter 21 of this volume; see also Prime Minister Justin Trudeau to Carolyn Bennett, Minister of Indigenous and Northern Affairs, *Minister of Indigenous and Northern Affairs Mandate Letter* (12 November 2015), online: *Office of the Prime Minister* https://pm.gc.ca/en/mandate-letters/2015/11/12/archived-minister-indigenous-and-northern-affairs-mandate-letter, and Chapter 6 of this volume.

are said to be driven by prime ministers and their "courtiers," with less collaboration among ministers and within Cabinet.[16]

The direction in ministers' mandate letters was broadly reflected in terms of reference for members of an expert panel who were appointed in August 2016 to conduct the promised review and report with recommendations to the minister of environment and climate change by 31 March 2017.[17]

## 2)  The Expert Panel

The Expert Panel for the Review of Environmental Assessment Processes (Expert Panel) was chaired by Johanne Gélinas, who had served as federal commissioner of the environment and sustainable development (an officer of Parliament, appointed by the auditor general of Canada) from 2000 to 2007 and as a member of Quebec's EA board, the Bureau d'audiences publiques sur l'environnement, from 1990 to 2000. Other Panel members included Renée Pelletier, who is originally from Canada's Atlantic region and practises Indigenous law; Rodney Northey, an Ontario environmental lawyer experienced in federal EA; and Doug Horswill, a former mining executive and former civil servant from British Columbia. The selection of the Panel reflected a range of expertise and background as well as gender equality and — always important in Canadian federal initiatives — broad regional representation.

---

16    See, for example, Donald J Savoie, *Democracy in Canada: The Disintegration of Our Institutions* (Montreal & Kingston: McGill-Queen's University Press, 2019), ch 8 at 219–38. Anonymous Liberal "MPs and senior Liberals" are reported as saying that although former Conservative prime minister "Stephen Harper took control of the cabinet, caucus, and the party to [an unprecedented] level in his 10 years of power, and despite promises to the contrary during the 2015 campaign, nothing has changed [in this respect] under Prime Minister Trudeau": see Abbas Rana, "'Nobody Calls Out the Prime Minister:' WE Charity Scandal 'a Truly Systemic Error,' Say Some Liberal MPs Who Also Wonder About PM's Advisors" *The Hill Times* (27 July 2020), online: www.hilltimes.com/2020/07/27/we-charity-scandal-a-truly-systemic-error-say-some-liberal-mps/257665.

17    Expert Panel for the Review of Environmental Assessment Processes, *Building Common Ground: A New Vision for Impact Assessment in Canada* (Ottawa: Canadian Environmental Assessment Agency, 2017) at 108, Annex 1, online (pdf): *Government of Canada* www.canada.ca/content/dam/themes/environment/conservation/environmental-reviews/building-common-ground/building-common-ground.pdf [*Building Common Ground*].

Despite the time constraints and ambitious assignment, the Expert Panel used a variety of methods to seek Canadians' views throughout autumn 2016, including in-person sessions in twenty-one cities across Canada.[18]

Although the Expert Panel report disappointed some who had advocated for bolder improvements, it set benchmarks for the *IAA* to meet.[19] Several scholars of EA declared that "the panel's recommendations have set the stage for Canada to become a world leader in sustainability."[20] Among the recommendations that would have meant significant reform of federal EA compared to practices under *CEAA 2012* were those involving sustainability criteria, the identity of the decision maker, and cumulative effects.

### a)  Sustainability Criteria

The Expert Panel recommended that criteria for sustainability be developed and that they be the basis for project decisions; a sustainability-based analytical framework for each assessment would be based on five sustainability pillars and "key questions."[21] While acknowledging the challenges and complexity involved, the Panel nevertheless recommended "that federal impact assessment *decide* whether a project should proceed *based on that project's contribution to sustainability.*"[22]

### b)  Quasi-judicial Decision Maker, Independent of Cabinet

The Panel recommended[23] that a single authority have the appropriate quasi-judicial powers to resolve disputes and hold formal and informal

---

18  *Ibid* at 87.

19  Even the process of allowing public review of the Panel's draft terms of reference was admirable and allowed an important broadening of focus. The original terms asked the Panel to consider only how to "renew EA processes associated with CEAA 2012." Following public comment, the terms required the Panel to "consider the goals and purpose of modern-day EA."

20  Jason MacLean et al, "A Plan that Promotes Environmental Sustainability" *Policy Options* (30 May 2017), online: https://policyoptions.irpp.org/magazines/may-2017/plan-promotes-environmental-sustainability.

21  *Building Common Ground*, above note 17. See, for example, section 2.1.3 and page 60.

22  *Ibid* at 22 [emphasis added]. The Panel noted, both during its engagement sessions and in its report, that many participants "expressed support for the concept of next-generation EA" (a concept with "contribution to sustainability" at its core), articulated in Gibson, Doelle & Sinclair, above note 5 at 1 and 19.

23  *Building Common Ground*, above note 17 at 50–55.

hearings and have the mandate to conduct and decide upon IAs on behalf of the federal government, subject to an extraordinary appeal[24] to the Governor in Council (Cabinet).[25]

### c) Cumulative Effects and Tiering

The Expert Panel recommended that "a tiered approach should be implemented whereby strategic and regional IAs produce the policy and planning foundations for improved and efficient project IAs" and "that IA legislation *require* the use of strategic and regional IAs to guide project IA" and "*require* regional IAs where there are potential consequential cumulative impacts to matters of federal interest."[26]

In addition to setting substantive standards, the Panel also set admirable procedural standards. It held public workshops and open-dialogue sessions on Indigenous themes in each city it visited and heard almost 400 presentations, almost one-third of which were made by Indigenous groups or organizations. The Panel received more than 520 written submissions and almost 3,000 responses to an online survey tool.[27] The high level of response and participation suggests that the Panel succeeded in reflecting Canadians' views and priorities.

The report includes explanations of how the Panel had reached each of its findings and recommendations. It summarizes what the Panel had heard from participants, followed immediately by the Panel's

---

24    *Ibid* at 51–52. The Panel described Canada's "longstanding experience of independent, quasi-judicial tribunals making final decisions, with perhaps the best-known example being the Canadian Radio-Television and Telecommunications Commission (CRTC)." The Panel did not mention the historic significance of this recommendation: in the landmark "Red Book" campaign manifesto from the 1993 election that returned them to power after nine years in opposition, the Liberals had committed that "[u]nder a Liberal government, the Canadian Environmental Assessment Act will be amended to shift decision-making powers to an independent Canadian Environmental Assessment Agency, subject to appeal to the Cabinet. The agency's relationship to government would be roughly similar to that between the CRTC and the Cabinet": Liberal Party of Canada, *Creating Opportunity: The Liberal Plan for Canada* (1993) ch 4, online: https://web.archive.org/web/19961109135908/http://www.liberal.ca/english/policy/red_book/chapter4.html.

25    Executive authority in Canada is vested in the Crown and exercised by the governor general, who acts on the advice of the Cabinet. See "The Canadian Parliamentary System," online: *House of Commons* www.ourcommons.ca/About/OurProcedure/ParliamentaryFramework/c_g_parliamentaryframework-e.htm.

26    *Building Common Ground*, above note 17 at 7, 22, and 80 [emphasis added].

27    *Ibid* at 87.

detailed "findings and recommendations" on each subject, allowing readers better insight into the conclusions.

## 3)   The Discussion Paper

The government solicited public comments in response to the Expert Panel report over a period initially spanning April 5 to May 5 and eventually extending into June 2017. It held seventy private in-person meetings in this period, but these were not announced or publicized.[28] A "what we've heard" document was published,[29] but it did not appear until roughly the time the government released its discussion paper. Moreover, unlike the Expert Panel report, which connects what was heard, recommendations, and their rationale, the "what we've heard" document and the discussion paper are separate and not explicitly linked. Consequently, read alone, the discussion paper gives little sense of the complexity of what the Expert Panel had considered, proposed, and explained in its report.

When the government's discussion paper was released on 29 June 2017,[30] it failed to propose, and in several cases even to acknowledge, central recommendations of the Expert Panel about IA legislation—recommendations that, in turn, had reflected "a clear message" and "a broad interest" from those participating in the reviews that sustainability should be the meaningful objective of IA.[31] The discussion paper nevertheless set a clear benchmark about the government's plans for new legislation. Its release would have required that officials in a variety of federal departments and agencies had at least agreed on its outline, representing in some cases important compromises by economic, resource exploitation, and environmental ministers and their departments. Unseen was whatever impact the more powerful economic

---

28   By contrast, anyone could give input to the Expert Panel, and such input was acknowledged and made public.

29   See Canadian Environmental Assessment Agency, *Summary of What We've Heard*, (2017) online: *Government of Canada* www.letstalkea.ca.

30   Government of Canada, Environment and Climate Change Canada, *Environmental and Regulatory Reviews: Discussion Paper* (Ottawa: Environment and Climate Change Canada, June 2017), online: *Government of Canada* www.canada.ca/en/services/environment/ conservation/assessments/environmental-reviews/share-your-views/proposed-approach/discussion-paper.html [*Environmental and Regulatory Reviews*].

31   *Building Common Ground*, above note 17 at 1 and 19.

lobbies, provincial governments, and Cabinet discussions had on the final product.

In terms of the three key issue areas, the discussion paper represented departures from the Expert Panel report.

### a) Sustainability Criteria

The government's discussion paper proposed "broadening the scope of assessment to include environmental, economic, social and health impacts to support holistic and integrated decision making" but was silent on requiring sustainability criteria or trade-off rules.[32] The *IAA* requires that decisions be "based on the [Agency's or a review panel's] report" and on five listed factors, one of which is "the extent to which the designated project contributes to sustainability."[33]

### b) Quasi-judicial Decision-Maker, Independent of Cabinet

Despite the Expert Panel's call for a quasi-judicial decision maker, the discussion paper said only that the government was "considering … establishing a single government agency responsible for guiding and conducting federal assessments."[34] The discussion paper declared that changes to laws including *CEAA 2012* were needed because "[currently,] decisions are not sufficiently explained so that Canadians can understand why a choice was made";[35] perhaps decisions would be considered legitimate if they were better explained. The government said nothing in response to the Panel about changing the decision maker; instead, the discussion paper said only this: "We are considering: … Decision making [to be] retained by Minister(s) or Cabinet [and to be] based on whether projects are in the public interest, to ensure accountable government."[36] This snippet, it will be noted, also dispenses succinctly with

---

32　*Environmental and Regulatory Reviews*, above note 30 at 11. The Expert Panel had recommended that trade-offs be "explained and justified" (*Building Common Ground*, above note 17 at 47, 51–52, and 64) but did not explicitly recommend that trade-off rules be binding.

33　*IAA*, s 63. Reports to the minister are required by *IAA* ss 28 (the Agency) and 51 (a review panel) and must reflect how the assessment takes into account an extensive list of factors listed in s 22, of which just one is "the extent to which the designated project contributes to sustainability" (s 22(1)(h)).

34　*Environmental and Regulatory Reviews*, above note 30 at 13.

35　*Ibid* at 6. The only explicit reference in the discussion paper to decision makers is contained in an infographic ("Project Decision: Minister or Cabinet") at 8.

36　*Ibid* at 13.

the possibility that sustainability criteria would be included. The eventual bill confirmed that as with the previous *CEAA* regimes,[37] responsibility for *IAA* decisions would remain with Cabinet ministers.

## c)  Cumulative Effects and Tiering

The discussion paper dedicated a full page, titled "Addressing Cumulative Effects," to the need for "collaborative processes with provinces and territories, Indigenous peoples and stakeholders [in order] to understand … the cumulative effects of development."[38] The government proposed what it called a "deliberate approach to the assessment and management of cumulative effects" that would include the following:

- **Conducting strategic assessments** that explain the application of environmental frameworks to activities subject to federal oversight and regulation, starting with one for climate change [and]
- **Regional assessments** to guide planning and management of cumulative effects (e.g. biodiversity and species at risk), identify the potential impacts on the rights and interests of Indigenous peoples, and inform project assessments.[39]

However, as explored in chapters 11 and 17,[40] the discussion paper did not propose, and the *IAA* has no mandatory language about, regional and strategic assessments. As a result, it seems unlikely that any such assessments will build strong foundations for subsequent project IAs.

The government did not respond directly to issues raised during the Expert Panel's public process. The discussion paper does not explicitly and clearly articulate which recommendations the government proposed to accept and which it would reject. Consequently, with some exceptions, the discussion paper also does not explain its proposals in terms that directly address the Expert Panel and what the Panel heard.

The confidential deliberations of government officials on assessment reform were critically important. The parameters of the Act were set out in memoranda to Cabinet confirming the contents of the discussion

---

37  *Canadian Environmental Assessment Act*, SC 1992, c 37 (as amended) and *Canadian Environmental Assessment Act*, 2012, SC 2012, c 19, s 52 (as amended).

38  *Environmental and Regulatory Reviews*, above note 30 at 9.

39  *Ibid* at 9.

40  Chapter 11 makes the case for "cumulative effects as the leading rationale for regional assessment." See Chapter 17 for the "strategic" connection.

paper and, later, drafting instructions for officials defining the contents of the bill.[41] One or more interdepartmental "task teams" of officials met regularly to discuss and resolve matters arising among their respective departments and agencies.[42] In any policy or law development process, the information available to outsiders is limited to what government officials are permitted to reveal. Such information may be considered (appropriately or otherwise) as Cabinet confidences,[43] conflicting with the public interest in more participatory democratic practices. It is also difficult to say with confidence how lobbying and other communications with government officials by various interests, notably provincial governments, industry, and capital, influenced the content of the discussion paper and, ultimately, the bill. Such interactions are cloaked in secrecy yet may have had the greatest impact on the shape and features of the *IAA*.

The ten-month period of sustained consultation, conducted both publicly and in private by the Expert Panel and then by the government, was followed by six months of government silence until Bill C-69[44] was introduced in the House of Commons[45] on 8 February 2018. The bill broadly reflected what the government had proposed in the June 2017 discussion paper.

### 4) Bill C-69 in Parliament

Some interesting but ultimately incremental changes were made to Bill C-69 in both houses of Parliament, allowing the government and various interests to claim success or express outrage. In the end, as

---

41   See, for example, Government of Canada, *A Drafter's Guide to Cabinet Documents* (Ottawa: Privy Council Office, 2013), online (pdf): *Government of Canada* www.canada.ca/content/dam/pco-bcp/documents/pdfs/dr-guide-eng.pdf, and related documents providing guidance for officials.

42   The author assisted environmental and conservation groups in arranging, attending, and providing advice relating to meetings involving members of the task teams and other officials from 2017 to 2020.

43   See Nicholas d'Ombrain, "Cabinet Secrecy" (2004) in 47 *Canadian Public Administration* 332 at 335.

44   *An Act to enact the Impact Assessment Act and the Canadian Energy Regulator Act, to amend the Navigation Protection Act and to make consequential amendments to other Acts*, 1st Sess, 42nd Parl, 2018 (assented to 21 June 2019), SC 2019, c 28, part 1.

45   See generally "Stages in the Legislative Process," online: *House of Commons* www.our-commons.ca/About/OurProcedure/LegislativeProcess/c_g_legislativeprocess-e.htm.

discussed in Section C, below in this chapter, the integrity of the *IAA* as conceived and constructed by the executive was never really threatened by legislative deliberations.

### a)  In the House of Commons

Debate on Bill C-69 began the second week of February 2018 in the House. Contention about the bill ranged from claims that it would stall development ("no new major energy infrastructure project will ever get built in Canada" became a familiar refrain[46]) to claims that it insufficiently tied decisions to Canada's commitments to reduce greenhouse gas emissions or assessment of cumulative effects. The Conservative Party, the official Opposition, claimed that assessments would take longer than under *CEAA 2012* and decried the proposed planning phase, whereas the New Democratic Party wanted assurances that planning was sufficiently open and transparent. Both complained that the bill would allow too much discretion in decision making at the political level. All opposition parties were unhappy that the *IAA* did not establish to which projects it would apply; this was eventually set out in the *Physical Activities Regulations* (Project List), released on 2 May 2019,[47] when senators were already considering possible amendments to the bill.[48] Prominent government themes included that it had conducted public consultations for fourteen months and that the proposed planning phase would improve the regime.[49]

These themes continued throughout much of the bill's progress through both houses and the committees assigned to study it.[50] The House of Commons and Senate committee study stages of Bill C-69,

---

46    See "Bill C-69, An Act to enact the Impact Assessment Act and the Canadian Energy Regulator Act, to amend the Navigation Protection Act and to make consequential amendments to other Acts," 2nd reading, *House of Commons Debates (Hansard)*, 42-1, vol 148 No 264 (14 February, 2018) at 1835 (Tom Kmiec), online: *House of Commons* www.ourcommons.ca/DocumentViewer/en/42-1/house/sitting-264/hansard#9977090 ["Bill C-69 Hansard"]. By mid-2020, media reports continued to refer to "Bill C-69" and its supposedly damaging economic effects relative to previous assessment regimes.

47    SOR/2019-285.

48    See Section B(5), below in this chapter.

49    See, for example, Hon Catherine McKenna, PC, MP; Arif Virani, MP; Mike Bossio, MP in "Bill C-69 Hansard," above note 46.

50    Details of the bill's odyssey through parliament can be traced at www.parl.ca/LegisInfo/ BillDetails.aspx?Language=E&billId=9630600&View=0.

where greater scrutiny and more productive discussion might be expected to occur, produced little of either.

The example of the House of Commons environment committee that was assigned the bill is particularly concerning. Partisanship generally prevailed over serious deliberation. Despite the rule that a committee is said to be "master of its own procedure" (subject to the rules and authority of the chamber to which it reports),[51] the mode of the Commons committee's study of the bill was essentially dictated by the government. For example, despite past practice, whereby a committee would hear from officials responsible for the detailed thinking behind a bill, in this case the committee heard from ministers, supported by senior officials, at the outset of its study. In addition to encouraging partisan attacks on ministers rather than serious, constructive discussion aimed at improving the bill, this deprived the committee of opportunities for reaching early, shared understandings. It also deprived parliamentarians from being able to build their collective trust in and better relationships with officials who were available throughout the later "clause-by-clause" consideration of proposed amendments.

Since considerable time had already been consumed by consultation and drafting, and since the government was determined that the bill should become law before the October 2019 fixed federal election date,[52] little time was left for discussion and debate in Parliament.[53] Consequently, the Liberal-majority committee passed a procedural motion that imposed tight timelines on consideration of the bill and, in particular, strict limits on consideration of amendments.[54] One result was

---

51    See, for example, Senate, *Companion to the Rules of the Senate of Canada*, 2d ed (Ottawa, November 2013) at 1, 2, 4–5, 7, 318, and 333, online (pdf): *Senate of Canada* https://sencanada.ca/media/106242/companion-rules-senate-2nd-nov13-e.pdf.

52    In March 2018, the aim was to enact the law before Christmas; in the end, Bill C-69 received royal assent on the last sitting day (21 June 2019) before the election, having cleared the final Senate vote one day earlier.

53    In fact, "[o]ver 100 briefs [from private interests and members of the public] recommending amendments to this bill were received after the deadline [for members of Parliament who were members of the committee] to submit [proposed] amendments" for the committee to vote on: Canada, Parliament, *House of Commons Debates (Hansard)*, 42-1, vol 148 No 308 (5 June 2018) at 20232 (Linda Duncan, MP), online: *Our Commons* www.ourcommons.ca/DocumentViewer/en/42-1/house/sitting-308/hansard.

54    See Standing Committee on the Environment and Sustainable Development, *Minutes of Proceedings*, 42-1, No 98 (20 March 2018), online: *House of Commons* www.ourcommons.ca/DocumentViewer/en/42-1/ENVI/meeting-98/minutes.

that members enjoyed little discussion of the substance or meaning of proposed amendments. The overall climate suggested that members mistrusted each other and the expert witnesses. No basis for consensus was built about why reform through possible amendments might be needed. The meetings where amendments proposed by members were discussed were chaotic and anything but constructive.[55] Time to discuss the merits of various amendments to a clause was severely limited, especially as the final, imposed deadline loomed. The fourth and final such meeting discussing amendments spanned over fourteen hours (elapsed time), ending past midnight. No fewer than twenty different MPs were substituted for the eleven regular committee members throughout that day.

In the end, of over 300 amendments to Bill C-69 proposed by MPs of all parties,[56] only one amendment proposed by an opposition MP received the support of the Liberals.[57] All other amendments made in committee were introduced by Liberals.

### b)  In the Senate of Canada

Following its deliberations on Bill C-69, the House of Commons sent the bill to the Senate on 20 June 2018 for the next stage of the legislative process.

Deliberations on the bill included Conservative and some other senators promoting positions and amendments that were similar and sometimes identical to those advanced by organized oil and gas industry

---

55   See, for example, Standing Committee on the Environment and Sustainable Development, *Evidence*, 42-1, No 111 (8 May 2018), online: *House of Commons* www.ourcommons.ca/DocumentViewer/en/42-1/ENVI/meeting-111/evidence.

56   The overwhelming majority of amendments proposed to Bill C-69 dealt with the *IAA* portion of the bill. Government members of the House committee proposed over 100 of these amendments.

57   This amendment (adding s 6(3), providing that federal authorities "must … exercise their powers in a manner that adheres to the principles of scientific integrity, honesty, objectivity, thoroughness and accuracy"; see Chapter 21) was made in committee by a unanimous vote following statements of support from members of the Conservative and New Democratic parties. Standing Committee on the Environment and Sustainable Development, *Evidence*, 42-1, No 112 (9 May 2018), online (pdf): *House of Commons* www.ourcommons.ca/Content/Committee/421/ENVI/Evidence/EV9856717/ ENVIEV112-E.PDF.

lobbies.[58] A declared desire on the part of Conservative senators, some provinces (Alberta in particular),[59] and some representatives of the oil and gas industry to "kill the bill" led to long delays in debate and a nine-city, cross-Canada tour by the Standing Senate Committee on Energy, the Environment and Natural Resources. Proponents insisted that a "listening tour" including public hearings in several locations was necessary because some interests had not been heard (despite the Expert Panel's extensive outreach efforts and despite another expert panel having simultaneously consulted on reforms to the National Energy Board that were proposed in Part 2 of Bill C-69[60]). Senate committee tours during study of a bill are historically rare (tours are more common when committees conduct studies not directly linked to a bill), but in the case of Bill C-69, emotions and rhetoric were running high, and calls by some senators for the committee to travel to "meet the people" overpowered those resisting the call. Media reports that the bill was "poorly-worded and vague"[61] and that "no new energy projects would ever be built"[62] if the bill passed took on a life of their own and were often repeated.

Although space does not allow a detailed account of amendments made in the Senate, the Independent Senators Group, which by then

---

58    See, for example, John Paul Tasker "Conservative, Independent Senators Are Aligned on Some of Bill C-69's Flaws and Possible Fixes" *CBC* (8 May 2019), online: www.cbc.ca/news/politics/tasker-senate-amendments-bill-c-69-1.5128593:

> [The Conservative] package included amendments that had been suggested by the Canadian Association of Petroleum Producers (CAPP) and the Canadian Energy Pipeline Association (CEPA), among other stakeholders, and was meant to put Alberta's oilpatch at ease. . . . The Conservatives said the federal Liberal legislation is so problematic it could only be fixed by adopting the group's proposed amendments in their entirety.

59    Most other provinces had a more nuanced position toward the bill, advocating for amendments rather than for killing the bill outright.

60    See "NEB Modernization Expert Panel Report," online: *National Energy Board* https://web.archive.org/web/20181105035911/https://www.neb-modernization.ca/neb-welcome, and the *Canadian Energy Regulator Act*, SC 2019, c 28, s 10, which repealed the *National Energy Board Act*, RSC 1985, c N-7.

61    See, for example, "Bill C-69 Gets a Rough Ride at Senate Committee Hearing in Calgary" *Canadian Press* (10 April 2019), online: www.cbc.ca/news/canada/calgary/calgary-senate-hearing-bill-c69-oilsands-energy-projects-pipelines-1.5091846.

62    See, for example, "Controversial Bill on Energy Project Assessment Passes Senate Heavily Amended" *Canadian Press* (6 June 2019), online: www.cbc.ca/news/canada/calgary/bill-c69-senate-vote-amendments-1.5165976.

held the greatest number of Senate seats,[63] introduced and attracted sufficient support for several amendments aimed at "[reducing] ministerial discretion in favour of the expert and accountable independent agency" (the renamed Impact Assessment Agency of Canada).[64]

Unable to break a stalemate that, had it continued into the summer, would have resulted in the bill dying with the dissolution of Parliament prior to the 2019 election campaign, the Senate instead approved large packages of sometimes conflicting amendments proffered by both the Conservative and Independent groups, referring an internally incoherent bill back to the House of Commons. With an election four months away and holding very few seats in Alberta and Saskatchewan[65]—two provinces rich in oil and gas—the majority Liberals in the House had to consider which amendments returned to it by the Senate should be accepted. Among other factors to consider was which amendments supported and which threatened their re-election prospects. Despite strong industry and provincial pressure,[66] the federal government opted to

63    Recent years, including when Bill C-69 was in Parliament, have seen dramatic changes in the Senate of Canada. For a snapshot of the Senate in 2018, see David Moscrop, "The Senate of Canada Is Up on Its Hind Legs. Will It Bite?" *Maclean's* (28 November 2018), online: www.macleans.ca/politics/ottawa/the-senate-of-canada-is-up-on-its-hind-legs-will-it-bite/.

64    Independent Senators Group, "ISG Senators to Release Bill C-69 Amendments Package" press release (7 May 2019), online: www.isgsenate.ca/single-post/2019/05/07/ISG-Senators-to-Release-Bill-C-69-Amendments-Package.

65    The Liberals had won a comfortable majority of seats nationally in 2015 but only four of thirty-four in Alberta and one of fourteen in Saskatchewan: Elections Canada, *Canada—The 42nd Parliament* (map) (April 2016) online (pdf): *Elections Canada* www.elections.ca/res/cir/maps2/images/parlimap_42_e.pdf. Following the 2019 election, they were left with no seats in Alberta and Saskatchewan: Elections Canada, *Canada—The 43rd Parliament* (map) (April 2020) online (pdf): *Elections Canada* www.elections.ca/res/cir/maps2/images/parlimap_43_e.pdf. In the third prairie province, Manitoba, the Liberals went from seven seats in 2015 to four in 2019.

66    Of ten provinces and three territories, "six dissenting premiers wrote a joint letter to Trudeau … threatening that if the government doesn't pass the bill with all Senate amendments, it would 'present insurmountable roadblocks for major infrastructure projects across the country and will further jeopardize jobs, growth and investor confidence.'" Nevertheless, "The government signaled … it had accepted 62 [of a total of 188] amendments [sent to the House by the Senate] verbatim, and a further 37 with alterations. However, roughly 90 per cent of the 89 remaining amendments that were rejected had been proposed by Conservative parliamentarians": see Carl Meyer, "Trudeau Liberals Refuse to 'Copy and Paste' Oil Lobby Plan into Law" *National Observer* (12 June 2019), online: www.nationalobserver.com/2019/06/12/news/trudeau-liberals-refuse-copy-and-paste-oil-lobby-plan-law. The six premiers represented Alberta,

hold the line and not to alter the main architecture of the *IAA* that had been decided prior to the introduction of the bill.

The official Opposition's delaying tactics were successful in ensuring that the bill did not pass the Senate until its second-last sitting day. Despite the possibility that a majority of senators might "insist on its amendments" following the message from the House of Commons stipulating which Senate amendments the House opposed, the Senate instead relented. This allowed for a rather anticlimactic vote that paved the way for the governor general to grant royal assent to the bill the following day.[67]

The *IAA* received royal assent on 21 June 2019, sixteen and a half months after the bill's introduction, following twenty-six days of deliberation in the House and committee and fifty-four days in the Senate and committee.[68] Opposition delaying tactics had forced five additional sitting days in both houses, allowing both Liberals and Conservatives to claim moral victory during that summer's federal election campaign.

Following royal assent, the ministers responsible for Bill C-69 declared that "our government is working to strengthen environmental protection, restore trust in how decisions are made, and grow the economy."[69]

---

Ontario, Saskatchewan, Manitoba, New Brunswick, and the Northwest Territories. The Province of Québec was also said to oppose the bill "as a federal power grab that would duplicate Quebec's own environmental assessment process and stall the development of its resources": Konrad Yakubuski, "What National Unity Crisis? Even Quebec Thinks C-69 Is a Bad Bill" *Globe and Mail* (12 June 2019), online: www.theglobeandmail.com/opinion/article-what-national-unity-crisis-even-quebec-thinks-c-69-is-a-bad-bill/. Like many of his colleagues and commentators in the mainstream media, the columnist claimed that "[i]f adopted as is, C-69 would all but ensure endless gridlock by leaving it to the courts to sort out a host of concepts the bill fails to define or circumscribe." Much of the posturing by provincial governments may have been calculated not to prevent the *IAA*'s passage but to resist federal assessment of individual projects later.

67 See "Government Business: Bills—Messages from the House of Commons" (Bill C-69) *Journals of the Senate* 42-1, vol 307 (20 June 2020), online: https://sencanada.ca/en/content/sen/chamber/421/journals/307jr_2019-06-20-e.

68 The longer period in the Senate can be attributed to the unique procedures and culture of the Senate, the Conservatives' strong opposition to the *IAA* (especially in their symbolic defence of *CEAA 2012*), and their strategic advantage of having the largest caucus able to use party discipline to its advantage, as well as the intervention of the 2018 summer and Christmas holiday breaks.

69 Impact Assessment Agency of Canada, *Better Rules for Major Projects Become Law in Canada: Canada's New Approach to Impact Assessments Is Designed to Protect the Environment and Grow the Economy* (News Release), (Ottawa, 21 June 2019), online:

A newspaper of national record, the *Globe and Mail,* meanwhile reported a statement by the environment and climate change minister that with its "better rules" (a phrase that ministers had repeated throughout the legislative process), the *IAA* "will provide certainty to business and show investors that Canada is the best place in the world to invest."[70]

### c) The Fate of Sustainability Criteria, Quasi-judicial Decision Maker, and Cumulative Effects and Tiering in the Parliamentary Process

As summarized in Section B(3) above, the government did not alter the main direction of the *IAA* respecting these themes following the release of its discussion paper (although some of the strongest pressures from the Senate tended in the opposite direction). Consequently, the *IAA* that was enacted in August 2019 retained the notion of "sustainability" with no criteria, decision making by the minister or Cabinet rather than by an expert body at arm's length from government, and a weak model for gathering and acting upon cumulative effects information, in contrast to what had been recommended by the Expert Panel and others.

### 5) The Elusive Project List

Rather than responding directly in the discussion paper to the Expert Panel's recommendations about "what should require impact assessment,"[71] the government elected to conduct a separate, two-stage public consultation on a new "project list," first in early 2018 and again in May

---

*Government of Canada* www.canada.ca/en/impact-assessment-agency/news/2019/06/better-rules-for-major-projects-become-law-in-canada-canadas-new-approach-to-impact-assessments-is-designed-to-protect-the-environment-and-grow-the.html. See also above note 11.

70  Shawn McCarthy, "Senate Passes Liberal Government's Contentious Environmental Assessment Bill" *Globe and Mail* (21 June 2019), online: www.theglobeandmail.com/politics/article-controversial-environmental-review-bill-receives-royal-assent.

71  See *Building Common Ground*, above note 17 at 56–57. The Expert Panel essentially recommended a project list approach plus two additional "triggering mechanisms": first, where a project not on the list might affect present or future generations in a "consequential" manner based on "clear criteria" and, second, discretion to conduct an assessment of a project not on the list, on request, or on the minister's own initiative. The *IAA* does not adopt the "additional criteria" approach. It does retain discretion for the minister to require an assessment on request, similar to the *CEAA 1995* and *CEAA 2012: IAA*, s 9.

2019.[72] Consequently, Bill C-69 was considered without a clear picture of the projects that would be subject to assessment, even though the Project List was integral to the Act's design and the Act could not come into force without it. The resulting lack of clarity attracted criticism from all sides, including from parliamentarians, industry, provinces, and others. For example, several environmental groups wrote to ministers in April 2018 urging them to release the project list prior to enactment of Bill C-69 and to disclose whatever approach had been taken to determine its contents,[73] to no avail.

One is left with the impression that the government was committed to a short project list early in the reform process. Worries expressed by the provinces and several industry sectors[74] that the range of projects to be subject to assessment would be broadened under the *IAA* compared to *CEAA 2012* turned out to be unfounded.

## C.  CONCLUSION: LEGITIMACY AS EXPLANATION FOR THE *IAA*

The new Liberal government pledged to enact in the eventual *IAA* a "new, comprehensive, timely, and fair process" of IA. It also pledged that the review would somehow both "regain public trust and help get resources to market."

As the *IAA* and its project list are not that different from *CEAA 2012*, it can be argued that the Act is not really "new." Its "comprehensiveness" may also be contested as the regime will apply to fewer projects than ever before. Timeliness was a major focus of the government as *IAA* timelines are shorter compared to *CEAA 2012*'s and subject to limited

---

72    See Chapter 7. See also *Consultation Paper on Approach to Revising the Project List* (June 2018), online: *Government of Canada* www.canada.ca/en/services/environment/ conservation/assessments/environmental-reviews/environmental-assessment-processes/ consultation-paper-approach.html; and *Discussion Paper on the Proposed Project List: A Proposed Impact Assessment System* (May 2019), online: *Government of Canada* www. canada.ca/en/services/environment/conservation/assessments/environmental-reviews/ environmental-assessment-processes/discussion-paper-proposed-project-list.html.

73    Letter to Hon Catherine McKenna, PC, MP (18 April 2018), online (pdf): https://cela.ca/ wp-content/uploads/2019/07/1188-L-McKenna-project-list-letter-april-2018.pdf.

74    One outlet reported that "80% of Senate lobbying over Bill C-69 ... stemmed from industry and related groups, primarily from the oil and gas industry": see Sharon J Riley, "'Deep State' Lobbying a Growing Tactic of Fossil Fuel Industry, Report Finds" *The Narwhal* (5 November 2019), online: https://thenarwhal.ca/deep-state-lobbying-a-growing-tactic-of-fossil-fuel-industry-report-finds.

available discretion to extend or temporarily suspend them. The new timelines can be seen as a direct response to provincial and industry claims that federal assessment takes too long, rendering Canada "uncompetitive" with other jurisdictions.

Taken together, the *IAA* and *Physical Activities Regulations* are marked more by their similarities to *CEAA 2012* than by their differences. This should come as no surprise if one presumes that the strategies of the most powerful sectors of society, notably capital and government, tend to be aligned and to conceal and serve entrenched interests and that regimes such as IA serve to underscore the legitimacy of business-as-usual developments rather than to critically assess or upset their direction.

The federal government did not respond explicitly to the Expert Panel report in key areas, nor did it explain why it chose a different approach. The composition and qualifications of the Panel might have tended to lend legitimacy to the review process while it was under way, but its members' expertise can be seen as squandered when much of the Panel's advice was ignored. Following the release of the report, officials were quick to say that the Panel's advice was "just one input"[75] to the process, when one might have expected that the report was a major "input." That the government was fighting a rearguard action throughout the process against the significant resistance of certain corporate interests, provincial and territorial governments, and opposition parties is not a complete answer to how the result came about. I discuss below two aspects of legitimacy as an explanation for why the process unfolded as it did.

## 1)  The Legitimizing Role of Environmental Assessment

Mark Winfield documented how the "streamlining" of EA law leading to *CEAA 2012* stripped the federal process of its "legitimating capacity," which had been "the central political rationale for establishing environmental assessment processes" originally.[76] For example, the United States Congress's enactment in 1969 of the first EA legislation, the *National Environmental Policy Act (NEPA)*,[77] coincided with moves by

---

75    Author's files.

76    Winfield, above note 1 at 7–8.

77    42 USC § 4321 et seq.

President Nixon—such as establishing the Environmental Protection Agency—to outflank Democrats, who had staked out the environment as a major issue in anticipation of the 1972 presidential election.[78] The profile of environmental problems had grown dramatically in the late 1960s.[79] Similarly, international and domestic environmental concerns explain Canada's declaration in 1972 that it would establish a process of screening projects, which led to the *CEAA*'s precursor, the Environmental Assessment and Review Process (EARP),[80] established in 1973. Prime Minister Pierre Trudeau, in a confidential letter to a minister in 1978, anticipated how the federal environment department was to function as a stand-alone department (separate from the department of fisheries for the first time). He ordered limitations on the powers exercised in the EARP: "[I]n developing the [EARP], you will need to ensure that the objectives ... to reduce the regulatory burden on the private sector is [sic] respected and emphasized ... avoiding red tape and delay. You should ... ensure that it continues to operate in this manner."[81] Recommending that EARP be given a legislative basis, the 1985 Macdonald Commission report "argued that environmental values needed to be better integrated into economic decisions, and that provisions for public input, intervener funding, and monitoring and compliance could improve the legitimacy of the [environmental] assessment process."[82]

The Liberals' emphasis on public dissatisfaction with assessments conducted under *CEAA 2012* and their proclamation that the review process alone would have the effect of regaining public trust and helping get resources to market, rather than setting out more substantive objectives for the *IAA*, also tend to support the notion that EA is used

---

78    "Whether Nixon grasped the true implications of NEPA are [sic] unclear, but it was obvious that he used the bill to advertise his own concern for the environment": Jim Kershner, "NEPA, the National Environmental Policy Act" (27 August 2011), online: www.historylink.org/File/9903.

79    Gerald Markowitz and David Rosner, *Deceit and Denial: The Deadly Politics of Industrial Pollution* (Oakland, CA: University of California Press, 2002) at 155.

80    G Bruce Doern and Thomas Conway, *The Greening of Canada* (Toronto: University of Toronto Press, 1994) at 192: "By the early 1970s a total lack of interest in [addressing such costs of development as displacement of Indigenous peoples, destruction of habitat and mercury contamination of fish resulting from dam diversions] became a much less feasible option."

81    *Ibid* at 201–2.

82    *Ibid* at 207, citing *Report of the Royal Commission on the Economic Union and Development Prospects for Canada* (Ottawa: Minister of Supply and Services Canada, 1985).

primarily as a tool of legitimacy. Whenever opposition parties asserted that Bill C-69 was being rushed through Parliament, the Liberals responded that the bill was the product of fourteen months of consultation. This is not to say the Liberals did not argue that the *IAA* had substantive merit, but the very fact of consultation could be held up to a greater or lesser extent as having satisfied the election campaign promise. Decision outcomes, for the most part, are now likely to come after the next election and (not least due to the coronavirus pandemic and accompanying financial crisis) to be relatively unimportant as an election issue. Meanwhile, assessments can be claimed as conducted in accordance with the law, as a complete response to objections that outcomes are unsatisfactory. Whether the *IAA* will "regain public trust" or be considered "fair" will depend somewhat on the conduct and outcomes of actual assessments and other implementation measures.

The *IAA* can thus be seen as continuing a tradition of serving various actors' pursuit of legitimacy for assessment regimes and as contributing to the maintenance of certain power relations integral to the Canadian model of a liberal political economy.[83]

## 2) The Legitimizing Role of Institutions and Practices in the Prevailing Order

Consistent with the idea that IA regimes themselves serve to legitimize government decisions and thereby protect the established order, political actors, the legislative process, and the laws they create can also be seen as performing legitimizing roles.

Political declarations can legitimize the political actor: the Trudeau government's constant refrain that "the environment and the economy go hand in hand"[84] as Bill C-69 progressed through Parliament summarizes a simultaneous pursuit of legitimacy for the bill and for the

83    See CB Macpherson, *The Real World of Democracy* (Toronto: Canadian Broadcasting Corporation, 1965) [*Real World*]. For a recent assessment of *Real World* in the context of its broadcast (as the Massey Lectures) and publication, see Ian McKay, "The Real World of Democracy? CB Macpherson's Critique of the Cold War Reification of 'Liberal Democracy,' 1965" (2019), online (pdf): *Canadian Political Science Association* www. cpsa-acsp.ca/documents/conference/2019/51.McKay.pdf: *Real World* is "a refreshingly 'clear-headed' re-evaluation of the simplistic notion that liberalism and democracy [are] inseparably linked" at 11.

84    See above note 11.

government's ultimate liberal agenda of pursuing greater economic efficiency and competitiveness. That particular phrase is aimed at accommodating a wider range of interests across a spectrum of expert but especially popular opinion in order to gain or retain political power.[85]

Both the legislative process for Bill C-69 and the *IAA* regime it established can be seen as conditioning the public and other participants to outcomes and norms aimed at legitimizing industrial or natural resources "development" despite the environmental, social, and economic costs.[86] Soon after the bill was tabled, it was suggested to the environment and climate change minister that certain changes to the bill enhancing transparency of decisions would tend to increase one's comfort with how an *IAA* assessment decision was arrived at, even if one found the decision itself unsatisfactory. This fit well into the official *IAA* narrative and seemed to be embraced by the government, perhaps because it did not threaten the fundamental *IAA* architecture whereby Cabinet is minimally constrained in its decision making.

Although the secretive and opaque nature of decision making in Canada's Westminster system makes it difficult to state with precision when and how key decisions were made, it can be argued that the process leading to the *IAA*'s enactment was in large part an effort at (re)claiming legitimacy for government decision making involving the approval of development projects. Time and events will determine whether the *IAA* itself represents "real change."

---

85　For observations about how "perceived legitimacy of the [policy] actor is seen ... as a source of power," see Douglas Macdonald, *Carbon Province, Hydro Province: The Challenge of Canadian Energy and Climate Federalism* (Toronto: University of Toronto Press, 2020) at 32.

86　The accommodation of environmental groups in both law making and policy making can also be seen as lending legitimacy to both institutions and outcomes.

# CHAPTER 5

# Federal Jurisdiction and the *Impact Assessment Act*: Trojan Horse or Rational Ecological Accounting?

*Anna Johnston*

## A. INTRODUCTION

Federal jurisdiction over impact assessment (IA) remains unsettled despite the 1992 decision *Friends of the Oldman River Society v Canada (Minister of Transport)*.[1] This seminal case provided much-needed guidance on the extent of federal power to assess the impacts of proposed undertakings that were federally regulated or under federal constitutional authority. However, the case left important questions unanswered respecting the extent of federal authority at the triggering, information-gathering and analysis, and decision-making stages of assessment. By taking the bold step from environmental assessment (EA) to an IA model that considers a broader range of positive and negative environmental, social, health, and economic effects and their distribution, the *Impact Assessment Act* (IAA)[2] has raised new questions about the limits of federal jurisdiction to carry out assessments of proposed undertakings or activities covered by the Act. Indeed, in September 2019, Alberta's Lieutenant Governor in Council referred two constitutional questions to the Alberta Court of Appeal respecting the constitutional validity of the *IAA* and the *Physical Activities Regulations*,[3] which at the time of writing were still before the court.

---

1    [1992] 1 SCR 3 [*Oldman*].

2    SC 2019, c 28, s 1, s 22.

3    *Judicature Act*, OC 160/2019, s 26; *Physical Activities Regulations*, SOR/2019-285.

This chapter explores key questions respecting federal jurisdiction with regard to the *IAA*, beginning with a discussion of the constitutional division of powers in Canada, federalism and Canada's political constitution, and the cooperative federalism model that has gained traction in the courts in recent decades. Having set out the federalism context, the chapter then lays out the key issues respecting federal jurisdiction over project-level assessment and examines the *IAA* in light of relevant case law and the academic literature. In doing so, it analyzes federal jurisdiction in three distinct stages of IA: triggering, information gathering and analysis, and decision making.

## B. CANADA'S UNIQUE MODEL OF FEDERALISM

### 1) The Division of Constitutional Powers

Neither the provinces nor the federal government[4] has exclusive jurisdiction over environmental matters. The environment is not explicitly enumerated under the *Constitution Act, 1867*[5] (Constitution) and has been described as a "constitutionally abstruse matter which does not comfortably fit within the existing division of powers without considerable overlap and uncertainty."[6] To illustrate, the federal government has power over trade and commerce, navigation and shipping, the sea coast[7] and inland fisheries, Indigenous peoples and their lands, and

---

4    The federal Parliament and provincial legislatures are commonly referred to as "orders" of government as the federal and provincial governments are generally considered equal in status: Peter W Hogg, *Constitutional Law of Canada*, 5th ed supplemented (Toronto: Thomson Reuters, 2016) at 5.17.

5    (UK), 30 & 31 Vict, c 3, reprinted in RSC 1985, App II, No 5 [*Constitution Act*].

6    *Oldman*, above note 1 at 64.

7    Canada has claimed a twelve-mile territorial sea (*Territorial Sea and Fishing Zones Act*, RSC 1985, c T-8, s 3). In *Reference re Ownership of Off Shore Mineral Rights (British Columbia)*, [1967] SCR 792, the Supreme Court of Canada held that the boundaries of British Columbia end at the low watermark. As a result, British Columbia does not have any property rights in or rights to explore or exploit the continental shelf. Thus, the federal government owns the seabed of the territorial sea and has legislative jurisdiction over it, including the resources of the continental shelf, as well as the right to explore and exploit those resources. Hogg stated that this holding likely applies to the Atlantic Canada provinces, although Newfoundland and Labrador may be an exception because it joined Canada in 1949 and claims that it had acquired international status and therefore rights over its territorial sea, which it claims to retain (Hogg, above note 4 at 30.7–9). Other exceptions include inland waters, harbours, bays, estuaries, and other waters lying "between the jaws of the land," including the water between

criminal law,[8] whereas the provinces have jurisdiction over forests, local works and undertakings, property and civil rights,[9] non-renewable natural resources, and the generation and production of electrical energy.[10] Both levels of government are granted taxation powers,[11] and the federal government may enact legislation "for the Peace, Order, and good Government of Canada" for matters that the Constitution does not assign to the provinces (known as the POGG power).[12]

Due to its overlapping, diverse, and important nature, environmental protection is considered to be an area of shared jurisdiction. Each order of government is able to regulate matters that come under their respective heads of power, and both orders share authority over overlapping areas as long as the laws are not in direct conflict.[13] For example, whereas the federal fisheries power authorizes Parliament to legislate with respect to pollution in fish-bearing waters as long as the law provides a link between the proscribed conduct and harm to fisheries,[14] the provinces regulate matters related to drinking water.[15] The federal Parliament may only legislate with respect to matters assigned to it under section 91 of the Constitution,[16] but in doing so, it may touch on or incidentally affect provincial authority.[17]

Any understanding of the extent of federal constitutional authority[18] would be incomplete without concurrent understanding of the broader

---

    mainland British Columbia and Vancouver Island, which belong to the provinces: *Reference re Strait of Georgia*, [1984] 1 SCR 388; Hogg, above note 4 at 30.6–8.

8    *Constitution Act*, above note 5, ss 91(2), (10), (12), (24), and (27).

9    This power includes most mining, manufacturing, and other industries that affect the environment: Peter W Hogg, "Constitutional Authority over Greenhouse Gas Emissions" (2009) 46:2 *Alberta Law Review* 507 at 510.

10    *Constitution Act*, above note 5, ss 92(5), (10), (13), and 92A(1)–(2); see also Hogg, above note 4 at 30.3.

11    *Constitution Act*, above note 5, ss 91(3) and 92(2).

12    *Ibid*, s 91.

13    Meinhard Doelle, *The Federal Environmental Assessment Process: A Guide and Critique* (Markham, ON: LexisNexis Canada, 2008) at 59.

14    *R v Northwest Falling Contractors Ltd*, [1980] 2 SCR 292 [*Northwest Falling*].

15    See, for example, British Columbia's *Water Sustainability Act*, SBC 2014, c 15; see also Doelle, above note 13 at 55.

16    Above note 5.

17    *General Motors of Canada Ltd v City National Leasing*, [1989] 1 SCR 641 at 669.

18    Both "jurisdiction" and "authority" may be used to refer to the power conferred by the Constitution on the federal Parliament or the provincial legislatures, and both terms are used throughout this chapter.

socio-political context of Canadian federalism within which the constitutional division of powers sits.[19] In *Canadian Western Bank v Alberta*, the Supreme Court of Canada described Canada's federalism as "the legal response ... to the political and cultural realities" of Confederation-era Canada, "a legal recognition of the diversity of the original members."[20] The division of constitutional powers under sections 91 and 92 of the *British North America Act*[21] was intended "to uphold this diversity within a single nation" by conferring broad powers on the provinces while ensuring national unity through assignment to the federal Parliament of "powers better exercised in relation to the country as a whole."[22] At Confederation, as well as now, the "fundamental objectives of federalism [are] to reconcile unity with diversity, promote democratic participation by reserving meaningful powers to the local or regional level and to foster co-operation among governments and legislatures for the common good."[23]

Conflict between the two orders of government has been especially pronounced with respect to natural resources and the need for environmental protection.[24] IA is especially vulnerable to jurisdictional tensions due to its application early on in decision making and because it requires assessment of a comprehensive suite of relevant information, regardless of whether the Constitution assigns the subject matter of that information to the assessing authority.[25] Canadian courts, when addressing questions of constitutional authority, will be alive to such tensions, as well as to "perceived provincial sensitivities" and intergovernmental relations.[26] As Lederman argued, the "cultural, social and

---

19  WR Lederman, "Unity and Diversity in Canadian Federalism: Ideals and Methods of Moderation" (1975) 53:3 *Canadian Bar Review* 597 at 601; William R MacKay, "Canadian Federalism and the Environment: The Literature" (2004) 17 *Georgetown International Environmental Law Review* 25 at 28.

20  2007 SCC 22 at para 22 [*Canadian Western Bank*].

21  1867, SS 1867, c 3 [*BNA Act*].

22  *Canadian Western Bank*, above note 20 at para 22.

23  *Ibid.*

24  Romanow, "Federalism and Resource Management" in J Owen Saunders, ed, *Managing Natural Resources in a Federal State: Essays from the Second Banff Conference on Natural Resources Law* (Toronto: Carswell, 1986) 2 at 1.

25  Steven A Kennett, "Federal Environmental Jurisdiction After Oldman" (1993) 38 *McGill Law Journal* 180 at 182.

26  Alastair R Lucas, "Harmonization of the Federal and Provincial Environmental Policies: The Changing Legal and Policy Framework" in J Owen Saunders, ed, *Managing Natural Resources in a Federal State: Essays from the Second Banff Conference on Natural Resources Law* (Toronto: Carswell, 1986) 33 at 35; MacKay, above note 19 at 26.

economic realities of the society for which [the sections 91 and 92 heads of power] were intended" are likely to influence judicial consideration of balance of power questions, along with the need to balance national standards with provincial autonomy and regional diversity.[27]

## 2)  Cooperative Federalism

Increasingly over the decades, courts in Canada have looked to the principle of cooperative federalism to guide their analyses of jurisdictional questions. Indeed, the courts "discovered" federalism as an unwritten principle to help guide division of powers cases.[28] In the 1980s and 1990s, the Supreme Court of Canada stressed the need to reject the "watertight compartments" model of federalism that viewed the enumerated heads of power as exclusive enclaves and indicated a preference for recognizing concurrent or overlapping powers.[29] After the appointment of McLachlin J as chief justice in 2000, the Court shifted more prominently toward encouraging cooperative federalism and intergovernmental dialogue, beginning with *Reference re Firearms Act (Can)*.[30] In that case, the Court held that "overlap of legislation [was] to be expected and accommodated in a federal state."[31] A few years later in the *Employment Insurance Reference*,[32] the Court cautioned against judicial activism when adjudicating on the division of powers as constitutional interpretation is subjective and political in nature.[33] Wright interprets this finding as an indication that the Court is concerned that judge-based assignments of power will be "informed by politics" rather than law and that "it is considerably more comfortable leaving such line-drawing exercises to the political branches, as much as possible."[34]

---

27    WR Lederman, "The Concurrent Operation of Federal and Provincial Laws in Canada" (1963) 9 *McGill Law Journal* 185 at 186–87.

28    *Reference re Secession of Quebec*, [1998] 2 SCR 217 at para 32; Hogg, above note 4 at 15.52.

29    See, for example, *Husky Oil Operations Ltd v Canada (Minister of National Revenue— MNR)*, [1995] 3 SCR 453 at para 162; *Ontario Public Service Employees Union v Ontario (Attorney General)*, [1987] 2 SCR 2 at para 18.

30    2000 SCC 31.

31    *Ibid* at para 26.

32    2005 SCC 56.

33    *Ibid* at para 10.

34    Wade K Wright, "Facilitating Intergovernmental Dialogue: Judicial Review of the Division of Powers in the Supreme Court of Canada" (2010) 51 *Supreme Court Law Review* 625 at 635.

Federalism has featured prominently in environmental cases involving the division of powers, wherein the courts have demonstrated a preference for respecting the division while maintaining a flexible approach that allows both orders of government to address emerging environmental issues. In his dissent in *R v Crown Zellerbach Canada Ltd*,[35] La Forest J expressed concerns with the majority's decision to uphold federal prohibitions against the dumping of substances at sea under the federal POGG power, stating that the provinces would have "no concurrent authority with the federal government" over marine pollution under the national concern branch of POGG.[36] To uphold the legislation under POGG, La Forest J held, would "create considerable stress on Canadian federalism as it has developed over the years"[37] as it risks allocating environmental pollution broadly and exclusively to the federal government and "sacrificing the principles of federalism enshrined in the Constitution."[38] In the subsequent *R v Hydro-Québec* case,[39] La Forest J (this time writing for the majority) addressed these concerns by upholding provisions of the *Canadian Environmental Protection Act (CEPA)*[40] under the criminal law power rather than POGG. As laws enacted under the criminal law power do not take jurisdiction away from the provinces, upholding *CEPA* under that power recognizes the "superordinate importance" of having both federal and provincial legislative measures to protect the environment.[41] Due to what he called the "sweeping" nature of environmental pollution, care must be taken to respect the division of powers and preserve the ability of both orders of government to "exercise leadership" in environmental protection.[42]

In *Oldman* (described below), La Forest J rejected the argument that projects should be classified as a "provincial project" or an undertaking "primarily subject to provincial regulation."[43] Each order of government may regulate with respect to aspects within its responsibility,

---

35    [1988] 1 SCR 401 [*Crown Zellerbach*].

36    William Lahey, "Justice Gérard v La Forest and the Uncertain Greening of Canadian Public Law" (2013) 54 *Canadian Business Law Journal* 223 at 233.

37    *Crown Zellerbach*, above note 35 at 451.

38    *Ibid* at 455.

39    [1997] 3 SCR 213 [*Hydro-Québec*].

40    SC, 1999, c 33.

41    *Hydro-Québec*, above note 39 at para 85.

42    *Ibid* at para 154.

43    *Oldman*, above note 1 at 68.

and as an information-gathering tool, the *Environmental Assessment and Review Process Guidelines Order* of 1984 (EARP 1984)[44] in question simply regulated how federal officials approach their regulatory decision making.[45] He noted the multifaceted nature of the environment and the need for both orders of government to share responsibility for it through their respective heads of power. Through this recognition, La Forest J advanced the notion that the courts should facilitate collaboration in advancement of federalism principles, as well as the need for an "integrated approach to environmental management … if environmental protection was to be effective."[46]

Thus, a key question when considering federal authority is whether, with regard to the *IAA* or assessments under it that affect or touch on provincial matters, the Act fosters federal–provincial cooperation in pursuit of what the Supreme Court of Canada has recognized as the "fundamental value" of protecting the environment.[47]

## C.  FEDERAL JURISDICTION AND THE *IAA*

As noted in the introduction, the Supreme Court of Canada first considered federal jurisdiction over EA in *Oldman*. The *IAA* differs from the EA process that was the subject of that case in key ways, and the law on the full extent of federal authority to require IAs of projects and activities in Canada is far from settled. At issue in *Oldman* was whether EARP 1984 applied to the Oldman River Dam, a Province of Alberta project that required a permit under the *Navigable Waters Protection Act*[48] (as it was then called). EARP 1984 required EAs of any "initiative, undertaking or activity for which the Government of Canada has a decision making responsibility" and that "may have an environmental effect on an area of federal responsibility,"[49] and required those EAs to consider socio-economic, health, and other impacts along with environmental ones.[50]

---

44   SOR/84-467.

45   *Oldman*, above note 1 at 71–72.

46   Lahey, above note 36 at 234.

47   *114957 Canada Ltée (Spraytech, Société d'arrosage) v Hudson (Town)*, 2001 SCC 40 at para 1 [*Spraytech*].

48   RSC, 1985, c N-22.

49   Above note 44, ss 2 and 6(b).

50   *Oldman*, above note 1 at 36–37 and 71–72.

Unlike the triggering approach used in EARP 1984 (as discussed in Chapter 7), which required EAs of projects that needed to obtain a separate federal regulatory approval, the *IAA* uses a project list approach to designating which projects should be subject to IA. Thus, *Oldman* does not answer the question of federal authority to trigger IAs of projects that may not require federal regulatory approval.[51] Furthermore, as detailed in Chapter 9, the *IAA* requires assessment of all positive and negative environmental, social, economic, and health effects,[52] whereas in *Oldman*, it appeared germane to La Forest J (who again wrote the majority decision) that EARP 1984 restricted the factors to be considered to effects on areas of federal environmental responsibility and impacts resulting from those federal effects.[53] *Oldman* therefore did not discuss the extent to which federal authorities could reject projects due to impacts that are provincial in nature or impose conditions on matters that relate to areas of provincial jurisdiction (such as air pollution). As a result, the key questions respecting federal jurisdiction over the *IAA* are (1) federal jurisdiction to require an IA; (2) the scope of factors that may be considered in an IA; and (3) the extent to which the minister and Governor in Council (as the case may be) can consider the broad list of section 22(1) factors when deciding whether to approve a project or the extent to which federal authorities can impose conditions on projects, where those conditions relate to provincial matters. Each of these issues is discussed in more detail below.

### 1) Federal Authority to Require an Impact Assessment

The academic literature and the jurisprudence lean in favour of a low jurisdictional "threshold" (requirement to prove federal jurisdiction) at the triggering stage. A low threshold suggests that the federal government has broad authority to designate a project under the *Physical Activities Regulations*[54] or through the minister's designation power under section 9(1) of the *IAA*. As a planning tool, IA occurs in the early stages of decision making, before information about potential impacts on areas

---


51    Doelle, above note 13 at 73.

52    *IAA*, above note 2, s 22(1).

53    *Oldman*, above note 1 at 73.

54    *Ibid.*

of federal jurisdiction may be known.[55] As La Forest J described in *Oldman,* EA is "essentially an information gathering process"[56] to inform decision making. The same is true for IA. Requiring federal authorities to obtain evidence of a project's effects prior to the assessment would be to put the cart before the horse and undermine the Act's objectives of precaution and protection of the environment.[57] The Supreme Court of Canada has looked to the precautionary principle in upholding environmental legislation in cases respecting the division of powers,[58] and a precautionary approach to IA would trigger assessments early, where there is simply a reasonable possibility — rather than proof — of federal effects.[59] In recent decades, the Court has tended to accord the federal government jurisdictional latitude to deal with environmental issues in recognition of the need for both orders of government to be at the table of environmental protection.[60]

The precautionary approach is reflected in section 9(1), which authorizes the minister to subject a project to the *IAA* if, in the minister's opinion, the project *may* impact on areas within federal authority. In other words, the Act does not require proof of federal effects to order an assessment — only the possibility of effects.[61] Additionally, when determining whether an assessment of a designated project is required, the Impact Assessment Agency of Canada (the Agency) need only consider the *possibility* of the project causing effects on areas of federal jurisdiction (federal effects)[62] rather than show proof of federal effects or even the likelihood of federal effects. It is also reflected in

---

55    Jason MacLean, Meinhard Doelle & Chris Tollefson, "Polyjural and Polycentric Sustainability Assessment: A Once-in-a-Generation Law Reform Opportunity" (2016) 30 *Journal of Environmental Law & Practice* 35 at 43; Bram Noble & Kelechi Nwanekezie, "Conceptualizing Strategic Environmental Assessment: Principles, Approaches and Research Directions" (2017) 62 *Environmental Impact Assessment Review* 165 at 166; Meinhard Doelle & Rebecca Critchley, "The Role of Strategic Environmental Assessments in Improving the Governance of Emerging New Industries: A Case Study of Wind Developments in Nova Scotia" (2015) 11 *McGill International Journal of Sustainable Development Law & Policy* 87 at 110; Robert B Gibson et al, *Sustainability Assessment: Criteria and Process* (London, UK: Earthscan, 2005) at 16.

56    *Oldman*, above note 1 at 71 and 75.

57    *IAA*, above note 2, ss 6(a) and (d) [JBOA, Tab L1]; *Oldman*, above note 1 at 16.

58    *Spraytech*, above note 47 at paras 31–32.

59    MacLean et al, above note 55 at 43; Doelle, above note 13 at 72.

60    MacLean et al, above note 55; MacKay, above note 19 at 27–28.

61    *IAA*, above note 2, s 9(1).

62    *Ibid*, s 16(1)(b).

the *Canadian Wildlife Federation Inc v Canada (Minister of the Environment)* case,[63] which suggested that effects on areas within federal jurisdiction need not be established at the time of an assessment trigger. In that case, the Federal Court of Appeal held that EARP 1984 applied to the Rafferty and Alameda dams on the Souris River system on the basis that it would have transboundary impacts. Although federal jurisdiction over the project was not at issue, the Court of Appeal noted that the responsible minister was not aware of the potential impacts on areas within federal authority before deciding that EARP 1984 did not apply but held that the order applied nonetheless.[64]

Indeed, courts have held that EA panel reports are not reviewable on the basis that no legal right or interest has yet been affected,[65] which suggests that there may be judicial preference to defer the question of federal authority to the decision-making stage. Although requiring designated projects to enter into the IA process does affect proponents' interests, the case law suggests that courts are inclined to wait until the decision stage, during which the decision maker can determine that he or she has no constitutional authority to reject or impose conditions on a project. Moreover, assessments tend to be scoped at the triggering stage to lessen burdens on proponents and minimize intrusion into provincial jurisdiction.[66] Where the jurisdictional hook is low (e.g., there is only uncertain potential for low-level impacts on limited areas of federal authority), the assessment can be scoped to focus only on significant or relevant potential effects.[67] Finally, it should be noted that triggering IA early on in project design facilitates the identification of alternatives to the project and alternative means of carrying projects out, as discussed by Arlene Kwasniak and Sharon Mascher in Chapter 10. Thus, federal authority to trigger assessments early, before information respecting federal effects may be known, may help proponents design their projects in such a way as to enable decision makers to find that federal effects, including direct or indirect effects, are in the public interest.

---

63    [1989] 3 FC 309 (TD), aff'd [1990] 2 WWR 69 (FCA).

64    *Ibid* at 325–26.

65    *Gitxaala Nation v Canada*, [2016] 2016 FCA 187 at para 125; *Alberta Wilderness Association v Canada (Minister of Fisheries and Oceans)*, [1997] FCJ No 1666 at paras 2 and 4.

66    Jamie Benidickson, *Environmental Law*, 3d ed (Toronto: Irwin Law, 2009) at 259; Doelle, above note 13 at 62–63.

67    *IAA*, above note 2, ss 18(1.2) and 22(2).

Regardless of the breadth of federal authority to require an IA, the *Physical Activities Regulations* are designed to capture projects with the greatest potential for federal effects,[68] a higher threshold than reasonable possibility of such effects. Where designated projects are already subject to provincial assessment processes, the *IAA*'s cooperation mechanisms,[69] as explained in Chapter 8, present opportunities to minimize duplication. In the event that an IA shows no likely federal effects (or exercise of federal authority or federal funding), the project may proceed. Moreover, the *IAA* only prohibits proponents from causing prescribed federal effects without an assessment,[70] meaning that where it is reasonably certain that no federal effects will occur, proponents may proceed with designated projects without assessment under the Act.

## 2)   Information Gathering and Analysis

The case law and literature suggest that once an IA is triggered, the scope of the assessment may be broad. As discussed in Chapter 10, "scope" refers both to the scope of the project (its components and related activities) that will be subject to the assessment and to the factors that will be considered.[71] For the scope of the project, described as "whether and how far the federal environmental assessment can look beyond the proposal that requires federal regulatory approval,"[72] the jurisprudence is instructive. In *Quebec (Attorney General) v Canada (National Energy Board)*,[73] the Supreme Court of Canada rejected the argument that the scope of the National Energy Board's (NEB) EA was limited to those project components within federal jurisdiction and determined that the NEB was authorized to consider the future effects of provincially regulated energy generation facilities when deciding whether to grant licences to export electrical power to the United States.[74]

Similarly, in *Sumas Energy 2, Inc v Canada (National Energy Board)*,[75] the Federal Court of Appeal held that the NEB has jurisdiction to

---

68   *Regulatory Impact Analysis Statement*, SOR/2019-285 [RIAS] at 5663.

69   IAA, above note 2, ss 29, 31, and 39(1).

70   *Ibid*, s 7(1).

71   *Ibid*, s 22(1).

72   Doelle, above note 13 at 74.

73   [1994] 1 SCR 159.

74   *Ibid* at 193–94.

75   2005 FCA 377.

consider the potential environmental effects within Canada of a power plant located outside Canada. Sumas Energy 2 had applied for a certificate of public convenience and necessity to construct an international power line from a proposed power plant located in Washington State to a BC Hydro substation just north of the Canadian border, a plant that would emit pollutants into British Columbia's airshed.[76] The court held that although the NEB did not have authority to consider the effects of the plant that occurred in the United States, it did have jurisdiction to consider the environmental impacts that occurred in Canada as a result of project components in the United States, and could refuse to issue the certificate on those grounds.[77]

In *Friends of the West Country Association v Canada (Minister of Fisheries and Oceans)*, the Federal Court of Appeal found that the possibility that construction or operation of roads or bridges over non-navigable waters could have cumulative adverse environmental effects "demonstrates why it is logical that a cumulative effects assessment under paragraph 16(1)(a) not be restricted to the scope of the federal project or to projects only under federal jurisdiction."[78] In *MiningWatch Canada v Canada*, the Supreme Court of Canada confirmed that the scope of the project to be assessed federally must include all components and activities proposed by the proponent.[79] These cases demonstrate that federal authorities may look beyond those project components that will impact federal matters, and include all related components and activities in the scope of assessment.

Regarding the scope of factors considered in an IA, the Act requires assessments to consider all positive and negative environmental, health, and socio-economic effects, not only effects on areas of federal authority.[80] The *Oldman* decision emphasized that EARP 1984 only required the assessment of environmental and socio-economic factors that impacted on areas of federal jurisdiction.[81] However, there do not appear to be jurisdictional limitations on what information the Agency

---

76   *Ibid* at paras 1 and 4.
77   *Ibid* at paras 12 and 14.
78   [2000] 2 FC 263 at para 35.
79   2010 SCC 2 at paras 40–41.
80   *IAA*, above note 2, s 22(1).
81   *Oldman*, above note 1 at 72.

or a review panel may require to be brought to light in an IA, although interpretations of *Oldman* vary on this point.

Justice La Forest stated that the scope of information a federal EA will consider varies depending on which head of power the authority to trigger and make decisions lies and distinguishes between federal authority over natural resources (e.g., fisheries) and activities (e.g., navigation).[82] Kennett argued that the decision intended for federal jurisdiction respecting activities to be comprehensive and for federal authority over resources or impacts to be restricted.[83] Doelle disagreed, pointing to other statements in the decision "suggesting a progressive interpretation of federal jurisdiction to enable integrated decision-making unless to do so would be an invasion of provincial jurisdiction."[84] Applying such a progressive interpretation, MacLean et al referred to powers over activities such as fisheries as "functional" and powers over federally regulated projects as "conceptual."[85] Indeed, La Forest J did not mention "restricted" versus "comprehensive" jurisdiction; conversely, he wrote that "it defies reason to assert that Parliament is constitutionally barred from weighing the broad environmental repercussions, including socio-economic concerns," of a project when making decisions under its heads of power.[86] If EARP 1984 is valid legislation that can be upheld under a head of federal power, "it would be immaterial that it also affects matters of property and civil rights."[87]

The distinction respecting the different heads of power stems from the Supreme Court of Canada decisions in *R v Fowler*[88] and *R v Northwest Falling Contractors Ltd,*[89] which together require an exercise of the federal fisheries power to be rooted in actual or potential harm to fisheries. That power does not extend to blanket prohibitions of activities that are "not sufficiently linked to any actual or potential harm."[90] Similarly, IA may only affect matters that are "truly in relation to an institution

---

82  *Ibid* at 67–68.

83  Kennett, above note 25 at 187–89 and 193.

84  Doelle, above note 13 at 68.

85  MacLean et al, above note 55 at 41.

86  *Oldman*, above note 1 at 66.

87  *Ibid* at 62.

88  [1980] 2 SCR 213.

89  *Northwest Falling*, above note 14.

90  *Oldman*, above note 1 at 67–68.

that is otherwise within [federal] legislative jurisdiction."[91] Where matters are truly in relation to an area of federal jurisdiction, federal authorities may consider all information relevant to that matter. For example, the federal power over railways includes the authority to consider the national and local social, environmental, and economic ramifications of decisions related to railways.[92] Although the federal fisheries and navigation powers relate to activities and resources rather than projects, it seems logical that when considering the impacts of undertakings on those activities, the federal government may ask proponents to provide information related to all of a project's positive and adverse effects in order to have a comprehensive picture to inform decision making.[93] Whether a federal head of power be with respect to an activity or a natural resource, the scoping rules remain the same: the effects assessed should be based on issues related to an area of federal authority. Although the *actual* scope of effects that may be considered will vary among the various heads of power, the basic scoping *rules* are the same.

Regardless of whether the courts will ultimately determine that there is a functional difference between federal IA authority where its jurisdiction is over a project (such as a railway) or an activity (such as a fishery), MacLean et al argued that there is likely no jurisdictional limit on the scope of information that may be considered in an assessment; jurisdictional limits are instead relevant at decision making.[94] The provisions in the *IAA* that allow for multi-jurisdictional cooperation may alleviate jurisdictional concerns. IA has multi-jurisdictional implications due to overlapping legislative environmental responsibilities, and intergovernmental coordination is required in order to minimize duplication, enhance certainty and efficiency, and advance sustainability.[95] The *IAA* recognizes this fact by providing opportunities for substitution,[96] delegation,[97] and joint review.[98] Through its multi-juris-

---

91    *Ibid* at 72, from *Devine v Quebec (Attorney General)*, [1988] 2 SCR 790 at 808.

92    *Oldman*, above note 1 at 66.

93    *Ibid* at 66–68 and 72; MacLean et al, above note 55 at 42.

94    *Ibid* at 44–45.

95    Patricia Fitzpatrick & A John Sinclair, "Multi-jurisdictional Environmental Impact Assessment: Canadian Experiences" (2009) 29 *Environmental Impact Assessment Review* 252 at 253; MacLean et al, above note 55 at 38, 49, and 52.

96    *IAA*, above note 2, s 31(1).

97    *Ibid*, s 29.

98    *Ibid*, s 39(1). See Chapter 8 for a detailed description of these powers.

dictional collaboration mechanisms, IA can act as a vehicle for federal and provincial cooperation in environmental decision making, which is one of the "fundamental objectives" of cooperative federalism.[99]

## 3) Decision Making

The decision stage of assessments likely requires the most careful attention to the extent of federal jurisdiction, as it is here that the federal government may reject projects that have been approved by provincial governments (or vice versa) or attach conditions of approval that affect matters of provincial jurisdiction. As noted above, unlike under EARP 1984, which employed a federal decision-making trigger, the *IAA* does not guarantee that a designated project requires an exercise of federal regulatory authority. Sections 60(1) and 62 require the minister of environment and climate change or Governor in Council (as the case may be) to determine whether a project's adverse federal effects, or its direct or incidental effects (hereinafter referred to collectively as federal effects),[100] are in the public interest regardless of whether the project requires regulatory approval under another federal statute. Thus, the two relevant questions for decision-making authority over project IA are whether the Act can impose stand-alone decision-making authority and, if so, what the scope of that authority is.

Of course, an assertion of federal regulatory authority (such as a requirement to obtain a *Fisheries Act*[101] authorization) is not in itself guaranteed to be a valid exercise of federal jurisdiction. Failure to have enacted the *Fisheries Act* would not have nullified the federal fisheries power, and Parliament would still have authority to assess projects based on potential impacts on fish. Accordingly, the jurisdictional basis

---

99 *Canadian Western Bank*, above note 20 at para 22.

100 Direct or incidental effects are defined in s 2 of the *IAA* as effects that are "directly linked or necessarily incidental to" the exercise of a federal duty or provision of federal funding. Whereas in division of powers cases "incidental" refers to secondary effects or objectives (*Canadian Western Bank, ibid* at paras 27–28), "incidental," for the purposes of the *IAA* refers to effects that are connected to or flow from an exercise of a duty or provision of funding, such as harm to grizzly bears as a result of harm to fish that those grizzly bears eat, which is authorized by the federal fisheries minister.

101 RSC, 1985, c F-14.

for a decision under the *IAA* cannot be dependent on whether a statutory or other decision-making function outside the Act exists. Where a project will impact areas of federal jurisdiction or where the project is federally regulated, the critical question is whether the minister and Governor in Council may consider all of a project's impacts, benefits, risks, and uncertainties when deciding whether federal effects are in the public interest.

The majority decision in *Oldman* appears to suggest that a decision maker may base decisions on broader environmental, social, or economic considerations than those that are directly related to a federal head of power.[102] Using the analogy of a railway line, La Forest J found that it would be appropriate to relocate the line to avoid air or noise pollution that would result in a nuisance.[103] He referred to the Australian *Murphyores* case,[104] in which the Court upheld a federal decision to inquire into the environmental impacts of mineral extraction when considering whether to approve the minerals' export. In Australia, state governments, not the Commonwealth, regulate mineral extraction, but it was within the federal minister's power to consider the environmental effects of extraction when exercising federal authority over exports. As La Forest J concluded, considerations that inform administrative decision making may be broad as long as the subject matter of the legislation is valid.[105]

According to Kennett, the practical implication of his distinction between what he called "comprehensive" jurisdiction over activities (such as railways) and "restricted" jurisdiction (such as over fisheries) is that where an assessment is based on restricted federal jurisdiction, the federal government is limited to only addressing the consequences of the project on that subject matter.[106] In other words, federal authorities may assess a dam that will impact fisheries or navigation, but there are restrictions on the extent of federal authority to reject the project or impose conditions on it.[107] As a result, Kennett argued that

---

102   *Oldman*, above note 1 at 72; Doelle, above note 13 at 75.

103   *Oldman*, above note 1 at 66.

104   *Murphyores Incorporated Pty Ltd v Commonwealth of Australia* (1976), 136 CLR 1 (HCA).

105   *Oldman*, above note 1 at 69–70.

106   Kennett, above note 25 at 189–90.

107   *Ibid* at 191.

the federal government only has authority to "veto or attach stringent conditions to certain projects" over which it has restricted jurisdiction where a "significant link has been established" between the reason for the veto or the conditions and a federal power.[108] However, it could not impose restrictions on the dam that are unconnected to a federal head of authority.[109]

Doelle suggested that Kennett's interpretation of *Oldman* "would give no weight to the very strong statements at the start of the [*Oldman*] decision suggesting a progressive interpretation of federal jurisdiction to enable integrated decision-making unless to do so would be an invasion of provincial jurisdiction."[110] Indeed, La Forest J's primary concern in *Oldman* was that assessments be rooted in federal authority, and he recognized that many projects requiring a federal authorization, such as dams or bridges, do not improve the matter over which the federal government has authority (e.g., waterway navigation).[111] In many (if not most) cases, it is unlikely that federal impacts will be positive. Thus, inherent in federal environmental decision making of all projects is the consideration of socio-economic benefits that will flow from a project and that will (or will not) outweigh the negative impacts on fish, navigation, or other areas of federal responsibility.[112] As La Forest J held,

> In legislating regarding a subject, it is sufficient that the legislative body legislate on that subject. The practical purpose that inspires the legislation and the implications that body must consider in making its decision are another thing. Absent a colourable purpose or a lack of *bona fides*, these considerations will not detract from the fundamental nature of the legislation. A railway line may be required to locate so as to avoid a nuisance resulting from smoke or noise in a municipality, but it is nonetheless railway regulation.[113]

Accordingly, although there must be a sufficient relationship between an IA decision and valid legislation, and an assessment authority cannot

---

108   *Ibid.*

109   *Ibid* at 193.

110   Doelle, above note 13 at 68.

111   *Oldman*, above note 1 at 67.

112   Marie-Ann Bowden & Martin ZP Olszynski, "Old Puzzle, New Pieces: *Red Chris* and *Vanadium* and the Future of Federal Environmental Assessment" (2010) 89 *Canadian Bar Review* 445 at 475–76 and 484.

113   *Oldman*, above note 1 at 69.

use assessment "as a colourable device to invade areas of provincial jurisdiction,"[114] where a sufficient nexus exists between valid legislation and a decision under that legislation, any intrusion into matters within provincial authority is incidental and therefore permissible.[115] Conversely, it is unlikely that where an IA reveals no impacts on a federal power the federal government would be able to reject or impose conditions on a project, as those decisions would fall outside its constitutional authority to do so.[116]

In other words, there is a distinction between legislating on a matter and making decisions under that legislation. So long as a statute is *intra vires*, La Forest J indicated that the considerations that may inform decision making under it are not restricted to the jurisdictional root anchoring that legislation. Accordingly, it would seem to be appropriate for decision makers to consider all of a project's adverse impacts when determining whether federal effects are in the public interest. The minister may decide, for example, that a mine's adverse impacts on fish, when considered together with air pollution and health effects, are not outweighed by the project's benefits. Similarly, she or he may impose conditions under section 64(2) that enhance the mine's benefits — for example, to ensure longer-lasting jobs for the local community — in order to find that the impacts on fish are in the public interest. So long as such conditions are rationally connected to the valid exercise of federal jurisdiction, it should be immaterial that the decision affects property or civil rights, the management of natural resources, or other matters of provincial authority.[117] As Doelle argued, "It does not serve to protect provincial jurisdiction to force the federal decision, whether or not to approve an impact on navigation, to be made in a partially blind manner."[118]

Authority to assess all of a project's relevant effects is consistent with the Supreme Court of Canada's decision in *British Columbia v Canadian*

---

114    *Ibid* at 72; MacLean et al, above note 55 at 42.

115    *Ibid* at 75.

116    Doelle, above note 13 at 75.

117    *Oldman*, above note 1 at 66; Martin Z Olszynski, "Chapter 16: Reconsidering Red Chris: Federal Environmental Decision-Making after MiningWatch Canada v. Canada (Fisheries and Oceans)" in William A Tilleman and Alistair Lucas, eds, *Litigating Canada's Environment: Leading Canadian Environmental Law Cases by the Lawyers Involved* (Toronto: Thomson Reuters Canada, 2017) at paras 33–35.

118    Doelle, above note 13 at 67.

*Forest Products Ltd.*[119] In that case, a majority of the Court recognized the value of ecosystem services, or "the services provided by the ecosystem to human beings, including food sources, water quality and recreational opportunities."[120] Federal matters, such as fisheries and waterway navigation, are examples of such services. Where projects affect those matters, proponents are in effect seeking permission to use up some of those ecosystem services. When the minister or Governor in Council determines whether a project's federal effects are in the public interest,[121] that determination may appropriately be viewed as deciding whether it is in the public interest to allocate — or even forsake, as the case may be — a federal ecosystem service to the project in question. Accordingly, it would be not only appropriate but also arguably necessary to consider all of a project's impacts, benefits, risks, and uncertainties in order to make an informed decision as to whether it is in the public interest for that project to cause federal effects. As Bowden and Olszynski argued, to suggest that jobs and revenue are within federal powers to consider, but broader environmental and social impacts are not, is "to suggest that the Constitution is inherently and permanently biased towards an out-dated and discredited model for economic growth — a seemingly untenable position."[122]

Decisions do not stop at project approval, however; where the minister or Governor in Council decides that a project's adverse federal effects, including direct or indirect effects, are in the public interest, section 64 requires the minister to impose "any condition that he or she considers appropriate in relation to" those effects. On the one hand, this condition-imposing authority seems broad — *any* conditions the minister *considers* appropriate — but, on the other hand, it is limited to only conditions *in relation to* federal effects, or direct or indirect effects. The question, then, is whether the minister can impose conditions respecting provincial matters where those matters are in relation to federal, direct, or indirect effects. Using the mine example above, could the minister impose conditions on the project respecting the pace and scale of mining operations to ensure lasting jobs for the community in exchange for permitting the mine to harm fish? And could she or

119  2004 SCC 38.
120  *Ibid* at paras 138 and 141.
121  *IAA*, above note 2, ss 60(1) and 62.
122  Bowden & Olszynski, above note 112 at 484.

he attach another condition respecting noise and dust pollution abatement, even where the noise and dust have no impact on (and do not flow from harm to) fish?

From a jurisdictional perspective, it would appear illogical not to authorize the minister to attach such conditions. If, as the case law suggests, it is within federal jurisdiction to determine that a project's federal effects are not in the public interest in light of that project's broader environmental, social, and economic effects, it seems absurd not to permit the minister to attach conditions respecting those broader effects in order to allow the project to proceed. Indeed, in La Forest J's words, it "defies reason" to hold otherwise.[123] What remains to be seen are the reasonable limits to federal authority to reject projects based on provincial effects, or attach conditions on those effects, such as where federal effects will be relatively minor and the intrusion into provincial matters is significant. These questions are best resolved on a case-by-case basis as the particular facts of each situation will be pertinent.

## D. CONCLUSIONS AND REMAINING QUESTIONS

In *Oldman*, a majority of the Supreme Court of Canada rejected the claim that EAs are a "constitutional Trojan horse enabling the federal government, on the pretext of some narrow ground of federal jurisdiction, to conduct a far-ranging inquiry into matters that are exclusively within provincial jurisdiction."[124] Rather, both orders of government have the power to affect the environment through action or inaction,[125] and each order may legislate matters pertaining to their respective authorities. There is no general doctrine of interjurisdictional immunity that shields provincial projects from valid federal legislation, and the federal government has a decision-making role with natural resource projects that affect areas of federal jurisdiction.[126] At the heart of the jurisdictional question is the extent to which federal authorities may require IAs without proof of federal effects, reject projects based on

---

123  *Oldman*, above note 1 at 66.

124  *Ibid* at 71–72; Nathalie J Chalifour, "Drawing Lines in the Sand: Parliament's Jurisdiction to Consider Upstream and Downstream Greenhouse Gas (GHG) Emissions in Interprovincial Pipeline Project Reviews" (2018) 23:1 *Review of Constitutional Studies* 129 at 160.

125  *Oldman*, above note 1 at 65.

126  *Ibid* at 68.

issues related to provincial concerns, or impose conditions respecting provincial matters.

Although federal authorities may be able to consider all of a project's impacts when deciding whether to issue an approval, that decision must be rooted in federal jurisdiction, either because the project is federally regulated (e.g., a railway) or because it will impact an area of federal authority.[127] Although there must be a sufficient nexus between the degree of impact on the area within federal authority and the degree of intrusion into the provincial arena, that particular alchemy remains to be worked out by the courts on a case-by-case basis. For example, would the federal government have the authority to refuse a dam on the basis of airborne pollution where the effects on navigation are avoidable or mitigatable to the point of null or insignificance and the air pollution does not result in any impacts on federal jurisdiction? What about where the dam will impact navigation and the air pollution will result in significant socio-economic effects that the federal government believes outweigh the project's benefits? Similarly, if a mining project's impacts on fish are negligible and the burden on the proponent to relocate facilities is insurmountable, a court may find that the federal government has overstepped its jurisdiction by requiring relocation of its tailings pond. But where the impacts on fish are proven, any intrusion into provincial jurisdiction by requiring an alternative means of carrying out the mine would likely be within federal authority.

It is clear from the substitution, delegation, and joint review provisions that the legislative drafters intended the *IAA* to encourage cooperation with the provinces, which is an obvious aid to the jurisdictional problem.[128] Where cooperation occurs, IAs should naturally assess both provincial and federal matters. But where IAs occur in the absence of provincial cooperation, it would be unreasonable not to extend decision-making authority to the consideration of all of a project's impacts, benefits, risks, and uncertainties. Indeed, where a project will cause adverse federal effects, the primary constraint on decision-making authority under the *IAA* may not be constitutional limitations but administrative law ones: it is well established that a decision maker cannot consider irrelevant factors when exercising discretion.[129] Accordingly, the

---

127   Kennett, above note 25 at 200.
128   *Ibid* at 202; Doelle, above note 13 at 63.
129   *Ontario (Public Safety and Security) v Criminal Lawyers' Association*, 2010 SCC 23 at para 71.

minister and Governor in Council may only consider relevant information when deciding whether a project's effects are in the public interest. Following the reasoning of *Oldman* and the other cases discussed in this chapter, as long as a matter is relevant, there is a strong argument that it would also be constitutional. At the very least, given that environmental protection is "one of the major challenges of our time,"[130] broad constitutional authority under the *IAA* certainly seems to be in our best interest.

---

130 *Oldman*, above note 1 at 3.

# CHAPTER 6

# *UNDRIP*, Decision Making, and the Role of Indigenous Peoples

*Sara Mainville and Renée Pelletier*

## A. INTRODUCTION: THE *UNITED NATIONS DECLARATION ON THE RIGHTS OF INDIGENOUS PEOPLES* AND REDISCOVERY OF A POST-COLONIAL CANADA

The *United Nations Declaration on the Rights of Indigenous Peoples* (*UNDRIP*) was adopted through resolution by the United Nations General Assembly in September 2007.[1] *UNDRIP*'s promise triggered certain decolonization efforts in Canada's Indigenous groups, including revitalizing Indigenous law and asserting Indigenous jurisdiction. Indigenous self-determination in Canada also had a domestic impetus. In 2012, the Idle No More movement was founded by four women who were leading webinars and teach-ins within Indigenous communities to explain the legislative changes that were being made by the federal government to key environmental protections. These included several pieces of legislation that many First Nations relied on to protect their section 35 Aboriginal and treaty rights under the Constitution,[2] which were being radically amended. The *Jobs and Growth Act, 2012* (Bill C-45) was the main target of the Idle No More round dances and other protests under its banner, in an effort to stop the legislative changes from

---

1    GA Res 61/295, UNGAOR, 61st Sess, UN Doc A/RES/61/295 (13 September 2007).

2    *Constitution Act, 1982*, being Schedule B to the *Canada Act 1982* (UK), 1982, c 11 [*Constitution Act, 1982*].

passing.[3] The federal government was accused of gutting the *Navigable Waters Protection Act* (as it was then called),[4] undermining efforts by Indigenous groups promoting water protection[5] and opposing fracking and pipeline developments on traditional lands of Indigenous peoples in regions across Canada.

Beyond the political and moral arguments for stronger water protection in Canada, the Idle No More protesters recognized that *UNDRIP* now required the federal governments to seek free, prior, and informed consent before making these legislative changes.[6] Leading activists explained to the media and others that Bill C-45 and other legislative amendments would impact the future protection of section 35 rights and that federal legislative changes disrespected the efforts of Indigenous peoples to revitalize their own laws and jurisdiction. This undermined a reconciliation project of national importance, which had been recommended by the Truth and Reconciliation Commission of Canada's Calls to Action and reflected in other nation-building efforts of Indigenous peoples in Canada.[7] All of this underscored the widening gap between Indigenous peoples' strongly held belief in the stewardship of lands, resources, and waters and the position of the federal government.

The 2012 renaissance, or knowledge transfer, was facilitated by years of grassroots movements, from communities to regional political

---

3    SC 2012, c 31.

4    RSC, 1985, c N-22.

5    Water keeping as a traditional responsibility of Indigenous women has been revitalized through the work of "Grandmother" Josephine Mandamin, also known as the "Water Walker," and Minnesota activist Tara Houska, as well as legal academic Aimee Craft. See Craft's work with the Grand Council Treaty #3's Women's Council: "NIBI Declaration of Treaty #3: Toolkit Draft" (May 2019), online (pdf): *Grand Council Treaty #3* http://gct3.ca/wp-content/uploads/2019/05/2019-TREATY3-NIBI-TOOLKIT-FINAL-DRAFT-May-2019.pdf.

6    See *Mikisew Cree First Nation v Canada (Minister of Aboriginal Affairs and Northern Development)*, 2014 FC 1244; *Mikisew Cree First Nation v Canada (Minister of Aboriginal Affairs and Northern Development)*, 2016 FCA 311; *Mikisew Cree First Nation v Canada (Governor General in Council)*, 2018 SCC 40.

7    Truth and Reconciliation Commission of Canada, *Honouring the Truth, Reconciling for the Future: Summary of the Final Report of the Truth and Reconciliation Commission of Canada* (2015), online (pdf): *Truth and Reconciliation Commission of Canada* www.trc.ca/assets/pdf/Honouring_the_Truth_Reconciling_for_the_Future_July_23_2015.pdf [Truth and Reconciliation Commission of Canada]; and *Report of the Royal Commission on Aboriginal Peoples: Restructuring the Relationship*, vol 2 (Ottawa: Supply and Services Canada, 1996), online (pdf): http://data2.archives.ca/e/e448/e011188230-02.pdf.

organizations, who also supported the international efforts by Indigenous peoples in Canada.[8] *UNDRIP* was a result of multiple decades of Indigenous diplomacy going as far back as Deskaheh (Levi General, a Haudenosaunee or Six Nations Chief) at the League of Nations and likely further back to the original Indigenous treaties with Europeans.[9] It is a testament to the diplomatic resiliency of Indigenous Nations that *UNDRIP* was achieved at the United Nations General Assembly despite the opposition and concerns shared by industry and/or state or regional governments — including Canada — voting in opposition to it in 2007.[10]

Despite this early opposition, the political and moral significance of *UNDRIP* is now clear to most state actors, including the federal government in Canada. The federal government's 2015 commitments to implement *UNDRIP*[11] and the 94 Calls to Action of the Truth and Reconciliation Commission were met with skepticism and disbelief by both mainstream media and Indigenous activists.[12] Yet some legal scholars are optimistic that the recognition of Indigenous rights as

---

8    In Alberta and Quebec, both the Treaty 7 organization and the James Bay Cree of Quebec have had decades of international experience prior to 2007.

9    See James (Sa'ke'j) Youngblood Henderson, *Indigenous Diplomacy and the Rights of Indigenous Peoples: Achieving UN Recognition* (Saskatoon, SK: Purich Publishing, 2008) at 24–36 for a good overview of the efforts of Indigenous peoples to achieve UN recognition that their rights should be protected human rights in international law.

10    The United States, Canada, Australia, and New Zealand opposed the resolution for *UNDRIP*, above note 1. Canada explained its opposition to *UNDRIP*:

> Canada has significant concerns with respect to the wording of the current text, including the provisions on lands, territories and resources; on free, prior and informed consent when used as a veto; on self government without recognition of the importance of negotiations; on intellectual property; on military issues; and on the need to achieve an appropriate balance between the rights and obligations of Indigenous peoples, Member States and third parties.

> See GAOR, 61st Sess, 107th plenary meeting, UN Doc A/61/PV.107 (13 September 2007). See also a very good analysis on the implementation of *UNDRIP* in Canada: Brenda L Gunn, "Overcoming Obstacles to Implementing the UN Declaration on the Rights of Indigenous Peoples in Canada" (2013) 31:1 *Windsor Yearbook of Access to Justice* 147.

11    Jorge Barrera, "Trudeau: A Liberal Government Would Repeal, Amend All Federal Laws That Fail to Respect Indigenous Rights" *APTN* (15 October 2015), online: *Aboriginal Peoples Television Network* https://aptnnews.ca/2015/10/15/trudeau-a-liberal-government-would-repeal-amend-all-federal-laws-that-fail-to-respect-indigenous-rights/.

12    Indigenous academics and some allies have started the Yellowhead Institute to push back against other "think tanks" and institutes on Indigenous rights issues for many of these reasons and concerns, including holding the government accountable for its promises. See their website: https://yellowheadinstitute.org/.

human rights may be a safeguard against unfettered development in settler-colonial economies.[13]

The immediacy of reform was the elephant in the room during *UNDRIP* discussions between Indigenous peoples and Crown officials. In this chapter, we review the push and pull between Indigenous peoples, the international legal experts, industry officials, and Crown governments in Canada that have paused concerted efforts to bring a consensus position forward on *UNDRIP*.

*UNDRIP* is not without its critics in Indigenous communities. Article 46 recognizes that the United Nations is still based in the protection of state sovereignty. Human rights, including Indigenous rights, are limited in that context.[14] This state-centric approach is a problem in the context of a "Nation-to-Nation" relationship. The history of Indigenous peoples in Canada bringing their claims to international forums is evidence that Indigenous peoples continue to hold fast to a Nation-to-Nation vision of treaty, as symbolized in the Two Row Wampum belt.[15] These two visions of sovereignty need reconciliation, but not the legal reconciliation one finds in common law courts and settler-colonial legal tests. The real project of reconciliation and decolonization means allowing Indigenous peoples to be one of Canadian law's architects going forward.

---

13    Siegfried Wiessner, "Re-enchanting the World: Indigenous Peoples' Rights as Essential Parts of a Holistic Human Rights Regime" (2012) 15:1 *UCLA Journal of International Law and Foreign Affairs* 239.

14    Article 46 states:

Nothing in this Declaration may be interpreted as implying for any State, people, group or person any right to engage in any activity or to perform any act contrary to the Charter of the United Nations or construed as authorizing or encouraging any action which would dismember or impair, totally or in part, the territorial integrity or political unity of sovereign and independent States.

15    "Two Row History," online: *Two Row Wampum Renewal Campaign* http://honorthetworow.org/learn-more/history:

In between the two rows of purple beads are three rows of white beads. The first row of white beads is "peace," the second row, "friendship," and the third row, "forever." As we travel down the road of life together in peace and harmony, not only with each other, but with the whole circle of life—the animals, the birds, the fish, the water, the plants, the grass, the trees, the stars, the moon, and the thunder—we shall live together in peace and harmony, respecting all those elements. As we travel the road of life, because we have different ways and different concepts, we shall not pass laws governing the other. We shall not pass laws telling you what to do. You shall not pass a law telling me and my people what to do.

Through this lens, one understands the difficulty that a majority government would have in creating the appropriate measures to implement *UNDRIP* through environmental assessment legislation. After the 2015 Truth and Reconciliation Commission's report ceremony, the Canadian government promised that assimilation and cultural genocide policies would end. In addition, the restoration of the tools of self-determination to Indigenous peoples is a risky national test of Canada's core promise as a constitutional democracy.

As an international document, *UNDRIP* is intended to set out the minimum standards for recognition of the collective and individual rights of Indigenous peoples. Although the document is intended to be read as a whole, several articles relate specifically to the field of impact assessment: right to self-determination (articles 3, 4, and 5)

- right to participate in decision making and maintain institutions (articles 18, 19, 34, and 40)
- right to set own priorities and strategies (Article 23)
- right to make decisions over traditional territory (articles 26 and 29)
- right to free, prior, and informed consent (Article 32)
- right to culture (articles 8, 11, and 25)
- right to maintain and protect Indigenous knowledge (Article 31)
- right to financial assistance (Article 39)

Domestically, its implementation requires a process of decolonizing Canadian law. This goes beyond simply operationalizing particular rights expressed in *UNDRIP* and instead relies on a shift in how Indigenous peoples participate in decision making and the respect and understanding accorded to their laws, traditional knowledge, and world views in those processes. The overarching goal of decolonizing Canadian law will be achieved only through direct collaboration with Indigenous peoples, as per the Truth and Reconciliation Commission's vision of transforming Canadian law:

> In Canada, law must cease to be a tool of dispossession and dismantling of Aboriginal societies. It must dramatically change if it is going to have any legitimacy with First Nations.... Until Canadian law becomes an instrument supporting Aboriginal peoples' empowerment, many Aboriginal people will continue to regard it as a morally and politically malignant force. A commitment to truth and reconciliation

demands that Canada's legal system must be transformed. It must ensure that Aboriginal peoples have greater ownership of, participation in, and access to its central driving forces. Canada's Constitution must become truly a constitution for all of Canada. Aboriginal peoples need to become law's architects and interpreters where it applies to their collective rights and interests.[16]

Indigenous peoples' vision and way of life are misunderstood in Canada, although our treaty relationships are older than Canada itself. As such, there should be a deeper and broader understanding of Indigenous knowledge, philosophy, and the nature of their claims to self-determination and sovereignty. An example is in Anishinabemowin, the language of the Anishinaabe people (also known as Ojibway, Saulteux, Chippewa, and Mississauga). There is no word in this language for sovereignty. Instead, knowledge keepers use the word *miinigoziwin*, which means "given to us" but is commonly understood to mean "what the Creator has given to us." This comes from teachings that Anishinaabe were planted in their territories by the Creator, with all the symbolism that entails. The Creator had given us *Inakonigaawin*, our laws and the Creator's values. *Miinigoziwin* is not an orientation to territory, peoples, culture, and languages that licenses unilateral, one-sided decision making, like the blanket veto that Canada feared would come from *UNDRIP*. Instead, relationships and responsibility figure strongly in *Inakonigaawin*, the Anishinaabe law.

Indigenous views on constitutionalism, the rule of law, and sovereignty therefore need to be better understood for a helpful conversation to begin.[17]

---

16   Truth and Reconciliation Commission of Canada, above note 7 at 205.

17   Wiessner, above note 13 at 275, shared an understanding of self-determination and Indigenous sovereignty that is helpful here:

> The claim to Indigenous sovereignty is essentially founded upon the aspiration to preserve inherited ways of life, change traditions as Indigenous peoples see necessary, and to allow their cultures to flourish. That goal drives the claim for independent decision-making on the basis of existing structures and functions of decision-making within the Indigenous community. Internal autonomy thus asks of modern nation-states to recognize structures of Indigenous government whether they are formally democratic or not, as long as they are essential to traditional ways of life.

## 1) The Role of Indigenous Peoples in Impact Assessment

When the independent Expert Panel for the Review of Environmental Assessment Processes (Expert Panel) conducted its cross-country tour to engage with Indigenous and non-Indigenous groups on the future of environmental assessment in Canada, the overwhelming response supported the implementation of *UNDRIP*. These calls were echoed in many of the more than 500 written submissions received by the Panel. Groups were calling for the implementation of *UNDRIP* for good reason. In its terms of reference, the Expert Panel was called upon to "reflect the principles of the Declaration in its recommendations, as appropriate, especially with respect to the manner in which environmental assessment processes can be used to address potential impacts to potential or established Aboriginal and treaty rights."[18] As such, Indigenous and non-Indigenous groups alike spent time, money, and creative energy coming up with innovative ways to operationalize things such as free, prior, and informed consent in the context of decisions on project applications.

The Panel heard about the need for shared decision making over lands and resources.[19] Many presenters had recommended that shared decision making be achieved by way of environmental assessment co-management agreements, similar to the harmonization environmental assessment agreements in place between Canada and some provinces.[20] There was also clear support for a joint determination of methodologies for the assessment of project impacts.[21] First Nations called for Nation-to-Nation collaborative roles in the writing of government environmental assessment reports and in the assessment of

---

18    See Canada, "Review of environmental assessment processes: Expert Panel Terms of Reference" (26 November 2020), online: *Government of Canada* www.canada.ca/en/services/environment/conservation/assessments/environmental-reviews/environmental-assessment-processes/final-terms-reference-ea.html.

19    See, for example, "Final Argument of the Mikisew Cree First Nation for the Hearing Regarding the Proposed Frontier Project" (24 November 24), online (pdf): *Impact Assessment Agency of Canada* https://iaac-aeic.gc.ca/050/documents/p65505/126352E.pdf.

20    Wabun Tribal Council written submission to the Expert Panel (23 December 2016) (on file with the authors).

21    Ktunaxa Nation presentation to the Expert Panel (15 December 2016) (on file with the authors).

impacts.[22] Some First Nation communities called for the establishment of a section 35 compliance office that would act as an oversight body throughout the life of approved projects to ensure the respect and protection of section 35 Aboriginal and treaty rights.[23] Others called for a move to a sustainability assessment for project review and that "contribution to reconciliation" be a central criterion.[24] The Expert Panel heard that consent from Indigenous peoples was needed prior to project approval and that such consent could be enabled through agreements between Indigenous groups and the Crown, proponents, or both. These agreements would provide for a significant and funded role for Indigenous groups in consensus-building activities during the impact assessment, decision-making, and approval process.[25] It was recommended that if consent has been obtained and a project is to be approved, proposed mitigation measures should meet the requirements of Indigenous groups.[26] Overwhelmingly, groups called for increased capacity to be able to meaningfully participate in impact assessment.

In the backgrounder that the federal government put out to accompany the *Impact Assessment Act (IAA)*,[27] it claimed that "[u]nder the legislation, the Government of Canada is committed to implementing the United Nations Declaration on the Rights of Indigenous Peoples ... through commitments to working in partnership with Indigenous peoples throughout impact assessments." The preamble of the Act restates this commitment.

Several provisions have the potential to grant Indigenous peoples powers under the Act and serve to foreground Indigenous knowledge and rights in impact assessment processes.

The preamble and purposes of the Act help frame the overall role of Indigenous knowledge, and the primacy of Indigenous rights

---

22    Taykwa Tagamou Nation presentation to the Expert Panel (15 November 2016) (on file with the authors).

23    Federation of Sovereign Indigenous Nations presentation to the Expert Panel (10 November 2016) (on file with the authors).

24    Innu Nation and Wabun Tribal Council written submissions to the Expert Panel (23 December 2016) (on file with the authors).

25    Innu Nation written submissions to the Expert Panel (23 December 2016) (on file with the authors).

26    Cowichan Tribes written submissions to the Expert Panel (12 December 2016) (on file with the authors).

27    SC 2019, c 28, s 1.

protection. The preamble states that "Canada recognizes that impact assessments provide an effective means of integrating scientific information and Indigenous knowledge into decision-making processes." It also makes other important statements, including a commitment to ensuring respect for the rights of Indigenous peoples, fostering reconciliation, and working in partnership with them. These commitments are reflected in the purposes of the Act at section 6(1), which include the following:

1)  To foster sustainability[28]
2)  To protect the components of the environment in federal jurisdiction[29]
3)  To ensure that projects are considered in a careful and precautionary manner to avoid adverse effects[30]
4)  To promote cooperation with Indigenous governing bodies[31]
5)  To promote communication and cooperation with Indigenous peoples[32]
6)  To ensure the respect of the rights of Indigenous peoples[33]
7)  To encourage the assessment of cumulative effects[34]
8)  To ensure that impact assessment takes into account Indigenous knowledge[35]

There is no clear hierarchy between these purposes, and they are listed with potentially incompatible purposes, such as enhancing Canada's competitiveness and economic development.[36] But read together with the preamble, they suggest that one of the dominant purposes of the Act is to promote reconciliation with Indigenous peoples.[37] This purpose should influence how the rest of the Act is interpreted and applied,

---

28   *Ibid*, s 6(1)(a). "Sustainability" is defined in s 2 as "the ability to protect the environment, contribute to the social and economic well-being of the people of Canada and preserve their health in a manner that benefits present and future generations."

29   *Ibid*, s 6(1)(b).

30   *Ibid*, s 6(1)(d) and (l).

31   *Ibid*, s 6(1)(e).

32   *Ibid*, s 6(1)(f).

33   *Ibid*, s 6(1)(g).

34   *Ibid*, s 6(1)(m).

35   *Ibid*, s 6(1)(j).

36   *Ibid*, s 6(1)(b.1).

37   Even economic development is qualified by "sustainable," which draws in the definition and its elements of environmental protection and consideration of future generations.

including the Indigenous knowledge provisions and opportunities for Indigenous-led assessment or partnerships, which we discuss in Section A(2), below in this chapter.

In terms of partnership opportunities, section 31 of the Act provides for the possibility that the minister may allow for the substitution of another jurisdiction's impact assessment process.[38] In other words, another jurisdiction can be given the authority to conduct the impact assessment on behalf of itself and the federal government. Substitution was available under the *Canadian Environmental Assessment Act, 2012* (*CEAA 2012*)[39] to a body established under a land claims agreement or under legislation relating to the self-government of Indians that had powers, duties, or functions in relation to an assessment of the environmental effects of a designated project. Under the *IAA*, the possibility of substitution has been extended to an Indigenous governing body[40] that has entered into an agreement with the minister. This would seemingly provide for the possibility of Nations such as Stk'emlúpsemc te Secwepemc and Tsleil-Waututh—both of whom have conducted large-scale impact assessments for major projects in their territory[41]—to be delegated the authority to conduct the assessment on behalf of Canada as well.

Section 21 of the *IAA* provides for consultation and cooperation with jurisdictions performing powers, duties, or functions in relation to an assessment of the environmental effects of a designated project. This provision would now extend to those Indigenous governing bodies who have entered into agreements with the minister.

Finally, section 114(1) provides that the minister may authorize an Indigenous governing body to exercise powers or perform duties or

---

38   See Chapter 8.

39   *Canadian Environmental Assessment Act, 2012*, SC 2012, c 19, s 52, s 32(2)(e) or (f) of the definition of *jurisdiction* in s 2(1) [*CEAA 2012*].

40   *IAA*, above note 27, s 2(1). Indigenous governing body means a council, a government, or another entity that is authorized to act on behalf of an Indigenous group, community, or people that holds rights recognized and affirmed by s 35 of the *Constitution Act, 1982*, above note 2.

41   For more information on Stk'emlúpsemc te Secwepemc Nation's assessment of the Ajax mine, see "KGHM AJAX Review Process" (2020), online: *Stk'emlupsemc te Secwepemc Nation* https://stkemlups.ca/process, and for more information on Tsleil-Waututh Nation's assessment of the Trans Mountain Expansion tanker and pipeline project, see "Assessment of the Trans Mountain Pipeline and Tanker Expansion Proposal" online (pdf): *Tsleil-Waututh Nation* https://twnsacredtrust.ca/wp-content/uploads/TWN_assessment_final_med-res_v2.pdf.

functions in relation to impact assessments under the Act. Guidance documents prepared by the Canadian Impact Assessment Agency (the Agency) contemplate joint drafting of assessment reports, the possibility of joint panels, and Indigenous-led assessment processes.[42]

The *IAA* does provide some opportunities for working with Indigenous people, although it is arguable whether these can be described as true partnerships. It falls short of fully implementing the *UNDRIP* rights of self-determination, participation in decision making, and making decisions about activities in traditional territory.

## 2) The Unfinished Business in Impact Assessments: Joint Decision Making

Although the *IAA* goes further than *CEAA 2012* by creating the possibility of extending certain responsibilities under the Act to Indigenous groups other than those who are signatories to modern treaties, one must remember that what is contemplated is the delegation of the procedural aspects of assessment, not final decision making. Indigenous groups may be included as partners in the assessment process and preparing of reports or even to lead the assessment process, but the ultimate decision on whether to issue approval will rest with the minister and Governor in Council. Additionally, although there may be room for an Indigenous group when assessing impacts or even conducting an assessment by way of substitution to do so in accordance with the group's own laws, customs, and traditions, it must also ensure that it is meeting all of the requirements under the Act.[43] In that sense, an Indigenous governing body is arguably doing little more than administering federal legislation on behalf of the government. This falls short of the *UNDRIP* provisions that recognize the rights of Indigenous peoples to participate in decision making in accordance with their own procedures and traditional (Indigenous) institutions

---

42   Impact Assessment Agency of Canada, "Practitioner's Guide to Federal Impact Assessments Under the Impact Assessment Act," online: *Government of Canada* www.canada.ca/en/impact-assessment-agency/services/policy-guidance/practitioners-guide-impact-assessment-act.html; Impact Assessment Agency of Canada, "Advisory Committees" online: *Government of Canada* www.canada.ca/en/impact-assessment-agency/advisory/advisory-groups.html.

43   *CEAA 2012*, above note 39, s 33.

and to make decisions regarding their traditional territory.[44] It may be that Canada will enter into agreements that provide for joint decision making with Indigenous peoples. But the absence of a statutory authorization for joint decision making in the Act, combined with the Act's public interest approval powers being exercisable only by the minister and Governor in Council, leaves such an arrangement vulnerable to legal challenge.

By way of contrast, the Province of British Columbia recently passed the *Declaration on the Rights of Indigenous Peoples Act*,[45] which expressly authorizes agreements with Indigenous governments on the joint exercise of statutory decision making. Section 7(1) of that Act provides for agreements whereby certain decisions can only be made jointly or with the consent of the Indigenous government.[46] This is the beginning process of removing settler-colonial policies and possibly decolonizing the laws of that province. Sarah Morales and Josh Nichols explained what the legislation will do:

> First, the government must take all measures necessary to ensure the laws of B.C. are consistent with the UNDRIP. Second, the government must prepare and implement an action plan in consultation with Indigenous peoples, to achieve the objectives of the UNDRIP. Third, the government must prepare annual reports on the progress that has been made towards implementing the measures. Finally, Bill 41 articulates that the Act's purpose is "to affirm the application of the Declaration to the laws of British Columbia."[47]

---

44    *UNDRIP*, above note 1, art 18.

45    SBC 2019, c 44.

46    "For the purposes of reconciliation, the Lieutenant Governor in Council may authorize a member of the Executive Council, on behalf of the government, to negotiate and enter into an agreement with an Indigenous governing body relating to one or both of the following:
    (a)  the exercise of a statutory power of decision jointly by
       (i)   the Indigenous governing body, and
       (ii)  the government or another decision-maker;
    (b)  the consent of the Indigenous governing body before the exercise of a statutory power of decision."

47    Sarah Morales & Josh Nichols, "UNDRIP Is a Step Towards Reconciliation" *Maclean's* (5 November 2019), online: www.macleans.ca/opinion/undrip-is-a-step-towards-reconciliation.

Unfortunately, the Act only expressly allows for sharing of powers and duties other than decision making. In this way, the Act highlights the inherent difficulty in attempting to implement *UNDRIP* in the context of federal decision making. *UNDRIP* calls for the right to make decisions about one's traditional territory. Administering the Act on behalf of the government may give Indigenous peoples the opportunity to participate in the impact assessment process, but the Act does not provide them with the type of decision-making rights contemplated by *UNDRIP*. There is no doubt that the principles and purposes of the Act and its provisions for Indigenous-led assessment will shape how public interest decisions are made in particular cases. But as long as these ultimate decisions still solely rest with the minister and Governor in Council, there will always be a risk that they will give primacy to the economic interests of non-Indigenous Canadians.

Special Rapporteur James Anaya has given guidance as to how states and industry can best appreciate the international norms and principles that have evolved into and through *UNDRIP*,[48] including free, prior, and informed consent, and that guidance found its way into several First Nation submissions to the Expert Panel. One way to get around the difficulty of trying to recognize Indigenous jurisdiction within the framework of federal decision making is to insist on the free, prior, and informed consent of Indigenous peoples before decisions to authorize development are made. Generally, the participatory rights given to others in reviewing projects and development plans must now be afforded to Indigenous peoples.[49] The special rapporteur was clear that freedom of expression for Indigenous groups to oppose development by extractive industries is important, as well as the decision by an Indigenous group not to engage in consultation on developments that the group opposes from the outset.[50] This would be contradictory to what is expected in Canadian law by Indigenous communities as they are generally advised to engage in consultations, despite the processes being narrowly scoped, aimed solely at "checking boxes," or otherwise flawed.[51]

---

48   S James Anaya, "Report of the Special Rapporteur on the Rights of Indigenous Peoples on Extractive Industries and Indigenous Peoples" (2015) 32:1 *Arizona Journal of International & Comparative Law* 109.

49   *Ibid* at 5.

50   *Ibid* at 7–8.

51   *Tsleil-Waututh Nation v Canada (Attorney General)*, 2018 FCA 153, was a case about Canadian officials implementing consultation in a flawed process that resulted in the need

If free, prior, and informed consent was a requirement under the Act, then the provisions aimed at cooperation could be relied on to fulfill the *UNDRIP* requirements that Indigenous peoples be entitled to their own decision-making institutions. Indigenous peoples could conduct their own assessments in accordance with their owns laws, traditions, and customs. The outcomes of those assessments would be more than factors that would be considered in the federal government's decision making: they would serve as the consent or rejection of a project. This was a recommendation of the Expert Panel in its report.[52] Of course, communities would require significant funding to have the capacity to conduct their own assessments and participate in this type of decision making. Funding would need to be on par with that provided to government agencies fulfilling the same functions.

The Assembly of First Nations proposed a Senate amendment to the *IAA* that would have required a decision maker to consider whether the government approval of a project would be consistent with the Government of Canada's commitment to implementing the *United Nations Declaration on the Rights of Indigenous Peoples*.[53] The amendment did not pass. Indigenous peoples advocated for a number of reforms in both Parliamentary and Senate committees despite being concerned that the compromises made in Bill C-69 were overly responsive to provincial governments and industry, at the expense of the implementation of *UNDRIP*.

Romeo Saganash, a New Democratic Party MP, attempted to implement *UNDRIP* through a private member's bill. His efforts were thwarted by criticism from industry, provincial governments, and legal academics about the purported false distinction between "consent"

---

to re-engage in "Phase III" of that consultation plan, which would properly engage the Indigenous groups and be meaningful dialogue about their concerns in a truer effort to reach accommodation.

52    See the recommendation in Expert Panel for the Review of Environmental Assessment Processes, *Building Common Ground: A New Vision for Impact Assessment in Canada* (Ottawa: Canadian Environmental Assessment Agency, 2017), online (pdf): *Government of Canada* www.canada.ca/content/dam/themes/environment/conservation/environ-mental-reviews/building-common-ground/building-common-ground.pdf.

53    Senate of Canada, Standing Committee on Energy, the Environment and Natural Resources, Evidence, 42-1, (4 April 2019), online: *Senate of Canada* https://sencanada.ca/en/Content/SEN/Committee/421/enev/54654-e.

and "veto" within the declaration.[54] The "v word" unnecessarily plagues *UNDRIP* discourse.[55] Free, prior, and informed consent is a standard for decision making by Indigenous groups that governments are required to facilitate within their processes, whether it's the Expert Panel's "conduct of assessment agreement" tool or a section 114(1)(e) agreement with Canada under the *IAA*.[56]

Special Rapporteur Anaya has reported that the free, prior, and informed consent standard has its limitations, citing legal standards such as necessity and "proportionality with valid public purposes": "More plausibly, consent may not be required when it can be established that the extractive activity would only impose such limitations on Indigenous peoples' substantive rights as are permissible within certain narrow bounds established under human rights law."[57]

However, this will require Crown governments to create more exacting rules on these limitations. Anaya has instructed states and the extractive industry that a valid public purpose "is not found in mere commercial interests or revenue-raising objectives, and certainly not

---

54   For example see the statements of Hon Cathy McLeod during the debates at Second Reading: "The minister has suggested it was not a veto and the position was supported by National Chief Bellegarde. However, he noted on three occasions that free, prior, and informed consent means the right to say yes and the right to say no. A number of lawyers have said the whole discussion is really a bit of semantics and whether it is veto or consent it has the same effect." "Bill C-262, An Act to ensure that the laws of Canada are in harmony with the United Nations Declaration on the Rights of Indigenous Peoples," 2nd reading, *House of Commons Debates*, 42-1, vol 148 No 245 (5 December 2017) at 1815 (Hon Cathy McLeod).

55   See *Coldwater Indian Band v Canada (Attorney General)*, 2020 FCA 34 at para 53: "At some juncture, a decision has to be made about a project and the adequacy of the consultation. Where there is genuine disagreement about whether a project is in the public interest, the law does not require that the interests of Indigenous peoples prevail."

56   According to s 114 (1)(e), the minister may

>   if authorized by the regulations, enter into agreements or arrangements with any Indigenous governing body not referred to in paragraph (f) of the definition jurisdiction in section 2 to
>
>   (i)   provide that the Indigenous governing body is considered to be a jurisdiction for the application of this Act on the lands specified in the agreement or arrangement, and
>
>   (ii)  authorize the Indigenous governing body, with respect to those lands, to exercise powers or perform duties or functions in relation to impact assessments under this Act—except for those set out in section 16—that are specified in the agreement or arrangement.

57   Anaya, above note 48 at 10.

when benefits from the extractive activities are primarily for private gain."[58] Legal academic guidance states that we need to remove aspects of settler colonialism that has plagued development for all of these years. The federal government has tried to do that through its controversial *Principles Respecting the Government of Canada's Relationship with Indigenous Peoples*,[59] which would be the federal bureaucracy's new standards in implementing *UNDRIP* in the relationship with Indigenous peoples in Canada. Many Indigenous groups have criticized these principles as being a rehashing by Crown lawyers of what they feel is common law limits to Indigenous rights rather than a reflection of *UNDRIP*.

Making space for Indigenous law to coexist on Indigenous-shared territory is a promise as old as Canada: it is the promise of treaty making before and after Canada's Confederation.[60] The implementation of *UNDRIP* is the "road map for reconciliation"[61] for Canada as it focuses on working in partnership with Indigenous peoples themselves to change Canadian law and to revitalize Indigenous law and Indigenous (traditional) institutions.

Brenda Gunn, a Métis professor from Manitoba who has studied the passage of *UNDRIP* and the domestic implementation issues in depth, has argued that there is a misunderstanding about the declaration as non-binding international law in Canada. Professor Gunn shared academic and international legal discourse to prove her point that these minimum standards are relevant in Canadian law and that courts should use *UNDRIP* so that Canadian law can meet these standards now and in the future.[62] The strongest arguments for the declara-

---

58    *Ibid* at 11.

59    These ten principles are posted on the Government of Canada website: Canada, Department of Justice, *Principles Respecting the Government of Canada's Relationship with Indigenous Peoples*, (2018), online: *Department of Justice* www.justice.gc.ca/eng/csj-sjc/principles-principes.html. The principles are arguably the Department of Justice's interpretation of s 35 rights in the common law, and Indigenous peoples do not want these principles themselves to replace the articles of *UNDRIP*, which are minimum standards and include an Indigenous usderstanding of the treaty relationship with nation-states. The ten principles were also created unilaterally by Canada.

60    Sara J Mainville, "Treaty Councils and Mutual Reconciliation Under Section 35" (2007) 6:1 *Indigenous Law Journal* 141.

61    National Grand Chief Perry Bellegarde quoted in Jorge Barrera, "AFN National Chief Says Senators Should Not Be 'Afraid' of Indigenous Rights Bill" *CBC* (21 December 2018), online: www.cbc.ca/news/indigenous/afn-undrip-indigenous-rights-1.4955076.

62    Gunn, above note 10 at 162.

tion is the way that it was created, through decades of dialogue between member states, Indigenous peoples, and UN parties, and the fact that the resolution itself has achieved near unanimity in its protection of Indigenous rights as *human rights* within member states. The language of rights in the declaration defines it as a legal document, capable of being implemented in Canada and regions within Canada, in partnership with Indigenous peoples.[63]

### 3) Moving Forward (Actions Needed to Ensure Effective Implementation of the Act as Nation-to-Nation Impact Assessments)

International law processes have been the preferred forum for Indigenous treaty spokespeople since colonization began. Deskaheh's appearance at the League of Nations is evidence of this familiarity with international diplomacy.[64] Carpenter and Riley explained how international channels have become legitimate for Indigenous peoples:

> During periods of intense domination by newly formed nation-states, Indigenous peoples continued to pursue international channels for the protection of their rights and brought claims to protest nation-states' assertion of domestic power over them. Indeed, while commentators suggest that historically international law often neglected Indigenous subjects per se, it is also apparent that some Indigenous peoples believed that the principles of international law applied to them. Moreover, Indigenous peoples presented their claims through advocacy reflecting their own experiences and values, albeit availing themselves of new forums, processes, and languages.[65]

Most recently, developments in British Columbia have been watched closely by the United Nations Committee on the Elimination of Racial Discrimination (CERD).[66] CERD has addressed the lack of free, prior, and informed consent achieved in projects such as Coastal

---

63   There are other notable in-depth reviews in legal journals, including Wiessner's article, above note 13 at 258.

64   Henderson, above note 9 at 24.

65   Kristen A Carpenter & Angela R Riley, "Indigenous Peoples and the Jurisgenerative Moment in Human Rights," (2014) 102:1 *California Law Review* 173 at 185.

66   CERD is the body of independent experts that monitors implementation of the Convention on the Elimination of All Forms of Racial Discrimination by its state parties. See the committee's website: www.ohchr.org/en/hrbodies/cerd/pages/cerdindex.aspx.

GasLink pipeline and the Site C dam.[67] In a decision under its Early Warning and Urgent Action Procedure, CERD called upon Canada to immediately cease all construction on these projects and to cancel or suspend all of their permits until free, prior, and informed consent was obtained through a robust process:

> Recommends that the State party establish, in consultation with Indigenous peoples, a legal and institutional framework to ensure adequate consultation with the view to obtain free, prior and informed consent regarding all legislation affecting Indigenous peoples;
>
> Urges the State party to take the necessary steps to incorporate free, prior and informed consent in domestic legislation, in consultation with Indigenous peoples, in compliance with international human rights obligations and jurisprudence, taking into account the Committee's general recommendation No. 23 on the rights of Indigenous peoples.[68]

This outside reproach was amplified by Indigenous activists and allies across Canada as solidarity protests were sparked by the television images of RCMP police enforcement of an injunction against the Indigenous Nation of Wet'suwet'en within their asserted Aboriginal title lands. The most symbolic of those images depicted the RCMP's use of a chainsaw to deconstruct a barrier, including the "Reconciliation" sign split in half, to open up a road for the Coastal GasLink construction. The BC government lost credibility when its new *Declaration on the Rights of Indigenous Peoples Act* legislation was absent from the discussions with the Wet'suwet'en Nation.[69]

The United Nations Permanent Forum on Indigenous Issues (UNPFII) was formed to be a high-level advisory body to the Economic and Social Council. After the news of the unconditional acceptance of

---

67    Laura Dhillon Cane, "Work Must Stop on Trans Mountain, Site C, LNG Pipeline Until First Nations Approval, UN Committee Says" *Canadian Press* (7 January 2020), online: www.cbc.ca/news/canada/british-columbia/un-racism-committee-trans-mountain-site-c-coastal-gaslink-pipeline-1.5417343.

68    Prevention of Racial Discrimination, Including Early Warning and Urgent Action Procedure, GA Dec 1, UNCERD, 100th Sess, (2019), online (pdf): https://tbinternet.ohchr.org/Treaties/CERD/Shared%20Documents/CAN/INT_CERD_EWU_CAN_9026_E.pdf.

69    Judith Sayers, "Horgan's Pipeline Push Betrays His Reconciliation Promise" *The Tyee* (15 January 2020), online: https://thetyee.ca/Opinion/2020/01/15/Horgans-Pipeline-Push-Betrays-Reconciliation-Promise-UNDRIP/.

*UNDRIP* by Canada, UNPFII meetings have been well attended by Canadian delegations, including Indigenous representatives supported by the federal government. Also, these meetings are reported in Canada for Indigenous peoples on APTN and through social media. Through all of these efforts, one critical fact has emerged in Canada: "International human rights law now serves as a basis for indigenous peoples' claims against states and even influences indigenous groups' internal processes of revitalization."[70]

A revitalization has begun, and the reality is that old colonial approaches will more often be rejected by Indigenous peoples in favour of Indigenous-led decision making and institutional development that will define how Indigenous Nations themselves will approve developments within their own traditional governments.

## B.  INSTITUTIONAL DEVELOPMENT

Canada should implement *UNDRIP* through a coordinated review of Canadian law by the federal government in partnership with Indigenous groups. Equally important is the investment in Indigenous institutional development by governments, such as the Department of Justice funding for Indigenous law development announced in late 2019.[71] Unfortunately, such approaches only help those who have the capacity to formulate a proposal, and a more global effort of coordinating and facilitating this work is required. Scholarship on this development is helpful:

> We see two interrelated dynamics occurring when Indigenous legal systems engage with international human rights law. First, we see the diffusion of international human rights norms in Indigenous communities. Second, and perhaps even more powerfully, we also see the recovery and revitalization of Indigenous peoples' own human rights norms.[72]

---

70 Carpenter & Riley, above note 65 at 175.

71 To meet Call to Action 50, which calls on governments to fund Indigenous law institutions, federal funding was announced in 2019 to seek proposals for Indigenous law revitalization projects. "Justice Partnership and Innovation Program" (2019), online: *Department of Justice Canada* www.justice.gc.ca/eng/fund-fina/jsp-sjp/pfo-pfc.html.

72 Carpenter & Riley, above note 65 at 217.

These central dynamics within Indigenous groups will continue to push and pull at the legislative processes, requiring some general accommodations within the federal system: a path toward co-decision making, room for Indigenous peoples to facilitate their own decision-making processes, and federal policy that recognizes Indigenous customs, principles, and laws.

Under the Act as it stands, Indigenous groups should be able to participate more fully in assessment processes and have their traditional knowledge and rights respected and prioritized. There is room for joint report writing, for Indigenous groups to appoint members to joint panels, and for fully Indigenous-led assessment processes. However, much of this remains within the discretion of the minister and subject to the goodwill of Agency officials. Ultimately, the decisions on the process and the ultimate outcome rest with Canada and not Indigenous peoples.

## C. CONCLUSION

The federal review of the environmental assessment legislation that resulted in the *IAA* was a process that both raised and frustrated the hopes of Indigenous peoples that their laws, treaties, and ways of life would finally be valued and accepted by federal, territorial, and provincial governments. This policy-making and legislative process also opened a dialogue about how *UNDRIP* could be implemented through domestic legislation but ultimately failed in its attempt to do just that.

Sakej Henderson explained that Indigenous peoples hold a responsibility to implement *UNDRIP* with Canada as a partner:

> With the passage of the Declaration, we cannot continue to hide our distaste for political engagement under an alleged need for independence, sovereignty, self-determination. We must understand that the genuine core of empowerment is human responsibility and reconciliation. We must improve our people, our selves, and our consciences. We must re-imagine and remake our traditional institutions, and reconcile them with our vision of human rights.[73]

The Act will have a role to play as *UNDRIP* is recognized in the preamble, and there is a high expectation from Indigenous groups

---

73 Henderson, above note 9 at 100.

that their own laws and institutions will play a leading role in regional planning and assessment. The Agency is a necessary arm of the federal government that may help Canada meet the *UNDRIP* standards.

The promise of recognizing the right to Indigenous-led assessment processes will allow Indigenous peoples, government, and industry to truly understand the concerns of Indigenous peoples and to join in their vision of sustainable territories across Canada. Indigenous-led assessments provide a way forward that respects Indigenous laws and traditional processes, as well as international legal standards. Recognition of these Indigenous laws and values is central to the right to self-determination of First Nations, Métis, and Inuit.

Indigenous peoples have a vantage point for impact assessment that should be highly valued. Indigenous laws and principles are focused on long-term sustainability and environmental responsibilities rather than rights. Relationships and trust building are the solution to less fractured processes, and good faith is a key ingredient going forward. The Act goes a long way to facilitating this in the context of planning and executing impact assessment processes. But in order to fully implement *UNDRIP*, the Act needs to expressly provide the opportunity for joint decision making.

# CHAPTER 7

# Project Impact Assessments: Triggering and Coverage

*Stephen Hazell*

## A. INTRODUCTION

Any law is effective only to the extent to which it is applied. Thus, any law that is directed primarily to assessing the impacts of proposed development projects is effective only to the extent to which that law is applied to projects that warrant assessment. The rules for determining which categories of projects are to be assessed under the law (triggering) and the breadth of application of the law to the wide variety of development projects being considered by proponents (coverage) are arguably as important as the rules for the assessment process itself.

Two questions guide this chapter. First, how effectively are the purposes of the *Impact Assessment Act (IAA)*[1] likely to be met given the triggering process and coverage of projects under the *IAA* and its regulations? Second, do the triggering and coverage provisions facilitate its use in practice in addressing the acknowledged crises of climate change and biodiversity loss?

This chapter addresses the process of triggering of projects for impact assessment under the *IAA*, considering how impact assessments are triggered and how the triggering process under the *IAA* differs from previous laws. Next, the chapter reviews the regulatory authority and key policies the government says it applied to designate projects for

---

1    SC 2019, c 28, s 1.

inclusion on the *Physical Activities Regulations* (Project List),[2] as well as the lack of transparency in applying these policies to the development of the Project List. Finally, the chapter reviews the categories of projects with related thresholds that are included on the Project List and assesses whether or not as written it advances the purposes of the *IAA* and efforts to address climate change and biodiversity loss.

The chapter focuses on triggering and coverage relating to the impact assessments of projects as well as to determinations by federal authorities of the significance of the adverse environmental effects of projects to be carried out on federal lands or outside Canada.[3] Triggering and coverage issues relating to strategic and regional assessment processes are addressed in chapters 11 and 17.

## B.  TRIGGERING IMPACT ASSESSMENTS OF PROJECTS

Triggering refers to the process for determining which categories of projects are subject to an impact assessment. Federal assessment laws have used one of two broad approaches to triggering. The first approach, "all in unless excluded," provides that all projects that have an aspect falling under federal jurisdiction are subject to impact assessment unless excluded by statute or regulation.

The *Canadian Environmental Assessment Act* (*CEAA 1995*)[4] used the "all in unless excluded" approach for triggering undertakings in relation to physical works. Undertakings in relation to physical works were excluded if they were to be carried out in response to emergencies, for reasons of national security,[5] or if they had insignificant environmental effects.[6] Physical activities not in relation to physical works (e.g., low-level flying

---


2    SOR/2019-285.

3    *IAA*, above note 1, ss 82–91.

4    SC 1992, c 37. The entry into force of the Act was delayed until 1995 to allow for key regulations to be developed and passed.

5    *Ibid*, s 59. See Meinhard Doelle, *The Federal Environmental Process: A Critique and Guide* (Toronto: LexisNexis Canada, 2008) at 83–84 and 86–87 for a more detailed discussion of triggering under *CEAA 1995*.

6    *CEAA 1995*, above note 4, s 59(c)(ii); *Exclusion List Regulations*, SOR2/2007-108 (repealed) (regulations prescribing those projects and classes of projects for which an environmental assessment is not required).

of military fixed-wing aircraft) were subject to assessment only if they were listed in regulations.[7]

The second approach, "only in if included," provides that a project is triggered only if it falls within a category of projects specifically described in the statute or regulation. The "only in if included" approach is used in the *IAA* as well as the Act it repealed, the *Canadian Environmental Assessment Act, 2012 (CEAA 2012)*.[8]

A Project List approach is the primary mechanism for triggering impact assessments of projects under the *IAA*. The Project List follows the "only in if included" model, itemizing the categories of designated projects that are subject to the *IAA*. For example, new diamond mines with an ore production capacity of 5,000 tonnes per day are subject to assessment under the *IAA* because they are included on the Project List but were not subject to assessment under *CEAA 2012* because they were not included in the *Regulations Designating Physical Activities*.[9]

Proposed projects that fall within categories designated on the Project List are required to be assessed under the *IAA* unless the Impact Assessment Agency of Canada (the Agency) determines that an assessment is not required.[10] Projects that do not fall within any of these Project List categories are not required to be assessed unless the minister of environment and climate change orders otherwise pursuant to the minister's discretionary authority under the *IAA*.[11] In so designating a physical activity, the minister must determine that "either the carrying out of that physical activity may cause adverse effects within federal jurisdiction or adverse direct or incidental effects, or public concerns related to those effects warrant the designation."[12]

The minister's discretionary authority to designate a physical activity by order has not been exercised since the *IAA* came into force in August 2019.[13] Between 1995 and 2019, environment ministers had similar, but

---

7    *CEAA 1995*, above note 4, s 59(b); *Inclusion List Regulations*, SOR/94-637 (repealed) (regulations prescribing physical activities and classes of physical activities not relating to physical works that may require an environmental assessment).

8    SC 2012, c 19, s 52.

9    SOR/2012-147, ss 15–17.

10    *IAA*, above note 1, s 16(1).

11    *Ibid*, s 9(1).

12    *Ibid*.

13    Petitions to designate a physical activity for impact assessment under the *IAA* that have been rejected by the minister of environment and climate change include the

rarely exercised, discretionary authority to require federal environmental assessments of projects not otherwise required by law to be assessed.

The Project List uses the same mechanism with entries similar to those used to trigger environmental assessments under *CEAA 2012*. The *Regulations Designating Physical Activities*[14] under *CEAA 2012*, in turn, included entries that bear even greater similarity to those in the *Comprehensive Study List Regulations*[15] under *CEAA 1995*. Note that these latter regulations were issued for the different purpose of determining which categories of projects required a comprehensive study carried out by the Canadian Environmental Assessment Agency as opposed to a more modest screening assessment.

Once triggered under the *IAA*, a designated project enters the planning process under which the proponent submits an initial project description to the Agency.[16] The Act provides a period of up to 180 days for the Agency to support early engagement and assessment planning. The early planning process is intended to support scoping of the assessment[17] and requires that the public has an opportunity to participate meaningfully.[18] If the Agency determines that an impact assessment is necessary,[19] the proponent then prepares a detailed project description along with a response to issues raised during the early engagement process.[20]

## 1)  Importance of the Legislated Changes to Triggering

The *IAA* approach to triggering is important in several ways. First, the "only in if included" approach applied through the Project List has, in

---

Coalspur Vista Coal Mine Expansion Phase II Project near Hinton, Alberta, and the Northern Pulp Effluent Treatment Facility Project near Pictou, Nova Scotia.

14  Above note 9.

15  SOR 94-638 (repealed) (regulations prescribing those projects and classes of projects for which a comprehensive study is required).

16  *IAA*, above note 1, s 10(1).

17  Meinhard Doelle & A John Sinclair, "The New *IAA* in Canada: From Revolutionary Thoughts to Reality" (2019) 79 *Environmental Impact Assessment Review* 1 at 3–4.

18  *IAA*, above note 1, s 11.

19  *Ibid*, s 16(1).

20  Under s 10(b) of *CEAA 2012*, above note 8, the Canadian Environmental Assessment Agency had similar discretion to decide that an environmental assessment of a designated project was not required following completion of the prescribed screening process. This discretion not to require an assessment of a screened project was exercised infrequently.

part, resulted in only a handful of projects being assessed in the first year of the law coming into force.[21] Initially, *CEAA 1995* was applied to several thousand projects annually on the basis that the environmental effects of environmentally significant projects requiring a federal decision should be assessed under the law. *CEAA 1995* identified four types of federal decisions that triggered project assessments: where a federal authority proposed a project itself, proposed to fund a project, proposed to transfer an interest in federal land to a project, or proposed to make a regulatory decision to approve a project.

*CEAA 2012* and now the *IAA* both discard this approach that ties the requirement for an environment assessment to a federal decision related to a project.

The result of these legislated changes is that there are no assessments of countless federal decisions to fund or issue regulatory approvals for proposed projects or authorize uses on or dispositions of federal lands to enable proposed projects to proceed. The environmental impacts of infrastructure projects currently being funded by billions of federal dollars are not assessed by the federal government. *Fisheries Act*[22] authorizations for projects that destroy fish habitat but are not listed on the Project List are not assessed for impacts other than those related to fisheries and fish habitat.

Projects on federal lands, including national parks and national wildlife areas, are also not required to be assessed unless they are on the Project List. Instead, as noted, the *IAA* merely requires that federal authorities such as Parks Canada make a determination as to whether or not projects being proposed are likely to cause significant adverse environmental effects.[23]

---

21　In theory, the number of projects assessed could be as many under the *IAA* as under *CEAA 1995*. However, changing the regulatory onus from identifying projects not subject to assessment to projects subject to assessment makes it much easier for a government disposed to a more limited application of the law to dramatically pare the number of categories and projects to assessment.

22　RSC, 1985, c F-14.

23　*CEAA 2012*, above note 8, s 67.

## C.  REGULATORY AUTHORITY AND POLICIES FOR DESIGNATING PROJECTS FOR ASSESSMENT

As noted above, the Project List is the primary mechanism for triggering impact assessments of projects under the *IAA*. This section first reviews the regulatory authority for designating project categories for inclusion on the Project List. Second, the government's key stated policies for deciding which project categories to designate are reviewed. The key policies include the following:

- a transparent, evidence-based approach to be used to designate Project List entries;
- only major projects with the greatest potential for adverse effects to be designated;
- only projects in areas of federal jurisdiction related to the environment to be designated; and
- thresholds, usually based on project production capacity, to be used to circumscribe project categories.[24]

### 1)  Regulatory Authority for the Project List

Section 109 of the *IAA* provides authority to the Governor in Council to "make regulations … for the purpose of the definition of *designated project* in section 2, designating a physical activity or class of physical activities."

Section 2 of the *IAA* defines a designated project as

one or more physical activities that
(a)   are carried out in Canada or on federal lands; and
(b)   are designated under regulations made under paragraph 109(b) or designated in an order made by the Minister under subsection 9(1).

It includes any physical activity that is incidental to those physical activities.

This regulatory authority to designate project categories on the Project List is broad, limited only by the condition that they are physical

---

24   Government of Canada, *Discussion Paper on the Proposed Project List: A Proposed Impact Assessment System*, (Ottawa: May 2019), online (pdf): www.canada.ca/content/dam/themes/environment/conservation/environmental-reviews/project-list-en.pdf [*Discussion Paper*].

activities (as opposed to intellectual or mental activities) and are carried out in Canada or on federal lands. The legislation does not limit projects to be designated on the Project List to those that are "major" or even those that have potential for significant adverse environmental effects.

## 2) A Transparent, Evidence-Based Approach

As part of its public consultations leading to the Project List regulations, the Government of Canada released the *Consultation Paper on Approach to Revising the Project List* in February 2018[25] and the *Discussion Paper on the Proposed Project List* in May 2019.[26] The discussion paper stated that "[t]he Government has committed to a transparent, evidence-based approach to creating a new Project List."[27] In fact, the approach was not transparent, and the extent to which it was evidence based cannot be determined based on publicly available information. The discussion paper included a draft Project List but provided no information in support of the categories of projects proposed for the Project List.

The earlier consultation paper claimed that the government holds relevant "experience to date" with respect to project listings.[28] Unfortunately, the government failed to publicly disclose any of this experience to date or any other evidence showing why certain categories of projects are or are not included on the Project List or to justify thresholds adopted for project entries.

For example, why does the *IAA* apply only to hydroelectric generating facilities with a generating capacity greater than 200 MW? Virtually any hydroelectric generating facility that obstructs river flows or includes a reservoir will have adverse effects on fish and other aquatic life that are significant for that watershed. Why does the *IAA* apply to any new tidal power generating facility that is not in-stream regardless of its generating capacity? On what basis is a 1 MW tidal power facility that is not in-stream required to be assessed but not a 199 MW hydroelectric generating facility?

---

25    Government of Canada, *Consultation Paper on Approach to Revising the Project List: A Proposed Impact Assessment System* (Ottawa: February 2018), online (pdf): www.canada.ca/content/dam/themes/environment/conservation/environmental-reviews/consultation-paper-approach-revising-project-list.pdf [*Consultation Paper*].

26    *Discussion Paper*, above note 24.

27    *Ibid* at 5.

28    *Consultation Paper*, above note 25.

Numerous requests were made to the minister of environment and climate change[29] and the Impact Assessment Agency of Canada to provide information justifying decisions to list or not list categories of projects in the regulations and the thresholds used for some categories of projects that are listed (e.g., the 200 MW production capacity threshold for hydroelectric generating facilities). Agency officials promised to disclose such information in May 2019,[30] but this has not happened as of this writing.

The government's failure to share information supporting its decisions with respect to entries on the Project List contrasts with the Agency's consultative approach to developing the *Comprehensive Study List Regulations* for *CEAA 1995*.[31] These regulations, also identifying "major" projects,[32] were developed based on input and recommendations from the Regulatory Advisory Committee (RAC), which included representatives of industry, environmental and conservation organizations, environmental lawyers, Indigenous groups, and federal and provincial governments.[33]

Due to the lack of transparency, it is not possible to determine the extent to which the Project List was developed based on policies set out in the discussion paper noted above. Until the evidence supporting decisions whether or not to include categories on the Project List is publicly released, it is fair to question whether project-listing decisions were not, in fact, quietly negotiated by officials of Environment and Climate Change Canada and their counterparts at Natural Resources Canada based primarily on industry submissions.

---

29 Letter from Nature and Environment Groups to Environment and Climate Change Minister Catherine McKenna (8 April 2018) at 3 (on file with authors).

30 Notes of meeting between Canadian Environmental Assessment Agency and Environmental and Nature Groups (May 2019) (on file with authors).

31 *Comprehensive Study List Regulations*, above note 15. The author was the director of regulatory affairs at the Canadian Environmental Assessment Agency between 1992 and 1995 when these regulations were developed.

32 *Comprehensive Study List Regulations*, above note 15. (These regulations identified projects that "are likely to have significant adverse environmental effects," which arguably carries a similar meaning to "major.")

33 See Stephen Hazell, *Canada v. The Environment: Federal Environmental Assessment 1984–1998* (Toronto: Canadian Environmental Defence Fund, 1999) at 63–79 for a history of the establishment of the RAC and its role in the development of the *CEAA 1995* regulations.

### 3) Major Projects with the Greatest Potential for Adverse Effects

The discussion paper also states that the federal government has chosen to include "*major* projects *with the greatest potential for adverse effects* in areas of federal jurisdiction related to the environment"[34] on the Project List.

In essence, this statement suggests that only those project categories with the worst of the worst impacts are to be designated for assessment. Even projects with very great adverse impacts that require federal decisions are not to be included on the Project List as long as there are other similar projects with even greater adverse effects. Such an approach only makes sense if the overriding federal objective in structuring the Project List is to minimize the number of impact assessments conducted in any given period of time under the *IAA*.

This statement limiting projects to be designated to those that are major and have the greatest potential for adverse effects is not required under the *IAA* and surely has the effect of potentially denying the federal government the tools to understand the environmental and sustainability impacts of major projects with great (but not the greatest) potential for adverse effects prior to making decisions about those projects.

Experience with the application of the *IAA* to date demonstrates that this is what is happening. Major projects that are not triggered under the *IAA* include two huge coal mine expansions. The Coalspur Vista thermal coal mine expansion near Hinton, Alberta, would potentially triple the mine's maximum coal extraction, produce up to 33 million tonnes (MT) of carbon emissions, and damage habitat of cutthroat trout, a federal species at risk. The 2,500-hectare Castle Mountain metallurgical coal mine expansion in southeastern British Columbia would destroy critical habitat for Rocky Mountain Bighorn Sheep, add significantly more selenium and other water pollutants to the Elk River watershed, and lock in decades of high carbon emissions.[35]

The discussion paper justifies limiting the Project List to major projects by claiming that "[i]mpact assessment is a key element of a mature regulatory landscape for addressing environmental effects, working

---

34   *Discussion Paper*, above note 24 at 3 [emphasis added].

35   Stephen Hazell, "This Ain't No Way to Phase Out Coal" (2 July 2020), online (blog): *Nature Canada* https://naturecanada.ca/news/blog/this-aint-no-way-to-phase-out-coal/.

alongside other regulatory processes at the federal, provincial, and territorial levels, with complementary roles."[36]

This statement is problematic given that this so-called mature regulatory landscape largely applies to the operations of existing industrial facilities, not to the planning and design of these facilities. Neither the *Canadian Environmental Protection Act, 1999*[37] nor the *Greenhouse Gas Pollution Pricing Act*[38] includes planning tools to ensure that facilities make use of the best available technologies to reduce, mitigate, or eliminate environmental harms in the design process before approvals are made. Most provincial impact assessment processes do not have the tools to ensure these outcomes either. Ontario's *Environmental Assessment Act*[39] does not even apply to private-sector resource development projects unless designated by the provincial environment minister—a rare occurrence.

The federal regulatory landscape has indeed changed since *CEAA 1995* came into force. The *Species at Risk Act*[40] was enacted in 2002. Amendments to the *Auditor General Act* requiring federal departments to prepare sustainable development strategies and creating the position of a commissioner for the environment and sustainable development were enacted in 1995.[41] Sustainable development strategies for the federal government as a whole were mandated by Parliament in 2008.[42] These laws have had a positive impact on federal efforts to foster sustainability. However, it is debatable whether they have had any impact on the development of the project list or the types of natural resource development projects (sustainable or otherwise) proposed by the private sector and approved by the federal government.

### 4)   Projects in Areas of Federal Jurisdiction Related to the Environment

Federal policy as stated in the discussion paper also limits Project List entries to "major projects with … adverse effects *in areas of federal*

---


36    *Ibid* at 4.

37    SC 1999, c 33.

38    SC 2018, c 12, s 186,

39    RSO 1990, c E.18.

40    SC 2002, c 29.

41    Bill C-83, *An Act to amend the Auditor General Act*, 1st Sess, 35th Parl, 1995.

42    *Federal Sustainable Development Act*, SC 2008, c 33.

*jurisdiction related to the environment.*[43] Why use the term *federal juris-diction?* Clearly, this term is intended to restrict designation of project categories but invites confusion because the *IAA* defines the term *jurisdiction* as a government authority, agency, or body.[44] In the sense used in the discussion paper, *jurisdiction* carries a different meaning, presumably referring to heads of federal legislative powers under the *Constitution Act, 1867* (e.g., sea coast and inland fisheries).[45]

The 2017 report of the Expert Panel for the Review of Environmental Assessment Processes (Expert Panel) supported an approach linked to federal interest rather than federal jurisdiction, declaring that "[f]ederal [impact assessments] should only be conducted on a project, plan or policy that has clear links to matters of federal interest."[46] The report indicated that these federal interests include, at a minimum,

- federal lands, federal funding, and the federal government as proponent;
- species at risk;
- fish;
- marine plants;
- migratory birds;
- Indigenous peoples and lands;
- greenhouse gas (GHG) emissions of national significance;
- watershed or airshed effects crossing provincial or national boundaries;
- navigation and shipping;
- aeronautics;
- activities crossing provincial or national boundaries and works related to those activities; and
- activities related to nuclear energy.[47]

---

43   *Discussion Paper* above note 24 at 3 [emphasis added].

44   *IAA*, above note 1, s 2.

45   (UK) 30 & 31 Victoria, c 3.

46   Expert Panel for the Review of Environmental Assessment Processes, *Building Common Ground: A New Vision for Impact Assessment in Canada* (Ottawa: Canadian Environmental Assessment Agency, 2017) at 18, online (pdf): *Government of Canada* www.canada.ca/content/dam/themes/environment/conservation/environmental-reviews/building-common-ground/building-common-ground.pdf.

47   *Ibid.*

The Expert Panel's recommendation for "clear links to matters of federal interest" recognizes that although some federal interest should be clear at the outset of an impact assessment, federal jurisdiction to make a decision in relation to the project may not emerge until the early planning process or assessment is under way. For example, federally listed species at risk may occupy habitats in the project study area (establishing a federal interest). But federal jurisdiction to exercise a duty to protect a species at risk may not be identified until the early planning phase of the assessment depending on whether recovery strategies or action plans have been developed and critical habitats have been designated.

Ensuring that a Project List category is linked to a matter of federal interest is thus different from ensuring that it has the "greatest potential for adverse effects in areas of *federal jurisdiction* related to the environment" [emphasis added]. To be clear, federal jurisdiction to make a decision in relation to a project may not be established at the beginning of the early planning process even where a federal interest is obvious. If no federal decision, such as the need for a *Fisheries Act* authorization, is determined to be needed during early planning, the Agency has discretion to decide that no impact assessment need be carried out.

The discussion paper states that "[w]here there are effects in only one area of federal jurisdiction related to the environment, consideration was given to whether those effects could be effectively managed by other regulatory regimes."[48] This statement is strange at best, suggesting that the federal government should not assess the impacts of major projects that relate to only one head of power—say fisheries. This criterion only seems to make sense if the government's primary objective is to keep the Project List as short as possible.

## 5)  Use of Thresholds to Circumscribe Project List Categories

Many of the entries on the Project List make use of so-called thresholds that circumscribe the application of the *IAA* to the largest projects in their respective categories.

Thresholds employed for Project List categories typically relate to the size of the production capacity or size of the project, not its

---

48  *Discussion Paper*, above note 24 at 7.

environmental effects. The prescribed threshold for hydroelectric generating facilities, for example, is 200 MW electricity production capacity. Thresholds other than production capacity are employed for some project entries. For example, the threshold for triggering the application of the *IAA* to the construction of new wind power–generating facilities is ten or more wind turbines.

Although only a proxy for environmental impacts, the production capacity/size approach to setting thresholds is simpler to determine than biophysical indicators early in the project planning phase. Proponents usually know the expected production or another metric of project size early in the planning phase. But calculating the air or water pollution to be released by a project or the extent of damage to wildlife habitat caused by a project prior to commencing the impact assessment is difficult. Furthermore, the very role of the impact assessment is to test the proponent's claims with respect to impacts such as levels of pollution or harm to wildlife habitat. These claims may be arguable or not well understood. Proponent claims with respect to project production capacity or size are likely to be more accurate. Hence, production capacity or size may provide more consistent metrics to use as thresholds.

Some Project List categories also contain conditions that exclude projects from designation for impact assessment. For example, an offshore exploratory well proposed in an area with a completed regional assessment that meets ministerial exemption conditions is not designated for impact assessment.[49] Similarly, new in situ oil extraction facilities are not designated where the province has legislation to limit the amount of GHG emissions to be produced by oil sand sites and where that limit has not been exceeded.[50]

Although biophysical indicators are employed infrequently as Project List thresholds (proximity to a natural water body is one example), the Project List does include additional categories of projects to be built in federal protected areas such as national parks and national wildlife areas.[51] These additional categories represent at least a partial recognition that the ecological integrity of federal protected areas merits

---

49    *Physical Activities Regulations*, above note 2, s 34.

50    *Ibid*, s 33.

51    *Ibid*, ss 1–11.

special consideration in assessing the impacts of proposed projects to be located in those protected areas.[52]

GHG pollution is one biophysical indicator, the magnitude of which is usually known early in the planning phase of any large project. Given that Parliament and the federal government have recognized the planetary climate emergency, it is surprising that no Project List category is included for projects with high GHG pollution. Federal jurisdiction to enact a binding scheme to reduce GHG emissions in Canada has been supported by two of three provincial courts of appeal, with a Supreme Court of Canada appeal pending. The lack of current federal legal authority to mandate access to data on GHGs to be released from proposed high-carbon polluting projects, such as cement plants, is clear. The environmental community has proposed a trigger for proposed projects with high GHG pollution for many years; a threshold of 50,000 tonnes $CO_2$ eq/year has been proposed to conform to the federal policy that ensures that only major projects are designated for *IAA* assessment.[53]

## D.  COVERAGE OF PROJECTS

Coverage refers to the extent to which impact assessment law applies to the range of development projects being advanced by proponents. The "only in if included" approach to triggering assessments of projects under the *IAA*, together with policies to limit designated projects to "major projects with the greatest potential for adverse effects in areas of federal jurisdiction relating to the environment" and mainly higher thresholds, seems designed to produce a shorter Project List. The result will be fewer impact assessments in practice.

This section provides an overview of project categories as set out in the *Physical Activities Regulations* (Project List), describes changes compared to *CEAA 2012*, and provides examples of gaps in coverage, including a more detailed discussion of two examples of egregious gaps.

Coverage may be considered in at least two ways. First, certain categories of projects can be said to be covered by the *IAA*, whereas others

---

52    See *Canada National Parks Act*, SC 2000, c 32, s 8.

53    See *ENGO Priorities Under the new Impact Assessment Act (IAA)*, Centre Québécois du droit de l'environnement, Nature Canada, WCS Canada, West Coast Environmental Law (31 October 2019).

are not. For example, construction of proposed new canals is subject to the *IAA* by virtue of having been designated for inclusion on the Project List; cement plants are not subject to the *IAA* by virtue of not having been so designated.[54]

Second, coverage can refer to the proportion of development projects within a category that are likely to be designated. For example, most proposed hydroelectric projects are not subject to the *IAA* because their electricity production capacity is less than the prescribed threshold of 200 MW.[55] The largest hydroelectric projects, such as Muskrat Falls in Labrador, are covered by the *IAA* where electricity production capacity is expected to exceed 200 MW.[56]

### 1) Overview of Coverage Under the *IAA*

Overall, the Project List represents a shorter list of major projects over which the federal government has a strong interest and jurisdiction than under the *CEAA 2012* regulations. Furthermore, the Project List has not been significantly updated since 1995 to include major project types, such as oil and gas fracking, railway infrastructure for transporting bitumen, and commercial spaceports,[57] that have emerged in the past twenty-five years. In other words, the Project List represents diminished coverage compared to previous environmental assessment regimes.

Goodday reviewed the coverage of projects subject to the *IAA* compared to *CEAA 2012*.[58] The number of unique project categories designated in the Project List has been increased by sixteen, from ninety-eight to 114, in the *Regulations Designating Physical Activities* of

---

54 *IAA*, above note 1, s 9 (1). (Section 9(1) of the *IAA* provides the minister with the discretion to order the designation of a physical activity that is not included on the project list "if, in his or her opinion, either the carrying out of that physical activity may cause adverse effects within federal jurisdiction or adverse direct or incidental effects, or public concerns related to those effects warrant the designation.")

55 *Physical Activities Regulations*, above note 2, s 42(a).

56 The electricity production of Muskrat Falls is expected to be 824 MW. The project was assessed by a joint review panel under *CEAA 1995*.

57 Note that ss 54 and 55 of the *Physical Activities Regulations*, above note 2, designate new and expanded railway yards with a total or expanded area of fifty hectares, which could affect railway transportation of bitumen.

58 Victoria Goodday, "Demystifying Bill C-69: The Project List" *Energy & Environmental Policy Trends* (December 2019), online (pdf): *The School of Public Policy, University of Calgary* www.policyschool.ca/wp-content/uploads/2019/12/Energy-Trends-Bill-C-69.pdf.

*CEAA 2012*.[59] Most of this increase (thirteen categories) represents projects in national parks and federal protected areas that were required to be assessed under *CEAA 1995* but not under *CEAA 2012*.[60] Important additional new project categories relate to renewable energy generation projects such as wind and tidal energy facilities.

The increase in the number of project categories can hardly be said to represent progress in achieving Canada's climate change and biodiversity objectives. Furthermore, the mainly higher thresholds for designating project types on the Project List run counter to achieving these objectives, as argued below.

**a) Natural Resource Projects**

The Project List under the *IAA* includes fewer oil and gas pipeline projects, according to Goodday.[61] The most important entry for new onshore pipelines is less stringent, with both a reduced threshold and a narrower scope. Only new pipelines requiring 75 km or more on a new right-of-way are listed under the *IAA*, compared to 40 km or more for new pipelines under *CEAA 2012*. Thus, a new pipeline to be constructed on an already established right-of-way would not be subject to impact assessment.

In situ oil sands facilities with a production capacity of 2,000 m³/day or more are a new addition to the Project List. However, no assessments are required for such facilities located in a province with a legislated GHG emissions limit for in situ oil sands sites that has not been exceeded. Alberta is the only province with in situ oil sands sites and the only province with a legislated GHG emissions limit not yet exceeded.

The threshold for designation of new coal mines on the Project List is increased to 5,000 tonnes of coal produced per day from 3,000 tonnes per day on the *CEAA 2012* regulations.[62]

Although the Project List requires fewer assessments of projects with high GHG emissions (e.g., pipelines, coal mines) than under the *CEAA 2012* regulations, impact assessments will now be required for larger wind and tidal power energy projects having low GHG emissions.[63]

---

59    *Ibid* at 1.
60    *Ibid.*
61    *Ibid* at 2.
62    *Physical Activities Regulations*, above note 2, s 18(a).
63    *Ibid*, ss 42–45.

The rationale for requiring assessments of low-carbon projects, and not requiring them for high-carbon projects such as the Coalspur Vista Coal Mine Phase II Expansion Project described in Section D(2), below in this chapter, is baffling to the extent that that rationale is not mere political convenience. The rationale and evidence for these Project List decisions should be made publicly available in any event.

With respect to mining and nuclear energy projects, Goodday observed that proponents are now less likely to face federal assessment.[64] Thresholds are raised for eleven of the thirteen mining projects listed, including both coal mine entries.[65] Uranium and apatite mines were also taken off the Project List. Any uranium mine, mill, or nuclear reactor triggered a federal assessment regardless of size under the *CEAA 2012* regulations; fewer of these project types will be assessed under the *IAA* given that the Project List now includes minimum production capacity thresholds for these projects.[66] For example, construction and installation of small modular nuclear reactors—which use new technology and have not been deployed in Canada—will not be assessed unless the minister exercises discretion to designate such projects pursuant to section 9(1).

### b)  Projects in National Parks and Federally Protected Areas

Under the *IAA*, as it was with *CEAA 2012*, federal authorities, including Parks Canada, are generally not required to assess the impacts of projects on federal lands but merely to make a determination as to whether or not projects are likely to cause significant adverse environmental effects.[67] Federal authorities are not required to consult the public in making these determinations. The rigour, and perhaps even the bona fides, of this determination process is in doubt. According to a 2016 Canadian Parks and Wilderness Society submission based on information supplied in response to an access to information request, Parks Canada determined that none of 1,533 projects approved between January 1, 2013, and October 2016 were likely to cause significant adverse environmental

---

64    Above note 58 at 2.
65    *Ibid.*
66    *Ibid.*
67    CEAA 2012, above note 8, s 67.

effects.[68] This seems too much like the dictator who wins 99 percent of the vote in an election.

As noted, physical works projects to be carried out in national parks and on other federal lands are no longer subject to mandatory impact assessment. Exceptions include oil and gas facilities, mines and mills, railway lines, public roads, and aerodromes and runways that are designated on the Project List.[69] Given that the minister of environment and climate change's first priority in managing national parks is the maintenance or restoration of ecological integrity through the protection of natural resources and natural processes,[70] why are new oil and gas pipelines, railway lines, public roads, and runways not prohibited altogether in national parks?

Oil and gas development, other than pipelines, is currently prohibited in national parks but may be permitted by the minister in national wildlife areas. In 2010, Encana's application for a permit under the *Canada Wildlife Act*[71] to construct 1,275 shallow natural gas wells in the Suffield National Wildlife Area was turned down by then environment minister Jim Prentice following a panel review under *CEAA 2012*.[72] Without this environmental assessment, the Encana development may well have been approved, further fragmenting endangered prairie grasslands.

Major projects in federal protected areas that are not designated on the Project List include tourist attractions such as the one-kilometre-long Columbia Icefield Skywalk in Banff National Park (which was built), the giant "Mother Canada" statue that had been proposed for Cape Breton National Park, tourist visitor centres, campgrounds, and parking lots. Commercial development projects in any of the four

---

68　CPAWS Submission to the Expert Review Panel on Environmental Assessment, *Restoring Legal Rigour to Environmental Assessments in National Parks* (23 December 2016) (on file with authors). This submission is no longer available electronically, but the same assertion can be found in a subsequent CPAWS submission, here: www.ourcommons.ca/Content/Committee/421/ENVI/Brief/BR9762370/br-external/CPAWS-e.pdf.

69　*Physical Activities Regulations*, above note 2, ss 1–11.

70　*Canada National Parks Act*, above note 52, s 8(2).

71　RSC, 1985, c W-9.

72　Energy Resources Conservation Board and Canadian Environmental Assessment Agency, *Report of the Joint Review Panel Established by the Federal Minister of the Environment and the Alberta Energy and Utilities Board: Decision 2009-008: EnCana Shallow Gas Infill Development Project* (27 January 2009), online: https://static.aer.ca/prd/documents/decisions/2009/2009-008.pdf.

contiguous mountain parks along the British Columbia–Alberta border are designated on the Project List, but only if they have not been subject to a strategic environmental and public review as part of a park management plan.[73]

### c)  Other Projects

The Project List includes lower thresholds for hazardous waste facilities (only those facilities not more than 500 m from a natural water body are designated)[74] and nuclear fuel and waste facilities (certain on-site storage facilities are not designated).[75] Project entries for water and military projects were not changed.

Goodday concluded that "it is not likely that the IAA will be a disabler of major infrastructure projects as compared to the outgoing CEAA."[76] Her analysis supports a stronger conclusion: the shrunken Project List means that fewer projects will benefit from the application of the *IAA*. Unassessed projects will be less likely to be sustainable and hence also less likely to generate the social licence needed to succeed.

The paucity of projects registered on the Canadian Impact Assessment Registry since the *IAA* came into force on 29 August 2019, reinforces the conclusion that the coverage of projects under the *IAA* is less than under *CEAA 2012*. In its first year, only eight projects were registered for assessment by virtue of the Project List. These projects include two in Alberta (Suncor Base Mine Extension Project, Prairie Lights Power Project), two in British Columbia (Cedar LNG Project, Tilbury Phase 2 LNG Expansion Project), two in Ontario (Marten Falls First Nation and Webequie First Nation road projects), and two in Quebec (Gazoduq Gas Pipeline Project, Wasamac Gold Mine Project). As noted, Environment and Climate Change Minister Jonathan Wilkinson also exercised his discretion to designate two additional projects for assessment: the Coalspur Vista Coal Mine Phase II Expansion in Alberta and the Castle Mountain Coal Mine in British Columbia.

---

73   *Physical Activities Regulations*, above note 2, ss 9 & 10.
74   *Ibid*, ss 56 & 57.
75   *Ibid*, s 58(a).
76   Goodday, above note 58 at 1.

## 2)  Two Examples of Coverage Gaps

The preceding overview has identified Project List coverage gaps for project categories or underinclusions within project categories due to higher thresholds. This section describes in more detail two projects (a coal mine expansion and a cement plant) that are not designated on the Project List despite demonstrably significant adverse environmental impacts.

## a)  Coalspur Vista Mine Phase II Expansion

Coalspur Mines Ltd proposes to expand the existing Vista coal mine to produce an average of 4.2 million additional tonnes of coal per year over a ten-year period. Phase II would increase overall annual production from the mine to 15 MT of thermal coal every year, making it one of the largest, if not the largest, in Canadian coal mining history.[77] Coalspur Vista produces thermal coal for export to Asia for use in coal-fired electricity-generating plants; previous phases of the Vista mine did not undergo any federal assessment.

On behalf of Environmental Defence, Keepers of the Water, and the West Athabasca Watershed Bioregional Society, Ecojustice petitioned the minister of environment and climate change to designate the Coalspur Vista Coal Mine Phase II Expansion Project for an environmental assessment under section 14(2) of *CEAA 2012*.[78] The petition includes a calculation that GHG emissions from the mined coal in the phase II expansion would range between 10.67 MT and 21.78 MT $CO_2$ eq/year based on the proposed increase in thermal coal from 5.2 MT per year to 10 or 15 MT per year. Canada's annual GHG emissions in 2018 were 729 MT $CO_2$ eq/year, so this project alone would increase Canada's GHG emissions by roughly 1.4 to 3 percent; however, Canada does not count pollution from burning Canadian coal overseas toward its national climate targets.

---

77    "RE: Coalspur Mines Ltd./Phase II Vista Coal Mine Project," information package created by Coalspur Mines (Operations) Limited for the Canadian Environmental Assessment Agency (9 August 2019), online (pdf): https://iaac-aeic.gc.ca/050/documents/p80731/134898E.pdf (attached as appendix B).

78    Letter from Fraser Thomson, Ecojustice, to Environment and Climate Change Minister Catherine McKenna (17 May 2019) (on file with authors). Letter is referred to in Impact Assessment Agency of Canada, "Analysis Report: Whether to Designate the Coalspur Mines Project in Alberta," online (pdf): https://iaac-aeic.gc.ca/050/documents/p80341/133221E.pdf.

In addition to GHG emissions, Environment and Climate Change Canada expressed concerns about environmental impacts from the Coalspur Vista mine project, such as impacts from air emissions on Aboriginal health, impacts on water quality from cumulative effects, the presence of selenium in wastewater and options for treatment, loss of wetlands habitat, and effects on migratory birds and species at risk.

On 20 December 2019, Minister Wilkinson rejected the petition, deciding that the Coalspur Vista mine expansion would not be designated for federal review under the *IAA* because it will be covered under the Alberta environmental assessment process.[79] The same day, Minister Wilkinson and Natural Resources Minister Seamus O'Regan announced that Canada will launch a strategic assessment to provide guidance on how future thermal coal mine projects (but not Coalspur Vista) could be assessed under the *IAA*.

At the time, Minister Wilkinson's decision was astonishing for several reasons. First, Coalspur Vista appears to have evaded an impact assessment because the area of mining operations was expanded by less than 50 percent even though the additional coal production capacity was far greater than the 5,000 t/day threshold for coal mine expansion on the Project List. Coalspur Vista clearly qualifies as a major project with the greatest potential for adverse effects with respect to carbon, air, and water pollution and damage to wildlife and habitat and so should be assessed. As well, the thermal (for electricity generation) coal mining industry is one that the federal government has committed itself to phase out through its membership in the Powering Past Coal Alliance.[80] It is difficult to imagine any project more deserving for *IAA* impact assessment than Coalspur Vista.

Indeed, a year later, the minister reversed his decision on 30 July 2020, at least in part in response to a second Ecojustice petition submitted on behalf of Keepers of the Water, Keepers of the Athabasca, and the West Athabasca Watershed Bioregional Society.[81] The primary

---

79 Minister Wilkinson's Response to Coalspur Vista Coal Mine Phase II Expansion Project (20 December 2019), online: https://iaac-aeic.gc.ca/050/evaluations/document/133222.

80 "Declaration, Powering Past Coal Alliance" (16 November 2017), online: *Powering Past Coal Alliance* https://poweringpastcoal.org/about/declaration.

81 Letter from Anna MacIntosh, Ecojustice, to Environment and Climate Change Minister Jonathan Wilkinson (1 May 2020), online (pdf): https://iaac-aeic.gc.ca/050/documents/p80731/134898E.pdf.

stated reason for the 20 July 2020 decision was that the proponent filed an additional provincial regulatory application proposing new underground mining operations.[82]

### b)  Colacem Cement Plant

Colacem Canada Inc proposes to build a cement plant in eastern Ontario near the Ottawa River 70 km upwind from Montreal. Colacem stated that in producing cement for export through the port of Montreal, the plant would produce roughly 1 MT of GHG emissions annually, as well as substantial sulphur dioxide, nitrogen oxides, and particulate emissions. The project's GHG emissions would measurably prejudice Canada's ability to meet its Paris Agreement climate targets, whereas the acid gas emissions could generate smog and otherwise adversely affect air quality in the Montreal area.[83]

No federal or Ontario provincial assessment was required under either *CEAA 2012* or the provincial *Environmental Assessment Act*,[84] nor did either level of government indicate any intention of exercising discretion under these laws to require an assessment of the project. As noted, the Project List of the *IAA* does not include cement plants.

Approval of construction of the cement plant was delayed by an appeal of the rezoning of the property to the Ontario Municipal Board (now the Local Planning Appeal Tribunal) by a local municipality and a citizens group. The hearing of the appeal was further delayed by the poor health of the French-speaking tribunal member who was to preside at the appeal.

On 2 October 2018, Nature Canada, Ontario Nature, Nature Québec, and the Vankleek Hill and District Nature Society petitioned Minister of Environment and Climate Change McKenna to convene a panel review under *CEAA 2012* to assess the environmental effects of the proposed cement plant and to propose mitigation measures to reduce adverse

---

82  Minister Wilkinson's Response to Coalspur Vista Coal Mine Phase II Expansion Project and Vista Coal Underground Mine Project (30 July 2020), online: https://iaac-aeic.gc.ca/050/evaluations/document/135632.

83  Golder Associates, "Air Quality Environmental Compliance Approval Cumulative Effects Study" (2017), Report Number: 1529718 submitted to Colacem Canada Inc, online (pdf): *Colacem* http://colacem.ca/orignal/download/2018/Air%20Quality%20Cumulative%20Effects%20Study%20Aug%202017.pdf.

84  Above note 39.

effects.[85] The minister's 1 April 2019 response to the petition[86] makes clear that the federal government was not proposing to even consider specific mitigation measures to reduce the adverse effects of the project, claiming only that effects would be "adequately managed" once the project is operating.

The minister asserted that the hearings relating to the appeal of the rezoning of the property would provide opportunities for public participation[87] even though the Local Planning Appeal Tribunal has no mandate to consider GHG emissions or acid rain falling mainly in Quebec as part of its decision making. The Ontario government is also not undertaking an environmental assessment.

As a result, neither the federal nor the Ontario government is in a position to determine if Colacem Canada is proposing to employ best available technologies to limit emissions.

Federal seriousness of purpose in reducing Canada's GHG emissions to meet Paris Agreement obligations is questionable when no federal assessments are being carried out for projects such as the Coalspur Vista coal mine expansion and the Colacem cement plant, which produce annual GHG emissions in the megatonnes, as well as harm air and water quality and wildlife habitats.

In summary, the Project List effectively exempts projects with significant GHG and other pollution, such as some oil and gas pipelines, some coal mines, and all cement plants, from impact assessment through higher thresholds or decisions not to list. Conversely, it requires assessment of low-carbon pollution projects such as wind and tidal energy plants. Only the largest nuclear reactors are required to be assessed, and Alberta in situ oil sands projects are not required to be assessed unless the province abandons its legislated GHG emissions limits for oil sands sites.

---

85  Letter from Nature Canada, Nature Québec, Nature Ontario, and the Vankleek Hill and District Nature Society to Environment and Climate Change Minister Catherine McKenna (2 October 2018) (on file with authors).

86  Minister McKenna's response to petition from Nature Canada, Nature Québec, Nature Ontario, and the Vankleek Hill and District Nature Society requesting environmental assessment panel review of proposed Colacem cement plant (1 April 2019) (on file with authors). See partial summary at: https://naturecanada.ca/news/blog/environment-minister-mckenna-refuses-to-assess-cement-plant-with-one-megaton-ghg-emissions/.

87  Ibid at 2.

## E.   CONCLUSIONS AND RECOMMENDATIONS

Is the *IAA* likely to be effective in meeting its legislated purposes given the narrowly focused triggering mechanism and the shrunken Project List? The answer is no. Although the *IAA* represents an improvement over *CEAA 2012* in terms of its statutory provisions, the Act will be no more useful than *CEAA 2012* in practice, given that it will assess fewer projects over which the federal government has a clear interest.

However, decisions by the federal minister of environment and climate change in the summer of 2020 to exercise his discretion to require assessments of the Coalspur Vista phase II and Castle Mountain coal mine projects do suggest that at least some major projects with the greatest potential to cause environmental harm but not included on the Project List may be assessed. Nonetheless, the shrunken Project List was no administrative error. That this is a major lost opportunity for the federal government to address the crises of climate change and biodiversity loss hardly needs restatement. Certainly, with regard to the second question set for this chapter, the *IAA*'s triggering and coverage approaches are not useful tools in practice to address these acknowledged crises.

Here is perhaps the greatest failure of the *IAA* legislation with respect to triggering and coverage: high-carbon projects are neither triggered nor assessed as a matter of law on the basis of their GHG emissions. The statute does not set out a constitutionally robust legislative framework to enable federal impact assessments of high-carbon projects (projects designed to produce more than 50,000 tonnes $CO_2$ eq/year) that may not be subject to other federal decisions. The Project List should, but does not, include high-carbon projects whether they are coal mines, oil pipelines, or cement plants.

A Supreme Court of Canada decision declaring that the *Greenhouse Gas Pollution Pricing Act*[88] is constitutionally valid may provide the federal government with the political opportunity to include GHG emissions as an environmental component under Schedule 3 of the *IAA* and to move forward with changes to the Project List to ensure that all high-carbon projects are assessed.

An open and transparent consultative process to review the Project List entries and thresholds should be commenced by the minister of

---

88   Above note 38.

environment and climate change. Multi-interest advisory committees for each of the different sectors (e.g., oil and gas, mining, transportation, water) could be established with representation from industry and environmental groups, Indigenous organizations, and different levels of government to gather and review the scientific and technical evidence on impacts of different categories of projects within their respective mandates. These committees would make consensus-based (to the extent possible), publicly available recommendations on proposed project entries and thresholds. The RAC established by the Mulroney government in the early 1990s to develop and recommend entries and thresholds for projects likely to have significant adverse environmental effects and hence subject to comprehensive study under *CEAA 1995* is a possible model to consider.

Prior to launching such a multi-interest process, the government should set clear environmental benchmarks for the multi-interest committees. For example, any high-carbon project (e.g., a project that proposes to release more than 50,000 tonnes of $CO_2$ eq/year) would be deemed to be a major project and designated for impact assessment. A second example could be any project that involves net destruction or damage to habitat of a species at risk. Setting such benchmarks would assist in aligning the Project List with the government's key environmental commitments as well as ensure a measure of fairness among different categories of projects.

# CHAPTER 8

# Putting Multi-jurisdictional Impact Assessment into Action Under the *Impact Assessment Act*

*Patricia Fitzpatrick, Arlene Kwasniak, and A John Sinclair*

## A. INTRODUCTION

Multi-jurisdictional impact assessment (MJIA) occurs where more than one jurisdiction requires an assessment of impacts[1] with respect to the same project or initiative. The challenge of how best to implement MJIA has vexed the Canadian federation for decades. The decision on who conducts an assessment can have profound implications for what impacts are assessed and how they are assessed, potentially affecting the proponent, the public, affected communities, the environment, and sustainability.[2] For over thirty years, governments, academics, practitioners, and others have attempted to improve MJIA in Canada. Avoiding negative implications, such as jurisdictional bullying or reducing assessments to the lowest common denominator, has been one part of the approach. The other has been to preserve the positives, such as respecting the

---

1    Impact assessment throughout Canada is commonly referred to as "environmental assessment" or "EA." However, since the federal *Impact Assessment Act* (SC 2019, c 28, s 1) [*IAA*] came into force in August 2019 (SI/2019-86), federal impact assessment is characteristically referred to as "impact assessment" or "IA," to recognize the range of impacts assessed under the Act in addition to environmental impacts.

2    See Patricia Fitzpatrick & A John Sinclair, "Multi-jurisdictional Environmental Assessment in Canada" in Kevin S Hanna, ed, *Environmental Impact Assessment: Process and Practice*, 3d ed (Toronto: Oxford University Press, 2014) 182 [Fitzpatrick & Sinclair, "Multi-jurisdictional"] and A John Sinclair, Gary Schneider & Lisa Mitchell, "Environmental Impact Assessment Process Substitution: Experience of Public Participants" (2012) 30:2 *Impact Assessment and Project Appraisal* 85.

responsibilities of the assessing jurisdictions, meeting their information needs so they can make informed, independent decisions, and facilitating public and Indigenous involvement. Although it is possible for each assessing jurisdiction to carry out its own assessment, critiques of this practice hold that this approach can result in inefficiency, delay, duplication, inconsistency, and excessive cost for the proponent and stress and confusion for the proponent and participants.[3] Accordingly, attempts to deal with MJIA situations have concentrated on a "one project, one assessment" approach (also known as a "one-window" approach).

This chapter continues in that direction, focusing on methods to implement MJIA that seek to achieve a single, comprehensive assessment for each project. It reviews, explains, and assesses traditional approaches to address MJIA in order to place and evaluate the methods set out in the *Impact Assessment Act (IAA)*.[4] Section B outlines the constitutional context in which MJIA occurs. Section C focuses on traditional methods to address MJIA situations. Section D delves into the development of the *IAA* in light of the traditional methods available to lawmakers and of the information rendered in the law reform process. Section E sets out how the *IAA* deals with MJIA. Section F analyzes and evaluates the *IAA* approaches and makes recommendations to improve them and to facilitate better practices as the *IAA* comes into use.

## B. MULTI-JURISDICTIONAL IMPACT ASSESSMENT: THE CONSTITUTIONAL CONTEXT

In Canada, the federal government and all provinces and territories have impact assessment legislation of some kind. Additionally, most Indigenous governing bodies also have impact assessment processes.[5] To understand why there is MJIA in Canada, one needs to consider how

---

3    See, for example, Fitzpatrick & Sinclair, "Multi-jurisdictional," above note 2, and the Expert Panel for the Review of Environmental Assessment Processes, *Building Common Ground: A New Vision for Impact Assessment in Canada* (Ottawa: Canadian Environmental Assessment Agency, 2017), online (pdf): *Government of Canada* www.canada.ca/content/dam/themes/environment/conservation/environmental-reviews/building-common-ground/building-common-ground.pdf [*Building Common Ground*], especially s 2.2.1.

4    *IAA*, above note 1.

5    This includes legislative processes involving Indigenous peoples, such as land claims agreements, co-management provisions, etc., and important work by Indigenous governments and organizations that codify and revitalize Indigenous legal traditions relating to the environment.

the federal *Constitution Act, 1867*[6] allocates "heads of legislative power" between the federal and the provincial governments. Each head of power gives a level of government (federal or provincial) the jurisdiction to regulate matters falling under it. Chapter 5 provides a detailed discussion of jurisdiction, but for the purposes of this chapter, suffice it to say that the allocation is exclusive in that if the Constitution gives one level of government the right to legislate a matter, it excludes the other level from legislating that specific matter. Although neither level of government has exclusive legislative power over environmental or sustainability impacts, a proposed project may touch upon stand-alone heads of legislative power belonging to both levels.

To illustrate, suppose that a proposed nickel mine will impact provincial land, as well as air and water quality (all provincial jurisdiction), and impact fisheries and migratory birds (federal jurisdiction). Moreover, it will impact Indigenous peoples' rights and interests (provincial, federal, Indigenous). Assume that, to proceed, the project requires permits or approvals under provincial and federal legislation that trigger provincial and federal assessments and that the affected Indigenous government body's practices require an environmental assessment. In this situation, we have MJIA among three jurisdictions.

## C.   MULTI-JURISDICTIONAL IMPACT ASSESSMENT PRINCIPLES AND METHODS

### 1)   The Principles of the Canadian Council of Ministers of the Environment

One way to address some MJIA issues is to have one standardized impact assessment process that applies across all federal, provincial, and territorial jurisdictions. However, early efforts to this end were quickly abandoned,[7] and other MJIA approaches continued as the de facto reality. Early direction to rationalize MJIA was provided through the 1998 Canadian Council of Ministers of the Environment (CCME)[8]

---

6    (UK) 30 & 31 Vict, c 3, ss 91, 92, & 92A.

7    Steven A Kennett, "Meeting the Intergovernmental Challenge of Environmental Assessment" in Patrick C Fafard & Kathryn Harrison, eds, *Managing the Environmental Union: Intergovernmental Relations and Environmental Policy in Canada* (Kingston, ON: School of Policy Studies, Queen's University, 2000) 107.

8    The CCME is made up of the fourteen environment ministers from federal, provincial, and territorial governments. See the CCME website: www.ccme.ca.

Canada-Wide Accord on Environmental Harmonization[9] and the Sub-agreement on Environmental Assessment.[10] The accord, signed by all Council members except Quebec's, pledged a one-window approach to MJIA. The sub-agreement committed to a process that "contribute[s] to the vision of the highest level of environmental quality in Canada, and to a future based on the principles of sustainable development."[11] It commits to the following principles:

> **Effectiveness:** A harmonized approach to environmental assessment will provide the information needed for sound project planning and decision-making ... that contribute to environmental protection and sustainable development.

> **Transparency and Public Accountability:** The integrity and credibility of a sound environmental assessment process will be built on a foundation of openness, transparency, accountability, and effective participation of interested parties and the general public.

> **Efficiency and Certainty:** Environmental assessment will be conducted in a timely way that protects the environment, promotes certainty of process, and makes the best use of public and private resources.[12]

These principles are central to what is called a "harmonized" approach to MJIA, or simply "harmonization," discussed in the next section.

Although these are sound principles, the policy environment has evolved over the last twenty years to question their completeness. For example, the CCME does not include representatives of Indigenous governments, and the accord and sub-agreement are missing key commitments, including those related to reconciliation and the *United Nations Declaration on the Rights of Indigenous Persons (UNDRIP)*.[13]

---

9 The accord is available on the CCME website: Canadian Counsel of Ministers of the Environment, "A Canada-Wide Accord on Environmental Harmonization" (1998) online (pdf): *CCME* www.ccme.ca/files/Resources/harmonization/accord_harmonization_e.pdf.

10 The sub-agreement is available on the CCME website: Canadian Counsel of Ministers of the Environment, "Sub-Agreement on Environmental Assessment" (1998) online (pdf): *CCME* www.ccme.ca/files/Resources/harmonization/envtlassesssubagr_e.pdf.

11 *Ibid* at 1.

12 *Ibid* at 3.

13 GA Res 61/295, UNGAOR, 61st Sess, UN Doc A/RES/61/295 (13 September 2007).

## 2)  Methods to Address Multi-jurisdictional Impact Assessments

### a)  Separate Assessments

As noted earlier, it is always possible for each assessing jurisdiction to carry out its own assessment. However, in light of problems with this approach, this chapter focuses on methods aimed at achieving one project, one assessment.

### b)  Harmonization

Using this approach, a jurisdiction harmonizes and coordinates its impact assessment process with that of another jurisdiction, but each jurisdiction retains its own decision-making authority under its own legislation regarding whether a project will go ahead. A critical component is that each jurisdiction meaningfully participates in the assessment process and does not unduly defer to another jurisdiction.

Ideally, the objectives of harmonization include the following:

- the coordination and integration of the impact assessment processes of all involved jurisdictions so that there is only one process and one report, and if there is a hearing, one hearing
- the reduction of duplication of requirements and the standardization of impact assessment elements
- each jurisdiction carrying out its legislative requirements in the cooperative process
- each jurisdiction fulfilling its information needs to enable an informed exercise of authority under its legislation

A well-designed harmonized approach can result in a number of positive outcomes, such as better ensuring one project, one assessment; avoiding duplication; allowing for consistency in scope, process, and timelines; strengthening opportunities for meaningful engagement, including access to funding and information;[14] providing redundancy

---

14    Fitzpatrick & Sinclair, "Multi-jurisdictional," above note 2; Derek Doyle & Barry Sadler, *Environmental Assessment in Canada: Frameworks, Procedures & Attributes of Effectiveness: A Report of the International Study of the Effectiveness of Environmental Assessment,* (London, UK: Macmillan Press, 1996) at para 2.2.12; Steven A Kennett, "Interjurisdictional Harmonization of Environmental Assessment in Canada" in Steven A Kennett, ed, *Law and Process in Environmental Management: Essays from the Sixth CIRL Conference on Natural Resources Law* (Calgary: Canadian Institute of Resources Law, 1993) 297; Patrick C Fafard, "Groups, Governments and the Environment: Some Evidence from

where each jurisdiction can review the other's work, minimizing the chance of error and decreasing gaps in analysis; and allowing for consistent, effective, and enforceable conditions.[15]

Unfortunately, harmonized approaches have not always been well designed in Canada, as outlined in the body of literature that discusses the strengths and weaknesses of harmonization.[16] This literature shows how, in some instances, jurisdictions collaborated and cooperated, resulting in smooth and successful harmonized assessments. However, it also shows that despite claims of harmonized processes, in some instances two separate assessments unfolded. Such was the case for the Manitoba-Minnesota Transmission Project, which triggered environmental assessments under provincial legislation[17] and the National Energy Board (NEB).[18] The provincial hearings were conducted in the spring of 2017, and the report by the review body was issued in September of that year.[19] Federally, the NEB did not seek oral evidence until June of 2018—one year after the provincial hearings. Resultant problems, such as confusion over the process, uncertainty regarding the role of the government, multiple public records, and the prolonged timelines, mirror weaknesses identified in other poorly harmonized reviews. These unfortunate results could have been avoided. Improved

---

the Harmonization Initiative" in Patrick C Fafard & Kathryn Harrison, eds, *Managing the Environmental Union: Intergovernmental Relations and Environmental Policy in Canada* (Kingston, ON: School of Policy Studies, Queen's University, 2000) 81; Arlene Kwasniak, *Harmonization in Environmental Assessment in Canada: The Good, the Bad and the Ugly* (Ottawa: Canadian Environmental Network, 2008), online: *Canadian Electronic Library* www.deslibris.ca/ID/224701.

15 Fitzpatrick & Sinclair, "Multi-jurisdictional," above note 2 at 153.

16 See, for example, Fitzpatrick & Sinclair, "Multi-jurisdictional," above note 2, and Gordon M Hickey, Nicolas Brunet & Nadège Allan, "A Constant Comparison of the Environmental Assessment Legislation in Canada" (2010) 12:13 *Journal of Environmental Policy and Planning* 315.

17 The provincial project file is available on the Manitoba EA public registry: Government of Manitoba, "Public Registry file 5750.00—Manitoba Hydro—Manitoba—Minnesota Transmission Project" (28 May 2020), online: *Government of Manitoba* www.gov.mb.ca/sd/eal/registries/5750mbhydrombminnesota/index.html.

18 The federal project file is available from: Canada Energy Regulator, "Manitoba Hydro—Manitoba-Minnesota Transmission Project," online: *Canada Energy Regulator* www.cer-rec.gc.ca/pplctnflng/mjrpp/mntbmnnst/index-eng.html. See also *Clean Environment Commission, Report on Public Hearings: Manitoba Minnesota Transmission Line* (Winnipeg: Clean Environment Commission, 2017), online (pdf): http://digitalcollection.gov.mb.ca/awweb/pdfopener?smd=1&did=25795&md=1.

19 See Clean Environment Commission Report, *ibid.*

coordination by the proponent with all jurisdictions, potentially affected and interested parties, and communities early in the process would have allowed for more harmonization. The jurisdictions themselves could have taken appropriate steps to work together early in the process, including communicating with each other and all participants to ensure common timelines, participating meaningfully, meeting responsibilities to Indigenous communities, and coordinating and harmonizing processes to avoid needless duplication. The results of this case, and others, show that as coordination and cooperation decrease, so too do the benefits of taking a harmonized approach.

Despite some poorly designed attempts, in our view harmonization remains the best approach to MJIA. Compared to the other methods, it has the highest potential to meet the legislative requirements of the involved jurisdictions, with each jurisdiction carrying out its requirements through one cooperative and coordinated process. Each jurisdiction can benefit from incorporating the requirements of the other (or others) into the joint assessment, thus providing opportunity for a broad yet efficient impact assessment on which to base individual decisions. Harmonization presents the best opportunity for consistent and effective conditions being imposed on approvals, which are managed by the jurisdiction with the clearest legislative authority. In addition, successful harmonization fosters and furthers cooperative federalism, reflecting different orders of government working together to realize their common goal of efficiently and effectively exercising their respective constitutional authority and legislative requirements.

### c)  Substitution

*Substitution* means that an impact assessment process of one jurisdiction (call it "A") is substituted for (replaces) an impact assessment process of another jurisdiction (call it "B"). For example, the impact assessment process of British Columbia has been substituted for the impact assessment of the federal government. In this example, British Columbia is jurisdiction A and the federal government is jurisdiction B.

With substitution, there is only one assessment, and it is under jurisdiction A's process. Jurisdiction B relies on jurisdiction A's assessment and makes its impact assessment and regulatory decisions based on it. Although substitution mandates that only one process apply, jurisdiction B's involvement in the assessment can vary from virtually no involvement to considerable involvement. The amount of involvement may depend on the requirements of legislation, policy, the circumstances of a particular assessment, and MJIA agreements.

Substitution has a shorter history than harmonization in Canada. The *Canadian Environmental Assessment Act* (*CEAA 1995*)[20] only permitted substitution within the federal family, for example, NEB process as a substitution for *CEAA 1995* reviews.[21] New regulations in 2009 permitted provincial substitution for some projects under the Building Canada Plan.[22] The *Canadian Environmental Assessment Act, 2012* (*CEAA 2012*) broadened the potential for substitution by permitting federal environmental assessment substitution both to provinces and Indigenous jurisdictions as defined by the Act.[23] *CEAA 2012* required the minister to approve a federal/provincial substitution (but not a federal/Indigenous one) if "of the opinion that a process for assessment of environmental effects of [the province] would be an appropriate substitute."[24]

It is critical to understand that, in our opinion and as supported by the literature, jurisdiction B, the jurisdiction that substitutes its impact assessment process, cannot simply rely on A's impact assessment investigations and expect to make a fully informed decision. Jurisdiction B would need to carry out its own investigations and assessment or at least participate fully in these activities.[25] To begin with, although there may be some overlap in interests, each jurisdiction needs to have an assessment of impacts within its own jurisdictional legislative competence—the matters that it regulates. For example, a province may assess a project for impacts on water quality generally, whereas the federal government assesses the same project for impacts on a fishery. The federal government's inquiries during the assessment process will necessarily

---

20   SC 1992, c 37. The entry into force of the Act was delayed until 1995 to allow for key regulations to be developed and passed.

21   *CEAA 1995*, ss 40(1)(d) and 43(1). For a critique of this process, see John Sinclair, Gary Schneider & Lisa Mitchell, "Environmental Impact Assessment Substitution: Experiences of Public Participants" (2012) 30:2 *Impact Assessment and Project Appraisal* 85.

22   *Infrastructure Projects Environmental Assessment Adaptation Regulations*, SOR/09-89.

23   SC 2012, c 19, s 52, ss 32–34.

24   *Ibid*, ss 32(1) & (2).

25   Arlene Kwasniak, "Environmental Assessment, Overlap, Duplication, Harmonization, Equivalency, and Substitution: Interpretation, Misinterpretation, and a Path Forward" (2009) 20 *Journal of Environmental Law and Practice* 1; Brenda Heelan Powell, *Environmental Assessment & the Canadian Constitution: Substitution and Equivalency* (Edmonton: Environmental Law Centre, 2014).

reflect its constitutional authority, and these interests have a different focus from a province's more general water quality interests. Moreover, jurisdictions have the experience and expertise relating to the areas they regulate. For example, the federal government has experts relating to its heads of powers, as discussed in Chapter 5 of this book. It would be both inefficient and unrealistic to expect a province that does not have the same regulatory focus to match that of the federal government. Given the different levels and areas of interests and expertise, all assessing jurisdictions must be at the table and actively involved in the process to avoid undue reliance on one jurisdiction's processes and investigations. But if all assessing jurisdictions must be at the table and each jurisdiction must ensure that its legislative requirements are met and constitutional mandates are satisfied, why not harmonize and coordinate assessments rather than going through an unreliable and less than fully informative substituted process?

An early test case from 2006 involving federal family substitution under *CEAA 1995* reveals issues. The case involved two federal authorities, the Canadian Environmental Assessment Agency and the NEB. The Emera Brunswick Pipeline Project involved the construction and operation of a liquefied natural gas (LNG) pipeline. As this was the first occurrence of an MJIA following a single process, one outside the *CEAA* norm, it was subject to significant scrutiny. Some commenters strongly criticized it on the basis that the NEB process challenged the ability of the public to be meaningfully involved.[26] It is important to appreciate that the narrow interpretation of the regulated NEB process itself posed barriers to meaningful participation. This was surprising given the NEB's extensive efforts to engage the public in the harmonized panel review of the Sable Gas Project, including hosting sessions about how to intervene and offering staff counsel for participants with no legal representation.[27]

One problem in the Emera case was that some members of the public had difficulty becoming familiar with the complex NEB process and found that the NEB attempts at providing assistance did not enable

---

26   See Sinclair, Schneider & Mitchell, above note 21.

27   See Patricia Fitzpatrick & A John Sinclair, "Learning Through Public Involvement in Environmental Assessment Hearings" (2003) 67:2 *Journal of Environmental Management* 161 [Fitzpatrick & Sinclair, "Learning"].

them to confidently or meaningfully participate.[28] These issues can pose an acute challenge for public participants in any substitution unless the participant is already familiar with the substituted process.

In an earlier harmonized assessment, participants found that the NEB process was so formal that in order to effectively participate, a member of the public needed to hire a lawyer to, for example, prepare and file motions, affidavits, and evidence; cross-examine witnesses; be prepared for cross-examination; produce and submit rebuttals; and prepare and file final arguments.[29] To generalize this problem, public participants who may be familiar with the federal process should not have to hire a lawyer to meaningfully participate and should not be expected to understand, internalize, and abide by the processes of any other jurisdiction whose process may be substituted for the federal one. This is especially important as non-compliance with assessment process requirements can result in public participation being disregarded or even rendered void.

Even though *CEAA 2012* added the potential for provincial and Indigenous assessments to be substituted for federal ones, ultimately only two jurisdictions' processes were substituted for those under *CEAA 2012*: British Columbia's and the one established under the Inuvialuit Final Agreement.[30] By February 2020, only four assessments were complete using process substitution.[31] That should be telling in itself.

Given the problems with substitution, especially when MJIA could be carried out through harmonization and coordination, substitution is not a defensible method for carrying out MJIA.

---

28   See Sinclair, Schneider & Mitchell, above note 21.

29   See Fitzpatrick & Sinclair, "Learning," above note 27.

30   Agreement between the Committee for Original Peoples' Entitlement, representing the Inuvialuit of the Inuvialuit Settlement Region, and the Government of Canada dated 5 June 1984, and amendments, known as the "Inuvialuit Final Agreement." The Agreement and amendments are available at: "The Inuvialuit Final Agreement As Amended" (April 2005), online (pdf): *The Inuvialuit Corporation* https://irc.inuvialuit.com/sites/default/files/Inuvialuit%20Final%20Agreement%202005.pdf. The Agreement was approved and given effect by the *Western Arctic (Inuvialuit) Claims Settlement Act*, SC 1984, c 24, s 3.

31   According to the public registry, maintained by the Canadian Impact Assessment Agency, nine additional substituted environmental assessments (all in British Columbia) are in progress, and four have been terminated.

## d)  Equivalency and Delegation

### i)  *Equivalency*

With equivalency, jurisdiction B deems the impact assessment law or process of jurisdiction A to be equivalent to its own law or process. With equivalency, the project reviewed by jurisdiction A is, in effect, exempted from review by jurisdiction B, and jurisdiction B does not retain its decision-making authority.

### ii)  *Delegation*

With delegation, jurisdiction B delegates part of an impact assessment to jurisdiction A. Jurisdiction A carries out that part of the assessment instead of jurisdiction B. Subject to legislation, delegation powers can be narrow or broad.

Only *CEAA 2012* permitted MJIA by equivalency (section 37), but, to our knowledge, it was never used. On the basis of our observations on substitution, equivalency is not a defensible method to deal with MJIA. In addition, we find it unpalatable and an unjustified divesting of federal jurisdiction to, in effect, delegate decision making to non-federal jurisdictions through equivalency.

Delegation of aspects of environmental assessment to any person was permitted in both *CEAA 1995* (section 17) and *CEAA 2012* (section 26), although both statutes prohibited delegation of the final decision. In our view, it is difficult to see how federal impact assessment can be conducted without the power to delegate some aspects of it: for example, minor administrative tasks or independent research. However, delegation powers should be clearly circumscribed so that they cannot be used to effect substitution or equivalency or to relinquish legislative responsibility or accountability.

## D.  MULTI-JURISDICTIONAL IMPACT ASSESSMENT IN THE DEVELOPMENT OF THE *IAA*

Given the history of MJIA in Canada, it is not surprising that it garnered considerable attention in the development of the *IAA*. The federal government's mandate letter to Catherine McKenna, then-minister of Environment and Climate Change Canada, underscored the importance of addressing MJIA challenges in indicating that any new Act must "restore robust oversight and thorough environmental assessments of areas under federal jurisdiction, while also working with provinces and territories to avoid duplication."[32]

The Canadian public expressed considerable interest in MJIA in over 600 submissions made to the Expert Panel for the Review of Environmental Assessment Processes (Expert Panel) struck by the federal government to assist with impact assessment law reform. The vast majority of these noted the need for cooperation and the advantages of the "one project, one assessment" principle, as is also supported in the literature noted above.[33]

The Expert Panel report[34] included two broad recommendations for achieving greater cooperation in MJIA situations:

- *That cooperation be the primary mechanism for coordination where multiple impact assessment processes apply.* The Panel noted existing and past cooperative agreements between the federal government and many provinces as evidence that cooperation is possible and clearly preferred a focus on cooperation and coordination on an assessment-by-assessment basis for project, strategic, and regional assessments. Apparently, the success of joint review panels in the past was a significant driver for the Expert Panel, which recognized that the cooperation achieved in joint review panels has served to produce the most efficient, effective, and fair assessments under the current and previous federal legislation. The literature on this topic in the Canadian context also supports project-by-project agreements being the preferred approach.[35]

---

32 Prime Minister Justin Trudeau to Catherine McKenna, Minister of Environment and Climate Change, "Minister of Environment and Climate Change Mandate Letter" (12 November 2015), online: *Office of the Prime Minister* https://pm.gc.ca/en/mandate-letters/2015/11/12/archived-minister-environment-and-climate-change-mandate-letter. These components are also included in the mandate letter of the current minister, Jonathan Wilkinson: Prime Minister Justin Trudeau to Jonathan Wilkinson, Minister of Enviornment and Climate Change, "Minister of Environment and Climate Change Mandate Letter" (13 December 2019), online: *Office of the Prime Minister* https://pm.gc.ca/en/mandate-letters/minister-environment-and-climate-change-mandate-letter.

33 Above notes 2 and 3, all citations.

34 *Building Common Ground*, above note 3. See also Meinhard Doelle, "The EA Expert Panel Report: A Preliminary Assessment" (9 April 2017), online (blog): *Dalhousie University* https://blogs.dal.ca/melaw/?s=Expert+Panel.

35 See, generally, Meinhard Doelle's Dalhousie University law blogs on impact assessment law reform, online: https://blogs.dal.ca/melaw/category/environmental-assessment;

- *That substitution be available on the condition that the highest standard of impact assessment would apply.* Although the advice commissioned by the Expert Panel recommended that substitution not be available in the new legislation,[36] the Panel decided to retain it. However, the Panel established a list of criteria for the application of substitution to ensure the principle of "harmonization upward" including the following:

  1. Sustainability-based scope of issues based on criteria identified in the Planning Phase.
  2. Transparent and accessible information.
  3. Comparable opportunities for public engagement.
  4. Active engagement of federal experts and federal regulators.
  5. Delegation of procedural aspects of the duty to consult.
  6. The principles of UNDRIP, specifically consent, reflected into decision-making.
  7. Integration of independent science throughout the impact assessment.
  8. Meeting existing commitments set out in co-management or consultation agreements.[37]

The Expert Panel found that the "principle of 'one project, one assessment' is central to implementing impact assessment around the five pillars of sustainability"[38] but explicitly rejected equivalency, which it regarded as unviable.[39]

The Multi-Interest Advisory Committee on impact assessment struck by the minister of environment and climate change to assist the assessment law reform initiative also discussed and made recommendations about MJIA. It concluded that the goal for project-level

---

Fitzpatrick & Sinclair, "Multi-jurisdictional," above note 2 at 354–72; and Patricia J Fitzpatrick & A John Sinclair, "Multi-jurisdictional Environmental Impact Assessment: Canadian Experiences" (2009) 29:4 *Environmental Impact Assessment Review* 252.

36  See Arlene Kwasniak's expert report commissioned by the Expert Panel, Harmonization, Substitution, Equivalency, and Delegation in Relation to Federal and Provincial/Territorial Environmental Assessment (2 January 2017), online (pdf): https://s3.ca-central-1.amazonaws.com/ehq-production-canada/file_answers/files/bf4443811c7d0ea1d18142c540d490a6ef845bad/004/773/373/original/Report_Harmonization-etc_AJKwasniak.pdf.

37  *Building Common Ground*, above note 3, s 2.2.2.

38  *Ibid*, s 2.2.1.

39  *Ibid*, s 2.2.3.

assessment, as well as strategic and regional assessment, is a single collaborative process with an appropriate level of involvement by all applicable authorities: federal, provincial, territorial, Indigenous; local governments; and land claims–based co-management organizations.

## E. MULTI-JURISDICTIONAL IMPACT ASSESSMENT IN THE *IAA*

### 1) Cooperation

The *IAA* offers four methods to deal with MJIA: coordinated review, substitution, delegation, and joint and integrated review panels. Each is discussed below. But sitting above these methods is the principle of cooperation.

Overall, the *IAA* promotes cooperation as an umbrella objective that applies to all methods of impact assessment.[40] The Impact Assessment Agency of Canada (the Agency) echoes this opinion.[41] This point should be kept in mind as although the term *cooperative review* may naturally lend itself to describe a harmonized review, for the *IAA* at least, it may apply to substitution and other methods dealing with MJIA.

### 2) Coordinated Review

Although an Agency objective in the *IAA* is "to promote harmonization in relation to the assessment of effects across Canada at all levels of government"[42] (restoring this Agency objective, which was last present in *CEAA 1995*), the *IAA* does not identify "harmonization" as an MJIA

---

40　For example, the purpose of the *IAA* (above note 1) is to "promote cooperation and coordinated action between federal and provincial governments" (s 6(e)) and "to promote communication and cooperation with Indigenous peoples of Canada with respect to impact assessments" (s 6(f)). Section 33(1)(c) states that a substitution may be approved only if the substituted jurisdiction has the capacity to cooperate with the other involved jurisdictions; s 18(1) states that the Agency must publish its MJIA cooperation plans and may extend time limits to facilitate cooperation; s 21 provides that for review panels, the Agency/minister must offer to cooperate with any jurisdiction also assessing; and ss 28(5) and (6) state that time may be extended to facilitate cooperation.

41　Impact Assessment Agency of Canada, "Cooperative Impact Assessments (Infographic)" (2019), online (pdf): *Government of Canada* www.canada.ca/content/dam/iaac-acei/documents/acts-regulations/cooperative-impact-assessment-eng.pdf ["Cooperative Impact Assessments"].

42　*IAA*, above note 1, s 155(c).

method. However, it is apparent that Agency materials use the term "coordinated" assessment or review to capture what was previously identified as harmonization.[43] Hence, in this section, we use "coordinated assessment" or "coordinated review" in the *IAA* to mean what prior to the *IAA* was referred to as "harmonized assessment" or "review."

Overall, the *IAA* reflects the intention to effect cooperation and coordination with jurisdictions in MJIA, standing in contrast to *CEAA 2012*, which attempted to limit federal involvement in MJIA through delegation, substitution, and equivalency.

Coordinated review begins in the planning phase. For this phase, section 12 of the *IAA* establishes the following:

> For the purposes of preparing for a possible impact assessment of a designated project, the Agency must offer to consult with any jurisdiction that has powers, duties or functions in relation to an assessment of the environmental effects of the designated project and any Indigenous group that may be affected by the carrying out of the designated project.

For coordinated review (but not for substitution), *IAA* regulations require the Agency to provide the proponent with a plan for cooperating with other jurisdictions.[44] The Agency's "Practitioner's Guide to Federal Impact Assessments Under the Impact Assessment Act" gives direction on developing the plan.[45] An Agency-developed template indicates that such a plan will include the approach to cooperation, timelines and time management, information-sharing, public participation and funding, Indigenous consultation and engagement, and cooperation during the drafting of the decision statement to better ensure consistency of conditions.[46]

---

43   "Cooperative Impact Assessments," above note 41, in which the Agency identifies four methods of cooperation: coordination, substitution, delegation, and panel reviews.

44   IAA, above note 1, s 18(1)(b); *Information and Management of Time Limits Regulations*, SOR/2019-283, s 5.

45   Impact Assessment Agency of Canada, "Practitioner's Guide to Federal Impact Assessments Under the Impact Assessment Act," online: *Government of Canada* www.canada.ca/en/impact-assessment-agency/services/policy-guidance/practitioners-guide-impact-assessment-act.html.

46   Impact Assessment Agency of Canada, "Impact Assessment Agency Cooperation Plan—Template," online (pdf): *Government of Canada* www.canada.ca/content/dam/iaac-acei/documents/policy-guidance/practitioners-guide/cooperation_plan_external_template_final_en.pdf.

### 3) Substitution

The *IAA* retains substitution. If a "jurisdiction" (meaning a provincial government or assessment agency or an Indigenous governing body that has powers, duties, or functions in relation to an assessment of the "environmental effects of the designated project" and is otherwise qualified as a jurisdiction under the *IAA*) requests a substitution, the minister may grant the request if, in the minister's opinion, it would be an appropriate substitute, and the substitution meets statutory criteria.[47]

The Agency must post public notice of any request and invite public comments, and the minister must consider public comments in making a decision on the substitution.[48] The minister's decision on the substitution request and reasons for it must be posted. The minister "may only approve a substitution … if satisfied that":

- "the process to be substituted will include a consideration of the factors set out in subsection 22(1)";
- federal authorities with "relevant specialist or expert information or knowledge will be given an opportunity to participate in the assessment"; and
- the substituted jurisdiction must be able to enter into an arrangement with any relevant Indigenous jurisdiction for cooperation in the assessment, and the substituted process must include consultations with any Indigenous group that may be affected by the project.[49]

The public will be given an opportunity to participate meaningfully in the assessment, provide comments on a draft report, and have access to assessment records. If the minister approves a substitution, the Act deems the substituted process to have met the *IAA* requirements.[50] A participant funding program does not need to be established for substituted processes.[51]

---

47 IAA, above note 1, ss 31(1) and 33(1).
48 *Ibid*, ss 31(2) & (3).
49 *Ibid*, s 33(1).
50 *Ibid*, s 34.
51 *Ibid*, s 75(2).

## 4)   Delegation

Section 29 of the *IAA* gives the Agency the authority to "delegate to any person, body or jurisdiction referred to in paragraphs (a) to (g) of the definition jurisdiction in section 2 the carrying out of any part of the impact assessment of the designated project and the preparation of the report with respect to the impact assessment of the designated project."

## 5)   Review Panel: Joint, Integrated, and Joint Integrated

When in the public interest, the minister may refer a designated project for assessment by an independent panel of experts appointed in accordance with the *IAA*. In determining the public interest in this context, the minister considers the extent to which the likely effects of the project are in federal jurisdiction, public concern relating to these effects, opportunities for interjurisdictional cooperation, and potential adverse impacts on Indigenous rights.[52] Historically, because of the independence of review panel members, comprehensiveness of review panel assessments, and opportunities for public involvement, review panels have been known as the "flagships"[53] and the "high water mark"[54] of federal assessment.

MJIA comes in where an assessment triggered by the *IAA* is also triggered by the processes of another jurisdiction, for example, a province under provincial assessment legislation. The *IAA* contains provisions regarding MJIA being carried out by a joint review panel. Section 39(1) gives the minister the discretion to enter into an agreement with any "jurisdiction," as defined by sections (a) to (d) in the definition of "jurisdiction," to jointly establish a review panel, known as a "joint review panel." A joint review panel will carry out an assessment in accordance with the agreement and terms of reference (TOR) having due regard to the legislative requirements of the involved jurisdictions.

---

52   *Ibid*, s 36.

53   Peter Usher & Frances Abele, "Strengthening Environmental Reviews of Major Projects" *Policy Options* (14 November 2017), online: https://policyoptions.irpp.org/magazines/november-2017/strengthening-environmental-reviews-of-major-projects.

54   Meinhard Doelle, "Panel Reviews Under the Proposed Federal Impact Assessment Act (IAA)" (4 March 2018), online (blog): *Dalhousie University* https://blogs.dal.ca/melaw/2018/03/04/panel-reviews-under-the-proposed-canadian-impact-assessment-act-ciaa.

The *IAA* contains special provisions for some Canadian energy regulators. "Energy regulators" refers to the following:

- Canadian Energy Regulator (CER), which regulates designated "pipeline, power line and offshore renewable energy projects within federal jurisdiction" under the *Canadian Energy Regulator Act (CERA)*[55]
- Canadian Nuclear Safety Commission (CNSC), which regulates the "development, production and use of nuclear energy, ... nuclear substances, prescribed equipment and prescribed information" under the *Nuclear Safety and Control Act (NSCA)*[56]
- Canada–Nova Scotia Offshore Petroleum Board (CNSOPB), which is a joint federal–provincial board that manages offshore petroleum resources in accordance with an agreement between the Government of Canada and the Government of Nova Scotia under the *Canada-Nova Scotia Offshore Petroleum Resources Accord Implementation Act*[57]
- Canada–Newfoundland and Labrador Offshore Petroleum Board (C-NLOPB), which is a joint federal–provincial board manages offshore petroleum resources in accordance with an agreement between the Government of Canada and the Government of Newfoundland and Labrador, under the *Canada–Newfoundland and Labrador Atlantic Accord Implementation Act*[58]

We sometimes refer to the last two mentioned energy regulators as the "offshore boards."

Section 39(2) of the *IAA* prohibits the minister from entering into a joint panel review agreement with the CNSC, if the designated project includes physical activities that are regulated under the *NSCA* and the CER if the designated project includes physical activities that are regulated under the *CERA*. However, section 43 requires the minister to refer a designated project to a review panel if the project includes physical activities regulated by the *CERA* or the *NSCA*. Accordingly, although the minister cannot enter into a section 39(1) joint review agreement with these two energy regulators, designated projects that fall under their

---

55  SC 2019, c 28, Preamble.
56  SC 1997, c 9, Preamble.
57  SC 1988, c 8, long title of the Act, and ss 9(1) and 18(1).
58  SC 1987, c 3, long title of the Act, and ss 9(1) and 17(1).

regulatory authority must be assessed by an *IAA* review panel. The Agency refers to such a panel as an "integrated review panel,"[59] although the term *integrated review panel* does not appear in the *IAA* itself. The Agency presumably introduced the term because the review integrates *IAA* and an energy regulator's requirements and to distinguish an integrated review panel from a joint review panel established under section 39(1). The *IAA* sets out specific rules for integrated review panels, including regarding the composition of members, TOR, and review panel duties.

Memoranda of understanding between the Agency and the CER and between the Agency and the CNSC recognize "joint integrated review panels" for joint integrated impact assessments.[60] With a joint integrated impact assessment, a joint integrated review panel would assess an *IAA* designated project that is regulated under the *CERA* or *NSCA*, which also requires assessment by another jurisdiction (e.g., a province). As stated in Annex 8 of each memorandum, the Agency and the CER or CNSC will implement an integrated review "in the context of a joint review panel with a jurisdiction … of the environmental effects of a designated project" regulated under the *CERA* or the *NSCA*.[61] The memoranda contemplate a joint integrated impact assessment agreement with the jurisdiction also conducting an assessment (called the "partner jurisdiction")

---

59   As stated in the proposed terms of reference for the Gazoduq Project Integrated Review at 3, "A review panel whose mandate covers both the IAA and the CERA is called an integrated review panel." *Gazoduq Project Integrated Review Panel Terms of Reference: Draft for Consultation* (15 May 2020), online (pdf): *Impact Assessment Agency of Canada* https://iaac-aeic.gc.ca/050/documents/p80264/134808E.pdf.

60   Impact Assessment Agency of Canada, *Memorandum of Understanding on Integrated Impact Assessments Under the Impact Assessment Act Between the Impact Assessment Agency of Canada and the Canadian Nuclear Safety Commission* (Memorandum), (21 October 2019), online: www.canada.ca/en/impact-assessment-agency/corporate/acts-regulations/legislation-regulations/memorandum-understanding-iaac-cnsc.html; and Impact Assessment Agency of Canada, *Memorandum of Understanding on Integrated Impact Assessments Under the Impact Assessment Act Between the Impact Assessment Agency of Canada and the Canadian Energy Regulator* (Memorandum), (15 November 2019), online: www.canada.ca/en/impact-assessment-agency/corporate/acts-regulations/legislation-regulations/memorandum-understanding-iaac-cer.html.

61   Annex 8 to *the Memorandum of Understanding on Integrated Impact Assessments Under the Impact Assessment Act Between the Impact Assessment Agency of Canada and the Canadian Nuclear Safety Commission*, above note 60, "Purpose," and Annex 8 to the *Memorandum of Understanding on Integrated Impact Assessments Under the Impact Assessment Act Between the Impact Assessment Agency of Canada and the Canadian Energy Regulator*, above note 60, "Purpose."

that addresses matters such as "appointments of review panel members and the development of the review panel's Terms of Reference."[62] Although, as mentioned, the *IAA* prohibits the CER and the CNSC from entering into such an agreement (section 39(2)), the memoranda require the Agency to consult with the relevant energy regulator regarding agreement terms. (Section F, below in this chapter, contains analysis and recommendations regarding joint integrated review panels.)

The offshore boards are "jurisdictions" as defined by the *IAA*[63] and therefore have capacity to enter into a section 39(1) review panel agreement with respect to projects designated under the *IAA*. They are different from the other energy regulators since the *IAA* does not prohibit them from entering into a section 39(1) agreement. However, House of Commons amendments to Bill C-69,[64] which, at the time of writing,[65] are still not proclaimed and accordingly are not in force, include provisions that prohibit the minister from entering into a section 39(1) joint assessment agreement with the CNSOPB with respect to designated projects regulated under the *Canada-Nova Scotia Offshore Petroleum Resources Accord Implementation Act* (under proposed *IAA* section 39(2)(a.1)) and with the C-NLOPB (under proposed *IAA* section 39(2)(c)) with respect to designated projects regulated under the *Canada–Newfoundland and Labrador Atlantic Accord Implementation Act*. These amendments are part

---

62    Annex 8 to the *Memorandum of Understanding on Integrated Impact Assessments Under the Impact Assessment Act Between the Impact Assessment Agency of Canada and the Canadian Nuclear Safety Commission*, above note 60, "Roles and Responsibilities," and Annex 8 to the *Memorandum of Understanding on Integrated Impact Assessments Under the Impact Assessment Act Between the Impact Assessment Agency of Canada and the Canadian Energy Regulator*, above note 60, "Roles and Responsibilities."

63    Section 2(a) of the *IAA* definition of "jurisdiction" is a federal authority, which includes the Canada-Nova-Scotia Offshore Petroleum Board and the Canada-Newfoundland & Labrador Offshore Petroleum Board (*IAA*, Schedule 1).

64    See Bill C-69, *An Act to enact the Impact Assessment Act and the Canadian Energy Regulator Act, to amend the Navigation Protection Act and to make consequential amendments to other Acts*, 1st Sess, 42nd Parl, 2019 (Royal Assent, 21 June 2019) [*IAA* amendments]. Sections 2-8.9 of the amendments are intended to make the offshore boards to be in the same position of the CER amd CNSC and accordingly be required to assess designated projects by integrated panel review. Relevant proposed amendments to the *IAA* include to ss 39(2)(a.1), 39(2)(c); 41(b.1), 41(2)(d), 43(a.1) and (c); 46; 48.1; 50(b.1) and (d); and 61(1.1)(a.1) and (c). See also G Todd Stanley & Elliott Bursey, "Canada: Bill C-69—A Slightly Unfinished Work in the Newfoundland and Labrador Offshore" (2018), online: *Mondaq* www.mondaq.com/canada/environmental-law/859164/bill-c-69-a-slightly-unfinished-work-in-the-newfoundland-and-labrador-offshore.

65    December 2020.

of a series that mirror the *IAA* provisions regarding the CER and the CNSC discussed above. Once the *IAA* amendments are proclaimed, the CNSOPB and C-NLOPB impact assessment processes will parallel those applying to the CER and the CNSC. Accordingly, the *IAA* will require all energy regulators' designated projects to be assessed by integrated panel review. We anticipate that after proclamation the CNSOPB and the C-NLOPB will enter into memoranda of understanding with Canada comparable to those between Canada and the CER and the CNSC, discussed above. The reader should bear in mind, however, that until the *IAA* amendments are proclaimed, CNSOPB and C-NLOPB designated projects will be subject to *IAA* processes that apply to a designated project by default where the Agency decides whether a designated project requires an assessment.[66]

## 6)  Cooperation Agreements

The *IAA* authorizes the federal government to enter into cooperation agreements with other jurisdictions regarding the assessment of effects.[67] Pursuant to this authority, in August 2019 the Government of Canada entered into a cooperation agreement with the Government of British Columbia, titled the *Impact Assessment Cooperation Agreement Between Canada and British Columbia*.[68] A previous harmonization agreement between the two parties had been operational under *CEAA 2012*, which provided the foundation for moving forward under the *IAA*. The 2019 agreement covers coordinated impact assessment, substitutions (including substitution to a third-party Indigenous body), and joint

66   IAA, above note 1, s 16. For a critique of the IAA's empowering treatment of the offshore boards, and of the proposed IAA amendment requiring the offshore boards' designated projects to be assessed by an integrated review panel, see the East Coast Environmental Law Association and Ecology Action Centre's *Impact Assessment and the Offshore Energy Boards Submission to the House of Commons Standing Committee on Environment and Sustainable Development Concerning Bill C-69, Part 1 – Impact Assessment Act* (April 2018), online: www.ourcommons.ca/Content/Committee/421/ENVI/ Brief/BR9809093/br-external/EastCoastEnvironmentalLawAssociation-e.pdf.

67   See, for example, IAA, *ibid*, ss 39 (review panel agreements), 114(1)(c) (with jurisdictions other than Indigenous) and 114(1)(e) (with Indigenous jurisdictions), in accordance with regulations.

68   *Impact Assessment Cooperation Agreement Between Canada and British Columbia* (Agreement), (August 2019), online: www.canada.ca/en/impact-assessment-agency/corporate/ acts-regulations/legislation-regulations/canada-british-columbia-impact-assessment-cooperation/canada-bc-cooperation-agreement.html.

panel reviews. It provides that the Agency and the BC Environmental Assessment Office will coordinate participant funding.

The agreement also deals with matters in the *IAA* that were absent from previous legislation, such as the early planning phase. Regarding this phase, the parties agree to coordinate public engagement and engagement with Indigenous peoples, local governments, and other levels of government. The parties also agree to harmonize timelines and prepare a single document that sets out comments received.[69] Local governments presumably were expressly included in the agreement since British Columbia's new *Environmental Assessment Act* requires the proponent to engage with Indigenous nations, municipalities, government agencies, and the public during the "early engagement phase" of an assessment.[70] Under the *IAA*, during the early planning phase, the Agency must offer to consult only with the public, potentially affected Indigenous groups, and "any jurisdiction that has powers, duties or functions in relation to an assessment of the environmental effects of the designated project."[71]

### 7)  Cooperative Assessments Under the *IAA*

Here are the cooperative assessments under the *IAA* at the time of writing.[72] The Cedar LNG Project in British Columbia (under way) is the first project to be assessed under the *IAA* by substitution. According to the news release, in addition to meeting the terms of section 7 of the *Impact Assessment Cooperation Agreement Between Canada and British Columbia*,[73] the substituted BC process will assess not only the impacts of the physical work but also the potential effects of marine shipping associated with the development. In addition, the assessment must follow the process outlined in the federal *Strategic Assessment of Climate Change*[74] for evaluating project impacts associated with greenhouse gas emissions. It is too early to provide comment on whether *IAA* section 22

---

69   *Ibid*, s 5.

70   SBC 2018, c 51 (in force 28 August 2019), s 13 [*Environmental Assessment Act*].

71   *IAA*, above note 1, ss 11 & 12.

72   9 July 2020.

73   *Impact Assessment Cooperation Agreement Between Canada and British Columbia*, above note 68.

74   Government of Canada, *Strategic Assessment of Climate Change* (Revised October 2020), online www.canada.ca/en/services/environment/conservation/assessments/strategic-assessments/climate-change.html.

factors will be appropriately addressed or to comment on other aspects of the substitution.

An integrated review panel for the proposed Gazoduq natural gas pipeline between northeastern Ontario and Saguenay, Quebec, is being linked with a coordinated approach under the *IAA*. Federally, this project triggers the *IAA* and the *CERA*, and as such, as discussed earlier, the assessment must be by a review panel known as an "integrated review panel." The Agency is the lead negotiator (on behalf of the CER). Provincially, the project triggers an assessment under Quebec's *Environment Quality Act*.[75] The provincial process will be conducted by the Bureau d'audiences publiques sur l'environnement (BAPE).

A proposed agreement between the governments of Canada and Quebec is aimed at coordinating aspects of the integrated review panel process with the provincial project review process. Coordinated aspects include matters relating to exchange of information, location and timing of public information sessions and hearings, holding joint sessions and hearings, and cost sharing. The agreement stipulates that the federal integrated review panel and provincial BAPE panel are to remain "independent, autonomous and distinct."[76] Accordingly, this is not a joint integrated review panel as described in Section E(5) of this chapter. This is an integrated review panel that is coordinating its processes with a separate provincial review panel. Although time will tell, this unique integrated review panel/provincial assessment cooperative approach may help alleviate uncertainties associated with poorly implemented harmonized assessment described in Section C(2) of this chapter. It will be interesting to see if, in practice, this unique arrangement is preferred over the joint integrated review panel model contemplated in the Canada/CER/CNSC memoranda of understanding, discussed earlier. The Canada/Quebec coordination approach appears to be more flexible than the joint integrated review panel model, especially given *IAA* requirements for integrated review panel composition and duties, which apparently were drafted in contemplation of integrated review panels, not joint integrated review panels.[77] However, flexibility can sacrifice cooperation and coordination.

---

75   SQ, c Q-2.

76   *Gazoduq Project Integrated Review Panel Terms of Reference*, above note 59 at 19.

77   *IAA*, above note 1, ss 44–54.

## F.  ANALYSIS AND RECOMMENDATIONS

Despite the attention MJIA received during the development of the *IAA* and in the literature over the years, we cannot conclude that the Act has provided definitive direction on MJIA. Nevertheless, two very positive outcomes include emphasis in the *IAA* on cooperative assessment and the absence of any reference to equivalency, meaning that this option is formally off the table.

With respect to our preferred option of harmonization/coordination, there is nothing in the *IAA* to compel the realization of the benefits of coordinated assessments or to deal with some of the shortcomings of this approach that we note above. The direction in the *IAA* for coordinated assessment is only notional; the Act has not established it as the default and preferred method of MJIA. The minister should use the discretionary power under section 114(1)(a) to provide guidelines and codes of practices to this effect. Such provisions could help avoid two separate assessments, as well as avoid substituted assessment, and could result in fewer court challenges.

The *IAA* also needs to include inducements for all jurisdictions to favour a coordinated assessment approach and to effectively and constructively cooperate and participate to ensure "one project, one assessment." Incentives might be achieved by requiring the Agency to establish an MJIA program to assist and encourage jurisdictions to negotiate cooperative agreements with the federal government and to develop and implement a coordination accord, in the style of the CCME accord previously discussed.

The *IAA* is also silent on the framework for cooperative agreements under the Act with other jurisdictions. The Expert Panel saw the great potential to build on past experience, especially regarding project-by-project agreements, as is also underscored in the literature. We are very concerned that the planning phase does not provide enough time to develop a robust cooperative agreement. We agree with the recommendation made in other chapters in this volume that more time needs to be allocated to the planning phase. We cannot imagine more than very broad-brush agreements being made in the time available. The establishment of a multi-interest planning committee, as suggested in Chapter 15, could help facilitate jurisdictional cooperation among jurisdictions on a project basis.

The first cooperative agreement under the *IAA*, as outlined above, underscores both positive and wanting aspects of the *IAA* in relation to drafting such agreements. We view the inclusion of multiple jurisdictions in the agreement, including municipalities, as a positive step. Municipalities, for example, are uniquely affected by projects, including their development, and have responsibilities to secure and maintain the well-being of their citizens, as well as the overall authority over local land use planning and development. Municipalities lobbied the federal government for specific inclusion in the *IAA* for consultation purposes, among others.[78] They were unsuccessful, and, accordingly, under the *IAA* they have no more status than anyone else. Moving forward, the minister could opt for a broad interpretation (part (d) of the definition of jurisdiction in section 2 of the *IAA*) and use this definition as an opportunity to enter into cooperation agreements with municipalities with impact assessment processes. However, at least when there is a British Columbia–federal impact assessment, municipalities will have some recognition and opportunity for early involvement in project impact assessment. Having said that, we believe that the policy guidance needs to be developed that clarifies and promotes the foundational value of both general bilateral MJIA agreements and agreements relating to individual assessments in the implementation of the *IAA*. The guidance should outline the elements that must be included in such agreements.

As is evident from our discussion above, we are disappointed that substitution is an option for MJIA under the *IAA* but not entirely surprised given that the Expert Panel, as well as industry and provincial governments, supported its inclusion. We point out, however, that the section 22(1) factors are considerably broader than *CEAA 2012*'s section 19 factors. A review of assessment legislation throughout Canada

---

78    See "Bill C-69, An Act to enact the Impact Assessment Act and the Canadian Energy Regulator Act, to amend the Navigation Protection Act and to make consequential amendments to other Acts," 2nd reading, *House of Commons Debates*, 42-1, vol 150 (30 October 2018) at 1635 (Hon Éric Forest), online: https://sencanada.ca/en/content/sen/chamber/421/debates/241db_2018-10-30-e#57; House of Commons, Standing Committee on Environment and Sustainable Development, *Evidence*, 42-1, No 108 (26 April 2018) at 1135 (Mr Brock Carlton), online: https://www.ourcommons.ca/DocumentViewer/en/42-1/envi/meeting-108/evidence; and Federation of Canadian Municipalities, "Making Environmental Assessment Work—Municipal Perspectives on Bill C-69" (6 April 2018), online (pdf): www.auma.ca/sites/default/files/3._fcm_submission_-_bill_c-69_-_april_6_2018.pdf.

indicates that it may be difficult for many provinces to consider the factors required to be considered under section 22(1) of the *IAA* in a substituted assessment; therefore, coordinated assessment is a better option.[79] Even the new British Columbia *Environmental Assessment Act*,[80] for example, is not currently underpinned by a sustainability approach as broad and does not include factors as extensive as those in the *IAA*, leading us to wonder how the province will have the capacity or expertise to comply with the *IAA* and fulfill the terms of the 2019 cooperation agreement in substituted assessments.

The *IAA* also does not require some of the conditions that the Expert Panel recommended be set when entering into substitution agreements, such as including the principles of *UNDRIP*. It does allow for substitution with jurisdictions other than provincial governments. However, the minister needs to promulgate regulations under section 114(1)(e) in order for an Indigenous governing body that does not otherwise fit the definition of a "jurisdiction" to be recognized as a jurisdiction for the purpose of substitution and other applications of the *IAA*. We recommend that such regulations be promulgated as soon as possible. In addition, the minister should exercise his or her powers under section 33(1)(i) and establish further conditions when entering into cooperation agreements with other jurisdictions that must be met in order to approve a substitution. These would include conditions that

- require that those advocating a substitution establish that it is preferable to coordinated assessment and that these arguments be open to public scrutiny
- require the minister's reasons for substitution to set out how public input was taken into account in making the decision
- address all of the safeguards set out by the Expert Panel for the use of substitution

Some issues can only be addressed through legislative reform. For example, the delegation power is unduly broad and does not even

---

79   See Arlene Kwasniak, "Re: Bill C-69, Part 1—Impact Assessment Act" (Submission to Standing Senate Committee on Energy, the Environment and Natural Resources) (4 April 2018), online (pdf): https://sencanada.ca/content/sen/committee/421/ENEV/Briefs/2019-04-04_BillC-69_ArleneKwasniak_e.pdf, n 3.

80   *Environmental Assessment Act*, above note 70.

clearly exclude delegating the final decision,[81] as previous legislation did. We recommend that the Act be amended to clarify that the final decision cannot be delegated and delegation powers be clearly circumscribed in the law so that delegation authorities cannot be used to effect substitution or equivalency or to relinquish legislative responsibility or accountability. It is also shocking that there are no provisions in the *IAA* for participant funding in the case of substituted processes. Therefore, we recommend that section 75(2) of the *IAA* be deleted, which states that Agency participant funding responsibilities do not apply to substituted impact assessment.

*Joint* review panels for assessments involving energy regulators' projects should be encouraged and facilitated by the *IAA*. Currently, the *IAA* does not specifically provide for such reviews. In fact, the language of the *IAA* provisions regarding energy regulators' integrated review panels has led experts to interpret the *IAA* (when it was in bill form) as if it prohibited joint integrated review panels.[82] Even though the 2019 Canada/CER/CNSC memoranda of understanding contemplate joint integrated review panels, there can be doubt as to whether the *IAA* permits them. There are also questions and concerns regarding implementation of the *IAA* with respect to a joint integrated review panel. For example, the *IAA* requires the minister to consult with the energy regulator in developing TOR for integrated panel reviews,[83] but no provision requires the minister to consult with the non-federal jurisdiction in developing TOR for a joint review panel. Assuming that there is only one set of TOR for a joint integrated review panel, the energy regulator

---

81  An argument could be made that under the *IAA* the final decision is not part of the assessment process and therefore does not fall under the delegation authority.

82  See, for example, Peter Usher & Frances Abele, "The New Impact Assessment Bill Doesn't Give Enough Time or Responsibility to Major Project Review Panels. The Result Could Be Worse than What Exists Now" *Policy Options* (26 March 2018), online: https:// policyoptions.irpp.org/magazines/march-2018/panels-compromised-environmental-assessment-bill/; Richard Lindgren, "The Proposed Federal Impact Assessment Act" (Submission to the Standing Senate Committee on Energy, the Environment and Natural Resources) (2 April 2019), online (pdf): https://sencanada.ca/content/sen/ committee/421/ENEV/Briefs/CELA_e.pdf at 16; and Meinhard Doelle & A John Sinclair, "The Proposed Federal Impact Assessment Act (IAA): Assesment & Reform Proposals" (Submission to the Standing Senate Committee on Energy, the Environment and Natural Resources) (12 April 2019) online (pdf): https://sencanada.ca/content/sen/ committee/421/ENEV/Briefs/MeinhardDoelle_Brief_e.pdf.

83  *IAA*, above note 1, ss 44(1) and 47(1); IAA amendments, above note 64, ss 46.1 and 48.1.

could have an inordinately prominent role in developing the TOR for the review. This seems to us wrong and imbalanced, especially insofar as the TOR apply to the non-federal jurisdiction's joint assessment with the federal government. Here is another example. The *IAA*'s rules for panel composition for an integrated review permit up to 50 percent of an integrated review panel to be appointed from the energy regulator's roster of potential members. How do these provisions apply to a joint integrated review panel? Can up to 50 percent of a joint integrated review panel review be from the energy regulator's roster? Surely this would be an imbalance in favour of the energy regulator's choices and could impair panel independence from the energy regulator in appearance if not in fact. As a final example, for CER and CNSC integrated review panels, the Agency must appoint at least two members,[84] and for joint review panels, the Agency must appoint at least one member.[85] So how many members must the Agency appoint to a *joint* integrated review panel — at least two or three? Would a court have to decide this and the other mentioned issues?

Because of the uncertainty surrounding joint integrated review panels and potential issues and imbalances from applying integrated panel review provisions to joint panel reviews, we recommend that the *IAA* be amended to include specific provisions on joint integrated review panels. We recommend that the new provisions fully recognize the non-federal partner jurisdiction, ensure that joint integrated review panels are appropriate for both joint reviews and integrated reviews, and encourage and facilitate joint integrated review panels.

Finally, we are witnessing a surge in Indigenous sovereignty work as Indigenous communities reclaim their inherent rights. For example, there is growing work by First Nations institutions to revitalize and codify First Nations laws, and these will include environmental decision making. To illustrate, the S̱ḵwx̱wú7mesh[86] recently employed its own process to review the Woodfibre LNG Project in British Columbia.

---

84    *IAA*, above note 1, ss 44(1) and 47(1).

85    *Ibid*, s 42(c).

86    Chief Ian Campbell Xalek/SekyuSiyam & Byng Giraud, *S̱ḵwx̱wú7mesh Nation Environmental Process: Swiyat-Woodfibre LNG* (March 2019), online (pdf): https://static1. squarespace.com/static/5849b10dbe659445e02e6e55/t/5c8bef7f4e17b616cf64cdfa/ 1552674700042/S%E1%B8%B5wx%CC%B1w%C3%BA7mesh+Nation+Environmental+ Process+Swiyat+-+Woodfibre+LNG+.pdf.

In fact, the Agency's forward regulatory plan commits to proposing or finalizing regulations that address Indigenous cooperation.[87]

As Canada moves to better respect its obligations to Indigenous peoples, there will be a need to consider impact assessment as it applies to Indigenous-led assessment processes. Ultimately, these processes may look very different from traditional impact assessment processes, and in accordance with the Constitution and obligations under it, assessment legislation may need to make special provisions that recognize the sovereignty and inherent rights of Indigenous peoples.

---

87    Impact Assessment Agency of Canada, "Indigenous Cooperation Regulations" (5 September 2019), online: *Government of Canada* www.canada.ca/en/impact-assessment-agency/corporate/acts-regulations/forward-regulatory-plan/forward-regulatory-plan-2019-2021/indigenous-cooperation-regulations.html.

# CHAPTER 9

# Introducing the *Impact Assessment Act*'s Sustainability-Based Agenda

*Robert B Gibson*

## A. INTRODUCTION

The *Impact Assessment Act (IAA)*[1] promises a significant expansion of the agenda for federal-level assessments in Canada. Simply stated, the expansion of scope and ambition is from assessments centred on the mitigation of significant adverse effects on the biophysical environment to assessments encouraging positive overall contributions to sustainability. On the surface, at least, that is a substantial leap.

The *IAA*'s federal predecessors—the policy-based Environmental Assessment and Review Process (EARP) in the 1970s and early 1980s, the unintentionally binding EARP guidelines order of 1982, and the 1995 and 2012 versions of the *Canadian Environmental Assessment Act*—all focused on the effects on the biophysical environment and their consequences.[2] Attention to cumulative environmental effects was included.

---

1    SC 2019, c 28, s 1.

2    *Environmental Assessment and Review Process Guidelines Order*, SOR/84-467 (22 June 1984); *Canadian Environmental Assessment Act*, SC 1992, c 37, ss 2 (definitions of "environment" and "environmental effect") and 16 [*CEAA 1995*]; and *Canadian Environmental Assessment Act, 2012*, SC 2012, c 19, s 52, ss 2 (definitions of "environment" and "environmental effects"), 5 and 19 [*CEAA 2012*]. The entry into force of the 1992 Act was delayed until 1995 to allow for key regulations to be developed and passed. *CEAA 2012* attempted to limit attention to narrowly specified areas of federal legislative jurisdiction.

In cases involving joint review panels established in cooperation with other assessment jurisdictions, assessments could be mandated to consider additional effects, in

However, the core agenda was to identify the potential adverse bio-physical effects of assessed projects, determine which adverse effects would be significant, and encourage mitigation of these effects.

The possibility of further breadth at the decision-making stage was incorporated in the earlier assessment laws through provisions that allowed decision makers to approve projects with predicted significant adverse environmental effects, if approval was "justified in the circum-stances."[3] What might be justifiable "in the circumstances" was not defined in law or policy, nor were the provisions for such approvals accompanied by requirements for publication of the reasons for decisions. Logically, the potentially relevant circumstances included anticipated positive eco-nomic, social, political, or other effects sufficiently desirable to justify acceptance of significant adverse environmental effects. However, these anticipated positive effects lay outside the typical scope of effects identi-fied and evaluated in an assessment process focused on adverse effects.[4] Because the associated decision making was not transparent, the actual scope and rigour of decision-makers' evaluations in these cases are not known. Even with these uncertain "in the circumstances" exceptions, however, the predominant focus of federal assessments prior to the *IAA* was on adverse biophysical effects and their mitigation or justification.

In contrast, the *IAA* explicitly embraces a broader and more ambi-tious agenda. Its core decision-making requirements include mandatory consideration of the extent to which a proposed project "contributes to sustainability."[5] The Act defines "sustainability" as "the ability to protect

---

a few cases extending to sustainability effects. See Robert B Gibson, "Sustainability Assessment in Canada" in Alan Bond, Angus Morrison-Saunders & Richard Howitt, eds, *Sustainability Assessment: Pluralism, Practice and Progress* (Abingdon, Oxon, UK: Routledge, 2013) 167.

3    *CEAA 1995*, above note 2, s 37; see also s 23; and *CEAA 2012*, above note 2, ss 31, 52, & 53.

4    The partial exception is that guidelines for the preparation of environmental impact statements issued under *CEAA 2012* typically required proponents to report on antici-pated "benefits to Canadians" in the event that significant effects were predicted and a "justified in the circumstances" decision was needed. See, for example, *Guidelines for the Preparation of an Environmental Impact Statement for an Environmental Assessment Conducted Pursuant to the Canadian Environmental Assessment Act, 2012: Murray River Coal Project* (30 July 2013) at 37, online (pdf): *Canadian Environmental Assessment Agency* www.ceaa.gc.ca/050/documents/p80041/94123E.pdf.

5    The "contribution to sustainability" requirement is the first of five core components of the public interest determination to be made by decision makers in each project assessment. See s 63 of the *IAA*, above note 1.

the environment, contribute to the social and economic well-being of the people of Canada and preserve their health in a manner that benefits present and future generations."[6]

To facilitate assessment of sustainability contributions, the Act establishes a scope of effects that covers the broad suite of matters that influence sustainability. It defines "effects" as "changes to the environment or to health, social or economic conditions and the positive and negative consequences of these changes."[7]

In addition to these broad fields, the Act's list of mandatory factors for attention in project assessments includes cumulative effects and interactions among effects.[8] At least with regard to "sex and gender [and] other identity factors," the Act also requires consideration of distributional effects.[9]

Finally, the Act's provisions for decision making establish the "contributions to sustainability" test as the first and most comprehensive of five considerations for the public interest determination to be made by decision makers in each project assessment. The four more specific considerations are the significance of adverse effects on matters of federal jurisdiction,[10] implementation of mitigation measures to lessen adverse effects,[11] impacts on Indigenous groups and the rights of Indigenous peoples,[12] and effects on meeting Canada's environmental obligations and climate change commitments.[13] Each is a stand-alone consideration, and the one on matters of federal jurisdiction is an obligatory nod to constitutional niceties. Arguably, however, the considerations on mitigation,

---

6   *Ibid*, s 2.

7   *Ibid*.

8   *Ibid*, s 22(1)(a)(iii).

9   *Ibid*, s 22(1)(s). The government has released "Interim Guidance: Gender-Based Analysis Plus in Impact Assessment" (21 August 2019), online: *Government of Canada* www.canada.ca/en/impact-assessment-agency/services/policy-guidance/practitioners-guide-impact-assessment-act/gender-based-analysis.html. However, the extent to which attention to identity factors can and will be used to cover the field of distributional effects remains uncertain. See Chapter 12 of this book.

10   *IAA*, above note 1, s 63(b).

11   *Ibid*, s 63(c).

12   *Ibid*, ss 22(1)(c) and 63(d). The attention of Indigenous rights, however, is limited to those recognized and affirmed by s 35 of the *Constitution Act, 1982*, being schedule B to the *Canada Act 1982* (UK), 1982, c 11. Other than in a non-binding statement in the preamble, the Act is silent on application of the *United Nations Declaration on the Rights of Indigenous Peoples (UNDRIP)*. See Chapter 6 of this book.

13   *Ibid*, ss 22(1)(i) and 63(e).

Indigenous rights, and meeting obligations and commitments are typically consistent with and likely to strengthen a sustainability-based approach to decision making in the public interest.

Although the Act's list of five core public interest considerations raises questions about how decision makers will deal with any tensions that may arise among them,[14] the enlarged scope of assessment and decision making puts into a largely open public process all of the core factors likely to affect whether assessment decision making "benefits present and future generations." As is discussed further in Chapter 14, the sustainability agenda provides a working base for the overall "public interest" test that decision makers must apply to designated projects under the Act.[15] That test and the associated requirement for published reasons for a decision[16] establish a much more comprehensive framework for transparent decision making in the public interest than was available under the preceding federal assessment laws.

All of this, however, is merely enabling. The expanded range of recognized effects — positive and adverse, direct and incidental, cumulative and interactive, environmental, health related, social, economic, distributional, concerning Indigenous peoples and their rights, and covering present and future generations — only makes far-sighted assessment decision making possible. Effective implementation depends heavily on the elaboration and specification of the legislated provisions in regulations, policies, and institutional practice.

The extent to which the *IAA* and its application complete the ambitious step to consistent delivery of contributions to sustainability centres on at least two additional factors. The first is how well *sustainability* is understood and explained for application under the Act. The second is how well other elements of next-generation sustainability-based assessment[17] are incorporated in the Act and applied in practice. That combination of sustainability understanding and sustainability-based process requirements is needed not only in assessments of designated projects but also throughout the range of other deliberations and

---

14    See the discussion in Chapter 14.

15    *IAA*, above note 1, s 63.

16    *Ibid*, ss 65 & 66.

17    See Robert B Gibson, Meinhard Doelle & A John Sinclair, "Fulfilling the Promise: Basic Components of Next Generation Environmental Assessment" (2015) 29 *Journal of Environmental Law & Practice* 251, and the initial chapters of this book.

decisions under the Act. These include decision making on what projects are to be assessed, how regional and strategic assessments will be initiated and carried out, whether assessments at all levels will be well designed to identify options with the greatest contributions to sustainability, and how the results will be monitored and improved. They will also be critical in efforts to complement and inform sustainability initiatives and decision making beyond assessments under the Act.

The following sections of this chapter draw on the available literature and lessons from experience to address four areas:

- the basics of what "contribution to sustainability" now means and entails and what that means for elaboration and application of the provisions of the Act
- the foundations for evaluating the Act and the initial regulations and policy guidance under the Act in light of the core requirements for a sustainability-based assessment regime
- the overall strengths and limitations of the law and initial guidance on sustainability-related matters
- openings and means for improvement in these areas

## B.  CONTRIBUTION TO SUSTAINABILITY AND THE AGENDA OF THE ACT

The *IAA* introduces "contribution to sustainability" as the initial public interest test, at least for major projects subject to federal assessments.[18] That step is potentially bolder than merely expanding assessment scope from effects on the biophysical environment to a more comprehensive set of public interest considerations, if only because sustainability objectives entail attention to long-term implications. What consideration of contribution to sustainability entails, however, depends on what sustainability is taken to mean and what qualifies as a contribution, including how trade-offs are considered and addressed.

Because the term *sustainability* has been used and misused in many ways, its essential character and requirements for application under the Act must be clarified. Otherwise, the diverse uses and misuses will confuse assessment processes, frustrate participants, and undermine the public interest potential of the law. The Act itself establishes

---

18    *IAA*, above note 1, s 63.

sustainability-based requirements in many key sections but provides few specifics beyond the definition quoted above. The guidance offered in initial policy documents[19] goes only a little further, chiefly in setting out some broad principles[20] and establishing that many of the Act's assessment purposes and factors for consideration in assessments and decisions are aspects of the sustainability-based approach to application.[21] The initial policy guidance documents on sustainability are labelled "interim," and further elaborations are expected.

Further clarification will be necessary, but this is perhaps less challenging than it would seem. The past and continuing confusions and misuses of *sustainability* reflect the fate of any term that is at the same time broadly attractive and potentially threatening to entrenched interests and practices. Adoption of *sustainability* in law adds incentives to those whose immediate interests favour selective interpretations. At the same time, however, we now have the benefit of over thirty years of experience and learning since the 1987 report of the World Commission on Environment and Development (WCED) popularized the term "sustainable development."[22] Through that time, the basic concept has retained support and gradually spreading and authoritative adoption. The *IAA* is only one illustration of a multitude of examples stretching from neighbourhood and sectoral initiatives to the global Sustainable Development Goals.[23]

---

19    Impact Assessment Agency of Canada, "Practitioner's Guide to Federal Impact Assessments Under the Impact Assessment Act," online: *Government of Canada* www.canada.ca/en/impact-assessment-agency/services/policy-guidance/practitioners-guide-impact-assessment-act.html, especially ss 2.2 & 2.3.

20    *Ibid*, s 2.2(2):

> The sustainability principles developed for the purpose of implementing the Act are:
> 1.  Consider the interconnectedness and interdependence of human-ecological systems;
> 2.  Consider the well-being of present and future generations;
> 3.  Consider positive effects and reduce adverse effects of a designated project; and
> 4.  Apply the precautionary principle and consider uncertainty and risk of irreversible harm.

21    *Ibid*, Annex I.

22    World Commission on Environment and Development, *Our Common Future* (New York: Norton, 1987).

23    United Nations Sustainable Development Goals Knowledge Platform, *Sustainable Development Goals*, online: https://sdgs.un.org/goals.

From the outset, sustainability was not merely about environmental stewardship or about long-term human interests. The WCED built its foundational conception of sustainable development on recognition that poverty could not be eliminated without protection of the environment and vice versa. Today, that basic understanding is enriched by much more advanced recognition of the interactions in and among complex socio-ecological systems.[24] The academic and professional literature that was once dominated by primitive depictions of sustainability at the conjunction of social, economic, and ecological pillars now features much deeper inquiries into how to pursue overall sustainability in a world of complex multi-scale interactions.[25] Advanced work, including in impact assessment, is now focused on how best to enhance the resilience of desirable systems and system characteristics and how to push transformation of undesirable and unsustainable systems and characteristics while protecting the most vulnerable and respecting uncertainty.[26]

Some of the advances in understanding are largely the product of the years of experience with more and less successful sustainability-based initiatives. That experience has demonstrated, for example, the interdependence of and interactions among social, economic, health, and biophysical factors, with adverse effects combining to deepen problems and positive effects combining to bring lasting gains.[27] Equally important, however, has been the mounting evidence of unsustainable

---

24  Jianguo Liu et al, "Systems Integration for Global Sustainability" (2015) 347:6225 *Science* 1258832; Mark Swilling, *The Age of Sustainability: Just Transitions in a Complex World* (Abingdon, Oxon, UK: Routledge, 2020).

25  Stephen Williams & John Robinson, "Measuring Sustainability: An Evaluation Framework for Sustainability Transition Experiments" (2020) 103 *Environmental Science & Policy* 58.

26  Alan Bond et al, "Managing Uncertainty, Ambiguity and Ignorance in Impact Assessment by Embedding Evolutionary Resilience, Participatory Modelling and Adaptive Management" (2015) 151 *Journal of Environmental Management* 97; Robert B Gibson, ed, *Sustainability Assessment: Applications and Opportunities* (London, UK: Earthscan/Routledge, 2017).

27  Kai Fang, Reinout Heijungs & Geert R De Snoo, "Understanding the Complementary Linkages Between Environmental Footprints and Planetary Boundaries in a Footprint– Boundary Environmental Sustainability Assessment Framework" (2015) 114 *Ecological Economics* 218; Jianguo Liu et al, "Complexity of Coupled Human and Natural Systems" (2007) 317:5844 *Science* 1513; John A Dearing et al, "Safe and Just Operating Spaces for Regional Social-Ecological Systems" (2014) 28 *Global Environmental Change* 227; Sylvia LR Wood & Fabrice DeClerck, "Ecosystems and Human Well-being in the Sustainable Development Goals" (2015) 13:3 *Frontiers in Ecology and the Environment* 123.

trajectories and their consequences. Accelerating climate change is the most obvious example.[28] It is accompanied by many others, including biodiversity decline, impairment of basic systems that deliver ecological services, deepening disparity between the richest and the poorest, and economic growth that increases ecological stresses while leaving perhaps two billion people without adequate nourishment or sanitation.[29]

Sustainability has always been essentially about establishing and preserving the conditions for lasting well-being—for humans as well as for the biophysical environment that is the foundation for all of Earth's inhabitants. In the current context, lasting well-being cannot be attained merely by mitigating adverse effects. The new sustainability-based agenda for federal assessment law moves the goal from less environmentally damaging projects to projects that help reverse unsustainable trajectories. Attention to transformational contributions is most explicitly required in the Act's provisions concerning climate change.[30] These provisions centre on whether proposed projects will hinder or contribute to meeting Canada's commitments, which the current government recognizes to entail reducing our greenhouse gas emissions to net zero by 2050. But the Act's sustainability agenda generally shifts the focus from mitigating adverse effects to encouraging positive contributions to sustainability. The possible contributions include combinations of many actions—rehabilitating damaged ecosystems, establishing foundations for lasting community livelihoods, and building viable alternatives to unsustainable socio-economic activities and practices. All of these are well beyond the scope and ambition of mitigating significant adverse environmental effects.

How ambitiously these positive contributions will be sought in deliberations and decision making under the Act remains to be seen. Much

---

28    Intergovernmental Panel on Climate Change, *Global Warming of 1.5 °C: Summary for Policymakers* (2018), online: *Intergovernmental Panel on Climate Change* www.ipcc.ch/report/sr15/.

29    Kate Raworth, *Doughnut Economics: Seven Ways to Think Like a 21st-Century Economist* (London, UK: Random House, 2017); William Steffen et al, "Planetary Boundaries: Guiding Human Development on a Changing Planet" (2015) 347 *Science* 1259855. S Díaz et al, *Global Assessment Report on Biodiversity and Ecosystem Services: Summary for Policy Makers* (Intergovernmental Science-Policy Platform on Biodiversity and Ecosystem Services, 2019), online: https://ipbes.net/global-assessment; Facundo Alvaredo et al, eds, *World Inequality Report 2018: Executive Summary* (Berlin: World Inequality Lab, 2018), online (pdf): https://wir2018.wid.world/files/download/wir2018-summary-english.pdf.

30    *IAA*, above note 1, ss 22(1)(i) and 63(e). See also chapters 13 and 14 of this book.

depends on further elaboration of the now-interim policy guidance on sustainability and on the expectations demonstrated over time in case practice. However, the nature and treatment of other components of the assessment regime established under the Act will also be influential.

## C. AN EVALUATION OF THE ACT'S SUSTAINABILITY AGENDA IN LIGHT OF THE CORE COMPONENTS OF A SUSTAINABILITY-BASED ASSESSMENT REGIME

The basic purpose of any sustainability-based assessment regime is to foster planning and implementing undertakings that make the most positive overall contributions to sustainability that can reasonably be expected in the circumstances. Establishing a contribution to sustainability test is a key prerequisite, but it needs to be accompanied by an integrated set of other components. Chief among these components are sustainability-based provisions determining the following:

- what undertakings are subject to assessment requirements under the law
- how undertakings subject to assessment are planned and evaluated
- how the credibility of assessment information, deliberations, and decision making is ensured
- how assessment predictions and approval conditions are followed up
- how continuous learning is facilitated throughout the process
- how the assessment process and its particular applications are to be linked to related sustainability initiatives and decision making, in Canada and beyond[31]

Most of these assessment process components are discussed in detail in other chapters of this book, and all involve matters of sustainability-based decision making that are examined in Chapter 14. The discussion here focuses only on the extent to which the relevant considerations are included in the Act's scope and ambition. For each matter, the following evaluation first presents what is required in

---

31  These factors are drawn from the key next-generation assessment considerations discussed in Chapter 2.

sustainability-based assessment and then discusses what is in the Act and initial regulations and policy guidance under the Act.

## 1)  Application

### a)  What a Sustainability-Based Agenda Requires

For sustainability purposes, assessment regimes should apply requirements to the undertakings most likely to affect lasting well-being and benefit from sustainability-based assessment. Undertakings subject to legislated assessment requirements normally include physical projects. Most project-level assessments, however, are ill-equipped to address major issues and opportunities—extensive cumulative effects, broad alternatives, and major policy concerns. Many assessment regimes now also apply assessment requirements at the regional and strategic level of policies, plans, programs, and other such undertakings.[32] The assessment requirements involved may include more or less demanding streams for undertakings of different levels of complexity and consequence. However, all decision making on how and when to require assessment should be transparent and guided by explicit sustainability-based criteria.[33]

To ensure that the relevant proponents and other participants know to address sustainability-based assessment requirements from the outset of planning, determination of what categories of undertakings will be subject to assessment should be anticipatory. Where the relevant undertakings arise unexpectedly, provisions for case-by-case application are needed. Case-by-case application processes may be especially important for regional and strategic assessments initiated to address emerging issues and policy or planning gaps.[34] In some cases, effective

---

32  Such higher-tier assessments are most common in member states of the European Union, operating under *Directive 2001/42/EC of the European Parliament and of the Council of 27 June 2001 on the Assessment of the Effects of Certain Plans and Programmes on the Environment* (2001), online: https://eur-lex.europa.eu/legal-content/EN/TXT/?uri=celex%3A32001L0042. However, experience in the rest of the world is also considerable. See, for example, Barry Sadler & Jiri Dusik, eds, *European and International Experiences of Strategic Environmental Assessment* (Abingdon, Oxon, UK: Routledge, 2016).

33  Robert B Gibson et al, *Sustainability Assessment: Criteria and Processes* (London, UK: Earthscan, 2005); Alan Bond, Angus Morrison-Saunders & Jenny Pope, "Sustainability Assessment: The State of the Art" (2012) 30:1 *Impact Assessment and Project Appraisal* 53; Serenella Sala, Biagio Ciuffo & Peter Nijkamp, "A Systemic Framework for Sustainability Assessment" (2015) 119 *Ecological Economics* 314.

34  See Chapter 17.

responses to these needs may include identification and assignment of suitable proponents as well as specification of assessment obligations.

### b) What Is in the Act and Associated Initial Regulations and Policy Guidance

The Act applies mostly to major projects in categories identified in the tightly constrained "project list" categories set out in the *Physical Activities Regulation*[35] or designated individually.[36,37] As well, the Act introduces, for the first time at the federal level, legislated provisions for regional and strategic assessments.[38] The Act is not clear about whether and to what extent the sustainability-based agenda applies to regional and strategic assessments and provides few specifics about the processes to be used or the products to be delivered. Early strategic assessment initiatives[39] and regional assessment policy guidance[40] indicate ambition well

---

35    SOR/2019-285. For comments on the limitations of the current project list, see Richard D Lindgren, "Submissions by the Canadian Environmental Law Association to the Government of Canada Regarding Discussion Paper on the Proposed Project List and Discussion Paper on Information Requirements and Time Management Regulatory Proposal" (29 May 2019), online (pdf): www.impactassessmentregulations.ca/8869/ documents/16566/download; and Sharon Mascher, "As Bill C-69 Receives Royal Assent, Will the Project List Deliver on the Promise?" (25 June 2019), online (blog): *Ablawg* http://ablawg.ca/wp-content/uploads/2019/06/Blog_SM_ProjectListC-69.pdf. See also Chapter 7 of this book.

36    *IAA*, above note 1, s 9.

37    *Ibid*, ss 81–91, also include a residual, biophysical effects assessment process for designated categories of projects on federal lands or outside Canada. The process is largely non-transparent, does not reflect the general sustainability agenda, and was mostly ignored in the debates leading to passage of the new Act. See Chapter 18 of this book.

38    *Ibid*, ss 92–103. See chapters 11 and 17 of this book.

39    See *Draft Strategic Assessment of Climate Change*, online: *Government of Canada* www.canada.ca/en/services/environment/conservation/assessments/environmental-reviews/get-involved/draft-strategic-assessment-climate-change.html; David V Wright, "Draft Strategic Assessment of Climate Change: Big Steps for Impact Assessment, Baby Steps for Climate Change" (25 June 2019), online (blog): *Ablawg* https://ablawg.ca/2019/ 12/13/draft-strategic-assessment-of-climate-change-big-steps-for-impact-assessment-baby-steps-for-climate-change. See also Environment and Climate Change Canada, *Canada Launches Strategic Assessment of Thermal Coal Mining* (News Release), (20 December 2019) online: www.canada.ca/en/environment-climate-change/news/2019/12/ canada-launches-strategic-assessment-of-thermal-coal-mining.html.

40    Impact Assessment Agency, "Regional Assessment Under the Impact Assessment Act" (19 December 2019), online: *Government of Canada* www.canada.ca/en/impact-assessment-agency/services/policy-guidance/regional-assessment-impact-assessment-act.html. The guidance indicates that many regional "assessments" will be studies to improve

short of consistency with the agenda for sustainability-based next-generation assessment, but the potential for improvement remains.

## 2) Planning and Evaluation of Undertakings Subject to Assessment

### a) What a Sustainability-Based Agenda Requires

If projects and other undertakings subject to assessment are to make the most positive feasible contributions to sustainability, the legislation must incorporate core requirements for sustainability-based planning (of new undertakings) and evaluation (of proposals and associated assessment findings).[41] Key components begin with the establishment of the sustainability scope and contribution to sustainability test discussed above.

No less important are clear obligations for proponents and reviewers. Both must know from the outset of deliberations that the proposal and assessment process must meet the following four requirements:

- to serve sustainability-based public interest purposes (as well as the proponent's narrower purposes);
- to address all potentially important effects and associated uncertainties;
- to identify and compare potentially reasonable options (alternatives), recognizing uncertainties and trade-offs and applying explicit, context-specified sustainability-based criteria; and
- to deliver the best option in the circumstances, from an overall contribution to sustainability perspective (the best combination

---

the information base for project assessments rather than assessments of options for plans or other regional undertakings with authoritative implications for project-level deliberations and decisions.

41  Alberto Fonseca & Robert B Gibson, "Testing an Ex-ante Framework for the Evaluation of Impact Assessment Laws: Lessons from Canada and Brazil" (2020) 81 *Environmental Impact Assessment Review* 106355; Bond, Morrison-Saunders & Pope, above note 33; Chris Joseph, Thomas Gunton & Murray Rutherford, "Good Practices for Environmental Assessment" (2015) 33:4 *Impact Assessment and Project Appraisal* 238; Expert Panel for the Review of Federal Environmental Assessment Processes, *Building Common Ground: A New Vision for Impact Assessment in Canada* (Ottawa: Canadian Environmental Assessment Agency, 2017), online (pdf): *Government of Canada* www.canada.ca/content/dam/themes/environment/conservation/environmental-reviews/building-common-ground/building-common-ground.pdf [*Building Common Ground*]; Multi-Interest Advisory Committee (MIAC), *Advice to the Expert Panel Reviewing Environmental Assessment Processes* (Ottawa: 2016) (on file with authors).

of mutually supporting and lasting positive effects while avoiding potentially serious adverse effects).

### b) What Is in the Act and Associated Initial Regulations and Policy Guidance

As has been established above, the Act is scoped broadly enough to cover the full range of sustainability-related effects.[42] On the other elements listed above, the Act and initially available guidance are less helpful. Although for project assessments the Act requires consideration of the "purpose of and need for the designated project,"[43] the clause does not tie purpose and need explicitly to sustainability or the public interest. Initial guidance generally preserves the tradition of focusing on the proponent's purposes and perception of need, but also encourages proponents to consider participant perspectives and establish "objectives that relate to the intended effect of the project on society."[44]

Similarly, although the Act requires consideration of "alternative means of carrying out the designated project" and "alternatives to the designated project," both are subject to narrowing constraints.[45] Also, the Act sets out no direct requirement to identify and evaluate alternatives in light of their contributions to sustainability and implications for the other key considerations for decision makers set out in section 63 of the Act. Initial guidance for proponents preparing Impact Statements under the Act provides some clarifications. For example, the guidance requires proponents to justify the selection of the preferred alternative in part by identifying and applying criteria for comparing the considered alternatives in light of the broad range of effects recognized in the Act, and considering trade-offs associated with the preferred

---

42  The Act could be more specific on some key sustainability matters. For example, the Act establishes a contribution to sustainability test (s 63(a)) and defines sustainability to include delivery of benefits to future as well as present generations (s 2). Those elements necessarily include the identification and evaluation of intergenerational effects; however, the Act does not say so directly.

43  *IAA*, above note 1, s 22(1)(d).

44  See Impact Assessment Agency of Canada, "Tailored Impact Statement Guidelines Template for Designated Projects Subject to the Impact Assessment Act," ss 4.1 & 4.2, online: *Government of Canada* www.canada.ca/en/impact-assessment-agency/services/policy-guidance/practitioners-guide-impact-assessment-act/tailored-impact-statement-guidelines-projects-impact-assessment-act.html#_Toc15652087 ["Tailored Impact Statement"].

45  *IAA*, above note 1, ss 22(1)(e) & (f).

and alternative means.[46] This guidance falls short of directly requiring application of sustainability-based criteria to establish whether or not the best option in the public interest has been selected in light of the core section 63 decision factors. However, such a requirement may be implicitly present in the combination of the existing guidance and section 63's mandatory considerations for decision makers.

In a sustainability-based assessment regime that aims to make decisions in the public interest; sets out mandatory considerations; and requires consideration of purposes, needs, and alternatives, rational justification for decisions on proposed projects would seem to depend on explicit application of defensible criteria in the comparative analysis of the alternatives. But as long as the implicit logic is not expressed clearly in policy guidance, uptake in practice is uncertain.

For regional and strategic assessments, the scope and ambition of planning and evaluation practice are largely undefined. Even application of the sustainability-based scope of factors for consideration is uncertain. Insofar as regional and strategic assessments are to provide credible and authoritative guidance for project assessments, both levels should adopt the Act's sustainability agenda. However, no commitment to that has yet been announced.

## 3) Ensuring the Credibility of Assessment Information, Deliberations, and Decision Making

### a) What a Sustainability-Based Agenda Requires

Assessment law has always aimed to induce change from established thinking and practice.[47] It has also always had to contend with resistance from those required to change and dissatisfaction from those who see the change as urgent. In the face of such tensions, effective application of the law has depended heavily on the credibility of its processes, analyses, and decision making. That was the case when Canadian assessment law focused on mitigation of adverse environmental effects;

---

46  See Impact Assessment Agency of Canada, "Tailored Impact Statement" above note 44, ss 4.3 & 4.4.

47  See, for example, the account of one of the architects of the first assessment law: Lynton Keith Caldwell, *The National Environmental Policy Act: An Agenda for the Future* (Bloomington, IN: Indiana University Press, 1998).

the larger scope and ambition of sustainability-based assessment law add to the credibility imperative.[48]

Credibility in assessments is best established and maintained through a package of law, policy, and implementation components. Of these, the most important include transparency, evident impartiality, soundness of information, independent expertise, inclusion of diverse perspectives, analytical rigour, capable adjudication, and published reasons for decisions based on explicit criteria.[49]

### b)  What Is in the Act and Associated Initial Regulations and Policy Guidance

The Act is the product of a law reform exercise initiated in large part in response to the perceived low credibility of assessments under the *Canadian Environmental Assessment Act, 2012*.[50] Steps to enhance impartiality and credibility were central to the recommendations of the Expert Panel for the Review of Federal Environmental Assessment Processes (Expert Panel) appointed by the government to hold cross-country public hearings as the first stage of the assessment reform process.[51] Not surprisingly, the Act includes provisions for a variety of credibility-enhancing measures:

- development of interjurisdictional cooperation plans early in project assessments[52]

---

48    Lesley Evans Ogden, "Canada Aims to Rewrite Environmental Law" (2016) 353:6307 *Science* 1480.

49    MIAC, above note 41; *Building Common Ground*, above note 41; Richard D Lindgren, *The Legal Path to Sustainability: The Top Five Reforms Needed for Next-Generation Assessments: Final Submissions of the Canadian Environmental Law Association to the Expert Panel Regarding the Canadian Environmental Assessment Act, 2012* (22 December 2016), online (pdf): *Canadian Environmental Law Association* https://cela.ca/wp-content/uploads/2019/07/CELA-Submissions-Expert-Panel.pdf; AR Westwood et al, "The Role of Science in Contemporary Canadian Environmental Decision Making: The Example of Environmental Assessment" (2019) 52:1 *UBC Law Review* 243; Bram F Noble, "Strategic Environmental Assessment Quality Assurance: Evaluating and Improving the Consistency of Judgments in Assessment Panels" (2004) 24:1 *Environmental Impact Assessment Review* 3.

50    *Building Common Ground*, above note 41, Annex I.

51    *Ibid.*

52    *IAA*, above note 1, ss 18(1)(b) and 21.

- specific consultations with potentially affected Indigenous groups[53] and preparation of "engagement and partnership" plans with Indigenous peoples[54]
- more opportunities for the public to participate meaningfully, including in regional and strategic assessments[55]
- a public process for requests for regional and strategic assessments[56]
- publication of reasons for decision based on specified considerations[57]
- a more central role for[58] and less political interference in[59] the new Impact Assessment Agency of Canada

All of these provisions are discussed elsewhere in this book. Although many fall short of the approaches recommended by the independent Expert Panel[60] and may be vulnerable to weak implementation, they nonetheless represent moves toward advanced assessment practice.

## 4) Following Up Assessment Predictions and Approval Conditions

## a) What a Sustainability-Based Agenda Requires

Like their environmentally focused predecessors, sustainability-based assessments centre on prediction of behaviours and effects in complex socio-ecological systems about which our understanding is limited. Also, they involve the legislated imposition of requirements on parties to act in ways that they have been disinclined to choose voluntarily. Assessment law with a sustainability-based agenda must therefore require and facilitate effective follow-up — monitoring the effects of assessed undertakings and the adequacy of compliance with commitments and conditions of approval and responding suitably to emerging problems and opportunities — both to improve implementation

---

53    *Ibid*, s 12.
54    *Ibid*, s 18(1)(b).
55    *Ibid*, ss 11, 27, 51(1)(c), and 99.
56    *Ibid*, s 97(1).
57    *Ibid*, s 65(2).
58    *Ibid*, ss 10 and 25.
59    *Ibid*, s 153(2).
60    *Building Common Ground*, above note 41.

of approved undertakings and to facilitate learning from experience.[61] Especially with a move into the unfamiliar territory of sustainability-based assessment, careful monitoring, response to findings, and reporting of lessons are likely to be crucial.

### b) What Is in the Act and Associated Initial Regulations and Policy Guidance

In addition to expanding the scope of effects to be considered and therefore monitored, the Act requires the approval conditions of all projects to include a follow-up program.[62] The Act provides few specifics about follow-up programs, but initial policy guidance on the contents of the tailored impact statements includes some details on what follow-up programs are to address.[63] Less clear are means of ensuring effective responses to monitoring findings and compliance with related conditions of approval. The Act and associated guidance documents reveal no inclination to abandon heavy reliance on self-monitoring by proponents and are mostly silent on the allocation of follow-up responsibilities to government authorities and/or other experts.[64] The Act does, however, require the participant funding program to support public engagement in "the design or implementation of follow-up programs."[65]

### 5) Facilitating Continuous Learning Throughout the Process

### a) What a Sustainability-Based Agenda Requires

Progress toward sustainability is unavoidably long term. On most if not all matters, it demands improved understanding, informed support, and broadly capable engagement. Sustainability-based assessment regimes must therefore be designed to facilitate broad participation in

---

61    Elise Pinto et al, "Distilling and Applying Criteria for Best Practice EIA Follow-up" (2019) 21:02 *Journal of Environmental Assessment Policy and Management* 1950008; Angus Morrison-Saunders et al, "Towards Sustainability Assessment Follow-up" (2014) 45 *Environmental Impact Assessment Review* 38; Carol Hunsberger, Robert B Gibson & Susan K Wismer, "Citizen Involvement in Sustainability-Centred Environmental Assessment Follow-up" (2005) 25:6 *Environmental Impact Assessment Review* 609.

62    *IAA*, above note 1, s 64(4)(b). See also the discussion in Chapter 16 of this book.

63    Above note 44, s 26.

64    See Chapter 16.

65    *IAA*, above note 1, s 75(1).

continuous learning.[66] Some of the needed opportunities lie in provisions to expand the range, depth, and quality of information available to individual assessments and to other assessment deliberations (e.g., concerning process application, regulations and policy guidance, strategic and regional assessment priority setting, and interjurisdictional collaboration models). Other key areas include measures to ensure that findings and lessons from these particular initiatives are conveyed for improvement of future deliberations and decisions in and beyond assessment practice.

### b)  What Is in the Act and Associated Initial Regulations and Policy Guidance

The innovative aspects of the Act, including the adoption of a sustainability-based scope and ambition, add important new opportunities for broad and better-integrated learning. More specifically, the Act strengthens prospects for learning in several areas. Particularly important are learning opportunities for all participants in areas of assessment in which Canada has limited experience, including sustainability-based evaluation, law-based regional and strategic assessments, greater emphasis on initial planning, attention to Indigenous rights and knowledge, and collaborative assessments. Other openings for broad learning are provided by the Act's improved provisions for mandatory publication and accessibility of documents, participant funding, and effects monitoring.[67] As in other areas, the extent to which these openings are used effectively will depend on elaboration in guidance and commitment in practice.

The Act and initial guidance could have gone further, including through more specific direction for sustainability-based evaluations and more clarity and ambition in its provisions for law-based regional and strategic assessments to address neglected big issues (e.g., regional cumulative effects, broad alternatives, and major policy concerns).[68] Establishment of a much more comprehensive and user-friendly open

---

66  See Chapter 22.
67  These provisions are discussed in other chapters of this book. See in particular Chapter 22.
68  See chapters 11 and 17.

data platform would also have enhanced prospects for learning.[69] But as a starting point for more advanced learning, the Act has potential.

### 6) Linking the Assessment Process and Its Particular Applications with Related Sustainability Initiatives and Decision Making, in Canada and Beyond

### a) What a Sustainability-Based Agenda Requires

Assessments of individual major projects, plus a handful of assessments at the regional and strategic levels, do not begin to cover the range and diversity of future undertakings likely to have cumulative consequences for lasting well-being. They also overlook the much larger and often more problematic realm of unsustainable existing activities. Transition to more sustainable socio-ecological systems and economies cannot be built with only one tool, applied to only some activities within one jurisdiction. Sooner or later, the sustainability agenda needs to be adopted and pursued comprehensively and in ways that are mutually supporting and linked from the local to the global.[70]

Numerous options are available. Well-designed and -implemented sustainability-based assessment can demonstrate the feasible applicability of necessary but disruptive ideas and practices.[71] Increased use of regional and strategic-level assessments could help establish sustainability-based plans and policies of general application to existing as well

---

69    The Act strengthens the impact assessment information registry and is accompanied by the development of a separate open data platform for some government materials but falls short of the Expert Panel's call for a large, well-integrated, open, and searchable data site. See *Building Common Ground*, above note 41.

70    Barry Sadler, *Environmental Assessment in a Changing World: Evaluating Practice to Improve Performance* (Ottawa: Canadian Environmental Assessment Agency and International Association for Impact Assessment, 1996); David P Lawrence, "PROFILE: Integrating Sustainability and Environmental Impact Assessment" (1997) 21:1 *Environmental Management* 23; Joseph, Gunton & Rutherford, above note 41; Andrew Macintosh, "Best Practice Environmental Impact Assessment: A Model Framework for Australia" (2010) 69:4 *Australian Journal of Public Administration* 401.

71    Christopher Luederitz et al, "Learning Through Evaluation—A Tentative Evaluative Scheme for Sustainability Transition Experiments" (2017) 169 *Journal of Cleaner Production* 61; Mark Winfield et al, "Implications of Sustainability Assessment for Electricity System Design: The Case of the Ontario Power Authority's Integrated Power System Plan" (2010) 38:8 *Energy Policy* 4115.

as new activities.[72] Evaluation and decision-making criteria developed for projects and regional and strategic assessments under the Act can be available for adoption in the planning and review of new and existing federal undertakings not subject to assessment under the Act and activities in other jurisdictions. Collaborations with other jurisdictions can extend understanding and capacity. Alignment with global sustainability objectives, such as the Sustainable Development Goals[73] and the Paris Agreement climate commitments,[74] can build and benefit from international contributions and allies. Similarly, assessment practice here can draw much from the broader world of sustainability experience. At the federal level, Canada is new to sustainability-based approaches and has much to learn from earlier applications in this country and from the variety of sustainability-based assessment and assessment-like processes that have been tested around the world over the past quarter-century.[75]

## b)  What Is in the Act and Associated Initial Regulations and Policy Guidance

The Act establishes a promising framework for serious sustainability-based assessment that could both serve and benefit from links to the broader world of applied sustainability. The Act's most evident links are revised versions of the established ones with the energy sector "life-cycle regulators," the Canadian Nuclear Safety Commission and the Canadian Energy Regulator (previously the National Energy Board), which have in the past demonstrated no serious interest in

---

72   For example, serious strategic assessment on how to translate the Paris Agreement and other Canadian climate chance commitments into clear implications for project-level assessments could serve many needs for policy clarity affecting decision making well beyond assessment. See Robert B Gibson, Karine Péloffy & Meinhard Doelle, "Challenges and Opportunities of a Forthcoming Strategic Assessment of the Implications of International Climate Change Mitigation Commitments for Individual Undertakings in Canada" (2018) 10:10 *Sustainability* 3747.

73   Above note 23. See also Theo Hacking, "The SDGs and the Sustainability Assessment of Private-Sector Projects: Theoretical Conceptualisation and Comparison with Current Practice Using the Case Study of the Asian Development Bank" (2019) 37:1 *Impact Assessment and Project Appraisal* 2.

74   United Nations Climate Change, "The Paris Agreement" (December 2015), online: https://unfccc.int/process-and-meetings/the-paris-agreement/the-paris-agreement.

75   Barry Dalal-Clayton and Barry Sadler, *Sustainability Appraisal: A Sourcebook and Reference Guide to International Experience* (Abingdon, Oxon, UK: Earthscan/Routledge, 2014).

sustainability. Much of the potential for positive links lies with other bodies involved in Indigenous rights, environmental obligations and climate change, regional and strategic assessment issues, and inter-jurisdictional assessment collaborations. None of these areas of assessment attention has yet been well elaborated, and initial guidance and application steps have been tentative. The hesitancies reflect the usual near-term political and administrative constraints as well as uncertainties about how best to proceed. However, these may be increasingly countered by expected pressures for more clarity about decision criteria and more efficient and effective use of available tools for collaborations and responses to big policy and planning concerns.

Further development of policy guidance on addressing the section 63 considerations for decision makings — especially on the contribution to sustainability test, respect for Indigenous rights, and implications for meeting Canada's environmental obligations and climate commitments[76] — will have to draw from and could influence federal and national law, policy, and practice in these areas. Similarly, most of the issues and opportunities needing exploration by regional strategic assessments also involve provincial, territorial, and/or Indigenous powers and responsibilities; will demand collaborative work; and have impacts beyond project assessments.[77]

## D. OVERALL STRENGTHS, DEFICIENCIES, AND OPENINGS FOR IMPROVEMENT

As is revealed by the brief review above of the *IAA*'s approach to advanced sustainability assessment regime components, the Act provides a foundation of scope and potential ambition that could be used to pursue a serious sustainability-based assessment agenda. Unfortunately, the initial elaborations and application steps have been mostly timid.

Potentially, the Act's requirements could be applied quite widely to projects and regional/strategic undertakings. However, the initial list of designated projects covers only a small number of big projects, and plans for broader assessments suggest that they will be few and will often not assess strategic or regional undertakings.

---

76 *IAA*, above note 1, ss 63(a), (d), & (e). See, in particular, chapters 6 and 13 of this book.
77 See Chapter 17.

The Act's scope of effects and other considerations for assessment and decision making is mostly adequate, though dependent on practice. Important uncertainties include how provisions for the specific scoping of mandatory factors for consideration will be interpreted, how effective attention to cumulative effects will be ensured in the usual absence of regional/strategic assessment guidance, how well assessments address intergenerational effects and distributional effects beyond those related to gender and other identity factors, and whether the mandatory factors for project assessments will also be applied to regional and strategic assessments.

Important matters of scope and potential ambition are ill-defined or lacking in areas central to the assessment of impacts, alternatives, and proposed undertakings. Major uncertainties include how effects on Indigenous rights, environmental obligations, climate commitments, and overall contributions to sustainability will be evaluated. Initial guidance on required assessment analyses is especially unclear on how general sustainability-based expectations will be translated into case-specific sustainability criteria for evaluations and on how such criteria will guide the comparative evaluation of alternatives needed to justify selection of the preferred option as the proposed project (or regional/ strategic undertaking). As is discussed in subsequent chapters, the Act's most promising advances include the section 63 requirements concerning decision making based on contributions to sustainability, effects on Indigenous rights, and effects hindering or contributing to meeting environmental obligations and climate change commitments. But progress in all of these areas will depend on clear, detailed, and well-informed guidance.[78]

The Act's great advantage is that it has useful basic provisions or at least leaves openings for ambitious elaboration and application in most areas crucial for advanced sustainability-based assessment. Although inclination to act on the law's potential in the near term has not been well demonstrated, opportunities for improvement remain in the further elaboration of regulations, policies, and administrative practice; in the negotiation of innovative collaborations with other jurisdictions (including Indigenous ones); and in committed efforts to take on difficult regional and strategic assessment challenges. As in the past, the

---

78   See especially chapters 6 and 10–13.

best short-term possibilities for precedent-setting good practice in individual assessments may lie in joint review panels or joint regional/strategic assessments that are established by two or more jurisdictions that may have enough independence to innovate positively.

# CHAPTER 10

# Purpose, Need, and Alternatives Through the Lens of Sustainability and the Public Interest

*Arlene Kwasniak and Sharon Mascher*

## A. INTRODUCTION

A primary tool to foster and achieve sustainability is the practice of impact assessment (IA). Through carrying out IA processes, regulators and other decision makers identify and assess the environmental, health, social, and economic consequences of proposed projects to assist in determining whether they should be approved and, if so, under what conditions. By implementing IA legislation, projects will ideally be better planned and more acceptable, have fewer adverse impacts and social costs, and confer greater positive societal benefits.

Canada's *Impact Assessment Act* (*IAA*),[1] regulations, and guidance material provide and inform IA processes for projects within federal jurisdiction that are designated for assessment under the Act. Central among these processes are consideration of the *IAA*'s section 22 factors, each of which must be taken into account in IA. This chapter focuses on four key section 22 factors: the purpose of the project, the need for the project, alternatives to the project, and alternative means of carrying out the project, which we sometimes abbreviate as purpose, need, and alternatives. The chapter shows how together these four factors play an essential role in the federal IA process, in particular with respect to the Act's objective to achieve more sustainable outcomes.

---

1    SC 2019, c 28, s 1.

This chapter begins with a general discussion (not specific to the *IAA*) of the role that purpose, need, and alternatives play in assessment processes. The chapter then focuses on the Act, regulations, and guidance material and purpose, need, and alternatives in the context of phases of the assessment process, including the planning phase, the assessment phase, and the decision-making phase. Then the chapter considers a hypothetical mining project example to illustrate how seeing and analyzing these factors through the lens of sustainability and the public interest in accordance with the *IAA* differs from dealing with these factors under previous assessment legislation. The chapter concludes with a summary and recommendations on how need, purpose, and alternatives might be better grounded in the *IAA*, regulations, and guidance material in order to advance sustainability and the public interest, as required by the Act.[2]

## B. ABOUT PURPOSE, NEED, AND ALTERNATIVES WITHIN THE ASSESSMENT PROCESS

### 1) Purpose and Need and Their Interrelationship

A statement of purpose provides what is to be achieved by the project and the project's objectives.[3] Purpose can be expressed in various ways, ranging from a narrow articulation to a broad one. For example, suppose that a proposed project is to build a bridge to connect two landforms separated by water. The project proponent might describe the purpose as simply that: to build a bridge to connect two landforms separated by water. Or the project proponent might frame the purpose more broadly, to include not only the descriptive purpose but also broader societal purposes: for example, to build a bridge to facilitate and increase commerce between two landforms separated by water.

The purpose forms the foundation to establishing the need for a project, which is the factual basis that explains and underpins the

---

2    See, for example, *ibid*, ss 6(1)(a), 6(3), 8(b), 22(1)(h), 60–64, and 106. See also the discussion in Section C(1), below in this chapter.

3    See, for example, Impact Assessment Agency of Canada, "Practitioner's Guide to Federal Impact Assessments Under the Impact Assessment Act," entries for "need for," "purpose of," "alternatives to," and "alternative means," s 2.4 at 2, online: *Government of Canada* www.canada.ca/en/impact-assessment-agency/services/policy-guidance/ practitioners-guide-impact-assessment-act.html ["Practitioner's Guide"].

purpose, and supplies the fundamental justification or rationale for the project.[4] Using the two expressions of purpose in the proposed bridge set out above, if the purpose is expressed narrowly as "to connect two landforms separated by water," the need might similarly be narrowly put forward — for example, "the people on both landforms have lobbied government to build a bridge so that they can easily get from one landform to the other." However, even here there is a call for an explanation of societal need: why do people need to easily get from one landform to the other? The second example more forcefully calls for an explanation of societal need to provide a rationale for the purpose. If the purpose of the bridge is to facilitate and increase commerce between the two landforms, then providing the need, the factual basis for the purpose, will require evidence of the societal need to increase commerce.

In the example, both expressions of purpose and need relate to the same project. This fact highlights that the assessor and the decision maker can have more or less information before them when considering purpose and need depending on how purpose and need are articulated. However, what they require is sufficient information to enable them to carry out their duties under IA law. Although any particular assessment law must be examined on its own, assessment law, by its nature, implicitly or explicitly requires them to have a clear understanding of societal purpose and need, which may well be in addition to whatever statement of purpose and need a proponent puts forward. After all, if the approval of a project tolerates some adverse environmental impacts and costs that affect society, the societal purpose and need must be clearly understood.

This example and others given in the next section are simple and are designed to introduce and illustrate the factor concepts. In Section D, after these concepts are described in general and as to how they function under the *IAA*, we present a more complex example, a mining proposal, which better reflects IA in practice.

## 2)  Alternatives and Their Interrelationship to Purpose and Need

IA legislation may require one or both of two alternatives analyses: alternatives to a project and alternative means of carrying out a project.

---

4    *Ibid.*

Alternatives to the project consider other kinds of projects that could meet the purpose of and need for the proposed project. Such analyses commonly consider the "no go alternative," meaning no project at all. The "no go alternative" is an essential consideration as it provides a status quo baseline and sets out the consequences of not proceeding with the project. Alternative means of carrying out a project include alternatives for "locations, development and/or implementation methods, routes, designs, technologies, mitigation, etc."[5]

How do alternatives relate to purpose and need? If together purpose and need relate to the end, alternatives describe potential ways and means by which to achieve that end.[6] The framing of the purpose and need determines the starting point for both developing and eliminating alternatives.[7] When properly embedded in the assessment, consideration of alternatives allows for "unbiased, proactive consideration of options, to determine the most optimal course of action."[8] But when statements of purpose and need are framed narrowly, alternatives may be improperly excluded, so more sustainable options may not be considered[9] because they fall out of the scope of the assessment. This could significantly diminish the value of the assessment or even the ability to fulfill administrative duties under assessment legislation.[10] To illustrate, the United States Court of Appeals Seventh Circuit observed in *Simmons v United States Army Corps of Engineers*[11] that it is possible to "contrive a purpose so slender as to define competing 'reasonable alternatives' out

---

5   *Ibid* at s 5.

6   Anne Steinemann, "Improving Alternatives for Environmental Impact Assessment" (2001) 21:1 *Environmental Impact Assessment Review* 3 at 4.

7   *Ibid* at 8.

8   Department of Environmental Affairs and Tourism, *Criteria for Determining Alternatives in EIA*, Information Series 11 (Pretoria: Department of Environmental Affairs and Tourism, 2004) at 4, online (pdf): aardlink.files.wordpress.com/2013/08/11-alternatives.pdf.

9   Steinemann, above note 6 at 11.

10   See, for example, Alexandra Jiricka-Pürrer, Martin Bösch & Ulrike Pröbstl-Haider, "Desired but Neglected: Investigating the Consideration of Alternatives in Austrian EIA and SEA Practice" (2018) 10:10 *Sustainability* 3680. These authors state that the "evaluation of alternatives is perceived as a precondition for transparent decision making and the selection of solutions, which are less harmful for the environment or human health" (at 1). See also Council of Environmental Quality, "National Environmental Policy Act, Implementation of Procedural Provisions: Final Regulations" (1978) 43 *Federal Regulation* 55978 at 55978, emphasizing that the regulations "stress that the environmental analysis is to concentrate on alternatives, which are the heart of the process."

11   120 F (3d) 664 (7th Cir 1997) [*Simmons*].

of consideration (and even out of existence)."[12] In that case, the court held that an environmental impact statement prepared by the Army Corps of Engineers under the *National Environmental Policy Act*[13] was inadequate because it defined the purpose of the project as to provide water to two water districts from a single source, thus necessitating the creation of a particular dam and lake to provide the water, even though "[a]t no time has the Corps studied whether this single-source idea is the best one — or even a good one."[14]

Here is an example of "alternatives to" a project. Assume that the stated purpose of a project is to provide direct transportation infrastructure to join two areas of a municipality. The statement of need provides that population in both areas is expanding, there is no direct transportation infrastructure between them (existing transportation routes go around the perimeter of the areas), and people need to get from one area to the other area efficiently. The proponent proposes a highway between the two areas to meet the stated purpose and need. An alternative to the highway might be a public transit corridor. This alternative may achieve the same purpose and meet the same need as stated but also allows for consideration of other societal benefits, namely fewer negative air quality and climate change impacts.[15]

Using the previous example, alternative means involving a highway could include an alternative route that avoids sensitive wetland areas, provides mitigation measures to permit wildlife passage over or under the highway, uses permeable pavement for the road to permit storm-water runoff to drain, and so on. But whether the proponent would

---

12    *Ibid* at 666.

13    42 USC § 4321 et seq.

14    *Simmons*, above note 11 at 667.

15    The Lower Churchill Review Panel provides an explicit example of how the identification of possible alternatives to the project depends on how the "need for" and "purpose of" the project are defined. As Meinhard Doelle explained, the panel considered the issue of alternatives in three steps. First, in order to identify possible alternatives to the project, the need for and purpose of the project had to be defined. Second, the panel considered whether there was one alternative or some combination of alternatives that could meet the need for and purpose of the project as defined. Finally, the panel asked whether any of the alternatives identified in step two could meet the need for and purpose of the project with a more desirable combination of effects, benefits, risks, and uncertainties. Meinhard Doelle, "The Role of EA in Achieving a Sustainable Energy Future in Canada: A Case Study of the Lower Churchill Panel Review" (2013) 25 *Journal of Environmental Law & Practice* 113 at 126.

put these alternative means forward depends on whether it is in the proponent's interests to do so. This observation brings to light how proper consideration of alternatives may be challenging if alternative assessment requirements are largely proponent driven. By the time the proposal is prepared, the proponent may have already rejected more environmentally sound alternatives and will have little or no motivation to raise them. The proponent may also have made capital commitments to a preferred alternative and may want to avoid bringing attention to others.[16]

## C. THE *IAA* AND PURPOSE, NEED, AND ALTERNATIVES

### 1) The Sustainability and Public Interest Lens

The objective of the *Canadian Environmental Assessment Act*[17] (CEAA 1995) and the *Canadian Environmental Assessment Act, 2012*[18] (CEAA 2012) was the avoidance of significant adverse environmental effects (SAEEs). The *IAA* took a different path, with the major objective being to "foster sustainability."[19] In the Act, "sustainability" means "the ability to protect the environment, contribute to the social and economic well-being of the people of Canada and preserve their health in a manner that benefits present and future generations."[20] This objective is to be achieved, at least in part, through assessment of the section 22 factors and in making the determination of whether a project is in the public interest, taking into account (among other factors) the extent to which the project contributes to sustainability.[21] The Act requires that "[t]he Government of Canada, the Minister, the Agency and federal authorities, in the administration of this Act, must exercise their powers in a manner that fosters sustainability."[22] This means that under the *IAA*, purpose, need,

---

16   John F Benson, "What Is the Alternative? Impact Assessment Tools and Sustainable Planning" (2003) 21:4 *Impact Assessment and Project Appraisal* 261.

17   SC 1992, c 37. The entry into force of the Act was delayed until 1995 to allow for key regulations to be developed and passed.

18   SC 2012, c 19, s 52.

19   The preamble to the *IAA*, above note 1, begins with "[w]hereas the Government of Canada is committed to fostering sustainability," and the first purpose of the *IAA* is to foster sustainability (s 6(a)).

20   *Ibid*, s 2, definition of "sustainability."

21   *Ibid*, ss 60, 61, and 63(a). See also chapters 9 and 14 of this book.

22   *Ibid*, s 6(2).

and alternatives, like other factors, must be assessed through what we abbreviate as "a sustainability and public interest lens." In other words, the *IAA* requires the assigned administrators in the Act to assess the project's purpose, need, and alternatives with a view to determining its potential to contribute to sustainability and, in part based on this assessment, whether a project is in the public interest.

The purpose, need, and alternatives provided by the proponent may not be sufficient for the assessor and decision maker to carry out legislated duties and to assess purpose, need, and alternatives through a sustainability and public interest lens. When this is so, in order to carry out their duties under the *IAA*, administrators must seek, acquire, and analyze the necessary information.

The next section sets out what the *IAA*, regulations, and guidance materials say about purpose, need, and alternatives in various assessment phases. In this discussion, we consider the extent to which the legislation and policy relating to these phases facilitate or require viewing purpose, need, and alternatives through a sustainability and public interest lens.

## 2)   The *IAA* Factors: Purpose, Need, and Alternatives

Section 22 of the *IAA* sets out the factors that must be considered in an IA. These include

(d)   the purpose of and need for the designated project;

(e)   alternative means of carrying out the designated project that are technically and economically feasible, including through the use of best available technologies, and the effects of those means;

(f)   any alternatives to the designated project that are technically and economically feasible and are directly related to the designated project.

Regarding alternatives, as introduced to Parliament, section 22(1)(f) read "alternatives to the designated project," but the House of Commons, in a flurry of amendments, added the words "that are technically and economically feasible and are directly related to the designated project." How the addition, especially the words "are directly related to the designated project," will limit the application of section 22(1)(f) has yet to be seen. Will proponents argue that alternatives must include the project itself—for example, the project at a lower production rate or the project with alternative components (which risks conflating alternatives to with alternative means)? If this is what the addition means, then what is to be made of the "no go" alternative, which excludes the project? Or perhaps the words limit the kinds of alternatives that may be considered—for example, alternatives to a coal mining project must be other comparable resource development projects. Perhaps the words add nothing at all, although in statutory interpretation it is assumed that Parliament's words are intended to have meaning. In the end, a court might have to decide what the words "directly related to the designated project" add to section 22(1)(f). In our view, given the uncertainty of interpretation, the added words risk unduly and inappropriately tying the hands of regulators in considering whether there are reasonable alternatives to the project that may better contribute to sustainability and are in the public interest.

### 3) The Planning Phase

### a) Initial Project Description

Under the *IAA*, a 180-day planning phase begins when the Canadian Impact Assessment Agency (the Agency) accepts and posts the initial project description[23] on the internet site it maintains for assessment purposes. The description is a document the proponent of a proposed designated project prepares that contains the information required by the *Information and Management of Time Limits Regulations* (IMTL Regulations).[24] The Agency uses the initial project description, and other acquired information, in its determinations on whether the proposed project will need to undergo an IA and, if an assessment is warranted, what process applies and what information has to be gathered to inform the assessment.

The IMTL Regulations require the initial project description to include "[a] statement of the purpose of and need for the project, including any potential benefits" and a list of

 (a) potential alternative means of carrying out the project that the proponent is considering and that are technically and economically

---

23 *Ibid*, s 18(1).

24 SOR/2019-283, s 3 and Sch 1, Pt A.

> feasible, including through the use of best available technologies; and
>
> (b)  potential alternatives to the project that the proponent is considering and that are technically and economically feasible and directly related to the project.[25]

One way of ascertaining purpose, need, and alternatives through a sustainability and public interest lens is through meaningful, broad-based consultation with persons and entities other than those acting for a private economic interest, such as the proponent. For example, as Anne Steinemann stated,

> [A]lternatives should better reflect societal goals, not just narrow agency goals. One way to help accomplish this is to involve the public more substantively in the development of alternatives …. Public involvement can be used to discover alternatives that may have been overlooked, to design new alternatives that are more widely supported, and to assist the implementation process. And public involvement for strategic decisions could create alternatives that reflect broader societal goals, rather than the traditional approach of piecemeal public meetings for individual projects.[26]

Broad-based consultation is most likely to happen if legislation requires it. Neither the *IAA* nor regulations under it require the proponent to consult with anyone when first establishing purpose, need, or alternatives. However, government policy, in the form of the "Guide to Preparing an Initial Project Description and a Detailed Project Description" (project description guide),[27] urges the proponent to consult with "other federal regulatory agencies, the provincial government(s) and any other relevant jurisdictions, regarding project information that may be required by these authorities."[28] Conspicuously absent from this list are persons or entities that would most obviously have information

---

25  *Ibid*, Sch 1, Pt B, ss 7 and 12.

26  Steinemann, above note 6 at 19.

27  Impact Assessment Agency of Canada, "Guide to Preparing an Initial Project Description and a Detailed Project Description" (13 July 2020), online: *Government of Canada* www.canada.ca/en/impact-assessment-agency/services/policy-guidance/practitioners-guide-impact-assessment-act/guide-preparing-project-description-detailed-project-description.html#_Toc1779470.

28  *Ibid*, "Prior to Submission of an Initial Project Description."

on societal purpose, need, and alternatives and would provide a public interest perspective. This absence is unfortunate. As Meinhard Doelle and John Sinclair wrote,

> [T]he whole idea of early planning is to be sure we have the right project to fit the societal need, purpose or rational[e] the project is intended to serve. It is not enough to consider alternative means by which the proponent could undertake its project....
>
> A key issue that should be clarified in this regard is who will identify the societal need, purpose and rational[e] of the project, and the alternative ways of achieving such societal goals to be considered in the assessment phase.[29]

The "Practitioner's Guide to Federal Impact Assessments Under the Impact Assessment Act" does at least mention the perspectives of others than the proponent with respect to establishing the purpose of and objectives of a project:

> Proponents should report the comments or views of Indigenous peoples, the public and other participants on the proponent's description of the need for a project.... The description of the "purpose of" a project should include any objectives a proponent has in carrying out the project. Proponents *are encouraged* to consider the perspectives of relevant participants (i.e. public, Indigenous groups, governments) in establishing objectives that relate to the intended effect of a project on society. This may help ensure that the process is guided from the outset towards finding mutually beneficial alternatives.[30]

Reporting comments and views, and encouraging the proponent to include societal perspective in the proponent's statement of purpose and objectives is a start, but it is a far cry from requiring the proponent to consult in such a manner so as to "identify the societal need, purpose and rational[e] of the project, and the alternative ways of achieving such societal goals to be considered in the assessment phase."[31]

---

29   Meinhard Doelle & A John Sinclair, "Discussion Papers on the Time Management Regulation Under the Impact Assessment Act (IAA)" at 2, online: www.impactassessmentregulations.ca/8866/widgets/34211/documents/16961/download.

30   Practitioner's Guide, above note 3, s 3, "Planning Phase Requirements, Initial Project Description Key Deliverable #1," sixth and ninth to eleventh sentences [emphasis added].

31   Doelle & Sinclair, above note 29.

If proponents were required to consult broadly in developing need, purpose, and alternatives, a sustainability and public interest perspective would more likely be reflected in the initial project description. The way the requirements now read, the proponent could just focus on its own views, which may be result oriented and self-interested. This is unfortunate as the initial project description forms the basis for the detailed project description that follows it, and the Agency decides whether an IA is required on the basis of the detailed project description.

As to Doelle and Sinclair's query regarding "who will identify the societal need, purpose and rational[e] of the project, and the alternative ways of achieving such societal goals," the answer is not in the IMTL Regulations. They are silent with respect to perspective on purpose and need but, as mentioned, specifically state that alternatives are those being considered by the proponent at the initial project description phase.[32] This is puzzling since nothing in the *IAA* provides that any of these factors be established from the perspective of the proponent. Indeed, as discussed earlier, the *IAA* requires its administrators to implement their statutory duties in a manner that fosters sustainability.[33] This suggests that even early articulations of purpose, need, and alternatives need to reflect a broader, societal perspective in addition to any private perspective of the proponent. Although time and chapter-length restrictions do not permit us to carry out a comprehensive statutory interpretation of the *IAA* of the issue, our initial investigations suggest that regulatory or policy limitations of perspective of alternatives or other factors to those of the proponent (e.g., those implicit in the guidance issued by the Agency) are an incorrect and potentially unreasonable interpretation of the *IAA*.

### b) Detailed Project Description

The project description guide requires the Agency to prepare a "summary of issues" raised in relation to the initial project description, and to inform the summary, the Agency must "engage and consult with provincial, territorial and Indigenous jurisdictions, Indigenous groups, the public, federal authorities and other participants."[34] This engagement is to take place in only twenty to thirty calendar days, although the Agency may modify the schedule. This period is astonishingly short,

---

32   IMTL Regulations, above note 24, Part C, s 12.
33   *IAA*, above note 1, s 6(2).
34   Above note 27, "Engagement on an Initial Project Description," first sentence.

and it is difficult to imagine how such consultation could be meaningful. Remarkably, the Agency has only about ten further days to prepare the summary of issues raised by participants.[35] The summary is then provided to the proponent, who uses it to prepare the detailed project description, due in thirty days unless the Agency approves a longer period. The IMTL Regulations provide that the detailed project description must include updated entries on purpose, need, and alternatives. Although the *IAA* and the IMTL Regulations are silent on consultation on these factors, guidance materials suggest that broad consultation could influence the updates.

After the Agency receives the detailed project description and accepts it as complete, the Agency posts it on the internet site and then proceeds to make a decision as to whether to require an IA.[36]

### 4) Tailored Impact Statement Guidelines and the Impact Assessment Phase

#### a) About the Guidelines and the Assessment Phase

An IA of a designated project that has not been substituted is conducted either by the agency or a review panel. In either case, the Agency must prepare Tailored Impact Statement (TIS) Guidelines, which provide instructions to the proponent in preparing an impact statement. The assessor (the Agency or a review panel) then uses the impact statement, and other information acquired in the IA stage, to prepare the impact assessment report. The report informs the minister's decision statement regarding whether the project is in the public interest. Although the Agency or a review panel may require further information during the assessment stage, including on need, purpose, and alternatives,[37] the TIS Guidelines set the agenda and focus of the assessment. Accordingly, it is important to consider what the TIS Guidelines may require with respect to purpose, need, and alternatives. The Agency determines the scope of a number of the factors, including purpose, need, and alternatives.[38] Accordingly, the Agency has discretion in the TIS Guidelines to require that these factors be assessed from a broad sustainability and

---

35 Above note 27, "Summary of Issues," third sentence.

36 *IAA*, above note 1, s 16.

37 *Ibid*, ss 26(2) and 52(2).

38 *Ibid*, ss 18(1.2) and 22(2).

societal perspective, not just from the perspective of the proponent. This broad scope could be implemented in a variety of ways under the *IAA*, including through mandating appropriate government departments or agencies to provide the societal purpose, need, and alternatives information and analysis.[39] However, as nothing in the *IAA* or regulations specifically requires anything in this regard, it is important to consider how guidance materials direct these matters.

## b)  The Tailored Impact Statement Guidelines and the Issue of Perspective in Determining Purpose, Need, and Alternatives

The *IAA* Practitioner's Guide entry on the TIS Guidelines template for designated projects subject to the *IAA* provides some direction on the issue of perspective in determining purpose, need, and alternatives. With respect to "purpose," the template mildly suggests that the proponent undertake a broader approach than simply using its own perspective in establishing societal purpose:

> **Purpose of the project**
>
> The Impact Statement must outline what is to be achieved by carrying out the project. The statement should broadly classify the project (e.g., electricity supply, mineral extraction/processing, etc.) and indicate the target market (e.g., international, domestic, local, etc.), where applicable. The *purpose of* statement should include any objectives the proponent has in carrying out the project.
>
> *Proponents are encouraged to consider the perspectives of participants (i.e. public, Indigenous groups, governments) in establishing objectives that relate to the intended effect of the project on society.*[40]

---

39  Opportunities under the *IAA* include provisions giving the Agency or a review panel the right to gather information in carrying out an assessment (for example ss 25–27), a federal authority's obligations to supply information (for example s 13), and the minister having regulatory authority under s 112(1)(b) "respecting the procedures, requirements and time periods relating to impact assessments."

40  Impact Assessment Agency of Canada, "Tailored Impact Statement Guidelines Template for Designated Projects Subject to the Impact Assessment Act," s 4.1, online: *Government of Canada* www.canada.ca/en/impact-assessment-agency/services/policy-guidance/practitioners-guide-impact-assessment-act/tailored-impact-statement-guidelines-projects-impact-assessment-act.html#_Toc15652087 [emphasis added]. See also "Tailored Impact Statement Guidelines Template for Designated Projects Subject to the Impact Assessment Act and the Canadian Energy Regulator Act," online: *Government of Canada* www.canada.ca/en/impact-assessment-agency/services/policy-guidance/practitioners-guide-impact-assessment-act/tailored-impact-statement-

However, in relation to the "need for" factor, the template focuses on the perspective of the proponent, with even the reporting of other views seemingly left as a matter of discretion:

**Need for the project**

The Impact Statement must describe the underlying opportunity or issue that the project intends to seize or solve and should be described from the perspective of the proponent. In many cases, the need for the project can be described in terms of the demand for a resource. The proponent should provide supporting information that demonstrates the need for a project. The information provided should make it possible to reasonably conclude that there is an opportunity or issue that warrants a response and that the proposed project is an appropriate approach (e.g. the output of an operation does not excessively exceed the projected demand). *The proponent may report the comments or views of Indigenous peoples, the public and other participants on the proponent's need statement.*[41]

Regarding "alternatives to the project," the template underscores that alternatives are identified from the proponent's perspective but requires that the proponent consider a broader perspective:

**Alternatives to the project**

In addressing alternatives to the designated project, the Impact Statement must provide a description of the functionally different ways that are technically and economically feasible to meet the project need and achieve the project purpose from the perspective of the proponent.... The process of identifying and considering alternatives to the project *must consider the views, information and knowledge from Indigenous peoples, the public and other participants, as well as existing studies and reports.*[42]

After tying the identification and consideration of the "alternative means" factor to the sustainability purposes of IA, the template

---

guidelines-template-impact-assessment-canadian-energy-regulator-act.html, and "Tailored Impact Statement Guidelines Template for Designated Projects Subject to the Impact Assessment Act and the Nuclear Safety and Control Act," online: Government of Canada www.canada.ca/en/impact-assessment-agency/services/policy-guidance/practitioners-guide-impact-assessment-act/tailored-impact-statement-guidelines-projects-impact-assessment-nuclear-safety-act.html#_Toc16256498.

41   *Ibid* at s 4.2 [emphasis added].

42   *Ibid* at s 4.3 [emphasis added].

narrowly requires the consideration of a broader perspective in determining how to compare alternative means:

> **Alternative means of carrying out the project**
>
> The Impact Statement must identify and consider the potential environmental, health, social and economic effects of alternative means of carrying out the designated project that are technically and economically feasible ....
>
> *The proponent must also consider the views or information provided by Indigenous people, the public and other participants in establishing parameters to compare the alternatives [sic] means.*[43]

In summary, the TIS Guidelines template makes some movement toward shifting perspective beyond the proponent in determining purpose, need, and alternatives, but, for the most part, such movement is limited, narrow, and tentative. It is difficult to see how following the template in establishing the TIS Guidelines to be used by a proponent in preparing an impact statement for a designated project would render the kind of information required for the assigned administrators of the Act to assess the project's purpose, need, and alternatives from a sustainability and public interest lens.

### c)  Tailored Impact Statement Guidelines and the Assessment Phase: Alternatives and the Preferred Alternative Through a Sustainability and Public Interest Lens

A critical question regarding alternatives concerns the nature and role of the preferred alternative in the assessment process. This is particularly important at the TIS Guidelines phase as the Guidelines direct how the assessment is to proceed and what it is to include.

Legal commentator Rod Northey explored the role of the preferred alternative with respect to pre-*IAA* assessment legislation.[44] He noted that there have been two regimes regarding alternatives. The first regime, used in the early days of IA in the United States and Canada,[45] evaluates

---

43  *Ibid* at s 4.4 [emphasis added].

44  Rod Northey, "Fading Role of Alternatives in Federal Environmental Assessment" (2016) 29 *Journal of Environmental Law & Practice* 41.

45  In the United States under the *National Environmental Policy Act* of 1969, above note 13, and in Canada under the 1973 Environmental Assessment and Review Process policy and the 1984 *Environmental Assessment and Review Process Guidelines Order*, SOR/84-467.

and compares alternatives, including their relative advantages and disadvantages (which could go beyond regarding environmental impacts), with the aim of identifying a preferred alternative given legislative and policy objectives (the "alternatives model"). The second regime is related to the overall objective of *CEAA 1995* and *CEAA 2012*, which was the avoidance or minimizing of SAEEs (the "significance model"). Judicial authority has indicated that the significance model does not require that the alternative with the least environmental impact be preferred. Rather, any alternative that avoids or minimizes SAEEs may be acceptable.[46] Northey pointed out that the shift from the alternatives to the significance model reflects a lessening of the role of alternatives analyses in IA. Northey suggested that were sustainability the objective of assessment, a switch back to the alternative model might well follow.[47]

As discussed earlier, the *CEAA* goal of avoidance of SAEEs is not the *IAA*'s goal with respect to assessment of designated projects. Therefore, the significance model is not relevant to the assessment of these projects. The *IAA*'s goal of assessing projects to foster sustainability clearly indicates a return to the alternatives model. Under the *IAA*, the alternative that best contributes to sustainability is the preferred alternative, whether that be an alternative to the project or an alternative means of achieving the project. This interpretation is somewhat supported by current guidance material, although guidance material could make the connection between the preferred alternative and the best contribution to sustainability more clear. The guidance material seems to struggle between accepting the connection and paying obeisance to the now-defunct god of the significance model.

The Practitioner's Guide chapter on interim guidance states the following:

> In a proponent's Impact Statement Report, proponents should describe the extent to which a project contributes to sustainability.... It is ... recommended *that a proponent apply the sustainability principles when assessing alternatives to a designated project that are technically and*

---


46   *Inverhuron & District Ratepayers' Assn v Canada (Minister of the Environment)*, 2001 FCA 203, leave to appeal refused, 2002 CarswellNat 414 (SCC). See also Northey, above note 44 at 59–60.

47   Northey, *ibid* at 55.

*economically feasible and are directly related to a project, as well as the alternative means of carrying out a designated project.*[48]

Sustainability principles for the purposes of implementing the *IAA* are as follows:

1. Consider the interconnectedness and interdependence of human-ecological systems;
2. Consider the well-being of present and future generations;
3. *Consider overall positive benefits and minimize adverse effects of a designated project*; and
4. Apply the precautionary principle and consider uncertainty and risk of irreversible harm.[49]

The TIS Guidelines template reflects these requirements and directs that the impact statement identify the preferred alternative to the project and preferred alternative means on the basis of their contribution to sustainability. However, differences in language between alternatives to the project and alternative means in the template suggest a greater deference to the proponent's perspective with respect to alternatives to the project, in contrast to alternative means. The preferred alternative to the project need only be "consistent with the aims of the *IAA*," whereas the alternative means must be based on consideration of sustainability factors:

**Alternatives to the project**
*... The analysis of alternatives to the project should serve to validate that the preferred alternative for the project is a reasonable approach to meeting the need and purpose and is consistent with the aims of the IAA.*[50]

**Alternative means of carrying out the project**
*...* The Impact Statement must *...* identify:
- the preferred alternative means of carrying out the *project based on the consideration of environmental, health, social and economic effects,*

---

48  Impact Assessment Agency of Canada, "Interim Guidance: Considering the Extent to which a Project Contributes to Sustainability," s 3, online: *Government of Canada* www.canada.ca/en/impact-assessment-agency/services/policy-guidance/practitioners-guide-impact-assessment-act/interim-guidance-considering.html [emphasis added].

49  *Ibid*, s 2 [emphasis added].

50  "Tailored Impact Statement Guidelines Template for Designated Projects Subject to the Impact Assessment Act," above note 40, s 4.3 [emphasis added].

*and of technical and economic feasibility and through the use of best available technologies;*

- the methodology and criteria used to determine the preferred alternative means and the unacceptability of excluded alternative means, including consideration of trade-offs associated with the preferred and alternative means; and
- criteria to examine the environmental, health, social and economic effects of each remaining alternative means to identify a preferred alternative.[51]

In closing this section, we note that although the guidance materials are tentative with respect to viewing and assessing alternatives through a sustainability and public interest lens, we must remember that guidance materials are policy at best and can easily change. What really matters is the *IAA*. In our view, given the shift from significance to sustainability in the *IAA* alternatives assessments, the preferred alternatives are those that objectively maximize overall positive benefits and minimize adverse ones. This shift provides further reason why government entities overseeing IA should not be confined to the proponent's determinations of purpose, need, and alternatives and why ample time and broad participation opportunities should be provided in the planning and assessment phases for development and consideration of these factors. Since proponents are naturally invested in their own purposes and needs and, accordingly, their own choice of alternatives, assessors and decision makers must look elsewhere for broader perspectives that focus through a sustainability and public interest lens. This new focus on sustainability also supports the conclusion that consideration of alternatives should not be scoped to restrict consideration of alternatives that are not technically and economically feasible *to the specific proponent*, as has been the practice under earlier IA regimes.[52] Even in light of this new direction, it is not clear whether, at the end of the assessment process, the discretion involved in exercising the public interest test is broad enough to support approval of a project that did not adopt the preferred alternative. See chapters 9 and 14 for further discussion.

---

51    *Ibid*, s 4.4 [emphasis added].
52    See, for example, *Alberta Wilderness Assn v Cardinal River Coals Ltd*, [1999] 3 FC 425, where the Federal Court was satisfied that consideration of "alternative means" of a proposed open-pit mine was properly restricted to underground mining because of the proponent's practical and economic concerns.

## 5)  Decision-Making Phase

At the decision-making phase, the decision maker—the minister or Cabinet—determines whether a project is in the public interest.[53] The *IAA* requires that the determination be based on the assessment report and the factors set out in section 63, including "(a) the extent to which the designated project contributes to sustainability." The report will set out how the section 22 factors, including purpose, need, and alternatives, were assessed. Accordingly, these will be the subject of a public interest determination. The assessment of purpose, need, and alternatives as part of the report that the decision is based on also will feature in the application of section 63 factors, which include the extent to which the project contributes to sustainability.[54] It is critical, therefore, that the consideration of purpose, need, and alternatives be developed through a sustainability and public interest lens. See chapters 9 and 14 for further discussion.

## D.  HYPOTHETICAL MINING EXAMPLE, BEFORE AND AFTER THE *IAA*

## 1)  Introduction

Based on the foregoing discussion, we provide a hypothetical example of how, in practice, purpose, need, and alternatives, analyses should be carried out under the *IAA*. The example is a mining project, a mainstay of IA. We consider how these factors would likely have been considered under pre-*IAA* legislation and then how the new Act has changed the way consideration should proceed. To inform the "before the *IAA*" discussion, we reviewed and focused on completed *CEAA 1995* comprehensive studies of mining projects.[55] We chose *CEAA 1995* comprehensive studies since *CEAA 1995* specifically required assessment of the purpose of and need for projects assessed by comprehensive study. *CEAA 1995* also required the consideration of alternative means for all assessments

---

53    *IAA*, above note 1, ss 60 & 61.

54    *Ibid*, s 63(a).

55    Assessment records are available from the Canadian Impact Assessment Registry on the Impact Assessment Agency of Canada's website: https://iaac-aeic.gc.ca/050/ evaluations.

and gave the Agency specific discretion to require the assessment of alternatives to the project.[56]

## 2)  The Hypothetical Example

This example is a hypothetical open-pit nickel mine proposed by Fortune Nickel. Fortune frames the purpose of its proposal as the construction, operation, and decommissioning of an open-pit mine to extract nickel from a deposit located at a specific site southwest of Sudbury, Ontario. The proponent plans to extract ore for twenty-one years. Regarding need, Fortune states that industry analysts anticipate a future increase in nickel consumption and predict that current nickel mining projects likely will not satisfy demand.

Adopting an approach common for mining projects subject to federal assessment under *CEAA 1995*, in relation to alternatives to the project Fortune contends that alternatives to the project are limited because the purpose is to mine the resource at a specific site where the ore exists. The purpose can only be carried out by mining the ore at its location. Fortune does consider the "no go" alternative—to abandon the project—although it condemns this alternative on the basis that it will deprive the region of the benefits the project will bring and deprive the proponent of profits. Although the need (the increasing demand for nickel) could be met through other companies mining deposits elsewhere, Fortune denounces this as having the same negative consequences as abandoning the project.

Fortune considered alternative means regarding tailings and other waste, water supply, waste water management, access and transportation, stockpile sites, and alternatives to open-pit mining. Fortune's objective is to identify technically and economically feasible alternative means that have fewer negative environmental impacts. Fortune provides many such alternatives but rejects some alternatives with significant environmental benefits, such as alternatives to open-pit mining, on economic grounds.

---

56   Above note 17, ss 16(1) and 16(1)(e). Of purpose, need, and alternatives, *CEAA 2012*, above note 18, only required assessment of purpose (s 19(1)(f)) and alternative means (s 19(1)(g)).

## 3)   Before the *IAA*

Would Fortune's statement of purpose and need be acceptable under pre-*IAA* legislation? As narrow and self-serving as they are, based on our review of comprehensive studies, the Agency likely would accept them. Our review did not find the Agency requiring a broader range of alternatives to the "no go" alternative, suggesting that it found acceptable proponents' ubiquitous claim that mining projects had limited alternatives to the project because the purpose is to mine at a certain location.[57] Regarding alternate means, we found that the Agency typically accepted the proponent's preferences provided that they were aimed at reducing environmental impacts. We assume, therefore, that pre-*IAA* the Agency would accept Fortune's choices. We also assume, as discussed earlier, that the Agency would not require Fortune to adopt the alternative means with the least environmental impact as long as the proponent's preferences would avoid or at least minimize SAEEs.

## 4)   After the *IAA*

As discussed above, analyzing purpose, need, and alternatives factors through a sustainability and public interest lens means that articulations of these factors must reflect a broad, societal perspective, not just the proponent's perspective, and must support the consideration of more sustainable options.

Statements of purpose must do more than just describe the project, as Fortune's does. How could it be appropriately broadened to reflect societal need? Among other ways, an addition could be made that a purpose of the project is to foster and effect sustainability for the community. This broadening of purpose opens the door to expanding the rest of the factors to be considered. For need, not only will the need for nickel be a factor, but so too is the community need for sustainability, including sustainable projects. Is there a need in this community for

---

57   See, for example, the comprehensive study reports of the following: Mining and Milling the Midwest Project (updated 20 May 2012) at 5.1; Dumont Nickel Mine Project (updated 19 May 2015) at 4.1; Arnaud Mining Project (updated 31 July 2015) at 4.1; Sisson Project (Tungsten and Molybdenum Mine) (updated 15 April 2016) at 4.1; and Hammond Reef Gold Project (updated 30 July 2018) at 5.1. All are accessible on the Registry, above note 55.

the benefits associated with this project? Is that need purely economic, or are there social and cultural needs that the proposed project will meet within the community? Community participation and input are essential to accurately frame both the purpose and the societal need for the project at the local level. For alternatives to the project, the broadening should enable participants to judge whether the Fortune mine will likely foster sustainability or whether an alternative is better able to do this. For example, an alternative to a nickel mining project might be a nickel recycling facility. Or a more sustainable option to meet the community sustainability need might include developing a community recreation centre or a solar facility to provide power to the community. The proponent might argue that these are out of its control,[58] but where the objective is sustainability, not just what the proponent wants to do, consideration of options other than the proponent's project is reasonable and critical. Focused on sustainable outcomes, the "no go" option must also examine the question of community needs more broadly to address how the project fosters, or impacts, not only the economic but also the social and cultural needs of the community.

As well, alternative means under the *IAA* should not centre on avoiding or mitigating SAEEs but rather should focus on fostering all of the objectives of sustainability. Thus, Fortune's alternative means analyses would have to be rewritten to show how the alternative means foster or impact all of the *IAA* sustainability elements. Preferred alternatives would be those that best meet sustainability objectives, not necessarily those preferred by the proponent. Greater economic costs alone cannot explain why one alternative means is preferred over another.

In summary, with this mining example, the factors, when seen through a sustainability and public interest lens, should play a considerably different role under the *IAA* than they played under previous assessment legislation. And, as pointed out earlier, there is no reason why the proponent should be the sole determiner of these factors and many reasons why they should not be.

As a final comment in this section, if there were a regional or strategic assessment in place before the Fortune proposal, at least some

---

58    See, for example, Impact Assessment Agency of Canada, *Sisson Project Comprehensive Study Report* (April 2016) at s 4.1, online: *Impact Assessment Agency of Canada* https://iaac-aeic.gc.ca/050/evaluations/document/117323#_Toc018.

sustainable alternatives for the project area likely would have been identified and evaluated. As Bram Noble and Kelechi Nwanekezie stated,

> As a strategic process, the consideration of alternatives, or strategic options, is at the heart of [Strategic Environmental Assessment (SEA)] (Gonzalez and Therivel, 2014). SEA is about exploring desirable outcomes, determining what is needed to achieve those outcomes, and identifying and assessing the potential implications of alternative strategic initiatives (Noble and Gunn, 2015). The focus is on building a more desirable or resilient future (Slootweg and Jones, 2011), as opposed to locking-in futures based on past trends, conditions or events (Noble and Gunn, 2015, Partidário, 2007).[59]

Regional and strategic assessment can be invaluable in identifying and considering sustainable alternatives rather than just carrying on "business as usual" and assessing projects in a piecemeal fashion. Nevertheless, every project proposal stands on its own, and although regional and strategic assessments can inform and guide alternatives analyses at the project level, they cannot replace them.

## E.   CONCLUSIONS AND RECOMMENDATIONS

We have concluded, based on the *IAA*, that to properly implement the Act, the factors of purpose, need, and alternatives must be developed, voiced, and assessed through a sustainability and public interest lens, in addition to any perspective of the proponent. We demonstrated how various phases of IA contribute to, or fail to contribute to, such

---

59   Bram Noble & Kelechi Nwanekezie, "Conceptualizing Strategic Environmental Assessment: Principles, Approaches and Research Directions" (2017) 62 *Environmental Impact Assessment Review* 165 at 167. In this article, the authors included regional assessments under strategic environmental assessment. Internal references: Ainhoa Gonzalez & Riki Therivel, "Alternatives in Strategic Environmental Assessment of Plans and Programs" *FasTips* No 7 March (Fargo, ND: International Association for Impact Assessment, 2014); Bram F Noble & Jill Gunn, "Strategic Environmental Assessment" in Kevin S Hanna, ed, *Environmental Assessment in Canada: Practice and Participation*, 3d ed (Don Mills, ON: Oxford University Press, 2016) 96; Roel Slootweg & Mike Jones, "Resilience Thinking Improves SEA: A Discussion Paper" (2011) 29:4 *Impact Assessment and Project Appraisal* 263; Maria do Rosário Partidário, *Strategic Environmental Assessment Good Practices Guide: Methodological Guidance* (Amadora, Lisbon: Portuguese Environment Agency, 2007). See Chapter 17 of this book for a detailed discussion of strategic assessments.

implementation. We also noted how the IMTL Regulations do not emphasize or require a sustainability and public interest lens for purpose, need, and alternatives.

We recommend that the IMTL Regulations be revised to clarify that both the initial project description and the detailed project description must set out purpose, need, and alternatives from a broad, societal perspective in addition to any unique to the proponent. We also recommend that the timelines in the IMTL Regulations and the *IAA* be revised to provide sufficient time for meaningful participant participation throughout the IA process, but in particular in the planning phase, so that purpose, need, and alternatives may be developed early from a sustainability and public interest perspective.[60] Furthermore, we recommend that the IMTL Regulations, when setting out what must be included in the initial and detailed project descriptions, specify that these factors must be set out from a societal perspective to enable the *IAA*'s intent and requirements to be met, in addition to any perspectives brought forward by a proponent. As well, the IMTL Regulations should specify that the preferred alternatives (to both the project and the means of carrying it out) be identified and that they are the ones that best meet the sustainability objectives of the *IAA*. We have argued that assessors and decision makers must look beyond the proponent for these factors to appropriately reflect the sustainability and public interest objectives of the Act. We recommend that opportunities in the *IAA* to assign these responsibilities to someone other than the proponent (e.g., an expert federal authority) be pursued. This may be particularly important for private, in contrast to public, proponents.

As well, we recommend that there be clear statements in regulation or at least in guidance that the aim of considering alternatives is not only to identify the preferred alternative but also to clarify that acting in the public interest requires that it be adopted. In addition, we recommend that the *IAA* be amended to delete the House of Commons addition to "alternative means."

Finally, the guidance materials need revision. They should be comprehensively reviewed and revised to require that purpose, need, and alternatives be set out from a sustainability and public interest lens.

---

60   See also Chapter 15.

# CHAPTER 11

# The Scope and Focus of Cumulative Effects and Regional Assessment

*Jill Blakley, Bram Noble, and Jason MacLean*

## A. INTRODUCTION

The assessment of cumulative environmental effects has been a requirement for project proponents since impact assessment legislation was first introduced in Canada in 1995. Simply defined, cumulative effects assessment (CEA) is a systematic process for identifying, analyzing, and evaluating the cumulative effects associated with a project.[1] The goals of CEA are somewhat more complex, but the overall thrust of practice within a regulatory context is to support project-based impact assessment and decision making. In principle, this is achieved by determining whether or not valued components of the biophysical or social environment likely to be impacted by a proposed project are also likely to be impacted by the effects of other known past, present, or future developments or disturbances in the project's regional environment.

A requirement for CEA has been included in each version of federal impact assessment legislation in Canada, but it is also routinely practiced in the context of non-regulatory, regional assessments and land use planning initiatives. Although the performance of CEA in Canada and abroad has tended to receive more criticism than praise, the need for effective CEA processes has never been stronger. This is due in part

---

1   "Canada-Wide Definitions and Principles for Cumulative Effects" (2014), online (pdf): *Canadian Council of Ministers of the Environment* www.ccme.ca/files/Resources/enviro_ assessment/CE%20Definitions%20and%20Principles%201.0%20EN.pdf.

to a growing awareness of novel, complex, and connected global risks (sometimes called "Anthropocene risks"[2]) and an increased policy and legal focus on issues such as climate change, ocean acidification, loss of biodiversity, freshwater pollution and shortages, and Indigenous rights.

Canada's *Impact Assessment Act (IAA)*[3] carries with it an expectation that CEA would be both strengthened for project-based reviews and more connected with both regional and strategic environmental assessments. This chapter examines the provisions for cumulative effects and regional assessment under the *IAA* in light of established standards and suggests actions needed to ensure effective implementation through regulations, policies, and guidance. In Section B, we summarize what the *IAA* says about cumulative effects and regional assessment. In Section C, we evaluate these provisions with respect to internationally peer-reviewed literature and other established guidance for good-practice cumulative effects and regional assessment. Finally, in Section D, we discuss both opportunities and challenges to strengthen implementation of the *IAA*, concluding that several steps can be taken to do so. In Chapter 17, we explore provisions for strategic environmental assessment more closely.

## B.  THE *IAA*'S CUMULATIVE EFFECTS ASSESSMENT AND REGIONAL ASSESSMENT SECTIONS

The Act contains several sections that directly mention both cumulative effects and regional assessment. The CEA-related provisions include the purposes of the Act[4] and the factors to be considered in impact assessment.[5] Cumulative effects are also indirectly referenced in the definition of "environment" in the *IAA*.[6] Provisions related to regional assessment include the Act's preamble, the purposes of the Act, section 6(1)(m), and sections 92 and 93(1), which outline the role of the federal

---

2    Victor Galaz, "Anthropocene Risks: Social Scientists Need to Step Up to the Challenge" *The Guardian* (12 November 2014), online: www.theguardian.com/science/political-science/2014/nov/12/anthropocene-risks-social-scientists-need-to-step-up-to-the-challenge.

3    SC 2019, c 28, s 1.

4    *Ibid* at s 6(1)(m).

5    *Ibid* at s 22(1)(a)(ii).

6    *Ibid* at s 2.

minister of environment and climate change in both regional and strategic assessments.

The preamble of the *IAA* states that the government of Canada is "committed to" and "recognizes the importance of" regional and strategic assessments. Furthermore, among the purposes of the *IAA*, section 6(1)(m) encourages "the assessment of the cumulative effects of physical activities in a region and the assessment of federal policies, plans or programs and the consideration of those assessments in impact assessments."

Among the factors to be considered in impact assessment, the *IAA* stipulates that the impact assessment of a designated project, whether it is conducted by the Impact Assessment Agency of Canada (the Agency) or a review panel, must take into account "any cumulative effects that are likely to result from the designated project in combination with other physical activities that have been or will be carried out."[7] Project effects to be considered are outlined in section 2 and include fish and fish habitat, aquatic species, migratory birds, Indigenous peoples of Canada, and other components of the environment, whereas

> **environment** means the components of the Earth, and includes
> (a)  land, water and air, including all layers of the atmosphere;
> (b)  all organic and inorganic matter and living organisms; and
> (c)  the interacting natural systems that include components referred
>      to in paragraphs (a) and (b).

The definition of environment in the *IAA* also implies the importance of assessing cumulative effects by emphasizing attention to "interacting" natural systems.

Later in the *IAA*, the federal minister of environment and climate change is enabled to authorize a committee or the Agency to conduct a regional assessment on federal lands[8] or enter into a partnership to perform a regional assessment that involves a region partly or entirely outside federal lands.[9] The Act states that the minister will consult an advisory council to make decisions about which regional and strategic assessments will receive priority.[10]

---

7    *Ibid* at s 22(1)(a)(ii).
8    *Ibid* at s 92.
9    *Ibid* at s 93(1).
10   *Ibid* at ss 117(2) & (3).

## C. EVALUATION OF THE *IAA*'S CUMULATIVE EFFECTS AND REGIONAL ASSESSMENT PROVISIONS

There is a long history of cumulative effects research and development in Canada at the federal level, dating back to the 1980s and the seminal works of Beanlands and Duinker[11] and the Canadian Environmental Assessment Research Council.[12] Yet cumulative effects have remained one of the most contested aspects of Canadian impact assessment and are increasingly politicized by those communities of interest opposed to project development.[13] Scholars[14] and practitioners[15] have noted the poor state of practice of CEA under federal impact assessment, characterized by Duinker and Greig as "doing more harm than good."[16] Duinker and Greig are referring to the conventional practice of assessing cumulative effects solely within the scope of a single project. In these cases, the focus is on minimizing the project's impact contribution to a proportionally acceptable level versus the established good practice of considering the total impacts of all activities (including those not subject to regulatory assessment) and the implications for the socio-ecological condition of a region.[17] Unfortunately, in several respects, the *IAA* falls short of meeting standards set forth in literature and offers little (if any) improvement over its predecessor legislation,

---

11    See, for example, Gordon E Beanlands & Peter N Duinker, *An Ecological Framework for Environmental Impact Assessment in Canada* (Halifax: Institute for Resource and Environmental Studies, Dalhousie University & Federal Environmental Assessment Review Office, 1983).

12    Canadian Environmental Assessment Research Council, *The Assessment of Cumulative Effects: A Research Prospectus* (Hull, QC: Canadian Environmental Assessment Research Council, 1988).

13    Bram Noble, "Cumulative Effects Research: Achievements, Status, Directions and Challenges in the Canadian Context" (2015) 17:1 *Journal of Environmental Assessment Policy and Management* 1.

14    See, for example, Michael P Gillingham et al, eds, *The Integration Imperative: Cumulative Environmental, Community, and Health Effects of Multiple Natural Resource Developments* (Basel, Switzerland: Springer International Publishing, 2016).

15    See, for example, George Hegmann and GA Yarranton, "Alchemy to Reason: Effective Use of Cumulative Effects Assessment in Resource Management" (2011) 31:5 *Environmental Impact Assessment Review* 484.

16    Peter N Duinker & Lorne A Greig, "The Impotence of Cumulative Effects Assessment in Canada: Ailments and Ideas for Redeployment" (2006) 37:2 *Environmental Management* 153 at 153.

17    "Canada-Wide Definitions and Principles for Cumulative Effects," above note 1.

the *Canadian Environmental Assessment Act, 2012 (CEAA 2012)*[18] regarding provisions for the assessment and management of cumulative effects.

One of the stated purposes of the *IAA* is "to encourage the assessment of the cumulative effects of physical activities in a region."[19] A stated purpose of *CEAA 2012* was similarly "to encourage the study of cumulative effects of physical activities in a region."[20] Notwithstanding the shift in language from "study" to "assessment," both Acts offer similar levels of encouragement. Sections 22(1)(a)(ii) and (iii) of the *IAA* do identify the cumulative effects that are likely to result from a designated project in combination with other physical activities that have been or will be carried out, and the result of any interaction between those effects, as key factors that must be taken into account by the Agency or review panel. *CEAA 2012* included a similar requirement (section 19(1)), but it also noted that the significance of any cumulative effects must be considered. Ehrlich and Ross pointed out that ecological significance "should not be confused with significance in [environmental impact assessments], which may not only include ecological significance but also considers social values."[21]

Interestingly, notwithstanding the stated purpose of the *IAA* to encourage the assessment of cumulative effects and a clear message from the Expert Panel for the Review of Environmental Assessment Processes (Expert Panel) on the need to strengthen CEA at the federal level,[22] there is no other mention of cumulative effects in the Act other than the two provisions noted above. There is no direction provided as to the scope of what may be included when assessing cumulative effects (i.e., spatial, temporal), including how that scope is to be determined, and no consideration of "growth-inducing infrastructure" that one would expect to find in leading-edge assessment legislation.[23] For

18    SC 2012, c 19, s 52.

19    *IAA*, above note 3 at s 6(1)(m).

20    *CEAA 2012*, above note 18 at s 4(1)(i).

21    Alan Ehrlich & William Ross, "The Significance Spectrum and EIA Significance Determinations" (2015) 33:2 *Impact Assessment and Project Appraisal* 87.

22    Expert Panel for the Review of Environmental Assessment Processes, *Building Common Ground: A New Vision for Impact Assessment in Canada* (Ottawa: Canadian Environmental Assessment Agency, 2017), online (pdf): *Government of Canada* www.canada.ca/content/dam/themes/environment/conservation/environmental-reviews/building-common-ground/building-common-ground.pdf [*Building Common Ground*].

23    Chris J Johnson et al, "Growth-Inducing Infrastructure Represents Transformative Yet Ignored Keystone Environmental Decisions" (2020) 13:2 *Conservation Letters* 1.

many large-scale infrastructure projects, such as major energy projects or transportation corridors, a range of future expansion and ancillary developments often follow, each of which carries its own adverse social and environmental impacts.[24] Of course, similar to *CEAA 2012*, it may be that such direction is forthcoming by way of supporting regulations, a cumulative effects policy statement, or updated practitioner guidance. The most widely used guidance for CEA in Canada remains the practitioner guidance manual developed by Hegmann et al,[25] updated by the Canadian Environmental Assessment Agency in 2018 as "interim technical guidance" under *CEAA 2012*.[26] The Impact Assessment Agency of Canada's "Practitioner's Guide to Federal Impact Assessments Under the Impact Assessment Act,"[27] at the time of writing, does not provide CEA guidance or direct proponents to the existing "interim technical guidance" that is available.

Presumably, the intent under the *IAA* is that cumulative effects will be addressed, at least in part, by way of regional assessments. However, there is no explicit reference to cumulative effects in the Act in relation to regional assessment,[28] and neither are there mechanisms to trigger or

---

24 Reginald C Tricker, "Assessing Cumulative Environmental Effects from Major Public Transport Projects" (2007) 14:4 *Transport Policy* 293; Bram Noble, *Getting the Big Picture: How Regional Assessment Can Pave the Way for More Inclusive and Effective Environmental Assessments* (June 2017), online (pdf): *Macdonald-Laurier Institute* https:// macdonaldlaurier.ca/files/pdf/Noble_Aboriginal%233Study_FinalWeb.pdf.

25 George Hegmann et al, *Cumulative Effects Assessment Practitioners Guide* (Hull, QC: Canadian Environmental Assessment Agency, 1999).

26 Canadian Environmental Assessment Agency, *Assessing Cumulative Environmental Effects Under the Canadian Environmental Assessment Act, 2012* (Interim Technical Guidance), Version 2 (Ottawa: Canadian Environmental Assessment Agency, 2018), online: www.canada.ca/en/impact-assessment-agency/services/policy-guidance/assessing-cumulative-environmental-effects-ceaa2012.html.

27 Impact Assessment Agency of Canada, "Practitioner's Guide to Federal Impact Assessments Under the Impact Assessment Act" (2020), online: *Government of Canada* www.canada.ca/en/impact-assessment-agency/services/policy-guidance/practitioners-guide-impact-assessment-act.html.

28 Not all regional assessments in Canada adopt cumulative effects assessment as a central focus. See Jill Blakley et al, *Lessons Learned, Best Practices and Critical Gaps in Regional Environmental Assessment: A Synthesis of Canadian and International Literature* (2020), Final report prepared for the Knowledge Synthesis Grant Program, Social Sciences and Humanities Research Council of Canada and Impact Assessment Agency of Canada, online: www.sshrc-crsh.gc.ca/funding-financement/programs-programmes/ksg_environmental_and_impact_assessments-ssc_evaluations_environnementales_et_impacts-eng.aspx.

mandate a regional assessment that includes CEA.[29] The Expert Panel's report makes explicit reference to cumulative effects as the leading rationale for regional assessment. This is consistent with persistent messages from scholars and practitioners on the need for a regional approach to properly assess and manage cumulative effects.[30] In principle, regional assessments can ensure that regional issues are addressed upfront, not at the time projects are proposed. This would mean a more effective assessment of broader planning issues—including cumulative effects—subsequently shorter timelines for project reviews, and a clearer focus for proponents and decision makers.[31] Regional assessment does not dismiss proponents from their responsibilities to identify and appropriately manage the effects of their projects that contribute to cumulative effects, but it is broadly recognized that CEA and management extend well beyond the scope, mandate, and ability of any single project proponent.[32]

Sections 92 and 93 of the *IAA* provide the minister with discretionary powers to establish a committee—or authorize the Agency—to conduct a regional assessment of the effects of existing or future physical activities carried out in a region. Similar provisions for regional assessment existed under *CEAA 2012* (e.g., sections 73(1) and 74(1)), referred to then as "regional studies," even though no such studies have been completed under that Act. That said, the current agreement between Canada and Newfoundland and Labrador to conduct a regional assessment of offshore oil and gas exploratory drilling east of the province was

---

29    There is, however, a new mechanism for requesting regional assessments, which the minister must respond to within a prescribed period of time. This is undoubtedly a step forward.

30    See, for example, Jill Gunn & Bram Noble, "A Conceptual Basis and Methodological Framework for Regional Strategic Environmental Assessment (R-SEA)" (2009) 27 *Impact Assessment and Project Appraisal* 258; Monique G Dubé et al, "A Framework for Assessing Cumulative Effects in Watersheds: An Introduction to Canadian Case Studies" (2013) 9:3 *Integrated Environmental Assessment and Management* 363; Cheryl Chetkiewicz & Anastasia M Lintner, *Getting It Right in Ontario's Far North: The Need for a Regional Strategic Environmental Assessment in the Ring of Fire* (Thunder Bay and Toronto: WCS Canada & Ecojustice, 2014), online (pdf): www.wcscanada.org/Portals/96/Documents/ RSEA_Report_WCSCanada_Ecojustice_FINAL.pdf; A John Sinclair, Meinhard Doelle & Peter N Duinker, "Looking Up, Down, and Sideways: Reconceiving Cumulative Effects Assessment as a Mindset" (2017) 62 *Environmental Impact Assessment Review* 183.

31    Noble, above note 24.

32    Gunn & Noble, above note 30; Hegmann & Yarranton, above note 15; *Building Common Ground*, above note 22.

initiated in April 2019 under the provisions of *CEAA* 2012. The point is that the mere inclusion of provisions for discretionary regional assessment in the *IAA* does not mean that their use is necessarily assured, and the provision for regional assessment by itself is not an improvement over *CEAA* 2012. Although the minister must respond in a timely fashion to any request for an assessment as per section 97(1), the exercise of this power is also informed and arguably constrained by sections 6(1) to (3). This is inconsistent with a key recommendation of the Expert Panel, which explicitly stated that federal impact assessment legislation require "regional [impact assessments] where cumulative impacts may occur or already exist ... or where there are potential consequential impacts to matters of federal interest."[33]

However, regional assessments under the Act may offer something new compared to the regional study provision of *CEAA* 2012. In principle, regional assessments are far more than "studies" (i.e., research undertakings, reviews, and reports): they are designed to estimate the extent, quality, and severity of impacts; explore alternatives, land use, and development scenarios; and, ideally, establish the context and direction for regional development strategies, land use, and environmental management frameworks.[34] Arguments in favour of regional assessment are not new,[35] and neither are they academic. The Joint Review Panel for the Site C hydroelectric power–generating project in British Columbia, for example, raised many issues that were beyond the scope of a single project-focused assessment. Included in the panel's recommendations was a recommendation that the governments of British Columbia and Canada consider a more proactive and regional approach to land use planning and decision making about resource development.[36] However, there is no indication under the *IAA* as to whether and how regional assessments will differ from more traditional regional studies provided for, though not enacted, under *CEAA* 2012.

---

33   *Ibid* at 7.

34   West Coast Environmental Law & Northwest Institute, *Regional Strategic Environmental Assessment for Northern British Columbia: The Case and the Opportunity* (Vancouver, BC: West Coast Environmental Law and Northwest Institute, 2016).

35   See, for example, AJ Kennedy, ed, *Cumulative Effects Assessment in Canada: From Concept to Practice* (Calgary: Alberta Society of Professional Biologists, 1995).

36   Joint Review Panel, *Report of the Joint Review Panel: Site C Clean Energy Project*, BC Hydro and Power Authority (May 2014), online (pdf): www.ceaa-acee.gc.ca/050/documents/ p63919/99173E.pdf.

The scope for CEA under the *IAA* is not necessarily broader than it was under *CEAA 2012* as the definition of *environment* in both Acts is very similar. Under the *IAA*, "environment" means the components of the Earth and includes land, air, water, and atmosphere, as well as organic and inorganic matter and living organisms and interacting natural systems (see section 2). This definition of environment is congruent with the best-practice scope of cumulative effects, which include changes in the environment attributed to the interactions among human activities and natural processes that accumulate across space and time.[37] The reference to "organic matter" and "living organisms" in the definition of environment creates latitude for consideration of a wide range of human impacts, including Gender-based Analysis Plus (GBA+) impacts (see Chapter 12). However, under *CEAA 2012*, section 5 limited the scope of environmental effects to those within federal jurisdiction: fish and fish habitat, aquatic species at risk, migratory birds, federal lands, and Aboriginal peoples.[38] Although there is no equivalent to section 5 in the *IAA*, which instead relies entirely on the interpretation of effects within federal jurisdiction (section 2), the focus on those elements and the limiting result is the same.

The *IAA* requires that project assessments take into account positive and adverse effects, as well as direct and incidental effects. This also lends itself to CEA and suggests a role for regional assessment, which is typically needed to discern incidental or indirect effects that may occur at some distance from the project site. In this sense, the *IAA* is a modest step forward from *CEAA 2012*, which does not require attention to positive effects and considers incidental effects only in the context of federal permits. The challenge is that there is little to no empirical research documenting the positive environmental effects of projects (other than economic benefits), particularly in a CEA context, and therefore little guidance available about how to assess such effects. It is also challenging for project proponents to assess anything other than direct, immediate effects given constraints to project assessment processes. Tight timelines, limited budgets, and other factors — not the

37  "Canada-Wide Definitions and Principles for Cumulative Effects," above note 1.

38  Brenda Heelan Powell, "The Difference a Year Makes: Changes to Canadian Federal Environmental Assessment Law in 2012" *LawNow* (28 February 2013), online: www.lawnow.org/canadian-federal-environmental-assessment-law.

least of which are proponents' vested interests[39]—can work against the assessment of delayed or dispersed effects or potentially distort the assessment of positive effects, and there are limits to what proponents can realistically accomplish in any one project assessment. Similar to the *IAA*'s provisions for strategic environmental assessment, discussed in Chapter 17, there are no explicit criteria as to the scope or types of issues that a regional assessment would address or guidance around how proponents might ultimately resource them. The Expert Panel's final report suggests that regional assessment should be used to assess the cumulative impacts of all activities in a region such as a watershed or airshed and can play a major role in addressing "cumulative impacts on Indigenous communities and their ability to exercise their constitutionally-protected Aboriginal and treaty rights."[40] Presumably, a high degree of federal leadership or partnership will be needed to perform regional assessments.

Should a regional assessment be undertaken, any such assessment that is relevant to a project (applies to the region in which the project is located) becomes a mandatory factor for consideration pursuant to section 22. However, the *IAA* does not require any particular outcome from this consideration. That said, there are heightened requirements for transparency (e.g., detailed reasons for decisions) that could prompt dialogue about regional assessment results. The Act is silent about whether and how the results of a regional assessment must inform regulatory reviews or decisions. The outputs of any regional assessment must form useful and meaningful inputs to subsequent project assessments or there is little benefit to undertaking them. This is an established good practice in the impact assessment literature, known as "tiering."[41] The final report of the Expert Panel recommended that regional assessments "will inform and streamline project [impact assessment]" and "establish thresholds and objectives to be used in project [impact assessment] and federal decisions."[42] These and other funda-

---

39    *Building Common Ground*, above note 22 at 6 and 14.

40    *Ibid* at 76.

41    Jos Arts et al, "EIA and SEA Tiering: The Missing Link" in "International Experience and Perspectives in SEA," Conference of the International Association of Impact Assessment (2005) 26–30; Luis E Sánchez & Solange S Silva-Sánchez, "Tiering Strategic Environmental Assessment and Project Environmental Impact Assessment in Highway Planning in São Paulo, Brazil" (2008) 28:7 *Environmental Impact Assessment Review* 515.

42    *Building Common Ground*, above note 22 at 6–7.

mental matters of regional assessment, such as considering the need for a project assessment, setting benchmarks and guidance for assessing cumulative effects, identifying priority valued components and indicators, and establishing regional monitoring programs to guide project compliance and mitigations, are not assured under the *IAA*.

An enduring challenge to regional assessments as a means to tackle cumulative effects is that rarely is there authority to implement recommendations or to carry forward the findings to project assessments and decisions.[43] As a result, given no specific mechanisms to ensure that the results of a regional assessment directly influence decisions about individual project actions, there is high risk that many, if not all, regional assessments, to the extent that the minister decides to conduct them, will be one-off "studies" rather than true assessments and remain largely separate from regulatory decision making about project approvals. There is a history of disconnection between regional studies and impact assessment in Canada. Some of the best regional-scale assessments and CEAs have had little influence on project assessments. For example, the Great Sand Hills regional environmental study in Saskatchewan resulted in a strategic management plan to guide the land use activities that cumulatively affected the long-term ecological integrity and sustainability of the region. Yet one member of the overseeing Scientific Advisory Committee identified a need for improved "institutional support and tiering mechanisms." The lack of these factors limited the influence of the study over time.[44]

Finally, the *IAA* separates regional and strategic assessments when often, where the goal is to influence a natural resource development program, a regional-scale impact assessment can and does include a strategic element that is future focused and analyzes the relative desirability of multiple future state options.[45] Regional assessments of cumulative effects without a deliberate focus on future conditions

---

43   John R Parkins, "Deliberative Democracy, Institution Building, and the Pragmatics of Cumulative Effects Assessment" (2011) 16:3 *Ecology and Society* 20.

44   Bram Noble, "Strategic Approaches to Regional Cumulative Effects Assessment: A Case Study of the Great Sand Hills, Canada" (2008) 26:2 *Impact Assessment and Project Appraisal* 78 at 89.

45   Christopher Wood & Mohammed Dejeddour, "Strategic Environmental Assessment: EA of Policies, Plans and Programmes" (1992) 10:1 *Impact Assessment* 3; Bram Noble, "Strategic Environmental Assessment: What Is It? What Makes It Strategic?" (2000) 2:2 *Journal of Environmental Assessment Policy and Management* 203.

are ultimately retrospective in nature instead of prospective. Although useful for understanding past change and current baseline conditions and benchmarks, such an approach limits the ability to understand system responses to disturbances in the future, including those directly attributable to the project in question and to other future projects and actions within the regional environment. The Manitoba Hydro Regional Cumulative Effects Assessment, for example, which addressed the impacts of fifty-plus years of hydroelectric development on the Nelson River complex, did not include any prospective analysis. This was despite the fact that a major question regarding the future welfare of the environment and communities in northern Manitoba is the potential for more hydroelectric dams.[46] This assessment was also not explicitly connected to subsequent project assessments or decision making in any way. The *IAA* does not limit proponents from including a prospective element in regional assessment, and connection between the regional and strategic assessments via the Act should be promoted. We return to this point in Chapter 17.

## D. ACTIONS REQUIRED TO ENSURE EFFECTIVE IMPLEMENTATION OF CUMULATIVE EFFECTS ASSESSMENTS

The development of supporting regulations and practice guidance is needed to ensure cumulative and regional assessments conducted under the *IAA*. To begin, an updated, comprehensive CEA guidance document for Canadian practitioners must be developed to replace the existing interim guidance. Implementation guidance should clearly direct practitioners to this document. Importantly, new CEA guidance should include directives about how to document positive environmental effects and effects of a socio-cultural nature. Impacts to Indigenous lands, cultures, and livelihoods should be an area of special consideration.

Minor or moderately severe project impacts may, in fact, be deemed unacceptable when considerations are based on ecological limits or the spatial and temporal accumulation of change in the regional environment. However, such impacts are easily and routinely dismissed within

---

46    Jill Blakley & A Olagunju, *Critical Review of the Regional Cumulative Effects Assessment (RCEA) for Hydroelectric Developments on the Churchill, Burntwood and Nelson River Systems*, Technical report prepared for the Public Interest Law Centre, (Winnipeg, MB: 2017).

the scope and scale of a single project assessment and not subject to CEA.[47] Not only does this suggest the need for greater guidance and clarity for CEA application and design, it also suggests that the significance determination of project impacts may have to be altered when considered in a regional context. The level of disturbance in some regions may call for higher levels of sensitivity when determining whether a project's impacts are justified. Revised CEA practitioner guidance should promote a tighter coupling of project assessment with regional assessment in terms of requiring demonstrated project adaptations responsive to regional assessment outcomes and consideration of the regional development context. The importance of cooperative regional monitoring efforts with clearer triggers for intervention should also be stressed in guidance as a means to improve the outcomes of CEA performed in project-level assessment.

Regional assessment must be subject to mandatory triggering mechanisms under the *IAA*. Absent a genuinely legislative approach to regional assessments based on an objective legal test as opposed to largely unfettered ministerial discretion, CEA will not achieve its full potential. Although a new request mechanism for regional assessment has been introduced, an objective legal test for the triggering of mandatory regional assessments is needed that also includes clear guidance with respect to how these types of assessment will be conducted and how they will be used to inform project-level assessments. The current guidance about regional assessment approach and types of regional assessment is both broadly stated and very brief.[48] Without these reforms, it is difficult to see how the *IAA* will improve project-level assessments, including their capacity to effectively deal with cross-cutting challenges such as cumulative effects, as well as alternatives and broader policy issues.

Many of Canada's most important environmental decisions and policies, both current and past, are not subject to CEA because they

---

47  Bram Noble & Jill Gunn, *Review of KHLP's Approach to the Keeyask Generation Project Cumulative Effects Assessment* (Winnipeg, MB: 2013), Research report prepared for the Public Interest Law Centre on behalf of the Consumers Association of Canada (Manitoba Branch).

48  Impact Assessment Agency of Canada, "Regional Assessment Under the Impact Assessment Act" (September 2020), online: *Government of Canada* www.canada.ca/en/impact-assessment-agency/services/policy-guidance/regional-assessment-impact-assessment-act.html.

do not trigger project impact assessments. This applies to both significant projects that fall outside regulatory triggers or are designed as such and to the many small, dispersed, and non-federal developments and decisions that incrementally lead to some of society's most pressing cumulative effects issues, including climate change and impacts to Indigenous lands, cultures, and livelihoods.[49] For this reason, it is important that *IAA* implementation guidance establish that regional assessment should capture this broad range of activity and how regional assessments will differ (i.e., process, outputs) from more traditional regional studies provided for, though never conducted, under *CEAA* 2012. Unless specific regulatory mechanisms are in place to ensure that the results of a regional assessment directly influence decisions about individual project actions, there is a high risk that regional assessments, to the extent that the minister decides to conduct them, will be one-off "studies" rather than true assessments. The results of regional assessments, where they are completed, must be explicitly linked or "tiered" to project-specific terms of reference for designated projects. That said, striking the right balance between ensuring that the results of regional assessment are not ignored and leaving flexibility at the project level will be important.

There will be a need for ongoing work to keep regional assessments current and relevant to other decision-making processes. A regional assessment, like a regional plan, can become out of date if, for example, it does not anticipate a type of new activity in the region or because another activity has stopped unexpectedly. Therefore, a regulation requiring that adaptive management and learning and periodic reviews be embedded within regional assessment design is necessary for them to properly inform or direct CEA at the project level.

The weak performance of CEA in Canada to date, notwithstanding its nominal requirement in legislation, suggests that it is honoured more in the breach than in observance. Although regulatory reform and improved practitioner guidance are important steps in creating the preconditions for more effective implementation of CEA in Canada, these alone will likely prove insufficient. Equally important is mainstreaming

---

49 Bram Noble, "Cumulative Effects and the Tyranny of Small Decisions: Towards Meaningful Cumulative Effects Assessment and Management" (2014), Occasional Papers Series, Natural Resources and Environmental Studies Institute, University of Northern British Columbia.

what Sinclair, Doelle, and Duinker characterized as the "CEA mindset."[50] They argued that rather than dismissing CEA as a thorny distraction from the usual business of project-level assessments, CEA should be at the core of every assessment of environmental systems and components affected by human activity. Ideally, CEA should be conducted at the regional and strategic levels, but whatever the given level of assessment — project, sectoral, regional, or strategic — it is essential to adopt a holistic approach capable of considering cumulative effects across all levels.[51] Crucially, this means altering, if not abandoning, the predominant major-project approach to assessment in Canada. Designating only "major" projects, while exempting a great many others,[52] creates a siloed, project-by-project assessment process.[53] This significantly hinders practitioners' ability to assess cumulative effects and use CEA to facilitate the transition toward greater resilience and sustainability. For example, in Canada, major oil pipeline projects are assessed on a pipeline-by-pipeline basis, precluding a broader assessment of regional, national, and international energy and economic strategies and their trade-offs with environmental and socio-economic conditions and related dimensions of sustainability across multiple scales. When such issues are raised and vetted within project-based reviews, they tend to frustrate the assessment process and disappoint all parties involved.

Addressing this challenge, of course, is easier said than done. It is unclear whether and to what extent government regulators, practitioners, and project proponents understand and are prepared to adapt to the emerging nature of cumulative environmental impacts in the Anthropocene epoch.[54] Formal debates about its stratigraphic starting point aside, the Anthropocene is widely accepted as denoting a new epoch in which human beings, as geological agents, are the primary

---

50    Sinclair, Doelle & Duinker, above note 30.

51    Jill Harriman & Bram Noble, "Characterizing Project and Strategic Approaches to Regional Cumulative Effects Assessment in Canada" (2008) 10:1 *Journal of Environmental Assessment Policy and Management* 25.

52    Impact Assessment Agency of Canada, "Designating a Project under the Canadian Environmental Assessment Act, 2012" (March 2015), online: *Government of Canada* www.canada.ca/en/impact-assessment-agency/services/policy-guidance/designating-project-under-canadian-environmental-assessment-act-2012.html.

53    Wendy J Palen et al, "Consider the Global Impacts of Oil Pipelines" (2014) 510:7506 *Nature* 465.

54    Patrick Keys et al, "Anthropocene Risk" (2019) 2 *Nature Sustainability* 667.

driver of planetary change. Anthropocene impacts and risks originate from anthropogenic changes in key Earth-system functions, including climate change, land use changes, and biodiversity loss. They co-evolve with globally intertwined socio-ecological systems, which are often characterized by socio-economic inequality and injustice. For example, as the Expert Panel observed, Indigenous peoples in Canada bear the disproportionate brunt of exploitative natural resource extraction and development. Importantly, these developments exhibit complex cross-scale interactions, ranging from local to regional to global and short term to long term, potentially involving Earth-system tipping points and regime changes, such as the transformation of forests into savannahs. Emerging and evolving Anthropocene risks call for precisely the kind of holistic, cross-scale assessment embodied by CEA—one that regulatory impact assessment may ultimately be impotent to address.

## E. CONCLUSION

In several respects, the *IAA* fails to meet established good practices for cumulative and regional assessment in the literature and offers few, modest improvements over *CEAA 2012*. Provisions under the *IAA* differ little from those offered under previous legislation, notwithstanding a clear message from the Expert Panel, scholars, proponents, practitioners, and affected interests that project-based impact assessment is, alone, inadequate for assessing and managing cumulative environmental effects. The ability to commission regional assessments under the *IAA* is again only a modest step forward from *CEAA 2012*, which also provided for regional "studies." Still missing are the serious commitments and regulatory scaffolding needed to properly assess and manage cumulative effects via regional assessments and ensure that the results of regional assessments directly inform and benefit project-level reviews and decision making and that project-based assessments and monitoring programs also "tier up" to inform improved regional understanding. Project proponents are likely to remain frustrated by the demands placed on them to solve regional cumulative effects issues, and project-based assessments will continue to come up short on addressing the needs of CEA.

# CHAPTER 12

# Assessing the Intersections of Sex, Gender, and Other Identity Factors in the New Canadian *Impact Assessment Act*

*Heidi Walker and Maureen G Reed*

## A.  INTRODUCTION

Researchers, practitioners, and nearby residents have long understood that the benefits and burdens of resource development projects are not shared equally or equitably.[1] For example, women and men, Indigenous peoples and settler populations, senior citizens and youth, high- and low-income earners, and people living nearby or far away from developments will all experience the benefits and burdens of such projects differently. Additionally, development projects are often introduced into regions where residents may already feel excluded from many of the benefits of economic and social life that are taken for granted in other parts of Canada. Because some groups may be more disadvantaged to begin with, blanket efforts to address the negative impacts or share the positive impacts of development projects will not be received in the same way across these different groups. Researchers have suggested that if we do not pay attention to existing social contexts and power relationships before new resource developments are introduced, new development

---

1    Linda Archibald & Mary Crnkovich, *If Gender Mattered: A Case Study of Inuit Women, Land Claims and the Voisey's Bay Nickel Project* (Ottawa: Status of Women Canada, 1999); Sara O'Shaughnessy & Naomi T Krogman, "Gender as Contradiction: From Dichotomies to Diversity in Natural Resource Extraction" (2011) 27:2 *Journal of Rural Studies* 134; Erik Kojola, "Indigeneity, Gender and Class in Decision-Making About Risks from Resource Extraction" (2019) 5:2 *Environmental Sociology* 130.

projects may simply exacerbate pre-existing inequalities (e.g., employment and income inequality, social marginalization, and exclusion) rather than reduce them.[2] This realization is at the heart of impact assessment (IA) that accounts for the "intersections of sex, gender, and other identity factors," as required in the Canadian *Impact Assessment Act (IAA)*.[3]

Canada has been committed to applying gender-based analysis to federal policies, programs, and legislation since at least 1995 when it ratified the United Nations' Beijing Declaration and Platform for Action for working toward gender equality.[4] The first formal requirement — though not a legislated requirement — for gender-based analysis in Canadian environmental assessment occurred in 1997 for a proposed nickel mine at Voisey's Bay, Newfoundland and Labrador. The designated environmental assessment panel for the project drafted the environmental impact statement guidelines, through which it required the proponent to consider how the project would differently affect men and women.[5] This was a progressive step, resulting in the inclusion of some gender-disaggregated data in the environmental assessment report. Several deficiencies, however, were noted: limited opportunities for women's organizations to meaningfully participate, the prioritization of men's traditional ecological knowledge, and "very little analysis or insight into how the differential impacts affect *Inuit* women."[6] From that time to the implementation of the *IAA*, gender-based analysis in Canadian assessments has been directed only on an ad hoc basis and without standardization from one project to the next.

Since the 1990s, Women and Gender Equality Canada (formerly Status of Women Canada) has clarified that other identity attributes of women and men, such as age, education, geography, culture, language,

---

2    See, for example, Amnesty International, *Out of Sight, Out of Mind: Gender, Indigenous Rights, and Energy Development in Northeast British Columbia, Canada* (London, UK: Amnesty International, 2016), online: www.amnesty.ca/outofsight; Christine Hill, Chris Madden & Nina Collins, *A Guide to Gender Impact Assessment for the Extractive Industries* (Melbourne: Oxfam, 2017), online: https://policy-practice.oxfam.org.uk/publications/a-guide-to-gender-impact-assessment-for-the-extractive-industries-620782; Elana Nightingale et al, "The Effects of Resource Extraction on Inuit Women and Their Families: Evidence from Canada (2017) 25:3 *Gender & Development* 367.

3    SC 2019, c 28, s 22.

4    Erin Skinner, "Lessons from the Field: Policy Matters and Gender-Based Analysis Tools in Canada" (Halifax: Maritime Centre of Excellence for Women's Health, December 1998).

5    Archibald and Crnkovich, above note 1.

6    *Ibid* at 23 & 24 [emphasis added].

and income, should also be considered in gender-based analysis. In 2015, the federal government renewed its commitments to Gender-based Analysis Plus (GBA+), a framework that recognizes the intersections of gender with diverse identity attributes, across federal departments, policy, legislation, and initiatives.[7] The key active section of the *IAA* related to gender and diversity specifies that an IA of a designated project must account for "the intersection of sex and gender with other identity factors."[8] This requirement was not without controversy and received vocal support and opposition throughout the review and consultation phases following the introduction of Bill C-69, the legislative proposal that replaced the former *Canadian Environmental Assessment Act, 2012*, with the new *IAA*. Despite the challenges, its passing provides opportunities for understanding and addressing a broad range of environmental and social effects of policies, plans, or projects.

In August 2019, the Impact Assessment Agency of Canada released an interim guidance document that provides initial direction for meeting section 22 requirements.[9] The guidelines reiterate that the GBA+ requirement, like other section 22 requirements, will be scoped through the Tailored Impact Statement Guidelines at the end of the early engagement phase,[10] although it also clarifies that GBA+ should be integrated throughout the entire IA process—from early planning to follow-up and compliance. The document does not prescribe a specific methodology for GBA+ in IA but does provide broad steps for its application, including understanding GBA+ and the context in which the proposed project is situated, early engagement with diverse social groups, establishing a baseline, and assessing potential effects across subgroups within communities. A list of best practices provides direction for ensuring that GBA+ is respectful, inclusive, critical, and context specific. The document outlines five expectations that will guide the determination of GBA+ completion: GBA+ findings are integrated

---

7   Status of Women Canada, "Government of Canada's Approach: Gender-based Analysis Plus" (4 December 2018), online: *Government of Canada* https://cfc-swc.gc.ca/gba-acs/ approach-approche-en.html.

8   Above note 3, s 22(1)(s).

9   Impact Assessment Agency of Canada, "Guidance: Gender-based Analysis Plus in Impact Assessment" (2019), online: *Government of Canada* www.canada.ca/en/impact-assessment-agency/services/policy-guidance/practitioners-guide-impact-assessment-act/gender-based-analysis.html ["Interim Guidance"].

10   *IAA*, above note 3, s 18(1.1).

throughout the impact statement; project effects have been considered for diverse subgroups; there has been a thorough presentation of data; where relevant, mitigation measures respond to GBA+ findings; and GBA+ findings inform indicators for follow-up.

The *IAA* requirement is a promising mechanism for more consistent application of gender and diversity analysis across designated projects. It provides a significant opportunity to ensure that the benefits of proposed projects are distributed more equitably and the burdens are minimized across a broader spectrum of society. Such outcomes, however, are possible only if analyses are employed not simply as stand-alone checkbox activities but as potentially transformative tools that can challenge existing inequalities and power relationships in the local context. In this chapter, we first draw from feminist and resource management scholarship to identify key trends important to the understanding and realization of good-practice gender and diversity analysis. As noted, the federal government uses the specific GBA+ framework to guide evaluation of its policies and programs with explicit recognition of gender and other intersecting social factors. Feminist scholars employ the term *intersectionality* (and multiple intersectional frameworks) to describe the intersections of social and structural factors that affect and are affected by resource developments. We have chosen to use the term *gender and diversity analysis* from a range of possibilities because we feel it will be best understood by the widest group of people. We then turn to frameworks and methodologies for undertaking gender and diversity analysis and identify several key considerations for its application in the context of the *IAA* requirements.

## B. THEORETICAL FOUNDATIONS FOR GENDER AND DIVERSITY ANALYSIS

Feminist theorists, whose work underlies gender and diversity analysis, have adopted the term *intersectionality* to describe the multiple intersecting factors that account for experiences of privilege and marginalization experienced by a range of social groups. The term is credited to Black feminist scholar Kimberlé Crenshaw,[11] who argued that Black

---

11  Kimberlé Crenshaw, "Demarginalizing the Intersection of Race and Sex: A Black Feminist Critique of Antidiscrimination Doctrine, Feminist Theory and Antiracist Politics" (1989) 1989:1 *University of Chicago Legal Forum* 139.

women face multiple *intersecting* axes of discrimination, and these factors are not "additive" but rather are experienced simultaneously. Her analysis of how gender intersects with other social attributes challenged feminist scholars to reconsider how privilege and power operate within feminism and within society at large. As Olena Hankivsky stated, "Intersectionality promotes an understanding of human beings as shaped by the interaction of different social locations [and identities] (e.g., 'race'/ethnicity, Indigeneity, gender, class, sexuality, geography, age, disability/ability, migration status, religion)."[12]

But intersectionality does not simply focus on intersections across social locations and identities. Hankivsky went on to say,

> [T]hese interactions occur within a context of connected systems and structures of power (e.g., laws, policies, state governments and other political and economic unions, religious institutions, media). Through such processes, interdependent forms of privilege and oppression shaped by colonialism, imperialism, racism, homophobia, ableism and patriarchy are created.[13]

Although intersections occur horizontally across multiple axes of social locations and identities, they also occur vertically across multiple axes of social structures, institutions, and norms. We consider these social structures, institutions, and norms both formal laws and informal "rules in use"[14] that structure our everyday lives. Often the informal rules and norms are most difficult to address because they are taken for granted and are often invisible. In the context of IA, this consideration of the vertical intersections across social structures, institutions, and norms marks the key point of departure from standard, and likely more familiar, social IA. Like gender and diversity analysis, social IA accounts for horizontal intersections through its attention to differing impacts on and the needs, interests, and values of diverse subgroups

---

12   Olena Hankivsky, *Intersectionality 101* (Vancouver, BC: Institute for Intersectionality Research & Policy, Simon Fraser University, 2014) at 2, online (pdf): *Violence Against Women Forum* http://vawforum-cwr.ca/sites/default/files/attachments/intersectionallity_101.pdf.

13   *Ibid* at 2.

14   Douglass C North, *Institutions, Institutional Change and Economic Performance* (Cambridge, UK: Cambridge University Press, 1990).

within communities as relevant to the proposed project.[15] Gender and diversity analysis can add value to such assessments through increased attention to complex and evolving local histories, social structures, and power dynamics that a project simultaneously shapes and is shaped by (i.e., its vertical intersections).[16]

Government frameworks seeking to adopt an intersectional approach, such as the federal government's GBA+ framework, have also typically placed greater emphasis on the first point, intersecting social factors,[17] although there is evidence that consideration of broader structures is now being introduced into the *IAA* guiding documents.[18] Contemporary gender and resource development literature reinforces the importance of paying attention to horizontal *and* vertical intersections. In this context, social structures, institutions, and norms across household, community, regional, national, and global scales contribute to inequalities in how diverse groups use natural resources, as well as the degree to which they can access employment and influence decision making about the resources.[19] We agree that effective gender and divers-

---

15 Frank Vanclay, "International Principles for Social Impact Assessment" (2003) 21:1 *Impact Assessment and Project Appraisal* 5; Ana Maria Esteves, Daniel Franks & Frank Vanclay, "Social Impact Assessment: The State of the Art" (2012) 30:1 *Impact Assessment and Project Appraisal* 34; Frank Vanclay et al, *Social Impact Assessment: Guidance for Assessing and Managing the Social Impacts of Projects* (Fargo, ND: International Association for Impact Assessment, 2015), online (pdf): www.iaia.org/uploads/pdf/SIA_Guidance_Document_IAIA.pdf.

16 Margarita Serje, "Social Relations: A Critical Reflection on the Notion of Social Impacts as Change" (2017) 65 *Environmental Impact Assessment Review* 139.

17 Carol Bacchi, "Gender/ing Impact Assessment: Can It Be Made to Work?" in Carol Bacchi & Joan Eveline, eds, *Mainstreaming Politics: Gendering Practices and Feminist Theory* (Adelaide, AU: University of Adelaide Press, 2010) 112.

18 Impact Assessment Agency of Canada, "Interim Guidance" above note 9.

19 Conny Roggeband & Mieke Verloo, "Evaluating Gender Impact Assessment in the Netherlands (1994–2004): A Political Process Approach" (2006) 34:4 *Policy & Politics* 615; O'Shaughnessy & Krogman, above note 1; Jane Stinson & Leah Levac, "Requiring Gender Based Analysis Plus (GBA+) and Participatory Research Principles in Environmental Assessments," FemNorthNet submission to the Expert Panel for the Review of Environmental Assessment Processes (December 2016), online: http://docplayer.net/159925390-Requiring-gender-based-analysis-plus-gba-and-participatory-research-principles-in-environmental-assessments-executive-summary.html; Carol J Pierce Colfer, Bimbika Sijapati Basnett & Markus Ihalainen, *Making Sense of 'Intersectionality': A Manual for Lovers of People and Forests* (2018) Occasional Paper 184, online (pdf): *Center for International Forestry Research* www.cifor.org/publications/pdf_files/OccPapers/OP-184.pdf; Deborah Stienstra et al, "Generating Prosperity, Creating Crisis: Impacts

ity analysis in IA must also consider the second point: intersecting structural factors.

To demonstrate, we use the example of employment. Women continue to be under-represented in resource industries. When they are employed, they are often consigned to lower-status positions that have traditionally been classified as "women's work" (e.g., cooking, housekeeping, and administration). Typically, these jobs are lower paid and offer less stable employment. Women who secure "non-traditional" jobs often face harassment or discrimination, as well as barriers to training and advancement.[20] Gender is not, of course, the only axis of identity that shapes these outcomes. Although non-Indigenous women are more likely to be represented in clerical and administrative positions, Indigenous women are often excluded from those jobs and are more likely to be represented in the lowest-status jobs, such as housekeeping and cooking.[21] Such jobs place Indigenous women at greater risk of sexual harassment or sexual violence because of the time spent in male-dominated living spaces. To explain these differential experiences, Manning, among others, explained that systems of power, such as racism, sexism, and colonization, affect employment opportunities and barriers.[22]

Formal and informal institutions operating at different scales also play a part in determining the employment prospects for women and men. A proposed project may also reinforce or alter existing gendered roles, norms, and relationships within households and, at a higher level of organization, within communities. Relationships at household and community levels affect one another and influence who is in a position

---

of Resource Development on Diverse Groups in Northern Communities" (2019) 54:2 *Community Development Journal* 215; Kojola, above note 1.

20 Joni Parmenter, "Experiences of Indigenous Women in the Australian Mining Industry" in Kuntala Lahiri-Dutt, ed, *Gendering the Field: Towards Sustainable Livelihoods for Mining Communities* (Canberra: ANU E Press, 2011) 67; Suzanne Mills, Martha Dowsley & Emilie Cameron, *Gender in Research on Northern Resource Development* (2013), online (pdf): *Yukon Research Centre* http://yukonresearch.yukoncollege.yk.ca/wpmu/wp-content/uploads/sites/2/2013/09/14-Gender-and-Res-Dev-Chapter-May-31-20132.pdf; David Cox & Suzanne Mills, "Gendering Environmental Assessment: Women's Participation and Employment Outcomes at Voisey's Bay" (2015) 68:2 *Arctic* 246.

21 *Ibid.*

22 Susan Manning, "Feminist Intersectional Policy Analysis: Resource Development and Extraction Framework" (2014), online: *Canadian Research Institute for the Advancement of Women* http://fnn.criaw-icref.ca/en/product/fipa-framework#.XebCbuhKjIU.

to take up employment opportunities. For example, higher wages and rates of employment secured by men in resource industries have, paradoxically, left women with whom they are in relationships with less influence on *household* decisions around how resources and revenues are used.[23] Job opportunities that have been offered to men, particularly those with extended shift-work schedules away from the home community, have also placed more pressure on women to continue to take on a greater proportion of caring and domestic responsibilities within their households.[24] In some cases, women may also take on additional civic and community responsibilities because their partners are not available.[25] Household dynamics, therefore, reinforce a highly gendered division of paid and unpaid labour in both households and communities and affect opportunities for women with children to seek paid employment in resource-based industries.

Although consideration of *all* systems of power and institutions falls well outside the scope of an IA, identifying and considering relevant axes can deepen analysis and point to more equitable mitigation and enhancement strategies. For example, resource developers operating in northern Canada might do well to consider how colonization and sexism have worked together to marginalize or exclude Indigenous women and men from different types of employment opportunities within their sector (Box 12.1).

---

23 Adriana Eftimie, Katherine Heller & John Strongman, *Gender Dimensions of the Extractive Industries: Mining for Equity* (Washington, DC: The World Bank, 2009); Deanna Kemp & Julia Keenan, *Why Gender Matters: A Resource Guide for Integrating Gender Considerations into Communities Work at Rio Tinto* (Melbourne: Rio Tinto, 2009); Hill, Madden & Collins, above note 2.

24 Jennifer Koshan, "Bills C-68 and C-69 and the Consideration of Sex, Gender and Other Identity Factors" (2 May 2018), online (blog): *ABlawg* https://ablawg.ca/wp-content/uploads/2018/05/Blog_JK_Bills_C68_69.pdf; Mills, Dowsley & Cameron, above note 20.

25 Alison M Gill, "Women in Isolated Resource Towns: An Examination of Gender Differences in Cognitive Structures" (1990) 21:3 *Geoforum* 347.

**BOX 12.1   DO SOCIAL FACTORS AND SYSTEMS OF POWER INFLUENCE THESE OUTCOMES?**

In the Canadian mining sector, an estimated 83 percent of Indigenous workers are in trades and labour, whereas only 8 percent act as supervisors, coordinators, or foremen and only 2 percent are in management roles. These numbers remain unchanged since 2001.[26] More than twice as many Indigenous women hold university degrees, trade school certificates, or college diplomas as Indigenous men. Yet Indigenous women are typically in underemployed positions (in forest nurseries or gathering forest products) and have the lowest median incomes in the forest sector. Women living on reserve make even less than those who live off reserve.[27]

How might structural factors such as racism, sexism, and gender norms account for some of these differences? Will an IA for a new resource development reinforce or address these inequalities? Can governments and industry work together to alleviate such adverse effects?

Structural and identity factors may enable some groups and disable others, although the factors will likely change over time and place. Employment is just one area of consideration. The introduction of projects, within the context of existing structures, institutions, and norms, may also result in differential social impacts (e.g., access to social services, health care, and affordable housing), cultural losses, and barriers for participation in decision making across and within communities. In the case of the latter, gender and diversity analysis in IA considers the factors that influence who supports and who opposes resource projects, what groups have the resources and ability to participate effectively, and how companies engage local communities. Structural barriers, such as norms about who should speak publicly about community concerns or which types of knowledge are valued over others, are built into the fabric of everyday life and are often invisible to those who benefit from them. These dynamics are context specific. If gender and diversity analysis frameworks employ a deeper analysis of structures, institutions, and norms, they can help build more inclusive IA processes and reveal historical and contemporary injustices so that new developments

26   Bipasha Baruah, *Barriers and Opportunities for Women's Employment in Natural Resources Industries in Canada* (Ottawa: Natural Resources Canada, 2018).

27   Sandrine Devillard et al, "The Power of Parity: Advancing Women's Equality in Canada" (21 June 2017), online: *McKinsey Global Institute* www.mckinsey.com/featured-insights/gender-equality/the-power-of-parity-advancing-womens-equality-in-canada#.

can be designed to avoid reinforcing pre-existing social inequalities. In the following section, we present a few select frameworks that support this deeper kind of analysis.

## C.  FRAMEWORKS AND METHODOLOGIES FOR GENDER AND DIVERSITY ANALYSIS

Several frameworks for gender and diversity analysis have been developed for broad application at regional, national, or international scales. Other frameworks have been developed specifically for application to IA and resource development projects.[28] Many of these frameworks provide suggested steps, as well as specific tools and methodologies, for conducting gender and diversity analysis in IA. We have provided a brief description of six of these frameworks in Table 12.1 and draw attention to a few examples below.

---

28  See, for example, Mieke Verloo & Conny Roggeband, "Gender Impact Assessment: The Development of a New Instrument in the Netherlands" (1996) 14:1 *Impact Assessment* 3; Marie Crawley & Louise O'Meara, *Gender Proofing Handbook: An Initiative of Six County Development Boards* (Dublin: Gender Equality Unit of the Department of Justice, Equality and Law Reform, 2002); Carol Bacchi & Joan Eveline, "Approaches to Gender Mainstreaming: What's the Problem Represented to Be?" in Carol Bacchi & Joan Eveline, eds, *Mainstreaming Politics: Gendering Practices and Feminist Theory* (Adelaide: University of Adelaide Press, 2010) 17; European Institute for Gender Equality, *Gender Impact Assessment: Gender Mainstreaming Toolkit* (Luxembourg: Publications Office of the European Union, 2017), online: https://eige.europa.eu/publications/gender-impact-assessment-gender-mainstreaming-toolkit; Status of Women Canada, above note 7.

**TABLE 12.1 GENDER AND DIVERSITY FRAMEWORKS FOR IA AND RESOURCE DEVELOPMENT PROJECTS**[29]

| Framework | Framework Purpose and Description |
| --- | --- |
| *Making Sense of 'Intersectionality': A Manual for Lovers of People and Forests*[30] | • *Purpose*: more effectively incorporate diverse voices, gender, and other equity concerns into forest management and research<br>• Suggests six steps for conducting an intersectional analysis |
| *A Guide to Gender Impact Assessment for the Extractive Industries*[31] | • *Purpose*: guidance for identifying and understanding the gender impacts of extractive industry projects in order to work toward gender equality<br>• Provides a four-step gender IA framework that includes templates and guiding questions |
| Inuit-specific, gender-based analysis[32] | • *Purpose*: outlines a tool for understanding unequal relationships between men and women in Inuit cultural contexts; the framework is situated within the ongoing socio-cultural and historical effects of colonization<br>• Applies framework to examine the gendered social impacts of resource extraction in Qamani'tuaq, Nunavut |
| *Feminist Intersectional Policy Analysis: Resource Development and Extraction Framework*[33] | • *Purpose*: help identify different impacts on women and other marginalized members of communities living at the intersection of multiple inequalities<br>• Outlines a framework for conducting a feminist intersectional policy analysis of a resource development or extraction project (primarily *ex post* evaluation based on review of documentation)<br>• Provides sensitizing questions and subquestions about how relationships of power operate within policy- and decision-making processes |

29  Adapted from Heidi Walker, Maureen G Reed & Bethany Thiessen, *Gender and Diversity Analysis in Impact Assessment* (February 2019), Report prepared for the Canadian Environmental Assessment Agency, online (pdf): *University of Saskatchewan* https:// research-groups.usask.ca/reed/documents/CEAA%20Report.FINAL.%20Walker%20 Reed%20Thiessen.%20Gender%20Diversity%20in%20IA.Feb%208%202019.pdf.

30  Colfer, Basnett & Ihalainen, above note 19.

31  Hill, Madden & Collins, above note 2.

32  Nightingale et al, above note 2.

33  Manning, above note 22.

| Framework | Framework Purpose and Description |
| --- | --- |
| Mainstreaming gender into extractive industries projects[34] | • *Purpose*: guidance for identifying ways that World Bank extractive industry projects impact men and women differently and understanding whether the benefits of a project outweigh the risks for both men and women<br>• Provides checklists of gender sensitizing of questions to ask throughout all project phases |
| *Why Gender Matters: A Resource Guide for Integrating Gender Considerations into Communities Work at Rio Tinto*[35] | • *Purpose*: "how to" guidance for integrating gender considerations through all stages and functions of Rio Tinto's work and projects<br>• Provides a four-part conceptual framework where inclusive engagement is a cross-cutting theme; includes sensitizing questions and checklists for guidance |

Some frameworks respond to the need for culturally relevant gender and diversity analysis. For example, Nightingale and colleagues explained that the experiences of Inuit women in northern Canada are "both broadly and deeply impacted by resource extraction activities, particularly at the intersection of gender with race, class, culture, and language."[36] They adopted an Inuit-specific, gender-based analysis framework to demonstrate how specific impacts across these intersections were influenced by broader structural factors associated with colonization. FemNorthNet, a project of the Canadian Research Institute for the Advancement of Women, informed IA practice through policy briefs that explained who benefits and who bears the cost of "sustainable" economic development in northern Canada.[37] They observed that there is now "compelling evidence that the negative effects of resource development are experienced most often and profoundly by women, Indigenous peoples, people living in poverty, people with disabilities, and other marginalized groups"[38] and "resource development that destroys or pollutes land also harms Indigenous communities

---

34  Eftimie, Heller & Strongman, above note 23.

35  Kemp & Keenan, above note 23.

36  Nightingale et al, above note 2 at 380.

37  See, for example, Manning, above note 22.

38  Barbara Clow et al, "Gender-Based Analysis Meets Environmental Assessment: Aligning Policy Mechanisms to Address the Resource Development in Canada's North" (2016) at 1, online: *Canadian Research Institute for the Advancement of Women* http:// fnn.criaw-icref.ca/en/product/gba-meets-environmental-assessment#.Xojyo4hKg2w.

by diminishing food sources and interfering with cultural and family practices."[39] Their framework specifically addresses how power relationships influenced decision making in this context.

Other frameworks explicitly integrate an institutional perspective into gender and diversity analysis.[40] For example, Colfer and colleagues considered how global and local structures and institutions marginalize or empower diverse groups in specific ways.[41] Their framework identified six steps by which institutions influence development, with the aim of generating more equitable policies and institutions. Hill and colleagues noted that diverse social institutions "discriminate against women (deliberately or not) and perpetuate gender inequality. Through their interactions with these institutions, mining, oil and gas companies may inadvertently condone or tolerate discrimination against women."[42] They suggested a two-part institutional analysis whereby the proponent identifies relevant institutions (e.g., family, community, market, state, religion) and asks questions about how a proposed project might interact with these institutions in ways that exacerbate or overcome gender inequality.


## D.  INCLUSIVE ENGAGEMENT

A common theme found in all frameworks is the need for inclusive engagement throughout an IA and for the life cycle of a project. Although much research has been done in relation to public participation in IA,[43] concerns remain about how consultation and engagement processes reinforce existing social inequalities and power relationships. Historically marginalized groups (e.g., women and girls, Indigenous peoples, seniors, recent immigrants) are generally more likely to be excluded from engagement processes, and this contributes to a lack of equity in the distribution of the benefits and negative impacts of resource development. It is important to recognize that these groups are not just passive victims of the negative impacts associated with

---

39  *Ibid* at 2.
40  Hill, Madden & Collins, above note 2; Colfer, Basnett & Ihalainen, above note 19.
41  Colfer, Basnett & Ihalainen, above note 19.
42  Hill, Madden & Collins, above note 2 at 12.
43  See, for example, chapters 15, 19, and 22.

resource development.[44] Indeed, although some people may be privileged in some contexts and marginalized in others, all are holders of important and relevant knowledge that can contribute to IA decision processes. Nevertheless, they may also experience barriers to participation that are structurally determined.[45]

Some studies note that consultation and engagement activities in IA, particularly those conducted in northern communities, often focus on concerns and impacts associated with what are typically considered male land-based activities, such as hunting, trapping, and fishing. Activities more typically associated with women, such as berry picking and medicine gathering, may be marginalized or omitted altogether.[46] Environmental impacts of resource development may also impact cultural and spiritual connections to the land, which can affect men and women in different ways.[47] The choice of focus shapes who and what knowledge are included in IAs, whose impacts are considered and mitigated, and the processes by which decisions are made. Gender and diversity analysis helps reveal effects that go beyond individual identity and focus on broader cultural norms and institutions.

In another example, Kojola's review of the assessment process for a copper-nickel mining project in northern Minnesota revealed logistical

---

44  See, for example, Roggeband & Verloo, above note 19; Kuntala Lahiri-Dutt & Nesar Ahmad, "Considering Gender in Social Impact Assessment" in Frank Vanclay & Ana Maria Esteves, eds, *New Directions in Social Impact Assessment: Conceptual and Methodological Advances* (Cheltenham and Northampton, UK: Edward Elgar, 2010) 117; Ciaran O'Faircheallaigh, "Women's Absence, Women's Power: Indigenous Women and Negotiations with Mining Companies in Australia and Canada" (2013) 36:11 *Ethnic and Racial Studies* 1789; Stienstra et al, above note 19; Sheena Kennedy Dalseg et al, "Gendered Environmental Assessments in the Canadian North: Marginalization of Indigenous Women and Traditional Economies" (2018) 47 *The Northern Review* 135.

45  Kojola, above note 1.

46  Mills, Dowsley & Cameron, above note 20; Kiri Staples & David Natcher, "Gender, Critical Mass, and Natural Resource Co-Management in the Yukon" (2015) 41 *The Northern Review* 139; Tara L Joly & Clinton Westman, "Taking Research Off the Shelf: Impacts, Benefits, and Participatory Processes Around the Oil Sands Industry in Northern Alberta," Final report for the SSHRC Imaging Canada's Future Initiative, Knowledge Synthesis Grants: Aboriginal Peoples (11 September 2017) [unpublished], online: https://artsandscience.usask.ca/cdprofile/download.php?fileid=192; Kojola, above note 1.

47  Konstantia Koutouki, Katherine Lofts & Giselle Davidian, "A Rights-Based Approach to Indigenous Women and Gender Inequities in Resource Development in Northern Canada" (2018) 27:1 *Review of European, Comparative & International Environmental Law* 63.

barriers that prevented Indigenous peoples, women, and those of lower socio-economic status from attending, while power dynamics at public hearings reduced the efficacy of the participation by those who did attend.[48] He noted that most meetings were held well away from Indigenous communities. Whereas workers in construction unions were provided with transportation to and from the meetings, none was provided to Indigenous groups that relied on wild rice harvesting in the affected area. All meetings were held in the evening, which required people to bring their children or find child care. People were expected to present fact-based arguments and evidence rather than political or moral claims. They were given three minutes to speak in front of a government panel and required to make only "short declarative statements."[49] One Ojibwe woman gave a passionate and emotional speech that "sparked applause from the crowd, but the moderator quickly asked the crowd to be quiet — it was a violation of rules and norms of being unemotional."[50] As a consequence of these restrictions, most people who spoke were representatives of environmental organizations or scientific and legal experts rather than community members.

These meeting norms and rules reinforced other gaps noted in the final environmental impact statement for this project. For example, the public health risks of the mining activity, particularly for Indigenous peoples who rely on fish that might be contaminated (including elevated risks to pregnant women and children), were not considered. Knowledge provided by Indigenous community members, including elders, women, wild rice harvesters, and fishers, was largely absent:

> Assessments of impacts to wild rice was largely based on government data and modeling, not the direct experiences of wild rice harvesters and elders ... Written comments from Ojibwe bands included alternative data about wild rice that was based on experiential knowledge but this was not incorporated into the official calculations or conclusions. The EIS stated that it was difficult to determine how Ojibwe people used the area because of a lack of specific data that limited quantitative analysis.[51]

---

48   Kojola, above note 1.
49   *Ibid* at 9.
50   *Ibid.*
51   *Ibid* at 10.

These findings suggest that gender and diversity analysis integrated early and throughout can help build inclusive IA processes that align with the core principles of meaningful public engagement and create opportunities for enhancing distributive justice.[52]

## E. MOVING FORWARD WITH GENDER AND DIVERSITY ANALYSIS IN CANADIAN IMPACT ASSESSMENT

There are still very few applications of gender and diversity analysis frameworks in IA processes, including in Canada. Newfoundland and Labrador is the only provincial jurisdiction that explicitly mandates gender-based analysis in IA, but even then it is limited to employment equity considerations.[53] Globally, there are a few examples of how specific resource development companies have applied gender and diversity analysis to their operations (e.g., Rio Tinto);[54] many of the frameworks in Table 12.1 also provide suggested tools and methods that can contribute to effective gender and diversity analysis. However, concrete examples of robust analyses in IA are extremely rare in the academic and grey literature. Most commonly, empirical studies undertake *ex post* assessments to explain how gender and diversity could have been integrated into IA processes.[55] Several of these restate the importance of documenting the experiences of women—most often Indigenous women—in resource development and IA processes. The observation by Stienstra and colleagues, however, remains true: "[T]he literature does not significantly address several groups including people with disabilities, immigrants, homeless populations, people who identify with LGBTQ or two-spirit communities, and men."[56] These groups have also typically been left out of IA. How they might be included remains important. For proponents, consultants, and regulators, this will require knowledge of emerging research, developing strong understandings of the local contexts in which they work, and building

---

52    See Chapter 15, Section A.

53    See Clow et al, above note 38.

54    See, for example, Kemp & Keenan, above note 23.

55    See, for example, Archibald & Crnkovich, above note 1; Cox & Mills, above note 20; Kennedy Dalseg et al, above note 44; Nightingale et al, above note 2; Melina Ey, "'Soft, Airy Fairy Stuff'? Re-evaluating 'Social Impacts' in Gendered Processes of Natural Resource Extraction" (2018) 27 *Emotions, Space, and Society* 1; Kojola, above note 1.

56    Stienstra et al, above note 19 at 6–7.

opportunities for sharing best practices and experiences in facilitating inclusive engagement.

As we have argued throughout this chapter, effective analysis should identify not just the horizontal intersections of static categories (e.g., men, women) and differences between them but also how designated projects play a role in shaping or reinforcing existing power dynamics and social inequalities. Encouragingly, the interim guidance for GBA+ in IA to some extent supports this direction. Its introduction, for example, emphasizes that

> historical and current power structures (e.g., laws, policies, governments and other institutions) have shaped society and created inequalities ... Recognizing this context is important to understand why impacts may be different for diverse groups of people and how projects have the potential to both reinforce and transform existing inequalities and unequal power relations in communities.[57]

It also clarifies that best-practice analysis under the *IAA* "should move beyond the descriptive (e.g., percentage of low-income people) to ask critical questions about social roles, relationships, relative power in communities and intersections among these factors that create disparities."[58] Despite this positive direction, the rubric outlining expectations for GBA+ in the interim guidance—to date the only publicly available criteria for the assessment of gender and diversity analysis completeness—focuses primarily on the horizontal intersections of identity. It asks for evidence that diverse subgroups have been considered throughout the IA process but does not explicitly ask for findings about how social structures, institutions, and norms may interact with the proposed project to produce differential (positive or negative) outcomes for diverse groups (i.e., the vertical intersections). As there is still limited experience with gender and diversity analysis within IA processes in Canada, particularly relating to these structural issues, strong enforcement, continual review, and adaptive learning will be needed as this component becomes more integrated into policy and practice. Some *ex post* gender and diversity analysis frameworks provide guiding questions for determining analysis completeness, including of

---

57    *Interim Guidance*, above note 9.

58    *Ibid.*

these vertical structural intersections.[59] Although it is vital to avoid rigid evaluation frameworks that transform gender and diversity analysis into a checkbox activity, regulators should clearly state the expectation that robust analyses be undertaken.

Gender and diversity analysis is most effective when integrated into the earliest stages of the IA process. The addition of the early planning phase under the *IAA* is an important mechanism for this integration. The interim guidance emphasizes that GBA+ should be integrated throughout every stage of the IA, from early planning to follow-up; it also provides broad steps for starting GBA+ during the early planning phase. Under the legislation, however, the scope of the gender and diversity analysis, along with other section 22 factors, is not formally decided upon until the development of the Tailored Impact Statement Guidelines near the *end* of the early planning phase. This leaves significant discretion about how gender and diversity are considered prior to the development of the Guidelines, such as in the initial project description and where IA is required under the *IAA*, and the development of participation and Indigenous engagement plans. Indeed, Women and Gender Equality Canada's assessment of the initial project description for the Webequie Supply Road Project—the first to enter the early planning phase under the newly implemented *IAA*—noted significant deficiencies, including insufficient disaggregated data and a lack of "information on socio-economic [and] cultural trends, including relevant laws and policies in order to obtain a context-specific analysis."[60] It is yet to be seen how these concerns and provided suggestions will inform the remainder of the early planning phase. Ultimately, undertaking gender and diversity analysis from the very beginning is vital to ensuring that diverse groups are represented in IA processes and that any barriers to their meaningful participation (e.g., social structures, institutions, and power relations) are identified and addressed.

---

59   Manning, above note 22 at 3, for example, asked, "How are colonization, racism, and other systems of power recognized and addressed?"; see also Joy L Johnson, Lorraine Greaves & Robin Repta, "Better Science with Sex and Gender: Facilitating the Use of a Sex and Gender-Based Analysis in Health Research" (2018) 8:1 *International Journal for Equity in Health* 14.

60   Women and Gender Equality Canada, "Federal Authority Advice Record—Webequie Supply Road Project" (28 November 2020) at 2, online: https://iaac-aeic.gc.ca/050/evaluations/proj/80183.

Additional uncertainties related to the gender and diversity analysis requirement in the *IAA* remain. For example, a lack of guidance remains on how to conduct strategic and regional assessments under the *IAA*,[61] resulting in a great deal of uncertainty about the role of gender and diversity analysis within these types of assessment. Careful consideration of gender and diversity analysis in future regulations, policies, and guidance at these levels is important as these higher-level processes would feed into section 22 considerations for project IA and are most conducive to influencing broad measures for social equity from ensuing developments. Also, the proposed legislation provides some allowance for coordination, delegation, or substitution of federal IA processes with those of other jurisdictions. Among other conditions for substitution, section 33(1) of the *IAA* indicates that "[t]he Minister may only approve a substitution if he or she is satisfied that … the process to be substituted will include a consideration of the factors set out in section 22(1)," and section 22(1)(s) includes "the intersection of sex and gender with other identity factors." Clow et al recently noted, however, that there is currently very little integration of gender-based analysis with IA processes in provincial jurisdictions in Canada.[62] Therefore, explicit attention to the capacity of other jurisdictions to fulfill the requirement for gender and diversity analysis will be needed when a substitution or delegation of IA activities is considered.

## F.  CONCLUDING REMARKS

The requirement for gender-based analysis in Canadian IA has been a long time coming. Over twenty years ago, Archibald and Crnkovich pointed out that "with guidelines in place, the application and use of gender-based analysis would not be something left to the discretion of each panel. Such guidelines should set out the obligation for the panel to incorporate gender-based analysis as an integral part of the process."[63] Hence, the *IAA* requirement for IAs to consider "the intersection of sex and gender with other identity factors" is a welcome step forward in advancing social equity in relation to development, particularly natural resource development.

---

61   See chapters 11 and 17.

62   Clow et al, above note 38.

63   Above note 1 at 34.

Integrating effective gender and diversity analysis in Canadian IA will require a great deal of commitment from proponents, practitioners, and regulators. We have identified some strengths and remaining uncertainties around the gender and diversity component of the *IAA* and its interim guidelines. Gender and diversity analysis will be most valuable when underpinned by intersectionality principles, paying attention to both the horizontal and vertical intersections of identity attributes, structures, institutions, and norms. By considering both identity and structural factors, such analysis can inform proponents and governments about cultural expressions and livelihood practices that are deeply rooted in the landscapes where developments are proposed. Such analysis can also reveal a broader range of social impacts, explain the needs of host communities, identify potential limitations of public engagement, and suggest alternatives to address these limitations. Ultimately, it can support equitable and capacity-enhancing resource development, ensuring that no one is left behind.

# CHAPTER 13

# Integrating Climate Change Mitigation into the *Impact Assessment Act*

*Meinhard Doelle**

## A. INTRODUCTION

The successful conclusion of the UN climate negotiations resulted in the Paris Agreement's entry into force on 4 November 2016. Most UN member states — including Canada — have committed to make all reasonable efforts to reduce their greenhouse gas (GHG) emissions and to become carbon neutral within the next few decades.[1] All parties have set some initial reduction targets that are to be enhanced over time.[2] Impact assessment (IA) is a critical tool for meeting both short- and long-term commitments as it provides an opportunity to ensure that decisions about new projects, proposals, and undertakings are consistent with decarbonization goals.

Integrating climate change into IA requires consideration of both mitigation and adaptation, along with the adverse impacts not prevented through mitigation and adaptation efforts (sometimes referred to as loss and damage). Although these areas are connected, each brings

---

* The research for this chapter was funded by the Social Science and Humanities Research Council (SSHRC) of Canada.

1 *Paris Agreement*, 22 April 2016, UNTS art 2 (entered into force 4 November 2016).

2 In the course of the 2019 election campaign, the current federal government committed to a target of net zero emissions by 2050 and has signalled a review of its 2030 target of reducing emissions to 30 percent below 2005 levels; see "A Net-Zero Emissions Future," online: *Liberal Party of Canada* www2.liberal.ca/our-platform/a-net-zero-emissions-future.

unique challenges. The focus of this chapter is on the mitigation element, which includes GHG emissions as well as impacts on natural sinks such as forests, soils, grasslands, and oceans. Adaptation, although equally important, has a more established role in assessment processes and is not considered here.

Many countries are in the process of making decisions about major energy, transportation, and building infrastructure that are expected to serve them for decades to come. Bad decisions can lead to emissions being locked in for many decades or to stranded assets in the billions of dollars for project proponents and difficulties for the individuals, communities, and economies that become dependent on these activities. Furthermore, making major changes in direction after projects are approved risks exposing countries that have entered into investor protection agreements to challenges by foreign investors affected by post-approval policy decisions that might impact the viability of approved projects.[3] Clearly, the stakes are high.

GHG emissions are unlike other adverse environmental impacts traditionally assessed and a challenge to incorporate into existing IA methodologies and processes. This is due in part to three key characteristics:

1) The effects of releasing GHG emissions are felt globally, with regional variations in the nature and scale of the effects.
2) The effects are delayed.
3) The emissions and effects on sinks are cumulative, with the result that a given effect cannot be traced back to a specific project beyond the increase in GHG concentrations in the atmosphere.

The resulting dilemma is that the climate impacts of proposed projects are distributed globally and over time, including to future generations, whereas the benefits of projects tend to be more local and immediate. It is perhaps understandable that before the entry into force of the Paris Agreement, IA practitioners and project decision makers sometimes preferred to ignore climate change altogether or summarily dismissed

---

3    See, for example, *Clayton and Bilcon of Delaware Inc v Government of Canada* (April 2008), PCA Case No 2009-04, 17 March 2015; *AbitibiBowater Inc v Government of Canada* (15 December 2010), ICSID Case No UNCT/10/1. Although they don't deal directly with a change in regulatory condition following environmental assessment approval, they both serve to illustrate the risk.

the climate change effects of individual projects as insignificant.[4] This approach, however, has contributed to a general failure to address climate change and is no longer supportable in a post-Paris Agreement world.[5]

Canada is among the jurisdictions seeking to improve the role of IA in climate mitigation efforts. The *Impact Assessment Act* (IAA) includes a requirement to consider whether proposed projects "hinder or contribute to the Government of Canada's ability to meet its environmental obligations and its commitments in respect of climate change."[6] Guidance on what information is to be gathered to support this part of the assessment process has recently been completed and is in the process of being translated into IA guidance.[7] In the meantime, the inadequacies of current approaches have been highlighted repeatedly, especially in the ongoing battles over various pipeline proposals for transporting bitumen from the Alberta oil sands to export markets.[8]

Initial recognition of the need to consider how to integrate climate change into IA goes back two decades. In Canada, climate change was considered in some project assessments in the 1990s.[9] In 2003, the Canadian

---

4      See, for example, the BC Woodfibre LNG project, discussed in some detail in Anthony Ho & Chris Tollefson, "Sustainability-Based Assessment of Project-Related Climate Change Impacts: A Next Generation EA Policy Conundrum" (2018) 32 *Journal of Environmental Law & Practice* 30 at 67.

5      See Robert B Gibson et al, *From Paris to Projects: Clarifying the Implications of Canada's Climate Change Mitigation Commitments for the Planning and Assessment of Projects and Strategic Undertakings* (Toronto: Metcalf Charitable Foundation, January 2019) [Metcalf Report].

6      SC 2019, c 28, s 22.

7      Government of Canada, *Discussion Paper: Developing a Strategic Assessment of Climate Change* (2018), online: www.strategicassessmentclimatechange.ca/5637/documents/11224. At the time of writing, some of this guidance was in the process of being released: Impact Assessment Agency of Canada, "Policy Context: Considering Environmental Obligations and Commitments in Respect of Climate Change Under the Impact Assessment Act," online: *Government of Canada* www.canada.ca/en/impact-assessment-agency/services/policy-guidance/practitioners-guide-impact-assessment-act/considering-environmental-obligations.html. A detailed review of Agency's guidance for the implementation of the new Act was not possible due to the publication deadline for the book. Rather, this chapter explores the principles that should guide the consideration of GHG emissions at the key steps in the process.

8      *Tsleil-Waututh Nation v Canada (Attorney General)*, 2018 FCA 153.

9      Canadian Environmental Assessment Agency et al, *The Joint Public Review Panel Report: Sable Gas Projects*, (October 1997), online (pdf): http://publications.gc.ca/collections/Collection/NE23-91-1997E.pdf.

Environmental Assessment Agency initiated a multi-jurisdictional process to develop a basic guide on the consideration of climate change in IA.[10] The guide has since been endorsed by a number of jurisdictions, but its use has not been widespread or effective. More recently, some provinces—particularly British Columbia, Ontario, Quebec, and Nova Scotia—have initiated internal efforts to develop their own guidance on climate change in IA. These efforts to more effectively integrate climate change into IA are very much in their infancy, but they provide an opportunity to fix a major shortcoming of IA in Canada.[11]

Canada is not alone in its struggle to integrate climate change into IA, as evidenced by efforts in many jurisdictions around the world. Significant activities include individual project assessments that have considered climate mitigation, court cases over the failure to adequately consider climate mitigation, and literature on these efforts in the United States, the European Union, Australia, and New Zealand.[12] Many other jurisdictions have gained valuable experience with climate adaptation, but experience with climate mitigation has been limited.[13]

10   The Federal-Provincial-Territorial Committee on Climate Change and Environmental Assessment, *Incorporating Climate Change Considerations in Environmental Assessment: General Guidance for Practitioners*, (November 2003), online: www.canada.ca/en/impact-assessment-agency/services/policy-guidance/incorporating-climate-change-considerations-environmental-assessment-general-guidance-practitioners.html.

11   Émilie Godbout-Beaulieu, "Climate Change in Canadian Environmental Assessment Legislation: Review and Recommendations for a Further Integration" (LLM thesis, Dalhousie University, 2018), discusses many provincial efforts, including Quebec's *Regulation respecting environmental impact assessment and review*, CQLR c Q-2, r 23, s 2; Nova Scotia's *Environmental Assessment Regulations*, NS Reg 26/95, s2(1)(1), which require an environmental assessment on projects that are generally known to have an impact on climate change; and Manitoba's definition of climate change within their environmental assessment legislation, *The Environment Act*, CCSM, cE125, s 1(1).

12   Jessica Wentz, Grant Glovin & Adrian Ang, *Survey of Climate Change Considerations in Federal Environmental Impact Statements, 2012–2014* (Sabin Center for Climate Change Law, Columbia Law School, 2016); Sabin Center for Climate Change Law, "Non-US Litigation Cases" (2018), online: *Climate Change Litigation Databases* http://climatecasechart.com/non-us-climate-change-litigation; New Zealand, Ministry for the Environment, *Climate Change Effects and Impacts Assessment: A Guidance Manual for Local Government in New Zealand*, 2d ed (Wellington, NZ: May 2008), online (pdf): www.mfe.govt.nz/sites/default/files/climate-change-effect-impacts-assessment-may08.pdf.

13   For a summary of case studies from around the world dealing mostly with adaptation, see Netherlands Commission for Environmental Assessment, ed, *Environmental Assessment for Climate Smart Decision Making: Good Practice Cases* (March 2017), online (pdf): http://api.commissiemer.nl/docs/mer/diversen/2017environmental-assessment-for-climate-smart-decision-making_good-practice-cases.pdf.

The focus of this chapter is on the consideration of the impacts of a proposed project on GHG emissions and carbon sinks at five critical stages of IA: triggering, information gathering, analysis, the project decision, and post-approval follow-up.[14] These stages are considered in turn in sections B to F below. In each section, the treatment of climate mitigation in the respective project IA stage under the *IAA* is first considered. This is followed with recommendations on how the effectiveness of efforts to integrate climate mitigation into the process can be improved through implementation, including ultimately through the development of a combination of regulations, policies, and guidance in line with the framework, principles, and issues explored below.

## B.  CLIMATE CHANGE MITIGATION AND IMPACT ASSESSMENT TRIGGERS

The *IAA* continues the basic approach under the *Canadian Environmental Assessment Act, 2012* (*CEAA 2012*)[15] with respect to the triggering of project assessments. At the core of the triggering process is a project list regulation. This process is complemented by a ministerial power under section 9 to designate projects not listed in the regulation. There is a separate requirement to assess the environmental effects of projects on federal land and outside Canada. Finally, the *IAA* provides for regional and strategic assessments.[16]

There is no indication that GHG emissions factored into the preparation of the initial designated projects list for the *IAA* based on the justification that accompanied the draft designated projects list regulation.[17] There is no legislative direction on the exercise of ministerial discretion under section 9 to require an assessment of a project not listed, and to date no guidance has been prepared. Similarly, the *IAA* is

---

14    The term *project* is used throughout as this is the term used in the current assessment process in Canada. Other processes use terms such as *undertaking* and *activities*. These terms are defined differently in assessment processes throughout the world. Unless otherwise noted, *project* is used as a generic term to refer to a proposed initiative that is subject to an assessment process.

15    SC 2012, c 19, s 52.

16    See chapters 11 and 17.

17    Government of Canada, *Consultation Paper on Approach to Revising the Project List: A Proposed Impact Assessment System* (February 2018), online: www.canada.ca/content/ dam/themes/environment/conservation/environmental-reviews/consultation-paper-approach-revising-project-list.pdf.

silent on whether and how GHG emissions may factor into decisions to carry out assessments of projects on federal land or outside Canada. The main legal requirement is a determination as to whether proposed projects on federal lands and outside Canada cause significant adverse environmental effects.[18]

With respect to regional and strategic assessments, the Act is similarly silent on criteria for determining when to carry them out. This makes it difficult to predict whether and how GHG emissions will factor into decisions to carry out regional and strategic assessments. Given the scale of the challenge to transition Canada to full decarbonization in the coming decades, both regional and strategic assessments are critical tools.[19]

From a climate mitigation perspective, triggering would ideally be designed to ensure that all proposed projects not likely to assist with full decarbonization are assessed. Annual GHG emission thresholds alone do not serve this purpose effectively as they ignore the duration of the activity and the alternatives its approval displaces. Life-cycle emission thresholds are similarly ineffective on their own as they tend to ignore the distribution of the emissions over time, indirect emissions, cumulative impacts, and the resulting effect on decarbonization efforts. Some projects with significant short-term GHG emissions may be quite compatible with a transition to GHG neutrality. Other projects, even though the direct GHG emissions are small, may nevertheless put jurisdictions on a track that is incompatible with decarbonization. This is not to suggest that annual and life-cycle thresholds cannot be used in combination with other considerations, but they are crude tools that risk missing many important projects.[20]

The goal of ensuring that activities with the potential to hinder the decarbonization of affected jurisdictions are assessed can only be met through the use of a combination of tools not currently part of the *IAA* or associated guidance. First, from a project IA perspective, a project list could be developed in each of the key sectors involved in the transition

---

18   *IAA*, above note 6, ss 82–84. See also Chapter 18.

19   *Ibid*, ss 92–103. See also chapters 11 and 17.

20   For a more detailed discussion of the issues raised in this paragraph, see the Metcalf Report, above note 5, at 168–69. It includes a full list of factors that could be considered in determining whether the GHG emission implications of a proposed project warrant triggering the assessment process.

to GHG emission neutrality, including electricity, resource extraction, transportation, manufacturing, forestry, and agriculture. For each sector, defined categories of projects that warrant an assessment in light of their potential to hinder the transition could be listed. The lists could be developed with a reverse onus approach so that all activities in identified climate risk categories would be assessed unless their proponents can establish that the activities would be consistent with the transition without the need for an IA.

Strategic assessments of key emitting sectors can serve to offer more specific guidance to prospective proponents to encourage innovation in project selection and design to help with this transition rather than propose projects that will hinder it.[21] With appropriate policy signals in the key sectors, proponents will know that projects that contribute to decarbonization will be welcome. Depending on the outcome of a strategic IA of a given sector, it can also serve to shorten the list of activities to be assessed at the project level. Strategic IAs should therefore be carried out in each sector identified. In some cases, where conditions within the sector warrant, they can be carried out at a national level. In other cases, a regional approach may be required in light of different regional circumstances.

Any of these approaches to triggering would be enhanced by a credibly and transparently developed national climate change mitigation policy that is regularly updated. It would include an implementation schedule with delineated pathways, allocated carbon budgets, graduated carbon pricing, and suitable social cost of carbon calculators. The pathways implications could then guide sectoral or regional carbon budget allocations and implications for particular categories of projects. This would make identification of whether projects are on or off the decarbonization path more feasible. In the absence of such a policy or set of policies, IA should apply to all projects that on their face may not be compatible with achieving the necessary reductions overall or not compatible with full decarbonization before 2050. That approach would add pressures on the relevant authorities to develop the needed overall plan.

Ultimately, the key will be to develop regulation and/or policy containing clear criteria for when the GHG emissions associated

---

21    See Chapter 17 for a more detailed discussion of strategic assessments.

with a proposed project warrant triggering an assessment. The overall goal should be clearly set out: to assess projects that on their face are not consistent with decarbonization. The criteria can be expected to include annual and lifetime thresholds for direct GHG emissions and for impact on natural sinks, but with more nuanced and specific criteria for each key sector, such as energy, transportation, buildings, mining, and manufacturing. This means that for each sector, careful consideration will have to be given to what projects are expected to contribute to decarbonization and what projects may not. The criteria, once developed, can then be used to implement various approaches to triggering, from project lists to the exercise of discretion.

## C.  CLIMATE MITIGATION INFORMATION NEEDS

The *IAA* does not directly identify what information has to be gathered or by whom. Rather, the information needs are expected to be identified during the course of the early planning process. This includes the specific needs of a given project, the concerns and priorities of those potentially affected, and the legislative assessment and decision-making criteria, particularly those in sections 22 and 63 of the *IAA*.[22] Key among these criteria for GHG emissions is the extent to which a proposed project contributes to sustainability and to meeting Canada's climate commitments.

Specific guidance from the Impact Assessment Agency of Canada (the Agency) on what information must be gathered to inform the project's GHG emissions assessment is still absent. The closest is the guidance to proponents resulting from the policy developed by Environment and Climate Change Canada (ECCC) through a process called a "strategic assessment of climate change."[23] (It is important to point out that the process followed for the development of this document is not what we have in mind in this book when we use the term "strategic assessment," and the process was commenced before the IAA came into force, so it is not a strategic assessment under the IAA.) The ECCC guidance is focused on the information required from

---

22  See chapters 9 and 14 for a more detailed discussion of ss 22 and 63 and their implications for the scope of assessments and decision making.

23  Environment and Climate Change Canada, *Strategic Assessment of Climate Change* (July 2020), online: *Government of Canada* www.strategicassessmentclimatechange.ca.

proponents. All proponents will be required to include a basic estimate of a project's direct emissions in their project description. Information for projects with net direct emissions below 500 kt/year will be limited to this basic information about direct net emissions and emissions intensity. For projects with direct emissions over 500 kt/year, more detailed information will be required. Proponents are not required to estimate downstream emissions, and information on upstream emissions is required only for projects with upstream emissions estimated to be over 500 kt/year.[24] Proponents of projects projected to exist beyond 2050 are required to demonstrate how they will be carbon neutral by then.

Unfortunately, the information required of proponents under the ECCC guidance is not adequate to make appropriate determinations either about a project's contribution to sustainability or its contribution to Canada's climate commitments. This leaves two options. Either the information provided by the proponent will be supplemented with information from other sources to ensure that appropriate analysis can be carried out or the information needed for assessing the sustainability and climate implications of proposed projects will not be available. The remainder of this section will consider the information needs for a proper assessment under the *IAA* of a proposed project's implications for climate change.

As an underlying principle for information gathering, as much information as reasonably possible should be gathered about the implications of the proposed project for decarbonization efforts. There may be a tendency to work back from the decision-making stage to first decide how to determine whether the project, in comparison with alternatives including the null option (no project), is acceptable from a climate perspective. In that case, only information that is needed for that determination — however conceived — would be gathered. Given the seriousness and complexity of the issue and our collective limited experience, it would be a mistake to limit the information gathered in this manner. Instead, it is critical to gather and publicly share as much information as possible about the potential implications of a proposed project on decarbonization efforts in affected jurisdictions. This offers the best opportunities for innovative approaches during the course of the assessment and will maximize learning opportunities after the project decision.

---

24    *Ibid.*

The starting point for any assessment is that it needs to be able to quantify the direct GHG emissions and any sinks impairment of the proposed activity over its life cycle. This information should be a basic requirement of the *IAA*. The more difficult step is identifying what else is needed to be able to properly analyze the climate mitigation implications of the project and, ultimately, to inform decision makers on whether the project will contribute to or hinder decarbonization efforts. These steps in turn can help identify the minimum information needs.

As discussed in more detail in Chapter 15, the *IAA* includes a new planning phase. This step in the assessment process provides an opportunity to consider, in a manner appropriate for the specific proposed project, the information needs of the assessment from a GHG emissions perspective. A good starting point for this planning phase (or the more traditional scoping process in other assessment processes) will be to pose key questions to guide decisions about the information needed to understand the GHG emission implications of the project. Among the key questions to consider at this stage are the following:

- What information is needed to consider whether the project, in comparison with reasonable alternatives, will contribute to or hinder efforts to decarbonize?
- What information is needed to consider whether the proponent has made all reasonable efforts to design the project to contribute to decarbonization?
- What information is needed to determine whether direct emissions associated with the project are justified because they will result in emission reductions elsewhere?
- Is there a risk of the project serving as a catalyst for emissions beyond those included in the life-cycle direct emissions analysis?
- Are there indirect emissions, such as upstream or downstream emissions, to consider?
- Are there provincial or national jurisdictional boundaries to consider? For example, do emissions outside the home province of the proposed project have to be tracked to allow for an assessment of whether emission reduction efforts within the province are hindering decarbonization efforts beyond? Conversely, would an increase in emissions within the province contribute to decarbonization efforts in line with the long-term goals of the

Paris Agreement outside the province that would otherwise not materialize?[25]

A good starting point for determining the scope of information needs would be a rebuttable presumption that the direct GHG emissions from a proposed activity are additional. In other words, the default conclusion would be that the life-cycle direct emissions from a proposed activity are solely attributable to the proposed activity as a negative environmental effect. This would then raise the question of whether it can be shown that the proposed activity will offset emissions elsewhere. If the proponent intends to demonstrate that the project will displace emissions elsewhere, additional information would be needed on the GHG emissions associated with reasonable alternatives, including the "no project" option, and on the upstream and downstream GHG emissions associated with the proposed activity. Under this scenario, a credible assessment of societal needs, alternative ways of meeting those needs, and cumulative effects will be particularly critical. The burden of making the argument would be on the proponent.[26]

Of course, a project may be responsible for an increase or a decrease in indirect (such as upstream or downstream) emissions independent of whether the proponent is claiming that the direct project emissions are warranted on the basis that they avoid emissions elsewhere. These upstream or downstream emissions may occur within or outside the jurisdiction in which the assessment is carried out. A key question arises as to when the consideration of potential indirect emissions associated with a proposed activity should be included in the assessment. The potential for upstream or downstream GHG emissions of the project to undermine efforts to decarbonize in affected jurisdictions might serve as the ultimate test. This means that the upstream and downstream effects must be considered unless it is clear that these concerns have been addressed.[27]

---

25  For a detailed discussion of the issues raised here, see the Metcalf Report, above note 5.

26  Of course, this is not to suggest that alternatives should be considered only in these circumstances. It also emphasizes the importance of considering carefully the appropriate sources of information as much of the information will have to come from sources other than proponents.

27  Jurisdiction here refers to both jurisdictions within Canada and foreign jurisdictions potentially affected. The focus here is on informed decision making, not on prejudging

As a starting point, the default presumption should be that these broader implications are included in the information-gathering phase of a project IA so that appropriate determinations can be made at the assessment stage. With experience, we may learn that this is not needed for certain types of activities.

IAs should, however, remain open to intervenors making the case (at the planning stage and beyond) that a project will have undesired consequences for efforts to decarbonize. This is a key function of IA, one that distinguishes it from regulatory processes. To achieve this goal, it is important for the information-gathering stage of the IA to err on the side of collecting more information rather than less. Strategic assessments can sometimes serve to identify situations where this broader exploration of indirect GHG emissions associated with a proposed activity is not warranted. For example, a strategic assessment of liquefied natural gas (LNG) could help resolve controversies about the life-cycle emissions of LNG and whether there are markets where LNG will serve to reduce emissions in the short and medium term. It could also consider when the nature of those markets can be expected to change such that LNG will no longer contribute to a reduction in GHG emissions in those markets because lower emitting options will have become viable.

Finally, it is important to design the information-gathering stage of IA with a full range of possible projects in mind. There has been a tendency in Canada to view the integration of climate change into IA largely through the lens of fossil fuel exploration and infrastructure projects. Although this is an important sector, not all of its challenges are applicable to other sectors. The approach, therefore, needs to be designed with all key sectors in mind, including transportation, buildings, mining, manufacturing, agriculture, and forestry. In addition to general guidance in line with the recommendations made here, specific guidance will likely be warranted for some sectors.

One key will be to ensure that the scope and substance of the information-gathering component of the assessment process under the *IAA* adequately inform the analysis needed to ensure a sound basis for decision making. It should also offer flexibility to do the analysis needed to understand whether the project contributes to or hinders efforts to meet Canada's climate commitments.

---

the decision to be made on this information. It is important for decision makers to know whether proposed projects contribute to global efforts to decarbonize or not.

## D.  CLIMATE MITIGATION ANALYSIS

The information requirements discussed in the previous section are closely connected to the required analysis. Sections 22 and 63 of the *IAA*, as discussed, offer the legislative direction on what analysis is needed. Ultimately, the analysis should support conclusions about the project's contribution to sustainability and to Canada's climate commitments.

As already explored in the previous section, the analysis needed will depend, at least to some extent, on the climate mitigation claims made by proponents. It will also depend on national and subnational policies and commitments to reduce emissions.

To carry out the analysis needed in the context of the *IAA* to understand a project's impact on efforts to decarbonize, the following information will have to be available:

- the project's direct life-cycle GHG emissions, including emissions embedded in the goods and services used for the project, along with any emissions due to impairment of sinks
- information to assess the credibility and impact of any proposed efforts to permanently sequester emissions or to offset emissions
- the project's indirect emissions in Canada
- the project's broader impact on emissions in Canada and beyond
- the emissions of a range of alternatives (including "best" climate/ sustainability options and the "no project" option) estimated in a manner that makes them comparable to the predicted project emissions

With this information in hand, the analysis can then focus on answering the following questions reflective of the complexity of determining whether a project will help or hinder Canada's efforts to meet its climate commitments:

- Is the project consistent with targets set in Canada's current Nationally Determined Contribution (NDC) and its long-term climate strategy?[28]

---

28    Government of Canada, *Canada's Mid-Century Long-Term Low-Greenhouse Gas Development Strategy* (Ottawa: Environment and Climate Change Canada, 2016), online (pdf): https://unfccc.int/files/focus/long-term_strategies/application/pdf/canadas_mid-century_long-term_strategy.pdf [Canada's Long-Term Strategy].

- Will the project contribute to or hinder efforts to increase ambition of the current NDC in response to the Global Stocktake every five years under the Paris Agreement and in light of the gap between NDCs and the long-term goal of the agreement as it is currently understood?[29]
- Is the project consistent with efforts to achieve enhanced GHG emission reduction targets for 2030 and 2040 that are consistent with Canada's commitments under the Paris Agreement?[30]
- Would the life-cycle project emissions help or hinder efforts to reach full decarbonization before or by 2050?[31]
- Does the project contribute to or hinder efforts to decarbonize as soon as possible?
- Does the project achieve emission reductions in Canada in the short term compared to reasonable alternatives?
- Does the project achieve emission reductions outside Canada in the short term?
- Does the project contribute to global efforts to decarbonize as soon as possible, in line with the long-term goals of the Paris Agreement?
- Is the project consistent with the GHG emission reduction plan of any affected jurisdiction that would stay within carbon budgets grounded in (global and/or intergenerational) equity?[32]
- Would the project be economically viable if it had to pay the social cost of carbon, estimated based on a discount rate that is appropriate to the climate crisis and the concept of intergenerational equity?[33]
- Would the project be economically viable in the face of carbon pricing at a graduated scale identified in the literature as

---

29　See UNFCCC Secretariat, "NDC Registry (Interim)" (all NDCs, 2018), online: http://www4.unfccc.int/ndcregistry/Pages/All.aspx, to find that Canada is committed to reduce GHG emissions by 30 percent below the 2005 levels by 2030 and to reduce black carbon; Paris Agreement, above note 1, art 14.

30　*Ibid*, art 4, ss 3, 5, and 11.

31　Metcalf Report, above note 5 at 54–59.

32　*Ibid* at 42–53. Jurisdictions could include other provinces in Canada as well as other states.

33　David Wright, "Carbonated Fodder: The Social Cost of Carbon in Canadian and U.S. Regulatory Decision-Making" (2017) 29:3 *Georgetown International Environmental Law Review* 513. See also David V Wright & Meinhard Doelle, "Social Cost of Carbon in Environmental Impact Assessment" (2019) 52:3 *UBC Law Review* 1007.

appropriate (or necessary) to meet the long-term goals of the Paris Agreement?[34]

- Given Canada's commitments and their implications for carbon budgets and emission reduction targets, to what extent would project approval constrain future development opportunities that are not carbon neutral?[35] In other words, what is the opportunity loss of allocating portions of any remaining carbon budgets to the proposed project?[36]

In what follows, some of the key issues that arise in carrying out the analysis needed to answer these questions are briefly highlighted and discussed. All, of course, warrant more detailed consideration in terms of their implications for the *IAA* than is possible here.[37]

If the proponent accepts that the life-cycle direct emissions are additional and constitute a negative effect of the project, then beyond these direct emissions, the GHG emissions analysis would have to consider next whether the project risks serving as a catalyst for indirect emissions. If not, a detailed assessment of indirect emissions will not be needed. If, however, the proponent takes the position that some or all of the project emissions are justified on the basis that they will result in emission reductions elsewhere, then a comprehensive analysis on the overall GHG emissions impact of the proposed project is warranted. Actions related to both options should be clearly identified.

An important design question is how the information gathered about the proposed activity's GHG emissions is to be used during the assessment phase of the IA. The default assumption should be that GHG emission levels that would hinder the transition to full decarbonization

---

34     Environment and Climate Change Canada, *Technical Update to Environment and Climate Change Canada's Social Cost of Greenhouse Gas Estimates* (Ottawa: Environment and Climate Change Canada, 2016), states that the central value should be $40.7 per tonne.

35     A John Sinclair, Meinhard Doelle & Peter N Duinker, "Looking Up, Down, and Sideways: Reconceiving Cumulative Effects Assessment as a Mindset" (2017) 62 *Environmental Assessment Review* 183 at 185.

36     The important point about these questions is that all have to be answered. It is not enough to determine that a project will not compromise Canada's current NDC or any one of the other elements. These questions are not proposed as a simple formula, where there is an automatic outcome depending on the answer to each of these questions. Rather, what is proposed is more clarity and transparency on the climate implication of proposed projects before decisions are made.

37     Metcalf Report, above note 5.

would preclude approval of a proposed project, and the burden should be on the proponent to demonstrate that the proposed activity contributes to this transition in spite of its life-cycle emissions.

Justification for the proposed project or activity could be made (for consideration by project decision makers) in a number of ways:

- The proposed activity (or the GHG emissions associated with the activity) has a short lifespan and is compatible with Canada's obligations to reduce emissions during that time period.
- The emissions are necessary to build infrastructure to assist with decarbonization efforts.
- The emissions are necessary to replace activities whose emissions are even higher, the proposed activity is the lowest emissions replacement, and it does not lock Canada into unnecessary future emissions.
- The emissions are being offset by investing in credible transformational emissions reductions elsewhere in Canada that would not be achieved without the project-induced investment.

A related issue is the design and application of appropriate methodologies for determining whether a proposed initiative will have a positive, negative, or neutral effect on Canada's global commitments. So far, I have expressed this determination in terms of Canada's transition to full decarbonization. Of course, there is no clear date for full decarbonization in the Paris Agreement itself or in Canada's NDCs. We do have Canada's emission reduction targets for 2020 and 2030 in combination with the quantified 2030 global emissions gap of upwards of 15 Gt and the long-term temperature and GHG neutrality goals in the Paris Agreement.[38] We also have Canada's mid-century strategy submitted under Article 4.19 of the agreement and the current government's commitment to achieve net zero emissions by 2050.[39]

What all this means for decision making under the *IAA* requires clear articulation. We know that Canada's 2020 and 2030 targets are a floor, not a ceiling, and that Canada will have to increase its commitment. We also know that Canada is among the parties to the UN climate regime with the highest capacity, the highest per capita emissions,

---

38    Above note 1.

39    Canada's Long-Term Strategy, above note 28. See also above note 2.

the highest historical emissions, and the highest potential to reduce emissions. Under any measure of equity, Canada will be expected to lead the effort to bridge the 2030 emissions gap and the global effort to reach GHG emissions neutrality. All of this points to the importance of a sound policy context for GHG emissions, one that recognizes that current provincial, national, and international commitments are a significant but inadequate first step. Whatever the approach, it needs to recognize that Canada's commitment under the Paris Agreement includes progress beyond its current NDC toward a fair contribution to the global goals.[40]

In short, more clarity is needed to turn these basic elements into a standard against which the GHG emission implications of individual projects can be measured in the context of an assessment under the *IAA*. Federal–provincial negotiations can assist with this process, as can strategic IAs of key sectors that need to lead the transition to GHG emissions neutrality. In the end, there will be some basic options on how to develop the standard against which projects can be measured. One approach will be to develop national, provincial, and sectoral carbon budgets (possibly with a domestic trading mechanism for provinces and sectors) for key stages in the transition, such as 2020, 2030, and 2040. Projects would then essentially have to compete against other existing and possible future activities for the limited carbon budget and should be expected to pay for the privilege of having some of that budget allocated to them.[41]

An alternative, or a complement, to a carbon budget approach would be to use best-available information to set prices for a tonne of GHG emissions at five- or ten-year intervals for the life of the project that would include the social cost of carbon. Projects could be required to internalize this cost in demonstrating the project's economic viability. A third option would be to require project proponents to purchase offsets from sources that are transformational in their contribution to full decarbonization, either for all emissions or for any that are deemed to be in excess of the budget allocation granted. These sources would need to be within Canada, on the assumption that the goal is to achieve

---

40    Metcalf Report, above note 5 at 60.

41    Of course, this approach will unduly favour existing facilities unless the costs of their GHG emissions are gradually internalized to level the playing field and there are adequate efforts to facilitate the innovation needed for full decarbonization.

GHG emission neutrality in Canada. Performance standards for sectors, potentially based on the social need being served by the sector, would be further alternatives to explore.[42]

## E.  PROJECT DECISION MAKING IN LIGHT OF CLIMATE MITIGATION ANALYSIS

Project decisions under the *IAA* involve two key steps.[43] First, a determination is required on the nature and scale of the project's impacts in areas of federal jurisdiction. Second, if the impacts on areas of federal jurisdiction warrant a federal project decision, the *IAA* requires a public interest determination informed by the assessment report of the Agency or a review panel, taking into account the decision-making considerations in section 63, including the project's contribution to sustainability and to Canada's climate commitments.[44]

It is here that the information gathered and the analysis carried out are translated into decisions about whether specific proposed activities are permitted to proceed and, if so, under what conditions. The focus remains on project IA as the general assumption is that regional and strategic assessments serve to inform project IAs. Although certain types of activities might be precluded by policies and plans adopted on the basis of regional or strategic assessments (which should include early policy decisions to refuse categories of projects that are clearly not consistent with Canada's climate goals), it is otherwise at the project IA stage that decisions are ultimately made.

To make a project decision in light of the analyses carried out in accordance with the approach discussed in the previous section, a number of key determinations will have to be made:

- What emissions will be attributed to the proposed project for the purposes of the project decision, and are they based on a clear and defensible rationale?
- Which alternatives to the project factor into the project decision based on a clear and defensible rationale, and how will decision

---

42   Any carbon pricing option would have to equally apply to existing facilities to avoid unduly favouring existing facilities over new projects.

43   *IAA*, above note 6, s 60.

44   See Chapter 14 for a more detailed discussion on project decisions in light of s 63.

makers determine whether they are better or worse from a climate mitigation perspective?

- Have all reasonable efforts been made to avoid negative climate impacts and contribute to decarbonization?
- Does the project help or hinder Canada's climate mitigation efforts in light of its Paris Agreement commitments?
- How should any remaining climate impacts be weighed against other adverse impacts, benefits, risks, and uncertainties to determine whether the impacts are justified, whether the project makes an overall contribution to sustainability, and whether the project is in the public interest?

Of course, these questions can be adequately addressed at the decision-making stage only if the information gathering and analysis provide an appropriate basis for their consideration. To be clear, all questions would have to be answered before a project decision is made. The analysis would lead to a range of possible conclusions about the proposed project's contribution to Canada's climate mitigation:

- The project does not involve GHG emissions.
- The project involves GHG emissions that are lower than those of all viable alternatives.
- The project will assist Canada in meeting its climate mitigation commitments and goals without undermining other nations' efforts.
- The project hinders efforts to meet or exceed Canada's 2020 and 2030 targets.
- The project hinders efforts for Canada to achieve GHG emission neutrality before 2050.
- The project involves GHG emissions that are higher than viable alternatives but also involves greater net benefits in other areas.
- The project can/cannot be accommodated in a suitable carbon budget, is/is not on a sectoral or regional pathway to meeting Canada's carbon commitments, and is/is not economically viable once it has fully internalized the cost of its GHG emissions over the life cycle of the project.

In addition to predicting whether the project will help or hinder Canada's efforts to mitigate climate change, it will be important to quantify the positive or negative contribution the project is predicted to make and to identify the risks and uncertainties associated with the predictions made in the IA. Regardless of the ultimate approach adopted, some basic principles for sound decision making can be identified:

- full transparency about the project's impact on Canada's commitment to work with other nations toward the long-term goal of keeping global temperatures to rising less than 2 degrees Celsius and striving for a rise of 1.5 degrees Celsius as a maximum, including Canada's 2030 NDC under the Paris Agreement, Canada's contribution to the global 2030 emission reduction gap of 15 GT, and Canada's contribution to full decarbonization in Canada and the global aspiration to keep temperatures from rising less than 2 degrees while striving to keep temperatures from rising no more than 1.5 degrees
- clear decision-making rules and accountability for decisions to approve projects that represent something less than Canada's best efforts to reach its global commitments and make an equitable contribution to the global goals in the Paris Agreement
- explicit decision-making criteria and full transparency about choices to allocate limited carbon budgets to approved projects while preserving the ultimate accountability for making the decision at a political level
- explicit decision-making criteria to encourage principled decision making in case of conflict between climate change mitigation goals and other societal values and benefits of proposed activities and accountability in cases where decisions are demonstrably inconsistent with decision-making principles and criteria[45]
- careful and thorough consideration of all viable alternatives to any project that hinders Canada's transition to GHG emission neutrality and a clear and demonstrable preference for alternative ways to meet societal needs, with approval only on strict conditions that ensure minimal adverse impact and only as a last resort under clearly defined circumstances
- mandatory monitoring, full transparency about the GHG emissions performance of approved projects during the full life cycle

---

45    See Chapter 19 on accountability.

of the project, and means of requiring corrections to resolve emerging problems

- clear rules that hold proponents accountable for any negative GHG emission consequences of approved projects that are beyond those predicted during the course of the IA[46]
- conditions for approval that preserve the rights of governments to impose more strict limits on GHG emissions of the project in the future, to require full offsetting, and to hold the proponent liable for the life-cycle emissions of the project, with a view to preserving the flexibility for approved projects to contribute to the progression of ambition required under the Paris Agreement and to prepare for possible investor challenges in case of more stringent future requirements[47]

## F.   POST-APPROVAL CONSIDERATIONS

The requirement to design a follow-up program is listed among the factors to be assessed under section 22 of the *IAA*. The final assessment report of the Agency or a review panel and the final project decision by the minister or Cabinet are similarly required to address follow-up requirements. There is limited direction, however, on the substantive requirements of the follow-up program, either generally or with respect to GHG emissions in particular. The details on the design requirements will have to be either provided through guidance or worked out during the new planning phase of the *IAA*. The implementation will have to be addressed under the terms and conditions of approval.

For approved projects, the post-approval (or follow-up) phase is critical for a number of reasons. It provides an opportunity to learn, particularly with respect to the accuracy of the predictions made about the GHG emissions of the project. This will be important for future assessments, allowing prediction errors to be reduced over time. The follow-up phase is also important for compliance and adaptive management purposes. The relevant issues are briefly highlighted here, separated into what needs to be tracked and monitored and what actions

---

46   Such as through offset requirements linked to approved transformational decarbonization projects in Canada or payment into a decarbonization fund.

47   For a more detailed discussion of these principles, see the Metcalf Report, above note 5.

may need to be taken in response to the information gathered during the follow-up phase.[48]

With respect to tracking, the focus from a GHG emission perspective should be on tracking direct emissions as well as any indirect emissions that were considered relevant in approving the project. Policy under the *IAA* should require proponents to track and report such emissions on a regularized schedule. In addition, it will be important to track compliance with any terms or conditions that relate to GHG emissions, such as mitigation measures, efforts to protect or enhance sinks, sequestration, promised offsets, and monitoring.[49]

The response to the information tracked through follow-up programs is critical. It will be important to be as clear as possible about the consequences of non-compliance within the terms and conditions of a project's approval as well as the consequence of predictions having underestimated emissions from the project or underestimated harm to sinks. A good starting point would be to require proponents to pay the equivalent of the social cost of carbon as compensation for any emissions over what was predicted during the assessment. Furthermore, to the extent possible, the adaptability of the approved project in light of concerns over its GHG emissions or impact on sinks should be clearly identified as part of the information, analysis, and decision-making phases of the process so that opportunities to adapt to the information gathered during the follow-up stage are clear and are pursued.

Finally, in order to facilitate the growth in ambition of Canada's GHG mitigation effort over time, and in line with its commitments under the Paris Agreement, the post-approval process should include a specific mechanism for strengthening the terms and conditions regarding the reduction of GHG emissions and the protection of sinks. This would make it clear to proponents of approved projects that there is no legal right to continue to emit at the rates permitted as part of the original approval and would provide a clear mechanism to adjust terms and conditions as Canada increases its ambition under its NDC.

---

48   See Chapter 16 on follow-up.

49   *Ibid.*

## G.  CONCLUSION

Ultimately, there are many difficult choices that will have to be made at a political level and for which decision makers will have to be accountable as part of the democratic process. One role of IA is to minimize the need for difficult political choices by seeking mutually supportive solutions. Where difficult choices are unavoidable, assessments must clearly identify these political choices. In addition, IAs must provide transparency and clarity about the decisions being made and the implications for climate change commitments and for a jurisdiction's contribution to the global effort.

More thought will have to be given to how best to guide those responsible for implementing the IA process and ultimate project decisions to ensure that progress toward climate commitments is facilitated, not hindered. Sound climate policy, rigorous and transparent strategic IAs, and project IAs with clear guidance for decision makers are all critical elements in this regard. Only through a coordinated approach can we hope to redirect innovation toward integrated solutions that meet societal needs for energy, employment, health, education, and general well-being while accelerating our transition to GHG neutrality.

What is clear from the analysis in this chapter is that more direction is needed at each of the five stages of the project assessment process under the *IAA* considered here. Clarity is needed in the project list regulation on how GHG emissions should factor into the development of the project list and changes to it over time. A combination of regulations, policy, and guidance is needed to ensure that appropriate information is gathered, and the responsibility to gather the information is clearly assigned and appropriately allocated among proponents, expert departments and agencies, and other sources. Similar clarity is needed for the analysis, decision making, and follow-up. The preferred approach would be a regulation specific to climate mitigation, in combination with guidance to proponents and government departments and agencies in line with the principles explored in this chapter. Memoranda of understanding being developed with provinces and federal departments can also play a critical role in implementation if they are designed to ensure effective application of section 63(e).

In short, effective integration of GHG emissions into project assessments is possible within the existing framework. What is needed is a careful consideration of the issues discussed in this chapter, implemented through a combination of carefully designed regulations and supplemented with policies and guidance. A key priority will be to properly guide the broad discretion currently left to decision makers in each of the five stages of the assessment process considered. Regulations should be considered the preferred tool for this as they offer the best combination of legal certainty and flexibility to be able to learn from experience. Although the focus of this chapter has been on the designated project assessment process, the same issues need to be considered for the process for projects on federal lands and projects outside Canada discussed in Chapter 18. Climate mitigation considerations also need to be effectively incorporated into strategic and regional assessments explored in detail in chapters 11 and 17.

# CHAPTER 14

# Sustainability-Based Decision Making

*Robert B Gibson*

## A.  INTRODUCTION

At the federal level, the *Impact Assessment Act* (*IAA*)[1] moves Canada from assessments focused on mitigating significant adverse environmental (biophysical) effects to assessments centred on contributions to sustainability. The shift is first signalled in the name of the Act, which no longer features "environmental assessment."[2] Then, the definitions section establishes that the scope of effects to be covered includes "changes to the environment or to health, social or economic conditions and the positive and negative consequences of these changes."[3] Finally, the sections on factors to be considered in project assessments, and decisions about designated projects, include "the extent to which the designated project contributes to sustainability."[4] As was discussed in Chapter 9, this new agenda represents a major expansion of scope and potential ambition. Decision making seriously committed to positive contributions to sustainability would certainly be an improvement over decisions that aim only to reduce adverse effects. However, many key aspects of the Act's positive agenda are left minimally specified or only

---

1   SC 2019, c 28, s 1.

2   Previous versions of federal assessment legislation were titled the *Canadian Environmental Assessment Act* – *Canadian Environmental Assessment Act*, SC 1992, c 37 and *Canadian Environmental Assessment Act, 2012*, SC 2012, c 19.

3   *Ibid*, s 2, definition of "effects."

4   *Ibid*, especially ss 22(1)(h) and 63(a).

implicit in the legislation, with little clarification in the initial regulatory or policy guidance. This chapter looks more closely at the role of sustainability considerations in decision making under the Act.

The bulk of the Act is concerned with the assessment and approval (or rejection) of proposed major projects. Accordingly, this chapter focuses on decision making on the major projects subject to assessment under the Act, including the key decisions required throughout the project assessment process and in the follow-up stage of project implementation. However, application of the Act also involves key decisions on many other matters. Among these are decisions about what processes are to be used in regional and strategic assessments and what to do with the products of these assessments; decisions on what projects must be assessed and when regional and strategic assessments will be initiated; decisions on the processes for and contents of regulatory and policy guidance; and decisions on the exercise of procedural and substantive discretion, the negotiation of collaborative agreements with other jurisdictions, and the ongoing establishment of administrative practices.[5]

Although few of these decisions are explicitly required to take the sustainability-based approach that the Act establishes for decision making on designated projects, most, if not all, of these decisions are expected in one way or another to serve sustainability-based project assessment. To be useful and credible for that purpose, decision making under the Act generally needs to respect the contribution-to-sustainability objective.

The following sections of this chapter consider the following:

- how and where sustainability-based decision making is needed in assessments
- what the Act and initial regulatory and policy guidance require for sustainability-based decision making on projects and other undertakings subject to assessment and on other key matters of implementation (e.g., decisions on application, development of regulations, policy making, and the use of discretion)
- the overall strengths and limitations of the law and initial guidance
- openings and means for improvement

---

5   The Act's overall approaches to all of these topics are covered in other chapters of this book.

## B. THE PROMISE AND CHALLENGES OF SUSTAINABILITY-BASED DECISIONS IN NEXT-GENERATION ASSESSMENTS

For assessments in Canada and elsewhere, a sustainability-based agenda is both realistic and challenging. The real world of interacting biophysical, socio-economic, cultural, and other effects requires decision making with a similarly broad and complex agenda. Assessments focusing only on adverse environmental effects have played a pivotal role in winning serious attention to biophysical effects in development decisions. Environmental protection will need to be a priority in sustainability-based assessments as well. However, assessments with a narrowly biophysical scope are not positioned to consider the interplay of positive and adverse effects that we now know to be instrumental in a world of entwined and complex human and environmental systems.[6] Similarly, assessments focused on mitigating adverse environmental effects are ill-equipped to identify best options for improvements in a world that at least since the 1980s has embraced the objective of positively sustainable — rather than merely less adverse — development.[7]

At the central assessment stage of determining whether proposed and assessed projects are to be rejected or approved (and with what conditions), mitigation-centred environmental assessment regimes perpetuate fragmented evaluations and leave overall decision making in the black box of government secrecy. When assessments contribute only conclusions related to adverse environmental effects, other decision-making considerations (e.g., perceived economic priorities, social implications, political acceptability) enter separately, get joint attention in only late-stage integrative analysis, and go to decision makers whose information base and reasoning are largely beyond public scrutiny.

6    Kai Fang, Reinout Heijungs & Geert R De Snoo, "Understanding the Complementary Linkages Between Environmental Footprints and Planetary Boundaries in a Footprint–Boundary Environmental Sustainability Assessment Framework" (2015) 114 *Ecological Economics* 218; John A Dearing et al, "Safe and Just Operating Spaces for Regional Social-Ecological Systems" (2014) 28 *Global Environmental Change* 227; Sylvia LR Wood & Fabrice DeClerck, "Ecosystems and Human Well-being in the Sustainable Development Goals" (2015) 13:3 *Frontiers in Ecology and the Environment* 123; Jianguo Liu et al, "Complexity of Coupled Human and Natural Systems" (2007) 317:5844 *Science* 1513.

7    World Commission on Environment and Development, *Our Common Future* (New York: Norton 1987). For the currently most salient global commitments, see United Nations Sustainable Development Goals Knowledge Platform, "Sustainable Development Goals," online: *United Nations* https://sustainabledevelopment.un.org/?menu=1300 [SDGs 2020].

In that context, the ambitious agenda of sustainability-based assessment promises a more comprehensive and better integrated approach and greater prospects for multiple, mutually reinforcing gains.[8] Combined with other elements of next-generation assessment[9] — especially explicit criteria and trade-off rules, mandatory comparison of alternatives, meaningful public participation, and explicit reasons for decisions — the sustainability-based agenda and rules for decision makers should also deliver more acceptable decisions. Next-generation sustainability-based assessment seeks positive options in a complex world of interactive problems and major threats to lasting well-being. Its more integrated approach promises better practice in the planning of projects and other undertakings and a stronger overall base of information and analysis for decision making. Also, because next-generation provisions for sustainability-based assessment facilitate early engagement, meaningful public participation, and effective scrutiny, the assessment regime can provide a more credible venue for planning, reviewing, approving (or rejecting), and implementing important new undertakings. Moving to a sustainability-based agenda is especially suitable now that assessments have become the most important public venues for the review and approval of major undertakings.

The challenges, however, are also significant. Moving from mitigating adverse effects to contributing positively to sustainability is a big step from established day-to-day practice. Although conventional practice in many fields of social, economic, and political decision making has delivered improvements for many people, it has also brought increasing stresses on biophysical systems and allocated most of the gains to those already most advantaged. The UN's Sustainable Development Goals indicate the global gap between what has resulted from conventional decision making and what is needed for sustainability.[10] Particular national data on persistent and worsening problems that undermine future prospects — for example, concerning unabated

---

8   Robert B Gibson, ed, *Sustainability Assessment: Applications and Opportunities* (London, UK: Routledge, 2017), especially ch 1.

9   See Chapter 2 in this book.

10   SDGs 2020, above note 7.

greenhouse gas (GHG) emissions,[11] biodiversity losses,[12] and deepening divides between the richest and the poorest[13] — also underline the inadequacies of conventional practice.

Climate change provides an especially clear illustration of the need for change and the difficult implications for assessments. The Canadian federal government has made a commitment to reduce GHG emissions to net zero by 2050.[14] Details on how the target is to be met have not yet been announced, but, clearly, any potentially adequate package will entail major departures from established practice in many sectors. Certainly, the 2050 deadline poses problems for the many conventional projects, in the hydrocarbon sector and elsewhere, that add rather than subtract net GHG loadings and have life expectancies beyond 2050. It is also evident that Canada needs reasonably quick delineation of a working strategy for meeting the 2050 deadline so that decision makers and others can determine the implications for particular initiatives, including assessment of new projects.

To meet climate commitments, overall Canadian strategy requirements seem likely to involve delineating viable national and sectorial pathways to net zero GHG emissions, defining and allocating Canada's remaining carbon budget, establishing graduated long-term carbon pricing regimes, and mobilizing other such tools for determining what activities — including assessed projects — are consistent with

---

11    "Greenhouse Gas Sources and Sinks: Executive Summary 2019" (19 September 2019) Figure ES-1, online: *Government of Canada* www.canada.ca/en/environment-climate-change/services/climate-change/greenhouse-gas-emissions/sources-sinks-executive-summary-2019.html.

12    World Wildlife Fund, "Living Planet Report Canada: A National Look at Wildlife Loss" (2017), online (pdf): wwf.ca/wp-content/uploads/2020/02/WEB_WWF_REPORT_v3.pdf.

13    Lars Osberg, *The Age of Increasing Inequality: The Astonishing Rise of Canada's 1%* (Toronto: Lorimer, 2018).

14    Governor General, *Moving Forward Together: Speech from the Throne to Open the First Session of the Forty-third Parliament of Canada*, 43-1 (5 December 2019) at 5, online (pdf): *Government of Canada* www.canada.ca/content/dam/pco-bcp/documents/pm/Speech-from-the-Throne_2019.pdf. Although this is considered an ambitious objective, it is by itself insufficient to meet Canada's climate change commitments under the Paris Agreement. See Robert B Gibson et al, *From Paris to Projects: Clarifying the Implications of Canada's Climate Change Mitigation Commitments for the Planning and Assessment of Projects and Strategic Undertakings* (Waterloo, ON: Paris to Project Research Initiative, January 2019), full and summary reports, online: *University of Waterloo* https://uwaterloo.ca/paris-to-projects/publications-o/reports-journal-papers-and-book-chapters.

sustainability and climate objectives.[15] However, for overall "contribution to sustainability" purposes, such a strategy would have to go beyond GHG reductions. The necessary steps include building the foundations for more sustainable livelihoods in a non-fossil fuel economy, assisting those displaced, and protecting the people and ecosystems most vulnerable to the turbulence of change.[16]

Climate change strategy needs are a particularly pressing example of a common challenge for sustainability-based assessments. In most areas of assessment application, taking sustainability objectives seriously entails examination of unconventional alternatives and adoption of new approaches to planning and decision making. As we have already seen in assessments under the old legislation, the space between conventional practice and more sustainable alternatives is difficult and contested. In that space, assessment decision making, and the processes supporting it, must be scrupulously impartial, rigorous, and open. The processes must respect diverse current interests and perspectives without compromising prospects for the future. They must engage the most informed and impartial expertise, attract willing collaboration, and build broad public awareness and understanding of the issues and options. As we have seen, even transitions clearly needed to secure lasting well-being face resistance from entrenched interests, fears about uncertain futures, and a shortage of easy win-win solutions. For sustainability-based assessment decision making, the credibility of process is as important as the quality of the decisions.

For decision making on project assessments, the key practical questions centre on how to determine the extent to which a proposed project, in comparison with reasonable alternatives, including the null option, will contribute to sustainability. The answers begin with establishing a "contribution to sustainability" test, identifying relevant general criteria and trade-off rules, determining how they should be specified for the case and context, and clarifying how they should be applied in project assessments. But given the distance between conventional and sustainability-enhancing practice, sustainability-based decision

---

15    Robert B Gibson, Karine Péloffy & Meinhard Doelle, "Challenges and Opportunities of a Forthcoming Strategic Assessment of the Implications of International Climate Change Mitigation Commitments for Individual Undertakings in Canada" (2018) 10:10 *Sustainability* 3747.

16    See Chapter 13 in this book.

making must also be informed by an understanding of how to proceed in realistic steps. As with the climate-centred transition, closing the gap between current practice and what is needed for sustainability overall may require targets and at least broadly delineated pathways as a basis for making decisions on projects.

Meeting these basic requirements for defensible sustainability-based project decision making involves assessment and decision making at the strategic level. Some issues may be candidate topics for regional and strategic assessments under the Act. Others may be addressed in different processes. The common need, however, is for authoritative and credible guidance based on respected processes and openly justified decisions.

## C. SUSTAINABILITY-BASED DECISION MAKING UNDER THE ACT

Chapter 9 of this book has outlined the key general prerequisites for comprehensive and credible application of a sustainability-based assessment agenda and has reviewed whether and how the needed scope and ambition of core prerequisites are addressed in the Act. In particular, Chapter 9 considered to what projects and other undertakings the Act applies, how well the assessment provisions for individual cases cover essential sustainability assessment needs, how expectations for process credibility are to be met, how the implementation of approved undertakings is to be followed up, and how the assessment process is to be linked to other sustainability-related initiatives and processes in Canada and beyond.

The discussion here focuses on sustainability-based decision making. It pays particular attention to the provisions of the Act that affect decision making on the approval (usually with conditions) or rejection of assessed undertakings at the project and strategic levels. However, it also considers decision making on other key aspects of implementing sustainability-based assessment law, especially decisions on application, regulatory and policy guidance, and negotiation of agreements with other jurisdictions. Accordingly, two core questions are addressed below in evaluating the key decision-making provisions of the Act: What is needed for credible and defensible sustainability-based decision making? To what extent are these needs met by the Act and associated initial regulations and policy guidance?

The six sections to follow cover the main determinants of adequate sustainability-based decision making under the Act. The first four sections consider the key foundations for sustainability-based decision making on assessed projects: sustainability's role in the context of other decision-making factors, the basic sustainability test and the role of alternatives, criteria for evaluation, and the information base and process. The fifth and sixth sections consider the extent to which these foundations are established for decision making on regional and strategic-level assessments and for decision making on other matters of assessment regime implementation, including decision making on application of assessment requirements, preparation of regulatory and policy guidance, and negotiation of collaborative arrangements with other jurisdictions.

### 1) Sustainability and Other Factors for Decision Making

### a) What Sustainability-Based Decision Making Requires

As an encapsulation of what is needed by present and future generations for lasting well-being, sustainability can represent the overall long-term public interest objective. For practical sustainability-based decision making, two kinds of elaboration of the general objective are needed. These are generic sustainability principles or criteria that are applicable everywhere and more specific criteria respecting the particular context of application.[17] Insofar as sustainability priorities or other considerations are to be addressed by decision makers, the statute and/or regulations or policy guidance need to clarify how potential tensions are to be resolved.

### b) What's in the Act and Associated Initial Regulations and Policy Guidance

As noted in Chapter 9, the Act establishes a "contribution to sustainability" test as the first of five core public interest considerations that decision makers must take into account.[18] The other four require attention to matters of federal jurisdiction, mitigation of adverse effects, impacts on Indigenous groups and rights, and implications for meeting Canada's environmental obligations and climate change commitments.

---

17    Both are addressed below in the section on criteria for decision making.

18    *IAA*, above note 1, s 63.

Since the sustainability test is the broadest, it could be taken as the umbrella concept under which the others are to be considered. However, the other, more specific considerations for decision makers represent priorities that the law makers found important to emphasize, in addition to integrated and long-term sustainability.

The Act does not say that "contribution to sustainability" is meant to be an umbrella concept for the other considerations. Nor does it indicate how decision makers are to combine attention to all five considerations and deal with any trade-offs. Also, it is not yet clear how fully the decision makers' deliberations will be reported to the public in the mandatory reasons for decision.[19] These deficiencies could be addressed in the short term through clarifying regulations and/or policy guidance and in the long term through revision of the statute. Such clarifications would be important for proponents, reviewers, and other assessment participants whose planning and engagement must anticipate how decision makers will treat the submitted evidence and analyses.

## 2) The Basic Sustainability Test and the Role of Alternatives in Decision Making on Assessed Undertakings at the Project Level

### a) What Sustainability-Based Decision Making Requires

Provisions for sustainability-based decision making in assessment law need to be clear about the basic nature of the test used to determine what may or may not be approved. Two broad approaches are available. The key factor is what role alternatives play in evaluations. In the first broad approach, the test question for assessment decision making is whether the project (or other undertaking) as proposed is or is not acceptable or could be acceptable if certain conditions were imposed. In the second broad approach, the test question is whether the proposed undertaking is the best option in comparison with feasible alternatives, including the null option.[20]

With the acceptability test, the assessed undertaking has to be examined in light of an acceptability standard of some sort: whether it is generally more positive than negative, whether it is on a defined pathway to meeting established goals, or whether it is sufficiently net

---

19    *IAA*, above note 1, ss 65–66.

20    Bram F Noble, *Introduction to Environmental Impact Assessment: A Guide to Principles and Practice*, 3d ed (Don Mills, ON: Oxford University Press, 2015).

positive to meet some valued non-sustainability objective (e.g., positive enough to make it politically attractive to the decision makers). For sustainability purposes, the best-option test is clearly preferable to any version of the acceptability test. A higher standard is set and potentially met. Proponents are encouraged to give serious and innovative attention to alternatives, and quicker progress toward sustainability may result. Adopting the best-option approach, however, forces assessment regimes to deal seriously with the long-standing weaknesses and challenges in alternatives assessment.

At the project level, ensuring meaningful assessment of a reasonable range of alternatives in light of public interest criteria has been difficult. To maximize sustainability contributions, the identification and comparison of reasonable alternatives must aim to serve the broad and long-term public interest. However, project proponents in the public and private sectors typically have narrowly focused purposes, mandates, motivations, and expertise. The common result is limited interest in considering options beyond their usual range. Also, the most attractive alternatives for contribution to sustainability purposes are often at the strategic level or require strategic-level action to become feasible. Consequently, commitment to seeking best options entails stronger emphasis on public interest purposes and alternatives in project assessments and, where the important promising alternatives involve strategic-level options, greater emphasis on the use of regional and strategic assessments to identify and compare alternatives that lie beyond the effective scope of project assessments.

### b) What's in the Act and Associated Initial Regulations and Policy Guidance

Just how a proposed project's contributions to sustainability will be assessed under the Act is not entirely clear. The Act establishes a suitably broad sustainability-oriented scope[21] and requires consideration of alternatives to the project[22] and alternative means of carrying it out.[23] Comparative evaluation of alternatives seems also to be expected. Although the Act does not include an explicit requirement to compare alternatives, there is no evident legislative rationale for mandatory

---

21    See Chapter 9.

22    *IAA* above note 1, s 22(1)(f).

23    *Ibid*, s 22(1)(e).

consideration of alternatives other than to enable comparison of the alternatives with the project as proposed.

The initial policy guidance following the enactment of the *IAA* generally failed to illuminate assessment of alternatives in light of sustainability-based public interest criteria. At one point, despite the Act's language about alternatives as factors that impact assessments "must take into account,"[24] the guidance presented consideration of alternatives as a discretionary matter that proponents must address in environmental impact statements only "[i]f required by the Agency."[25] Where alternatives assessment was required, the initial guidance encouraged proponents to do an alternatives assessment as "a process for optimizing the project"[26] and to compare project alternatives using explicit criteria.[27] However, the guidance did not state whether the criteria are to be sustainability based or whether the comparison is to establish that the best option has been selected in light of the legislated core decision factors.[28] No instruction on how to assess and avoid trade-offs was included. Also, the initial guidance tied relevant alternatives to the proponent's purposes rather than to public interest purposes.[29]

### 3) Criteria for Decision Making on Assessed Undertakings at the Project Level

### a) What Sustainability-Based Decision Making Requires

Decisions on the approval or rejection of assessed projects inevitably rest on some type of criteria for evaluation. Where the criteria are ill-defined or unstated, the assessment process is hampered by

---

24  *Ibid*, s 22(1).

25  Impact Assessment Agency of Canada, "Practitioner's Guide to Federal Impact Assessments Under the Impact Assessment Act" (2020) part 2.5, online: *Government of Canada* www.canada.ca/en/impact-assessment-agency/services/policy-guidance/practitioners-guide-impact-assessment-act.html ["Practitioner's Guide"]. The suggestion that consideration of alternatives in project assessments is not mandatory seems to be inconsistent with s 22(1) of the Act.

26  *Ibid*, part 2.4.

27  *Ibid*.

28  Comparison of alternatives and justification of the proposed project are addressed briefly, *ibid*, part 1.2, ss 4.3 & 4.4. The legislated core decision factors are in the *IAA*, above note 1, s 63.

29  Impact Assessment Agency of Canda, "Practitioner's Guide," above note 25, parts 2.4 & 2.5.

uncertain expectations, inconsistent practice, and minimal account-ability. Especially for sustainability-based assessments, application of well-conceived and explicit criteria is important.[30]

Although sustainability-based assessments, or the equivalent (e.g., broadly scoped public inquiries into long-term issues and options), have been undertaken in Canadian jurisdictions for several dec-ades,[31] most practice has been ad hoc, and reviews of the lessons to be drawn from these experiences have been rare.[32] Especially during the early years under the new Act, decision makers and other partici-pants will need guidance on how proposed projects will be evaluated, with and without possible conditions of approval and in comparison with alternatives. Also, because of the great proliferation of different and often misleading definitions and interpretations of sustainability, assessment regimes with sustainability-based agendas need to provide a reasonably clear base for understanding how the "extent to which a designated project contributes to sustainability"[33] is to be determined.

Establishing the necessary base begins with providing a suitable definition of sustainability, setting out associated basic principles, and listing especially important relevant considerations. These elements help clarify fundamental understandings and the major categories of effects and other considerations that will be covered. But for informed application and defensible decisions, the legislation or associated regu-lations and policy also need to provide proponents, decision makers, and other assessment participants with guidance on how the defin-itions, principles, and categories of considerations are to be elaborated

---

30    David Lawrence, "Integrating Sustainability and Environmental Impact Assessment" (1997) 21:1 *Environmental Management* 23.

31    Examples of Canadian assessments or similar processes with an effectively sustaina-bility-based agenda include the Mackenzie Valley Pipeline Inquiry (1974–77), Ontario's Class Environmental Assessment of Timber Management on Crown Lands (1987–1994), development of the Regional Growth Strategy for British Columbia's Capital Regional District (1996–2003), the Voisey's Bay Mine and Mill Environmental Assessment (1997–2002), Kemess North Copper-Gold Mine Environmental Assessment (2005–2007), and the Mackenzie Gas Project Environmental Assessment (2004–2009). See Robert B Gibson, "Sustainability Assessment in Canada" ch 11 in Alan James Bond, Angus Morrison-Saunders & Richard Howitt, eds, *Sustainability Assessment: Pluralism, Practice and Progress* (Abingdon, Oxon, UK: Routledge, 2013) 167.

32    *Ibid.*

33    *IAA*, above note 1, s 63(a).

and organized into a sustainability-based framework with explicit criteria for evaluating proposed projects.[34]

Guidance on sustainability-based criteria must address two key challenges. The first is to identify the broad categories of needed contributions to sustainability that apply everywhere and must be addressed in all cases. The second is to clarify how to recognize and incorporate attention to the much more specific and variable concerns and opportunities that affect how sustainability objectives can be pursued in particular cases and contexts.

Identifying appropriate generic sustainability criteria for assessment purposes does not demand blueprints for a sustainable future or even agreement on what qualifies as sustainable. It can rest adequately on a solid understanding of what is required for progress toward sustainability in general. Those requirements are not difficult to identify. After decades of deliberations, advances in sustainability science, and lessons from serious application efforts, the generic requirements for progress are quite evident. Box 14.1 provides a condensed version of the key requirements drawn from the broad sustainability literature.[35]

---

**BOX 14.1  KEY GENERIC REQUIREMENTS FOR PROGRESS TOWARD SUSTAINABILITY**

- *Life support:* establish and maintain the long-term integrity and irreplaceable functions of ecological and socio-biophysical systems
- *Livelihoods:* ensure that everyone and every community has enough for a decent life and opportunities to seek improvements
- *Intragenerational equity:* reduce inequities in sufficiency and opportunity between the advantaged and the disadvantaged
- *Intergenerational equity:* preserve or enhance the opportunities and capabilities of future generations to live sustainably
- *Resource maintenance and efficiency:* reduce extractive damage, avoid waste, and cut overall material and energy use per unit of benefit

---

34 Alan Bond, Angus Morrison-Saunders & Jenny Pope, "Sustainability Assessment: The State of the Art" (2012) 30:1 *Impact Assessment and Project Appraisal* 53; Robert B Gibson, ed, *Sustainability Assessment: Applications and Opportunities* (London, UK: Earthscan Publications/Routledge, 2017).

35 Adapted from Robert B Gibson et al, *Sustainability Assessment: Criteria and Processes* (London, UK: Earthscan, 2005) ch 5.

- *Understanding, commitment, and engagement:* build the capacity, motivation, and habitual inclination of individuals, communities, and other bodies to pursue lasting well-being
- *Precaution and adaptation:* respect uncertainty, plan to learn, design for surprise, and manage for adaptation
- *Immediate and long-term integration:* act on all requirements for sustainability at once, seeking mutually supportive benefits and multiple gains

Setting out these basic requirements in the form of generic criteria in authoritative guidance is important both to clarify expectations and to provide a foundation for consistent practice. But generic criteria are not sufficient by themselves. Assessment decision making in Canada involves many different kinds of undertakings across a country of great human and biophysical diversity. Suitable frameworks for evaluation must respect the specifics of case and context—the particular options, limitations, possibilities, and potential effects of different undertakings and the particular needs, opportunities, resources, capacities, valued components and interrelations, stresses, vulnerabilities, and uncertainties of different places.[36] Essentially, this entails setting out generic sustainability criteria and establishing appropriate processes for specifying the criteria for case and context.[37]

To specify sustainability-based criteria for a particular application, assessment participants must prepare an integrated set of criteria that combine the generic requirements for progress toward sustainability with recognition of the key case and context considerations. For each assessment, adequate information on these matters is needed, along with a credibly open and participative process for drafting and reviewing the specified criteria for evaluations and decisions. For overall consistency and rigour, the specification for context must not be allowed to compromise the generic requirements.

Finally, because progress toward sustainability depends on mutually supportive advances in all of the interconnected areas of concern (e.g., sustainable livelihoods, healthy ecological and socio-biophysical systems, greater efficiencies in resource use, greater equity in opportunities), avoiding or minimizing trade-offs is important. For trade-offs,

---

36  Jenny Pope et al, "Reconceptualising Sustainability Assessment" (2017) 62 *Environmental Impact Assessment Review* 205.

37  Gibson, above note 34.

the needed approach parallels the one for sustainability-based assessment criteria: establishing authoritative generic rules for avoiding or minimizing trade-offs and processes for specification of these rules for the case or context of particular applications.[38] As with the sustainability-based criteria, the specification of trade-off rules must not be allowed to compromise the generic requirements.

### b)  What's in the Act and Associated Initial Regulations and Policy Guidance

As reported in Chapter 9, the Act establishes the broad foundations for sustainability-based assessment but provides little elaboration. For decision making on designated projects, section 63 requires the minister and the Governor in Council to base their decisions on consideration of the assessment report and five public interest factors. As noted above, the first factor is the extent to which a proposed project "contributes to sustainability." The other four concern federal jurisdiction, implementation of mitigation measures, impacts on Indigenous groups and the rights of Indigenous peoples, and impacts on meeting Canada's environmental obligations and climate change commitments.[39] Listing these factors complements and clarifies the proper scope of the Act's sustainability-based public interest test. Further clarification is provided in section 22(1), which lists more specific sustainability-related factors for particular consideration, including positive and negative effects on environmental, social, economic, and health conditions; distributional effects related to identity factors; and cumulative and interactive effects. Finally, the Act requires decision makers to publish their reasons for decisions, based on the assessment report and mandatory public interest considerations.[40]

Arguably, these required factors for consideration and reasons for decisions entail transparent application of something that approximates a set of sustainability-based criteria. However, the Act does not say so explicitly. The word *criteria* does not appear in the Act's provisions on decision making — nor does *trade-offs*. Initial policy guidance on

---

38  Gibson et al, above note 35, ch 6; Angus Morrison-Saunders & Jenny Pope, "Conceptualising and Managing Trade-offs in Sustainability Assessment" (2013) 38 *Environmental Impact Assessment Review* 54.

39  *IAA*, above note 1, s 63.

40  *IAA*, above note 1, ss 65(2) and 66.

"considering the extent to which a project contributes to sustainability" provided a well-articulated but very basic set of fundamental principles. These were accompanied by helpful illustrations of implications for assessments, but the guidance stopped short of setting out generic criteria or considering how such criteria would be specified for particular applications.[41] Assessment authorities have plenty of documented experience from earlier sustainability-based assessments from which to draw good guidance on sustainability-based criteria development.[42] In their initial guidance, however, they chose not to make use of it.

### 4) Other Prerequisites for Effective and Credible Sustainability-Based Decision Making on Assessed Undertakings at the Project Level

### a) What Sustainability-Based Decision Making Requires

In addition to clear direction on the matters of purpose, basic test, alternatives, and criteria discussed above, good sustainability-based decision making depends on the law's provisions for application and information. These provisions determine what cases and what quality of documentation and analyses the decision makers receive.

As discussed in Chapter 9, the rules and practices that determine what proposed projects are subject to assessment should aim to cover all sustainability-significant projects, though with different assessment streams for more and less demanding cases. Also, the application provisions should be anticipatory, predefining the categories and kinds of projects subject to assessment so that proponents and planners can address assessment expectations from the conception of the project. Neither of these ideals can be met fully. Especially in Canada, assessment application is constrained by the complexities of separate though overlapping constitutional jurisdictions. Anticipatory application is at best difficult where innovations in project characteristics or context are involved. Also, there is no easily identified line between categories of projects that do or do not merit assessment, and there is limited capacity for doing assessments. Nevertheless, the basic principle holds. Anticipatory application should be the main approach, and application

---

41    Impact Assessment Agency of Canada, "Practitioner's Guide," above note 25, part 2.3.

42    For example, Joint Review Panel for the Mackenzie Gas Project, *Foundation for a Sustainable Northern Future* (December 2009), especially chapters 5 and 19, online: *Canadian Environmental Assessment Agency* www.acee-ceaa.gc.ca/default.asp?lang=En&n=155701CE-1.

decisions should clearly prioritize project categories that pose the greatest risks to lasting well-being and, consequently, the greatest need for and potential for benefit from assessment.

The quality of assessment information and analyses and the credibility of the assessment process determine the value of the assessment material upon which the decision makers rely. The core prerequisites are the sustainability-based scope and ambition examined in Chapter 9 and the matters of purpose and criteria discussed above. Other factors include provisions for obtaining information from diverse sources and perspectives; mobilizing independent expertise; ensuring rigorous public review with impartial analyses and evaluations; and learning from experience through effective follow-up, accessible reporting, and collaborations with other assessment and assessment-like bodies and jurisdictions.

### b)   What's in the Act and Associated Initial Regulations and Policy Guidance

The Act's sustainability-based scope, purposes, and requirements for decision making on designated projects are not accompanied by explicit provisions requiring sustainability-based decision making on what projects are to be assessed. Categories of projects subject to assessment under the Act are set out in the *Physical Activities Regulations*, commonly called the "Project List,"[43] which came into force along with the Act.[44] While drafting the Project List, the government initiated public consultations as well as discussions with other Canadian assessment jurisdictions and stakeholders. The decision making on project categories to include in the Project List, however, seems not to have applied the equivalent of the section 63 factors for consideration in project assessments and was not accompanied by detailed reasons for the decision. The resulting list restricts application more severely than did the previous federal assessment law, omits important categories of projects likely to have important sustainability implications,[45] and appears to have been influenced more by short-term political imperatives

---

43    SOR/2019-285.

44    See Chapter 7.

45    For example, the Project List does not include categories for projects such as cement plants with substantial lifetime GHG emissions, hydropower dams and new nuclear reactions with less than 200 MW of generating capacity, expansion of hydrocarbon pipeline capacity within the same right-of-way, and coal mines with less than 5,000 tonnes/day production capacity.

than by careful identification of project categories most likely to have significant implications for progress toward sustainability.[46]

The Act also empowers the minister of environment and climate change to designate physical activities (projects) not covered by the Project List.[47] The legislated grounds for such designations do not mention sustainability but are quite broad. Designation by the minister is allowed "if, in his or her opinion, either the carrying out of that physical activity may cause adverse effects within federal jurisdiction or adverse direct or incidental effects, or public concerns related to those effects warrant the designation."[48] If the case involves a designation request (rather than the minister's own initiative), the minister must respond with published reasons.[49]

On matters of information quality and process credibility, the initially available guidance left many big questions unanswered about the likely adequacy of the assessment reports that would inform project decision making. The guidance failed to describe the extent to which independent expertise would be used to enhance the reliability of data, interpretation, and analysis[50] or direct the Impact Assessment Agency of Canada (the Agency) and review panels on how to use their discretion in determining what is required to facilitate "meaningful public participation."[51] Nor did the initial guidance establish how the Agency and review panels would do their overall evaluations and justify the recommendations in their reports to decision makers. The Act requires project decisions to be based on these assessment reports and the five core considerations in section 63. But how that will be accomplished remains a mystery in the absence of clear guidance on how assessment reviewers are to evaluate proposed projects in light of their alternatives and the section 63 considerations.

---

46   See Chapter 7.

47   *Ibid.*

48   *IAA*, above note 1, s 9(1).

49   *Ibid*, s 9(4).

50   Impact Assessment Agency of Canada, "External Technical Reviews," online: *Government of Canada* www.canada.ca/en/impact-assessment-agency/services/policy-guidance/external-technical-reviews.html. See also Chapter 21 in this book.

51   *IAA*, above note 1, especially ss 11, 27, 51(1)(c), and 99.

## 5) Decision Making on Assessed Undertakings at the Regional and Strategic Levels

### a) What Sustainability-Based Decision Making Requires

Experience in Canada and internationally has repeatedly confirmed that project-level assessments have serious limitations when they raise issues involving major cumulative effects, broad alternatives, or unresolved policy questions.[52] Assessments at the regional and strategic levels are commonly advocated responses but have been used only occasionally and inconsistently in Canada.[53] Provisions for both regional and strategic assessment are included in the Act. The extent to which these provisions will be used, however, remains unclear.[54]

To some extent, regional and strategic assessments parallel project assessments but at a larger scale and with potentially broader influence. For decision making, they benefit similarly from sustainability-based scope and ambition, with public interest purposes, a clear sustainability test, and comparative evaluation of a reasonable range of alternatives in light of sustainability-based public interest criteria, specified for the case and context. To be credible, both regional and strategic assessments need to obtain information from diverse sources and perspectives, mobilize independent expertise, ensure rigorous public review with impartial evaluation, specify expectations for analyses, learn from experience through effective follow-up, incorporate accessible reporting, and facilitate collaborations with other assessment and assessment-like bodies and jurisdictions.

At the same time, sustainability-based decision making at the regional or strategic level has its own set of challenges, possibilities, and considerations for design and implementation. Regional and strategic undertakings and associated assessments are typically meant to provide responses to big issues in ways that guide deliberations and decision

---

52 Peter N Duinker & Lorne A Greig, "The Impotence of Cumulative Effects Assessment in Canada: Ailments and Ideas for Redeployment" (2006) 37:2 *Environmental Management* 153; Canadian Council of Ministers of the Environment, *Regional Strategic Environmental Assessment in Canada: Principles and Guidance* (Winnipeg: Canadian Council of Ministers of the Environment, 2009); Barry Sadler et al, eds, *Handbook of Strategic Environmental Assessment* (London, UK: Earthscan, 2011).

53 Bram Noble, "Promise and Dismay: The State of Strategic Environmental Assessment Systems and Practices in Canada" (2009) 29:1 *Environmental Impact Assessment Review* 66.

54 See chapters 11 and 17.

making on multiple individual activities, including projects subject to assessment requirements. Usually, they are government-led initiatives with the scope and mandate not only to address complex matters at the policy, plan, and program scale but also to compare significantly different response options and deliver decisions, or recommendations for decisions, that can be acted upon with authority and credibility. Less ambitious regional and strategic studies are sometimes labelled as assessments, but unless they lead to implementable guidance (e.g., in policy, plans, or programs), the label seems inappropriate.

Properly, assessment is incorporated into the development of regional and strategic undertakings much as it should be in project planning: with attention to alternatives and other mandatory factors for consideration folded into the process from the outset. Project assessments, however, typically centre on undertakings with established proponents. Regional and strategic assessments, in contrast, may be most necessary in situations where there is no immediately evident proponent. Especially where they are initiated to address major issues that have emerged in project assessments, regional and strategic assessments may be called upon to address problems and/or opportunities that do not fit within the mandate and capacity of any one agency or jurisdiction and that have been neglected in part because of the absence of clear responsibility and authority. That is often the case, for example, where there are unmet needs to address the cumulative ecological and socio-economic effects of ongoing or anticipated regional development. In such circumstances, the first step for a regional or strategic assessment may be to identify and assign a suitable proponent or team of proponents, perhaps through building collaborations with other jurisdictions, as well as clarifying purposes, options, and process specifics.

For decision-making purposes, the key characteristic of regional and strategic assessments is their role in producing a regional or strategic undertaking (a policy, plan, program, or the equivalent) that provides credible and authoritative direction for more specific activities, including projects subject to assessment requirement. For such applications, regional and strategic assessments need to be designed to deliver guidance with a scope and ambition that are equivalent to that expected at the project level and sufficiently comprehensive to cover the range of concerns and response needs raised by the regional and strategic issues involved. Especially where the project-level agenda is sustainability based, regional and strategic assessments must be sustainability based as well.

## b) What's in the Act and Associated Initial Regulations and Policy Guidance

The Act includes a concise set of provisions for regional and strategic assessments that enable rather than specify rules and processes for application.[55] Although the Act's sustainability-based agenda for project assessment decisions seems likely to influence the scope of regional and strategic assessments, nothing in the Act clearly establishes the basic scope of effects and other considerations to be addressed in these assessments. The assessments are to be initiated at the discretion of the minister and carried out by the Agency or a committee appointed by the minister.[56] The Act does not say what role or roles the Agency or an appointed committee could be assigned in a regional or strategic assessment (e.g., to develop and propose a strategic response to the identified issue, to assess the proposals of some other proponent or team of proponents, or merely to undertake or supervise studies) or what factors they would be expected to consider and what analyses they would be expected to carry out (e.g., of effects on Indigenous rights and on meeting environmental obligations and climate change commitments). Similarly, the Act leaves undefined the processes to be used by the Agency or committee, except that they must take into account scientific information and Indigenous knowledge, ensure appropriate opportunities for meaningful public participation, and make the information used available to the public.[57]

The product of a regional or strategic assessment is a report to the minister.[58] The Act requires reports to set out how Indigenous knowledge was taken into account[59] and requires the Agency to post all reports online.[60] But the Act is silent as to what the minister or other decision makers might do with a report once it has been submitted. Despite the strategic promise, the Act does not indicate whether report

---

55    *IAA*, above note 1, ss 92–103. See also Chapter 17.
56    *Ibid*, ss 92, 93, 95, & 96.
57    *Ibid*, ss 97(2), 98, & 99.
58    *Ibid*, s 102(1).
59    *Ibid*, s 102(2).
60    *Ibid*, s 103.

recommendations could be adopted as authoritative new policies, plans, or program, and, if so, what further deliberations, consultations, and decision making might be involved.

Early guidance for regional and strategic assessments provided little further clarification. The initial documents identified a range of potential roles for regional assessments, including data-gathering and trend analysis efforts that might provide useful information but would contribute only marginally to resolving major strategic issues facing project assessments. Although the initial guidance recognized a role for regional and strategic assessments in guiding project assessments,[61] it did not address aligning these assessments with the sustainability-based agenda for project assessments or anticipate application of the section 63 factors for consideration by decision makers. Also, it devoted little attention to other means of ensuring that regional or strategic guidance for project assessments is based on credibly rigorous, impartial, and participative processes.

For effective sustainability-based decision making, the Act's bare-bones regional and strategic assessment provisions need to be filled out by policy guidance and regulations. The most important contents would set out core expectations for credible processes, confirm that the section 22(1) scope and section 63 decision considerations apply to these assessments and establish means for decisions based on regional and strategic assessment reports to provide authoritative direction for planning and assessment at the project level. These components are priority candidates for entrenchment in law when the Act is next revised.

## 6) Decision Making on Other Key Matters of Assessment Regime Implementation

### a) What Sustainability-Based Decision Making Requires

In addition to rulings on proposed projects and regional and strategic-level issues and undertakings, legislated assessment regimes involve decision making on many other matters of implementation. Of these, the most important include application of assessment requirements,

---

61    Impact Assessment Agency of Canada, "Policy and Guidance: Regional Assessment Under the *Impact Assessment Act*," online: Government of Canada www.canada.ca/en/ impact-assessment-agency/services/policy-guidance/regional-assessment-impact-assessment-act.html.

preparation of regulatory and policy guidance, and negotiation of collaborative arrangements with other jurisdictions. All of these decisions ought to serve the lasting public interest. Especially in regimes that explicitly adopt a sustainability scope and ambition, application of sustainability-based criteria is appropriate, as are associated expectations for transparency and accountability, meaningful public participation, independent expertise and rigorous approaches to evidence, publication of detailed reasons for decisions, impartial administration, and commitment to continuous learning.[62]

### b) What's in the Act and Associated Initial Regulations and Policy Guidance

As with decision making on assessed regional and strategic undertakings, the Act is mostly silent about the extent to which sustainability-based considerations and criteria are to be applied in decision making on matters of application, regulatory and policy guidance, and collaborative arrangements with other jurisdictions.

As discussed above, the Act specifies some grounds for individual project-level designation decisions (including public concerns and potential for adverse effects, including on the rights of Indigenous people).[63] These considerations could be applied in ways roughly equivalent to a sustainability-based approach. However, the Act includes no specified grounds for making regulations (including the one that establishes the Project List), drafting policy guidance, or initiating regional and strategic assessments. The Act's provisions for entering into assessment-related agreements with other jurisdictions also include no mention of sustainability-based considerations or criteria.[64]

The Act's provisions on many of these matters include requirements for public notice and opportunities to comment (e.g., on "draft guidelines, codes of practice, agreements, arrangements or criteria"[65]). In addition, all decision making under the Act is broadly subject to its legislated purposes, the first of which is "to foster sustainability."[66] However, decision making on applications, important regulations, and

---

62  See chapters 15, 19, 21, & 22.
63  *IAA*, above note 1, s 9.
64  *Ibid*, s 114.
65  *Ibid*, s 114(3).
66  *Ibid*, s 6(1)(a).

agreements with other jurisdictions have long been treated as part of the political arena. In the absence of clear requirements for application of sustainability-based considerations and criteria, shorter-term political imperatives seem likely to prevail.

## D. CONCLUSIONS

The Act takes a large step toward establishing foundations for sustainability-based assessments and decisions. The core framing for that move is relatively well developed in the central portions of the Act concerning project-level assessments. However, the Act lacks specifics in many key areas and leaves many decisions open to the exercise of ministerial and/or Cabinet discretion. Much of the initial policy guidance for application of the project assessment provisions is timid, incomplete, and inclined to overuse "flexibility" as an excuse for vagueness about how expectations will be defined and how proposals will be evaluated by reviewers and decision makers. Especially problematic gaps include missing guidance on comparative evaluation of alternatives and the establishment of specified sustainability-based criteria for evaluations.

The most evident decision-related deficiencies in the Act lie within the provisions for decision making on the application of assessment requirements at the project and regional/strategic levels, on the processes for and products of regional and strategic assessments, and on the development of regulations, policy guidance, and agreements with other jurisdictions. In all of these areas, the Act provides general grounds for sustainability-based decision making but fails to establish specific requirements.

New and better regulations and policy guidance could address most of the identified gaps and deficiencies concerning decision making under the Act. Some of the current deficiencies may be due in part to uncertainties about the sustainability-based agenda and other key components of the Act (e.g., regional and strategic assessment), which are new in federal legislation. Consequently, there is an argument for beginning with clear but flexible policy guidance (that would continuously be improved) and moving to the greater firmness of regulations as experience and confidence build. However, continued reliance on the weak initial policy risks entrenchment of habitual low-performance implementation of a promising law.

In the absence of further specification and broader application of requirements for sustainability-based decision making, the Act remains vulnerable to poor implementation, even by otherwise reasonably forward-looking governments. Without clear and consistent presentation and application of a sustainability-based public interest test, the many key decisions made under the Act are likely to be inconsistent and unpredictable, plagued by interest-based interpretations of sustainability and easily influenced by voices favouring immediate political advantage and short-term convenience.

# CHAPTER 15

# Considering the Potential for Meaningful Public Participation Under Canada's *Impact Assessment Act*

*A John Sinclair and Alan P Diduck*[*]

## A. INTRODUCTION

Ensuring that the general public, stakeholder organizations, and other levels of government have a voice in decisions around development activities has long been a goal of the Canadian government.[1] For many, a high watermark in this regard was the Berger Inquiry, which took place in the 1970s in relation to a proposal to build a gas pipeline along the Mackenzie Valley.[2] Thomas Berger and his team did many new things, particularly in terms of public involvement, that were a departure from the past and set a benchmark for the future:

- Environmental and Indigenous organizations received funding to present their own expert witnesses at the formal hearings held in Yellowknife — a first.

[*] Research supporting this chapter was funded by the Social Science and Humanities Research Council of Canada (SSHRC).

1 Meaningful public participation involves objectives, principles, methods, and outcomes that are broadly applicable in Canada. For specific principles, rights, issues, and institutional arrangements pertaining to Indigenous peoples and governments, see chapters 6 and 9.

2 DJ Gamble, "The Berger Inquiry: An Impact Assessment Process" *Science* 199:4332 (3 March 1978) 946; Robert Page, *Northern Development: The Canadian Dilemma* (Toronto: McClelland and Stewart, 1986).

- Hearings were organized in more than thirty Dene, Inuit, and non-Aboriginal communities across the Northwest Territories so that residents could offer testimony.
- The Canadian Broadcasting Corporation created an Aboriginal news team that broadcast nightly reports from the inquiry in six languages.
- Hearings were also organized in cities across southern Canada so that all Canadians could express their views.
- The inquiry's final report, released on 9 May 1977, was a bestseller, with 10,000 copies in circulation by the end of the first week.[3]

Since the late 1970s, many reports, journal papers, and other publications have been written about the important role that environmental assessment (EA) processes can play in ensuring sound participation in decision making.[4] There are now also many practice manuals, regulatory guidance documents, and policy briefs that provide direction on public participation in assessments.[5] These recognize that the role of the public in EA has evolved significantly, especially as the focus has shifted from a technical exercise of predicting biophysical impacts of

3   First Nations Study Program, "Berger Inquiry," online: *University of British Columbia* https://indigenousfoundations.arts.ubc.ca/berger_inquiry/; "Hundreds Testify Before Berger" *CBC*, online: www.cbc.ca/player/play/1722833856.

4   Ciaran O'Faircheallaigh, "Public Participation and Environmental Impact Assessment: Purposes, Implications, and Lessons for Public Policy Making" (2010) 30:1 *Environmental Impact Assessment Review* 19; Richard K Morgan, "Environmental Impact Assessment: The State of the Art" (2012) 30:1 *Impact Assessment and Project Appraisal* 5; David P Lawrence, *Impact Assessment: Practical Solutions to Recurrent Problems and Contemporary Challenges* (Hoboken, NJ: John Wiley & Sons, 2013); A John Sinclair & Alan P Diduck, "Public Participation in Canadian Environmental Assessment: Enduring Challenges and Future Directions" in Kevin S Hanna, ed, *Environmental Impact Assessment: Practice and Participation* (Toronto: Oxford University Press, 2016) 65.

5   International Association for Public Participation, "IAP2 Core Values" (2014), online (pdf): www.iap2canada.ca/Resources/Documents/0702-Foundations-Core-Values-MW-rev1.pdf; Canadian Environmental Assessment Agency, "Public Participation Guide," online: www.canada.ca/en/impact-assessment-agency/services/policy-guidance/practitioners-guide-impact-assessment-act/guidance-public-particaption-impact.html; Organization of Economic Cooperation and Development, *OECD Due Diligence Guidance for Meaningful Stakeholder Engagement in the Extractive Sector* (2017), online: www. oecd.org/publications/oecd-due-diligence-guidance-for-meaningful-stakeholder-engagement-in-the-extractive-sector-9789264252462-en.html; Asian Development Bank, *Strengthening Participation for Development Results: An Asian Development Bank Guide to Participation* (2012), online: www.adb.org/documents/strengthening-participation-development-results-asian-development-bank-guide-participation.

proposed undertakings to impact assessment (IA) processes that consider a full range of social, economic, health, and cultural impacts of proposals.[6] This recognition has led to calls for participation in IA to be meaningful and based on principles such as including opportunities for dialogue and providing participant funding.[7]

Despite all of the attention that has been placed on creating meaningful opportunities for public participation in IA, many participants and those who have reviewed participation processes find the practice to be seriously flawed in many cases.[8] In the Canadian context, participation processes in IA now tend to focus on opportunities for passive involvement (e.g., letter writing) offered to those participants directly affected, with any participation events being run and reported on by the proponents of the undertaking being assessed.[9] Hearing panels and other tribunals are, of course, still in place in Canada, but, for the most part, their use is limited. Our purpose here is to consider the extent to which the *Impact Assessment Act (IAA)*[10] incorporates the principles of and opportunities for meaningful participation.

Federally, the need for meaningful public participation was first formally recognized when it was included as a stated purpose of EA in the now-repealed *Canadian Environmental Assessment Act, 2012 (CEAA*

6   John F Devlin, Nonita T Yap & Robert Weir, "Public Participation in Environmental Assessment: Case Studies on EA Legislation and Practice" (2005) 26:3 *Canadian Journal of Development Studies* 482; A John Sinclair, Alan P Diduck & Patricia J Fitzpatrick, "Conceptualizing Learning for Sustainability Through Environmental Assessment: Critical Reflections on 15 Years of Research" (2008) 28:7 *Environmental Impact Assessment Review* 415; Carla Lostarnau et al, "Stakeholder Participation Within the Public Environmental System in Chile: Major Gaps Between Theory and Practice" (2011) 92:10 *Journal of Environmental Management* 2470.

7   Jennifer MP Stewart & A John Sinclair, "Meaningful Public Participation in Environmental Assessment: Perspectives from Canadian Participants, Proponents, and Government" (2007) 9:2 *Journal of Environmental Assessment Policy and Management* 161; National Consumer Council, *Deliberative Public Engagement: Nine Principles* (2008), online (pdf): www.involve.org.uk/sites/default/files/uploads/Deliberative-public-engagement-nine-principles1.pdf; Sinclair & Diduck, above note 4; Ariana J McKay & Chris J Johnson, "Confronting Barriers and Recognizing Opportunities: Developing Effective Community-Based Environmental Monitoring Programs to Meet the Needs of Aboriginal Communities" (2017) 64 *Environmental Impact Assessment Review* 16.

8   O'Faircheallaigh, above note 4; Morgan, above note 4; Sinclair & Diduck, above note 4.

9   Robert B Gibson, "In Full Retreat: The Canadian Government's New Environmental Assessment Law Undoes Decades of Progress" (2012) 30:3 *Impact Assessment and Project Appraisal* 179.

10   SC 2019, c 28, s 1.

2012).[11] In initiating their review of federal decision processes in 2016, the Liberal government recognized, however, that federal EA law and policy needed to be updated to ensure that such participation occurs throughout the process. In fact, one of four key expectations of the review process, as expressed by the federal government itself, was to "provide ways for Canadians to express their views and opportunities for experts to meaningfully participate," as indicated in the mandate letter to Catherine McKenna, Minister of Environment and Climate Change.[12] To assist with the law reform process, McKenna struck the Expert Panel for the Review of Environmental Assessment Processes (Expert Panel), which travelled across Canada getting input from Canadians on needed reforms.[13] She also formed the Multi-Interest Advisory Committee (MIAC),[14] which met many times in Ottawa.

Reflecting views expressed by the people they consulted and some of the literature noted above, the Expert Panel concluded that significant improvements were needed to achieve the goal of meaningful public participation in EA in Canada.[15] Borrowing from Arnstein's (1969) classic ladder of citizen participation,[16] they noted the following:

> Current practices in Canada situate public participation in federal EA in the "Inform" and "Consult" categories. Current engagement practices, while varied, lean toward information dissemination rather than

---

11   SC 2012, c 19, s 52.

12   Prime Minister Justin Trudeau to Catherine McKenna, Minister of Environment and Climate Change, "Minister of Environment and Climate Change Mandate Letter" (12 November 2015), online: *Office of the Prime Minister* https://pm.gc.ca/en/mandate-letters/2015/11/12/archived-minister-environment-and-climate-change-mandate-letter.

13   Expert Panel members included Johanne Gélinas (Chair), Doug Horswill, Rod Northey, and Renée Pelletier.

14   The MIAC was chaired by the then vice president of policy of the Canadian Environmental Assessment Agency and included eighteen members with representation from Indigenous organizations, environmental non-governmental organizations, and industry associations, as well as additional participants from within the federal government, such as the Canadian Nuclear Safety Commission. The lead author was a member of the MIAC.

15   Expert Panel for the Review of Environmental Assessment Processes, *Building Common Ground: A New Vision for Impact Assessment in Canada* (Ottawa: Canadian Environmental Assessment Agency, 2017), online (pdf): *Government of Canada* www.canada.ca/content/dam/themes/environment/conservation/environmental-reviews/building-common-ground/building-common-ground.pdf [*Building Common Ground*].

16   Sherry R Arnstein, "A Ladder of Citizen Participation" (1969) 35:4 *Journal of the American Institute of Planners* 216.

mutual learning and inclusive dialogue, and information gathering rather than clear integration of this information into project design or approval requirements.[17]

The Panel offered three key recommendations on how to improve public participation in the assessment process:

1) IA legislation requires that IA provide early and ongoing public participation opportunities that are open to all. The results of public participation should have the potential to impact decisions.
2) The participant funding program for IA should be commensurate with the costs associated with meaningful participation in all phases of IA, including monitoring and follow-up.
3) IA legislation requires that IA information be easily accessible and permanently and publicly available.[18]

The MIAC itself spent considerable time developing a set of ten overarching principles for meaningful participation in federal EA that they felt would set a foundation for strong and meaningful participatory processes and that, if properly applied, would help restore trust and faith in federal EA. The principles encompass timing, impacts, inclusivity, formality, accessibility, fairness, and other important attributes of meaningful participation (Box 15.1).

---

**BOX 15.1   MIAC PRINCIPLES OF MEANINGFUL PUBLIC PARTICIPATION**[19]

- Participation *begins early in the decision process, is meaningful,* and builds public confidence.
- Public input can *influence* or *change the outcome or project* being considered.
- Opportunities for public comment are *open to all interested parties,* are varied and flexible, *include openings for face-to-face discussions,* and involve the public in the design of an appropriate participation program.
- Formal processes of engagement, such as hearings and various fora of dispute resolution, are specified, and *principles of natural justice and procedural fairness are considered in formal processes.*
- Adequate and *appropriate notice* is provided.

---

17   *Building Common Ground,* above note 15 at 44.
18   *Ibid* at 45, 47, and 49.
19   MIAC, *Advice to the Expert Panel Reviewing Environmental Assessment Processes from the Multi-Interest Advisory Committee* (Ottawa: 2016) at 41–42 (on file with authors) [MIAC Report].

- *Ready access to the information and the decisions at hand* is available and in languages spoken, read, and understood in the area.
- *Participant assistance and capacity building* are available for informed dialogue and discussion.
- Participation programs are *learning oriented* to ensure outcomes for all participants, governments, and proponents.
- Programs *recognize the knowledge and acumen of the public.*
- Processes need to be *fair and open* in order for the public to be able to accept a decision.

The recommendations of the Expert Panel and the MIAC reflect quite closely calls in both the national and international literature for more meaningful participation in EA.[20] Importantly, they establish that the EA playing field is not balanced and that special care needs to be taken to accommodate various actors and their interests throughout the assessment process. They also recognize the importance of moving beyond the default or "go to" approaches to participation now common to EA, such as open houses and letter writing, to more deliberative forms of participation.[21]

## B.  PROVISIONS FOR MEANINGFUL PARTICIPATION IN THE *IAA*

The federal government noted that the *IAA* includes sixteen sections related to meaningful participation.[22] Perhaps one of the most significant reforms, however, relates to what is not in the *IAA*. The statute does not create standing requirements, such as were found in *CEAA 2012*, thereby restoring the right of any interested member of the public to

---

20    Stewart & Sinclair, above note 7; O'Faircheallaigh, above note 4; National Consumer Council, above note 7; Sinclair & Diduck, above note 4.

21    Thomas Webler, Hans Kastenholz & Ortwin Renn, "Public Participation in Impact Assessment: A Social Learning Perspective" (2005) 15:5 *Environmental Impact Assessment Review* 443; Hans Wiklund, "In Search of Arenas for Democratic Deliberation: A Habermasian Review of Environmental Assessment" (2005) 23:4 *Environmental Impact Assessment Review* 281; A John Sinclair & Alan P Diduck, "Reconceptualizing Public Participation in Environmental Assessment as EA Civics" (2017) 62:1 *Environmental Impact Assessment Review* 174 [Sinclair & Diduck, "Reconceptualizing"].

22    Impact Assessment Agency of Canada, "Interim Framework: Public Participation Under the Impact Assessment Act," online (pdf): *Government of Canada* www.canada.ca/content/dam/iaac-acei/documents/policy-guidance/pp-pp/public-participation-framework-en.pdf ["Interim Framework: Public Participation"].

participate in an assessment. Other provisions in the Act dealing with public participation include the preamble and various sections covering notice requirements, opportunities for public input in the various phases of an assessment, access to information, and participant funding.

The preamble to the *IAA* states that the Government of Canada "is committed to providing Canadians with the opportunity to participate in [the assessment] process and with the information they need in order to be able to participate in a meaningful way." Section 6(1)(h) goes on to state that a purpose of the *IAA* is "to ensure that opportunities are provided for meaningful public participation during an impact assessment, a regional assessment or a strategic assessment." Furthermore, section 6(1)(j) states that a purpose of the Act is "to ensure that an impact assessment takes into account scientific information, Indigenous knowledge and community knowledge." Additionally, section 22 indicates that the IA of a designated project "must take into account ... community knowledge provided with respect to the designated project [and] comments received from the public."

The actual process for the assessment of designated projects under the *IAA* can be broken into key phases, including planning, assessment by the Impact Assessment Agency of Canada (the Agency) or a review panel, decision making, and follow-up. The planning phase will be carried out for all projects assessed. Section 11 ensures that the public will have an opportunity to participate meaningfully in early planning "in a manner that the Agency considers appropriate." The *IAA* sets out 180 days for the planning phase, during which a decision will be made about whether an assessment is necessary. This decision must consider comments received from the public. If an assessment is required, section 18 calls on the Agency to post a copy of the designated project description and provide the proponent with a notice of commencement and any documents, such as plans for public participation. The decision whether to refer the assessment to a review panel is to be made within forty-five days of the notice of commencement. This decision must be based on the potential for adverse effects on areas of federal jurisdiction, public concern, opportunities for collaboration with other jurisdictions, and any impact on the rights of Indigenous peoples, but the final decision is discretionary and left in the hands of the minister.

If the IA is Agency led, section 27 requires the Agency to "ensure that the public is provided with an opportunity to participate meaningfully, in a manner that [it] considers appropriate, within the time period specified by the Agency." The Agency must also ensure that a draft IA report that includes any comments received from the public be posted and that the public has an opportunity to provide comments on the draft report (section 28). If the assessment proceeds by way of a review panel, section 51 outlines various obligations, such as the need for the panel to "hold hearings in a manner that offers the public an opportunity to participate meaningfully." Timelines have been set for assessments led by the Agency (300 days) and the panel (600 days). If the minister is considering a request that an assessment be permitted to proceed by way of substitution, section 31 of the *IAA* requires that the request be posted, that the public be given the opportunity to comment on it, and that public comments be taken into account in making any decision. If a substitution is approved, the minister must be satisfied that "the public will be given an opportunity to participate meaningfully in the assessment and provide comments on a draft report" and have access to information "in relation to the assessment to enable its meaningful participation" (section 33).

The only mention of the follow-up phase of assessment with regard to public participation comes in section 75, which is related to participant funding programs. This section indicates that the Agency must provide participant funding for the design and/or implementation of follow-up programs. This section also extends the Agency's participant funding obligations to preparations for a possible IA and the IA of a designated project. These opportunities for participant assistance also apply to regional and strategic assessments.

In terms of information sharing throughout all phases of assessment, section 105 states that the "Agency must establish and maintain an Internet site that is available to the public." The site must include records relating to designated projects, notices requesting public participation in an assessment, a description of the factors to be taken into account in the assessment and the scope of those factors, any scientific information received or a summary of the information and an indication of how the information may be obtained, the IA report, a description of the follow-up program and any results as well as any public comments received, and other documents or information.

Since the passage of the *IAA*, the Agency has produced information on implementing public participation. This includes a fact sheet on public participation in IA[23] and an interim framework and interim guidance on public participation under the IAA, both of which are contained in the "Practitioner's Guide to Federal Impact Assessments Under the Impact Assessment Act,"[24] which is directed at proponents.

The fact sheet provides the only definition of meaningful participation, indicating that it

> means that members of the public who want to engage in public consultations have an opportunity to do so. It means that they have access to the information they need to take part in an informed way, and that their perspectives inform and influence decisions. Meaningful public participation means that consultation processes are open, transparent and inclusive and that they occur in a timely manner.[25]

The fact sheet and the interim framework document also establish a list of overarching principles that are meant to guide the Agency's approach to public participation. These principles largely echo those put forward by the MIAC (Box 15.1), although this set includes a reference to prioritizing the participation of those who are *most affected* by a proposed project, which was not part of the MIAC principles. Nor does this set refer to the principles of natural justice and procedural fairness, provide an assurance that programs should be open, or recognize the knowledge and acumen of public participants.

The fact sheet and framework also provide examples of the methods and tools for implementing public participation, including ways of *sharing* information, for example, through social media and open houses, and ways of *gathering* information, such as through workshops, informal meetings, and other in-person events. The framework repeatedly establishes that timelines for assessment are set in legislation and that the

---

23    Impact Assessment Agency of Canada, "Public Participation in Impact Assessment," online: *Government of Canada* www.canada.ca/en/impact-assessment-agency/services/policy-guidance/public-participation-impact-assessment-fact-sheet.html.

24    Impact Assessment Agency of Canada, "Practitioner's Guide to Federal Impact Assessments Under the Impact Assessment Act," online: *Government of Canada* www.canada.ca/en/impact-assessment-agency/services/policy-guidance/practitioners-guide-impact-assessment-act.html; Impact Assessment Agency of Canada, "Interim Framework: Public Participation" above note 22.

25    Above note 23.

Agency or a Review Panel may take measures to prioritize the allocation of time at an in-person event to those individuals or groups that, in the view of the Agency or Review Panel, are the most likely to be impacted by the project, or to those most likely to have relevant expertise or information to provide.[26]

The framework goes on to note the importance of access to information and the role of the Public Registry[27] and the Open Science and Data Platform being developed by Natural Resources Canada and Environment and Climate Change Canada. A general outline of how meaningful participation can proceed is also provided. The importance of public participation during the planning phase is noted because participation in this phase is viewed as being critical to "build awareness and trust in the process," setting "clear objectives for public participation," and allowing "for issues and concerns to be identified early."[28]

The interim guidance document is designed as a compendium to the framework, and in addition to establishing tools for meaningful participation and emphasizing timelines, as noted above, the document goes on to provide information on how participation may occur in each phase of the assessment and who is responsible for various activities in each phase. In terms of the planning phase, for example, it is noted that, "[p]ublic participation opportunities and methods will be established in consideration of community needs, the complexity of the project, legislated timelines and consultation timelines set by the Agency."[29] As part of this phase, a public participation plan is to be developed and what could be contained in that document is established, including the following:

- a summary of how the public's comments were considered in the development of the public participation plan
- details about how the public can learn more about the project or sign up to receive notifications when new information is made available
- dates, times, locations, and methods for public participation planned for each phase of the IA and how notifications will be publicized

---

26  "Interim Framework: Public Participation," above note 22 at 6.

27  See Chapter 19.

28  "Interim Framework: Public Participation," above note 22 at 8.

29  *Ibid.*

- information about how public comments will be considered in the IA
- an overview of potential techniques that will be used to engage participants throughout the review, such as public hearings or online questionnaires
- information on participant funding and the application process for financial support to facilitate public participation

The Agency responsibilities at this phase are noted as relating to engaging the public, considering feedback, preparing a summary of issues, and posting documents to the registry. Activities related to participation and associated responsibilities are outlined for each of the five key phases of assessment under the *IAA* noted above, with the exception of follow-up.

## C. ANALYSIS OF THE PROVISIONS FOR MEANINGFUL PUBLIC PARTICIPATION IN THE *IAA*

As others have established,[30] whether public participation is meaningful and whether the benefits of participation are realized depend, to a large extent, on the legislation and policy applicable to a particular IA system. Although the *IAA* calls for meaningful public participation and includes provisions for early involvement, participant funding, and access to information, other attributes of meaningful participation are not addressed. There is nothing in the Act to ensure that the opportunities for participation that unfold during an IA will, in fact, be meaningful. Moreover, the call for meaningful participation in the purposes section of the *IAA* mirrors *CEAA 2012*, which is concerning given that the implementation of that Act was so problematic and resulted in considerable loss of public trust in the process.[31] Additionally, in the course of replacing *CEAA 2012*, input from many sectors called for meaningful

---

30 Judith Petts, "Public Participation and Environmental Impact Assessment" in Judith Petts, ed, *Handbook of Environmental Impact Assessment. Volume 1: Environmental Impact Assessment: Process, Methods and Potential* (Oxford, UK: Blackwell Science, 1999) 145; A John Sinclair & Alan P Diduck, "Public Involvement in Environmental Assessment in Canada: A Transformative Learning Perspective" (2001) 21:2 *Environmental Impact Assessment Review* 113; O'Faircheallaigh, above note 4; Morgan, above note 4; Sinclair & Diduck, "Reconceptualizing," above note 21.

31 Gibson, above note 9.

participation to be defined in the new statute in order to provide clear legislative direction. The MIAC, for example, suggested that "[m]eaningful public participation refers to processes that incorporate all of the essential components of participation, from the opportunity to provide input to active and critical exchange of ideas among proponents, regulators, and participants."[32]

However, because meaningful participation is not defined in the *IAA*, implementing it when called for in an IA will be left to discretion, as it was in the past,[33,34] and to policy and guidance documents with no legislative standing. The definition and principles for meaningful participation contained in the framework and guidance for proponents are, of course, helpful as they signal administrative intent. But taken in the context of the other direction provided in those documents, as discussed below, there is reason to question how meaningful participation will be achieved.

The establishment of the planning phase, and the call for meaningful participation within it, is a very important innovation of the *IAA*. Proponents of more meaningful participation have long called for earlier engagement, especially before irrevocable decisions are made.[35] As outlined above, this phase is critical because it is here that the decision will be made as to whether or not to proceed with an assessment, and if so, requirements for public notice and the development of assessment guidelines come into play. Having the opportunity to provide input to these decisions set forth in legislation is an important advancement from previous IA regimes. Perhaps most importantly for the assessment itself, this stage will result in the development of a public participation plan. The development of such a plan is important for both Agency-led assessments and panel reviews because it can be an effective way to

---

32    MIAC Report, above note 19 at 41.

33    Meinhard Doelle, "CEAA 2012: The End of Federal EA as We Know It?" (2012) 24:1 *Journal of Environmental Law & Practice* 1.

34    Gibson, above note 9.

35    Md Arif Hasan, Kh Md Nahiduzzaman, & Adel S Aldosary, "Public Participation in EIA: A Comparative Study of the Projects Run by Government and Non-governmental Organizations" (2018) 72:1 *Environmental Impact Assessment Review* 12; Sinclair & Diduck, "Reconceptualizing," above note 21; Thomas Meredith, "Assessing Environmental Impacts in Canada" in Bruce Mitchell, ed, *Resource and Environmental Management in Canada: Addressing Conflict and Uncertainty* (Don Mills, ON: Oxford University Press, 2004) 467.

encourage the use of a wide range of public engagement tools rather than defaulting to formal hearings and written submissions as the only ways to engage. Unfortunately, the *IAA* is not clear on when or how the development of the plan will occur, nor is the guidance material that has been produced to this point.

Recent discussions about the Webequie Supply Road Project[36] (associated with the Ring of Fire mine development[37]) provide the first window into how the planning phase could unfold. A major focus of the planning phase, according to the guidance documents, is on understanding the "concerns" people have about the designated project. In this case, the Agency indicated that after it issued notice of receiving an initial project description, there would be twenty days available for public consultations. The Agency also said that at or before the eighty-day point, a decision would be made about whether to proceed with an assessment. If the decision is affirmative, draft assessment guidelines will be prepared and public consultation on the guidelines will occur. Also, if the decision is made to proceed with an assessment, the forty-five-day period would begin for the minister to decide if the assessment will proceed by way of a panel review. It is not clear from this approach to the 180-day planning phase when the public participation plan will be developed. These timelines are obviously very tight, especially for receiving initial concerns about a project or an undertaking.

In the case of a decision to refer the assessment to a panel, the *IAA* is not clear on how the public participation plan developed during the planning phase will be implemented by the panel and how the panel will be given the time and capacity to do so. The central point is that the decision to refer to a panel should not predetermine the form of engagement. It will be critical for the panel to move ahead with the public participation plan, especially since the plan may encourage use of diverse engagement tools, and for the panel to carefully consider the time needed to implement the plan effectively. A panel-led assessment should not rely primarily on formal hearings as the challenges of doing so are well known (e.g., strict standing requirements, cost barriers, procedural formality) and are often magnified for Indigenous

---

36    Impact Assessment Agency of Canada, "Webequie Supply Road Project," online: *Government of Canada* www.ceaa-acee.gc.ca/050/evaluations/proj/80183?culture=en-CA.

37    Ontario, Ministry of Energy, Northern Development and Mines, "Ring of Fire," online: *Government of Ontario* www.mndm.gov.on.ca/en/ring-fire.

communities because of insufficient attention given to their legal and decision-making traditions. Additionally, the requirement for assessments to include broader social, health, and economic considerations makes the use of engagement tools that are appropriate for affected communities more urgent than ever.[38]

Timelines are often mentioned in the *IAA* and especially in the guidance material developed to this point in relation to the planning and assessment phases, as outlined above. The literature suggests that strict timelines often put serious limitations on the engagement techniques used and the ability to deliver on meaningful participation.[39] For example, the twenty–day period noted above to get input on public concerns about a project proposal is very short and likely led to reliance on online comments (an impersonal and somewhat inaccessible technique) to gather input. In the context of the planning (180 days) and assessment (300 or 600 days) stages, it is not unreasonable to think that the Agency or a panel may need more time if they wanted to engage in deliberative forms of involvement with participants, which is increasingly likely given the new requirement in the *IAA* to undertake gender and diversity analysis.[40] Likewise, ensuring the meaningful engagement of affected communities and finding the needed capacity for such engagement could be valid reasons for stopping the clock. Another important reason for stopping the clock would be to provide time for the provision of information responses, particularly by government actors in other jurisdictions or other parties that are not responding in a timely way. It also seems reasonable to think that a proponent may

---

38   Patricia J Fitzpatrick & A John Sinclair, "Learning Through Public Involvement in Environmental Assessment Hearings" (2003) 67:2 *Journal of Environmental Management* 161; Susan Rutherford & Karen Campbell, *Time Well Spent? A Survey of Public Participation in Federal Environmental Assessment Panels* (Vancouver, BC: West Coast Environmental Law, 2004), online: www.wcel.org/publication/time-well-spent-survey-public-participation-federal-environmental-assessment-panels-0.

39   Mark S Reed et al, "A Theory of Participation: What Makes Stakeholder and Public Engagement in Environmental Management Work?" (2017) 26:S1 *Restoration Ecology* S7; Meinhard Doelle & A John Sinclair, "Mediation in Environmental Assessment in Canada: Unfulfilled Promise?" (2010) 33(1): *Dalhousie Law Journal* 117; Alan P Diduck, Maureen G Reed & Colleen George, "Participatory Approaches to Resource and Environmental Management" in Bruce Mitchell, ed, *Resource and Environmental Management in Canada: Addressing Conflict and Uncertainty*, 5th ed (Toronto: Oxford University Press, 2015) 142.

40   See Chapter 12.

need to request suspension of a timeline to resolve in a satisfactory manner highly vexing or contentious issues.

Trying to deal with all of these potential time management considerations, along with incorporating deliberative engagement techniques, within a strict timeline seems at odds with the goal of achieving meaningful public participation. Compounding this problem is that the *IAA* and available guidance material make it clear that decisions with regard to the time available for participation will be at the discretion of the minister and Agency and in terms of what they "consider appropriate and within the time period specified."[41] Experience suggests that this discretion will more than likely be exercised against extending timelines in aid of achieving meaningful participation. Furthermore, there is no explicit provision for deliberative forms of engagement, such as alternative dispute resolution, scenario workshops, and nominal group techniques, despite calls for this in the literature.[42] Importantly, however, section 54 does allow panels some flexibility in the conduct of hearings, which may allow for alternative approaches to be used.

Beyond the assessment phase, a key shortcoming of the *IAA* concerns involvement in and accountability for the post-approval process.[43] Other than section 75, which indicates that the Agency must provide participant funding for the design and implementation of follow-up programs, there are no specific requirements in the *IAA* for public participation in follow-up. Moreover, there is no clarity on the allocation of responsibility for follow-up (particularly when multiple jurisdictions are involved), how communities will be involved, what happens when predictions made during the assessment turn out to be wrong, and when mitigation measures are not effective in achieving the expected outcomes.[44] These gaps are problematic for several reasons, not the least of which is the missed opportunity for legislating and thereby advancing community-based monitoring. This form of monitoring presents opportunities for integrating local and Indigenous understanding into follow-up and enables mutual learning among scientific, local, and

---

41    "Interim Framework: Public Participation," above note 22 at 11.

42    Doelle & Sinclair, above note 39; Sinclair & Diduck, "Reconceptualizing," above note 21.

43    Lawrence, above note 4; *Federal Environmental Assessment Reform Summit* (Vancouver: West Coast Environmental Law, 2016) online (pdf): www.wcel.org/sites/default/files/publications/WCEL_FedEnviroAssess_ExecSum%2Bapp_fnldigital.pdf.

44    Lawrence, above note 4; Angus Morrison-Saunders et al, "Towards Sustainability Assessment Follow-up" (2014) 45:1 *Environmental Impact Assessment Review* 38.

Indigenous knowledge holders.[45] Also absent are provisions to ensure that the results of follow-up are permanently available to the public, for both accountability and learning purposes for future assessments, as called for by the Expert Panel and in the literature.[46]

The *IAA* generally rates well on access to information and the need to publish reasons for key decisions during the assessment process. The Agency is in the midst of improving its internet site to make it easy to navigate and to ensure that it contains all of the necessary information, such as the various notices required by the *IAA*. This is in keeping with calls in the literature for transparency and easy opportunities to review and comment on documents.[47] Such improvements will need to be ongoing as the Gazoduq liquefied natural gas case[48] is revealing problems with the system, such as the type of information available on a case depending on how one enters the registry site (i.e., which page you land on) and how documents such as public comments are organized, among other issues. According to the guidance documents, the Agency is also looking to use social media in all phases of the assessment to help keep people informed and engaged. The *IAA* itself does specifically address communications requirements, and it is unclear if the sorts of innovative communication called for in the literature (e.g., using cloud environments) will be implemented through guidance.[49]

The provisions respecting participant funding programs are also strong in section 75 and require funding opportunities to be provided in all of the key phases of the process; as such, they are in line with the literature[50] and what civil society organizations have been requesting

---


45    McKay & Johnson, above note 7.

46    Webler, Kastenholz & Renn, above note 21; Sinclair et al, above note 6; Sinclair & Diduck, "Reconceptualizing," above note 21; *Building Common Ground*, above note 15.

47    Lisa Odparlik, "Are Agencies Turning a Blind Eye to Public Access to Environmental Assessment Information?" (2015) 17:03 *Journal of Environmental Assessment and Policy Management* 1.

48    "Gazoduq Project," online: *Impact Assessment Agency of Canada* https://iaac-aeic.gc.ca/050/evaluations/proj/80264.

49    A John Sinclair, Timothy J Peirson-Smith & Morrissa Boerchers, "Environmental Assessment in the Internet Age: The Role of E-Governance and Social Media in Creating Platforms for Meaningful Participation" (2017) 35:2 *Impact Assessment and Project Appraisal* 148.

50    Sinclair & Diduck, above note 4; Sarah Lynn & Peter Wathern, "Intervener Funding in the Environmental Assessment Process in Canada" (1991) 6:3 *Project Appraisal* 169.

for years.[51] Funding is also available for participation in regional and strategic assessments, but no direction is offered on how to implement meaningful participation for these types of assessment. The literature is quite clear on the benefits of participation in strategic assessments[52] and that it is most often not done well, so the lack of direction with regard to meaningful participation in regional and strategic assessments is a serious gap in the *IAA*.[53] Of course, the amount of participant funding in any type of assessment, and how to access funding, will likely continue to be issues of concern for public intervenors, as they have been in the past. For example, there is no direction in the current guidance material about the timing of funding awards. In the past, awards have often been made with insufficient time to do the work being funded. The strict timelines in the *IAA* will mean that practice in this regard will have to improve.

It is also important to note that there are some concerning aspects to the framework and guidance material. Non-government organizations and academics have raised concerns about overemphasizing participation activities for those designated as "directly affected," while leaving out others who may have very legitimate concerns about a project or undertaking.[54] For example, both the framework and guidance documents indicate that the Agency or review panel may take measures to "prioritize the allocation of time at an in-person event" to individuals and groups that are most likely to be impacted by the project and may focus in-person participation events "on those nearest the project." Furthermore, they may limit input to other means to allow "the process to handle high participation rates."[55] This guidance suggests that electronic means of participation may be relied on for those who

---

51    West Coast Environmental Law, above note 43; Environmental Planning and Assessment Caucus, *A Federal Environmental Assessment Process: The Core Elements* (Ottawa: Canadian Environment Network, 1988).

52    See Chapter 17.

53    Carlo Rega & Giorgio Baldizzone, "Public Participation in Strategic Environmental Assessment: A Practitioners' Perspective" (2014) 50 *Environmental Impact Assessment Review* 105; Bram F Noble, "Promise and Dismay: The State of Strategic Environmental Assessment Systems and Practices in Canada" (2009) 29:1 *Environmental Impact Assessment Review* 66.

54    A John Sinclair & Patricia J Fitzpatrick, "Provisions for More Meaningful Public Participation Still Elusive in Proposed Canadian EA Bill" (2002) 20:3 *Impact Assessment and Project Appraisal* 161; Gibson, above note 9.

55    "Interim Framework: Public Participation," above note 22 at 6.

are not "directly affected" and as a general default. Furthermore, as established above, the guidance documents are also silent on how the plan for meaningful participation is going to be developed. It is clear that the Agency will hold the pen in writing the participation plan but not how the public will be engaged in this activity.

## D.  CONCLUSIONS AND ACTIONS NEEDED

The federal government created high expectations regarding meaningful participation during its recent reform of the EA process. After the introduction of Bill C-69, however, it became clear that there was strong opposition to such provisions from some provinces and industry sectors. In particular, there was vocal opposition to broad public participation.[56] Ultimately, meaningful public participation under the *IAA* is left mostly to the discretion of the Agency and the minister. Without clear legislative direction that provides the necessary incentives, meaningful participation will likely continue to be elusive.[57]

In relation to the principles established by the federal government and the MIAC (above), many are reflected in the *IAA*, such as the provision of notice of a project or an undertaking being considered, participant funding, access to information, early participation, and the potential for input to influence decisions. The federal government has worked to achieve these principles in the past, so it is not surprising that they are reflected in the *IAA*. Still, issues are likely to arise in relation to the implementation of these principles, as suggested in the discussion above. Where the *IAA* and the principles differ is in relation to who is engaged and how. The interim framework indicates as a principle that participation activities are "designed to prioritize those most affected."[58] This was not suggested by the MIAC, the Expert Panel, or the literature;[59] in fact, the literature specifically indicates that this should be avoided.

As well, the MIAC principles and the literature promote the use of a variety of tools and techniques for engaging the public, whereas

---

56    See, for example, Hall Findlay & Orenstein, online: *Canada West Foundation* https://cwf.ca/research/publications. Bill C-69 was the precursor to the IAA.

57    Judith Petts, "Barriers to Deliberative Participation in EIA: Learning from Waste Policies, Plans and Projects" (2003) 5:3 *Journal of Environmental Assessment and Policy Management* 269; Sinclair & Fitzpatrick, above note 54; Meredith, above note 35.

58    "Interim Framework: Public Participation," above note 22 at 4.

59    West Coast Environmental Law, above note 43; Gibson, above note 9.

the principles articulated by the government prioritize "methods that are flexible, innovative and *consider the assessment context and legislated timelines.*"[60] The concern is that context and timelines will more often than not be used in the name of efficiency to justify overreliance on passive and impersonal techniques rather than deliberative and interactive ones. Additionally, the MIAC principles and the literature specifically call for the use of various forms of dispute resolution, which is also absent from the *IAA* and guidance.[61] This, again, leaves the adoption of innovative tools and techniques highly discretionary, as has been the case throughout the history of federal EA in Canada. One positive aspect of the guidance material is recognition of two main considerations with respect to methods and techniques: how to *share information* (e.g., social media, open houses) and how to *gather information* (e.g., workshops, technical meetings, informal meetings). Since the predominant approach to participation in federal assessment currently leans mostly toward the sharing of information, this distinction could become important in the development of public participation plans that aim for meaningful participation.

Past experience suggests that no amount of voluntary guidance on its own will ensure that meaningful participation is achieved. There has been quite good guidance available from the Agency under previous federal assessment legislation, yet we have mostly fallen short of meaningful participation. Given that further statutory changes are at this stage unlikely, we recommend that the shortcomings discussed in this chapter be addressed through regulations. First, the federal government should establish, in a participatory manner, a robust regime under section 112(1)(d) of the *IAA* (permitting regulations "respecting a participant funding program established under section 75"). Furthermore, section 112(1)(b) of the *IAA* (permitting regulations "respecting the procedures, requirements and time periods relating to impact assessments, including the manner of designing a follow-up program") should be used to create regulations that define meaningful participation and provide details about the following matters:

---

60    "Interim Framework: Public Participation," above note 22 at 4. See also Petts, above note 30; Environmental Planning and Assessment Caucus, above note 51 [emphasis added].

61    Doelle & Sinclair, above note 39; A John Sinclair, Alan P Diduck & Morgan Vespa, "Public Participation in Sustainability Assessment: Essential Elements, Practical Challenges and Emerging Directions" in Angus Morrison-Saunders, Jenny Pope, & Alan Bond, eds, *Handbook of Sustainability Assessment* (Camberley, UK: Edward Elgar, 2015) 349.

- how to ensure meaningful public participation in each of the key phases of the IA process, including planning, assessment by the Agency or a review panel, decision making, and follow-up
- the key purposes of participation in the planning phase (e.g., participation in development of the final project plan, development of guidelines, and establishment of a public participation plan) and a plan of action for carrying them out, such as through establishment of a multi-interest planning committee (MIPC)
- how to ensure meaningful public participation in each of the key phases (planning, assessment, decision making, and follow-up) of regional and strategic assessments
- how to ensure meaningful public participation that is culturally appropriate and tailored to the regional and local circumstances
- how to protect fundamental procedural rights in hearings, such as the right to cross-examine witnesses while avoiding what participants often find to be undue intimidation during cross-examination and allowing for deliberative processes that promote learning about the values, priorities, and aspirations of affected communities
- the manner in which information relevant to the assessment and all follow-up data and information will be made permanently and publicly accessible

These recommended regulatory changes should be considered for statutory amendment on the required review of the *IAA* in ten years or at any opportunity before the review period. For example, the definition of meaningful participation should be included in the definitions section of the *IAA*, and provisions for meaningful participation in follow-up should be part of the Act. If there were an opportunity to consider statutory changes before the required review of the *IAA*, then consideration should be given to modifying the timeline requirements. Such amendments should allow for the 180-day planning phase to be replaced with a project-specific timeline to be set based on advice from a MIPC or similar body. As well, the 300-day timeline for Agency-led assessments should be set as a default, allowing the appropriate timeline to be set by the Agency, again on advice from an MIPC or a similar body, at the conclusion of the planning phase of the assessment.

# CHAPTER 16

# Monitoring, Follow-Up, Adaptive Management, and Compliance in the Post-decision Phase

*Martin Olszynski*

## A. INTRODUCTION

This chapter considers the critical and yet often overlooked "post-decision phase" of impact assessment,[1] following planning, assessment, and decision making.[2] Section B briefly explains monitoring, follow-up, adaptive management, and compliance in the impact assessment context and sets out the manner in which these are treated under the *Impact Assessment Act (IAA)*.[3] Where useful for comparison, this section also considers how they were treated under Canada's previous assessment

---

1   See, for example, Carol A Hunsberger, Robert B Gibson & Susan K Wismer, "Citizen Involvement in Sustainability-Centred Environmental Assessment Follow-Up" (2005) 25:6 *Environmental Impact Assessment Review* 609 at 610: "In Canada, ... follow-up monitoring has been well recognized as a crucial component of environmental assessment but, at least until recently, seldom required or allocated potentially sufficient resources."

2   Alana Westwood et al, "The Role of Science in Contemporary Canadian Environmental Decision Making: The Example of Environmental Assessment" (2019) 52:1 *UBC Law Review* 243 at 249 (describing the post-decision phase as the fourth and final phase in impact assessment). For its part, the Canadian Impact Assessment Agency has taken to describing this as the fifth phase, adding a proponent-led "impact statement" phase between planning and assessment; see Impact Assessment Agency of Canada, "Impact Assessment Process Overview," online: *Government of Canada* www.canada.ca/en/impact-assessment-agency/services/policy-guidance/impact-assessment-process-overview.html.

3   SC 2019, c 28, s 1.

regimes, the *Canadian Environmental Assessment Act (CEAA 1995)*[4] and the *Canadian Environmental Assessment Act, 2012 (CEAA 2012)*.[5] Section C then considers the federal government's track record with respect to these matters, including the findings and recommendations of the Expert Panel for the Review of Environmental Assessment Processes (Expert Panel).[6] Although much was said during the *IAA*'s development about increasing the quality, transparency, and accessibility of monitoring and follow-up results, as well as addressing the misuse of adaptive management, the Act itself is only marginally distinguishable from *CEAA 1995* and *CEAA 2012* with respect to most of these issues. The one exception appears to be with respect to adaptive management, which has been reintroduced following its deletion from *CEAA 2012*. Section D considers some of the steps that could be taken to bolster the implementation of the post-decision phase under the *IAA* to bring it closer to best practice.

## B. THE POST-DECISION PHASE UNDER THE *IAA* AND PREVIOUS REGIMES

### 1) Monitoring

In the impact assessment context, there are at least three kinds of monitoring that we are concerned with, all of which can and do overlap: (1) traditional compliance monitoring, for example, to determine whether a given condition is being met; (2) monitoring for the purposes of confirming predicted effects (as part of a follow-up program or adaptive management plan), contributing to project management or broader learning;[7] and (3) ambient environmental monitoring, including collaboration in the context of regional efforts.[8] Ambient environmental monitoring is "the monitoring of . . . the state of the environment at the

---

4    SC 1992, c 37. The entry into force of the Act was delayed until 1995 to allow for key regulations to be developed and passed.

5    SC 2012, c 19, s 52.

6    Expert Panel for the Review of Environmental Assessment Processes, *Building Common Ground: A New Vision for Impact Assessment in Canada* (Ottawa: Canadian Environmental Assessment Agency, 2017), online (pdf): *Government of Canada* www.canada.ca/content/dam/themes/environment/conservation/environmental-reviews/building-common-ground/building-common-ground.pdf [*Building Common Ground*].

7    See also Chapter 22.

8    See also Bram F Noble, *Introduction to Environmental Impact Assessment: A Guide to Principles and Practice*, 2d ed (Don Mills, ON: Oxford University Press, 2010), describing

local, regional, national, or global scale.... Ambient monitoring usually requires measurements over a larger temporal and geographic scale than compliance monitoring."[9]

Neither the *IAA* nor its predecessors contain any detailed provisions with respect to monitoring. The only provisions that even referred to monitoring under the prior legislation were those setting out the Impact Assessment Agency of Canada's (the Agency) objects.[10] These provisions have been carried over to the *IAA* almost verbatim, although the Act now also refers to "monitoring committees" in the context of follow-up and adaptive management:

> **155** The Agency's objects are ...
>
> (f)  to promote, *monitor* and facilitate compliance with this Act;
>
> (g)  to promote and *monitor* the quality of impact assessments conducted under this Act
>
> **156 (2)** In carrying out its objects, the Agency must ...
>
> (e)  establish research and advisory bodies for matters related to impact assessment and *monitoring committees for matters related to the implementation of follow-up programs and adaptive management plans,* including with respect to the interests and concerns of Indigenous peoples of Canada, and appoint as a member of any such bodies one or more persons. [emphasis added]

The only other section relevant to monitoring and introduced in the *IAA* is found within the registry provisions. As with the previous regimes, the Agency must establish an internet site available to the public, now named the Canadian Impact Assessment Registry (the Registry).[11] Pursuant to section 105(2), among the records and information that the Agency must post to the Registry are "(d) any *scientific information* that the Agency receives from a proponent or federal authority, *or a summary*

---

a similar typology: compliance monitoring, progress monitoring, and monitoring for understanding.

9   Eric Biber, "The Problem of Environmental Monitoring" (2011) 83 *University of Colorado Law Review* 1. For a Canadian example, see "Canada-Alberta Oil Sands Environmental Monitoring," online: *Government of Canada* www.canada.ca/en/environment-climate-change/services/oil-sands-monitoring.html.

10   *CEAA 1995*, above note 4, s 62(e); *CEAA 2012*, above note 5, s 105(e).

11   As required by the *IAA*, s 105. The Registry is available online: www.ceaa.gc.ca/050/evaluations/050?culture=en-CA.

*of the scientific information* and an indication of how that information may be obtained" [emphasis added]. Although "scientific information" is not defined in the Act, monitoring data presumably falls within this definition.[12]

As a general rule, then, and notwithstanding recent recommendations to the contrary (as further discussed in Section C), monitoring requirements have been, and will continue to be, governed first and foremost by the conditions of individual project approvals, whether within a project's decision statement or pursuant to any other related authorization or permits.[13] As one example of what such requirements could look like, the decision statements for the Brucejack Gold Mine Project, Site C Clean Energy Project, Woodfibre LNG Project, and Kemess Underground Project all contain the following condition: "The Proponent shall monitor mortality of Little Brown Myotis (*Myotis lucifugus*) and Northern Myotis (*Myotis septentrionalis*) and their usage at buffer-zones and of roosting structures, to determine the effectiveness of the mitigation measures during construction and operation."[14]

Absent from this condition — and many others — are any specifications with respect to monitoring methodology, including duration, frequency, and sampling protocols.[15]

## 2)  Follow-Up Programs

As with monitoring, the *IAA* adopts the previous regimes' basic approach to follow-up programs. These are defined almost identically across these regimes as programs for "verifying the accuracy of the impact assessment of a designated project and determining the effectiveness of any mitigation measures."[16] Mitigation or mitigation measures have consistently been defined as "measures to eliminate, reduce, control or

---

12    See Chapter 21.

13    A commonly associated federal permit is a *Fisheries Act*, RSC, 1985, c F-14, s 35(2) authorization for "any work, undertaking or activity that [results] in the harmful alteration, disruption or destruction of fish habitat."

14    This condition and over 200 others were recently reviewed by Kyle Havert-Krans, University of Calgary JD Program (2020), as part of a directed research project: "Formulation of Approval Conditions in Canadian EA: Do They Make the Grade?" (May 2020) (on file with the author).

15    *Ibid* at 32–33.

16    *IAA*, above note 3, s 2.

offset the adverse effects of a project or designated project, and includes restitution for any damage caused by those effects through replacement, restoration, compensation or any other means."[17]

As they were under *CEAA 2012*, follow-up programs are a mandatory factor to be taken into account as part of the assessment phase: "The impact assessment of a designated project … must take into account … the requirements of the follow-up program in respect of the designated project."[18] None of these provisions, however, specify when or for what kinds of environmental effects such programs will be required. Ultimately, whether one or more are required will depend on the recommendations of the Agency or a review panel, as reflected in the Agency's draft assessment report or a review panel's report[19] and the minister's subsequent decision statement:

> The conditions [in a decision statement] must include
> (a) the implementation of the mitigation measures that the Minister [or Governor in Council] takes into account in making [their public interest] determination … and
> (b) the implementation of a follow-up program and, if the Minister considers it appropriate, an adaptive management plan.[20]

In other words, follow-up programs are programs for monitoring and analyzing specific environmental effects (as selected by the Agency or a review panel) with two distinct objectives: to determine whether the predictions made during the assessment phase were accurate (presumably with a view toward improving assessment practice going forward) and to determine if any required mitigation measures are functioning effectively (presumably with a view toward requiring corrective measures, but also potentially informing mitigation planning for future projects with similar impacts).

Where the *IAA* differs from *CEAA 2012* in its approach to follow-up programs but aligns with the original *CEAA 1995* is with respect to the registry. To understand this difference, it is important to note that in addition to the public registry, the Agency has always been — and continues to be — under an obligation to maintain internal and generally

---

17   *Ibid.*

18   *Ibid*, s 22(1)(k).

19   *Ibid*, ss 28(3.2) and 51(1)(d)(iv), respectively.

20   *Ibid*, s 64(4).

more comprehensive "project files."[21] Under *CEAA 2012*, records related to follow-up programs were restricted to the Agency's internal project files; the Agency was not required to post *any* information with respect to follow-up programs on the public registry. Under the *IAA*, "records relating to the design or implementation of any follow-up program" and "any records relating to the implementation of any mitigation measures"[22] must be included within a project's files, but the public registry must at least include "a description of the results of the follow-up program that is implemented with respect to that designated project or a summary of the results and an indication of how such a description may be obtained."[23]

Like both of its predecessors, then, the *IAA* explicitly—and problematically—contemplates an information gap between the public registry and the Agency's internal project files. The rationale for this gap has never been formally articulated. Some indication, however, can be derived from the inclusion, across all regimes, of a series of rules referencing the federal *Access to Information Act*[24] that set out which records have to be made publicly available.[25] Most of these rules refer to third-party information (e.g., monitoring data provided by an environmental consultant company on behalf of a proponent) and the circumstances in which such records could be disclosed. As a general matter, such records are not to be disclosed where they have been treated as confidential by the generating third party or where doing so could result in financial loss or gain to a third party, subject always to public interest exceptions. Setting aside Indigenous knowledge,[26] however, it is not clear why or how environmental data with respect to air, land, and water can or should ever be treated as confidential.[27]

---

21    *Ibid*, s 106.

22    *Ibid*, s 106(3)(d) & (e).

23    *Ibid*, s 105(2)(e).

24    RSC, 1985, c A-1.

25    For the *IAA*, see s 107.

26    See discussion in Chapter 21.

27    The Multi-Interest Advisory Committee struck by the federal government to assist both it and the Expert Panel recommended a "searchable database for accessing, or at least determining how to access, *all of the information gathered in [environmental assessment]*, including follow-up, adaptive management, and information gathered as a consequence of conditions of approval": Multi-Interest Advisory Committee, *Advice to the Expert Panel for the Review of Environmental Assessment Processes* (Ottawa: 2016) (on file with authors).

One final comment is merited here. Because most litigation involves a challenge to the assessment and decision-making phases, and follow-up programs play their greatest role in the post-decision phase, there is no jurisprudence interpreting these provisions directly. Rather, the existence of follow-up provisions has been used indirectly—and perversely—to dismiss challenges to the adequacy of impact assessments. Perhaps the most cited case on this front is *Alberta Wilderness Assn v Express Pipelines Ltd* (1996), where the Federal Court of Appeal upheld as reasonable a review panel's deferral of "certain further studies and ongoing reports."[28] The court decided that "[b]y its nature the panel's exercise is predictive and it is not surprising that the statute specifically envisages the possibility of 'follow up' programmes."[29] To be sure, the existence of follow-up provisions in no way supports deferring the assessment of a project's impacts; on the contrary, there can be no prediction verification without first making a prediction, nor can there be any evaluation of mitigation effectiveness without first identifying mitigation. If anything, the presence of follow-up provisions augments the case for rigorous assessment, without which follow-up programs are bound to fail.

### 3) Adaptive Management

Originally coined "adaptive environmental assessment and management" by CS Holling in the 1970s,[30] adaptive management has become ubiquitous in Canadian impact assessment practice and law.[31] At a high level, adaptive management can be understood simply as learning by doing.[32] However, there are long-standing concerns that the practice of adaptive management diverges—sometimes drastically—from the

28  137 DLR (4th) 177 (FCA) at para 13 [*Express Pipelines*]. This decision has been cited thirty-one times according to CanLII.

29  *Ibid.*

30  CS Holling, ed, *Adaptive Environmental Assessment and Management* (Chichester, UK: John Wiley and Sons, 1978).

31  A 2017 survey of the Canadian Environmental Assessment Registry revealed that 91 percent of the projects listed there contained at least one reference, and usually several, to adaptive management: see Martin Olszynski, "Failed Experiments: An Empirical Assessment of Adaptive Management in Alberta's Energy Resources Sector" (2017) 50:3 *UBC Law Review* 657.

32  Holly Doremus, "Adaptive Management, the Endangered Species Act, and the Institutional Challenges of "New Age" Environmental Protection (2001–2002) 41:1 *Washburn Law Journal* 50 at 55.

theory.[33] Defined by the Canadian Environmental Assessment Agency in a 2009 operational policy statement (OPS) as "a planned and systematic process for continuously improving environmental management practices by learning about their outcomes,"[34] in the Canadian context adaptive management is often neither planned nor systematic and rarely results in changes to management practices. Not surprisingly, it seldom contributes to learning (further discussed in the next part).[35]

Although definitions vary at the margins, genuine adaptive management is generally understood as involving the following six-step iterative cycle (Figure 16.1),[36] with each step often consisting of several substeps. For example, steps 1 and 2 (assess and design) require identifying relevant uncertainties, developing hypotheses, selecting indicators, and designing monitoring programs. In the impact assessment context, the "problem" is usually a predicted adverse environmental effect for which no proven mitigation measures exist, and the "actions" to be tested are mitigation measures that may or may not prove effective. In other words, adaptive management can be considered a very specific kind of follow-up program where the goal is not merely to verify impact predictions or mitigation effectiveness for their own sake or as part of a broader learning effort but to determine the need for adaptation (i.e., the implementation of alternative mitigation measures).

Viewed this way, the adaptive management cycle spans all four phases of impact assessment. Like follow-up programs, the need for and design of any proposed applications of adaptive management should occur during the planning and assessment phases, where it can benefit from Indigenous, public, expert, and federal authority input. In addition to scrutinizing the various elements of the proposed application, these phases should also include a discussion as to why adaptive management is even appropriate in the circumstances, bearing in mind

---

33  Olszynski, above note 31 at 658.

34  Canadian Environmental Assessment Agency, *Operational Policy Statement Adaptive Management Measures Under the Canadian Environmental Assessment Act* (Ottawa: Government of Canada, 2009), online: www.canada.ca/en/impact-assessment-agency/services/policy-guidance/adaptive-management-measures-under-canadian-environmental-assessment-act.html.

35  Olszynski, above note 31 at 666.

36  Carol Murray & David R Marmorek, "Adaptive Management: A Spoonful of Rigour Helps the Uncertainty Go Down" (Paper submitted to the 16th International Conference for Ecological Restoration, Victoria, Canada 24–26 August 2004) at 1.

that it does not and cannot guarantee that effective measures will be found.[37] Both appropriateness and design should also be reflected in the decision-making phase, including conditions in relation to monitoring, evaluation, and adaptation. The bulk of actual implementation, including several possible iterations of the cycle, occurs in the fourth phase.

**FIGURE 16.1   THE ADAPTIVE MANAGEMENT CYCLE**

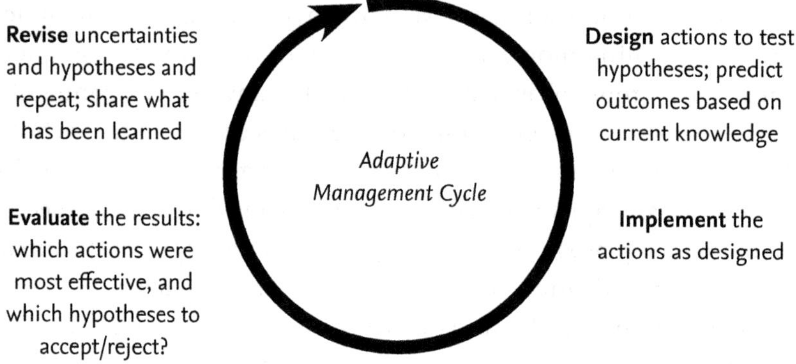


CEAA 1995 made only a cursory, undefined reference to adaptive management that reinforced its association with follow-up programs: "The results of follow-up programs may be used for implementing adaptive management measures or for improving the quality of future environmental assessments."[38] Nevertheless, in *Pembina Institute for Appropriate Development v Canada (Attorney General)*,[39] a 2008 decision involving a challenge to the Joint Review Panel report for Imperial Oil's Kearl Oil Sands Project, the Federal Court elevated adaptive management to the status of a "guiding tenet" in the interpretation

37   Olszynski, above note 31 at 670 (and associated references).

38   *CEAA 1995*, above note 4, s 38(5).

39   2008 FC 302 [*Pembina Institute*].

of the Act,[40] holding that it "permits projects with uncertain, yet potentially adverse environmental impacts to proceed based on flexible management strategies capable of adjusting to new information regarding adverse environmental impacts *where sufficient information regarding those impacts and potential mitigation measures already exists.*"[41] In the context of the Kearl Oil Sands Project, this meant upholding as reasonable the panel's findings that significant adverse environmental effects were not likely with respect to the destruction of thousands of hectares of peatlands and the creation of end-pit lakes, even though effective mitigation measures for addressing both of those issues did not exist, and Imperial Oil failed entirely to complete any of the steps of the adaptive management cycle at the assessment phase.[42] In other words, the *Pembina Institute* decision's approach to "sufficient information" appeared to set a very low bar.[43]

For reasons that are not clear, *CEAA 1995*'s singular reference to adaptive management was removed with the passage of *CEAA 2012*. Nevertheless, proponents and the federal government continued to rely on it to support findings of non-significance. Fortunately, in *Taseko Mines Limited v Canada (Environment)*,[44] the Federal Court tempered at least some of the earlier jurisprudence's shortcomings. In that case, the proponent, Taseko Mines, invoked adaptive management with respect to its tailings plans but, citing *Pembina Institute* and *Express Pipelines*, refused to provide the federal review panel with any pertinent details, arguing that these could and would be finalized in conjunction with regulators in what Taseko Mines called the "post EA permitting" stage.[45] The federal review panel disagreed, a position that was subsequently upheld as reasonable by the Federal Court:

---

40   *Ibid* at para 33.

41   *Ibid* at para 32 [emphasis added].

42   Olszynski, above note 31 at 758–59.

43   The decision was widely criticized for other reasons as well. See Arlene Kwasniak, "Use and Abuse of Adaptive Management in Environmental Assessment Law and Practice: A Canadian Example and General Lessons" (2010/11) 12:4 *Journal of Environmental Assessment Policy and Management* 425; Nathalie J Chalifour, "Case Comment: A (Pre) Cautionary Tale about the Kearl Decision" (2009) 5:2 *McGill International Journal of Sustainable Development Law and Policy* 251.

44   2017 FC 1099, aff'd 2019 FCA 319 [*Taseko*].

45   Submission to the panel of closing remarks from Taseko Mines Limited (23 August 2013) at 10–11, available on the Canadian Impact Assessment Registry on the Government of Canada website: https://iaac-aeic.gc.ca/050/evaluations/exploration?projDocs=63928.

> It was reasonable for the Panel not to accept Taseko's "vague assurances" that it would engage in adaptive management in order to deal with adverse environmental effects. The Panel sought information on environmental effects and mitigation measures, and Taseko refused to provide this information. It was entirely reasonable, and in line with the Panel's (reasonable) interpretation of the precautionary principle, for the Panel to conclude that the concentration of water quality variables in Fish Lake (Teztan Biny) and Wasp Lake would likely be a significant adverse environmental effect.
>
> Indeed, acceptance of vague adaptive management schemes in circumstances such as these would … tend to call into question the value of the entire review panel process — if all such decisions could be left to a later stage, then the review panel process would simply be for the sake of appearances.[46]

Although the *Taseko* decision does not address all of the problems in the jurisprudence with respect to adaptive management,[47] the Federal Court did recognize that adaptive management should not be invoked to avoid or circumvent the work of assessing a project's environmental effects, including proposed mitigation measures, and that its proposed use requires some specificity, including the selection of indicators, thresholds for adaptation, and proposed mitigation measures.[48] In *Pembina Institute* terms, *Taseko* appropriately raises the bar in terms of the "sufficient information" required before adaptive management can be relied upon in making predictions with respect to a project's effects (additional limitations are discussed below and in Section D).

With respect to the *IAA*, the term *adaptive management* has been reintroduced as part of the contents of a decision statement, with the addition of the word *plan*: "The conditions referred to in subsections (1) and (2) must include … the implementation of a follow-up program and, *if the Minister considers it appropriate, an adaptive management plan*."[49] Several observations can be made. First, the reintroduction of adaptive management alongside follow-up programs harkens back to its original reference in *CEAA 1995* and further reinforces the relationship between

---

46 *Taseko*, above note 44 at paras 123 & 124 [emphasis added].

47 Below note 48. See also Kwasniak, above note 43, and Chalifour, above note 43.

48 New Prosperity Mine Federal Review Panel Supplemental Information Request 15/19/25/49, above note 45.

49 *IAA*, s 64(4)(b) [emphasis added].

these concepts. Second, the addition of the term *plan*, that is, "a detailed formulation of a program of action" or "an orderly arrangement of parts of an overall design or objective,"[50] is significant as it speaks to one of the previously noted deficiencies in Canadian impact assessment practice: the invocation of adaptive management without sufficient attention being paid to its various requirements. The reference to adaptive management *plans* in the decision-making phase also implies consideration of the various steps of the adaptive management cycles during the planning and assessment phases in order for such consideration to feed into the subsequent plan and decision statement. Although adaptive management plans are not specifically mentioned in the list of mandatory factors to be considered in the assessment phase—in contrast to follow-up programs—this omission makes sense when one recalls that follow-up programs are mandatory, whereas adaptive management plans are not (i.e., only "if the Minister considers it appropriate"). Where adaptive management is being proposed, it presumably falls under "any other matter relevant to the impact assessment that the Agency requires to be taken into account"[51] in the assessment phase. Finally, that the minister must consider adaptive management "appropriate" appears to address the remaining problems in the jurisprudence alluded to in the preceding paragraph, namely that adaptive management is not "fail-safe" (e.g., no successful mitigation measures may ultimately be found) and is not appropriate for every kind of environmental problem (there are spatial and temporal limits to experimentation in the natural world).[52] These two limitations are particularly salient in light of the minister's duty to apply the precautionary principle and adhere to the principles of scientific integrity, respectively.[53] The minister should have to grapple with these limitations in determining whether adaptive management is appropriate, as further discussed in Section D.

The *IAA* also contains new provisions authorizing the minister to modify the conditions of a decision statement (including adding or removing conditions), subject to the limitations that such modification cannot change the decision regarding the project, cannot increase the adverseness of any impacts, and must be preceded by notice, an

---

50    Merriam-Webster Dictionary, *sub verbo* "plan."

51    *IAA*, above note 3, s 22(1)(t).

52    Olszynski, above note 31 at 683.

53    *IAA*, above note 3, ss 6(2) & 6(3). See also Chapter 21.

opportunity for comment, and the minister's reasons for the amendment.[54] These provisions should facilitate the adaptive management process by allowing the minister to amend the relevant adaptive management plan in response to monitoring data and evaluation, which otherwise may have been prohibited by administrative law principles, especially the doctrine of *functus officio*.[55] For example, the adaptive management plan may yield positive results at the outset, in which case the mitigation measures that were proven to be effective could be made final and the adaptive management plan terminated. Alternatively, the results may be consistently negative, in which case an entirely new suite of measures may be required.

### 4) Compliance and Enforcement

In his landmark work on non-compliance in environmental law, Professor Daniel Farber observed that although in "all areas of the law, there are gaps between the 'law on the books' and the 'law in action,'" in environmental law, "this gap is sometimes a chasm."[56] Applying this metaphor to the Canadian context a few years later, Professor David Boyd suggested that the gap is more like the Grand Canyon.[57] As further discussed in Section C, this appears to have been the case with respect to *CEAA 2012*; the Expert Panel certainly heard "concerns that proponents are not being held accountable for all conditions set out

---

54   *Ibid*, ss 68 & 69.

55   J Benidickson et al, "Practicing Precaution and Adaptive Management: Legal, Institutional and Procedural Dimensions of Scientific Uncertainty," Report to the SSHRC and Law Commission of Canada (Ottawa: Institute of the Environment, University of Ottawa, 2005) at F-7:

> Adaptive management raises most distinctly the divergence between administrative decision-making and science with regard to their visions of finality. As we have seen, adaptive management calls for decisions taken in the face of uncertainty to be taken as hypotheses, to be tested and re-evaluated as additional information becomes available. By contrast, administrative decision-makers and reviewing courts have as one of their primary goals the *final* resolution of disputes or determination of matters before them. Fundamental legal principles such as the rule of precedent, *res judicata*, and *functus officio* all indicate the quest, at least in the traditional view to date, of administrative tribunals and courts for certainty and finality.

56   Daniel A Farber, "Taking Slippage Seriously: Noncompliance and Creative Compliance in Environmental Law" (1999) 23 *Harvard Environmental Law Review* 297 at 297.

57   David Boyd, *Unnatural Law* (Vancouver, BC: UBC Press, 2004) at 238.

in environmental assessment approvals" and of "a lack of capacity for compliance and enforcement."[58]

The *IAA*'s provisions for "administration and enforcement" are set out in sections 120 to 152. Although there are similarities with *CEAA 2012*, there are also several significant changes. While under *CEAA 2012*, enforcement officers and analysts were designated by the minister, these are now designated by the president of the Agency;[59] they are also for the first time immunized from civil liability for anything done or not done in the exercise of their duties in good faith.[60] Enforcement officers' powers are more or less the same as under the previous regime,[61] except that the *IAA* also makes clear that, when entering a place, enforcement officers may be accompanied by anyone necessary to assist them in exercising their powers and duties.[62] As under the prior legislation, the owner or person in charge of a place has a duty to assist such officers as well.[63]

In the event of non-compliance, enforcement officers have the power to issue an order for the person or entity to take certain measures,[64] but under the *IAA* an officer may also, or in the alternative, issue a notice of non-compliance, which simply sets out the sections of the statute alleged to have been contravened and a statement of the relevant facts.[65] A new feature of the federal assessment regime but a long-existing one of Canada's flagship environmental statute, the *Canadian Environmental Protection Act, 1999*,[66] proponents may request the president of the Agency for a review of any enforcement order,[67] upon receipt of which the president must appoint a review officer.[68] Orders are not automatically suspended by such a request, but a review officer may suspend them upon

---

58  *Building Common Ground*, above note 6.

59  *IAA*, above note 3, s 120.

60  *Ibid*, s 121.

61  *Ibid*, s 122. These include entering a place in which they have reasonable grounds to believe a designated project is or was being carried out or a record or anything relating to a designated project is located and related powers on entry, including examining records, taking photographs, and prohibiting access to the place.

62  *Ibid*, s 122(3).

63  *Ibid*, s 122(5).

64  *Ibid*, s 127.

65  *Ibid*, s 126.

66  SC 1999, c 33, ss 243–71 [*CEPA*].

67  *IAA*, above note 3, s 130.

68  *Ibid*, s 131.

application.[69] After conducting the review, a review officer may confirm or cancel the order, amend or suspend a condition of the order, add a condition to it or delete a condition from it, or extend the order's duration.[70] In doing so, a review officer must provide reasons for the decision, which are appealable to the Federal Court.[71]

The remaining compliance and enforcement provisions are roughly similar to the previous regime, with two important exceptions. First, fines have been significantly increased, drawing a distinction between large and small corporations that was first introduced to several other federal environmental laws over a decade ago.[72] Second, the *IAA* contains new "whistle-blower" provisions.[73] Unlike those other federal environmental laws, however, and notwithstanding the recommendations of the Expert Panel, no provision has been made for an administrative monetary penalty regime, which is essentially a ticketing regime for non-criminal offences that is widely regarded as a useful additional enforcement tool.[74]

## C.  ASSESSING THE *IAA*'S COMMITMENT TO THE POST-DECISION PHASE

Having set out the *IAA*'s requirements in relation to monitoring, follow-up, adaptive management, and compliance, this section gauges the Act's

---

69    *Ibid*, s 132.

70    *Ibid*, s 134.

71    *Ibid*, s 138. Such an appeal would be reviewed on the appellate standard of correctness with respect to questions of law and palpable and overriding error with respect to errors of fact: *Canada (Minister of Citizenship and Immigration) v Vavilov*, 2019 SCC 65.

72    *An Act to amend certain Acts that relate to the environment and to enact provisions respecting the enforcement of certain Acts that relate to the environment*, SC 2009, c 14 (commonly known as the *Environmental Enforcement Act*). The Act established new minimum and higher maximum fines and required fines to be doubled for second and subsequent offences for nine different federal environmental laws, including *CEPA, 1999*. See also Shaun Fluker, "Oversight and Enforcement in Bill C-69 regarding the *Impact Assessment Act* and the *Canadian Energy Regulator Act*" (26 February 2018), online (blog): *ABlawg* http://ablawg.ca/wp-content/uploads/2018/02/Blog_SCF_BillC69.pdf.

73    *IAA*, above note 3, s 141.

74    *Building Common Ground*, above note 6 at 71: "Administrative monetary penalties are widely used across all governments for different types of offences, ranging from minor to serious non-compliance. In situations where non-compliance falls short of criminal behaviour but may still warrant financial penalty, administrative monetary penalties are an effective option."

provisions against what is — and was — known about these aspects of the post-decision phase at the time that the *IAA* was making its way through the legislative process. The goal is to assess the extent to which the federal government has sought to address existing opportunities and challenges as well as to determine what more could or should be done.

## 1)  Monitoring and Follow-Up

Following a review of all audits related to monitoring by the federal commissioner for the environment and sustainable development (CESD), only one audit (2009) directly focused on the implementation of *CEAA 1995*.[75] It found that the Agency had established what was then the Canadian Environmental Assessment Registry[76] and that project files were created "for most environmental assessments."[77] No audit findings were reported with respect to the quality of the monitoring data and follow-up programs contained within the Agency's project files. However, under the original *CEAA*, the requirements of monitoring and the implementation of follow-up programs were generally the responsibility of the various federal departments whose regulatory regimes triggered the application of the Act in the first place. For example, Fisheries and Oceans Canada was responsible for a *Fisheries Act* section 35 authorization to impact fish habitat.[78] This authorization would then contain the relevant conditions in relation to monitoring and follow-up. Some sense of their implementation can be gleaned from the CESD audits of those departments. In the same year that the CESD audited *CEAA*, it also audited Fisheries and Oceans Canada's implementation of its fish habitat protection program.[79] The CESD's findings are relevant and troubling in several respects:

---

75  "2009 Fall Report of the Commissioner of the Environment and Sustainable Development," ch 1, online: *Office of the Auditor General of Canada* www.oag-bvg.gc.ca/internet/ English/parl_cesd_200911_01_e_33196.html#hd5l.

76  *Ibid* at 1.53.

77  *Ibid* at 1.55. Under the original *CEAA*, there were three tiers of assessment of increasing rigour: screenings, comprehensive studies, and panel reviews.

78  Above note 13.

79  "2009 Spring Report of the Commissioner of the Environment and Sustainable Development," ch 1, online: *Office of the Auditor General of Canada* www.oag-bvg.gc.ca/ internet/English/parl_cesd_200905_01_e_32511.html#hd5g.

> Proponents are normally required to carry out project monitoring activities, and the Department may monitor projects directly or rely on monitoring by the proponent. We found that the Department does not have a risk-based approach to monitoring proponents' compliance with the terms and conditions of ministerial authorizations .... For example, we found that proponents had carried out the required monitoring in only 6 of 16 (38 percent) sample items involving ministerial authorizations .... We found no documentation to show that the Department had followed up or evaluated the effectiveness of its decisions.[80]

Other monitoring-related audits have also consistently revealed weaknesses in federal efforts. In a 2010 audit of Environment Canada's monitoring of water resources, the CESD concluded that

> Environment Canada is not adequately monitoring the quality and quantity of Canada's surface water resources.... The Department has not established many of the essential management practices needed to plan, implement, assess, and improve its long-term monitoring programs.... As a consequence, the Department has no objective basis on which to identify opportunities for improvement or take corrective actions to improve these programs.[81]

Similarly, a 2011 audit focusing on the assessment of cumulative effects of oil sands projects found "[i]ncomplete environmental baselines and environmental data monitoring systems needed to understand changing environmental conditions in northern Alberta."[82] This latter audit preceded the launching of two expert panels (one federal and one provincial) into the quality of monitoring in Alberta's oil sands region, both of which concluded that then-current monitoring efforts were seriously deficient.[83]

---

80 *Ibid* at 1.38.

81 "2010 Fall Report of the Commissioner of the Environment and Sustainable Development," ch 2, online: *Office of the Auditor General of Canada* www.oag-bvg.gc.ca/internet/English/parl_cesd_201012_02_e_34425.html.

82 "2011 October Report of the Commissioner of the Environment and Sustainable Development," ch 2, online: *Office of the Auditor General of Canada* www.oag-bvg.gc.ca/internet/English/parl_cesd_201110_02_e_35761.html.

83 Liz Dowdeswell et al, *A Foundation for the Future: Building an Environmental Monitoring System for the Oil Sands* (Government of Canada Oil Sands Advisory Panel, 2010); Alberta Environmental Monitoring Panel, *A World Class Environmental Monitoring,*

Simply put, the past decade of monitoring practice has generated considerable concern about the effectiveness of project monitoring that is not reflected in the relatively marginal changes to these issues under the *IAA*. This phenomenon is not restricted to the federal government but rather appears to plague most government agencies and departments. A 2011 audit of British Columbia's Environmental Assessment Office (EAO) concluded that the EAO's "oversight of certified projects is not sufficient to ensure that potential significant adverse effects are avoided or mitigated."[84] Specifically, the EAO was "not evaluating the effectiveness of environmental assessment mitigation measures to ensure that projects are achieving the desired outcomes," nor was it "making appropriate monitoring, compliance and outcome information available to the public to ensure accountability."[85] More recently, Ontario's auditor general also concluded that the province's Ministry of Environment "does not have effective processes to ensure that projects are implemented as planned. Such processes could include field inspections during project implementation or requesting data, after projects are implemented, that shows their environmental impact."[86]

Not surprisingly, the Expert Panel devoted considerable time and effort to the issues of monitoring and follow-up, and its findings were generally negative:

> Participants were concerned about the federal government's lack of attention to monitoring and follow-up after a decision has been made and emphasized the importance of verifying the conclusions of EA predictions. There were also a number of concerns about proponent self-monitoring, with some participants suggesting that third parties should be contracted to conduct monitoring activities. Some participants felt that insufficient effort is being put into monitoring and

---

*Evaluation and Reporting System for Alberta* (Edmonton, AB: Alberta Environmental Monitoring Panel, 2011), online: *Wood Buffalo Environmental Association* https://wbea.org/news/alberta-environment-monitoring-panel.

84　BC Auditor General, "An Audit of the Environmental Assessment Office's Oversight of Certified Projects," (2011, Victoria: Government of BC) at 6, online (pdf): www.bcauditor.com/sites/default/files/publications/2011/report_4/report/OAGBC-Environmental-Assessment-Office.pdf.

85　*Ibid.*

86　Auditor General of Ontario, "2016 Annual Report," online: www.auditor.on.ca/en/content/annualreports/arbyyear/ar2016.html.

would like to see increased oversight by the federal government to ensure monitoring is taking place. Local communities and Indigenous Groups want a role in monitoring but are currently limited in how they can be involved.

Participants said that the lack of trust related to monitoring and follow-up is related to a lack of transparency in the monitoring and follow-up phase. They want all monitoring data to be posted publicly in real time in order to show clearly that monitoring is taking place and that the local environment is not being put at risk.[87]

Viewed against the foregoing track record, the *IAA's* commitment to improved monitoring and follow-up appears limited. There will be more information available on the public registry, especially with respect to follow-up programs, but in and of themselves the Act's monitoring and follow-up provisions do not reflect a significant shift toward greater quality, transparency, and accountability with respect to these elements. Some improvement may be expected from the *IAA's* new and related duty of scientific integrity,[88] especially with respect to the quality of monitoring and follow-up programs, but further gains will depend on the government's exercise of its regulatory authorities (e.g., to promulgate regulations or guidelines to standardize monitoring methodology) and a correspondingly appropriate allocation of Agency resources.

## 2) Adaptive Management

As noted in Section B, there is widespread concern that the practice of adaptive management diverges significantly from the theoretical ideal. A recent study of Canada's energy resource sector (including joint review panels for oil sands mines under *CEAA 1995* and *CEAA 2012*) found that definitions and conceptions of adaptive management varied widely, with most proponents mistaking it as a general strategy that guarantees the effectiveness of mitigation measures in virtually any and every context.[89] There was also little or no attention paid to experimental design (i.e., completing the steps and substeps of the adaptive management

---

87　*Building Common Ground*, above note 6.

88　See Chapter 21.

89　Olszynski, above note 31.

cycle) (Figure 16.2),[90] and there was often little to no follow-through in terms of implementation.[91]

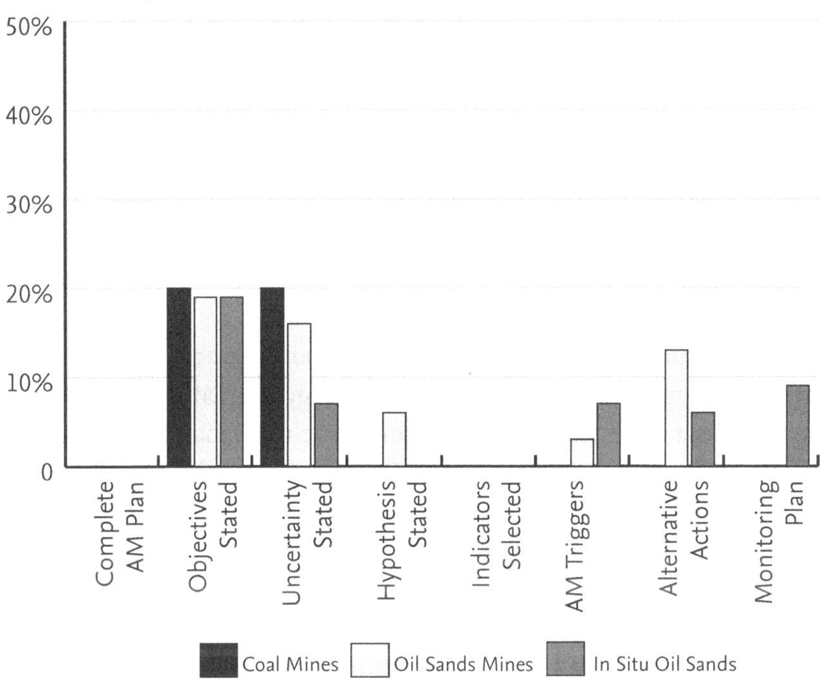

**FIGURE 16.2  COMPLETENESS OF ADAPTIVE MANAGEMENT (AM) AT ENVIRONMENTAL ASSESSMENT STAGE BY PROJECT TYPE (% OF PROPOSED AM APPLICATIONS)**



Concern about the misuse of adaptive management is also reflected in the Expert Panel's report: "Participants identified that adaptive management is being used by proponents inappropriately as an alternative to mitigation, instead of applying the precautionary principle and identifying mitigation even in cases where there is uncertainty in predictions."[92] This is essentially what the proponent was attempting to do in *Taseko*. In fairness, however, such an approach is the predictable result of jurisprudence that, until only recently (i.e., *Taseko*), reflected a relatively superficial understanding of adaptive management.

---

90   *Ibid.*

91   *Ibid.*

92   *Building Common Ground*, above note 6 at 42. The Expert Panel also noted warnings that adaptive management "is sometimes used as an excuse to not meet the requirements of the current assessment process."

Viewed this way, the provisions with respect to adaptive management may represent the most significant improvements in the *IAA*. The requirement for an actual plan, which implies completion of the adaptive management cycle and the need to determine that such a plan is "appropriate," especially in light of the minister's duty to apply the precautionary principle, could address most of the major deficiencies currently plaguing its application and related jurisprudence. The one notable omission is a clear definition of adaptive management in the Act, which is regrettable bearing in mind that the Canadian Environmental Assessment Agency already had a relatively decent definition in its 2009 OPS on adaptive management.[93]

### 3) Compliance and Enforcement

Returning one last time to the CESD's reports, a 2015 audit of the National Energy Board (now the Canada Energy Regulator), one of three responsible authorities under *CEAA 2012*, concluded that its compliance tracking efforts were "inadequate."[94] Of relevance to this chapter were the findings that the board had only "tracked condition implementation adequately in 25 of the 49 cases."[95] In those 25 instances (roughly 50 percent), "the Board had updated its tracking records, had received and recorded submissions provided by the company, and had documented its analysis and final conclusion as to whether the condition had been implemented to the Board's satisfaction."[96] In the remaining 50 percent of cases, however, "the conditions had not been adequately tracked and documented. The type of inadequacies varied: ... Board analysis or conclusion on company compliance was missing; or the desired end result of a condition had not been achieved or properly documented."[97] The CESD concluded that the board "faced significant, system-wide challenges with the information management tools it used to track company compliance."[98] With respect to public access to infor-

---

93   Above note 34.

94   "2015 Fall Report of the Commissioner of the Environment and Sustainable Development," ch 1, online: *Office of the Auditor General of Canada* www.oag-bvg.gc.ca/internet/ English/parl_cesd_201601_02_e_41021.html.

95   *Ibid* at 2.29.

96   *Ibid.*

97   *Ibid* at 2.30.

98   *Ibid.*

mation on compliance, the audit found that the board had taken steps to improve such access, but that this was being "hindered by the way the information was presented."[99] Ultimately, the CESD recommended that the board "provide the public with improved access to information about company compliance with pipeline approval conditions" by ensuring "that its website incorporates a user-centered design that the public can access and use efficiently."[100]

There have been no similar audits of the Agency's compliance program, the contours of which were laid out in its 2017 "Compliance and Enforcement Policy for the *Canadian Environmental Assessment Act, 2012.*"[101] As with most such policies, the Agency's policy lays out the principles that continue to guide its approach to compliance and enforcement, including fairness, predictability, and consistency. It lists the types of information that enforcement officers will consider in the event of an alleged contravention, including the nature of the circumstances and the alleged offender's history of compliance. It also sets out the different tools available to enforcement officers, including warnings (oral and written), orders, injunctions, and prosecutions.

Figure 16.3 shows the number of inspections (on- and off-site/report auditing), warnings, orders, and injunctions issued in the three years preceding the passage of the *IAA*, which the Agency posts on its website (although the relevant original documents have to be searched for through the Registry).[102] Although there were roughly 200 projects on the project registry during this period, most of this activity was related to roughly a handful of projects (for on-site inspections, an average of six projects/year; for off-site inspections, an average of eleven projects/year; and for other enforcement actions, four projects over four years),[103] including the controversial Site C Dam in British Columbia. No prosecutions were ever initiated under *CEAA 2012.*

---

99  *Ibid* at 2.55–2.56.

100  *Ibid.*

101  Online: *Government of Canada* www.canada.ca/en/impact-assessment-agency/corporate/compliance-promotion-enforcement/compliance-enforcement-policy.html.

102  See Impact Assessment Agency of Canada, "Compliance Promotion and Enforcement," online: *Government of Canada* www.canada.ca/en/impact-assessment-agency/corporate/compliance-promotion-enforcement.html#pr.

103  *Ibid.*

**FIGURE 16.3   COMPLIANCE AND ENFORCEMENT ACTIVITY (2016–2019)**

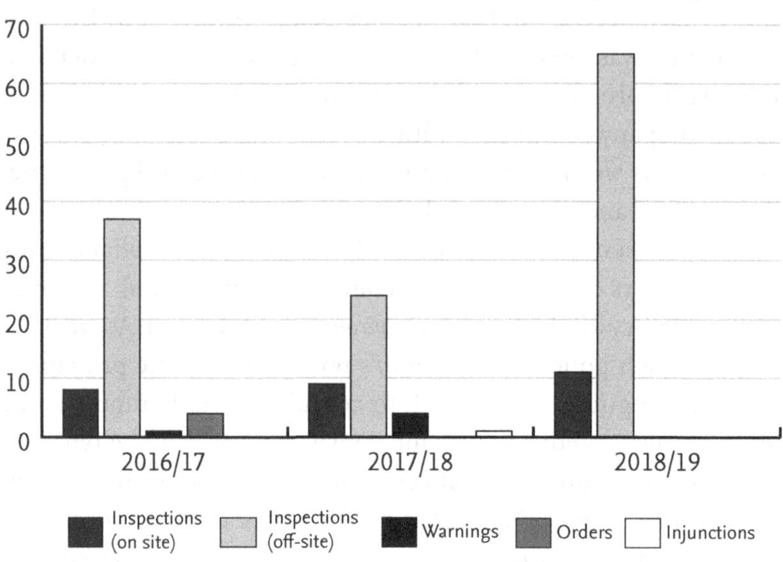


Bearing in mind the number of projects on the public registry, these numbers—and the total absence of any prosecutions—do suggest low compliance and enforcement activity, as reflected in the Expert Panel's report.

## D.  MOVING FORWARD

Moving forward, the best course would be for the Agency, the minister, and the Government of Canada to make up for the shortfall between the *IAA* and the Expert Panel's recommendations with respect to the post-decision phase. Regulations or guidelines should be promulgated (pursuant to section 112 or 114, respectively) to standardize monitoring and follow-up program design and methodology. The Agency should also embrace open science and post original proponent monitoring data as a general rule, relying on summaries of data only in exceptional cases where the need for confidentiality has clearly been established. Indigenous and other community involvement in monitoring, including through monitoring committees, should be encouraged whenever possible, but especially when a project has been determined to have a potential impact on Aboriginal or treaty rights and interests.

With respect to adaptive management, the Agency should update its 2009 OPS to reflect the legislative changes in the *IAA* and the requirements for the preparation of an adaptive management plan. A new OPS should also set out the considerations that the minister will consider when determining whether an adaptive management plan is "appropriate." At a minimum, this should include recognition that adaptive management cannot be applied to all environmental problems (e.g., those for which there are too many variables to control for or whose control would require participation from other parties or jurisdictions that are not willing or that would be cost-prohibitive) and that it is not fail-safe. This latter aspect has led some practitioners to suggest that adaptive management should not be applied where failure would result in serious or irreversible harm, which raises the question of the relationship between adaptive management and the precautionary principle and what role, if any, these concepts should play in decision making in the impact assessment context.

To suggest, as some Canadian courts have, that adaptive management "counters the potentially paralysing effects of the precautionary principle on otherwise socially and economically useful projects"[104] is to fundamentally misconceive of both concepts and the basic mechanics of impact assessment laws generally. The precautionary principle *does not* require "that a project should not be undertaken if it may have serious adverse environmental consequences,"[105] and even if it did, it is clear that no such limitation has ever existed in Canadian impact assessment law; politicians have approved all kinds of projects, including those deemed likely to result in serious or irreversible harm (or "significant adverse environmental effects"). Rather, the precautionary principle is a response to the invocation of uncertainty, specifically, as an excuse for not addressing or mitigating significant environmental risks: "Where there are threats of serious or irreversible damage, *lack of full scientific certainty should not be used as a reason* for postponing measures to prevent environmental degradation."[106] Confronted with such

---

104 *Canadian Parks and Wilderness Society v Canada (Minister of Canadian Heritage)*, 2003 FCA 197 at para 24.

105 *Ibid* [emphasis in the original].

106 *114957 Canada Lteé (Spraytech, Société d'arrosage) v Hudson (Town)*, 2001 SCC 40 at para 31, citing the definition of the precautionary principle from the Bergen Ministerial Declaration on Sustainable Development (1990) [emphasis added]. See also *Castonguay Blasting Ltd v Ontario (Environment)*, 2013 SCC 52 at para 20: "[S]ince there are inherent limits in being able to determine and predict environmental impacts with scientific certainty, environmental policies *must anticipate and prevent environmental degradation*"

uncertainty, it would hardly seem precautionary to respond with mitigation measures that are themselves uncertain, which is the driver for adaptive management in the first place. To comply with the precautionary principle, the required measures should have proven effectiveness in preventing or reducing the potential environmental harm (should it materialize) to the level deemed acceptable by the decision maker(s). That is what makes such an approach precautionary.[107] Conversely, where serious or irreversible damage is relatively certain (within the bounds of environmental science), the precautionary principle becomes less relevant, and other considerations and values, including social and economic ones, determine the extent to which environmental harms will be permitted.

This latter situation more accurately reflects the facts in *Pembina Institute*. In the absence of any proposed mitigation, there would have been little uncertainty about the Kearl Oil Sands Project's likely impacts on peatlands, which were bound to be deemed significant (as they eventually were in the context of a subsequent oil sands project proposal five years later).[108] These impacts only became notionally uncertain because Imperial Oil invoked adaptive management, that is, mitigation that was itself uncertain. Viewed this way—and contrary to the precautionary principle—Imperial Oil *did* invoke uncertainty and adaptive management to dissuade the review panel from requiring demonstratively effective mitigation or from making a finding that significant adverse effects were likely, which, under the then-applicable regime, would have required further justification. Adaptive management and uncertainty were thus used to obscure the actual risk of harm and, subsequently, the real trade-offs that project approval entailed.

Genuine adaptive management is not a response to the precautionary principle; it is essentially an admission that the effectiveness of the mitigation measures proposed and potentially being taken into account in impact prediction is uncertain. Where the uncertainty regarding effectiveness is low, it may be appropriate to factor in such measures in impact prediction. But where the uncertainty is moderate to high, the measures should be excluded altogether, even though they may

---

[citations omitted; emphasis added]. In some formulations, measures are qualified as those that are cost-effective.

107  See also Chalifour, above note 43 at 272.

108  Olszynski, above note 31 at 719–21.

still be included in the subsequent decision statement as part of an adaptive management plan. Consequently, the primary role for adaptive management in decision making is to assist in improving the overall acceptability of a given project on the basis that, although it may still result in significant adverse environment effects, the proponent is at least committed to learning and the potential for improvement that comes with that.

Finally, with respect to compliance and enforcement, increased availability of proponent data (as discussed at the outset of this part) should be expected to have a positive effect on implementation. The Agency should also devote considerably more resources to compliance and enforcement activities, especially on-site inspections, and improve the accessibility and functionality of the public registry with respect to these matters. Finally, efforts should be undertaken to enable the establishment of an administrative monetary penalty regime to remove the economic incentives for non-compliance that falls short of criminal behaviour.

# CHAPTER 17

# Strategic and Regional Environmental Assessments

*Jason MacLean, Bram Noble, and Jill Blakley*

## A. INTRODUCTION

Strategic environmental assessment (SEA) is based on the understanding that many of the decisions that help ensure sustainability outcomes occur long before project proposals are assessed. In Canada, SEA was formally established in the early 1990s through a Cabinet directive. It emerged independently of project-based environmental assessment (EA), making Canadian SEA among the "first of the new generation of SEA systems that evolved in the 1990s."[1] The federal Cabinet Directive on the Environmental Assessment of Policy, Plan and Program Proposals mandates a SEA whenever a federal agency or department submits a policy, plan, or program (PPP) proposal to a minister or Cabinet for approval. The performance to date of federal SEA in Canada, however, is at best mixed, and its ability to help achieve sustainability objectives is questionable.[2] The federal SEA paradigm has been deeply rooted in and restricted by its use as an impact assessment (IA) tool reflecting the

---

1    Barry Dalal-Clayton & Barry Sadler, *Strategic Environmental Assessment: A Sourcebook and Reference Guide to International Experience* (London, UK: Earthscan, 2005) at 61.

2    Bram Noble et al, "Effectiveness of Strategic Environmental Assessment in Canada Under Directive-Based and Informal Practice" (2019) 37:3–4 *Impact Assessment and Project Appraisal* 344. See also Government of Canada, "The Cabinet Directive on the Environmental Assessment of Policy, Plan and Program Proposals" (Ottawa: Privy Council Office & Canadian Environmental Assessment Agency, 2016), online: *Government*

traditional principles and practices of project EA. This is not surprising. Globally, SEA was originally conceived as a tool for assessing environmental impacts at the time when PPPs are proposed, with current motivation for its application often being compliance and the delivery of an EA report.[3] Most systems of SEA that have emerged over the last thirty-plus years, including in Canada, reflect this traditional approach and are built largely on project-based EA thinking.[4]

The recently implemented *Impact Assessment Act (IAA)*[5] introduces a potentially new role for SEA in Canada. SEA provisions in the legislation do not replace the SEA Cabinet directive, effectively introducing a dual-track system, but the *IAA* may provide an opportunity to shift SEA thinking and practice beyond the traditional EA-like mindset. SEA is fundamentally about shaping the formulation and implementation of PPPs, enabling them to proceed in a more sustainable manner, and ensuring that development choices align with desired outcomes.[6] The exploration of strategic options, including alternative PPP scenarios, is thus central to how SEA informs and guides planning and decision-making processes. Providing direction to both higher and lower tiers of decision making, good SEA is integrated with the legislative, administrative, and institutional contexts in which PPPs are conceptualized, formulated, and implemented, thus informing and improving institutional decision-making culture and processes.[7] Assessing the impacts of PPPs is a necessary feature of SEA but is not sufficient.[8] Ultimately, the true test of SEA is whether it serves to identify opportunities for and facilitate transitions toward a more sustainable future.

---

    *of Canada* www.canada.ca/en/impact-assessment-agency/programs/strategic-environmental-assessment/cabinet-directive-environmental-assessment-policy-plan-program-proposals.html.

3    Vincent Lobos & Maria Partidario, "Theory Versus Practice in Strategic Environmental Assessment (SEA)" (2014) 48 *Environmental Impact Assessment Review* 34.

4    Bram Noble, "Transforming IA from the Outside in: Capacity and Levers for Strategic Assessment" (2020) 38:2 *Impact Assessment and Project Appraisal* 122. Note that throughout this chapter we refer to both EA and IA, and for the purposes of the discussion here, we consider these terms interchangeable.

5    SC 2019, c 28, s 1.

6    Noble et al, above note 2.

7    *Ibid.*

8    Bram Noble & Kelechi Nwanekezie, "Conceptualizing Strategic Environmental Assessment: Principles, Approaches and Research Directions" (2017) 62 *Environmental Impact Assessment Review* 165.

This chapter introduces the SEA provisions of the Act, including an examination of the strengths and weaknesses of each provision. Our assessment is informed by established scholarship on effective SEA, what we have learned from SEA practice under the Cabinet directive, and the recommendations of the federally appointed Expert Panel for the Review of Environmental Assessment Processes (Expert Panel).[9] The chapter concludes with recommendations to ensure effective implementation of SEA under the *IAA*.

## B. STRATEGIC ENVIRONMENTAL ASSESSMENT PROVISIONS OF THE *IAA*

The *IAA* allows the minister to initiate SEAs under section 95, the core SEA provision, which provides as follows:

**Strategic Assessments**

*Assessments*

**95** (1) The Minister may establish a committee — or authorize the Agency — to conduct an assessment of

(a) any Government of Canada policy, plan or program — proposed or existing — that is relevant to conducting impact assessments; or

(b) any issue that is relevant to conducting impact assessments of designated projects or of a class of designated projects.

*Minister's power*

(2) The Minister may deem any assessment that provides guidance on how Canada's commitments in respect of climate change should be considered in impact assessments and that is prepared by a federal authority and commenced before the day on which this Act comes into force to be an assessment conducted under this section.

The Act, however, neither defines nor requires SEA. The remaining provisions spell out in very broad and general terms the procedures that

---

9    Expert Panel for the Review of Environmental Assessment Processes, *Building Common Ground: A New Vision for Impact Assessment in Canada* (Ottawa: Canadian Environmental Assessment Agency, 2017), online (pdf): *Government of Canada* www.canada.ca/content/dam/themes/environment/conservation/environmental-reviews/building-common-ground/building-common-ground.pdf [*Building Common Ground*].

may be required of SEAs, as well as regional assessments,[10] including establishing SEA committees and terms of reference (section 96); the minister's responsibility for responding to a request for a SEA (section 97); public disclosure of information relevant to the conduct of a SEA (section 98); public participation in SEAs (section 99); obligations of other federal authorities possessing information relevant to a SEA to disclose it upon request of the relevant SEA committee or the Impact Assessment Agency of Canada (the Agency) (section 100); and the modified application of section 53 — a review panel's powers to summon witnesses — to a committee established in relation to section 95 (section 101). Other procedural obligations relate to SEA committee reports to the minister, including, as the case may be, the use of Indigenous knowledge (section 102) and public disclosure of section 102 reports (section 103).

The *IAA* makes a number of other, isolated mentions of SEA. The preamble expresses the federal government's overarching commitment to "fostering sustainability" (a core goal of SEA) and, more specifically, the government's recognition of "the importance of strategic assessments in assessing federal policies, plans or programs that are relevant to conducting impact assessments." Other mentions include public participation in SEA (section 6(1)(h)); SEA as a potential decision-making factor (section 16(2)(e)); existing SEAs as a factor to be considered in project assessments, where a SEA has been referred to (section 22(1)(p)); participant funding for SEAs (section 75(c)); the minister's authority to make regulations with respect to the procedures and requirements of SEAs (section 112(1)(a.3)), which highlights the discretionary nature of the Act's SEA power and provisions; the minister's obligation to establish an advisory council relating to the implementation of SEAs under the *IAA* (sections 117 to 119); and the Agency's obligation to establish an expert committee to advise it on issues relating to SEAs (section 157).

---

10　We discuss regional assessment in relation to cumulative effects assessment (CEA) practices in Chapter 11.

## C. ASSESSMENT OF THE *IAA*'S STRATEGIC ENVIRONMENTAL ASSESSMENT PROVISIONS

### 1) An Added Layer of Terminology

The *IAA* introduces a new provision for federal SEA but does not adopt the same SEA name tag used under the Cabinet directive, referring instead to "strategic assessment." The Cabinet directive will likely continue to serve as the primary vehicle for SEA to assess the impacts of PPPs. Presumably, the *IAA* provides for a more strategic approach to SEA that extends beyond the limitations and constraints of the Cabinet directive. However, the Act does not integrate, or even mention, the SEA Cabinet directive or clarify this relationship.[11] This new terminology is introduced without any explanation as to whether strategic assessment under the *IAA* is intended to signal the adoption of an instrument other than SEA, one with different strategic principles, methodology, and objectives, or whether it is simply an effort to align a label with the title of the new Act, emphasizing that the scope of strategic assessment under the *IAA* considers more than "environmental" matters — even though the term *environment* is broadly understood in international SEA systems and practices to include more than the biophysical realm.

The terminology adopted under the Act not only differs from standard SEA terminology used globally, but the dual labels (strategic assessment under the *IAA* and SEA under the Cabinet directive) also risk adding unnecessary confusion about an assessment approach that is already poorly understood in Canada.[12] Internationally, scholars have noted that the growing list of assessment types and terminology[13] creates silos and even poses challenges to meaningful practice. This is especially problematic for advancing a common understanding of federal SEA as

---

11    Meinhard Doelle & A John Sinclair, "The New IAA in Canada: From Revolutionary Thoughts to Reality" (2019) 79 *Environmental Impact Assessment Review* 106292.

12    See Bram F Noble, "Promise and Dismay: The State of Strategic Environmental Assessment Systems and Practices in Canada" (2009) 29:1 *Environmental Impact Assessment Review* 66; Bram Noble et al, "Strategic Environmental Assessment Opportunities and Risks for Arctic Offshore Energy Planning and Development" (2013) 39 *Marine Policy* 296.

13    Angus Morrison-Saunders et al, "Strengthening Impact Assessment: A Call for Integration and Focus" (2014) 32:1 *Impact Assessment and Project Appraisal* 2.

considerable diversity already exists among the policy and practitioner communities about what SEA is and what it should accomplish.[14]

## 2)  Legislative Provisions

The lack of legislative provisions for SEA in Canada has long been criticized.[15] Canada was one of the first countries to introduce a directive-based SEA system, but unlike many international SEA systems, Canada's directive-based approach is not based in legislation. This discrepancy continued under the *IAA*, which does not integrate the SEA Cabinet directive. Canada did not sign the UN Economic Commission for Europe Protocol on Strategic Environmental Assessment (Kyiv Protocol), the international agreement introduced in 2003 to all United Nations member states.[16] It provides for legal obligations and a procedural framework for the implementation of SEA in countries that are parties to it. More than thirty countries have signed the protocol, which requires its member states to, among other things, enact legislative and regulatory provisions for SEA, ensure that a SEA report is prepared, and demonstrate that the conclusions of the SEA report are accounted for in plan or program adoption.

For the first time in Canada, SEA provisions now exist in federal IA legislation under the *IAA*. However, the provisions do not establish a triggering mechanism whereby a SEA must be undertaken. Instead, as explained above, it only provides that the minister "may establish a

---

14    See Noble et al, above note 2; A John Sinclair et al, "Looking Up, Down, and Sideways: Reconceiving Cumulative Effects Assessment as a Mindset" (2017) 62 *Environmental Impact Assessment Review* 183; Olivia Bina, "A Critical Review of the Dominant Lines of Argumentation on the Need for Strategic Environmental Assessment" (2007) 27:7 *Environmental Impact Assessment Review* 585.

15    See Hugh Benevides et al, "Law and Policy Options for Strategic Environmental Assessment in Canada" (2009) [unpublished], online: https://ssrn.com/abstract=1660403 [dx.doi.org/10.2139/ssrn.1660403]; Robert B Gibson et al, "Strengthening Strategic Environmental Assessment in Canada: An Evaluation of Three Basic Options" (2010) 20:3 *Journal of Environmental Law & Practice* 175.

16    UN Economic Commission for Europe, *Protocol on Strategic Environmental Assessment: Facts and Benefits* (UNECE Secretariat to the Protocol on Strategic Environmental Assessment to the Convention on Environmental Impact Assessment in the Transboundary Context, 2017), online (pdf): www.unece.org/fileadmin/DAM/env/eia/Publications/2016/ Protocol_on_SEA/1609217_UNECE_HR.pdf.

committee — or authorize the Agency — to conduct [a strategic] assessment."[17] The *IAA* thus provides significant ministerial discretion with respect to whether a SEA is conducted and for what reasons. This discretion allows for careful case-by-case consideration of the need for SEA, ensuring efficient use of SEA processes and resources and providing an opportunity to potentially focus on the most complex and controversial environmental issues. At the same time, such discretion could mean that SEAs are completed only when convenient and provides little guarantee that SEAs will be completed at all, especially for the most controversial and politically contested matters. By nature, SEA is a politically sensitive instrument,[18] and policy makers and political decision makers can be reluctant about its full integration.[19] Section 117 provides some assurance on SEA application in that the minister must establish an advisory council to advise on issues related to the implementation of SEA, as well as IA and regional assessment regimes under the Act. However, the council's terms of reference are extremely broad, and its governance structure does not alter or otherwise guide the minister's absolute discretion with respect to SEA under the Act.

### 3) Scope of Application

Effective SEA is about more than assessing and mitigating the impacts of proposed and existing PPPs or informing project-based EA; it is also about shaping policies and institutional priorities, informing strategic-level decisions on an ongoing basis, and facilitating transitions in institutions and decision-making practices toward the achievement of more sustainable futures.[20] The *IAA* provides the minister with the ability to establish a committee or instruct the Agency to conduct a SEA. As noted above, section 95(1) stipulates that a SEA can assess any policy, plan, program, or designated project that is relevant to conducting impact assessments.

---

17    *IAA*, above note 5, s 95(1).

18    Lobos & Partidario, above note 3.

19    Noble, above note 4.

20    Monica Fundingsland Tetlow & Marie Hanusch, "Strategic Environmental Assessment: The State of the Art" (2012) 30:1 *Impact Assessment and Project Appraisal* 15; Maria Partidario, "A Strategic Advocacy Role in SEA for Sustainability" (2015) 17:1 *Journal of Environmental Assessment Policy and Management* 1; Noble & Nwanekezie, above note 8; Noble et al, above note 2.

In principle, the Act provides an opportunity to advance SEA beyond the EA-like approach of the SEA Cabinet directive. A constraint introduced under the *IAA*, which does not appear in the SEA Cabinet directive, is that the PPPs or issues being assessed must be relevant to the conduct of *project* IA. Of course, as discussed below in terms of tiering, good SEA informs next-level decisions;[21] however, limiting the relevance of SEA to known projects and project-based assessments is unduly restrictive. It significantly diminishes the potential of SEA and its role as a mechanism for innovation and transformation with respect to policies and governance practices.[22]

What is meant by "relevant" under section 95(1) is not defined, and the *IAA* does not specify how the minister—advised by an advisory council—will make decisions about which SEAs will receive priority. This introduces the potential for a broad range of issues to be considered in SEA, and there may be significant discretion for the minister to commission SEAs for matters that are not *directly* related to projects or ongoing assessments but that are certainly relevant in shaping future projects through policy influence or other strategic-level actions. This might include several pressing issues in Canada, including renewable-energy transitions in remote regions, Canada's nuclear power road map, so-called energy corridors, agricultural land conversion, international climate commitments, and flood risk management, to name only a few.

Limiting the relevance of SEA to known projects and project-based assessments also creates a potential issue with respect to timing. SEA is meant to influence project options and decisions, but if a SEA must be relevant to designated projects under the *IAA*, then the SEA may be occurring well after early planning decisions have been made. Significant project infrastructure investments may also have been made by the time the SEA is undertaken. This situation can easily diminish any influential benefits of SEA.

---

21    Denis Kirchhoff et al, "Strategic Environmental Assessment and Regional Infrastructure Planning: The Case of York Region, Ontario, Canada" (2011) 29:1 *Impact Assessment and Project Appraisal* 11.

22    Fundingsland Tetlow & Hanusch, above note 20; Noble & Nwanekezie, above note 8.

## 4) Relationship to Regional Assessment

As discussed in Chapter 11, the *IAA* makes provisions for regional assessment in addition to strategic assessment. Both types of assessment are treated in much the same way: the minister has the discretion to call for each in circumstances deemed warranted, the minister will rely on an advisory council to determine which regional and strategic assessments will receive priority, and the Act encourages the consideration of the results of both types of assessment in project-based EA. The *IAA* casts regional and strategic assessment as entirely separate entities; their potential relationship or interaction is not alluded to in any way, and the nature and scope of a regional assessment are not explained.

Section 92 states that a regional assessment is an "assessment of the effects of existing or future physical activities carried out in a region." Sinclair et al explained that the term *regional assessment* has been used in many contexts, creating confusion in the literature and among practitioners.[23] Unfortunately, the *IAA* provides no further direction or clarification on regional assessment, such as *why* it would be carried out, *what* it would focus on, and *who or what* it would inform. The Expert Panel was much clearer, explaining that regional assessments would gather baseline information (including traditional land use studies), establish valued-components and associated criteria, provide an understanding of the state of the environment (including regional stressors and trends), assess cumulative impacts, set a preferred direction for achieving sustainability in a region through the evaluation of alternative development scenarios, and inform and streamline project assessment. The views of the Expert Panel closely align with scholarship on the topic,[24] as well as a 2005 research and development report published by the former Canadian Environmental Assessment Agency that discussed the different models for and approaches to regional and strategic assessments.[25]

---

23    Sinclair et al, above note 14.

24    *Ibid*; Jill AE Harriman & Bram F Noble, "Characterizing Project and Strategic Approaches to Regional Cumulative Effects Assessment in Canada" (2008) 10:1 *Journal of Environmental Assessment Policy and Management* 25.

25    Bram F Noble, *Regional Cumulative Effects Assessment: Toward a Strategic Framework*, Research supported by the Canadian Environmental Assessment Agency's Research and Development Program (Ottawa: Canadian Environmental Assessment Agency, 2005).

Given the growing interest in various forms of regional assessment across Canada, guidance is needed under the *IAA* to clarify its intent and approach at the federal level and its relationship to SEA. In practice, for example, many regional assessments conducted under provincial jurisdiction are strategic in nature and intended to explore alternative scenarios and guide policy making, planning, and project-level decision making toward specified sustainability goals or outcomes.[26] In 2009, the Canadian Council of Ministers of the Environment (CCME) endorsed regional strategic environmental assessment (RSEA) as a framework to address impacts associated with the development of strategic, sustainable initiatives on a regional scale. RSEA has been the basis for recent on-the-ground practice in the Elk Valley, British Columbia, and the South Athabasca Oil Sands.[27] The CCME guidance,[28] in part, also prompted the inclusion of regional and strategic assessment in the *IAA*. However, the Act ignores the often fruitful relationship between regional and strategic assessment and the signalling of environment ministers themselves who identified the synergies as a key area of interest for government, industry, Indigenous communities and organizations, and other leaders.

## 5) Tiering and Influence

The limited tiering and influence of SEA over project assessments have been a long-standing topic in SEA scholarship[29] and a major criticism of SEA practice in Canada.[30] At a minimum, legislation must set out

---

26   Jill AE Gunn & Bram F Noble, "Sustainability Considerations in Regional Environmental Assessment" in Angus Morrison-Saunders, Jenny Pope & Alan Bond, eds, *Handbook of Sustainability Assessment* (Cheltenham, UK: Edward Elgar, 2015) 79.

27   *Ibid.*

28   Canadian Council of Ministers of the Environment, *Regional Strategic Environmental Assessment in Canada: Principles and Guidance* (2009), online (pdf): www.ccme.ca/files/Resources/enviro_assessment/rsea_principles_guidance_e.pdf.

29   Thomas B Fischer, "Strategic Environmental Assessment in Post-modern Times" (2003) 23:2 *Environmental Impact Assessment Review* 155; Riki Therivel, *Strategic Environmental Assessment in Action*, 2d ed (London, UK: Earthscan, 2010); Lisa White & Bram Noble, "Strategic Environmental Assessment in the Electricity Sector: An Application to Electricity Supply Planning, Saskatchewan, Canada" (2013) 30:4 *Impact Assessment and Project Appraisal* 284.

30   Bram F Noble, "Promise and Dismay: The State of Strategic Environmental Assessment Systems and Practices in Canada" (2009) 29:1 *Environmental Impact Assessment Review* 66.

clear expectations for how project initiatives and decisions are to be responsive to SEA.[31] As indicated above, the *IAA* requires the results of an applicable SEA to be considered by the minister when determining whether to designate a project that is not on the federal Project List and by the Agency during the planning phase of a project when determining whether an EA is required. SEAs are also identified under the Act as a factor to be considered in the EA of a designated project, where an existing SEA is applicable and referenced in the project review. Furthermore, the "Practitioner's Guide to Federal Impact Assessments Under the Impact Assessment Act" instructs proponents to refer to "regional studies" and "strategic assessment" when developing their baselines studies and assessing alternatives to and alternative means of carrying out a project.[32]

These provisions all indicate a clear intention under the Act for SEA (and regional studies) to tier toward and inform project-level EA. This is consistent with the views of the Expert Panel in that "a tiered approach should be implemented whereby strategic and regional IAs produce the policy and planning foundations for improved and efficient project IAs."[33] However, the legislation is silent on the nature and authority of decision making and on guidance regarding how the results are to be used in future project decisions.[34] Specifically, the *IAA* stops short of providing details on what factors stemming from a SEA must be considered in a project assessment and how, including whether SEA results are to shape the terms of reference for EAs for designated projects and

---

31    Meinhard Doelle, "Role of Strategic Environmental Assessments in Energy Governance: A Case Study of Tidal Energy in Nova Scotia's Bay of Fundy" (2009) 27:2 *Journal of Energy & Natural Resources Law* 112.

32    Impact Assessment Agency of Canada, "Practitioner's Guide to Federal Impact Assessments Under the Impact Assessment Act" (2020), online: *Government of Canada* www.canada.ca/en/impact-assessment-agency/services/policy-guidance/practitioners-guide-impact-assessment-act.html. The Practitioner's Guide consistently refers to "regional studies," the terminology used under the *Canadian Environmental Assessment Act, 2012* (SC 2012, c 19, s 52), versus "regional assessment," adding further uncertainty to the role of regional studies under the *IAA* and how they differ from regional studies under the former Act.

33    *Building Common Ground*, above note 9 at 22.

34    Meinhard Doelle, "Regional & Strategic Assessments in the Proposed Federal Impact Assessment Act (IAA)" (25 February 2018), online (blog): *Environmental Law News* https://blogs.dal.ca/melaw/2018/02/25/regional-strategic-assessments-in-the-proposed-canadian-impact-assessment-act-ciaa/.

establish common monitoring parameters for multiple projects operating in the same region.

Other opportunities for tiering are also missing. Various scholars report that the key to effective SEA is how it relates to the various planning and decision processes it is intended to inform, both from higher to lower and lower to higher tiers of decision making.[35] Of particular importance, given past debates about the burden that strategic issues can place on project assessment,[36] are windows of opportunity to conduct a SEA when a series of project EAs — perhaps in a given region or economic sector — reveal a policy gap[37] or other strategic-level issues that need to be resolved to ensure informed project-level decision making.

## 6)  Strategic Principles and Guidance

Multiple methodological frameworks for SEA have emerged, and it is often described as "one concept, multiple forms"[38] or "a family of approaches."[39] However, scholarly thinking about SEA has shifted from viewing it as a formal IA process designed solely to assess and mitigate PPP impacts to a strategy-oriented approach to (a) better understand the complex institutional arena and governance conditions of strategic-decision processes,[40] (b) assess viable environmental and sustainability options that will help achieve strategic objectives, and (c) facilitate strategic transitions toward a more sustainable future.[41]

Methodological guidance to accompany SEA application is missing from the legislation, including the foundational principles and steps for conducting a SEA. It is anticipated that a policy framework will provide detail around the steps, activities, roles, and responsibilities in SEAs.

---

35    Doelle, above note 31; Jenny Pope et al, "Advancing the Theory and Practice of Impact Assessment: Setting the Research Agenda" (2013) 41 *Environmental Impact Assessment Review* 1; Sinclair et al, above note 14; Noble et al, above note 2.

36    Government of Canada, *Jobs, Growth and Long-Term Prosperity: Economic Action Plan 2012* (29 March 2012), online (pdf): www.budget.gc.ca/2012/plan/pdf/Plan2012-eng.pdf.

37    Robert B Gibson, Meinhard Doelle & A John Sinclair, "Fulfilling the Promise: Basic Components of Next Generation Environmental Assessment" (2015) 29 *Journal of Environmental Law & Practice* 251.

38    RAA Verheem & JAMN Tonk, "Strategic Environmental Assessment: One Concept, Multiple Forms" (2000) 18:3 *Impact Assessment and Project Appraisal* 177.

39    Dalal-Clayton & Sadler, above note 1 at 12.

40    Noble & Nwanekezie, above note 8.

41    Fundingsland Tetlow & Hanusch, above note 20.

However, the current baseline on the "how to" of SEA is the SEA Cabinet directive, which approaches SEA largely as an IA tool and is deeply entrenched in traditional, project-based EA principles and design.[42] In the absence of accompanying methodological principles and guidance that emphasize strategic thinking, the practice of SEA under the *IAA* is likely to resemble "studies" with little ability to influence key policy agendas or entrenched development trajectories. Methodological guidance for SEA under the Act is needed to instill the principles of strategic thinking in SEA and redirect its practice away from a "product-oriented" approach focused on delivering an assessment report to one based on providing strategic direction and fostering sustainability transitions.[43] Without further development as a strategic process, and in the absence of clear methodological guidance, the SEA regime under the *IAA* will likely come up short on meeting its strategic intent and potential.

## D.　ACTIONS REQUIRED TO ENSURE EFFECTIVE IMPLEMENTATION OF STRATEGIC ENVIRONMENTAL ASSESSMENT

Six actions are required to ensure effective implementation of SEA under the *IAA*. First, the Act provides an opportunity to introduce "strategic thinking" to federal SEA; however, section 95(1) constrains the scope of SEA to *proposed* or *existing* PPPs that are relevant to conducting IAs. The scope of section 95(1) should be expanded to include the *formulation* of PPPs. Once PPPs are proposed, or if they already exist, the opportunity for SEA to set a strategic direction and help achieve more sustainable outcomes is already restricted. Broadening the scope of SEA application will open the door for it to be far more influential in not only *how* PPPs are implemented but also in *what* PPPs are formulated and the factors considered in their development.

Second, and closely related, introducing strategic thinking into SEA requires supporting guidance on *how* this is to be achieved. Currently, there is no guidance at the federal level on how to conduct SEA, posing a high likelihood that practice will resemble the EA-like approach adopted under the SEA Cabinet directive. Shifting SEA mindsets requires more than legislating that something *must* be done; it requires practical methodological principles on *how* to do it.

---

42　Noble et al, above note 2.

43　Lobos & Partidario, above note 3.

Third, there is a need for stronger legislative and regulatory requirements on *when* SEA (and regional assessment) must be done. The current approach is entirely at the discretion of the minister. Similar in approach to the European SEA directive, regulations are needed to identify the types of strategic issues and actions for which SEA will be mandatory under the Act. We have not developed a comprehensive list of what strategic initiatives should be subject to SEA since scoping such a list may be one of the initial tasks of the advisory committee referred to in section 177 of the Act. However, such initiatives may include the formulation and implementation of strategic-level policies and action plans, along with the setting of federal targets and programming regarding such matters as renewable energy transitions, national climate strategies or international climate and sustainability commitments, the development of agricultural policy and technology innovation, investments in nuclear energy, marine fisheries and habitat protection, the development and implementation of national initiatives to conserve biodiversity, and the development of national environmental emergency and disaster programs. Such a list need not be exhaustive of all matters and should be complemented by the discretionary provisions that already exist under the *IAA* for the minister to conduct SEA on a case-by-case basis. However, discretionary provisions should be guided by clearly stated, transparent screening criteria, such as matters relating to the national interest regarding water, energy, and food security, as well as climate and biodiversity. There should also be a requirement for publicly disclosed reasons for a decision on the need for SEA.

Fourth, tiering is essential to good SEA, although not all SEAs may immediately tier to other regional or project-level actions. Strategic and regional assessments can set the policy and planning foundations for more effective and more efficient project EAs. Although the practitioner's guidance for federal assessments under the Act instructs proponents to consider regional and strategic assessments when preparing an impact statement, clearer authoritative guidance is needed to ensure that the results of strategic and regional assessments inform the terms of reference for a project assessment. Proponents should also have to demonstrate how their projects comply with or contribute to the strategies, trends, or thresholds set out under strategic and regional assessments.

Fifth, the nature and role of regional assessment under section 92 need to be better defined through supporting regulation or guidance.

The *IAA* simply refers to regional assessment in the context of assessing the effects of existing or future physical activities carried out in a region. Consistent with the recommendations of the Expert Panel,[44] the purpose and scope of regional assessment need to be clearly explained, with a focus on understanding baseline trends and conditions, assessing potential cumulative effects, identifying thresholds or acceptable levels of change, and establishing the criteria and indicators that will direct — through project-specific terms of reference — the nature of project assessments within those regions. Regional assessment also provides an important opportunity to strengthen follow-up and monitoring under the *IAA*, yet requirements that regional assessment directly inform the conditions for post-approval project monitoring under the legislation are absent.

Finally, the federal government must clarify the relationship of "strategic assessment" initiated under the *IAA* to "strategic environmental assessment" initiated in response to the Cabinet directive. This need not require legislative changes but rather an operational policy statement clarifying their respective roles, scope, and function. Arguably, there is an opportunity to focus SEA under the Act on the more "strategic" issues and matters that set policy direction and enable meaningful implementation of PPPs while reserving SEA under the Cabinet directive for the more routine appraisals or assessments of the impacts of PPPs once they are proposed. Of course, in recent years, governments have sought to streamline EA processes to counter concerns over costs and administrative burden,[45] and, indeed, the perceived need to streamline EA in Canada was one of the primary drivers behind the pared-down *Canadian Environmental Assessment Act, 2012.*[46] Perhaps if "strategic assessment" is made mandatory under the *IAA* it can meet *both* the EA-like and the strategic-thinking functions of SEA, and the Cabinet directive can be rendered superfluous and eliminated, either formally or by implication.

---

44    Above note 9.

45    Alan Bond et al, "Impact Assessment: Eroding Benefits Through Streamlining?" (2014) 45 *Environmental Impact Assessment Review* 46.

46    Above note 32.

## E.  CONCLUSION

In Canada, SEA is sorely needed and underutilized. In this chapter, we have endeavoured to describe the framework of effective SEA, assess its potential application under the *IAA*, and suggest a series of proposed enhancements to the federal SEA regime that are largely technical in nature.

We would be remiss, however, if we concluded on a purely technical note. As discussed in this volume's earlier chapter on EA law reform, the nature of EA in Canada is intensely ideological and political. Without unduly diminishing the technical challenges associated with the improvements we propose to the application of SEA under the *IAA*, the larger challenge is political.[47] Indeed, in the final design of the *IAA*, the federal government made a decision to dismiss many of the key recommendations of its own Expert Panel, including the Panel's recommendations relating to the uses of SEA and regional assessment. This illustrates the core obstacle to effective environmental law reform in Canada: the outsized influence of the special interests of Canada's natural resource extractive sectors.[48] The conclusion of the canonical assessment of Canadian environmental law made in 2010 remains just as true today: sustainability will arise in Canada only if Canadians choose and demand from their leaders and governing laws "a fundamentally different economic model in which maintenance of ecological integrity is a precondition to all development."[49] The SEA provisions of the new Act, and the *IAA* more generally, strongly suggest that Canadians are not yet prepared to make this choice.

---

47    See, for example, Jason MacLean, "Regulatory Capture and the Role of Academics in Public Policymaking: Lessons from Canada's Environmental Regulatory Review Process" (2019) 52:2 *UBC Law Review* 479; Jason MacLean, "The Crude Politics of Carbon Pricing, Pipelines, and Environmental Assessment" (2019) 70 *University of New Brunswick Law Journal* 128; Jason MacLean, Meinhard Doelle & Chris Tollefson, "Polyjural and Polycentric Sustainability Assessment: A Once-in-a-Generation Law Reform Opportunity" (2016) 30:1 *Journal of Environmental Law & Practice* 36.

48    Jason MacLean, "Striking at the Root Problem of Canadian Environmental Law: Identifying and Escaping Regulatory Capture" (2016) 29 *Journal of Environmental Law & Practice* 111.

49    Stepan Wood, Georgia Tanner & Benjamin J Richardson, "What Ever Happened to Canadian Environmental Law?" (2010) 37 *Ecology Law Quarterly* 981 at 1039–40.

# CHAPTER 18

# Impact Assessment for Projects on Federal Lands and Outside Canada: The "Federal Projects" Process

*Jamie Kneen*

## A.  INTRODUCTION

One vexing issue for next-generation impact assessment (IA) processes is ensuring the proper assessment of projects and undertakings that the government either undertakes itself or funds in other jurisdictions. Along with projects receiving federal funding, projects on federal lands and Canadian overseas development assistance are clearly within federal jurisdiction for implementing the IA process. Projects on federal lands could include activities such as work in ports, in national parks, and on Indian reserves. Projects outside Canada could include infrastructure or initiatives in the areas of agriculture or aquaculture, for example, directly funded or implemented by the Canadian government elsewhere in the world.[1] Ensuring that such projects undergo IA is part of the federal government's role as guardian and custodian of the public good, but it

---

1    In s 2 of the *Impact Assessment Act*, SC 2019, c 28, s 1, "federal lands" is defined as

    (a)    lands that belong to Her Majesty in right of Canada, or that Her Majesty in right of Canada has the power to dispose of, and all waters on and airspace above those lands, other than lands under the administration and control of the Commissioner of Yukon, the Northwest Territories or Nunavut;

    (b)    the following lands and areas:

        (i)    the internal waters of Canada, in any area of the sea not within a province,

        (ii)    the territorial sea of Canada, in any area of the sea not within a province,

        (iii)    the exclusive economic zone of Canada, and

        (iv)    the continental shelf of Canada; and

also provides the opportunity for public participation and improved decision making, as well as the potential to set a positive example for other jurisdictions, both nationally and internationally. The *Impact Assessment Act* (*IAA*)[2] makes specific provisions for the assessment of projects on federal lands and projects outside Canada; however, as detailed in this chapter, these provisions are flawed and are further weakened by the absence of any linkage between them and the rest of the Act.

Specifically, this chapter explores the process set out in the Act for the assessment of projects on federal lands and projects outside Canada; how this process differs from the rest of the Act and from previous generations of federal environmental assessment legislation; the practical and policy reasons for this; the benefits and drawbacks of this approach; and, finally, what can be done to address identified shortcomings.

## B.  A DIFFERENT ASSESSMENT PROCESS

Essentially, the *IAA* sets out a completely different and separate process for the assessment of projects on federal lands and projects outside Canada. I call it the "federal projects" process to differentiate it from the Act's standard process for designated projects.[3] In recognition of the clear federal authority in these areas, all projects on federal lands and federally funded projects outside Canada are captured, and in sections 81 to 91, the Act prescribes a specific IA process for them. The federal projects process and the standard assessment process established in the Act have surprisingly little in common, although they are administered by the same agency and incorporated into the same public registry. The federal projects process applies to many more projects than the standard assessment process, but with greatly reduced timelines and process requirements in areas such as opportunities for public participation. It even has different factors to consider in decision making, as outlined below.[4]

---

    (c)   reserves, surrendered lands and any other lands that are set apart for the use and benefit of a band and that are subject to the Indian Act, and all waters on and airspace above those reserves or lands. (*territoire domanial*)

2    *Ibid.*

3    The less-than-illuminating heading in the Act is "Duties of Certain Authorities in Relation to Projects."

4    To be clear, even if designated projects—those falling within the definitions of the *Physical Activities Regulations* (SOR/2019-285)—are covered by the federal projects process, they would still be subject to the standard impact assessment regime under the *IAA*.

The key features of the federal projects process that differentiate it from the Act's standard assessment process are as follows:

- it has much broader application: all projects on federal lands and projects federally funded or executed outside Canada;
- it requires public notification of projects being assessed, via the online Canadian Impact Assessment Registry (the Registry);
- it has no planning phase and no requirement for public engagement or Indigenous engagement beyond notification;
- there is no access to participant funding;
- there is no timeline except for a public comment period that must be at least thirty days;
- assessments are done by the federal authority (FA), meaning the department or agency with primary regulatory decision making over the project, whether that be Heritage, Transport, Fisheries and Oceans, Indigenous and Northern Affairs, Environment and Climate Change, or the Canadian Nuclear Safety Commission;
- the factors to be considered in an assessment are more limited;
- decisions are made on the basis of whether there are likely to be significant environmental effects and whether they are deemed to be justified in the circumstances; and
- final decisions are made by the federal authority unless they refer the matter to Cabinet.

These provisions are outlined in Table 18.1, along with comparisons to previous generations of federal environmental assessment law: the *Canadian Environmental Assessment Act* (CEAA 1995)[5] and its 2012 rewrite, *CEAA 2012.*[6]

---

5    SC 1992, c 37. The entry into force of the Act was delayed until 1995 to allow for key regulations to be developed and passed.

6    SC 2012, c 19, s 52.

**TABLE 18.1 THREE GENERATIONS OF FEDERAL ENVIRONMENTAL ASSESSMENT LAW**

| | CEAA 1995 | CEAA 2012 | IAA |
|---|---|---|---|
| **Application of assessment** | Projects in Canada and projects outside Canada funded (in whole or in part) by a federal authority (FA) | Projects in whole or in part on federal lands, or outside Canada if carried out or funded (in whole or in part) by an FA | Unchanged from CEAA 2012 |
| **Responsible authority** | Responsible authority (RA): the primary federal decision maker on the project | FA same as RA in all but name | Unchanged from CEAA 2012 |
| **Trigger (which projects and activities are captured)** | Federal proponent, disposition of lands, or licence/permit; federal funding | FA to carry out any project, exercise any power, perform any duty or function to permit a project to be carried out; for projects outside Canada: federal funding (federal government no longer considered to act as proponent) | Same as CEAA 2012, but for projects on federal lands, it calls for financial assistance, enabling a project to be carried out |
| **Public notice** | Public (internet) registry | Annual report to Parliament | Public (internet) registry |
| **Public comment** | 15 days minimum on screening report if no public participation in screening; otherwise, other additional comment and participation; greater public involvement requirements under comprehensive study and panel reviews | None | 30 days minimum |

|  | CEAA 1995 | CEAA 2012 | IAA |
|---|---|---|---|
| **Assessment considerations** | Same as any other assessment: (a) environmental effects of the project (b) significance of effects (c) public comments (d) mitigation measures (e) need and alternatives (Community knowledge and Aboriginal traditional knowledge may also be considered) | None | For projects on federal lands: (a) adverse impact on rights of Indigenous peoples (b) Indigenous knowledge (c) community knowledge (d) public comments (e) mitigation measures For projects outside Canada, only (d) and (e) |
| **Determination/ decision** | (a) RA determines project not likely to cause significant adverse environmental effects or (b) RA determines project likely to cause significant adverse environmental effects that can be justified in the circumstances | (a) FA determines project not likely to cause significant adverse environmental effects or (b) FA determines project likely to cause significant adverse environmental effects; Governor in Council (GIC) decides that effects are justified in the circumstances | Unchanged from CEAA 2012 |
| **Exclusions** | GIC may designate projects or classes of projects exempted due to national security reasons, having insignificant environmental effects, or having a total cost below prescribed amount and meeting prescribed environmental conditions | Requirements do not apply in cases of national security, national emergency, or other emergency (no designation necessary) | As in CEAA 2012, plus minister may designate a class of projects deemed to cause only insignificant adverse environmental effects |

As can be seen, the *IAA*'s federal projects process generally follows *CEAA 2012* with small but significant changes with respect to public comment and factors to be considered. Federal projects must now be part of the public registry, and there is a minimum thirty-day public comment period. Although still minimal, this is a significant improvement over *CEAA 2012*, which provided no public notification or comment opportunity; departments merely filed cursory annual reports. There are also changes in the factors to be considered in the assessment. Only some of the standard process's expanded factors apply under the federal projects process, although *CEAA 2012* did not specify any factors to be considered.

## C. PURPOSE AND SCOPE OF FEDERAL ASSESSMENT OF PROJECTS ON FEDERAL LANDS AND PROJECTS OUTSIDE CANADA

Although provincial governments have claimed federal environmental assessment to be an intrusion on their jurisdiction (currently the subject of a constitutional reference case filed by Alberta) and that they can do whatever IA they feel is appropriate, federal authority over federal lands and spending is uncontested by other jurisdictions (not including the northern territories, Yukon, Northwest Territories, and Nunavut, where administration has been devolved to territorial governments). Indian reserve lands are also clearly federal responsibility, although Indigenous title and jurisdiction may eventually supersede the assertion of federal authority on reserve lands and beyond those boundaries, possibly as part of the implementation of the *United Nations Declaration on the Rights of Indigenous Peoples* (*UNDRIP*), addressed in Chapter 6. Co-management regimes established under comprehensive Indigenous land claims agreements represent a limited co-governance approach to assessment, where the federal government still makes the final decision.

The purpose of applying IA to projects on federal lands and projects outside Canada is stated in the purposes of the *IAA*:

[T]o ensure that projects, as defined in section 81, that are to be carried out on federal lands, or those that are outside Canada and that are to be carried out or financially supported by a federal authority, are considered in a careful and precautionary manner to avoid significant adverse environmental effects.[7]

This purpose is unchanged from *CEAA* 2012. As discussed below, this is noteworthy because the *IAA* introduces broader sets of factors to be considered in IA (*IAA* section 22(1)) and decision making (section 63), but these are not applied to projects on federal lands or projects outside Canada. Omitting or limiting the application of those considerations would seem to undermine many of the Act's other purpose provisions, especially in the absence of any clear link, rationale, or criteria for doing so. It may be that the intent is simply to make the process less onerous by narrowing the requirements, but there has been no explanation of why specific factors should not be considered—and if they are not applicable, no harm done—or why the decision-making criteria should not be consistent.

Those policy objectives are stated in the purposes of the *IAA*, ensuring that there be consideration of the environmental effects of projects on federal lands or outside Canada that are "carried out or financially supported by a federal authority." In this context, it is worth noting that the consistent implementation of the broader purposes of the Act is undermined by the more limited federal projects process described in sections 81 to 91. The purposes in the Act, such as

(f) to promote communication and cooperation with Indigenous peoples of Canada with respect to impact assessments; ...

(k) to ensure that an impact assessment takes into account alternative means of carrying out a designated project, including through the use of best available technologies; ... [and]

(m) to encourage the assessment of the cumulative effects of physical activities in a region and the assessment of federal policies, plans or programs and the consideration of those assessments in impact assessments,[8]

are all likely to be frustrated by the abbreviated federal projects process.

Beyond this, the federal government may seek to set direction for IA policy and implementation across Canada to lead other jurisdictions

---

7    *IAA*, above note 1, s 6(1)(l). In s 81, a "project" is "a physical activity that is carried out on federal lands or outside Canada in relation to a physical work."

8    *Ibid*, s 6(1).

(especially the provinces, but potentially also municipalities and Indigenous governments) and to establish best practices for proponents and other jurisdictions. Additionally, the federal government may wish to meet (and be seen to meet) the broad public expectation or assumption that the impacts of industrial development are being appropriately considered and competently managed and that Canadians will not be collectively held morally responsible for the effects of poor development decisions and irresponsible projects.

## D.  KEY FEATURES OF THE FEDERAL PROJECTS PROCESS

### 1)  Public Participation

Public participation is the area where the differences between the federal projects process and the standard assessment process under the *IAA* are the most significant. Meaningful public participation is heavily emphasized in the Act, even if, as discussed in Chapter 15, its realization is less than ideal. It is highlighted in the Act's preamble and in its purposes (section 6(1)). The purposes include ensuring that "opportunities are provided for meaningful public participation during an impact assessment."[9] For the federal projects process, this is expressed as a public notification requirement regarding the determination of whether a project is likely to cause significant adverse environmental effects:

- A responsible authority must post a notice on the Registry indicating that it intends to make a determination and inviting public comments.[10]
- No sooner than 30 days after posting that notice, the responsible authority "must post a notice of its determination, including any required mitigation measures."[11]

This is a very limited opportunity for public involvement. Conceivably, members of the public could somehow discover these notifications

---

9   *Ibid*, s 6(1)(h).

10   *Ibid*, s 86(1). See also Expert Panel for the Review of Environmental Assessment Processes, *Building Common Ground: A New Vision for Impact Assessment in Canada* (Ottawa: Canadian Environmental Assessment Agency, 2017), online (pdf): *Government of Canada* www.canada.ca/content/dam/themes/environment/conservation/environmental-reviews/ building-common-ground/building-common-ground.pdf [*Building Common Ground*].

11   *IAA*, above note 1, s 86(2).

on their own, but there is no commitment to proactively providing public involvement opportunities. Public interest groups with paid or volunteer staff may be in a better position to monitor automatic electronic notifications, assuming that these will also be generated. But they will be challenged to find the capacity to comment on the proposals, especially given the thirty-day deadline. As a result, it is difficult to see how the requirement to consider community knowledge and Indigenous knowledge can be meaningfully met.

Furthermore, funding to facilitate public participation in federal project assessments is not available, even where the thirty-day comment period does not make it completely impracticable. Participant funding is a necessity in getting the public involved in more complex projects. A federal authority could also decide that projects with potentially greater impacts should have a public comment period that is much longer than the minimum.

For projects outside Canada, public comments must be taken into consideration, although not community knowledge and Indigenous knowledge. It is hard to imagine how affected communities, local organizations, or even national or international non-governmental organizations working with them would be able to respond to or engage with this process in the time available and under these conditions.

### 2) Decision-Making Criteria

Under the standard *IAA* assessment process, projects on the designated projects list now have to be determined to be "in the public interest" to proceed, and that determination has to consider a more comprehensive set of criteria that nudge the process toward sustainability assessment. This is reflected in the change in nomenclature to *impact* assessment.[12] By contrast, the determination under the federal projects process remains more narrow and includes whether there are "significant adverse environmental effects" and whether these are "justified in the circumstances." This framework has been unchanged since *CEAA* 1995, as shown in Table 18.1. Effects other than environmental ones that could be used to assess sustainability are thus excluded; in fact, the determination for projects on federal lands drops the consideration

---

12 See Chapter 14 for a discussion of these criteria.

found in the standard process of both sustainability and climate change. The remaining factors to be considered are adverse impact on the rights of Indigenous peoples, Indigenous knowledge, community knowledge, public comments, and mitigation measures.[13] This is even more limited for projects outside Canada: only public comments and mitigation measures need to be taken into consideration.[14]

It remains to be seen whether the "public interest" test will be any more clear, specific, or meaningful than the "justified in the circumstances" test. Regardless, the *IAA* can be seen as having missed an opportunity in terms of bringing more comprehensive criteria and a sustainability framework to projects on federal lands or outside Canada. This would have potentially created an integrated process applying proportional levels of effort and scrutiny to small projects under direct federal jurisdiction, as discussed below.

### 3) Designation for Assessment: Physical Activities or Classes of Activities

There is provision in section 87 for the minister to designate a physical activity or class of physical activities that are not caught as "projects" under the federal projects process if they are not in relation to a physical work and are not on the designated projects list, to be assessed under the federal projects process. This can occur if, in the minister's opinion, the activity may cause significant adverse environmental effects. The standard process, on the other hand, allows the minister to designate a project for assessment—but not a class of projects—if she or he judges that it will have "adverse effects within federal jurisdiction or adverse direct or incidental effects," but also if "public concerns related to those effects warrant the designation."[15] The federal projects process includes no such consideration for public concern.

It is not clear how effective this provision is likely to be given the minimal public notice and public comment period. It seems fairly obvious that any such project would have to be identified long enough before it starts the assessment process for it to be designated by the minister. This provision would seem to be more useful as a proactive

---

13    *IAA*, above note 1, s 84(1).

14    *Ibid*, s 84(2).

15    *Ibid*, s 9(1).

mechanism to identify and designate projects, especially classes of projects, that are expected to be filed based on past experience.

### 4) Class Exclusion

There is also a provision for class exclusion (section 88), where the minister may designate a class of projects to be excluded from assessment if, in his or her opinion, they will cause only insignificant adverse environmental effects. Such an exclusion is not necessary in the standard process, where only designated projects are considered in the first place.

### 5) Triggering Assessments

The federal projects process casts a wide net. A large number of projects on federal lands have already been registered since the *IAA* came into force (377 as of 7 August 2020) and only two projects outside Canada, for the reasons discussed below. They are generally small projects with limited potential for significant impacts. However, if any of them did require more rigorous assessment, the Act does not provide a pathway to escalate or "bump up" projects to more intensive levels of scrutiny as appropriate, in the manner of the original *CEAA*. As noted in Chapter 7, the *IAA* also failed to do this with projects having clear federal interests with respect to navigable waters and fish habitat, which was especially notable given the public concern that those projects be subject to precisely this kind of oversight. Given the difficulty of identifying projects in time for the minister to designate them for assessment under section 9(1), the only other way to address this would seem to be to try to identify classes of projects to be added to the designated projects list.

The separate federal projects process was introduced in *CEAA 2012* in order to ensure that all identified projects on federal lands, as well as projects outside Canada that are carried out or directly funded by the federal government, would be subject to federal IA because they would not be captured by that Act's project list approach. This approach was necessitated by the need to ensure that all such projects were captured by the Act. It was also a response to the absence of either a process or mechanism for triggering assessments outside of the designated projects list or a provision for a scaled-down process for smaller or less disruptive projects as an option within the standard assessment process.

In this respect, the failure to link the federal projects process to the standard assessment process (for projects on the designated projects list) is a lost opportunity. The federally appointed Expert Panel for the Review of Environmental Assessment Processes, reflecting concerns heard in many of the submissions it received, recommended an integrated assessment process that would apply the same criteria and considerations to all projects, but also clearly set out different levels of effort to be applied to projects with smaller or larger potential sustainability implications. This would allow the possibility of identifying projects early on that are not on the designated projects list but that may have serious potential sustainability implications and moving them into a more intensive assessment process. This could be done without having to wait for a response to a request to the minister, including projects on federal lands and projects outside Canada:

> The Panel considered the role of section 67 of *CEAA* 2012 [now section 82 of the *IAA*] in the IA process and concluded that it is not consistent with the Panel's vision for IA as it lacks transparency and meaningfulness.... The Panel concluded that projects currently subject to section 67 meet the new project definition of affecting one or more federal interests and should therefore trigger IA where they meet the new proposed tests for triggering IA.[16]

*CEAA* 2012 created a restrictive list-based approach to triggering assessments for "large" projects. At the same time, it took a more inclusive approach to projects on federal lands and projects outside Canada, encompassing a much larger number of generally smaller projects with presumably smaller impacts on the environment or sustainability. The *IAA* does nothing to address this contradiction. The two approaches need not have identical process requirements, but, as discussed above, the federal projects process is less demanding and rigorous in terms of the scoping and criteria to be applied in decision making, as well as in terms of public participation and information, without any apparent rationale for why these elements should be varied. Nor does the Act create any explicit links between the two processes such that federal projects could be "bumped up" to the standard assessment process if they have the potential to have significant impacts. The *IAA* only allows

---

16   *Building Common Ground*, above note 10 at 57.

for a case-by-case ministerial decision to designate projects for assessment under the standard process as described in section 9(1) of the Act.

The *IAA* could have created a more consistent assessment regime by providing a mechanism to bump up projects on federal lands or outside Canada and moving to more intensive levels of scrutiny as appropriate, in recognition that issues may be identified during an assessment that require deeper investigation. The only option provided by the *IAA* is to allow the minister to designate individual projects for assessment that are not on the designated projects list. This is fraught with difficulties, ranging from the limited notification that would allow the public or Indigenous groups to be well enough informed of a project to decide if they should ask for a ministerial designation to the delays and uncertainty inherent in such a process. A bump-up provision would also allow the federal projects process to be consistent with the standard process under the *IAA* with the application of more comprehensive criteria (factors to consider in the assessment and in decision making) and a sustainability assessment framework, although in a proportionally more limited scope for smaller projects.

By way of background, *CEAA 1995* did not have a separate process for projects on federal lands and projects outside Canada. The Act only applied to these projects as part of the overall application of the environmental assessment process to any project funded, undertaken, or authorized by the federal government or requiring any change in the disposition of federal lands. It did, however, contain provisions to ensure that projects with potential transboundary impacts would be assessed if they were not otherwise caught under its triggering mechanism. Under *CEAA 1995*, there was a recognition of the distinct realities of such projects given the strong federal role in their execution, and specific regulations were developed to adapt the process. Although these were not without controversy, there was nonetheless a reasonable level of transparency and accountability. There was also a high level of continuity and coherence within the process. Although projects on federal lands and projects outside Canada were treated differently based on practical considerations of their circumstances, they were still part of the same legislative and policy framework.

## E.  PROJECTS ON FEDERAL LANDS

### 1)  Application of the *IAA* to Projects on Federal Lands

The Act's treatment of projects on federal lands is distinct from its treatment of projects outside Canada in that it requires the consideration of a broader set of factors, although still narrower than the full set of "factors to consider" under the standard process. Specifically, in section 84(1), the *IAA* introduces new requirements to take into consideration impacts on Indigenous rights, Indigenous and community knowledge, public comments, and mitigation measures for projects on federal lands. However, the rest of the standard process's innovative factors to be considered in conducting an assessment (section 22(1)) and factors to be considered in making decisions (section 63), including sustainability and the impact on Indigenous rights, are not referenced with respect to projects on federal lands.

The assessment of projects on federal lands has always been a core component of federal IA, although it has not necessarily attracted a lot of public or even academic attention. *CEAA 1995* required responsible authorities to do screenings of projects under their authority, including disposing of or changing the use of federal lands. Many projects on federal lands were assessed, and several classes of such projects were also included on the Comprehensive Study List (e.g., national parks, military facilities, and marine terminals).[17] Model class screenings for routine projects were also developed, for example, for projects in developed areas in and around the town of Banff in Banff National Park.

*CEAA 2012* eliminated screenings as a type of assessment process, redefining "screening" as a step in the assessment of designated projects to determine whether an assessment was required or, for example, if the project had already undergone an assessment or was otherwise ineligible. Nonetheless, *CEAA 2012* maintained self-assessment by federal authorities for projects on federal lands and projects outside Canada, although it was no longer integrated into the Registry, and departments (responsible authorities) were only required to report a summary of their determinations under the Act annually to Parliament. As a result, it is impossible to evaluate the utility of those assessments without filing an Access to Information request for the relevant files

---

17    *Comprehensive Study List Regulations,* SOR/94-638.

and/or interviewing the individuals responsible, if it is even possible to find them and assuming that they would be allowed to talk. The report for 2018–2019 is not yet available, but from 2012 until 2018, no projects from any federal assessment had been found to be likely to cause significant environmental impacts and therefore required to be referred to the Governor-in-Council for a determination of whether the project was "justified in the circumstances." At the same time, and reflecting the adoption of the *CEAA 1995* Comprehensive Study List as the designated projects list under *CEAA 2012* virtually unmodified, the above-mentioned classes of projects on federal lands were still subject to assessment.

Maintaining so much of *CEAA 2012*'s application to federal lands in the *IAA*, as shown in Table 18.1, represents a lost opportunity to bring these more comprehensive considerations to bear on a much broader range of projects. For many minor projects, most of those considerations might be marginal or even irrelevant. However, having them included as part of the assessment and decision-making framework makes it much more feasible to link the assessments to those of larger or more disruptive projects (e.g., designated projects), as well as regional assessments or any review, study of cumulative effects, or comparative study of differential effects across the more comprehensive set of considerations. Opportunities for institutional and shared learning are thus restricted to the "significant environmental effects" and related mitigation and regulatory measures.

### 2)  Public Participation in Assessments of Projects on Federal Lands

Many of the assessments of projects to be undertaken on federal lands will be more or less routine and/or uncontroversial, and many could be dealt with by way of a class assessment if such a provision existed. However, it is also likely that some will touch on sensitive ecosystems or attract more public interest for whatever reason, such as being in a national park. Although it would require a discretionary decision on the part of the federal authorities, it would be helpful if those authorities had the option of invoking a more active public involvement protocol. Where the federal authority is of the opinion that the proposal may attract greater interest from the public, it would actively inform and engage the public, using a range of mechanisms and following the best-practice principles and procedures promulgated by the Canadian Impact Assessment Agency (the Agency) and discussed in Chapter 15.

Both neighbouring communities and "communities of interest," that is, people or groups with a known interest in the physical area or the type of development being proposed, could be directly informed via social media, traditional media, and even physical notices (posters, mail, or household flyers) and thus be assured of at least being notified of an assessment. Fortunately, the thirty-day comment period prescribed in the Act is a minimum, so it would be relatively easy for the Agency to develop guidelines and performance standards to indicate the circumstances under which federal authorities should formally extend it. This would be done, for example, where it coincides with holidays or seasonal activities, where communications are difficult, or where there is likely to be increased public interest.

Regardless of the limited opportunities for public involvement, the new public notification requirement has the important effect of creating a public record of projects and decisions regarding projects on federal lands. This will allow the public, government agencies, other interested parties, and researchers to review and follow up on them, to learn from the application of the IA methodology and possibly even to identify potential problem areas, cumulative impacts and areas for further investigation, and opportunities for improved efficiency and effectiveness. It also provides an accountability mechanism insofar as specific agencies and offices within government will be identifiable as having signed off on their determinations. Although there is no specific accountability mechanism attached to the legislation, this transparency can be expected to have a marked effect on public confidence that the process and the determinations are being taken seriously.

## F.  PROJECTS OUTSIDE CANADA

### 1)  Application of the *IAA* to Projects Outside Canada

Projects outside Canada are subject to the same process as projects on federal lands, as described above, with a few variations. The federal projects process requires the consideration of public comments, community knowledge, and mitigation measures for projects outside Canada (section 84(2)) but not impacts on Indigenous rights and Indigenous knowledge, as it does for projects on federal lands, as noted in Table 18.1 (see "Assessment considerations"). As with projects on federal lands, the *IAA*'s innovative factors to be considered in conducting a standard assessment (section 22(1)) and factors to be considered in making decisions (section 63) are not referenced with respect to projects outside Canada.

Likewise, as can be seen in Table 18.1 (see "Determination/decision"), the final determination remains one of whether significant environmental impact is likely and, if so, whether it is justified in the circumstances, following *CEAA 2012* rather than the *IAA*'s standard process.

It is not clear how this provision is to be applied given that the federal government has moved away from building infrastructure[18] or other industrial development projects itself. Domestically, public-private partnerships or other forms of financial support to private proponents are preferred. For international projects, official development assistance (ODA) is channelled either into program support or, in the case of physical works, to recipient governments as bilateral aid (making the recipient state responsible for any assessment) or through multilateral agencies that tend to have their own IA processes. The World Bank, for example, introduced an environmental assessment policy, Operational Directive (now Operational Policy) 4.01, in 1989; this applies to "any Bank-financed or implemented project if there is the potential for that project to result in adverse environmental impact."[19]

Outside of ODA, the federal government does provide significant financial support for projects outside Canada through Export Development Canada (EDC), which is exempt from the Act. This Crown corporation provides financial services — loans, loan guarantees, and political risk insurance — to international businesses (not necessarily Canadian) and administers the so-called Canada Account funds directly authorized by the minister of international trade for investment in major infrastructure projects. This fund was recently used to finance

---

18   David R Morrison, *Aid and Ebb Tide: A History of CIDA and Canadian Development Assistance* (Waterloo, ON: Wilfrid Laurier University Press, 2006) at 19.

19   Road Development Agency, "Improved Rural Connectivity Project: Rehabilitation of Primary Feeder Roads in Eastern Province" (September 2020) at v, online (pdf): http://documents1.worldbank.org/curated/en/206811600167199098/pdf/Environmental-Project-Brief-for-Rehabilitation-of-Primary-Feeder-Roads-in-Eastern-Province.pdf.

the federal government's CAD$4.5 billion purchase of the controversial Trans Mountain Pipeline.

Some other countries' export finance agencies also have environmental IA requirements, and some are significantly more rigorous than EDC, notably the Export-Import Bank of the United States (EXIM).[20] Yet there is little reporting from the Organisation for Economic Co-operation and Development (OECD) on requirements to assess the potential impacts of overseas development projects undertaken or funded directly by member countries, as opposed to through multilateral institutions such as the World Bank or regional development banks. Such projects may be expected to be subject to the assessment requirements of the host country, and, ideally, these would be both rigorous and responsive to local needs and public involvement. Obviously, this is not always the case, and it becomes important to reinforce those processes and back them up with clear requirements and support to meet those requirements. The International Finance Corporation (IFC), the equity investment branch of the World Bank Group, has such safeguards in place, including an ombudsman's office to monitor compliance. Although these have also been criticized as being inadequate, they have an impact. For example, after Goldcorp Inc merged with Glamis Gold and acquired the Marlin gold mine in Guatemala, it bought out the IFC's share in the project. The IFC's compliance advisor ombudsman had found that Glamis Gold violated Indigenous consultation requirements. In this way, Goldcorp no longer had to respond to pressure from the IFC. At the same time, donor pressure and a commitment to delivering predetermined results on the part of both donor and recipient may impede or preclude an open assessment of the need for a given project, alternative means of implementing it, or alternatives to the project.

At the other end of the scale, Canadian embassies still have a discretionary "Canada Fund" for small projects, and those projects—and the communities and environments that host them—would arguably benefit from being included in an IA framework developed under the

---

20    RIAS Inc and Gartner Lee Limited, "Comparative Analysis of Impacts on Competitiveness of Environmental Assessment Requirements" Canadian Environmental Assessment Agency (September 2000), s 5, online: http://web.archive.org/web/20040107135816/https://www.ceaa-acee.gc.ca/017/0004/report_e.htm ["Comparative Analysis"].

*IAA.* Without such direction, whether it is in policy or regulation, such projects will continue to be funded without the scrutiny they may deserve. As of April 2021, ten months into the implementation of the *IAA*, there are three projects outside Canada on the Registry (compared to 466 projects on federal lands and ten designated projects). Historically, considerable effort went into developing regulations and guidance for projects outside Canada under *CEAA 1995*, and although it was uneven in quality and application, there are certainly lessons to be learned that could be applied in the present context.

### 2)　Learning from History

Under *CEAA 1995*'s self-assessment regime, responsible authorities were required to do screenings of projects under their authority, whether as regulator, funder, or proponent, domestically or internationally. The law's application to projects outside Canada was to be specified in a separate regulation, which was promulgated in 1996,[21] albeit in a much more limited form than had been recommended by the multi-stakeholder Regulatory Advisory Committee (RAC) appointed by the minister of environment.[22] Official guidance was developed and promulgated for projects carried out by the Canadian International Development Agency (CIDA), for example (including those in the Philippines[23]), and projects supported by Canadian embassies' discretionary Canada Fund for small projects.[24]

At the time, Canada's efforts involved designing and implementing an assessment process that would hold ODA projects to a higher standard of technical justification as well as public access and accountability

---

21　*Projects Outside Canada Environmental Assessment Regulations*, SOR/96-491.

22　The RAC was appointed to advise the minister of environment on the formulation of regulations under *CEAA 1995* and last met in 2008. It included representatives from industry associations, environmental groups, and national Indigenous organizations, as well as independent academics and legal experts.

23　Elmer Mercado, "Environmental Assessment Resource Kit: A Resource Kit for CIDA Projects in the Philippines," Canadian International Development Agency (March 2008), online: www.academia.edu/6435537/Guidebook_for_Integrating_Environmental_Assessment_and_Safeguards_for_CIDA_Projects_in_the_Philippines.

24　Canadian International Development Agency, *Manual on the Canadian Environmental Assessment Act (CEAA): The Canada Fund and Mission-Administered Funds* (August 1996), online: www.academia.edu/6862896/Manual_on_the_Canadian_Environmental_Assessment_Act_CEAA_The_Canada_Fund_and_Mission-administered_Funds.

for Canadians as donors. At the same time, they were working to help recipient countries provide similar participation opportunities and accountability for their own people by helping strengthen their own assessment and administrative processes. The assessment of ODA can skirt the legal question of extraterritorial application of Canadian law by not placing any obligations on recipient governments or providing their residents with special privileges, although it may still be seen as an additional burden. Environmental law has been applied extraterritorially in the context of pollution prevention and transboundary impacts,[25] and there is a growing body of law and practice when it comes to the assessment of transboundary impacts (such as the Espoo Convention[26]). There is little evidence of other countries applying a formal IA process to their overseas aid projects, although there has been consideration of it, for example, contemplating extraterritorial application of the United States' *National Environmental Protection Act.*[27] More effort has been focused on strategic level assessment internationally, for example, through the OECD,[28] especially following the 2005 Paris Declaration on Aid Effectiveness. This called for a commonly agreed framework to strengthen and harmonize the use of strategic environmental assessment in support of international development policies, plans, and programs.

Large projects were less effectively incorporated into *CEAA 1995*, with those supported by EDC—a Crown corporation—ignored completely, as noted above. Crown corporations were deemed not to be federal authorities, despite EDC's administration of so-called Canada Account funds underwriting major projects, most notably a CANDU nuclear reactor in Romania.

---

25 See, for example, Roger R Martella Jr and James W Coleman, *International Environmental Law: A Guide for Judges* (2015), online (pdf): *Federal Judicial Center* www.fjc.gov/sites/default/files/2015/INTL%20ENVTL%20LAW%20GUIDE%20FINAL.pdf.

26 United Nations Economic Commission for Europe, "Convention on Environmental Impact Assessment in a Transboundary Context" (1991), online (pdf): www.unece.org/fileadmin/DAM/env/eia/documents/legaltexts/Espoo_Convention_authentic_ENG.pdf.

27 42 USC § 4321 et seq. See also Joan R Goldfarb, "Extraterritorial Compliance with NEPA amid the Current Wave of Environmental Harm" (1991) 18:3 *Boston College Environmental Affairs Law Review* 543.

28 Barry Sadler, "Report of Short Term Assignment DFID Contract Number: ESD/14: Comparative Analysis of OECD/DAC Guidance and Other Internationally Important SEA Regimes" (30 August 2006), online (pdf): www.commissiemer.nl/docs/os/sea/approach/comparison_sea_oecd_06_dfid_sadler.pdf.

For its own part, EDC published its voluntary environmental review framework in May 1999. Although it has many of the features of an environmental assessment process, the framework does not allow for public participation, and it is impossible to verify its application with the sparse public reporting that is made available. Despite serious criticism from civil society,[29] there has been little improvement to date. A study commissioned by the Canadian Environmental Assessment Agency ahead of the five-year review of *CEAA 1995* hinted that this is due to fears of creating a competitive disadvantage for EDC clients vis-à-vis other export lending agencies with non-burdensome environmental assessment requirements. The study found that "company representatives urged the federal government not to impose the requirement that export credit financing be subjected to *CEAA*, nor to any other EA regime that placed them at a competitive disadvantage."[30]

The *Export Development Act*[31] is currently undergoing a Parliamentary review, so there is an opportunity to amend it to either make EDC subject to the *IAA*—perhaps with appropriate modifications to reflect the nature of its business—or to incorporate a mandatory, transparent, participatory, and rigorous environmental review framework.

## G. STRATEGIC ASSESSMENT IN RELATION TO PROJECTS ON FEDERAL LANDS AND PROJECTS OUTSIDE CANADA

The kind of incongruity in policy development and application observed in the *IAA*'s treatment of projects on federal lands and projects outside Canada could be usefully addressed by carrying out strategic assessments of the plans, programs, and policies that direct them. However, as noted in Chapter 17 of this volume, the Act provides for a fairly narrow application of strategic assessment that would seem to provide little support in this area. Expenditures at the program and policy

---

29    Linda Nowlan, *Environmental Standards and the Export Development Corporation of Canada*, (September 1999), online (pdf): *West Coast Environmental Law* www.wcel.org/sites/default/files/publications/Environmental%20Standards%20and%20the%20Export%20Development%20Corporation%20of%20Canada.pdf; NGO Working Group on the Export Development Corporation, *Environmental Assessment and EDC: The Shock of the Possible*, Halifax Initiative (March 2001), online: http://web.archive.org/web/20041128001407if_/http://www.halifaxinitiative.org:80/updir/EDC_EA.pdf.

30    "Comparative Analysis," above note 20.

31    RSC, 1985, c E-20.

levels should also be subject to strategic assessment. At least in principle, this should be possible under the existing Cabinet Directive on the Environmental Assessment of Policy, Plan and Program Proposals,[32] first introduced in 1990, although this has never been done. Federal spending is only subject to IA at the project level, where projects are on the designated projects list. In fact, federal spending on individual projects has mostly not been subject to IA since the 2010 exclusion of infrastructure projects outside national parks and protected areas.[33]

Canada's international trade and investment agreements are also subject to environmental assessments under the Cabinet directive, and Global Affairs Canada has developed both a framework for conducting environmental assessments of trade negotiations[34] and a handbook[35] to supplement it. There is no indication that this policy has changed with the introduction of the *IAA* or that there is any intent of revising it. However, the assessments themselves[36] are far from rigorous and of limited use. There is very limited public involvement for Canadians and effectively none for the partner country or countries, much less an informed, well-nourished deliberative process oriented toward learning. Sinclair and Diduck described such a process as reframing public participation as "EA civics" and building a more robust consensus, in this case around policy directions.[37] The application of the Cabinet directive, and therefore its utility, is further limited by the diminished number of formal policies and plans (e.g., white papers) being

---

32    Privy Council Office and the Canadian Environmental Assessment Agency, *The Cabinet Directive on the Environmental Assessment of Policy, Plan and Program Proposals: Guidelines for Implementing the Cabinet Directive* (2010), online (pdf): *Government of Canada* www.canada.ca/content/dam/iaac-acei/documents/strategic-environmental-assessment/ cabinet-directive-environmental-assessment-policy-plan-program-proposals/cabinet_ directive_on_environmental_assessment_of_policy_plan_and_program_proposals.pdf.

33    *CEAA 1995*, above note 5, s 7.1(2).

34    Global Affairs Canada, "Framework for Conducting Environmental Assessments of Trade Negotiations" (February 2001), online: www.international.gc.ca/trade-agreements-accords-commerciaux/env/framework-cadre.aspx?lang=eng.

35    Global Affairs Canada, "Handbook for Conducting Environmental Assessments of Trade Negotiations" (March 2008), online: www.international.gc.ca/trade-agreements-accords-commerciaux/env/handbook-guide.aspx?lang=eng.

36    Global Affairs Canada, "List of Environmental Assessments of Trade Negotiations," online: www.international.gc.ca/trade-agreements-accords-commerciaux/env/EAlist-listeEE.aspx?lang=eng.

37    A John Sinclair & Alan P Diduck, "Reconceptualizing Public Participation in Environmental Assessment as EA Civics" (2017) 62 *Environmental Impact Assessment Review* 174.

developed by government and to what the directive can be applied. An effective strategic assessment regime applied to federal programs, plans, and policies would include ODA and infrastructure spending.

## H. CONCLUSION

The *IAA*'s application to projects on federal lands and projects outside Canada—despite the mostly unnecessary and inappropriate exclusion of most of the Act's innovative considerations and its more sustainability-oriented decision criteria—promises greater public accountability and with it the potential for better decision making. In a historical context, *CEAA 1995* produced mixed outcomes with respect to projects on federal lands in terms of whether it was applied consistently and effectively and with respect to projects outside Canada in terms of which projects got assessed. It also lacked effective monitoring and follow-up, but it did generate data and create opportunities for research and learning. *CEAA 2012* removed those opportunities by condensing public involvement and reporting requirements to aggregate annual reports. In the absence of specific examples of success or failure and the diminished collection and availability of information on projects, decisions, and outcomes, it is impossible to gauge its effectiveness. The *IAA* restores at least a basic level of information gathering and reporting.

Public interest advocates have long pleaded for a requirement to at least document and publish the likely environmental impacts of the exercise of any federal power. The *IAA* accomplishes this with respect to federal lands and projects outside Canada and provides at least a thirty-day public comment period before a determination is made, although there is no proactive notification or public comment opportunity. It reinstates the link to the online Registry, and such assessments are now being reported to the public more or less in real time.

In this, and in the slightly expanded considerations for making a determination, the *IAA* represents a distinct but very limited advance on *CEAA 2012* (see Table 18.1). Arguably, the assessment of "non-designated" projects on a more limited scope of factors is an appropriate and useful application of assessment requirements. Yet this would be more meaningful if the process escalated or "bumped up" potentially significant environmental impacts to a more comprehensive review process with broader considerations rather than just to a Governor-in-Council

(Cabinet) decision on whether the damage is "justified in the circumstances." It is precisely that justification that needs to be part of the assessment process, not applied post hoc, under Cabinet secrecy. The Act missed an opportunity to provide appropriate public engagement opportunities and to integrate the factors to consider across all federal assessment processes. It also failed to incorporate the small-project screening of projects under direct federal jurisdiction (and, ideally, all federal decision making with respect to development projects and activities affecting sustainability on a local or regional scale) into a single comprehensive federal IA regime. Given the absence of any definition of "justified in the circumstances," there may be some potential to broaden the scope of assessments under the federal projects process. Unfortunately, the rest of these elements are baked into the legislation and would require amendments to the *IAA* itself.

As a move toward improving assessment of projects on federal lands and those outside Canada, the Act is a good first step, as they say, but an extremely small one. At least the limited requirements should be relatively easy for federal authorities to comply with, and recording projects and their respective determinations will at least allow the outcomes to be monitored, including identifying cumulative effects.

# CHAPTER 19

# Transparency and Accountability in Decision Making: Does the *Impact Assessment Act* Support Credible Decision Making?

*Jason Unger*

## A. INTRODUCTION

Decision making in impact assessment (IA) processes is governed by enabling law and regulation, informed by evidence gathered during the assessment, and influenced by a host of environmental, social, economic, and political pressures. Part of the driving motivation for the passage of the federal *Impact Assessment Act* (*IAA*)[1] was to build trust with the public by making "environmental assessments credible again" by engaging a "new, fair process" that would ensure "that decisions are based on science, facts, and evidence, and serve the public's interest" and by providing for meaningful public participation.[2]

Does the *IAA* succeed in creating a credible IA regime? Credibility in IA must attempt to bridge the knowledge gained in the assessment process and the remaining uncertainties in that knowledge with the various decisions that are to be made throughout the IA process. A credible process should result in what are perceived as credible decisions, characterized as impartial, independent, and informed by the evidence. Ideally, the statutory framing of the process will legitimize decisions

---

1    SC 2019, c 28, s 1.

2    Liberal Party of Canada, "Real Change: A New Plan for a Strong Middle Class" (2015) at 41–42, online (pdf): www.liberal.ca/wp-content/*uploads*/2015/10/New-plan-for-a-strong-middle-class.pdf. The document further commits to "[ensuring] that decisions are based on science, facts, and evidence, and serve the public's interest" (at 42).

in the view of most if not all stakeholders: proponents; the public; Indigenous groups; and provincial, territorial, and federal authorities.

This chapter considers the central decision points in the *IAA* to determine the extent to which the Act codifies mechanisms to provide for transparency and accountability in decisions. The chapter first provides a brief review of the challenges of arriving at credible decisions that are accountable to both the enabling statute and the evidence. Second, the chapter reviews how the *IAA* provides for access to information and transparency in decisions, sets out prescriptive criteria to guide decisions, and requires decision makers to provide reasons for decisions. Finally, the chapter discusses the ability to review IA decisions, specifically through judicial review.

As is discussed, all four of these aspects — access to information, decision criteria, reasons for decisions, and the review of decisions — are viewed as crucial to ensuring an adequate amount of transparency and accountability in decision making.

## B.  DECISION MAKING IN AN ERA OF EVOLVING ASSESSMENTS

The Supreme Court of Canada recently observed that "reasoned decision-making is the lynchpin of institutional legitimacy."[3] In the context of IA, "reasoned decision making" will be embodied by a clear linkage between evidence of project effects across environmental, social, and economic factors and the reasoning for specific decisions.[4] As such, the legitimacy of a decision can be undermined

---

3   Supreme Court of Canada quoting the *amici curiae* factum in *Canada (Minister of Citizenship and Immigration) v Vavilov*, 2019 SCC 65 at para 74 [*Vavilov*].

4   See David Cash et al, "Salience, Credibility, Legitimacy and Boundaries: Linking Research, Assessment and Decision Making" (2003), KSG Working Papers Series, online: *Digital Access to Scholarship at Harvard* https://dash.harvard.edu/bitstream/handle/1/32067415/Salience_credibility.pdf?sequence=4. The authors identified the importance of considering knowledge in decision making in the context of "three pillars": salience, credibility, and legitimacy. Within these three pillars are further complicating factors of uncertainty in information being considered as well as the need to ensure that public participation is meaningfully considered. Underlying these pillars as well is the need to ensure that information systems are transparent, both for provision of effective engagement by stakeholders but also for the purpose of clearly understanding the rationale for and justification of how decisions are being made.

- where decisions are made, or appear to be made, from a biased position (i.e., where decision makers appear to be assigning certain types of evidence more relevance and weight)
- where decisions appear to ignore relevant information
- where decisions are made in situations where there is significant uncertainty
- where decisions appear to be contrary to statutory purposes and objectives

Where statutory language is inherently vague and/or requires an assessment of value-laden trade-offs, the determination of "legitimate" or "good" decision making becomes increasingly challenging. A credible decision-making regime can only be realized through the deployment of a variety of statutory checks and balances that reveal the decision maker's analysis of the evidence and reasoning behind decisions.

For its part, the *IAA* reorients assessments in Canada toward sustainability[5] and requires decisions to consider specific factors, including to what extent projects align and support the tenets of sustainability, gender considerations, and climate considerations. The Act also places a heightened emphasis on the consideration of project impacts of Indigenous groups and related constitutional rights.

In this regard, the *IAA* is reorienting assessments from an empirical base of assessing the potential adverse biophysical environmental effects of a project toward consideration of broader social and economic impacts.[6] This broadening of the scope of assessment may greatly expand the types and nature of evidence and information a decision maker must consider and may result in decision makers facing additional challenges in how evidence is weighed and used to justify decisions.[7] These evidentiary challenges, both present and future, fun-

---

5    See Chapter 9.

6    In this regard, institutional bias toward empirical environmental effects assessment may need to be overcome, and decisions must embrace a broader conception of assessment.

7    See Robert B Gibson, "Beyond the Pillars: Sustainability Assessment as a Framework for Effective Integration of Social, Economic and Ecological Considerations in Significant Decision-Making" (2006) 8:3 *Journal of Environmental Assessment Policy and Management* 259, and Jenny Pope et al, "Reconceptualising Sustainability Assessment" (2017) 62 *Environmental Impact Assessment Review* 205. See also Robert B Gibson with Selma Hassan et al, *Sustainability Assessment: Criteria and Processes* (New York: Earthscan, 2005); Richard K Morgan, "Environmental Impact Assessment: The State of the Art" (2012) 30:1 *Impact Assessment and Project Appraisal* 5.

damentally affect the perceived legitimacy of decisions. The publication of reasons and the methodology and thoroughness that led to the decision will become increasingly important.

The challenges faced by decision makers under the traditional environmental assessment process have been identified in the literature. Reteif and colleagues noted several challenges in relation to environmental assessment, including "dealing with complexity and uncertainty," efficiency, significance determinations, and communication and participation.[8] Similarly, Sinclair and Diduck observed the need to revise and reconceptualize public participation in environmental assessment to better reflect and deal with uncertainties and complexities and to mitigate conflict.[9]

It has been recognized that uncertainty, in particular, will pose significant challenges for assessment practitioners and decision makers.[10] This includes uncertainty in the baseline environmental condition, the prediction of effects (through the use of models or expert opinion), and the effectiveness of mitigation actions. Leung and colleagues noted that "acknowledging, understanding, and considering uncertainty is ... essential to ensuring good IA."[11]

These challenges around historic approaches to IAs necessitate an evolution in assessment process to one that is more open, more participatory, and more adaptive.[12] There are indications that some evolution has been occurring. Bond and colleagues observed that as assessment approaches have become more open, inclusive, and transparent, the legitimacy of knowledge gained through the process and its evaluation

---

8   François Retief, et al, "Global Megatrends and Their Implications for Environmental Assessment Practice" (2016) 61 *Environmental Impact Assessment Review* 52.

9   A John Sinclair & Alan P Diduck, "Reconceptualizing Public Participation in Environmental Assessment as EA Civics" (2017) 62 *Environmental Impact Assessment Review* 174.

10  See Wanda Leung et al, "A Review of Uncertainty Research in Impact Assessment" (2015) 50 *Environmental Impact Assessment Review* 116; Alan Bond et al, "Managing Uncertainty, Ambiguity and Ignorance in Impact Assessment by Embedding Evolutionary Resilience, Participatory Modelling and Adaptive Management" (2015) 151 *Journal of Environmental Management* 97; and Aud Tenney, Jens Kværner & Karl Idar Gjerstad, "Uncertainty in Environmental Impact Assessment Predictions: The Need for Better Communication and More Transparency" (2006) 24:1 *Impact Assessment and Project Appraisal* 45.

11  Leung et al, above note 10 at 121.

12  Bond, et al, above note 10.

become increasingly complicated, subjected to bias and manipulation.[13] In light of these knowledge challenges, the authors recognized the need to reframe how knowledge is integrated and considered in the assessment process and in decision making.[14]

How can this evolving system of increasingly diverse forms of knowledge and information be integrated, in a credible fashion, into IA decisions? In the absence of co-management or a higher level of shared decision making, it would appear that what is required is codification of measures to ensure that decisions are as transparent as possible and are compliant with the legislation and that the reasons for decisions reflect the accountability of decisions makers to the suite of participants in the process.

## C. FOUNDATIONS OF TRANSPARENT AND ACCOUNTABLE IMPACT ASSESSMENT DECISIONS

The various decisions that are to be made under the *IAA* will be informed by a wide variety of quantitative and qualitative sources of evidence. They will be further directed by institutional, cultural, and political drivers that may either act in support of or contradict the making of "good" IA decisions. What, then, are the statutory aspects of IA that will ensure that a decision is accountable to the Act and to the evidence?

Meaningful public participation, as described in Chapter 15, and procedural fairness are inherently bound up together in ensuring a level of accountability for IA decisions.[15] Many of these aspects of procedural

---

13    Alan Bond et al, "On Legitimacy in Impact Assessment: An Epistemologically-Based Conceptualisation" (2018) 69 *Environmental Impact Assessment Review* 16.

14    *Ibid.* The authors categorized various dimensions of knowledge that should be considered, including accuracy (reliability and uncertainty), restrictions to knowledge (ambiguity and ignorance), diffusion of knowledge, and the spectrum of knowledge (i.e., implicit knowledge).

15    See Angus Morrison-Saunders & Gerard Early, "What Is Necessary to Ensure Natural Justice in Environmental Impact Assessment Decision-Making?" (2008) 26:1 *Impact Assessment and Project Appraisal* 29. This is also reflected at the global level in Principle 10 of the 1992 Rio Declaration on Environment and Development, *Report of the United Nations Conference on Environment and Development*, Annex I, Vol I (New York: United Nations, 1993), and the *Convention on Access to Information, Public Participation in Decision-Making and Access to Justice in Environmental Matters* (25 June 1998), online (pdf):

fairness are reflected in "good environmental assessment practices," as described by Joseph and colleagues, including practices that ensure that

- decisions are informed
- decisions are independent and rationally linked to the evidence before the decision maker
- public and community participation is meaningfully considered and reflected in decisions (and reasons for decisions)
- financial and information resources enable equitable participation in decision making
- there is an ability to seek review or appeal the decision[16]

Ensuring that decisions are transparent and accountable to both the process and evidence requires legislation that provides a safety mechanism to minimize bias (institutional, cultural, and political bias) while fostering rational and logical reasons for decisions. This can be achieved through the codification of the central pillars of good assessment practice when it comes to decision making under the *IAA*. These pillars are

- access to information used in decisions
- codified decision-making criteria that constrain the discretion of the decision maker,
- a codified obligation to provide written reasons with a decision
- a codified review or appeal mechanism for key decisions

In the following section, I discuss how the *IAA* codifies aspects of decision making around the first three pillars, whereas the review of decisions is left to judicial review, which is governed by other federal court rules statutory and common law.

---

*United Nations Economic Commission for Europe* www.unece.org/fileadmin/DAM/env/pp/documents/cep43e.pdf.

16  Chris Joseph, Thomas Gunton & Murray Rutherford, "Good Practices for Environmental Assessment" (2015) 33:4 *Impact Assessment and Project Appraisal* 4 238, Table 1 at 240–43.

## D.  THE *IAA*'S APPROACH TO REASONS, STATUTORY DISCRETION, AND DECISION TRANSPARENCY

The preamble of the *IAA* indicates that transparency and accountability are relevant to the Act's processes, highlighting the intent of IA to integrate science and Indigenous knowledge into decision making, the importance of providing reasons, the commitment to upholding section 35 of the *Canadian Charter of Rights and Freedoms*,[17] and to implementing the *United Nations Declaration on the Rights of Indigenous Peoples (UNDRIP)*.[18] The purpose of the *IAA* also highlights the importance of taking into account scientific and Indigenous knowledge in decision making.[19]

The purposes section of the Act (section 6) also sets out the overall direction in how the government administers the Act. Specifically, section 6(2) notes that the "Government of Canada, the Minister, the Agency and federal authorities … must exercise their powers in a manner that fosters sustainability, respects the Government's commitments with respect to the rights of Indigenous peoples of Canada and applies the precautionary principle." Section 6(3) further states that "the principles of scientific integrity, honesty, objectivity, thoroughness and accuracy" must be applied in government administration of the Act. This section will be relevant to how specific decisions are made as well as to any judicial review of decisions (as is discussed below).

These general directions feed into a suite of additional decisions through the IA process, leading to the ultimate decision to approve or reject a proposed project. I do not deal with them all. Rather I have focused on the following central IA decisions to determine how the *IAA* deals with access to information, statutory criteria to constrain discretion, and the obligation to provide reasons in decision making, including the following:

1)  The designation of a physical activity that is to be subjected to the Act (section 9)

---

17  Part I of the *Constitution Act, 1982*, being Schedule B to the *Canada Act 1982* (UK), 1982, c 11.

18  GA Res 61/295, UNGAOR, 61st Sess, UN Doc A/RES/61/295 (13 September 2007). See Chapter 6 for a discussion of UNDRIP, decision making, and the role of Indigenous Peoples in impact assessment.

19  *IAA*, above note 1, s 6(1)(j).

2) Whether to require an IA of an activity (section 16)
3) The scope of factors and studies to be considered in an assessment (section 18)
4) The determination of effects and recommendations set out in an agency report (section 28)
5) The decision, where applicable, regarding a substitution (section 31)
6) The determination of effects and recommendations of a review panel (section 51)
7) The minister's decision regarding the project (section 60)
8) The final decision regarding the project by the Governor in Council (section 62)

Table 19.1 highlights the various aspects of transparency and accountability provisions related to these decisions under the Act. There is no statutory review of decisions in the *IAA*; rather, any review of a decision must rely on judicial review, a subject dealt with later in this chapter.

**TABLE 19.1  TRANSPARENCY AND ACCOUNTABILITY MEASURES AT KEY DECISION POINTS UNDER THE IAA**

| Decision Point | Access to Information & Transparency | Criteria to Guide Decisions | Reasons for the Decision |
| --- | --- | --- | --- |
| • Ministerial decision to designate a physical activity that is to be subjected to the Act (s 9) | • The response to a request to require an IA must be posted on the internet site (s 9(4))<br>• Information considered in the decision need not be posted | • Discretionary: the minister considers the project's adverse effects on federal jurisdiction, adverse direct or incidental effects, and public concern (s 9(1)) and (2)) | • Ministerial response to the request for an IA requires reasons (s 9(4)) |
| • Agency decision as to whether to require an IA of an activity (s 16) | • Agency must post decision on the internet site (s 16(3)) | • Mandatory consideration of factors set out in s 16(2) | • Reasons must be provided (s 16(3)) |
| • The scope of factors and studies to be considered in an assessment (s 18) | • Notice of commencement of IA must be posted on the internet site (s 18(2))<br>• Information considered in determining scope of information and studies required need not be posted | • Agency must consider factors set out in s 22(1) in determining required information and studies (s 18(1.1))<br>• Scoping of prescribed factors is at the discretion of the Agency (s 18(1.2)) | • Reasons for the scoping of information and studies are not required |
| • The determination of effects and recommendations set out in an Agency report (s 28) | • Draft report must be posted on the internet site (s 28(1))<br>• Final report must be posted on the internet site (s 28(4)) | • Discretionary determination is made by Agency regarding the effects caused and the extent of adverse effects on federal jurisdictions (s 28(3)) | • The Agency's "rationale and conclusions" must be provided in the report (s 28(3.2)) |

| Decision Point | Access to Information & Transparency | Criteria to Guide Decisions | Reasons for the Decision |
| --- | --- | --- | --- |
| • The decision regarding substitution (s 31) | • Request for substitution must be posted on the internet site (s 31(2))<br>• Decision and reasons must be posted on the internet site (s 31(4)) | • Minister must consider public comments<br>• Minister must be satisfied that preconditions set out in s 33 are met<br>• Discretionary decision is made regarding whether substitution is "appropriate" (s 31(1)) | • Reasons for substitution decision are required (s 31(4)) |
| • The determination of effects and recommendations of a review panel (ss 51, 53 & 57) | • Information used when conducting IA must be publicly available (s 51(1)(a))<br>• Hearing must be public (s 53(3)), and a summary of public comments must be included in the report<br>• Non-disclosure of records or evidence can be invoked where harm may occur (s 53(4) & (5))<br>• Information and records that may reveal panel deliberations may be treated as confidential by the Agency (s 57) | • Report preparation is discretionary in terms of determination of project effects, adverse effects on federal jurisdiction, the extent to which those effects are significant, and how Indigenous knowledge was taken into account (s 51(1)(d)) | • Report must include the review panel's rationale, conclusions, and recommendations, including conclusions and recommendations with respect to any mitigation measures and follow-up program (s 51(1)(d)) |

| Decision Point | Access to Information & Transparency | Criteria to Guide Decisions | Reasons for the Decision |
|---|---|---|---|
| • The final decision regarding the project by the minister (ss 60, 63, 65 & 66) | • Minister's decision statement must be posted on the internet site (s 66) | • The responsible minister's public interest determination must consider s 63 factors | • Minister must provide reasons for the determination, and those reasons "must demonstrate" that the minister based the determination on the report and s 63 factors (s 65(2)) |
| • The final decision of the Governor in Council (ss 62, 65 & 66)[20] | • Minister's decision statement must be posted on the internet site (s 66) | • The responsible Governor in Council's public interest determination must consider s 63 factors (s 62) | • Cabinet must provide reasons for the determination (s 65), and those reasons "must demonstrate" that the Governor in Council based the determination on the report and s 63 factors |

20  The Governor in Council makes the final decision where there is a reference made by the minister or where the IA was conducted by a review panel; see *IAA*, above note 1, s 62.

## 1) Access to Information

Access to information is an essential component to any notion of legal or, more generally, political accountability. Yet providing meaningful access to information can be a significant challenge. The method and nature of communicating information matter: in what information is monitored and conveyed, the "accessibility and comprehensibility" of the information conveyed, and the ability to use the information in a tangible way to evaluate decisions and progress.[21] The scope and nature of information exchange are highly relevant, as is the perceived legitimacy of the process.[22] Providing transparency to complex scientific information often requires further technical or scientific analysis, which requires expertise and funding. The evidence and predictions of effects can have high levels of uncertainty. This uncertainty is rarely effectively communicated as part of the assessment process.[23] Data gaps, statistical analysis, and assumptions that are used in forming opinions or supporting modelling are often not clearly dealt with. This has led to a call for increased transparency and communication around uncertainty itself.[24]

For its part, the *IAA* does not significantly change the approach to accessing information from that found in previous iterations of federal environmental assessment legislation. The Act maintains the central public information platform in the form of an assessment registry.[25] The Impact Assessment Agency of Canada (the Agency) is charged with maintaining the Canadian Impact Assessment Registry (the Registry), which includes an internet site and project files.[26] For further discus-

---

21  Klaus Dingwerth & Margot Eichinger, "Tamed Transparency: How Information Disclosure Under the Global Reporting Initiative Fails to Empower" (2010) 10:3 *Global Environmental Politics* 74 at 83. The authors noted that the contribution of transparency to "enhanced accountability deserves further scrutiny." See also Virginia Haufler, "Disclosure as Governance: The Extractive Industries Transparency Initiative and Resource Management in the Developing World" (2010) 10:3 *Global Environmental Politics* 53.

22  See Alan Diduck & A John Sinclair, "Public Involvement in Environmental Assessment: The Case of the Nonparticipant" (2002) 29:4 *Environmental Management* 578.

23  Sinclair & Diduck, above note 9.

24  *Ibid.*

25  This includes the *Canadian Environmental Assessment Act*, SC 1992, c 37 (*CEAA 1995*), and the *Canadian Environmental Assessment Act, 2012*, SC 2012, c 19, s 52 (*CEAA 2012*). The entry into force of the 1992 Act was delayed until 1995 to allow for key regulations to be developed and passed.

26  *IAA*, above note 1, s 104.

sion of the importance of access to information to meaningful public participation, see Chapter 15.

The *IAA* itemizes various pieces of information that must be posted on the internet site and outlines the duty of the Agency to maintain the Registry.[27] The Registry includes relevant information regarding the project description; the scope of information and studies that must be provided by the proponent; the impact statement; notice of various decisions of the Agency, the minister, and Cabinet; reasons where required; and the posting of any public comments received during the assessment. The Act indicates that the Registry must be maintained in a "manner that ensures convenient public access" and that records are to be provided in a timely fashion upon request.[28] The *Information and Management of Time Limits Regulation* further dictates that prescribed information provided by the proponent must be machine readable and must include a plain-language summary in English and French.[29]

In this regard, the Registry provides a significant level of access to information that is relevant to the assessment and the decisions under the Act. The information may not be fit for purpose, however, as the volume and complexity of information provided may require significant resource capacity to review and critique, including by scientific, economic, social, and/or legal experts.

IA reports and information on which they are based are often lengthy and composed of both quantitative and qualitative data. Where models are used to forecast or predict project impacts, an understanding of the underlying assumptions and inner workings of the model may be required to properly evaluate the project impacts and related recommendations and conclusions. Modelling of this nature will become increasingly relevant in relation to topics such as climate change, a factor for consideration under the *IAA*, as modelling scales and modelling assumptions will all drive outputs. This, in turn, will challenge those evaluating the projections and conclusions that make up part of the impact statement.[30] Furthermore, how such complexity can be made

---

27    *Ibid*, s 105.

28    *Ibid*, s 104.

29    SOR/2019-283, s 6.

30    See, for example, Parisa Hosseinzadehtalaei, Hossein Tabari & Patrick Willems, "Uncertainty Assessment for Climate Change Impact on Intense Precipitation: How Many Model Runs Do We Need?" (2017) 37:S1 *International Journal of Climatology* 1105, and

into "plain-language summaries" while clearly representing the scope of assumptions and uncertainties will undoubtedly be a challenge.

The *IAA*'s constraints on access to information are primarily focused on instances where disclosure of the information may cause harm. Specifically, the Agency or a review panel may refuse to disclosure information used in the assessment process that may cause harm to Indigenous rights, the environment, or people.[31]

The potential of harm to economic interests may also limit Registry content through application of the federal *Access to Information Act*.[32] The *IAA* notes that only information that has otherwise been made publicly available may be included in the Registry or where the minister determines that it should be disclosed.[33] The minister may disclose information where it is determined that the information would have otherwise been disclosed under the *Access to Information Act*, including disclosure that is deemed to be in the public interest.[34]

The minister may also disclose information where "there are reasonable grounds to believe that it would be in the public interest to disclose it because it is required for the public to participate effectively" in the preparation for an IA or the IA itself.[35] However, records that are not disclosed under section 20 of the *Access to Information Act* are not subject to disclosure under this provision. This means that information pertaining to trade secrets of a third party, "financial, commercial, scientific or technical information that is confidential information supplied to a government institution by a third party and is treated consistently in a confidential manner by the third party," and "information the disclosure of which could reasonably be expected to result in material financial loss or gain to, or could reasonably be expected to prejudice the competitive position of, a third party" may not be subject to disclosure.[36] This type of information would only be disclosed if the

---

Patrick Willems et al, "Climate Change Impact Assessment on Urban Rainfall Extremes and Urban Drainage: Methods and Shortcomings" (2012) 103 *Atmospheric Research* 106.

31  *IAA*, above note 1, ss 30 and 53(4) & (5).

32  *Ibid*, s 107, and *Access to Information Act*, RSC, 1985, c A-1. Note that this was the case with the past two federal environmental assessment statutes, *CEAA 1995* and *CEAA 2012*.

33  *IAA*, above note 1, s 107.

34  *Ibid*, s 107(1)(b)(i).

35  *Ibid*, s 107(1)(b)(ii).

36  *Access to Information Act*, above note 32, s 20(1).

minister was of the view that it would have been disclosed as being in the public interest at the time the Agency received it.[37]

In looking at the codification of access to information and transparency of decision making within the *IAA*, there are a variety of positives and negatives. The Registry system provides a central hub of online information, although the ability to readily access it can certainly be questioned. The *IAA* and its regulations do require plain-language summaries for proponent-provided information.

Furthermore, the requirement of how Indigenous knowledge is considered in decision making ensures that there is transparency in how Indigenous knowledge is integrated and considered by the Agency and subsequent decision makers.[38] Unfortunately, a lack of clarity remains about how this knowledge will be gathered and effectively integrated into the IA process.[39]

The Act also fails to address concerns around access to information that may be claimed as confidential for reasons of competitiveness or trade secrets. This can impede disclosure and frank discussions around the economic aspects of a project in particular. The overall value of projects and uncertainty in economic predictions may fail to be disclosed, potentially biasing the evidence available to the decision maker in favour of project proponents.

In addition, the *IAA* does not specifically deal with uncertainty in the context of information and decision making. There is a need to understand the level of uncertainty in the evidence if one is to evaluate the validity of how decision makers grant weight to specific evidence. For example, proponent forecasts for the economic benefits of a project may be subject to significant uncertainty, which should be included in any decision-making process.

---

37  *IAA*, above note 1, s 107. Furthermore, where the Agency intends to include information regarding third-party information that may relate to trade secrets or other aspects of sensitive information, the Agency will follow the notice and waiver process under the *Access to Information Act*.

38  *IAA*, above note 1, ss 28(3), 51(1), and 59(3).

39  For further discussion of this issue, see Expert Panel for the Review of Environmental Assessment Processes, *Building Common Ground: A New Vision for Impact Assessment in Canada* (Ottawa: Canadian Environmental Assessment Agency, 2017), online (pdf): *Government of Canada* www.canada.ca/content/dam/themes/environment/conservation/ environmental-reviews/building-common-ground/building-common-ground.pdf [*Building Common Ground*]. See also chapters 6 and 21 for further information regarding the *IAA* and Indigenous knowledge.

## 2) Decision Criteria Under the *IAA*

Decision makers are clearly constrained by their enabling statute. The scope and nature of decisions are bounded by the intentions of Parliament as reflected in the law. Administrative decision making, to be legitimate, must respect these legal bounds. In the absence of these legislative directions, the discretion of the decision maker is open-ended. This makes the reviewability of decisions very difficult as there are few legal constraints on the final decision. As a result, having statutory criteria that create the goalposts for valid decisions is essential to ensure democratic accountability.

The Agency, federal authorities, the minister, and the Governor in Council all must be clearly mindful of provisions of the *IAA* that constrain and/or direct how they exercise their discretion. Codifying clear criteria around decision making provides the opportunity for increased accountability. Clear and concise decision-making criteria provide the guideposts of what evidence to consider, how it is weighed, and how a decision may be justified, by both the decision maker and, perhaps more importantly, a reviewing court. Where criteria are too vague or open-ended, the value of the criteria is diminished.

As highlighted in Table 18.1, various sections of the *IAA* set out criteria that must be considered in specific decisions. The Act also provides the overall direction in how it is to be administered. As noted above, the purposes section of the Act provides some guiding principles and direction. This includes the Government of Canada, the minister, the Agency, and other federal authorities exercising "their powers in a manner that fosters sustainability, respects the Government's commitments with respect to the rights of the Indigenous peoples of Canada and applies the precautionary principle."[40] Section 6(3) states that "the principles of scientific integrity, honesty, objectivity, thoroughness and accuracy" must be applied in administration of the Act. This section will be relevant to how specific decisions are made as well as to any judicial review of decisions (as discussed below).

For example, in the context of the federal *Species at Risk Act*,[41] courts have highlighted the relevance of the "precautionary principle" in the

---

40    *IAA*, above note 1, s 6(2).

41    SC 2002, c 29.

legislation in how government makes decisions under that Act.[42] Similarly, the precautionary principle has been recognized as relevant to decisions under previous environmental assessment laws. This is illustrated by the case of *Taseko Mines Limited v Canada (Environment)*, where a panel's interpretation of the precautionary principle in determining whether a project might result in significant adverse effects, and its final decision was found to be reasonable.[43]

Beyond this general direction in section 6, the *IAA* provides more specific guidance for certain decisions, including the factors in section 16 that guide the Agency's determination of whether an assessment must be conducted and those in section 22 that guide the content and scope of information and studies that must form part of an impact statement.

Furthermore, the final "public interest" determination, whether made by the minister or the Governor in Council, must be based on the assessment report and on a list of factors set out in section 63. Specifically, section 60 requires the minister to determine whether a project's adverse effects on areas of federal jurisdiction that are identified in a report are, in light of the section 63 factors and the extent of the effects, in the public interest. The same obligation lies with the Governor in Council, which is charged with making a final project decision under section 62.

The section 63 factors include how the project "contributes to sustainability," the extent to which the adverse effects are significant (i.e., the gravity of the effects), mitigation measures, impacts on Indigenous groups and the extent of adverse effects on Indigenous rights (as set out in section 35 of the *Constitution Act, 1982*[44]), and "the extent to which the effects of the designated project hinder or contribute to the Government of Canada's ability to meet its environmental obligations and its commitments in respect of climate change."

It is important to note, however, that the focus of the *IAA* is on creating mandatory *considerations* rather than mandating strict compliance with any clear definitions or regulatory standards. In this regard, the decisions contain a significant level of discretion in how different

---

42     See *Alberta Wilderness Association v Canada (Environment)*, 2009 FC 710, *Western Canada Wilderness Committee v Canada (Fisheries and Oceans)*, 2014 FC 148, and *Centre Québécois du droit de l'environnement v Canada (Environment)*, 2015 FC 773.

43     2017 FC 1099 at para 123.

44     Being Schedule B to the *Canada Act 1982* (UK), 1982, c 11.

evidence is considered and valued. For example, the Agency is charged with scoping the studies and the information needed to be provided in an impact statement, including the Tailored (project-specific) Impact Assessment Guidelines for the IA; the extent to which some factors are relevant; and the scope and depth of public participation, engagement with Indigenous nations, and engagement with other jurisdictions.[45]

This raises the risk of the Agency inappropriately limiting the information or studies required as part of the IA process and the potential that information provided by the proponent is deemed sufficient by the Agency notwithstanding apparent gaps in information to make an optimally informed decision. Where assessment information is too narrowly scoped, there may be insufficient evidence to properly assess effects within federal jurisdiction. This danger of excluding relevant information is increased further where a proponent's initial project description fails to appropriately capture the scope of the project. Appropriate scoping of assessments has been an area of conflict in the past as proponents and responsible government departments may seek to minimize the scope and nature of assessment that must be conducted.[46]

Similarly, where a review panel undertakes an assessment, significant discretion is embedded in the process notwithstanding a panel's duties being prescribed by the Act. This includes how evidence is managed in the hearing process and whether certain procedural rights are granted to participants.

The final determination of whether a project is in the public interest also has significant discretion. The public interest determination is guided by high-level direction in relation to how the project "contributes to sustainability," how effective a mitigation measure might be, the extent to which effects are significant, and the determination of the impact on Indigenous groups. Although regulatory standards, definitions, and guiding policy considerations may be forthcoming, these areas are currently very discretionary.

Could the *IAA* have provided more statutory direction to decision makers? Certainly, that would have assisted in ensuring transparent and more accountable decisions. The greater the discretion, the greater the

---

45   *IAA*, above note 1.

46   See, for example, *Prairie Acid Rain Coalition v Canada (Minister of Fisheries and Oceans)*, 2006 FCA 31, and *MiningWatch Canada v Canada*, 2010 SCC 2.

risk that decision makers will be swayed by political pressure or fail to come to impartial conclusions. The broader and more value laden the legislative direction is, the more discretion a decision maker has. This is reflected in past decisions around whether a project is in the "public interest." Specifically, the Federal Court of Appeal in *Gitxaala Nation v Canada* has noted that a high level of deference is required in a final public interest determination (in relation to a pipeline) that involves "broad public interest considerations, along with economic and policy considerations, and [weighs] them against detrimental effects."[47] The court further noted that

> [t]he Supreme Court itself has recognized that "[a]s a general principle, increased deference is called for where legislation is intended to resolve and balance competing policy objectives or the interests of various constituencies." In its view, "[a] statutory purpose that requires a tribunal to select from a range of remedial options or administrative responses, is concerned with the protection of the public, engages policy issues, or involves the balancing of multiple sets of interests or considerations will demand greater deference from a reviewing court." See *Dr. Q. v. College of Physicians and Surgeons of British Columbia*, 2003 SCC 19, [2003] 1 S.C.R. 226, at paragraphs 30-31.[48]

Insofar as meeting climate obligations and fostering sustainability often involve balancing competing policy objectives and could be reasonably achieved through multiple alternative paths, a high level of discretion in the final decisions remains.

### 3) Reasons and Rationale of Decisions Under the *IAA*

The relevance of providing reasons for specific government decisions was recently highlighted by the Supreme Court of Canada in *Canada (Minister of Citizenship and Immigration) v Vavilov*:

> Reasons explain how and why a decision was made. They help to show affected parties that their arguments have been considered and demonstrate that the decision was made in a fair and lawful manner.

---

47    2016 FCA 187 at para 150 [*Gitxaala Nation*].

48    *Ibid* at para 151. See also *Raincoast Conservation Foundation v Canada (Attorney General)*, 2019 FCA 224 at para 44.

Reasons shield against arbitrariness as well as the perception of arbitrariness in the exercise of public power.... And as Jocelyn Stacey and the Hon. Alice Woolley persuasively write, "public decisions gain their democratic and legal authority through a process of public justification" which includes reasons "that justify [the] decisions [of public decision makers] in light of the constitutional, statutory and common law context in which they operate."[49]

Reasons also "facilitate meaningful judicial review by shedding light on the rationale for a decision."[50] Where reasons are required, they are the primary mechanism by which administrative decision makers show that their decisions are reasonable — that is, they "demonstrate 'justification, transparency and intelligibility'" to both the affected parties and a reviewing tribunal (whether it is through a statutory appeal or an application for judicial review). [51]

The need to provide reasons "encourages administrative decision makers to more carefully examine their own thinking and to better articulate their analysis in the process."[52] The validity and appropriateness of a decision can only be tested where a reviewing court or tribunal has an understanding of the considerations and rationale for a given decision. The obligation to provide written reasons for a decision, particularly when considered in conjunction with review or appeal provisions, is central to accountability in the IA process.

The *IAA* prescribes the need to give reasons in relation to key decisions under the Act. The logic underpinning decisions can, theoretically at least, be revealed, either through the requirement to set out written reasons or the need to include a decision maker's rationale and conclusions. This is the case for the majority of central decision points under the Act, with the major exception being the Agency decision regarding the studies and information required to be provided by a proponent to inform the assessment. This deficiency in providing reasons early in the IA process may undermine the scope of the evidence and the final decision.

Specifically, the need to publish reasons for a decision include

---

49    Above note 3 at para 79 [citations omitted].
50    *Ibid* at para 81.
51    *Ibid.*
52    *Ibid* at para 80.

- the ministerial decision to designate a physical activity that is to be subjected to the Act
- the Agency decision as to whether to require an IA of an activity
- the decision regarding substitution
- the final decision made by either the minister or the Governor in Council

In addition, the *IAA* requires the decision maker's rationale and conclusions for the determination of effects and recommendations set out in an Agency report and the determination of effects and recommendations of a review panel.

The requirement to provide reasons and the rationale and conclusions for the determination of effects should allow for both an outside evaluation of decision justifications and, if well drafted, an understanding of how differing evidence is weighed in light of the purposes of the Act.

Relative to past iterations of environmental assessment law in Canada, the approach taken in the *IAA* increases the number of decision points for which the rationale of the decision should be revealed. The requirement to provide reasons ensures that the decision maker will have to be at least aware of the relevant evidence and the statutory criteria that are to guide their decision.

By way of example, the final public interest decision must be accompanied by detailed reasons that "demonstrate that the Minister or the Governor in Council, as the case may be, based the determination on the report with respect to the impact assessment of the designated project and considered each of the factors referred to in section 63."[53] Unfortunately, these factors are not currently accompanied by regulatory or policy guidance that might help delineate acceptable versus unacceptable impacts on areas of federal jurisdiction and therefore reflect an area of significant discretion. Although a general definition of "sustainability" is provided,[54] there is no accompanying statutory guidance as to how it should be evaluated, as discussed in chapters 9 and 14. In this regard, the detailed reasons are the only basis by which stakeholders might measure or evaluate the legitimacy and logic of the final decision and glean an understanding of how the decision-making

---

53    *IAA*, above note 1, s 65(2).
54    *Ibid*, s 2.

factors are valued. Nevertheless, the decision maker must clearly put his or her mind to both the assessment report and decision factors in providing the rationale for a given outcome.

The requirement to provide written and detailed reasons should lead to decisions that are representative of the recommendations of the assessment itself. However, the risk remains that the legitimacy of decisions will be undermined where the assessment report and/or the reasons are too vague or contain significant uncertainty. It is in this area that significant concern arises as poor reasons may be legally compliant but will undermine the legitimacy of the decision. Furthermore, the use of judicial review, rather than a more efficient and specialized statutory appeal tribunal, is likely to mean that many, if not most, reasons will avoid any type of review.[55]

## E.  JUDICIAL REVIEW OF IA DECISIONS

The *IAA* does not include a statutory review or an appeal mechanism. The review of decisions made by the Agency, other federal authorities under the Act, the minister, and the Governor in Council must therefore proceed via applications for judicial review.

This is a significant deficiency in the legislation. Reliance on a formal, adversarial role of the courts with limited scope and grounds to review decisions is a narrow, inefficient, and overly legalistic way to review decisions. The failure to include an independent statutory review mechanism for decisions and the de facto reliance on judicial review run counter to most conceptualizations of meaningful public participation.

The alternative approach, supported by the Expert Panel for the Review of Environmental Assessment Processes, would have seen the set-up of an independent and specialized quasi-judicial review tribunal.[56] The grounds and type of review of decisions of a tribunal are dictated by their enabling statute. In this regard, these tribunals offer the ability to provide a more efficient way to review the legality of decisions but also a more substantive review of decisions (as the statutory language allows). This, in turn, would have elevated the transparency and accountability of the whole process and would facilitate public participation. Instead,

---

55   A specialized quasi-judicial tribunal was proposed by an expert panel. See *Building Common Ground*, above note 39 at 51.

56   *Ibid* at 50.

through its silence on statutory appeals, the *IAA* relies on judicial review to provide oversight for decisions.

Judicial review of specific decisions may be limited as a result of the following:

1) The procedural limitations and limited grounds of judicial review
2) A limit on the type of decisions that are reviewable
3) The level of deference that a court will provide a decision maker

Each of these limitations is addressed further below.

## 1) Procedural Limitations

The process of bringing an application for judicial review in relation to the *IAA* will generally be governed by the *Federal Courts Act*[57] and related rules. The ability to review a specific decision is time limited by a requirement to file an application for review within thirty days of the decision or order of the federal board, commission, or other tribunal.[58]

A judicial review is also limited to reviewing a decision based on the record; hence, a court can only consider evidence that was before the original administrative decision maker through affidavits and cross-examination. The parties are not entitled to broad, relevance-based documentary disclosure. There is also no viva voce evidence.[59] Also, remedies arising from a judicial review are discretionary, and even a successful applicant may be refused the remedy they seek.[60]

Furthermore, the grounds for review of a federal decision are limited by section 18.1(4) of the *Federal Courts Act*, which prescribes where a federal court may grant relief. Specifically, this includes

- acting without jurisdiction, beyond its jurisdiction or refusing to exercise jurisdiction
- failure to observe a principle of natural justice and procedural fairness
- making an error in law in making a decision or order
- where a decision is made based on "an erroneous finding of fact that [the decision maker] made in a perverse or capricious manner"

---

57    RSC, 1985, c F-7.

58    *Ibid*, s 18.1. "Federal board, commission, or other tribunal" is broadly defined in the Act.

59    *Canada (Attorney General) v TeleZone Inc*, 2010 SCC 62 at para 26.

60    See *Canadian Pacific Ltd v Matsqui Indian Band*, [1995] 1 SCR 3 at para 30.

Any review of a decision made under the *IAA* will therefore be limited to issues of legality, in the sense of fitting within the prescribed grounds of review. A substantive review of the facts is not available under the Act, except to the extent that a court may find a substantive factual element to be determinative of the overall legality of the decision.

The federal court process is legalistic and adversarial, and engaging the process is likely to require retention of legal counsel. This raises concerns around the ability to review a given decision due to both time limitations and legal costs. This is in contrast to a less formal and adversarial approach that could be provided through a statutory-based appeal to a reviewing expert tribunal, which may provide for alternative dispute resolution and other forms of independent review.[61] This is particularly relevant for decisions that occur earlier in the process, such as whether to require an IA or decisions regarding the scoping of information to conduct the assessment. Failure to address potential deficiencies in early decisions may result in a fundamentally flawed final decision, and this, in turn, is likely to result in significant costs to all of those involved.

## 2) The Types of Decisions That Can Be Reviewed

Not all decisions will be subject to judicial review. Specifically, courts have found that only a decision that affects "'legal rights, impose[s] legal obligations, or cause[s] prejudicial effects'" is appropriate for review.[62] Where a decision lacks "any independent legal or practical effect," the decision will not be reviewable.[63]

Insofar as an IA report is merely a source of advice to inform the public interest decision made by the minister or Cabinet, it will not generally be reviewable.[64] However, this does not immunize the report from judicial scrutiny, as illustrated by the case of *Tsleil-Waututh Nation v Canada (Attorney General)*.[65] In that case, the Federal Court of Appeal indicated that a National Energy Board (NEB) report related to the Trans

---

61   An independent review process has been cited as "good practice" by Joseph et al, above note 16.

62   See *Taseko Mines Limited v Canada (Environment)*, 2019 FCA 319 at para 36 [*Taseko*]. See also *Gitxaala Nation* above note 47.

63   *Taseko*, above note 62 at para 36.

64   *Ibid* at paras 36 and 37.

65   2018 FCA 153 [*Tsleil-Waututh Nation*].

Mountain Pipeline expansion project under *CEAA 2012* was not subject to review.[66] Despite this, the court still undertook a review of the scoping decisions and rationale presented in the report in reference to marine shipping and its impacts on the "at risk" southern resident killer whales. The court held that the NEB in that case was unjustified in scoping out marine shipping (due to its error in limiting its scope of assessment) and that this resulted in a fundamentally flawed report.[67] The court overturned the subsequent decision by Cabinet about the project as its decision was based on "unreasonable reliance on the board's report."[68]

This case illustrates that although some decisions will not be subject to a review by the court per se, the fact that the final decision is reviewable has implications for decisions earlier in the process, even if those decisions are merely advisory in nature. For the *IAA*, this means that review of the final ministerial and Cabinet public interest decision will implicate any errors or failures that occur earlier in the IA process.[69] The question becomes whether the earlier error is of such a nature as to undermine the fundamental validity of the advice and thereby the final decision.

Nevertheless, it seems that several of the key decisions considered in this chapter are not readily reviewable in isolation. Case law has clearly stated that an IA report is not reviewable as it carries no direct legal consequence.[70] Similarly, a scoping decision regarding what is included in the assessment may not be reviewable as it would require establishing that the scope of the assessment itself has a direct impact on one's right, which may be difficult to establish. Scoping decisions may still have implications for the validity of the final decision, as discussed above.

Decisions on whether to require an IA for a designated project also pose a challenge. The failure to require an IA may be viewed merely as a procedural omission and not a decision on the project itself. In instances where a project-based decision is still required by the exercise of authority of a federal department, it would appear that the federal authorization should be reviewed, not the decision regarding whether an IA is required.

---

66    *Ibid.*

67    *Ibid.*

68    *Ibid* at paras 472 & 473.

69    *Ibid* at para 473.

70    *Taseko*, above note 62.

In this regard, the Act provides no statutory criteria to compel a specific decision about whether an IA must be conducted. This can be contrasted with the case of *Friends of the Oldman River Society v Canada (Minister of Transport)*,[71] where the statutory duties under the *Navigable Waters Protection Act*[72] and the mandatory nature of the *Environmental Assessment and Review Process Guidelines Order*[73] meant that a federal assessment was required with respect to a dam on the Oldman River.

Depending on the circumstances, valid arguments may still arise about the reasonableness of a decision not to require an IA, as happened recently in relation to provincial environmental assessment laws in *Newfoundland and Labrador (Environment and Climate Change) v Atlantic Salmon Federation (Canada)* (highlighted further below).[74] For example, where a project clearly impacts on federal jurisdiction and there is no alternative avenue to assess and mitigate project impacts by a federal authority, it seems that the reasonableness of the decision may be validly challenged for failing to live up to the principled approach mandated by section 6 of the *IAA*.

## 3) The Standard of Review and the Level of Deference Given to Decision Makers

The standard of review used by a court for the vast majority of decisions under the *IAA* will be that of reasonableness.[75] The focus on whether a specific government decision or order is "reasonable" guides the court to "give effect to the legislature's intent to leave certain decisions with an administrative body while fulfilling the constitutional role of judicial review to ensure that exercises of state power are subject to the rule of law."[76] A reasonable decision "is one that is based on an internally coherent and rational chain of analysis and that is justified in relation

---

71 2018 NLCA 53.

72 RSC, 1985, c N-22.

73 SOR/84-467.

74 2018 NLCA 53 [*Newfoundland and Labrador*].

75 Pursuant to the *Vavilov* framework for the standard of review, the decisions under consideration in this chapter do not rebut the underlying presumption of a "reasonableness" review, nor does the *IAA* create any statutory appeal mechanisms that would attract an alternative standard of review. See above note 3.

76 *Ibid* at para 82.

to the facts and law that constrain the decision maker."[77] To determine if a given decision is reasonable, "the reviewing court asks whether the decision bears the hallmarks of reasonableness—justification, transparency and intelligibility—and whether it is justified in relation to the relevant factual and legal constraints that bear on the decision."[78]

In determining whether a decision maker has displayed an internally coherent and rational chain of analysis, the court will be guided by the nature of duties and criteria set out in the Act. A court will look at the legislative context as a whole in determining whether a decision is "reasonable."[79]

This contextual analysis will include the *IAA*'s mandate and principles that guide administration of the Act as set out in sections 6(2) and 6(3), as highlighted above. For example, the application of the precautionary principle has guided several courts in how they interpret the exercise of statutory duties.[80] This is particularly the case where more prescriptive duties are found, such as those in the federal *Species at Risk Act*.[81]

The precautionary principle has also contextualized statutory interpretation in decisions regarding environmental assessment. A notable recent case involving a provincial environmental assessment regime is *Newfoundland and Labrador*.[82] The court held that a minister's decision to exclude an aquaculture undertaking from an environmental assessment was unreasonable. In this case, the regulation mandated that where the minister determined that where an undertaking may result in "significant negative environmental effects" or where there "is significant public concern, the minister shall require an environmental impact statement."[83] Notwithstanding the clear discretion of the minister to make the determination of significance under the regulation, the court found that the ministers' determination was not supported by the evidence. Both the superior and appellate courts highlighted the precautionary principle in contextualizing the reasonableness of the minister's statutory interpretation as well as the minister's determination of whether the project was the subject of a high level of public

---

77   *Ibid* at para 85.
78   *Ibid* at para 99.
79   *Ibid* at paras 108–24.
80   *Ibid*.
81   Above note 41.
82   Above note 74.
83   *Environmental Assessment Regulations*, 2003, NLR 54/03, s 25.

concern and the likelihood that the undertaking would have significant effects on the environment.[84]

In this regard, the precautionary principle, the rights of Indigenous peoples, and sustainability will be relevant to contextualizing the reasonableness of decisions under the *IAA*. The boundaries of deference should be constrained where the evidence or a given decision appears to be contrary to fundamental tenants of these principles and other legal obligations. This is particularly the case for impacts on the rights of Indigenous people and the precautionary principle, where there are contextual directions already reflected in jurisprudence. It is less so for "sustainability," where the context remains laden with trade-offs.

Similarly, administration of the Act in line with the enumerated principles of section 6(3) will contextualize a court's review. The need for government actors to apply principles of "scientific integrity, honesty, objectivity, thoroughness and accuracy" should elevate the courts' scrutiny in relation to whether a specific decision is "justified, transparent and intelligible." This should result in an increased willingness of the courts to review and assess the scientific integrity of given decisions, as well as to scrutinize the level of uncertainty in the evidence and assessment predictions, in an effort to understand whether decisions are thorough and accurate. This effectively adds a layer of review that will encourage courts to dive deeper to evaluate the integrity of a decision.

It is in this general context that other specific decisions should be assessed for reasonableness, that is, with a heightened scrutiny of how discretion is exercised in the context of decision-specific criteria. For example, section 65 of the *IAA* states that the final decision statement and reasons for the decision "must demonstrate that the Minister or the Governor in Council ... based the determination on the report with respect to the impact assessment of the designated project and considered each of the factors referred to in section 63." The language of section 65 of the *IAA* appears to provide both a factual and a legal constraint on the final decision.

The language also increases the relevance of the assessment report itself as the decision must clearly reflect the report's conclusions. The quality of the assessment report is very important, as are the decision makers' response and interpretation of the section 63 factors, particularly

---

84    *Atlantic Salmon Federation (Canada) v Newfoundland (Environment and Climate Change)*, 2017 NLTD(G) 137.

in light of the section 6 mandate and principles (described above). This can be contrasted with previous environmental assessment legislation in Canada, where a decision statement had to include conditions but did not have to provide detailed reasons or articulate how the authorization of significant adverse effects was justified.[85]

Nevertheless, the section 63 factors remain heavily discretionary and involve the type of policy trade-offs that courts have previously stated as involving matters "very much outside of the ken of the courts."[86] It remains to be seen if courts will use the directional language of the Act to take a new level of oversight over what are otherwise extremely discretionary decisions.

The overall justification around the project effects, mitigation, environmental and climate change commitments, and contributions to sustainability will still require decision makers to weigh various aspects of the evidence and make value judgments. As long as the decision adheres to a coherent and rational analysis, a court will likely defer to the decision maker's analysis. The *IAA* does not establish a substantive reference state of the public interest (or a process to evaluate sustainability), and as such, the impact of the legislation appears to, at most, create a need for the decision maker to provide a reasoned justification that addresses the section 63 factors with the level of precaution and scientific rigour mandated by section 6.

In this regard, it is likely easier to identify what may be viewed as unreasonable as opposed to cataloguing the range of reasonableness for a given project. Decisions that may raise the potential of being unreasonable include the following:

- where the justification and rationale of the project rely heavily on effects not identified in the report
- where the conclusions of a report regarding adverse effects are ignored by the decision maker or appear to be arbitrarily underplayed
- where mitigation measures are identified and relied upon that, on their face, fail in addressing an adverse effect or are otherwise not supported by the evidence

---

85   *CEAA* 2012, above note 25, ss 52–54.
86   *Gitxaala Nation*, above note 47 at para 157.

- where a project infringes on Indigenous rights in a manner that is contrary to section 35 jurisprudence
- where the reasons appear to be based on significant leaps of logic or appear irrational, and these aspects of the reasons are relied upon for the final determination
- where the evidence of project effects is ignored or minimized due to errors in interpretation of the scope of statutory duties[87]

What is determined as reasonable in a given circumstance will likely continue to be quite deferential. However, the evolution of the obligation to give reasons, the legislative mandate and principles, and the linkage of the decisions to the assessment report and other enumerated factors will encourage courts to ensure that decisions are operating within and representative of the factual and legal constraints provided by statutory criteria. It is likely that courts will still be restrained in evaluating assessment reports themselves, but they will be challenged by some of the directional language around scientific integrity and thoroughness.

## F.  CONCLUSION

The *IAA* creates the foundations for transparency and accountability in decision making, but its effectiveness in this regard has yet to be determined. Future decisions and judicial reviews will shed light on the effectiveness of the provisions and how they are considered by decision makers.

The Act provides, as did its predecessor legislation, the assessment registry, which includes a significant amount of access to information and transparency relevant to decision making. Concerns remain around when some information will be treated as confidential and not be publicly disclosed and the lack of clear indication of the types of economic, environmental, and social information that should be disclosed to allow for effective public participation in the process. Furthermore, although current regulations provide for plain-language summaries of project assessments, the ability of the public to effectively and critically scrutinize the proponent-provided data and other evidence (and any uncertainty therein) remains in question.

The conundrum of how uncertainty is treated in decisions remains a major challenge for decision makers and stakeholders alike. The

---

87    As was seen in *Tsleil-Waututh Nation*, above note 65.

guiding principles and mandate set out in section 6 of the *IAA* should lead to greater judicial scrutiny of how uncertainty is handled by a given decision maker and how this is reflected in the reasons for a given decision, but this too remains to be seen. The issue could be resolved through regulatory or policy guidance on the treatment of uncertainty, directing decision makers to communicate the uncertainty in evidence and models and how that uncertainty weighs in the decision.

Overall, the *IAA* has arguably increased the level of accountability through providing criteria to direct some key decisions and, more importantly, expanding when and how written reasons for a decision are required. However, in the absence of further binding definitions, thresholds, and standards, these decisions remain inherently discretionary in nature. Sufficient discretion remains to draft reasons that are legally sound but not fit for the legislative purpose. In this regard, the importance of strategic and/or regional IAs to delineate more discrete objectives that can guide decisions is elevated.[88]

Furthermore, not all decisions are required to be accompanied by reasons, to the detriment of the overall accountability of the new assessment regime under the *IAA*. Specifically, a requirement to provide reasons relating to the nature of the information that is required as part of the assessment and regarding the nature and scope of public participation would assist in the overall transparency and accountability of the process.

Finally, the lack of an independent statutory appeal mechanism significantly diminishes accountability under the Act as reliance on judicial review brings with it several limitations, including the fact that a variety of decisions are likely to avoid scrutiny. Although the directing language of the *IAA* is likely to bring increased judicial scrutiny of decisions, the overall ability of courts to provide sufficient accountability of decisions taken under the Act will need to be played out in jurisprudence—a slow, inefficient, and potentially arduous process.

Despite these criticisms, the language of the *IAA* provides an opportunity to elevate the rigour and rationale of IA decisions in Canada. The *IAA* can enable an evolution of environmental assessment law if decision makers and the courts embrace the opportunity.

---

88   See chapters 11 and 17 regarding regional and strategic assessments.

# CHAPTER 20

# Human Rights and the *Impact Assessment Act*: Proponents and Consultants as Duty Bearers

*Adebayo Majekolagbe, Sara L Seck, and Penelope Simons**

## A.  INTRODUCTION

The case for the explicit consideration of human rights in impact assessments (IAs) was made long before the 2011 United Nations' Guiding Principles on Business and Human Rights (UNGPs) were developed.[1] The UNGPs confirm that states have a duty to protect human rights from harmful business conduct and that businesses are expected to respect human rights wherever they operate.[2] Central to businesses' fulfillment of their responsibility to respect human rights is the requirement that they engage in human rights due diligence (HRDD).[3] Although human

---

*    The authors are grateful to the Social Sciences and Humanities Research Council of Canada (SSHRC) for funding support in the form of a Knowledge Synthesis Grant: Informing Best Practices in Environmental and Impact Assessments. Further information on this project is available on the Schulich School of Law digital commons project site, "Responsible Business Conduct and Impact Assessment Law," online: https://digitalcommons.schulichlaw.dal.ca/ialawrbc.

1    United Nations Human Rights, *Guiding Principles on Business and Human Rights: Implementing the United Nations "Protect, Respect and Remedy" Framework* (New York & Geneva: United Nations, 2011). See Nora Götzmann, "Introduction to the *Handbook on Human Rights Impact Assessment*: Principles, Methods and Approaches" in Nora Götzmann, ed, *Handbook on Human Rights Impact Assessment* (Cheltenham, UK: Edward Elgar, 2019) 2 at 5–9 for an overview of the origin and elements of human rights IA in relation to business activities.

2    UNGPs, above note 1, principles 1, 11, and 23.

3    *Ibid*, Principle 17.

rights impact assessment (HRIA) is not synonymous with HRDD, it has become a tool deployed to fulfill HRDD's objectives.[4] The more recent Framework Principles on Human Rights and the Environment (Framework Principles) affirm that the duty of a state to protect human rights entails requiring prior assessment of environmental impacts of projects and policies, including their potential effects on the enjoyment of human rights.[5] HRIA is a process for identifying, understanding, assessing, preventing, mitigating, and accounting for actual and potential human rights impacts of the activities and operation of businesses.[6] Although some Canadian extractive companies have employed HRIA and other HRDD tools with respect to projects abroad,[7] the application has been flawed and controversial,[8] and these tools have rarely been used in relation to proposed projects or operations within Canada. There is no law expressly requiring that Canadian companies assess and/or address the human right impacts of their domestic activities, beyond compliance with the limited expectations of national and provincial human rights commissions. And although different countries now impose HRDD reporting obligations on businesses,[9] Canada has so far failed to do likewise.

---

4    Götzmann, above note 1 at 7. Various tools, including the HRIA, can be used to achieve the objective of HRDD under the UNGPs. The UNGPs do not explicitly require businesses to conduct HRIA.

5    United Nations General Assembly, "Report of the Special Rapporteur on the Issue of Human Rights Obligations Relating to the Enjoyment of a Safe, Clean, Healthy and Sustainable Environment—Framework Principles on Human Rights and the Environment," UN Doc A/HRC/37/59 (24 January 2018), Annex, Framework Principle 8.

6    Götzmann, above note 1 at 4. Götzmann further noted that an inclusive definition of HRIA encompasses HRIAs commissioned by companies, whether integrated or "standalone," as well as those commissioned by communities (which may be led or driven by non-governmental organizations or civil society organizations), collaborative multistakeholder approaches, and sector-wide assessments; see Götzmann, above note 1 at 9.

7    See, for example, Penelope Sanz & Robin Hansen, "The Political Life of a Human Rights Impact Assessment: Canadian Mining in the Philippines" (2018) 7:1 *Canadian Journal of Human Rights* 97; Motoko Aizawa, Daniela C dos Santos & Sara L Seck, "Financing Human Rights Due Diligence in Mining Projects" in Sumit K Lodhia, ed, *Mining and Sustainable Development: Current Issues* (London, UK: Routledge, 2018) 99 at 105.

8    See, generally, Daniela Chimisso dos Santos & Sara L Seck, "Human Rights Due Diligence and Extractive Industries" in Surya Deva & David Birchell, eds, *Research Handbook on Human Rights and Business* (Northampton, UK: Edward Elgar, 2020) 151.

9    See, for example, *LOI n° 2017-399 du 27 mars 2017 relative au devoir de vigilance des sociétés mères et des entreprises donneuses d'ordre*, JORF, 28 March 2017, no 0074 [*Corporate Duty of Vigilance Law*]; EC, *Commission Regulation (EC) 2017/821 of 17 May 2017 laying*

Whereas the UNGPs reflect the international human rights law obligations of states to protect human rights and the expectation that businesses will respect human rights, the obligations of IA consultants are not as clear. IA consultants have been described as a community of practice, an epistemic community, and administrative entrepreneurs.[10] This community of practice, however, remains largely amorphous. It is loosely composed of experts and environmental practitioners employed or contracted by IA participants (proponents,[11] responsible authorities, rights-holders, or stakeholders) to carry out an assessment—wholly or in part—or to play an advisory role in an assessment process. The roles of IA consultants in screening, scoping, and drafting environmental impact statements are emphasized in the literature.[12] These early-phase activities are critical to the IA process. Existing literature has, however, highlighted the problems of corruption and the lack of independence among consultants.[13] Although ethical codes have been proposed to address these problems,[14] the effectiveness of such codes is doubtful.[15] We argue here that consultants have a responsibility to respect human rights

---

*down supply chain due diligence obligations for Union importers of tin, tantalum and tung-sten, their ores, and gold originating from conflict-affected and high-risk areas,* [2017] OJ, L130/1; *Modern Slavery Act 2018* (Austl), 2018/153; *Modern Slavery Act 2015*, 2015, c 30 (UK).

10 See Richard K Morgan, "Conceptualising Best Practice in Impact Assessment" (2017) 66 *Environmental Impact Assessment Review* 78 at 82; Neil Craik, *The International Law of Environmental Impact Assessment: Process, Substance and Integration* (New York: Cambridge University Press, 2008) at 207 and 219–21.

11 Section 2 of the *Impact Assessment Act*, SC 2019, c 28, s 1, defines *proponent* as "the person or entity—federal authority, government or body—that proposes the carrying out of, or carries out, a designated project." We, however, focus on businesses as proponents in this chapter.

12 See Tim Snell & Richard Cowell, "Scoping in Environmental Impact Assessment: Balancing Precaution and Efficiency" (2006) 26:4 *Environmental Impact Assessment Review* 359 at 363 ("planning officers and developers' consultants are key gatekeepers to the relatively closed world of scoping discussions"). See, generally, Erik Mostert, "Subjective Environmental Impact Assessment: Causes, Problems, Solutions" (1996) 14:2 *Impact Assessment* 191.

13 See, for example, Aled Williams & Kendra Dupuy, "Deciding Over Nature: Corruption and Environmental Impact Assessments" (2017) 65 *Environmental Impact Assessment Review* 118.

14 See Álvaro Enríquez-de-Salamanca, "Stakeholders' Manipulation of Environmental Impact Assessment" (2018) 68 *Environmental Impact Assessment Review* 10 at 15; Tim Richardson, "Environmental Assessment and Planning Theory: Four Short Stories About Power, Multiple Rationality, and Ethics" (2005) 25:4 *Environmental Impact Assessment Review* 341.

15 See Williams & Dupuy, above note 13 at 121.

under the UNGPs and that states, as part of their obligation to protect human rights under international human rights law, must ensure that private actors, including consultants, adhere to this responsibility. Properly implemented, this framing suggests that states have a duty to impose enforceable human rights obligations on consultants and proponents.

In this chapter, we make a case for a human rights approach to the interpretation and operationalization of the provisions of the *Impact Assessment Act (IAA)*,[16] emphasizing the role of IA proponents and consultants as duty bearers. As recently noted by Gibson, the success of the *IAA* will be in part dependent on strong elaboration of its innovative provisions in regulations and guidance.[17] We argue that it is both effective and efficient to adopt and adapt existing responsible business guidance tools in designing human rights-oriented regulations and guidelines under the *IAA*. The federal government has already been encouraging Canadian companies to apply these tools in operations abroad, but success has been limited. The use of these tools will also promote reconciliation and rights-respecting projects. Elsewhere, we have identified about 100 of such relevant tools, including those developed by Indigenous governments.[18] In Section B, we consider the *IAA*'s provisions on human rights and the roles of proponents and their consultants. Section C focuses on how existing responsible business conduct (RBC) tools can be used in the design of regulations and guidelines to improve the *IAA*. We conclude in Section D.

## B. HUMAN RIGHTS AND THE ROLES OF PROPONENTS AND CONSULTANTS IN THE *IAA*

The *IAA* is a marked improvement on previous IA legal regimes as it relates to human rights. The requirement in the *IAA* for businesses to undertake Gender-based Analysis Plus (GBA+) is one of the major wins for the human rights movement.[19] The Act also requires the con-

---

16   Above note 11.

17   See Robert B Gibson, "An Initial Evaluation of Canada's New Sustainability-Based Impact Assessment Act" (2020) 33:1 *Journal of Environmental Law and Practice* 1 at 31.

18   See Sara Seck et al, "Impact Assessment and Responsible Business Guidance Tools in the Extractive Sector: Implications for Human Rights, Gender and Stakeholder Engagement," Draft Final Report for the SSHRC Knowledge Synthesis Grant: Informing Best Practices in Environmental and Impact Assessments (13 April 2020).

19   See *IAA*, above note 11, s 22(1)(s). See also Chapter 12.

sideration of changes to health, social, or economic conditions when assessing projects.[20] However, it stops short of explicitly requiring the consideration of human rights impacts when projects are assessed. It is worth noting that the assessment of human rights impacts is not confined to GBA+. Social or socio-economic IA also differs from HRIA both substantively and procedurally.[21] Distinctively, HRIA emphasizes the participation of rights holders (not just stakeholders), the recognition of duty bearers, empowerment of rights holders and duty bearers, transparency with deference to the security of rights holders and human rights defenders, and accountability.[22] HRIA is also benchmarked against internationally recognized human rights standards and principles (not just domesticated rights), includes cumulative human rights impacts in its scope, discourages trade-offs between human rights and other project gains, and requires the availability of legal and non-legal grievance mechanisms.[23] In this section, we consider the extent to which the human rights-related provisions in the *IAA* align with HRIA and permit the inclusion of other rights not explicitly covered. We also make a case for a rights-based framing of the responsibilities of proponents and their consultants.

## 1)   The *IAA* and Human Rights

The provisions on Indigenous rights, GBA+, and right of access are the most explicit human rights-related provisions in the *IAA*.[24] The Indigenous rights referenced in the Act are rights "recognized and affirmed by section 35 of the Constitution Act."[25] However, John Borrows has criticized the Supreme Court of Canada's (SCC) narrow interpretation

---

20    *Ibid*, s 22(1)(a).

21    See, generally, Nora Götzmann, Frank Vanclay & Frank Seier, "Social and Human Rights Impact Assessments: What Can They Learn from Each Other?" (2016) 34:1 *Impact Assessment and Project Appraisal* 14; Deanna Kemp & Frank Vanclay, "Human Rights and Impact Assessment: Clarifying the Connections in Practice" (2013) 31:2 *Impact Assessment and Project Appraisal* 86.

22    See Götzmann, above note 1 at 13–14.

23    *Ibid* at 15–16.

24    Above note 11, ss 22(1)(c), 22(1)(s), 63(d), and 104(2). For further exposition on GBA+, Indigenous rights, Indigenous knowledge, and access to information provisions in the *IAA*, see chapters 6, 12, 19, and 21.

25    *Ibid* at Preamble.

of section 35 rights[26] as solely historical rights instead of being more broadly framed as human rights.[27] According to Borrows, the SCC's construction of section 35 rights excludes essential rights such as rights to child welfare, education, clean drinking water, and health.[28] Yet the *United Nations Declaration on the Rights of Indigenous Peoples* (*UNDRIP*) affirms the right of Indigenous peoples to the full enjoyment of all human rights and fundamental freedoms collectively or individually.[29] Although the *IAA* refers to the commitment of the Government of Canada to *UNDRIP* in its preamble, this commitment was not entrenched in any of the substantive provisions of the Act. It could, however, be argued that other *IAA* provisions on Indigenous knowledge, Indigenous culture, and the recognition of Indigenous governing bodies,[30] to various degrees, embed rights under *UNDRIP*, including cultural rights and the right to self-determination.[31]

The *IAA*'s requirement that studies or assessments by an Indigenous governing body be considered in an assessment process provides an opportunity to consider rights-based issues not otherwise covered by section 35 rights.[32] This potential is confirmed in the interim guidance on collaboration with Indigenous peoples, which states, in part, that studies (and Indigenous IAs) could cover impacts "on their

---

26 See *Mitchell v MNR*, 2001 SCC 33 at para 63 (identifying Aboriginal rights protected under s 35 as "those practices, customs and traditions integral to the distinctive cultures of aboriginal societies"); *R v Van der Peet*, [1996] 2 SCR 507 at para 63 (describing s 35 rights as "practices, customs and traditions which can be identified as having continuity with the practices, customs and traditions that existed prior to contact"). More recently, the SCC reaffirmed that "[t]o establish a s. 35 violation, a party must first demonstrate that it holds an Aboriginal right that remains unextinguished as of the enactment of the *Constitution Act, 1982* ... or a treaty right"; see *Mikisew Cree First Nation v Canada (Governor General in Council)*, 2018 SCC 40 at para 154 [citations omitted].

27 See John Borrows, *Freedom and Indigenous Constitutionalism* (Toronto: University of Toronto Press, 2016) at 130–31; John Borrows, "Challenging Historical Frameworks: Aboriginal Rights, the Trickster, and Originalism" (2017) 98:1 *The Canadian Historical Review* 114 at 115.

28 *Ibid* at 116.

29 GA Res 61/295, UNGAOR, 61st Sess, UN Doc A/RES/61/295 (13 September 2007) art 1.

30 See *IAA*, above note 11, ss 22(1)(g) and 22(1)(q)–(r).

31 See *UNDRIP*, above note 29, arts 3–5, 8, and 11–15. For more on *UNDRIP* and the *IAA*, see Chapter 6.

32 See *IAA*, above note 11, ss 22(1)(q)–(r).

territory, rights or community wellbeing."[33] The guidance further states that Indigenous communities may participate in the development of conditions at the decision-making stage to address "a project's potential impacts on their rights or interests."[34] The use of the phrase "rights or interests" in the guidance appears to appreciate the position of Indigenous peoples both as rights holders, with rights, and stakeholders, with interests. Importantly, the rights referenced in the guidance are not limited to section 35 rights and should be read to include rights under the *Charter*,[35] *UNDRIP*, and other sources of international human rights law. Yet although the minister or Governor in Council is mandated under the *IAA* to consider section 35 rights in determining public interest,[36] there is no such requirement to consider Indigenous IA and the broader rights recognized in the guidance.

The requirement for GBA+ provides another vehicle in the *IAA* for the consideration of human rights. Beyond gender, GBA+ entails the consideration of intersecting identities, including race, ethnicity, religion, age, mental ability, and physical ability.[37] The interim guidance describes GBA+ as an analytical framework that recognizes multiple identity factors "that intersect with sex and gender to affect how people may experience projects differently and be differently impacted by projects."[38] Although the *IAA*'s broad approach to GBA+ is laudable, it seems to have uncoupled the analysis from the human rights framework. The guidance, for example, makes no reference to human rights. A gender-based analysis must be rights based and consistent with international

---

33 Impact Assessment Agency of Canada, "Interim Guidance: Collaboration with Indigenous Peoples in Impact Assessments" (2019), online: *Government of Canada* www.canada.ca/en/impact-assessment-agency/services/policy-guidance/practitioners-guide-impact-assessment-act/collaboration-indigenous-peoples-ia.html.

34 *Ibid.*

35 *Canadian Charter of Rights and Freedoms*, Part I of the *Constitution Act, 1982*, being Schedule B to the *Canada Act 1982* (UK), c 11.

36 See *IAA*, above note 11, s 63(d).

37 See Status of Women Canada, "Government of Canada's Approach: Gender-based Analysis Plus," online: *Government of Canada* https://cfc-swc.gc.ca/gba-acs/approach-approche-en.html?wbdisable=true. See also Chapter 12.

38 Impact Assessment Agency of Canada, "Gender-based Analysis Plus in Impact Assessment (Interim Guidance)" (2019), online: *Government of Canada* www.canada.ca/en/impact-assessment-agency/services/policy-guidance/practitioners-guide-impact-assessment-act/gender-based-analysis-plus.html.

human rights law.[39] This is even more critical given the context of a broadly conceived notion of GBA+. A human rights approach premises the consideration of sex-, gender-, and identity-based issues on the right of all people, regardless of race, national or ethnic origin, colour, religion, sex, age, mental disability, physical disability, or other status, to be treated with equal protection and benefits, without discrimination.[40] It is further underpinned by other identity-specific international human rights instruments on the rights of women, workers, children, migrants, and the disabled, among others. The GBA+ provision is an opportunity to consider a vast array of human rights, particularly the rights of the most vulnerable. Requirements and provisions in international human rights law should be part of the GBA+ scoping and baseline data collection. When potential human rights-related GBA+ impacts are identified and measures are proffered to address the impacts, failure to address them could ground recourse to judicial or non-judicial grievance mechanisms individually and collectively.

The right of access to information is deemed a prerequisite to the meaningful participation that underpins Indigenous rights and rights-based GBA+, as well as procedural environmental rights more generally.[41] Transparency within an HRIA framework is ensured, in part, by the right of access to information.[42] The Framework Principles state that "[t]he human right of all persons to seek, receive and impart information includes information on environmental matters" and supports the exercise of additional rights, "including the rights to expression, association, participation and remedy."[43] The *IAA* guarantees the right of access to the Canadian Impact Assessment Registry (the Registry; internet site and project files) alongside other existing rights of access

---

39 See, for example, Christina Hill, Chris Madden & Nina Collins, *A Guide to Gender Impact Assessment for the Extractive Industries* (Melbourne: Oxfam, 2017) at 7.

40 See *Canadian Human Rights Act*, RSC, 1985 c H-6, ss 3(1) and 5(a)(b).

41 See Lisa F Odparlik & Johann Köppel, "Access to Information and the Role of Environmental Assessment Registries for Public Participation" (2013) 31:4 *Impact Assessment and Project Appraisal* 324; Framework Principles, above note 5 at Principle 7. See also Chapter 19.

42 See, for example, Nora Götzmann et al, *Human Rights Impact Assessment: Guidance and Toolbox* (Copenhagen: Danish Institute for Human Rights, 2020) at 25, online (pdf): www.humanrights.dk/sites/humanrights.dk/files/media/dokumenter/udgivelser/ hria_toolbox_2020/eng/dihr_hria_guidance_and_toolbox_2020_eng.pdf.

43 Above note 5 at Principle 7.

to information provided for under federal statute.[44] Thus, the right of access also applies to documents that could be obtained under the *Access to Information Act* (*AIA*).[45] This is important given the flaws of the Registry (under the repealed *Canadian Environmental Assessment Act, 2012* [*CEAA 2012*][46]), which include the non-availability of comprehensive documentation and the tendency of proponents and consultants to hold back documents by relying on copyright claims.[47] These flaws remain. For example, of the seventeen hydroelectric projects currently listed as completed in the online Registry, documents such as the environmental impact study, comprehensive study or assessment report, and other technical documents are only available with respect to four projects.[48] Although it is arguable that these projects were commenced under *CEAA 2012* and not the *IAA*, the *CEAA* requirement that the IA report and other enumerated project information be made available in the online Registry[49] has been reproduced in the *IAA*.[50] In any case, the Agency (and Review Panel) retain the same obligations with respect to projects under *CEAA 2012* as though the Act has not been repealed.[51]

The *Copyright Act* provides that a disclosure made pursuant to the *AIA* does not constitute a copyright infringement.[52] The *AIA*, however, prohibits disclosures including records containing trade secrets, scientific and technical information treated as confidential, and information that could result in material financial loss or gain.[53] The subjection of access rights under the *IAA* to copyright protection and the broad prohibitions

---

44   See *IAA*, above note 11, ss 104(1) & (2).

45   RSC, 1985, c A-1, s 4(1).

46   SC 2012, c 19, s 52.

47   See, for example, Kevin Hanna & Bram F Noble, "The Canadian Environmental Assessment Registry: Promise and Reality" (2011) 25:4 *UVP-report* 222 at 225. See, generally, A John Sinclair & Alan Diduck, "Public Participation in Canadian Environmental Assessment: Enduring Challenges and Future Directions" in Kevin S Hanna, ed, *Environmental Impact Assessment: Practice and Participation*, 2d ed (Don Mills, ON: Oxford University Press, 2009) 58.

48   See Canadian Impact Assessment Registry, "Hydroelectric Energy," online: *Government of Canada* https://iaac-aeic.gc.ca/050/evaluations/exploration?showMap=true&search=.

49   *CEAA 2012*, above note 46, ss 79(2) & 79(3), as repealed by *An Act to enact the Impact Assessment Act and the Canadian Energy Regulator Act, to amend the Navigation Protection Act and to make consequential amendments to other Acts*, SC 2019, s 9, c 28.

50   See *IAA*, above note 11, ss 105(2) & (3).

51   *Ibid*, ss 179–183.

52   RSC 1985, c C-42, s 32.1(1).

53   *AIA*, above note 45, ss 20(1)(a)–(d).

of the *AIA* considerably incentivize proponents and consultants to refuse to authorize either the publication or the disclosure of information. Compared to *CEAA 2012*, the right of access to information under the *IAA* is less robust. Under *CEAA 2012*, the Canadian Environmental Assessment Registry was to facilitate public access to assessment records and provide notice of environmental assessments in a timely manner.[54] This should be distinguished from the obligation of the Agency to provide a copy of any record in a timely manner when requested.[55] The obligation to facilitate public access and provide notice in a timely manner applies, in part, to the availability of relevant information in the online registry in a timely manner. Considerable time lag in posting of information has been found.[56] The *IAA*'s failure to mandate timely posting will further adversely affect the timeliness of documents provided on the online registry. Taken together, it is difficult to see how the *IAA* will effectively guarantee the timeliness, accessibility, and completeness that are crucial to exercising the right of access to information in the IA context.[57]

## 2)  Responsibilities of Proponents and Consultants

The *IAA* clearly spells out instances when proponents are prohibited from embarking on or doing anything with respect to a designated project, except as permitted after going through prescribed processes in the Act.[58] Prohibited acts include acts that may cause change to aquatic species, fish, fish habitat, or migratory birds; change of environment on federal lands, outside the province where the act was committed, or outside Canada; change to the environment that has an impact on Indigenous peoples; or change to a health, social, or economic matter under federal jurisdiction.[59] The *IAA* makes no reference to consultants, through whom proponents often fulfill their obligations.[60] The draft

---

54  Above note 49, s 78(1).

55  *Ibid*, s 78(3); see also *IAA*, above note 11, s 104(3).

56  See "2009 Fall Report of the Commissioner of the Environment and Sustainable Development: Chapter 1—Applying the Canadian Environmental Assessment Act" (2009), online: *Office of the Auditor General of Canada* www.oag-bvg.gc.ca/internet/ English/parl_cesd_200911_01_e_33196.html.

57  See, for example, Hanna & Noble, above note 47 at 225. See also Chapter 19.

58  See *IAA*, above note 11, s 7(1).

59  *Ibid*, s 7(1)(a)–(e).

60  *Ibid*.

guidance on Indigenous knowledge, which is part of the practitioner's guide under the *IAA*,[61] however, refers to consultants.[62] It expects consultants (and proponents) to understand whom they are meeting in communities, the roles of community members, whether individuals need the agreements of community leaders to share Indigenous knowledge, and whether such agreements were received.[63] Also, consultants should pay attention to the imperative of Indigenous knowledge holders sharing Indigenous knowledge using Indigenous language and do their utmost to get exact descriptions rather than one-word translations.[64] The practitioner's guide contains a description of processes, required contents of assessment documents, guidance, and policy contexts.[65] The extent to which the guide is binding is unclear. Some of the guidance contains the cautionary statement that the documents are for "information purposes only," while also stating that when inconsistent with the *IAA* and its regulations, the Act and regulations will prevail.[66]

The Agency's external technical reviews guide speaks relatively directly to the roles and responsibilities of experts.[67] The guide applies to external technical reviews of complex scientific questions and is designed to ensure that the evidence used in IAs is "rigorous, credible, and transparent."[68] The reviews are to be carried out by independent experts with

---

61    Impact Assessment Agency of Canada, "Practitioner's Guide to Federal Impact Assessments Under the Impact Assessment Act," online: *Government of Canada* www.canada.ca/en/impact-assessment-agency/services/policy-guidance/practitioners-guide-impact-assessment-act.html ["Practitioner's Guide"].

62    See, for example, Impact Assessment Agency of Canada, "Indigenous Knowledge Under the Impact Assessment Act: Procedures for Working with Indigenous Communities," online: *Government of Canada* www.canada.ca/en/impact-assessment-agency/services/policy-guidance/practitioners-guide-impact-assessment-act/indigenous-knowledge-under-the-impact-assessment-act.html.

63    *Ibid.*

64    *Ibid.*

65    Above note 61.

66    See, for example, Impact Assessment Agency of Canada, "Interim Guidance: Considering the Extent to which a Project Contributes to Sustainability," online: *Government of Canada* www.canada.ca/en/impact-assessment-agency/services/policy-guidance/practitioners-guide-impact-assessment-act/interim-guidance-considering.html.

67    Impact Assessment Agency of Canada, "External Technical Reviews" at para 2, online: *Government of Canada* www.canada.ca/en/impact-assessment-agency/services/policy-guidance/external-technical-reviews.html-_Toc19627763 ["External Technical Reviews"].

68    *Ibid*, s 2.

"no direct conflict of interest."[69] An external technical review is equated to a peer review, which is described as a review of technical merit by individuals with "qualifications and expertise equivalent to those of the researcher whose work they review."[70] Technical reviews are framed as dealing with "the most difficult science issues," with "science" understood as including natural sciences, social sciences, and engineering.[71] However, a rights-compliant framework recognizes that non-mainstream bodies of knowledge such as Indigenous knowledge are not less scientific or technological. Hence, *UNDRIP* recognizes the manifestations of Indigenous sciences and technologies.[72] Lawrence has argued that IA practitioners should "reject the false dichotomy between expert and layperson" and "recognize the value of local knowledge and experience."[73] This is especially true with respect to Indigenous knowledge and laws.

Although the external technical review guidance does not directly apply to a proponent's consultants,[74] its description of technical reviewers as experts with qualifications and expertise equivalent to "researchers" whose work they review suggests an expectation that consultants should have requisite qualifications and expertise. The EU directive on environmental impact assessment, more explicitly, mandates that "the developer shall ensure that the environmental impact assessment report is prepared by competent experts."[75] Codes of conduct and practice standards promoted by professional associations are the most well-known sources of the duties of IA practitioners. Integrity, sustainable practices, competence, continued education, full disclosure when there is a conflict of interest, freedom from bias, and compliance with the law are

---

69   *Ibid.*

70   *Ibid.*

71   *Ibid.*

72   Above note 29, art 31(1).

73   David P Lawrence, "The Need for EIA Theory-Building" (1997) 17:2 *Environmental Impact Assessment Review* 79 at 92.

74   "External Technical Reviews," above note 67, s 4.3 and 5 (comments will be sought from project proponents on the science question(s) to be posed to the independent experts, and proponents are permitted to submit written responses to the results of an external technical review to be considered by a review panel).

75   *Directive 2014/52/EU of the European Parliament and of the Council of 16 April 2014 amending Directive 2011/92/EU on the assessment of the effects of certain public and private projects on the environment*, L124/1 Official Journal of the European Union, art 5(3)(a).

common requirements in codes of conduct.[76] The International Association for Impact Assessment and the Environmental Careers Organization (ECO) Canada stand out for their requirement that all assessments must be underpinned by respect for human rights and must not violate the human rights of others.[77] Despite the usefulness of codes of conduct by professional bodies and advanced accreditation programs such as the Institute of Environmental Management & Assessment's Quality Mark scheme,[78] IA consultancy remains an unregulated, loosely bound profession. Promoted codes are limited in reach, and their effect on the quality of IA is unknown.

We argue that the UNGPs impose human rights responsibilities on companies and their consultants during IA processes. The recognition of these human rights obligations has informed the increasing number of HRDD laws. France's *Corporate Duty of Vigilance Law* requires designated companies to establish and implement an effective human rights vigilance plan for the identification of risks and prevention of the violations of human rights resulting from the operations of the company, its subsidiary companies, subcontractors, and suppliers.[79] There is a complaint process under the law through which individuals or organizations can seek a court order requiring a company to improve and implement its due diligence plan. Canada does not have an HRDD law. Nevertheless, the SCC recently held in *Nevsun Resources Ltd v Araya* (*Nevsun*) that it was not "plain and obvious" that corporations enjoy a blanket exclusion under customary international law and that direct remedy could be sought when customary international law or

---

76  See, for example, Environmental Institute of Australia and New Zealand, "Code of Ethics and Professional Conduct" (2012), online (pdf): www.eianz.org/document/item/2672; National Association of Environmental Professionals, "Code of Ethics and Standards of Practice for Environmental Professionals," online: www.naep.org/index.php?option= com_content&view=article&id=43:code-of-ethics&catid=19:site-content&Itemid=95; Institute of Environmental Management & Assessment, "Code of Professional Conduct" (2018), online: www.iema.net/iema-code-of-professional-conduct/the-code.

77  International Association for Impact Assessment, "Vision, Mission, Values, Professional Code of Conduct and Ethical Responsibilities," online (pdf): www.iaia.org/pdf/ Code-of-Ethics.pdf; ECO Canada, "Environmental Professional: Guidelines for Ethical Practice" (2019), online (pdf): www.eco.ca/wp-content/uploads/ECO-EP-Guidelines-for-Ethical-Practice-2018.pdf.

78  See Institute of Environmental Management & Assessment, "EIA Quality Mark," online: www.iema.net/eia-quality-mark.

79  Above note 9, art 1.

*jus cogens* norms (e.g., forced labour, slavery, torture, and crimes against humanity) are breached.[80] The Court also found that "the Canadian government has adopted policies to ensure that Canadian companies operating abroad *respect* these norms."[81] These policies include a range of RBC tools, including the UNGPs, the Organisation for Economic Co-operation and Development (OECD) guidelines,[82] and the International Finance Corporation performance standards,[83] among others.

Within the context of the *IAA*, human rights must be understood as extending to environmental human rights as articulated in the 2018 Framework Principles.[84] In a recent work, Seck shows how these mostly state-centric principles apply to businesses.[85] Furthermore, Boyd observes that the human right to a "safe, clean, healthy and sustainable environment" is now recognized in law by 156 of the 193 United Nations member states—more than 80 percent.[86] Even in the absence of a constitutionally protected substantive right to a healthy environment, it is important to recognize the interdependence of the environment and human rights. Without a "safe, clean, healthy and sustainable environment," it is impossible to fully enjoy a vast range of human rights, including rights to life, health, food, and water, yet in order to protect the environment, it is vital to exercise human rights, including rights to information, freedom of expression and association, participation, and remedy.[87] The responsibility of proponents and consultants to respect human rights is essential for environmental protection, and

---

80  2020 SCC 5 at paras 113–14 and 128.

81  *Ibid* at para 115 [emphasis in original].

82  Organisation for Economic Co-operation and Development, *OECD Guidelines for Multinational Enterprises* (Paris: OECD Publishing, 2011).

83  International Finance Corporation, "Performance Standards on Environmental and Social Sustainability" (2012), online (pdf): www.ifc.org/wps/wcm/connect/24e6bfc3-5de3-444d-be9b-226188c95454/PS_English_2012_Full-Document.pdf?MOD=AJPERES&CVID=jkV-X6h.

84  Above note 5.

85  Sara L Seck, with Akinwumi Ogunranti, Stephanie Robinson & Claire Lingley, "Overarching Concept Memo: Business Responsibilities for Environmental Human Rights" (2020) UN Environment: Environmental Rights Initiative [unpublished].

86  See *Report of the Special Rapporteur (David Boyd) on the Issue of Human Rights Obligations Relating to the Enjoyment of a Safe, Clean, Healthy and Sustainable Environment*, HRC, 43rd Sess, UN Doc A/HRC/43/53 (2020).

87  Framework Principles, above note 5 at 7.

the state's duty to protect human rights from harmful non-state actor conduct extends to environmental human rights.

The most basic and enforceable duty of proponents and their consultants is the duty to respect human rights both substantively and procedurally in all phases of an assessment process, including post-assessment. For the consultant, this duty includes the following:

1) The prioritization of the rights of rights holders over the interest of contracting proponents
2) Awareness of and compliance with domestically and internationally recognized human rights
3) Prioritizing human rights when faced with conflicting requirements
4) Timely and transparent communication of prospective and actual human rights infringement to rights holders
5) Prevention and timely address of infringement
6) Obtaining consent when personal or collective proprietary and privacy rights are involved
7) Clearly identifying rights holders and engaging them meaningfully all through an assessment process, including the follow-up and monitoring phase
8) Rightly identifying, assessing, and advancing measures to prevent or mitigate adverse human rights impacts

All of these components comprise the obligation of proponents and their consultants to, at a minimum, do no harm to individual and collective human rights. Apart from the substantive and procedural implications of this duty, this is also a mindset that should actuate every type of assessment. Although a stand-alone guidance under the *IAA* specifically detailing the components and processes of HRIA could be useful, the human rights dimension of other factors (e.g., Indigenous governance; GBA+; social, economic, and health impacts; access to information) could be addressed through other regulations and guidance.

Ethical assessment is, fundamentally, an assessment rooted in respect for human rights. Respect for human rights is at the core of RBC.[88] Hence, we argue for the development and/or improvement of

---

88 See, for example, Global Affairs Canada, "Responsible Business Conduct Abroad," online: *Government of Canada* www.international.gc.ca/trade-agreements-accords-commerciaux/topics-domaines/other-autre/csr-rse.aspx?lang=eng. (RBC is about

*IAA* regulations and guidance through the incorporation or adaptation of RBC tools. Although such regulations and guidance are not in themselves explicit codes of conduct for proponents and their consultants, the responsibility to respect human rights embedded in them has the potential to effectively compel IA practice that is both responsible and centred on human rights. Another reason for incorporating RBC tools into *IAA* regulations and guidance is the relative familiarity of Canadian multinational companies with these tools as they are expected to adhere to various RBC standards in their operations abroad.[89] Some of these standards are now understood to apply within Canada. RBC tools can be used to improve the *IAA* regime, and the potential effect on the conduct of proponents and their consultants is considered below.

## C.  REGULATIONS AND GUIDANCE: IMPROVING THE *IAA* REGIME WITH RESPONSIBLE BUSINESS CONDUCT TOOLS

The idea of using HRIA as a mechanism through which Canadian extractive companies meet corporate social responsibility (CSR) and human rights standards was proposed as far back as 2005 by the Parliamentary Standing Committee on Foreign Affairs and International Trade.[90] This

---

"conduct that demonstrates respect for human rights and is consistent with applicable laws and internationally recognized standards.")

89   See Global Affairs Canada, *Doing Business the Canadian Way: A Strategy to Advance Corporate Social Responsibility in Canada's Extractive Sector Abroad* (2014), online (pdf): www.international.gc.ca/trade-agreements-accords-commerciaux/assets/pdfs/ Enhanced_CS_Strategy_ENG.pdf [GAC, "Revised CSR Strategy"]. See also Global Affairs Canada, "Canada's Enhanced Corporate Social Responsibility Strategy to Strengthen Canada's Extractive Sector Abroad," online: *Government of Canada* www.international.gc.ca/trade-agreements-accords-commerciaux/topics-domaines/ other-autre/csr-strat-rse.aspx?lang=eng.

90   "FAAE Committee Report" (2005) 38th Parl, 1st Sess, online: *House of Commons* www.ourcommons.ca/DocumentViewer/en/38-1/FAAE/report-14. (The committee recommended that incentives be put in place for Canadian mining companies to conduct their activities outside Canada responsibly: "Measures in this area must include making Canadian government support ... conditional on companies meeting clearly defined corporate social responsibility and human rights standards, particularly through the mechanism of human rights impact assessments.") See also Charis Kamphuis, "Building the Case for a Home-State Grievance Mechanism: Law Reform Strategies in the Canadian Resource Justice Movement" in Isabel Feichtner, Markus Krajewski & Ricarda Roesch, eds, *Human Rights in the Extractive Industries: Transparency, Participation, Resistance* (Switzerland: Springer, 2019) 455 at 485–86 (referring to various recommendations

led to the release of Canada's first CSR strategy in 2009 and a revised policy in 2014.[91] Both documents focus on ensuring that Canadian extractive companies abroad operate in an economically, socially, and environmentally sustainable manner.[92] The 2009 CSR strategy established the Office of the Extractive Sector CSR counsellor to "assist stakeholders in the resolution of CSR issues" and incorporated in the strategy the already existing office of the OECD National Contact Point, designed to promote the OECD Guidelines for Multinational Enterprises.[93] Although the CSR counsellor has now been replaced by the Canadian Ombudsperson for Responsible Enterprise, the focus on the overseas operation of Canadian companies remains.[94] The 2014 revised CSR strategy refers to the OECD guidelines and UNGPs as "two fundamental documents" to be promoted to Canadian companies.[95] The CSR implementation guide, however, lists over seventy CSR standards and tools, with thirteen of them described as "[e]ndorsed by the Government of Canada."[96]

Following the endorsement of the UNGPs in 2011, human rights were incorporated into the OECD guidelines. Contrary to Canada's exclusive focus on overseas operations, the OECD National Contact Point has now recognized that the OECD guidelines apply domestically.[97]

---

for the Canadian government to monitor the human rights impacts of Canadian companies abroad and require them to undertake HRIA of proposed projects).

91  For more on the history of CSR in Canada, see Sara Seck, "Climate Change, Corporate Social Responsibility, and the Extractive Industries" (2019) 31:3 *Journal of Environmental Law & Practice* 271 at 274–78.

92  See Global Affairs Canada, "Building the Canadian Advantage: A Corporate Social Responsibility (CSR) Strategy for the Canadian International Extractive Sector" (2009), online: *Government of Canada* www.international.gc.ca/trade-agreements-accords-commerciaux/topics-domaines/other-autre/csr-strat-rse-2009.aspx?lang=eng [GAC, "CSR Strategy"]; GAC, "Revised CSR Strategy," above note 89.

93  GAC, "CSR Strategy," above note 92; Organisation for Economic Co-operation and Development, above note 82.

94  See Office of the Canadian Ombudsperson for Responsible Enterprise, online: *Government of Canada* https://core-ombuds.canada.ca/core_ombuds-ocre_ombuds/index.aspx?lang=eng .

95  GAC, "Revised CSR Strategy," above note 89 at 6.

96  Industry Canada, *Corporate Social Responsibility: An Implementation Guide for Canadian Business* (2014) at 67–73, online (pdf): *Government of Canada* www.ic.gc.ca/eic/site/csr-rse.nsf/vwapj/CSRImplementationGuide.pdf/$file/CSRImplementationGuide.pdf.

97  See Global Affairs Canada, "Canada's National Contact Point's Final Statement—Seabridge Gold and the Southeast Alaska Conservation Council" (13 November 2017), online: *Government of Canada* www.international.gc.ca/trade-agreements-accords-commerciaux/ncp-pcn/final_stat-seabridge-comm_finale.aspx?lang=eng.

The UNGPs also apply to businesses "wherever they operate."[98] Hence, both proponents and their consultants, jointly and severally, have responsibilities under standards such as the OECD guidelines when planning, assessing, and implementing projects. Furthermore, the UNGPs recognize the duty of states to protect human rights.[99] This duty includes clearly setting out the expectation that all businesses respect human rights and providing guidance to businesses on "how to respect human rights throughout their operations."[100] A requirement for the consideration of human rights in the *IAA* is one way to make this expectation clear. In the absence of such a requirement, guidance and regulations under the *IAA* should be published under existing provisions. As already noted, the guidance and regulations would also serve the purpose of setting out standards for human rights that proponents and their consultants should adhere to in different contexts.

In Section B, we referred to Indigenous rights, GBA+, and the right of access to information to demonstrate opportunities for the consideration of human rights in the *IAA*, despite not being expressly provided for. No doubt, gaps remain. For example, although the Framework Principles require the protection of human rights defenders and the consideration of rights to freedom of expression and association, including peaceful assembly, as well as the right to housing and children's rights, there is no readily available provision under the *IAA* through which these rights are required to be considered.[101] In the absence of an express human rights provision, the new requirement to consider social impacts provides an opportunity for a comprehensive assessment of potential human rights impacts. Although social IA is considered distinct from HRIA, Vanclay has argued that human rights is one of social IA's core values and that social IA seeks to defend and uphold human rights.[102] Requiring the consideration of human rights impacts in Agency guidance further to section 22(1)(a) of the *IAA* could therefore go a long way towards integrating human rights into IA practices in Canada.

---

98  UNGPs, above note 1, principles 11 and 23.

99  *Ibid*, Principle 1.

100  *Ibid*, principles 2 and 3(d).

101  See Framework Principles, above note 5 at paras 10–11, 13, 21, and 45.

102  See Frank Vanclay, "International Principles for Social Impact Assessment" (2003) 21:1 *Impact Assessment and Project Appraisal* 5 at 9.

It is arguable that the Agency could require that a project's impact on human rights be considered under its omnibus authority in section 22(1)(t) of the *IAA*, albeit on a case-by-case basis. This is, however, discretionary. Short of an amendment, one of the most viable options for making the consideration of human rights impact under the *IAA* mandatory is through the power of the minister through regulations, to prescribe information that a proponent must provide in the planning phase (e.g., in its project description).[103] The current regulation, however, does not address human rights.[104] Although there is no regulation-making power under section 22 of the Act, the Agency uses guidance to clarify its expectations on the requirements of the Act.[105] Human rights have largely been left out of existing guidance under the *IAA*.[106]

Although RBC tools are diverse, cover issues ranging from Indigenous relations to water stewardship, and are designed by entities including international organizations, Indigenous governments, and industry associations, one of their primary objectives is, arguably, to assist businesses to fulfill their responsibility to respect human rights. Canadian businesses already have responsibilities under a range of sector- or place-specific RBC tools on subjects covered under the *IAA*. Rather than further proliferating guidance, common requirements in various RBC tools, per subject, could be condensed into *IAA* guidance. Table 20.1 shows some subject areas under the *IAA* and provides examples of existing RBC tools that could be used in designing *IAA* guidance and regulations. Although we have included tools in Table 20.1 to show the relevance of RBC tools to the *IAA*, further detailed analysis of these tools is needed to identify and analyze the best in class.

---

103  *IAA*, above note 11, ss 15(1) and 112(1)(a).
104  See the *Information and Management of Time Limits Regulations*, SOR/2019-283.
105  See *IAA*, above note 11, s 22.
106  For guidance current at the time of writing, see the "Practitioner's Guide," above note 61.

**TABLE 20.1 IAA AND RBC TOOLS**

| IAA Subject Area | RBC Tools |
| --- | --- |
| Indigenous Rights, knowledge, culture, and governance (ss 22(1)(c), (g), (l), (q), & (r)) | • Kluane First Nation, *Proponents Engagement Guide* (2012)<br>• Gitanyow Hereditary Chiefs, *Gitanyow Engagement Framework* (2013)<br>• Yukon Chamber of Mines, *Yukon First Nations Engagement and Consultation Tool* (2019) |
| Meaningful stakeholder engagement (*IAA*, ss 11, 27, and 99) | • OECD, *OECD Due Diligence Guidance for Meaningful Stakeholder Engagement in the Extractive Sector* (2017) |
| GBA+ (*IAA*, s 22(1)(s)) | • Prospectors & Developers Association of Canada, *Gender Diversity and Inclusion: A Guide for Explorers* (2019)<br>• Global Mining Guidelines Group, *Women in Mining: Steps, Strategies and Best Practices for Gender Diversity* (2014)<br>• Danish Institute for Human Rights, *Towards Gender-Responsive Implementation of Extractive Industries Projects* (2019) |
| Social, health, and economic impact (*IAA*, s 22(1)(a)) | • Mining Association of Canada, *TSM Protocols and Framework* (2019)<br>• UNICEF, *Children's Rights and Businesses Principles* (2012)<br>• OECD, *OECD Due Diligence Guidance for Responsible Business Conduct* (2018) |
| Right of access (*IAA*, s 104(2)) | • International Finance Corporation, *Access to Information Policy* (2012) |

Although linked to specific subject areas, RBC tools such as the *OECD Due Diligence Guidance for Responsible Business Conduct* and the *OECD Due Diligence Guidance for Meaningful Engagement in the Extractive Sector* touch on all the subject areas. The guidance on meaningful engagement, for example, includes annexes on engaging with Indigenous peoples, women, and workers and trade unions.[107] It requires, among other things, proper identification and distinguishing of stakeholders and rights holders, the involvement of stakeholders and rights holders

---

107 See Organization for Economic Co-operation and Development, *OECD Due Diligence Guidance for Meaningful Stakeholder Engagement in the Extractive Sector* (Paris: OECD Publishing, 2017) annexes B, C, & D.

in the implementation of findings, monitoring and follow-up, and external verification of engagement activities.[108] The extensive provisions of the OECD guidance would further advance the current *IAA* guidance on meaningful participation, which, among other things, fails to recognize rights holders and provides no guidelines for meaningful participation at the monitoring and follow-up phases. The extensive recommendations for corporate planning, management, and on-the-ground personnel in the OECD stakeholder engagement guidance would also go a long way in making clear how proponents and consultants should conduct themselves when engaging with rights holders and stakeholders.[109]

The right of access to information is another example of how RBC tools could improve the *IAA* regime. The International Finance Corporation's Access to Information Policy operates on the presumption in favour of disclosure absent a compelling reason not to disclose such information and considers whether the benefit of disclosure (e.g., for health, safety, and the environment) outweighs likely harm to specific parties.[110] The policy also allows for partial disclosure to balance public and private rights; permits delayed disclosure considering market, legal, or regulatory concerns; requires proponents to disclose information on risks and impacts directly to specific communities that will be affected; and mandates early disclosure and updates throughout the investment life cycle.[111] These requirements address some of the previously identified flaws of the *IAA*'s right of access to information provision.

The *IAA* provides opportunities to ensure that Canada complies with its duty to respect, protect, and fulfill human rights and for businesses to respect human rights by identifying, assessing, preventing, and addressing actual and potential human rights impacts. We have briefly discussed how this could be done under the Indigenous rights, GBA+, social impacts, and rights of access provisions of the *IAA*. There are, however, possible challenges. Within Canada, Wanvik notes that upon completion of IA processes, the perception of a possible bias in favour

---

108   *Ibid*, Annex A.

109   *Ibid* at 23–83.

110   See International Finance Corporation, *Access to Information Policy* (1 January 2012), online (pdf): www.ifc.org/wps/wcm/connect/6810c62b-2a5d-47f2-97ba-06193bba4e42/ AIP_English_2012.pdf?MOD=AJPERES&CVID=kiIXyKw.

111   *Ibid.*

of industry development is high.[112] HRIA (or HRDD) is, however, not a silver bullet for addressing such bias or the actual or potential risks posed by proponents and/or their consultants.[113] As suggested by Coumans, RBC guidance tools could, in fact, be captured by companies and used in a manner that may in the end be harmful.[114] In the context of Canadian companies operating abroad, Simons and Macklin proposed the establishment of an independent expert-led CSR agency as part of a comprehensive regulatory framework that would have the mandate of overseeing and assessing pre-investment HRIAs and monitoring post-investment conduct.[115] In lieu of the proposed CSR agency, the *IAA's* provision that a specialist federal authority in possession of expert information or knowledge with respect to a designated project make such information or knowledge available provides a window for leveraging the expertise of federal and provincial human rights commissions in the consideration of the human rights impacts of assessed projects.[116]

Other likely roadblocks include the scoping of the human rights to be considered in HRIAs and jurisdictional questions attending the consideration of human rights in IA processes. Although we cannot deal with these issues comprehensively here, we make a few general statements. The identification of "internationally recognized rights" is foundational to HRIA.[117] What constitutes internationally recognized rights is, however, not clear and settled.[118] Although *Nevsun* is generally laudable,

---

112 See Tarje I Wanvik, "Governance Transformed into Corporate Social Responsibility (CSR): New Governance Innovations in the Canadian Oil Sands" (2016) 3:2 *The Extractive Industries and Society* 517 at 524.

113 See, for example, Rajiv Maher, "Managerialism in Business and Rights: Lessons on the Social Impacts of a Collaborative Human Rights Impact Assessment of a Contested Mine in Chile" in Matthew Mullen et al, eds, *Navigating a New Era of Business and Human Rights* (open access project commissioned by Mahidol University and Article 30, 2019) 63 at 67; Catherine Coumans, "Do No Harm? Mining Industry Responses to the Responsibility to Respect Human Rights" (2017) 38:2 *Canadian Journal of Development Studies* 272 at 278.

114 *Ibid* at 285.

115 See Penelope Simons & Audrey Macklin, *The Governance Gap: Extractive Industries, Human Rights, and the Home State Advantage* (London, UK: Routledge, 2014) at 277 and 320–28.

116 *IAA*, above note 11, s 23.

117 Götzmann et al, above note 42 at 24.

118 Arguably, the rights, at a minimum, include those contained in the nine core international human rights treaties. See United Nations Human Rights, "The Core International Human Rights Instruments and Their Monitoring Bodies," online: *Office of the High Commissioner* www.ohchr.org/EN/ProfessionalInterest/Pages/CoreInstruments.aspx.

with regard to human rights norms, its emphasis on a particular sub-set of *jus cogens* customary international law is narrow. Nevertheless, it is crucial to appreciate that fundamental rights such as the rights to life, liberty, security, and equality, recognized in the Charter,[119] are more contingent than autonomous. The factors necessary for the enjoyment of these rights must necessarily be read as part of the rights. This is the approach taken in the Framework Principles, which state that a "safe, clean, healthy and sustainable environment is necessary for the full enjoyment of human rights including the right to life."[120] On the issue of jurisdictional constraints,[121] we note briefly that the validity of the exercise of human rights jurisdiction depends on whether such an exercise falls under an allocated head of power in the Constitution. This also applies to the consideration of human rights in IA.

## D. CONCLUSION

The rights of rights holders differ substantially from the interests of stakeholders that are the typical focus of Canadian IA processes. Integrating human rights into the IA context would not only help ensure consideration of rights that might otherwise be overlooked but also may impose enforceable obligations on proponents and their consultants as duty bearers. An expansive understanding of human rights must necessarily include a right to a clean, healthy, and sustainable environment. We do not consider the argument on whether an HRIA is best carried out alone or within a comprehensive IA.[122] Instead, we emphasize that beyond being a mode of IA, human rights are a requirement that must actuate all aspects of an IA process. Consultants play an integral role in IA processes. There are, however, no clear-cut, generally applicable, and binding obligations or ethical standards that govern these key players. As shown in this chapter, as duty bearers, IA proponents and their consultants are, at the very least, obligated to actively ensure that they do no harm.

---

119  Above note 35, ss 7 and 15(1).
120  Above note 5, Principle 2.
121  For a more extensive consideration of federal IA jurisdiction, see Chapter 5.
122  See Götzmann et al, above note 42 at 26–28.

# CHAPTER 21

# Science and Indigenous Knowledge as the Evidentiary Basis for Impact Assessment

*Martin Olszynski and Justina Ray*

## A.  INTRODUCTION

In this chapter, we consider the *Impact Assessment Act's (IAA)*[1] approach to science and Indigenous knowledge. We begin by setting out the roles that science and Indigenous knowledge play in establishing the evidentiary basis for impact assessment and decision making. We also consider the unsatisfactory manner in which science and Indigenous knowledge have been applied over the past four decades of Canadian impact assessment law and practice and some of the factors that have been identified as contributing to this state of affairs. Having set the stage, we then consider the specific provisions contained in the Act with respect to science and Indigenous knowledge. Regarding science, much was said by the Liberal government— supported by their appointed Expert Panel for the Review of Environmental Assessment Processes (Expert Panel), which led to the *IAA's* focus on the need for increased transparency and scientific rigour.[2] Although the *IAA* does reflect important gains on this front, including a new duty of scientific integrity, these alone are

---

1    SC 2019, c 28, s 1.

2    Expert Panel for the Review of Environmental Assessment Processes, *Building Common Ground: A New Vision for Impact Assessment in Canada* (Ottawa: Canadian Environmental Assessment Agency, 2017), online (pdf): *Government of Canada* www.canada.ca/content/dam/themes/environment/conservation/environmental-reviews/building-common-ground/building-common-ground.pdf [*Building Common Ground*].

unlikely to yield the transformative change envisioned by the Expert Panel. Many observers anticipated these changes, seeing them as key to improving confidence in decision making regarding development projects. The improvements with respect to Indigenous knowledge are more significant but similarly do not address all of the impediments to its meaningful use in impact assessment. We end by considering some of the steps that must be taken to improve the application of science and Indigenous knowledge under the *IAA* to best ensure a strong evidentiary basis for decision making.

## B. SCIENCE AND INDIGENOUS KNOWLEDGE IN IMPACT ASSESSMENT

### 1) The Roles of Science and Indigenous Knowledge

Broadly speaking, scientific information and Indigenous knowledge are critical foundations for any impact assessment, and deficiencies in their collection (e.g., baseline data) or creation (e.g., impact predictions) can have profound and cascading consequences throughout all four phases of assessment (planning, assessment, decision making, and monitoring). Science and scientific information in this context are more inclusive than those found in the natural sciences. Rather, they should be understood as "the body of knowledge resulting from experiments, systematic observations, statistical data collection and analysis, theory and modeling, and including information from a range of fields in the physical and biological sciences, social sciences, health sciences and engineering."[3] This broader definition is in line with the *IAA*'s expanded breadth, including not only biophysical but also social, health, and economic impacts.[4] The core scientific task of impact assessment has been

---

3   We have borrowed this definition from the Scientific Integrity Project at the University of British Columbia, "Statement of Principles for Sound Decision-Making in Canada," online (pdf): www.zoology.ubc.ca/~otto/SIP2015/documents/SIP_Statement_of_Principles.pdf. See also the definition adopted by the United Kingdom's Science Council: "Science is the pursuit and application of knowledge and understanding of the natural and social world following a systematic methodology based on evidence." See "Our Definition of Science," online: https://sciencecouncil.org/about-science/our-definition-of-science.

4   *IAA*, above note 1, s 2.

described as impact prediction,[5] akin to the conventional scientific method. As recently explained by Westwood et al,

> Conventionally, the scientific method includes identifying a hypothesis to be tested, including associated predictions and assumptions, making observations, and analyzing whether the observed results match the predictions. In the [impact assessment] context, hypothesis testing manifests through the predicted necessity or effectiveness of mitigation measures. For example, if … mitigation is prescribed, and the proponent deems a project to have negligible (that is, non-significant) residual impacts, it is because the mitigation is hypothesized to work in the manner predicted by the proponent. Equally relevant to hypothesis testing, in both a purely scientific and [impact assessment] context, are evaluations of data reliability (for example, accuracy, precision, independence, and efforts to reduce sampling biases), sample size, effect size vis-à-vis statistical significance, and statistical power. Scientific methods are also used to estimate the costs and consequences of negative environmental impacts on species, ecosystems, and communities, as well as the expected costs to humans.[6]

By virtue of their extensive and intimate contact with the local environment, Indigenous peoples possess detailed knowledge acquired and transmitted over lengthy periods of time that is both unique and essential to the place-based decision making that characterizes impact assessment and, in some circumstances, the sole source of information.[7] "Traditional knowledge," as it is also called, is prominent in legislation

---

5   Lorne Greig & Peter Duinker, "A Proposal for Further Strengthening Science in Environmental Impact Assessment in Canada" (2011) 29:2 *Impact Assessment Project Appraisal* 159.

6   Alana Westwood et al, "The Role of Science in Contemporary Canadian Environmental Decision Making: The Example of Environmental Assessment" (2019) 52:1 *UBC Law Review* 243 at 249.

7   See Mark G Stevenson, "Indigenous Knowledge in Environmental Assessment" (1996) 49:3 *Arctic* 278; Peter J Usher, "Traditional Ecological Knowledge in Environmental Assessment and Management" (2000) 53:2 *Arctic* 183; Annie L Booth & Norman W Skelton, "Improving First Nations' Participation in Environmental Assessment Processes: Recommendations from the Field" (2011) 29:1 *Impact Assessment and Project Appraisal* 49; Maria Tengö et al, "Connecting Diverse Knowledge Systems for Enhanced Ecosystem Governance: The Multiple Evidence Base Approach" (2014) 43 *Ambio* 579; Lauren E Eckert et al, "Indigenous Knowledge and Federal Environmental Assessments in Canada: Applying Past Lessons to the 2019 Impact Assessment Act" (2020) 5:1 *FACETS* 67.

and associated guidance governing all three northern impact review systems.[8] Within these regimes, Indigenous knowledge is generally considered to encompass the comprehensive knowledge base derived from the experience and traditions of Indigenous and local peoples over millennia through direct contact with the environment. This includes not only specialized, localized information concerning the environment and how it is used and managed (e.g., important cultural sites and traditional uses of land and resources) but also the value system in which such knowledge is held.[9] The *IAA*, as further discussed below, defines Indigenous knowledge simply—but also comprehensively—as the "Indigenous knowledge of the Indigenous peoples of Canada."[10]

Aspects of Indigenous knowledge can be quite compatible with science and readily combined. That being said, these are fundamentally different knowledge systems that arise from different world views and must be considered on their own terms with appropriate institutional frameworks.[11] Authentic inclusion of this kind of information requires the active participation of knowledge holders that goes beyond simply sharing information.[12] It must involve active engagement in the process

---

8   *Nunavut Planning and Project Assessment Act*, SC 2013, c 14, s 2, ss 73(1) (defining trad-
    itional knowledge), 103(3), 122(3), and 197(1); *Mackenzie Valley Resource Management Act*,
    SC 1998, c 25, ss 60.1, 115.1, 144.35, 146, and 150(a); *Yukon Environmental and Socio-eco-
    nomic Assessment Act*, SC 2003, c 7, ss 2(1) (defining traditional knowledge), 33, 39, 67,
    74, and 121.

9   Usher, above note 7 at 184, 186, 187, & 188; Julia Christensen & Miriam Grant, "How
    Political Change Paved the Way for Indigenous Knowledge: The Mackenzie Valley
    Resource Management Act" (2007) 60:2 *Arctic* 115.

10  *IAA*, above note 1, s 2. Although this chapter is primarily focused on Indigenous
    knowledge's evidentiary contribution to impact assessment, we acknowledge that this
    approach does not adequately capture this and many other considerations relevant
    to Indigenous participation in impact assessment processes, including the relevance
    of Indigenous jurisdictions and traditions as decision-making frameworks. See also
    Chapter 6.

11  Fikret Berkes, "Evolution of Co-management: Role of Knowledge Generation, Bridg-
    ing Organizations and Social Learning" (2009) 90:5 *Journal of Environmental Manage-
    ment* 1692; Janelle Marie Baker & Clinton N Westman, "Extracting Knowledge: Social
    Science, Environmental Impact Assessment, and Indigenous Consultation in the Oil
    Sands of Alberta, Canada" (2018) 5:1 *The Extractive Industries and Society* 144.

12  Eckert et al, above note 7 at 73, identified the "risk of extraction of knowledge" as a
    barrier to the meaningful inclusion of Indigenous knowledge into the federal environ-
    mental assessment process, and Baker & Westman, above note 11, wrote of "traditional
    knowledge extraction" as a "form of negative reciprocity. Once knowledge is extracted
    from Aboriginal peoples, it is refined and distilled to meet consultation requirements."

of determining how this information will be documented, interpreted, shared, and applied in the impact assessment process.[13] The manner by which these different knowledge systems are brought together is increasingly the focus of discussion and debate. This is not only because science and Indigenous knowledge are often simply not comparable and can occasionally provide contradictory insights but also because the natural tendency is for Indigenous knowledge to be subsumed into scientific findings and Western-style processes.[14] The process of bridging, defined as "maintaining the integrity of each knowledge system while creating settings for two-way exchange of understanding for mutual learning,"[15] in a type of knowledge exchange paradigm is the ideal. A multiple evidence-based approach was recently devised in the context of the global assessment work of the Intergovernmental Science-Policy Platform on Biodiversity and Ecosystem Services (IPBES)[16]. Individual knowledge systems are considered complementary, with each speaking for itself in its own context, in a manner that best ensures that one dominant knowledge system will not serve in the role of external validator:

> [I]t is essential to keep in mind that different knowledge systems have always cross-fertilized and benefitted from each other and have rarely developed in isolation. However, in the context of knowledge-policy processes ... where power inequities and epistemological differences between diverse knowledge systems are brought to the fore, it is important to differentiate among (a) integration of knowledge, (b) parallel

---

Usher, above note 7 at 192, noted that "[t]here is a risk that any knowledge, taken out of the context in which it was generated, can be misinterpreted or even deliberately misused."

13   Stevenson, above note 7 at 279; Usher, above note 7 at 189 and 192.

14   Eckert et al, above note 7. For a recent example of this tension, see *Makivik Corporation v Canada (Environment and Climate Change)*, 2019 FC 1297 at paras 181–96 (assessing whether the minister gave sufficient regard to Nunavik Inuit knowledge when making a decision regarding the total allowable take of polar bears). Of course, multiple scientific inquiries into the same phenomena also can—and do—often result in contradictory insights.

15   Kaitlyn Joanne Rathwell, Derek Armitage & Fikret Berkes, "Bridging Knowledge Systems to Enhance Governance of the Environmental Commons: A Typology of Settings" (2015) 9:2 *International Journal of the Commons* 851 at 853.

16   Viola Hakkarainen, Christopher B Anderson, Max Eriksson, Carena J van Riper, Andra Horcea-Milcu & Christopher M. Raymond, "Grounding IPBES Experts' Views on the Multiple Values of Nature in Epistemology, Knowledge and Collaborative Science" (2020) 105 *Environmental Science and Policy* 11 at 16–17.

approaches to developing synergies across knowledge systems, and (c) co-production of knowledge.[17]

Although science, scientific information, and Indigenous and other forms of knowledge do not and cannot dictate impact assessment decisions, there is broad cross-sectoral support for the notion that, in order to be perceived as credible, outcomes should be derived from a rigorous process that transparently considers available evidence and knowledge.[18]

## 2) A Brief History of Science and Indigenous Knowledge

It has been almost forty years since Canada first codified a formal impact assessment regime.[19] By that time, Canada already had considerable experience with impact assessment. This included what is still often regarded as a high watermark in assessment practice, Thomas Berger's inquiry into the original Mackenzie Valley Pipeline project that legitimized the inclusion of Indigenous knowledge.[20] As early as 1983, however, concerns were already being expressed about the application of science in assessment. More specifically, although impact assessment had evolved "into a fairly complicated sociopolitical phenomenon … the scientific requirements and implications of such highly developed administrative procedures have not received similar attention," and it risked "degenerat[ing] into an exercise in public relations and government lobbying."[21]

Three decades later, and notwithstanding subsequent changes to impact assessment law and policy, including the passage of the original *Canadian Environmental Assessment Act* in 1995 (*CEAA 1995*),[22] leading Canadian practitioners suggested that where the scientific basis of assessment was concerned, "implementation still lag[ged] significantly behind

17    Tengö et al, above note 7 at 580–82.
18    Aerin L Jacob et al, "Cross-sectoral Input for the Potential Role of Science in Canada's Environmental Assessment" (2017) 3:1 *FACETS* 512 at 516, 518, and 523.
19    *Environmental Assessment and Review Process Guidelines Order*, SOR/84-467.
20    Thomas R Berger, *Northern Frontier, Northern Homeland: The Report of the Mackenzie Valley Pipeline Inquiry* (Ottawa: Ministry of Supply and Services Canada, 1977), online: *Prince of Whales Northern Heritage Centre* www.pwnhc.ca/exhibitions/berger/documentation.
21    Gordon E Beanlands & Peter N Duinker, "An Ecological Framework for Environmental Impact Assessment in Canada" (Halifax: Institute for Resource and Environmental Studies, Dalhousie University & Federal Environmental Assessment Review Office, 1983) at 1–2.
22    SC 1992, c 37. The entry into force of the Act was delayed until 1995 to allow for key regulations to be developed and passed.

the ideal."[23] Most recently, Mackinnon et al concluded that assessment processes are still not succeeding in providing decision makers with critical knowledge of impacts to better ensure protection of important environmental values.[24] More broadly, although knowledge and understanding of the biophysical and social impacts of human development activities have been steadily advancing, scientific practice associated with impact assessment in particular has lagged well behind.[25] Problems include the following:

- insufficient scientific rigour in the studies, surveys, and predictions found in proponent impact statements[26]
- production of lengthy but superficial documentation[27]
- mitigation strategies based on insufficient experience[28]
- inadequate treatment of cumulative effects through piecemeal, project-based assessments and inadequate project scoping[29]
- failures to adequately characterize, communicate, and reduce key uncertainties[30]
- myriad weaknesses of post-approval monitoring and adaptive management that contribute to failures in fostering adequate learning[31]

---

23 Greig & Duinker, above note 5 at 159.

24 See, generally, Aaron J MacKinnon, Peter N Duinker & Tony R Walker, *The Application of Science in Environmental Impact Assessment* (London, UK: Routledge, 2018).

25 *Ibid.*

26 Beanland & Duinker, above note 21 at 41; Greig & Duinker, above note 5 at 159–60; C Clarke Murray et al, "The Insignificance of Thresholds in Environmental Impact Assessment: An Illustrative Case Study in Canada" (2018) 61:6 *Environmental Management* 1062; Mac A Campbell et al, "Quantifying the Impacts of Oil Sands Development on Wildlife: Perspectives from Impact Assessments" (2020) 128:2 *Environmental Reviews* 129.

27 Ray Hilborn & Carl J Walters, "Pitfalls of Environmental Baseline and Process Studies" (1981) 2:3 *Environmental Impact Assessment Review* 265; Mackinnon et al, above note 24.

28 See, for example, Rosemary-Claire Collard, Jessica Dempsey & Mollie Holmberg, "Extirpation Despite Regulation? Environmental Assessment and Caribou" (2020) 2:166 *Conservation Science and Practice* 1.

29 See, for example, Peter N Duinker & Lorne Greig, "The Impotence of Cumulative Effects Assessment in Canada: Ailments and Ideas for Redeployment" (2006) 37:2 *Environmental Management* 153.

30 Wanda Leung et al, "Disparate Perceptions About Uncertainty Consideration and Disclosure Practices in Environmental Assessment and Opportunities for Improvement" (2016) 57 *Environmental Impact Assessment Review* 89.

31 See, for example, Martin Olszynski, "Failed Experiments: An Empirical Assessment of Adaptive Management in Alberta's Energy Resources Sector" (2017) 50:3 *UBC Law Review* 657; Peter N Duinker & Lisa M Trevisan, "Adaptive Management: Progress and Prospects

Over roughly this same period, the legacy of tensions between Indigenous peoples and resource development on their traditional lands led to negotiations aimed at increasing Indigenous participation in resource decision making.[32] The specific practice of including and applying Indigenous, traditional, or local knowledge in impact assessment in Canada was kick-started by—and contributed to the success of—the aforementioned Berger Inquiry, which "set a precedent of consultation with local Aboriginal people," allowing for the knowledge and values of Indigenous residents to be effectively communicated to environmental decision makers.[33] Subsequently, the inclusion of Indigenous knowledge in impact assessment law and policy has been most evident in the context of modern land claims agreements, for example, project impact assessments undertaken by the Nunavut Impact Review Board and the Mackenzie Valley Environmental Impact Review Board. Absent the formal co-management regimes rooted in the comprehensive land claims of the north, that is, where historic treaties with First Nations have been "settled" for almost a century or remain unsettled, processes for bringing Indigenous knowledge into development and land use decision making have lagged much further behind.[34] Indeed, the consideration of Indigenous knowledge in impact assessment south of the 60th parallel

---

for Canadian Forests" in Vic Adamowicz et al, eds, *Towards Sustainable Management of the Boreal Forest: Emulating Nature, Minimizing Impacts and Supporting Communities* (Ottawa: NRC Press, 2003) 857. For similar problems in Australia, see Angus Morrison-Saunders, Bryan Jenkins and John Bailey, "Chapter 7: EIA Follow up and Adaptive Management" in Angus Morrison-Saunders & Jos Arts, eds, *Assessing Impact: Handbook of EIA and SEA Follow-up* (London, UK: Earthscan, 2004) at 326. See also Chapter 16.

32    Nicolas Houde, "The Six Faces of Traditional Ecological Knowledge: Challenges and Opportunities for Canadian Co-management Arrangements" (2007) 12:2 *Ecology and Society* 34.

33    Nigel Vidler & Elias Elhaimer, "Indigenous Traditional Knowledge in Canadian Federal Environmental Assessment" (Submission to the Expert Review Panel, 2016). See also Chapter 15.

34    Modern land claim agreements negotiated shared authority (and corresponding co-management regimes) between Indigenous and federal governments, in contrast to historic treaties (1701–1923): see David C Natcher et al, "Implications of Tenure Insecurity for Aboriginal Land Use in Canada" (2009) 68:3 *Human Organization* 245. In their review of environmental assessment processes in the Arctic, Noble and Hanna observed that through "various co-management boards and committees, [environmental assessment] in Canada's Arctic is arguably more integrated into regional resource development planning than it is in the country's southern jurisdictions": Bram Noble & Kevin Hanna, "Environmental Assessment in the Arctic: A Gap Analysis and Research Agenda" (2015) 68:3 *Arctic* 341 at 343.

has only become mandatory with the passage of the *IAA*, as further discussed in Section C.

As readers will know by now, the *IAA* is Canada's fourth assessment regime in as many decades, replacing the short-lived *Canadian Environmental Assessment Act, 2012 (CEAA 2012)*,[35] passed as part of omnibus budget legislation that sought to overhaul most of the federal environmental and regulatory regime. Rather than address what by then were well-understood deficiencies in relation to science and Indigenous knowledge, however, that legislation was essentially silent on these issues and represented a significant regression in Canadian impact assessment.[36] The subsequent election of Prime Minister Justin Trudeau and the Liberal Party of Canada in the fall of 2015 marked the beginning of a long and often contentious law reform process that culminated in the passage of Bill C-69 (which included the *IAA*). For the purposes of this chapter, the most significant aspects of this government-led reform process were promises of "more transparency and certainty that decisions will be based on robust science, evidence and Indigenous knowledge" as key aspects of the government's self-imposed mandate for law reform and the establishment of the Expert Panel referred to in the introduction to this chapter.[37] Following several months of public consultations, during which it heard from numerous scientists, practitioners, and experts, including Indigenous ones,[38] the Expert Panel produced its report. *Building Common Ground: A New Vision for Impact Assessment in Canada* placed significant emphasis on "science, facts and evidence" as essential underpinnings of a well-functioning impact assessment process and stressed that "the quality of science contributes to a trusted process and credible outcomes."[39] The Expert Panel made several important recommendations, which focused on new legislative requirements for science, the importance of considering

---

35    SC 2012, c 19, s 52.

36    Meinhard Doelle, "CEAA 2012: The End of Federal EA as We Know It?" (2012) 24:1 *Journal of Environmental Law & Practice* 1; Chris Turner, *The War on Science: Muzzled Scientists and Wilful Blindness in Stephen Harper's Canada* (Vancouver, BC: Greystone Books, 2013).

37    "A Proposed New Impact Assessment System," online: *Government of Canada* www.canada.ca/en/services/environment/conservation/assessments/environmental-reviews/environmental-assessment-processes.html.

38    Jacob et al, above note 18 at 517.

39    *Building Common Ground*, above note 2 at 4 and 41.

Indigenous and community-based knowledge, and provisions aimed at ensuring that evidence is unbiased.[40]

## 3)  Understanding Gaps and Weaknesses in Implementation

In order to assess the *IAA*'s efforts toward ameliorating the conditions under which science and Indigenous knowledge can meaningfully contribute to impact assessment and to recognize what more will be required, it is useful to understand not only the deficiencies but also the reasons for them. Here we briefly discuss three factors that have been identified in the literature: the nature of Canada's economy, the legacy of colonialism, and insufficient judicial oversight.

As a starting point, Canada's economy is relatively dependent on natural resources development.[41] This creates several tensions within impact assessment. The first is for government regulators and decision makers tasked with ensuring some basic level of environmental protection while at the same time promoting economic development and the royalties, employment, taxes, and other revenues associated with it.[42] In addition, the globalized nature of our economy means that proponents are constantly seeking to reduce regulatory burdens and uncertainty in order to attract investment.[43] The result is a long-standing tension "between needs for improvement and pressures for faster, easier and

---

40   *Ibid.*

41   "Natural resources contribute greatly to Canada's economy and society, directly and indirectly accounting for 1.82 million jobs (10% of all jobs) and 17% of Canada's nominal GDP in 2017. Many regional economies rely on natural resources, and supply chains for goods and services extend across the country" [citation omitted]: Council of Canadian Academies, *Greater than the Sum of Its Parts: Toward Integrated Natural Resource Management in Canada* (Ottawa: The Expert Panel on the State of Knowledge and Practice of Integrated Approaches to Natural Resource Management in Canada, 2019) at 14.

42   As noted over two decades ago by the Newfoundland and Labrador Court of Appeal, "governments themselves, even strongly pro-environment ones, are subject to many countervailing social and economic forces, sometimes legitimate and sometimes not. Their agendas are often influenced by non-environmental considerations": *Labrador Inuit Association v Newfoundland (Minister of Environment and Labour)*, [1997] 155 Nfld & PEIR 93 at para 11. For a discussion of these issues, see Eric Biber, "Too Many Things to Do: How to Deal with the Dysfunctions of Multiple-Goal Agencies" (2009) 33 *Harvard Environmental Law Review*.

43   Council of Canadian Academies, above note 41 at 14.

cheaper approvals."[44] Perhaps the most obvious recent manifestation of this dynamic was the introduction, first as part of *CEAA, 2012*, of time limits on assessment — notwithstanding evidence that proponents are responsible for the vast majority of delays.[45] Proponents' desire to reduce costs and uncertainty also creates a conflict of interest, or at least the appearance of one, for the consultants who are hired to prepare impact statements on their behalf.[46]

Development of Canada's natural resources is also inextricably tied to colonialism.[47] Initially, the federal government adopted policies intended to "divest itself of its legal and financial obligations to Aboriginal people and gain control over their land and resources."[48] Although recent decades have seen some progress, including constitutional protection for Aboriginal and treaty rights and the settlement of modern land claims,[49] there is still considerable work to be done, including acknowledging the value and legitimacy of Indigenous knowledge and world views.[50]

A final factor is insufficient judicial oversight. In contrast to their American counterparts, who long ago recognized that the judiciary plays an important role in ensuring that impact assessment laws "are not lost or misdirected in the vast hallways of the federal bureaucracy,"[51]

---

44 Robert B Gibson, Meinhard Doelle, & A John Sinclair, "Fulfilling the Promise: Basic Components of Next Generation Environmental Assessment" (2016) 29 *Journal of Environmental Law & Practice* 251 at 251; Beanlands & Duinker, above note 21 at 1–2.

45 Grant Bishop & Grant Sprague, "A Crisis of Our Own Making: Prospects for Major Natural Resource Projects in Canada" (2019) CD Howe Institute Commentary No 534 at 25 (see Figure 12 in particular), online (pdf): *CD Howe Institute* https://dev.cdhowe.org/sites/default/files/attachments/research_papers/mixed/Commentary_534.pdf.

46 *Building Common Ground*, above note 2 at 45. See also below note 75.

47 Eckert et al, above note 7 at 74.

48 Truth and Reconciliation Commission of Canada, *Honouring the Truth, Reconciling for the Future: Summary of the Final Report of the Truth and Reconciliation Commission of Canada* (2015) at 3, online (pdf): www.trc.ca/assets/pdf/Honouring_the_Truth_Reconciling_for_the_Future_July_23_2015.pdf.

49 In *R v Sparrow* [1990] 1 SCR 1075, the Supreme Court of Canada endorsed the notion that s 35 "calls for a just settlement for aboriginal peoples" (at 1106). See also Chapter 6.

50 Eckert et al, above note 7; Truth and Reconciliation Commission of Canada, above note 48.

51 *Calvert Cliffs' Coordinating Committee v United States Atomic Energy Commission*, 449 F (2d) 1109, District of Columbia Circuit, 1971 at 1111. The Supreme Court of the United States has held that the *National Environmental Policy Act*, 42 USC § 4321 (1970) [*NEPA*], requires agencies to take a "hard look" at the environmental impacts of their actions: *Robertson v Methow Valley Citizens Council*, 490 US 332 (1989).

Canadian courts have adopted an exceedingly deferential approach to judicial review in this context.[52] In *Ontario Power Generation Inc v Greenpeace Canada*, for example, the Federal Court of Appeal held that a review panel will only be found to have given insufficient consideration to an environmental effect "if it is demonstrated that [it] gave *no consideration at all*" to that effect.[53] In *Gitxaala Nation v Canada*,[54] the same court dismissed in one paragraph all of the challenges to the then National Energy Board's (now Canada Energy Regulator) assessment report for a pipeline project on the basis that ruling otherwise "would be to second-guess [the government's] appreciation of the facts, its choice of policy, its access to scientific expertise and its evaluation and weighing of competing public interest considerations."[55] In the absence of meaningful judicial scrutiny, it is unsurprising that deficient assessment practices have persisted.

## C. SCIENCE AND INDIGENOUS KNOWLEDGE IN THE *IAA*

A statute's language and architecture can be keys to establishing the role of science and Indigenous knowledge throughout the assessment process and in decision making, as well as the respective obligations of those responsible for the statute's implementation. For example, both the *Canadian Environmental Protection Act, 1999*[56] and the *Species at Risk Act (SARA)*[57] contain sections on science, emphasizing the importance of evidence and the role of uncertainty in decision making.[58] *SARA* explicitly distinguishes between various products of science, decisions, and roles that consider scientific information alone and those that include

---

52    See Jocelyn Stacey, "Environmental Law" in Martine Valois et al, eds, *The Federal Courts at Fifty: Equity, Droit, Admiralty* (Toronto: Irwin Law, forthcoming in 2021); Martin Olszynski & Meinhard Doelle, "Ontario Power Generation Inc. v Greenpeace Canada: Form over Substance Leads to a 'Low Threshold' for Federal Environmental Assessment" (22 September 2015), online: *ABLawg* https://ablawg.ca/2015/09/22/ontario-power-generation-inc-v-greenpeace-canada-form-over-substance-leads-to-a-low-threshold-for-federal-environmental-assessment.

53    2015 FCA 186 at para 130 [emphasis added] [*Ontario Power Generation*].

54    2016 FCA 187 [*Gitxaala*].

55    *Ibid* at para 157.

56    SC 1999, c 33; see Preamble, s 2(1)(i), and s 76.1.

57    SC 2002, c 29, see Preamble, ss 2(1), 15(2), and 38.

58    Westwood et al, above note 6 at 250–52.

socio-economic factors, providing a helpful focus to implementation.[59] Similarly, all three northern assessment regimes, the *Nunavut Planning and Project Assessment Act*, the *Mackenzie Valley Resource Management Act*, and the *Yukon Environmental and Socio-economic Assessment Act*,[60] explicitly refer to both science and traditional knowledge, mandating their consideration for various decisions.

It may surprise some readers, then, that neither *CEAA 1995* nor *CEAA 2012* contained any explicit references to the words "science" or "scientific information," whereas other terms, such as "knowledge," "information," and "expertise," were largely limited to describing the various parties involved in the process.[61] "Aboriginal traditional knowledge" was referred to, but only as a discretionary consideration.[62]

### 1) New References to Science and Indigenous Knowledge in the *IAA*

The *IAA* contains several new references to science or scientific information and Indigenous knowledge (Table 21.1). In many cases, science and scientific information are mentioned alongside Indigenous knowledge, but each receives a unique and more substantive treatment in two distinct provisions, further discussed below: a duty of scientific integrity (section 6(3)) and rules regarding the confidentiality and disclosure of Indigenous knowledge (section 119).

---

59 These distinctions have been instrumental in a number of court decisions over the past decade; see, for example, *Alberta Wilderness Association v Canada (Environment)*, 2009 FC 710.

60 Above note 8.

61 For example, federal authorities, interested parties, and members of a review panel were all described as having expert knowledge.

62 *CEAA, 2012*, above note 35, s 19(3).

**TABLE 21.1  SCIENCE AND INDIGENOUS KNOWLEDGE UNDER THE *IAA***

| Section | Text [emphasis added] |
| --- | --- |
| Preamble | Whereas the Government of Canada recognizes that impact assessments provide an effective means of integrating *scientific information* and Indigenous knowledge into decision-making processes |
| Definitions (s 2) | Indigenous knowledge means the Indigenous knowledge of the Indigenous peoples of Canada |
| Purpose (s 6(1)(j)) | (j)  to ensure that an impact assessment takes into account *scientific information, Indigenous knowledge and community knowledge* |
| Purpose (s 6(3)) | [Duty of *scientific integrity*, excerpted in Section C(2), below in this chapter] |
| Factors to be considered (s 22) | (g) *Indigenous knowledge* provided with respect to the designated project |
| Agency report (s 28) | (3.1)  Subject to section 119, the report must set out how the [Impact Assessment Agency of Canada (the Agency)], in determining the effects that are likely to be caused by the carrying out of the designated project, took into account and used any *Indigenous knowledge* provided with respect to the designated project |
| Substitutions (s 33) | (2.1)  [With respect to substituted impact assessments, the subsequent report must] set out how … in determining the effects that are likely to be caused by the carrying out of the designated project, took into account and used any *Indigenous knowledge* provided with respect to the designated project |
| Review panel duties (s 51(1)) | (ii.1)  subject to section 119, sets out how the review panel, in determining the effects that are likely to be caused by the carrying out of the designated project, took into account and used any *Indigenous knowledge* provided with respect to the designated project |
| Agency completion (s 59(3)) | (3)  Subject to section 119, the report must set out how the Agency, in determining the effects that are likely to be caused by the carrying out of the designated project, took into account and used any *Indigenous knowledge* provided with respect to the designated project |
| Projects on federal lands (s 84) | (b) *Indigenous knowledge* provided with respect to the project |

| Section | Text [emphasis added] |
| --- | --- |
| Regional and strategic assessments (s 97(2)) | (2) When conducting an assessment referred to in section 92, 93 or 95, the Agency or committee, as the case may be, must take into account any *scientific information and Indigenous knowledge*—including the knowledge of Indigenous women—provided with respect to the assessment |
| Canadian Impact Assessment Registry (s 105(2) & (3)) | (d) *any scientific information* that the Agency receives from a proponent or federal authority, or a *summary of the scientific information* and an indication of how that information may be obtained |
| Indigenous knowledge (s 119) | [Confidentiality, excerpted in Section C(3), below in this chapter] |
| Expert committee (s 57(1)) | The Agency must establish an expert committee to advise it on issues related to impact assessments and regional and strategic assessments, *including scientific*, environmental, health, social or economic issues. |

With respect to science, then, the *IAA*'s references acknowledge, for the first time, the kind of information that is considered and listed on the project registry and, consequently, bolster the case for paying some attention to the manner in which this information (i.e., scientific) is gathered, created, and analyzed. This is further supported by the inclusion of the duty of scientific integrity (discussed below), all of which suggests a greater commitment to scientific rigour in impact assessment in Canada, even if it still falls short of the expectations generated by the Expert Panel and the reform process more generally.

Missing from the legislation, however, are provisions that would ensure implementation of several other promised reforms, such as mechanisms for the transparent consideration and weighing of available evidence, independent peer review for issues marked by a high degree of uncertainty or of strong public concern, and increased online access to data related to monitoring, follow-up programs, adaptive management, compliance, and enforcement.[63] As discussed in Chapter 16, the *IAA* is essentially unchanged from its predecessors in not requiring the publication of complete records submitted to the Agency. In and of itself, then,

---

63   See, for example, "Better Rules to Protect Canada's Environment and Grow the Economy" (2018), online: *Government of Canada* www.canada.ca/content/dam/themes/environment/conservation/environmental-reviews/infographic-canadians-e.png.

the *IAA* fails to meet the standards of open access to information—an emerging trend in modern scientific practice to support transparency in decision making made in the public interest.[64] That being said, there is nothing in the legislation that prevents the Agency from striving toward an open science approach if it chooses to do so.

With respect to Indigenous knowledge, the *IAA*'s provisions do elevate its status in impact assessment from a discretionary consideration to a mandatory one, bringing the Act more in line with existing northern regimes. The *IAA*'s requirement for relevant authorities to explain how they took such knowledge into account, subject to the confidentiality provisions (further discussed below), coupled with provisions that should increase capacity for Indigenous participation in assessment, also responds to some long-standing obstacles to the meaningful use of Indigenous knowledge in impact assessment.[65]

## 2) A Duty of Scientific Integrity

An amendment to include a duty of scientific integrity, proposed by then-leader of the Green Party Elizabeth May, was passed unanimously by the Standing Committee for Environment and Sustainability prior to Bill C-69's third reading:

> The Government of Canada, the Minister, the Agency and federal authorities must, in the administration of this Act, exercise their powers in a manner that adheres to the principles of scientific integrity, honesty, objectivity, thoroughness and accuracy.[66]

In moving this amendment, Ms May cited several US examples of such a provision.[67] Under regulations promulgated for the *National*

---

64 Jacob et al, above note 18 at 515, 518, 522, & 523. Canada's chief science advisor recently published "Roadmap for Open Science" (February 2020), online: *Government of Canada* www.ic.gc.ca/eic/site/063.nsf/eng/h_97992.html#8, which acknowledges the importance of open science in ensuring accountability, among other benefits.

65 Eckert et al, above note 7 at 72 and 81. The six categories of obstacles identified are resource limitations, legal obstacles, historical obstacles, epistemological obstacles, political obstacles, and procedural obstacles, for a total of eighteen obstacles. Eckert et al suggested that the *IAA* is responsive to three of them.

66 *IAA*, above note 1, s 6(3).

67 House of Commons, Standing Committee on Environment and Sustainable Development, Evidence, 42-1, No 112 (9 May 2018) at 9–10 (Hon Elizabeth May), online: www.ourcommons.ca/DocumentViewer/en/42-1/ENVI/meeting-112/evidence.

*Environmental Policy Act,*[68] agencies must ensure "the professional integrity, including *scientific integrity,* of the discussions and analyses in environmental impact statements."[69] It will therefore be useful to consider how this provision has been interpreted by American courts. In *Fund for Animals v Mainella,* the US District Court for Massachusetts cited with approval earlier decisions that held that an agency must go "beyond mere assertions and indicate its basis for them" and "must explicate fully its course of inquiry, its analysis and its reasoning."[70] In *National Audubon Society v Department of Navy,* the US Court of Appeals held that this provision precluded the Navy from relying on "anecdotal evidence" with respect to environmental effects.[71] In *Idaho Sporting Congress v Thomas,* the same court interpreted these regulations as requiring "that the public receive the underlying environmental data from which a Forest Service expert derived her opinion."[72] Although obviously not binding, these and other cases should inform the federal government's approach to this duty, as well as that of Canadian courts when called upon to ensure its fulfillment. Along these lines, the judiciary's hands-off approach to substantive review, as exemplified by the *Ontario Power Generation* and *Gitxaala* decisions discussed in Section B(3), above in this chapter, appears to be no longer tenable.[73] Indeed, to the extent that the approach in *Ontario Power Generation* hinged upon "the absence of any specific stipulation [as to] the type and level of consideration ... required,"[74] section 6(3) appears to be a full legislative response.

*Hansard* also refers to recent media reports describing instances where environmental consultants had their analyses challenged and

---

68    *NEPA,* above note 51.

69    40 CFR § 1502.24 [emphasis added]. The provision goes on to state that agencies "shall identify any methodologies used and shall make explicit reference by footnote to the scientific and other sources relied upon for conclusions in the statement. An agency may place discussion of methodology in an appendix."

70    D Mass 2003, 283 F Supp (2d) 418 at 429.

71    (2005) 422 F (3d) 174 at 194.

72    (1997) 137 F (3d) 1146, USCA 9th Cir at para 10. See also Holly Doremus, "Scientific and Political Integrity in Environmental Policy" (2008) 86:7 *Texas Law Review* 1601.

73    The Supreme Court of Canada's recent decision in *Canada (Minister of Citizenship and Immigration) v Vavilov,* 2019 SCC 65, which updated the general framework to judicial review in Canada, has also been widely received as signalling more robust review of administrative action. The Court explicitly affirmed the "need to develop and strengthen a culture of justification in administrative decision making" in Canada (at para 2).

74    *Ontario Power Generation,* above note 53 at para 127.

even changed by the proponents who hired them.[75] Although this new duty does not directly apply to proponents and their consultants, these examples do shed some light on the "problem" that it is intended to address.[76] It must also be recalled that although proponents are responsible for preparing the impact statement that forms the basis for assessment,[77] the Government of Canada, the Agency, and federal authorities (including life-cycle regulators) are ultimately responsible for the assessment and drafting the assessment report and are subject to this duty.[78] The Agency is also tasked with providing direction to proponents and ensuring that initial project descriptions and impact statements are reviewed by those with appropriate expertise and that proponents adapt their plans and projects accordingly. Simply put, "subsection 6(3) can be expected to have indirect upward (in terms of

75    See, for example, Anne Casselman, "Who Is Watching B.C.'s Environmental Watch Dogs?" *BC Business* (14 July 2015), online: www.bcbusiness.ca/who-is-watching-bcs-environmental-watch-dogs; Jimmy Thompson, "We Spoke to Consultants Forced to Alter Their Work to Benefit Industry on How to Fix Canada's Broken Environmental Laws" *The Narwhal* (7 May 2018), online: https://thenarwhal.ca/we-spoke-consultants-forced-alter-their-work-benefit-industry-how-fix-canada-s-broken-environmental-laws.

76    *Interpretation Act*, RSC 1985, c I-21, s 12: "Every enactment is deemed remedial, and shall be given such fair, large and liberal construction and interpretation as best ensures the attainment of its objects."

77    Although this is not clear from the legislation, it is apparent from Agency guidance that refers to five phases of impact assessment: (1) planning; (2) impact statement; (3) impact assessment; (4) decision making; and (5) post decision. See Impact Assessment Agency of Canada, "Impact Assessment Process Overview," online: *Government of Canada* www.canada.ca/en/impact-assessment-agency/services/policy-guidance/impact-assessment-process-overview.html.

78    With respect to designated projects, relevant provisions include ss 13 (federal authorities' obligations in the planning phase), 14 (the Agency's summary of issues), 16 (the Agency's decision on assessment), 18 (notice of commencement), 22 (factors to be considered), 23 (federal authority's obligations during the assessment), 26 (information), 28 (the Agency's draft report), and 60–65 (decision making). For reasons that are not clear, s 6(3) does not explicitly refer to review panels but would apply to the minister's formulation of a review panel's terms of reference (s 42). One obvious way to discharge the duty in this context would be to include the same or a similar duty within the panel's terms of reference, as is often done with the precautionary principle (s 6(2)), which also does not refer to review panels and may explain the omission in s 6(3); see, for example, "Amended Agreement between the National Energy Board and the Minister of the Environment concerning the Joint Review of the Northern Gateway Pipeline Project" (3 August 2012) online: https://apps.cer-rec.gc.ca/REGDOCS/Item/View/843294: "6.3 The Panel will review the project in a careful and precautionary manner."

quality) effect on nongovernment actors participating in the impact assessment process."[79]

Finally, although broader in both scope and application, the Office of the Chief Science Advisor in Canada has also issued a model policy defining "scientific integrity" as "the condition resulting from adherence to concepts of transparency, openness, high quality work, avoidance of conflict of interest and ensuring high standards of impartiality and research ethics,"[80] which the Agency has adopted in its own tailored policy on scientific integrity.[81] Although separate initiatives, these policies may also inform the scope of section 6(3); indeed, Ms May cited a similar policy by the US Geological Survey in moving her amendment.[82]

### 3)   Indigenous Knowledge: Confidentiality and Disclosure

Although transparency is the ideal for scientific data and other information, it can be problematic when dealing with Indigenous knowledge. Following a systematic review of the literature examining obstacles to the meaningful inclusion of Indigenous knowledge in impact assessment, Eckert et al found that

> [e]ight papers (42%) cited the historical extraction of [Indigenous knowledge] ... by state governments or scientific researchers for its role in Indigenous hesitation to offer their knowledge in the context of EA processes.... Many examples of this extraction of knowledge exist (e.g., Nadasdy 1999; Agrawal 2002; Berkes 2012), and no [previous] legislated safeguards assure participants that knowledge contributed to the

79   Westwood et al, above note 6 at 281.

80   Office of the Chief Science Officer, "Model Policy on Scientific Integrity" (2018), online: *Government of Canada* www.ic.gc.ca/eic/site/052.nsf/eng/00010.html. The model policy "was created to assist departments and agencies with making good on the commitments made under the 2016 memorandum of agreement between Treasury Board and Professional Institute of the Public Service of Canada, and to support them in implementing related guidelines."

81   Impact Assessment Agency of Canada, "Agency Policy on Scientific Integrity" (2018), online: *Government of Canada* www.canada.ca/en/impact-assessment-agency/corporate/transparency/agency-policy-scientific-integrity.html.

82   Above note 66. See Department of Interior, US Geological Survey Policy on "scientific integrity," which requires employees to "communicate the results of scientific activities clearly, honestly, objectively, thoroughly, accurately, and in a timely manner": www2.usgs.gov/usgs-manual/500/500-25.html.

EA process will not be de-contextualized or misused in the hands of western scientists or decision-makers.[83]

Consequently, the *IAA* has specific provisions for dealing with this issue. Pursuant to section 119(1), any Indigenous knowledge that is provided to the minister, the Agency, a committee for regional and strategic assessments, or a review panel in confidence must not knowingly be disclosed without written consent. The only other exceptions are if such knowledge is publicly available, its disclosure "is necessary for the purposes of procedural fairness and natural justice or for use in legal proceedings," or the disclosure "is authorized in the prescribed circumstances" (see section 119(2)). Furthermore, before disclosing Indigenous knowledge for the purposes of procedural fairness and natural justice, the minister, the Agency, a committee, or a review panel must consult the person or entity who provided the Indigenous knowledge and the person to whom it is proposed to be disclosed about the scope of the proposed disclosure and potential conditions attached to it (section 119(3)). Section 119(4) requires the persons to whom such knowledge is disclosed to comply with such conditions.

In terms of the letter of the law, these provisions and the related ones requiring some explanation as to how Indigenous knowledge was taken into account bring the *IAA* into line with Canada's northern assessment regimes. However, in the absence of any formal co-management arrangements for impact assessment and natural resources, considerable efforts will be required to overcome the legacy of obstacles to bringing Indigenous knowledge to bear in impact assessment.[84] Although practitioners can and should learn as much as possible from experience with the northern regimes and tailor guidance accordingly,[85] that experience demonstrates that even "the most sincere and sustained efforts to bring [Indigenous knowledge] into their operations" cannot

---

83 Eckert et al, above note 7 at 73.

84 Eckert et al, above note 7.

85 See, for example, Mackenzie Valley Environmental Impact Review Board, *Guidelines for Incorporating Traditional Knowledge in Environmental Impact Assessment* (July 2005), online: http://reviewboard.ca/file/618/download?token=70Zz2Cx4; Nunavut Impact Review Board, "Inuit *Qaujimajatuqangit*," online: www.nirb.ca/inuit-qaujimajatuqangit.

overcome what are fundamentally ill-aligned governance processes and bureaucratic characteristics of Euro-Canadian systems.[86]

### 4)  Other Aspects Related to Science and Indigenous Knowledge

In addition to the above, some promising indications of enhanced review and advice by experts outside of the Agency are evident from the addition of the Technical Advisory Committee on Science and Knowledge[87] and guidance issued almost immediately after the law came into force on external technical reviews,[88] both of which are intended to provide advice to the Agency during implementation. The former is composed of "experts working in their personal capacity" convening regularly and providing non-project-specific advice related to the new impact assessment regime, including topics associated with Indigenous knowledge. The latter outlines the process for engagement with individual experts to "resolve major issues of concern" related to specific project assessments, which the Agency views "as a form of peer review."[89]

The ETR policy recognizes that science in the *IAA* is broader than the natural sciences and includes social sciences, engineering, and other technical topics. Indeed, it is quite possible that external reviews will be applied just as frequently to these other areas (e.g., economics) as to natural sciences issues, bearing in mind that there is less experience with them in the formal impact assessment context. It is also worth noting that selected experts must have no direct conflict of interest: at the very least, this would seem to require no current financial relationship with the project proponent. Finally, as noted above, the policy makes clear that whether or not ETR will be initiated is a matter of Agency or

---

86 Graham White, "Cultures in Collision: Traditional Knowledge and Euro-Canadian Governance Processes in Northern Land-Claim Boards" (2006) 59:4 *Arctic* 401 at 412.

87 *IAA*, above note 1, s 157(1); see also Impact Assessment Agency of Canada, "Technical Advisory Committee on Science and Knowledge," online: *Government of Canada* www.canada.ca/en/impact-assessment-agency/advisory/advisory-groups/technical-a dvisory-committee-science-knowledge.html.

88 Impact Assessment Agency of Canada, "External Technical Reviews," online: *Government of Canada* www.canada.ca/en/impact-assessment-agency/services/policy-guidance/external-technical-reviews.html.

89 *Ibid.*

review panel discretion; in contrast to regional and strategic assessments,[90] there is no mechanism for requesting such reviews.

Although not directly related to science or Indigenous knowledge, two of the *IAA*'s procedural innovations can be expected to have considerable bearing on their application in impact assessment: the new planning phase and legislated timelines, as discussed in Section D.

## D.  MOVING FORWARD

At the outset of this chapter, we noted the fundamentally important role that science and Indigenous knowledge play in impact assessment, but also the unsatisfactory manner in which both have been applied over four decades of Canadian impact assessment law and practice. We also discussed some of the factors that have been identified as contributing to this state of affairs. Although some of these, such as the resource-dependent nature of the Canadian economy, may be immutable (at least for the foreseeable future), others are not. In particular, the resulting tensions for government regulators and environmental consultants and the nature of impact assessment itself are all amenable to adjustment, as are at least some of the obstacles to the meaningful inclusion of Indigenous knowledge.

In our view, the *IAA* can be regarded as an important course correction on many of these fronts — one that must be further bolstered by strong guidance and learning from practice to realize true improvements. The new duty of ensuring scientific integrity, in particular, has the potential to act as an important bulwark against what are likely to be persistent calls for faster, easier, and cheaper assessments. Where science-based processes and information are concerned, these should be marked by objectivity, thoroughness, integrity, and honesty (as set out in section 6(3)). Similarly, the mandatory consideration of Indigenous knowledge, including a requirement to explain how it was considered and protections against its unintended extraction and misuse, is a welcome improvement to the prior status quo.

Concretely, the *IAA* should provide a platform for strengthening both the evidentiary basis of impact assessment and predictive science.

---

90   *IAA*, above note 1, s 97.

We conclude this chapter by suggesting what that could look like in each phase of assessment.

At the planning phase, the goal should be more rigorous study and survey design (e.g., with respect to baseline studies, traditional land use studies, surveys, and potential adaptive management initiatives), with the benefit of diverse expertise brought together at the ideation phases of project development. This phase is currently the most timeline-constrained part of the Act.[91] Scientists with relevant expertise, both independent and within government, should participate closely in the design of initial studies, the selection of valued ecosystem components, and the consideration of alternatives. Early and formal consultation and engagement with affected Indigenous peoples are also prerequisites to meaningful and efficient participation, including the selection of valued ecosystem components and the need for and design of traditional use studies. All of this will take time but is entirely consistent with the advice of scholars and practitioners to invest in early planning before other significant investments have been made and where alternatives can still be seriously considered.[92]

At the assessment phase, the goal should be incisive impact predictions capable of testing and demonstrably effective mitigation measures and strategies. Alternatively, there should be clear acknowledgements of uncertainties (especially where adaptive management is being contemplated), data gaps, and their implications for impact prediction, including degrees of confidence. This will require a considerably strengthened Agency that sets clear expectations for proponents (and their consultants) through robust and steady oversight and guidance tailored to the particular circumstances of each project. It will also require more collaborative, creative, and proactive engagement with external scientists in the review of impact assessment studies and mitigation measures.[93] Improvements in the scientific enterprise in impact assessment will rely on the establishment of collaborative research networks that are clearly linked to assessment practice:

---

91   *IAA*, above note 1, s 18(1) states that the Agency must, within 180 days after the day on which it posts a copy of the description of the designated project, provide the proponent of that project with a notice of commencement.

92   John Sinclair et al, "Implementing Next Generation Assessment: A Case Example of a Global Challenge" (2018) 72 *Environmental Impact Assessment Review* 166 at 172.

93   Greig & Duinker, above note 5 at 160–63.

> In this way, [environmental impact assessment] is understood as an ongoing, collaborative and focused approach to development design and environmental decision making, rather than a reactive, fragmented and descriptive approach to evaluating a single preferred development design…. The long-term management of environmental effects and the ongoing reduction of scientific uncertainty through monitoring are therefore considered to be a single integrated endeavour, requiring close collaboration between researchers and practitioners.[94]

At the decision-making phase, it will be important to transparently consider and weigh available evidence, including both scientific and Indigenous knowledge. For authentic and equitable consideration of Indigenous knowledge as a line of essential evidence intertwined with that of scientific knowledge, Eckert et al called for "extensive consideration of the assumptions, cultural biases, and power structures that have shaped western [impact assessment]—and an increased acceptance of the essential ways in which [Indigenous knowledge] and associated worldviews differ."[95]

At the post-decision phase, the goal should be effective monitoring requirements, follow-up programs, and adaptive management plans that enable prediction verification and foster learning in a transparent manner.[96] Although the *IAA* does not contain any legislated standards on this front (notwithstanding recommendations for such from the Expert Panel),[97] the minister should use her or his regulatory authority to develop monitoring standards and other guidelines where possible.[98]

As with most Canadian environmental laws, whether or not these improvements will materialize will largely depend on the formulation and implementation of regulations and policies (e.g., for external technical reviews), capacity funding amounts and allocations, and whether the necessary shifts in the culture and practice of impact assessment take place in what essentially remains a proponent-driven process. It

---

94   MacKinnon et al, above note 24 at 20.

95   Eckert et al, above note 7 at 79.

96   See Chapter 16.

97   *Building Common Ground*, above note 2 at 42–43.

98   Pursuant to *IAA*, above note 1, s 112(1)(b), the minister may make regulations "respecting the procedures, requirements and time periods relating to impact assessments, including the manner of designing a follow-up program."

will also depend on Canada's judiciary, who should recognize within the *IAA*'s provisions and architecture Parliament's desire that it no longer abdicate its unique function in "conditioning the ... ethos of public administration."[99]

---

99  SA de Smith, *Judicial Review of Administrative Action* (London and New York: Stevens/ Oceana, 1959) at 3. It should also be noted that the Standing Senate Committee on Energy, the Environment and Natural Resources proposed several privative clauses during its review of Bill C-69; see "Report of the Committee" (28 May 2019) (Chair: Rosa Galvez), online: *Senate of Canada* https://sencanada.ca/en/committees/ report/74834/42-1. But they all were ultimately rejected by Parliament.

# CHAPTER 22

# A Learning-Focused Analysis of Canada's *Impact Assessment Act*

*Alan P Diduck and A John Sinclair*

## A. INTRODUCTION

The opportunities for learning during an impact assessment (IA), and from one assessment to another, are well recognized in academic, practical, and policy circles.[1] Learning from the evidence presented during the course of an IA can help optimize decision making about approvals and conditions. As well, public and Indigenous participation programs can be structured to enable opportunities for learning among the people, groups, organizations, and governments that are involved. Such learning can help build common ground and legitimatize decisions that are based on common interests.

Learning through experience is essential for improving IA practice over time. Suitably structured follow-up can improve future planning and design, impact predictions, and mitigation measures. Similarly, ongoing or regular legislative reviews can assist in refining or transforming legal,

---

1    Heli Saarikoski, "Environmental Impact Assessment (EIA) as Collaborative Learning Process" (2000) 20 *Environmental Impact Assessment Review* 681; A John Sinclair, Alan P Diduck & Patricia J Fitzpatrick, "Conceptualizing Learning for Sustainability Through Environmental Assessment: Critical Reflections on 15 Years of Research" (2008) 28 *Environmental Impact Assessment Review* 415; Anna Johnston, *Federal Environmental Assessment Reform Summit Proceedings* (Vancouver, BC: West Coast Environmental Law, 2016); Fabia Bozzola Cruz, Fernanda Aparecida Veronez & Marcelo Montaño, "Evidence of Learning Processes in EIA Systems" (2018) 36:3 *Impact Assessment and Project Appraisal* 242.

policy, and administrative measures that implement an assessment regime. In short, learning from each other, from the successes and failures in an IA, and from one assessment to another can improve the capacity of IA actors and regimes to achieve sustainability and related public policy goals. If IA requirements are to be more than just hoops for proponents to jump through in order to gain project approval, assessment must be centred on learning. To achieve this, the potential for learning by all participants must be recognized throughout the assessment process, from the earliest preplanning phases through to the monitoring of effects and outcomes.

The purpose of this chapter is to analyze the learning potential presented by the *Impact Assessment Act (IAA)*.[2] We appraise the Act in search of provisions that enable or block opportunities for learning. We adopt a multilevel approach in that we examine opportunities for learning at multiple levels of social organization; that is, we employ varying social units of analysis, all of which are highly relevant in the context of IA. In particular, we examine opportunities for learning by people, communities of practice (small groups with shared interests and/or concerns), organizations, and governments. Given that communities of practice, organizations, and governments do not learn in the same sense that individuals do, we employ different conceptualizations and definitions of learning processes, each suitable to its particular social unit of analysis. Others have employed similar analytical approaches in IA studies.[3]

The principal aspects of the statute that we appraise deal with meaningful public participation, knowledge development (and, in particular, using multiple knowledge bases), follow-up programs, and continuous improvement (including legislative review and evolution). The appraisal relies on best practices identified in the literature and recommendations made by experts[4] during the development and review of the

---

2   SC 2019, c 28, s 1.

3   Thomas B Fischer et al, "Learning Through EC Directive Based SEA in Spatial Planning? Evidence from the Brunswick Region in Germany" (2009) 29:6 *Environmental Impact Assessment Review* 421; Luis E Sánchez & Ross Mitchell, "Conceptualizing Impact Assessment as a Learning Process" (2017) 62 *Environmental Impact Assessment Review* 195; Cruz et al, above note 1.

4   Expert Panel for the Review of Environmental Assessment Processes, *Building Common Ground: A New Vision for Impact Assessment in Canada* (Ottawa: Canadian Environmental Assessment Agency, 2017), online (pdf): *Government of Canada* www.canada.ca/

bill leading to the *IAA* (Bill C-69). We conclude with recommendations for practical ways to optimize the learning opportunities in the current legislation, as well as suggestions for amendments to enhance the learning potential going forward.

## B.  KEY TERMS AND CONCEPTS

Although we distinguish among four different social units of analysis and associated conceptions of learning, there are fundamental linkages and overlaps connecting the units and concepts, as described below.

### 1)  Learning by Individuals

With respect to learning by the wide array of individuals typically involved in an IA, we adopt a broad definition from the adult education literature. Learning by people, in particular adults, involves processes through which a person's knowledge, skills, beliefs, perspectives, or behaviours are changed as a result of experience.[5] Various theories have been developed to describe and explain these processes,[6] including transformative learning theory,[7] which has been applied in several IA studies.[8] For Mezirow, influential learning processes for adults include taking part in dialogue under what he called the "ideal conditions of learning." These include having accurate and complete information, being free from manipulation or control, and having opportunities to participate and to critically reflect upon presuppositions. Sinclair and Diduck operationalized the ideal conditions of learning for application as criteria in the appraisal of IA processes.[9]

---

content/dam/themes/environment/conservation/environmental-reviews/building-common-ground/building-common-ground.pdf [*Building Common Ground*].

5    Sharan B Merriam, Rosemary S Caffarella & Lisa M Baumgartner, *Learning in Adulthood: A Comprehensive Guide*, 3d ed (San Francisco, CA: John Wiley & Sons, 2007).

6    *Ibid.*

7    Jack Mezirow, *Transformative Dimensions of Adult Learning* (San Francisco, CA: Jossey-Bass, 1991); Jack Mezirow, *Learning as Transformation: Critical Perspectives on a Theory in Progress* (San Francisco, CA: Jossey-Bass, 2000).

8    Sinclair et al, above note 1; Sánchez & Mitchell, above note 3.

9    A John Sinclair & Alan P Diduck, "Public Involvement in EA in Canada: A Transformative Learning Perspective" (2001) 21:2 *Environmental Impact Assessment Review* 113.

## 2) Social Learning in Communities of Practice

Individual learning is the foundation for the social learning that occurs in communities of practice—groups of people with common concerns and/or interests who interact over a sustained period of time and thereby develop shared resources, practices, and understandings of both problems and solutions.[10] IAs often involve communities of practice such as coalitions of environmental activists and networks of resource management practitioners. Social learning has long been of interest in environmental governance research,[11] including in the field of IA.[12] Of note is the seminal work of Webler et al,[13] which revealed the extent to which carefully facilitated public participation programs can enable the development of shared understandings, interests, and norms among stakeholders. This study and others in the broader environmental governance literature echo Mezirow's ideal conditions of learning, revealing that influential social learning processes include bringing together differing perspectives, attending to power imbalances among participants, and creating trusting environments and opportunities for deliberation.[14]

---

10  Etienne Wenger-Trayner & Beverly Wenger-Trayner, "Learning in a Landscape of Practice: A Framework" in Etienne Wenger-Trayner et al, eds, *Learning in Landscapes of Practice: Boundaries, Identity, and Knowledgeability in Practice-Based Learning* (Heidelberg: Springer 2015) 13.

11  Andrea K Gerlak et al, "Learning Our Way Out of Environmental Policy Problems: A Review of the Scholarship" (2017) 51:3 *Policy Sciences* 335; Monika Suškevič et al, "Learning for Social-Ecological Change: A Qualitative Review of Outcomes Across Empirical Literature in Natural Resource Management" (2018) 61:7 *Journal of Environmental Planning and Management* 1085; Javier Gonzales-Iwanciw et al, "Learning in Multi-level Governance of Adaptation to Climate Change—A Literature Review" (2020) 63:5 *Journal of Environmental Planning and Management* 779.

12  Sánchez & Mitchell, above note 3.

13  Thomas Webler, Hans Kastenholz & Ortwin Renn, "Public Participation in Impact Assessment: A Social Learning Perspective" (1995) 15:5 *Environmental Impact Assessment Review* 443.

14  Ryan Bullock, Derek Armitage & Bruce Mitchell, "Shadow Networks, Social Learning, and Collaborating Through Crisis: Building Resilient Forest-Based Communities in Northern Ontario, Canada" in Bruce Evan Goldstein, ed, *Collaborative Resilience: Moving Through Crisis to Opportunity* (Cambridge, MA: MIT Press, 2012) 309; Georgina Cundill & Romina Rodela, "A Review of Assertions About the Processes and Outcomes of Social Learning in Natural Resource Management" (2012) 113 *Journal of Environmental Management* 7; Romina Rodela, "The Social Learning Discourse: Trends, Themes and Interdisciplinary Influences in Current Research" (2013) 25 *Environmental Science & Policy* 157.

### 3) Organizational Memory and Learning

Individual and social learning form the basis of organizational learning, but what sets the latter apart is the role played by organizational memory.[15] For our purposes, organizational learning involves processes through which aspects of organizational memory, such as routines, practices, procedures, plans, norms, and cultures, are created, changed, or removed. As with individual and social learning, organizational learning has received attention in IA research.[16] Studies have revealed, among other things, that organizational learning by stakeholders (such as proponents, interveners, and regulators) is influenced by cultural, strategic, and structural arrangements. Important arrangements include cross-functional communication, participative decision making, transformational leadership, cognitive diversity, and positive organizational support.

### 4) Government Learning

Policy change can, of course, be explained in numerous ways, with learning being only one of several potentially relevant analytical frameworks, along with models that place greater emphasis on power, conflict, and

---

15    Chris Argyris & Donald A Schön, *Organizational Learning: A Theory of Action Perspective* (Boston: Addison-Wesley, 1978); Chris Argyris & Donald A Schön, *Organizational Learning II: Theory, Method, and Practice* (Boston: Addison-Wesley, 1996); Barbara Levitt & James G March, "Organizational Learning" (1988) 14 *Annual Review of Sociology* 319; Fernando Olivera, "Memory Systems in Organizations: An Empirical Investigation of Mechanisms for Knowledge Collection, Storage and Access" (2000) 37:6 *Journal of Management Studies* 811.

16    Ernesto Sánchez-Triana & Leonard Ortolano, "Organizational Learning and Environmental Impact Assessment at Colombia's Cauca Valley Corporation" (2001) 21 *Environmental Impact Assessment Review* 223; Patricia J Fitzpatrick, "In It Together: Organizational Learning Through Participation in Environmental Assessment" (2006) 8:2 *Journal of Environmental Assessment Policy and Management* 157; Paola Gazzola et al, "Enhancing Environmental Appraisal Effectiveness: Towards an Understanding of Internal Context Conditions in Organisational Learning" (2011) 12:2 *Planning Theory & Practice* 183; Luis E Sánchez & Angus Morrison-Saunders, "Learning About Knowledge Management for Improving Environmental Impact Assessment in a Government Agency: The Western Australian Experience" (2011) 92:9 *Journal of Environmental Management* 2260; Megan Jones & Angus Morrison-Saunders, "Understanding the Long-Term Influence of EIA on Organisational Learning and Transformation" (2017) 64 *Environmental Impact Assessment Review* 131.

political dynamics.[17] Moreover, there are various conceptualizations and typologies of policy learning,[18] some of which have received attention in environmental policy and governance.[19] We adopted the concept of government learning because of its emphasis on *state organizations*, which matches well with the other analytical units we adopted in the chapter. Government learning is the process through which governments improve the effectiveness of their policies and programs.[20] Government learning has received little attention in the IA literature, although similar forms of policy learning have received consideration, such as Ruddy and Hilty's study of complementarity between two European Commission IA policies.[21]

## C.  SALIENT ASPECTS OF THE LEGISLATIVE REGIME

Our analysis focuses on selected features of the *IAA* most applicable to learning. These echo the features highlighted by the Expert Panel for the Review of Environmental Assessment Processes (Expert Panel) and the federal Multi-Interest Advisory Committee (MIAC): meaningful public participation, knowledge development (and using multiple knowledge bases), follow-up programs, and continuous improvement (including legislative review and evolution). Each of the social units of analysis and their related concepts of learning presented in the previous section are pertinent to each of the selected features of the regime examined here. However, to focus attention on the most important implications and

---

17　Wayne Parsons, *Public Policy: An Introduction to the Theory and Practice of Policy Analysis* (Aldershot, UK: Edward Elgar, 1995); Richard Common, "Organisational Learning in a Political Environment" (2004) 25:1 *Policy Studies* 35; John W Kingdon, *Agendas, Alternatives, and Public Policies* (Boston: Longman, 1995).

18　Colin J Bennett & Michael Howlett, "The Lessons of Learning: Reconciling Theories of Policy Learning and Policy Change" (1992) 25:3 *Policy Sciences* 275; Claire A Dunlop & Claudio M Radaelli, "Systematising Policy Learning: From Monolith to Dimensions" (2013) 61:3 *Political Studies* 599; Stéphane Moyson, Peter Scholten & Christopher M Weible, "Policy Learning and Policy Change: Theorizing Their Relations from Different Perspectives" (2017) 32:2 *Policy and Society* 161.

19　Andrea K Gerlak et al, "Learning Our Way Out of Environmental Policy Problems: A Review of the Scholarship" (2017) 51:3 *Policy Sciences* 335.

20　Lloyd Etheredge & James Short, "Thinking About Government Learning" (1983) 20:1 *Journal of Management Studies* 41; Bennett & Howlett, above note 18.

21　Thomas F Ruddy & Lorenz M Hilty, "Impact Assessment and Policy Learning in the European Commission" (2008) 28:2–3 *Environmental Impact Assessment Review* 90.

because of chapter-length restrictions, in each section we highlight the most relevant social units of analysis.

First, it is important to recognize that learning was a recurring theme in recommendations made by the Expert Panel and MIAC during the development and review of Bill C-69. For example, MIAC was of the view that a core purpose of IA should be "to enhance the capability, credibility and learning outcomes" of IA-related deliberations and decision making.[22] Similarly, the committee thought that public participation programs need to be "learning oriented" so as "to ensure outcomes for all participants, governments, and proponents."[23] For its part, the Expert Panel linked learning to effective and efficient participation and identified participation as a learning process.[24] It also established the importance of learning for quality assurance and underscored the importance of interactive learning processes as a part of follow-up and monitoring. Although the Panel did not make separate recommendations regarding learning, it did provide direction in the four areas mentioned above to ensure that learning was considered in the new law.

Despite its prominence in the lead-up to Bill C-69, learning was not included as an explicit purpose in the bill or stated as a purpose of the *IAA*. That being said, aspects of learning are implicitly recognized in several subclauses of the Purposes section. Section 6(1)(h) states that a purpose of the Act is to ensure opportunities for "meaningful public participation," 6(1)(j) covers taking into account multiple knowledge bases (scientific information, Indigenous knowledge, and community knowledge), and 6(1)(n) refers to encouraging improvements to IAs through the use of follow-up programs.

## 1)   Meaningful Public Participation

This section is particularly relevant to people and communities of practice. Opportunities for meaningful public participation that are appropriately designed and implemented can be excellent forums for both individual learning and social learning in communities of practice. What follows in this section is a brief analysis of the extent to which

---

22   Multi-Interest Advisory Committee, *Advice to the Expert Panel Reviewing Environmental Assessment Processes* (Ottawa: 2016) at 5 (on file with authors).

23   See Chapter 15.

24   *Building Common Ground*, above note 4.

the *IAA* and draft guidance material respecting meaningful public participation create or could create the context and process conditions that optimize individual and social learning. The analysis covers information management; opportunities for early, ongoing, and deliberative involvement; and participant funding. As described in Chapter 15, the legislation and draft guidance include features supportive of meaningful public participation as well as aspects that should be improved.

### a)  Information Management

Sections 104 and 105 of the Act require the Impact Assessment Agency of Canada (the Agency) to establish an online public registry, and the range of required contents is fairly comprehensive.[25] In addition, guidance documents establish that one of the Agency's overarching principles for participation under the Act is that it be transparent and that information be available and accessible on the public registry, subject to certain exceptions set out in the Act.[26] Furthermore, guidance materials indicate that the Agency may use social media in all phases of an assessment to help keep people informed and engaged. Overall, the legislative and guidance framework governing information management is generally in keeping with calls in the literature for accountability, transparency, and opportunities to easily review and comment on documents.[27] The framework creates potential for the establishment of an important condition for optimizing learning, namely access to accurate and complete information. With that said, the devil, of course, is in the details. How the registry is implemented (e.g., see the early glitches described in Chapter 15) and how the Agency exercises its discretion in implementing its guidance materials will determine the extent to which accurate and complete information is provided in a timely and effective manner. To make the best use of the registry for the purpose

---

25  See Chapter 19.

26  Impact Assessment Agency of Canada, "Practitioner's Guide to Federal Impact Assessments Under the Impact Assessment Act" (2019), online: Government of Canada www.canada.ca/en/impact-assessment-agency/services/policy-guidance/practitioners-guide-impact-assessment-act.html ["Practitioner's Guide"].

27  Lisa Friederike Odparlik, "Are Agencies Turning a Blind Eye to Public Access to Environmental Assessment Information?" (2015) 17:03 *Journal of Environmental Assessment and Policy Management* 1550028; M Bucci & Tamer El-Diraby, "The Functions of Knowledge Management Processes in Urban Impact Assessment: The Case of Ontario" (2018) 36:3 *Impact Assessment and Project Appraisal* 265.

of supporting learning, all information used in the assessment, along with all monitoring and follow-up information, should be accessible to anyone who is interested.

## b) Participant Funding

This feature is included because it is important not only for developing knowledge—the subject of Section C(2)—but also for creating opportunities for meaningful and effective participation.[28] Moreover, participant funding can support the enabling conditions for individual and social learning by reducing the power imbalances and associated risks of manipulation and control in IA deliberations. Consistent with recommendations from practitioners and in the academic literature,[29] section 75 of the Act requires the Agency to establish a participant funding program applicable in all phases of IA, as well as in regional and strategic assessments. Again, the details have not yet been worked out either in regulations[30] or guidance materials. Moving forward, it is clear that adequate and timely funding must be made available and clear procedures for accessing the funding must be established in order to optimize the potential participation and learning benefits of such programs. Inequity in capacity to test the accuracy of claims made by others can unfairly privilege the knowledge and values of economically and politically powerful participants. This would obviously subvert opportunities for learning and, perhaps more importantly, undermine the legitimacy of the IA process.

## c) Early, Ongoing, and Deliberative Involvement

The legislation and guidance materials are mixed with respect to how they support early, ongoing, and deliberative involvement. Establishment of the planning phase (sections 10 to 15) and requirements for meaningful participation (section 11) in that phase clearly support early involvement. It is also supported by the requirement in section 18(1)(b) for the Agency to develop plans for engagement and partnership with

---

28   *Building Common Ground*, above note 4.

29   Johnston, above note 1; A John Sinclair & Alan P Diduck, "Public Participation in Canadian Environmental Assessment: Enduring Challenges and Future Directions" in Kevin S Hanna, ed, *Environmental Impact Assessment: Practice and Participation* (Toronto: Oxford University Press, 2016) 65.

30   The authority to establish regulations respecting the participant funding program created under s 75 is found in s 112(1)(d).

Indigenous peoples and for public participation. These provisions create opportunities for participants to advocate for ongoing, diverse, and deliberative involvement free from manipulation or control, which optimize chances for individual learning and learning by communities of practice. Furthermore, such conditions not only enhance the potential for improving the efficacy of assessment processes, they can also help instigate more profound or deep-seated types of learning outcomes.[31] These types of outcomes can help decision makers break from deeply entrenched inequitable or unsustainable approaches. On the other hand, the Act and guidance material are not clear on when or how development of the participation plans mentioned in section 18 should occur and do not require the use of deliberative mechanisms, such as the nominal group technique, scenario workshops, and backcasting. The Act also places considerable emphasis on timelines, which could easily pose challenges to the establishment of legitimate mechanisms for ongoing involvement and the use of deliberative methods.[32] For example, section 18(1) provides 180 days for the development of participation plans, which, in some instances, could restrict opportunities

---

31    The literature on learning and IA is quite rich when it comes to frameworks, types, and specific examples of learning outcomes; see, for example, Sinclair et al, above note 1; Sánchez & Mitchell, above note 3; Jones & Morrison-Saunders, above note 16. An example of an influential framework that encompasses profound or deep-seated types of learning outcomes is "loop learning." Developed in the organizational development and management literatures (see, for example, Argyris & Schön, 1978, 1996, above note 15; Mark Easterby-Smith, Mary Crossan & Davide Nicolini, "Organizational Learning: Debates Past, Present and Future" (2000) 36 *Journal of Management Studies* 783–96), the framework has been widely adopted in the environmental governance literature, including in the realm of IA (see, for example, Graeme Hayward, Alan Paul Diduck & Bruce Mitchell, "Social Learning Outcomes in the Red River Floodway Environmental Assessment" (2007) 9 *Environmental Practice* 239–50; Cruz et al, above note 1). Single-loop learning is incremental and involves getting better at fulfilling existing purposes, but it does not include questioning underlying presuppositions. Double-loop learning is more profound in that it involves evaluating presuppositions, although it falls short of questioning the overarching value-normative framework. Triple-loop learning is transformational, or structural, as it involves interrogating formative values, beliefs, perspectives, and world views.

32    Mark S Reed et al, "A Theory of Participation: What Makes Stakeholder and Public Engagement in Environmental Management Work?" (2017) 26:Supp 1 *Restoration Ecology* 7; Alan P Diduck, Maureen G Reed & Colleen George, "Participatory Approaches to Resource and Environmental Management" in Bruce Mitchell, ed, *Resource and Environmental Management in Canada: Addressing Conflict and Uncertainty*, 5th ed (Toronto: Oxford University Press, 2015) 142.

for public engagement in developing the plan itself. Finally, as described in Chapter 15, the guidance material indicates that public participation opportunities could prioritize directly affected people and communities at the expense of those who have broader but still legitimate interests.[33] This would run counter to involving diverse perspectives, which supports the conditions for individual and social learning and increases opportunities for profound or deep-seated outcomes, as explored in more depth in the next section.

## 2) Knowledge Development

This section is relevant to people and communities of practice but highlights the potential implications for organizational and government learning. The Expert Panel recognized that IA must place a heavy reliance on knowledge or evidence inputs of various kinds throughout almost all stages of the process.[34] The Panel viewed such inputs as being critical to learning and understanding the accuracy and full implications of the outcomes of any IA process. Furthermore, the Panel recognized that these inputs should come from a variety of sources, including traditional Indigenous and non-Indigenous sources and Western science. Relying on diverse knowledges in this manner is in keeping with insights being developed under what is being called the multiple evidence base approach to connecting knowledge systems. This approach, which emphasizes complementarity and equitable and transparent processes for connecting across knowledge systems, shows potential for generating new insights and innovations for environmental governance.[35] Moreover, as noted above, cross-functional communication and cognitive diversity are important cultural and strategic enablers of organizational learning.

The Act mandates the inclusion of scientific, Indigenous, and community knowledge in IA (e.g., Preamble, sections 6(1)(j) and 22(1)(g) and (m)) and provides for participant funding (section 75). In doing so,

---

33    "Practitioner's Guide," above note 26.

34    *Building Common Ground*, above note 4.

35    Maria Tengö et al, "Connecting Diverse Knowledge Systems for Enhanced Ecosystem Governance: The Multiple Evidence Base Approach" (2014) 43 *Ambio* 579; Maria Tengö et al, "Weaving Knowledge Systems in IPBES, CBD and Beyond—Lessons Learned for Sustainability" (2017) 26 *Current Opinion in Environmental Sustainability* 17.

it supports the conditions for organizational learning and increases opportunities for profound or deep-seated outcomes. Sharing, comparing, and respecting different knowledges (especially if combined with other features of meaningful participation) create opportunities and motivations for participants to interrogate the presuppositions of their goals and strategies, question formative values and beliefs, and generate insights respecting sustainability. If such insights were to be institutionalized by being adopted into the memories of organizations participating in IA, including government agencies, they could contribute to two of Canada's great historic projects: reconciliation with Indigenous peoples and achieving sustainable development. The adoption of such outcomes in this manner is not a sure thing, but the chances of it occurring are probably improved because the knowledge would have a certain legitimacy for having been created in formal IA processes and decisions.

### 3) Follow-Up

As above, this section is relevant to each of our social units of analysis, but here we emphasize individuals, communities of practice (such as IA practitioners and regulators), and governments. With respect to people and communities of practice, as discussed in Chapter 15, the follow-up provisions in the Act are a mixed bag when it comes to firmly establishing in post-approval processes opportunities for meaningful public participation and the associated forums for learning. On one hand, section 75 of the Act requires the Agency to provide participant funding for the design and implementation of follow-up programs, offering the potential learning benefits of such programs noted above. There are also reporting (section 28(3.2)) and public registry (section 105(2)(e)) requirements pertaining to follow-up that support some of the conditions for individual learning (e.g., having accurate and complete information). Additionally, section 156(2)(e) permits the Agency to establish "monitoring committees for matters related to the implementation of follow-up programs and adaptive management plans." On the other hand, the Act does not explicitly require public participation in these committees or other aspects of follow-up, nor does it recognize community-based monitoring, which, as noted in Chapter 15, can create conditions conducive to individual and social learning, such as bringing together differing perspectives and offering opportunities for deliberation.

With respect to communities of practice and governments, the Expert Panel recognized that the follow-up phase can help ensure that IA is an iterative learning process.[36] When done well, follow-up programs can help governments make adjustments in the terms and conditions of approval in any given IA. Furthermore, follow-up offers a critical opportunity for practitioners and governments to learn beyond the assessment process and thereby enhance the efficiency and effectiveness of assessments over time. By tracking and assessing the effectiveness of mitigation measures and the accuracy of impact predictions, it is possible to "learn from past successes and mistakes in order to improve future project design, predictions and decision-making."[37] Consistent with this view, as noted earlier, a purpose of the Act, as established in section 6(1)(n), is "to encourage improvements to impact assessments through the use of follow-up programs." The requirements related to follow-up are documented fully in Chapter 16, but these requirements do not explicitly mention learning. This is a missed opportunity to optimize ways to learn from one IA to another. Elsewhere, we and others have argued for the development of an accessible, well-organized, and searchable electronic database of IA case materials, encompassing impact predictions, follow-up results, administrative decisions and reasons, and associated judicial reviews, if any.[38] Such a database would be a valuable shared resource for communities of practice—IA practitioners, environmental activists, and regulatory officials—looking to improve their methods, assessments, and decisions. It would also be an authoritative source for evidence-based decision making by governments wanting to improve IA law and policy. To be sure, the Act requires establishment of a comprehensive registry, including an internet site and project files (sections 104 to 107), but it does not ensure that follow-up results and other key documents will be publicly available on a permanent basis. As well, public registries can be notoriously incomplete and difficult to access. Clear regulatory requirements for deposits of information and good guidance materials for searching will

---

36    *Building Common Ground*, above note 4.

37    *Ibid* at 66.

38    Sánchez & Morrison-Saunders, above note 16; A John Sinclair & Alan P Diduck, "Reconceptualizing Public Participation in Environmental Assessment as EA Civics" (2017) 62:1 *Environmental Impact Assessment Review* 174; *Building Common Ground*, above note 4.

no doubt be required to make the most effective use of the registry's capacity to support learning from one assessment to another. As mentioned in other chapters of this book, the Canadian government has also committed to creating an open science and data platform. It is possible that this platform could be used in the way we have described above specifically for IA, but the architecture and contents of the platform are still very much under discussion. Overall, with respect to follow-up and taking advantage of learning from experience over time, practice in Canada has been less than stellar. In the absence of clear legislative requirements, there is little reason to think that practice will improve in this regard.

### 4) Continuous Improvement (Including Legislative Review and Evolution)

This final section focuses on government learning. The Expert Panel recognized the need for government agencies to monitor application of IA processes for successes and limitations (including with respect to impact predictions, Indigenous and public engagement, sustainability trade-offs, and compliance and effects monitoring) in order to ensure learning and to modify IA processes as needed.[39] The Panel noted that any new assessment agency

> would require strong quality assurance programs, as well as audit functions covering both cost control and process. The role of the quality assurance program would be to assess the quality of IAs conducted by the [agency] and to ensure that continuous learning and improvement takes [sic] place within the organization. Cross-cutting issues would be studied, such as the accuracy of predictions of certain impacts, the effectiveness of mitigation measures and the implementation and effectiveness of follow-up programs. Program analyses would be publicly available.[40]

We agree wholeheartedly with this position, and we note that the Act contains provisions that are supportive of such government learning. Again, however, the provisions create a less than perfect legislative framework

---

39    *Ibid* at 53.
40    *Ibid.*

when it comes to learning. Section 6(1)(n), dealing with encouraging improvements to IAs through the use of follow-up programs, was noted earlier. Section 155(g) includes among the Agency's duties the promotion and monitoring of the quality of IAs conducted under the Act. However, there is no associated duty placed on the Agency to involve Canada's chief science advisor,[41] interested members of the public, or IA communities of practice and organizations in any consideration of the quality of assessments, nor is there a duty to report any findings.

Section 167 requires that a comprehensive review of the provisions and operations of the Act be initiated ten years after the Act comes into force by a committee of the Senate, the House of Commons, or both houses. This is a positive feature of the Act, and since review processes by parliamentary committees are normally public, this can enhance opportunities for inclusion of diverse values and knowledges and for broader learning at others levels of society. On the other hand, the highly partisan nature of parliamentary reviews can, of course, detract from the effectiveness of the review process and result in invidious compromises and poor decisions.

That being said, an inclusive review of federal assessment provisions was undertaken by the Canadian Environmental Assessment Agency during the legislated five-year review of the *Canadian Environmental Assessment Act* (*CEAA 1995*)[42] and included some positive features. The review incorporated the development of expert reports in focus areas in order to generate dialogue and discussion, as well as cross-Canada consultations.[43] Participants in that review also recognized the need to develop opportunities for government learning, particularly related to lessons resulting from consideration of the quality and accuracy of IA predictions that are made. This last point highlights a gap in the Act, namely, a lack of specific mechanisms and criteria for connecting the

---

41    The mandate of the chief science advisor includes providing advice to ensure that scientific analyses are considered when the government makes decisions and identifying ways to improve the science advisory function within the federal government (Office of the Chief Science Advisor, "Mandate" (2019), online: *Government of Canada* www.ic.gc.ca/eic/site/063.nsf/eng/h_97646.html).

42    SC 1992, c 37. The entry into force of the Act was delayed until 1995 to allow for key regulations to be developed and passed.

43    A John Sinclair & Patricia J Fitzpatrick, "Provisions for More Meaningful Public Participation Still Elusive in Proposed Canadian EA Bill" (2002) 20:3 *Impact Assessment and Project Appraisal* 161.

results of section 155(g) evaluations to the ten-year review mandated by section 167. Work will be needed in the coming years to fill this gap to ensure that learning through consideration of the quality of assessments helps guide revision of legislation and policy.

At a more fundamental level, one is left to question the efficacy of placing too much emphasis on the ten-year review if the goal is continuous improvement in IA practice, law, and policy. For this to occur, we obviously need more regular reviews and ongoing efforts to learn from every assessment. The challenge is to properly link post-decision processes with continuous improvement. To help address this challenge, we suggest that requirements for more frequent reviews and emphases on continuous improvement be adopted in regulations and guidance materials.

## D. IMPLICATIONS: IMPROVING THE LEARNING POTENTIAL IN THE *IAA*

Our consideration of selected features of the Act that are directly relevant to learning, that is, meaningful public participation, knowledge development (using multiple knowledge bases), follow-up programs, and continuous improvement (to IAs and the Act itself), indicates a patchy foundation for learning-oriented assessment. On the positive side, each of these features is recognized in section 6, which sets out the purposes of the Act. With regard to meaningful public participation, sections 104 and 105 of the Act and the guidance material are supportive of accountability, transparency, and opportunities for the public to review and comment on documents. Section 75 requires establishment of a participant funding program, which can help reduce power imbalances and associated risks of manipulation and control in IA deliberations. The provisions regarding the planning phase (sections 10 to 15) and meaningful participation (section 11) in that phase support early involvement, as does the requirement in section 18(1)(b) for the Agency to develop plans for engagement, partnerships, and participation. With respect to knowledge development, the Act mandates the inclusion of scientific, Indigenous, and community knowledge (sections 22(1)(g) and (m)) and, as noted above, provides for participant funding. Concerning follow-up, positive features include the provisions concerning participant funding, reporting (section 28(3.2)), the public registry (section

105(2)(e)), and monitoring committees (section 156(2)(e)). Respecting continuous improvement, section 155(g) requires the Agency to promote and monitor IA quality, and section 167 mandates a comprehensive review of the Act be done ten years after the law comes into force.

On the other hand, many of these legislative features fall short in some important way in creating optimal conditions for learning by people, IA communities of practice and organizations, and governments. Far too often the legislation is vague, contains important gaps, or lacks clear regulatory or policy guidance, as we established above. In fact, a number of these features were in place for years in earlier federal legislation, yet Canada failed to achieve significant progress toward a learning approach to IA. We therefore see the need for remedial efforts to each of the features noted above, as well as to related elements of IA covered elsewhere in this volume. Without such efforts, the Act will not fully establish learning as important to, and a critical outcome of, IAs as envisioned by the Expert Panel[44] and MIAC.[45]

First and foremost, learning needs to be included in section 6(1) as a purpose of the Act, and this new provision should explicitly recognize both learning *in* and *from* IA. At the very least, such recognition needs to be made in regulation and guidance material. Specifically, the legislative and guidance framework should recognize opportunities for learning among the array of people, groups, organizations, and governments involved in any given IA, as well as opportunities for learning from one IA to another for the purpose of improving assessment practice, the legal and policy regime, and administrative measures.

Second, since learning by people is at the heart of learning by communities of practice, organizations, and governments, reforms are needed to shore up the legislation and policy guidance pertaining to meaningful public participation (which, as noted above, provides excellent opportunities for individual learning). We made detailed recommendations about improving the provisions for meaningful public participation in Chapter 15, so we will not present them in full here. However, several key points bear repeating.

It is critical to clarify ways to implement "meaningful participation," as defined in the Act and elsewhere, and the related principles that have been outlined in guidance material. It will be especially important

---

44   *Building Common Ground*, above note 4.

45   MIAC, above note 22.

to recognize that timelines can impede meaningful participation and limit opportunities for learning. Furthermore, we see the need to go beyond policy guidance by implementing new regulatory provisions covering meaningful participation. Regulations are needed that establish roles in and responsibilities for participation programs (especially in the planning phase), create opportunities for deliberative participation (using the full range of methods in the participation toolbox, including forward-looking tools such as scenario building and visioning), and specify ways that alternative dispute resolution could be used. At this stage, it is still not even clear how the public participation plan for a project will be developed. What is clear is that there is very little time to develop such a plan, limiting opportunities for learning following the planning phase.

With respect to knowledge development, as noted earlier, sharing and using multiple knowledge bases not only helps create suitable conditions for learning (at multiple social levels) but also enhances opportunities for profound or deep-seated outcomes. However, the Act gives scant attention to the incorporation of community and Indigenous knowledge and scientific information into IA, beyond the recognition of the need to do so. Although section 22 does recognize that community and Indigenous knowledge must be taken into account, it is not clear how broadly *community* and *Indigenous* will be interpreted, especially when taken in combination with guidance material suggesting a bias toward including those directly affected.[46] Greater specificity with respect to the diversity of knowledge inputs is thus needed in regulations and policy guidance. This would not only help advance the potential learning functions of the Act but also would support other important provisions, such as the new Gender-based Analysis Plus (GBA+) requirement, as explored in Chapter 12.

Follow-up is not only conducive to learning in the context of a given IA, it also supports learning from one assessment to the next, as outlined above. Chapter 16 describes reforms needed to the Act when it comes to follow-up. For promoting learning within an IA, the most important of these reforms relate to ensuring that follow-up includes opportunities for meaningful public participation, which are detailed further in Chapter 15. The ability to track compliance and monitoring

---

46   See Chapter 15.

is also particularly important for creating learning opportunities. The most important reforms for supporting learning from one IA to the next—especially relevant to governments and IA communities of practice—pertain to establishment and maintenance of the database of IA case materials referred to earlier in the chapter. It would also be helpful for the Act to explicitly state, beyond what is said in section 6(1)(n), that a goal of follow-up is to harness the potential to learn across assessments. Such learning is something we have not been able to achieve in an effective manner despite years of IA experience at the federal level.

A learning approach also underpins effective actions to improve both the quality of IAs and the governing legal and policy regime. Supplementing section 6(1)(n), which deals with improvements to IAs through follow-up, section 155 requires the Agency to monitor the quality of IAs. In addition, as noted previously, section 167 requires a comprehensive legislative review be initiated ten years after the Act comes into force. In the first instance, a major gap is that there is no associated provision for the development of a quality assurance program that would institutionalize IA improvements, thereby ensuring some level of government learning. Second, neither are there specific mechanisms for linking government learning about IA improvements to regular modifications to law and policy (as was the case under the 2003 version of the *Canadian Environmental Assessment Act*[47]) or to the ten-year review. If such a quality assurance program included opportunities for meaningful participation of interested individuals and organizations and IA communities of practice, there would be a substantial opportunity for broad learning that could result in important adjustments to how the Act is implemented. At a minimum, regulations and policy guidance will be needed to ensure the implementation of quality assurance and that it includes feedback and improvement mechanisms so that mistakes are not repeated. This ongoing consideration of process will also allow for the development of new regulations and policy guidance to be linked to implementation experiences.

With respect to the ten-year review itself, we have little confidence that it will be learning oriented if it is not supported by a participatory quality assurance program such as the one noted above. It will also be necessary to identify key subject areas for deliberation well before the

---

47    *An Act to amend the Canadian Environmental Assessment Act*, SC 2003, c 9.

review starts. The review otherwise risks focusing on recent concerns rather than being a comprehensive and robust review of IA implementation over time and any consequent needed improvements. Ten years also seems to be a very long window. Previous reviews were carried out at five- and seven-year intervals, either of which seem more appropriate, especially in terms of the potential to document and act on any lessons learned over the period of implementation.

In conclusion, we feel that in many respects the Act represents a missed opportunity for creating a truly learning-oriented assessment regime, as was called for by both the Expert Panel[48] and MIAC.[49] Adopting such an approach would have put Canada at the forefront of IA law and practice and would have increased our national capacity to make IA decisions that are consistent with the principles and objectives of sustainability.

---

48  *Building Common Ground*, above note 4.
49  MIAC, above note 22.

# PART III

# Overall Assessment of the *Impact Assessment Act*

# CHAPTER 23

# Entering the Next Generation of Impact Assessment in Canada

A John Sinclair and Meinhard Doelle

## A.  INTRODUCTION

Chapter 2 established a next-generation assessment framework that incorporated international learning, as well as key themes in Canadian deliberations surrounding the assessment law and policy reform process that led to the *Impact Assessment Act* (*IAA*).[1] The framework recognizes both global learning and Canadian considerations captured in fourteen components. As noted in previous chapters, a basic package of the components and various configurations of each were very much in play during the federal government's assessment reform discussions. In fact, the report of the Expert Panel for the Review of Environmental Assessment Processes (Expert Panel) reflects many of the components.[2]

Our purpose here is to consider each component in relation to the *IAA* evaluations made by the authors contributing to Part II of this book. We have taken their analysis and conclusions in developing our own assessment of what the *IAA* achieves and where further reform is needed. In addition to the work of the authors contributing to Part II,

---

1    SC 2019, c 28, s 1.

2    Expert Panel for the Review of Environmental Assessment Processes, *Building Common Ground: A New Vision for Impact Assessment in Canada* (Ottawa: Canadian Environmental Assessment Agency, 2017), online (pdf): *Government of Canada* www.canada.ca/content/dam/themes/environment/conservation/environmental-reviews/building-common-ground/building-common-ground.pdf.

we have also reflected on our own analysis of the *IAA* in relation to the criteria as reflected in recent publications.[3]

## B. APPROACHING EACH OF THE NEXT-GENERATION COMPONENTS

### 1) Sustainability-Based Purpose, Scope, and Criteria for Evaluations and Decisions

As established in Chapter 9, the *IAA* includes provisions that focus assessments on sustainability outcomes, including a purpose statement: "to foster sustainability." The broadening of the scope of federal assessment beyond biophysical considerations to include consideration of social, cultural, health, and economic impacts is very significant in its own right. The *IAA* falls short, however, with respect to providing basic criteria and other direction on how to make decisions related to a project's implications for sustainability. The provisions related to the contribution to a sustainability test merely provide a promising basis for elaboration in policy and guidance.[4]

One important new consideration in relation to sustainability is the requirement to assess the intersections of sex, gender, and other identity factors in impact assessment (IA), known as Gender-based Analysis Plus (GBA+). As indicated in Chapter 12, Canada has been committed to applying gender-based analysis to federal policies, programs, and legislation since at least 1995, and the *IAA* is one avenue for fulfilling this commitment. An important outcome of this provision could be that it provides a foundation for the identification and evaluation of both equal and unequal effects more generally. However, the *IAA* provides little direction on implementation and guidance to this point and requires further refinement. It is critical to recognize that gender and diversity analysis will be most valuable when underpinned by intersectionality principles, paying attention to both the horizontal and vertical intersections of identity attributes, structures, institutions, and norms.

---

3   Robert B Gibson, "An Initial Evaluation of Canada's New Sustainability-Based Impact Assessment Act" (2020) 33:1 *Journal of Environmental Law & Practice* 1; Meinhard Doelle & Andrew John Sinclair, "The New IAA in Canada: From Revolutionary Thoughts to Reality" (2019) 79 *Environmental Impact Assessment Review*.

4   As established in Chapter 9.

The consideration of an undertaking's impact on climate is another important change in support of sustainability introduced in the *IAA* by way of a requirement to consider the extent to which a project contributes to or hinders the government's climate commitments. There is, however, little direction in the *IAA* about how climate should be considered at each phase of an assessment. Effective attention to greenhouse gas emission implications in project assessment is now possible under the Act, but the *IAA* and associated guidance so far provide little direction on how this will be achieved. As explored in Chapter 13, inadequate attention is also paid to how greenhouse gas emissions should factor into the key steps of the process, particularly triggering, information gathering, decision making, and follow-up.

The *IAA* also has provisions requiring that scientific information, Indigenous knowledge, and community knowledge be considered in assessments. Government agencies are also required to exercise their powers in a manner that adheres to the principles of scientific integrity, honesty, objectivity, thoroughness, and accuracy—all critical aspects when considering sustainability impacts and outcomes. This is part of the government commitment to improving the science and evidence basis for decisions, with noted improvements related to Indigenous knowledge, as outlined in Chapter 21. This chapter also reveals, however, that the *IAA* has not established a platform for strengthening the scientific basis of assessments and that some essential required elements for rigorous scientific and knowledge-based IAs are absent. These include targeted evidence gathering, robust designs with testable predictions, and recognition of uncertainty and risk.

## 2)  Application in Integrated, Tiered Assessments Covering All Potentially Significant Undertakings with Federal Jurisdiction or Involvement at the Regional, Strategic, and Project Levels

Application of the *IAA* is directed principally by the *Physical Activities Regulations*[5]—the Project List. As concluded in Chapter 7, the *IAA* has narrow triggering provisions and a diminished project list compared to its predecessors. This means that many major, environmentally harmful, and sustainability-blocking projects with implications for matters of federal interest are not likely to be assessed. Compounding this, the minister of environment and climate change has to date been hesitant to exercise his discretion to designate for assessment any projects not on the Project List. One such designation has occurred now with the Vista mine assessment, but this decision is being challenged in court.[5] Not using ministerial discretion to designate means, for example, that numerous proposed projects with high greenhouse gas emissions (e.g., in situ oil sands projects and cement plants) are not, and likely will not be, assessed under the *IAA*. Petitioning the minister for such designations also requires a significant amount of time and effort—yet another drain on resources.

In addition to project assessments, the *IAA* does provide for regional and strategic assessments, as discussed further below. However, it falls short on provisions for triggering such assessments or for integrative links among the tiers of assessment, despite many interventions outlining the importance of both.[6] Linkages noted are limited to a requirement that project assessments take into account any associated regional and/or strategic assessments while remaining silent on provisions related to the nature and authority of products from these broader assessments and their potential use in future project planning and assessments.

The *IAA* also recognizes the need to assess projects under federal jurisdiction but to be undertaken outside Canada. The Act's process provisions for assessment of such projects are weak, but many projects could be covered, and the coverage does not rely on a list approach. As outlined in Chapter 18, "triggers" are used to establish what needs to be assessed. This includes, for example, decisions by a federal authority, such as issuing a permit, projects on federal lands, and federal financial assistance. Unfortunately, the opportunity to reintroduce a comprehensive, flexible, project-appropriate approach to triggering that could, once tested, provide a model for application of assessment requirements to projects under federal regulatory authority was missed. Also, the *IAA* only requires an abbreviated approach to undertaking triggered assessments that does not reflect the assessment provisions in the *IAA*. This limits, for example, the opportunity for public participation and focused attention on projects with serious sustainability implications.

---

5    *Coalspur Mines (Operations) Ltd v Canada (Minister of Environment and Climate Change)* Ottawa T-1008-20 (FC) (Notice of Application); Ainslie Cruickshank, "Alberta Coal Miner Launches Legal Challenge Against Federal Environmental Assessment" *The Narwhal* (2 September 2020), online: https://thenarwhal.ca/coalspur-vista-coal-mine-alberta-legal-challenge-launched.

6    See chapters 11 and 17.

## 3) Interjurisdictional Cooperation, Collaboration, and Upward Harmonization

To avoid inefficiencies and other negative implications of multiple assessments being carried out by different affected jurisdictions, there were calls during the reform process for a cooperative approach to multi-jurisdictional assessment. As Chapter 8 outlines, governments in Canada have adopted different methods of working together over the last thirty years of experience, including harmonization (coordination), substitution, delegation, and equivalency. Important steps forward in the *IAA* relate to the recognition of cooperation as the desired means for moving forward and the removal of the provisions for equivalency contained in the *Canadian Environmental Assessment Act, 2012 (CEAA 2012).*[7]

To facilitate cooperation, the *IAA* contains provisions allowing four pathways: coordinated assessment, substitution, joint panel review, and delegation. Despite the attention cooperation received during the law reform process and the identification of these four pathways, the *IAA* has not provided definitive direction on multi-jurisdictional assessment. As a result, uncertainty of process remains. Although the Act espouses cooperation, there are no provisions to encourage it. In fact, most of the *IAA* wording deals with implementing substitution and delegation, approaches that actually promote the avoidance of cooperation. The Act is also silent on a key aspect of cooperation noted by the Expert Panel and in the literature: that all cooperation should adopt the highest possible assessment standard among the jurisdictions involved.

## 4) Respect for Indigenous Rights, Facilitation of Reconciliation, and Encouragement of Co-governance with Indigenous Governing Bodies

There are important but tentative steps in the *IAA* with respect to Indigenous rights and communities, commitments that are considerably stronger than what was present in earlier legislation. The recognition of the need to implement the *United Nations Declaration on the Rights of Indigenous Peoples (UNDRIP)*[8] means that the Act may have a role to play in recognizing rights and implementing federal

---

7    SC 2012, c 19, s 52.

8    GA Res 61/295, UNGAOR, 61st Sess, UN Doc A/RES/61/295 (13 September 2007).

*UNDRIP* requirements through IA. It has also created high expectations among Indigenous groups that their own laws and institutions can have authoritative roles in regional planning and, if required, project planning as established in Chapter 6. Indigenous-led assessments can provide a way forward that respects Indigenous laws and traditional processes as well as international legal standards. The provisions for the establishment of an Indigenous advisory committee lend some hope to the prospect of effectively using the considerable discretion in the Act from the planning phase through to follow-up to implement *UNDRIP*. More work will also be needed to ensure that commitments to reconciliation that can be addressed through IA are met.

### 5) Streams for Assessments of Projects and Regional and Strategic Undertakings of Different Character and Significance

The *IAA* offers only two process streams for designated projects: a standard assessment undertaken by the Impact Assessment Agency of Canada (the Agency) and panel reviews. Selection between the streams is decided on a case-by-case basis. Both streams are fairly flexible in terms of process and scope of consideration, except for strict legislated timelines, which threaten to undermine the effectiveness and fairness of assessments for larger projects and complex assessments. Missing from these two process options is adequate legislated direction on the range of options that can be used in appropriate circumstances to make the IA process fit the project and affected communities. These include the use of alternative dispute resolution tools; efforts to develop consensus among affected parties; and other innovative forms of public engagement, information gathering, analysis, and decision making.

The *IAA* provides no defined processes, much less process options or streams, for regional and strategic assessments. In fact, the wording in available policy guidance may add confusion because regional assessments are called "studies," leading some authorities to refer to "regional studies."[9] The *IAA* only spells out in very general terms the procedures that may be required for strategic and regional assessments.[10] The lack of any legislative provisions on when to carry out these types of

---

9  See Chapter 11.

10  See chapters 11 and 17.

assessments and silence on the basic design of the process are clear weaknesses. The Act is also silent on whether the broad scope of factors for consideration in project assessment apply as well to regional and strategic assessments.

## 6)  Meaningful Public Participation

The federal government set high expectations for building public trust in assessment processes through more meaningful participation. The government noted that sixteen sections of the *IAA* relate to meaningful participation.[11] Despite these provisions, Chapter 15 concludes that decisions about implementing meaningful participation are left to the discretion of the Agency and the minister, missing an important opportunity to establish specific expectations regarding participatory processes.

The one new provision that has significant potential, depending on how it is implemented in the future, relates to the planning phase and requirements to consult the public during this phase and to develop a public participation plan. Unfortunately, early practice and guidance do not indicate that the benefits some expected from this phase, such as greater opportunity to influence early project planning and develop meaningful approaches to participation, are emerging. Instead, short timelines have resulted in the Agency seeking input through passive means, such as the internet. Chapter 15 also establishes that although other provisions of the *IAA*, such as notice, access to information, and participant funding, are welcome, these have been an important part of federal environmental assessment in Canada for many years.

In the final analysis, concrete requirements to ensure that public participation will be meaningful are absent, and the emphasis that the *IAA* places on strict timelines may subvert attempts to implement more meaningful participation. The history of assessment in Canada has also shown that policy guidance has failed as a tool for implementing meaningful participation.

---

11    Impact Assessment Agency of Canada, "Interim Framework: Public Participation Under the Impact Assessment Act," online: *Government of Canada* www.canada.ca/en/ impact-assessment-agency/services/policy-guidance/practitioners-guide-impact-assessment-act/framework-public-participation.html.

### 7)  Full-Process Learning

The importance of taking a learning-centred approach to the design of IA processes is outlined in Chapter 22, which also notes support for this from the Expert Panel, the Multi-Interest Advisory Committee, and other participants to the IA reform process, as well as the literature. All of these establish that a focus on learning and a significantly enhanced post-approval process are needed to ensure that learning is embedded in assessment practice. The authors noted that although there are supportive provisions in the *IAA*, such as those for meaningful participation, knowledge exchange, and follow-up, these provide only a patchy foundation for learning-oriented assessment. Too often the legislation is vague, contains important gaps, or is not backed by clear regulatory or policy guidance. As a result, the conclusions drawn in Chapter 15 indicate that the Act represents a missed opportunity for creating a truly learning-oriented assessment regime that would have put Canada at the forefront of IA law and practice. It would also have increased our national capacity to make IA decisions consistent with the principles and objectives of sustainability.

### 8)  Early Process Initiation

The planning phase is an important new addition to federal assessment processes, as pointed out in various chapters in Part II. In fact, during initial development of the Act, this phase was called the "early planning phase." However, "early" was later dropped, and the length of time to carry out an assessment was reduced from the time allowed under *CEAA 2012*. Together these steps may signal how early and effective the planning phase will actually be. A number of concerns have been raised related to this phase in the chapters cited above, particularly in relation to the number of activities that need to be completed in a very short time frame (180 days), ranging from jurisdictional cooperation to developing involvement plans and introducing the project concept. In addition, there are concerns about the need for a fairly advanced project description, which will likely limit serious consideration of alternatives and encourage proponents to trigger the process later rather than earlier. Chapter 15 also identifies concerns with how this phase is currently being implemented from the perspective of public participants.

## 9) Rigorous and Credible Impact Assessments Focused on Cumulative and Interactive Effects and Uncertainties

The *IAA* has two provisions related directly to cumulative effects. Unfortunately, as outlined in Chapter 11, these fall short of meeting standards set forth in the literature and offer no improvement over its predecessor legislation. There is no direction provided as to the scope of what may be included when assessing cumulative effects (e.g., spatial, temporal, interactive), including how that scope is to be determined, and no consideration of "growth-inducing infrastructure," which one would expect to find in leading-edge assessment legislation. There is also no linkage made between cumulative effects and regional or strategic assessments. Yet the Expert Panel and others suggested this as an explicit reason for regional assessment, especially given the well-known challenges of trying to undertake an effective assessment of cumulative effects at the project level.

## 10) Comparative Evaluation of Reasonable Alternatives, Including the Null Option

Under the *IAA*, the consideration of alternatives must include the "no action alternative," as well as alternative means of carrying out a project. Given the need to inform the ultimate public interest determination, these should be understood from a societal rather than a private, proponent-driven perspective.[12] The basic approach under the *IAA* similarly suggests that the purpose and need for a project should be framed broadly and reflect societal purpose and need. If an approval tolerates some adverse environmental impacts and societal costs, the societal purpose and need must be clearly understood before a public interest determination can be made. Clarity is needed, however, on how appropriate alternatives are to be identified and compared and who will be involved in both processes, as well as to whether the consideration of alternatives is required in regional and strategic assessments. Without attention to these issues, the references to alternatives in the *IAA* are not likely to take us far beyond provisions contained in previous versions of the Act.

---

12   See Chapter 10.

### 11) Credible, Accountable, and Authoritative Decision Making for Assessed Undertakings, Policy Making, and Other Core Initiatives Under the Act

Guiding the exercise of discretion provided to the minister and the Agency with legislated criteria and accountability is central to the successful implementation of the *IAA* and the trust people place in the decisions taken through its application. Section 63 decisions, particularly the first factor—the extent to which a proposed project "contributes to sustainability"—and section 22(1), which lists specific sustainability factors to be considered, are critically important to decisions under the Act. As established in Chapter 14, although these factors for consideration must be applied and reported on, the word *criteria* is never used, nor is *trade-off*. Guidance in this regard is also currently wanting as it does not draw on the documented experience of previous sustainability-based assessments, is incomplete, does not establish how independent expertise might be used to inform decisions, and is inclined to overuse "flexibility" as an excuse for vagueness. Also absent are any provisions on how these decisions will be made in the context of cooperative assessments and strategic and regional assessments.

### 12) Follow-Up of Compliance with Conditions, Effect Predictions, and Effective Response to Monitoring Findings

Chapter 16 notes that experience over the past decade has generated considerable concern about the effectiveness of auditing follow-up and monitoring practice. However, that concern is not reflected in the marginal changes in provisions addressing these issues in the *IAA*. For example, provisions to ensure that actual effects are compared to predicted effects are still missing. On a more positive note, it is likely that more information will be available on the Canadian Impact Assessment Registry with respect to follow-up programs and participant funding than was available under *CEAA* 2012. Yet the *IAA*'s monitoring and follow-up provisions do not reflect a significant shift toward greater quality, transparency, and accountability. There is a lack of clarity, for example, on the allocation of responsibility to ensure the implementation of the various elements of follow-up for approved projects (particularly with multiple jurisdictions involved). It is also unclear as to what happens when predictions made during the assessment turn out to be wrong or when mitigation measures do not achieve the expected outcomes. Also, the potential for learning beyond a single assessment through follow-up and monitoring continues to be limited, as noted above. The enforcement provisions backing approval conditions are reasonably strong and in line with the literature but need to be used effectively as part of a well-designed, integrated approach to the post-approval process.

## 13) Independent and Impartial Administration and Assessment Review

Access to information is a key foundation of ensuring transparent decisions, and transparency on many aspects of project assessment implementation is facilitated in the *IAA* through the registry. Challenges remain in relation to decisions about access to confidential and proprietary information as well as the provision of plain-language summaries of information.[13] The Act rates well on providing criteria to direct some key decisions and for expanding the obligation to give written reasons for key decisions. However, as noted in Chapter 19, the absence of binding definitions, thresholds, standards, and criteria in the *IAA* means that many key decisions still lack the specific direction needed, meaning that they will likely attract review by the courts. This is particularly so in relation to broad discretion in the *IAA* around decisions under section 6. In this regard, the lack of an independent statutory appeal mechanism significantly diminishes accountability under the Act. Reliance on judicial review brings with it several limitations, including the fact that a variety of decisions are likely to avoid scrutiny as well as being a barrier to effective participation and accountability (i.e., cost, timing, efficiency, need for lawyers).

## 14) Effective, Efficient, and Fair Process

As established in Chapter 2, effectiveness, fairness, and efficiency are interdependent. Lasting effectiveness depends on the assessment processes being both fair and efficient. Aspects of each attribute are distributed throughout the components of next-generation assessment, as we discussed above. However, any consideration of the character and

---

13   See Chapter 19.

nature of these attributes depends on how each is independently met and integrated through an assessment process. For example, there was obvious support from some sectors and governments for the *IAA* to be governed by strict timelines, likely to encourage efficiency in terms of time and needed resources. But as the analysis above reveals, such strict timelines can negatively impact both fairness and effectiveness if not implemented in a flexible and case-sensitive way. Likewise, the *IAA's* requirement to consider impacts beyond biophysical ones broadens the scope and potential effectiveness of the review process, but proper implementation will require time to do the necessary science and other analyses in order to understand the impacts of a project or regional or strategic undertaking. Fairness garnered the least attention in the reform process, and although provisions for the involvement of the public in the planning phase, for example, are meant to improve on past shortcomings, how this will be achieved is vague, and the early implementation is worrisome. Recognition in the *IAA* of Indigenous interests and rights, although imperfect, does, however, help improve fairness considerations. Lastly, the vagueness and uncertainty of the *IAA* in relation to strategic and regional assessment processes and outcomes compromise prospects for effectiveness, efficiency, and fairness.

It is important to emphasize that efficiency cannot be assessed in isolation of effectiveness and fairness. Whether the time and resources spent on an assessment process are warranted depends on the value that it offers and on the improvements it makes to decision making and, ultimately, to the sustainability of human societies and natural systems. An assessment process that meets firm timelines but undermines the goal of improving decision making cannot be considered efficient.

The nature of the outcomes related to each of the examples above obviously depends on how the Act is implemented and how the broad discretion contained in it is exercised. Regulatory and policy clarifications, as well as guidance, could help.[14]

---

14 See Chapter 24.

## C.  THE NEXT GENERATION OF ASSESSMENT IN CANADA

The *IAA* includes provisions that speak in some way to each of the next-generation components and contains promising innovations in relation to the next-generation frame itself, but we cannot conclude that it is revolutionary in this regard. In the Canadian context, as established above and in Part II, there are certainly provisions for positive innovations. These include the planning phase; the sustainability-based approach; the stronger recognition of Indigenous rights and interests; the need to consider the intersection of sex, gender, and other identity factors; and recognition of the need to meet Canada's climate commitments and environmental obligations, such as those related to the protection of biodiversity. There are, however, troubling concerns related to how the *IAA* satisfies each component. The Act largely enables an assessment process that could address important aspects of all fourteen components of next-generation IA, but it does not ensure significant gains. For example, deep uncertainties remain about the following:

- what core criteria will be used in considering the sustainability implications of a project or regional or strategic undertaking
- to what extent impact predictions and approaches to mitigation will be based in rigorous science and analyses
- how real cooperation among jurisdictions will be achieved
- what meaningful public participation will be delivered
- how broad-based learning can be achieved
- how the process will ensure that projects help us meet Canada's climate commitments and environmental obligations
- how the process will become compliant with *UNDRIP*

In the next chapter, we consider the sorts of reforms that are needed to ensure that the *IAA* continues to move us toward the next generation of assessment in Canada. Making progress on each component of the next-generation framework is particularly warranted in the context of the *IAA* because, as currently crafted, the Act only applies to a very small number of the projects under federal jurisdiction that could have significant sustainability outcomes. Although this focus on a small number of significant projects may make it easier to ensure efficiency, it also offers the opportunity to ensure that the process is thorough, effective, and fair. Given the low number of assessments being carried out, the standard should be high and reflect the next-generation components as closely as can be achieved through assessment process reform. Once we have gained valuable experience with high-quality assessments, it will be important to find ways to make this process work effectively, efficiently, and fairly for a larger number of projects.

# CHAPTER 24

# The Path Forward

*Meinhard Doelle and A John Sinclair*

## A. INTRODUCTION

In this final chapter, we focus on law reform and key changes in the implementation of the *Impact Assessment Act (IAA)*[1] that are needed to complete the transition of the federal assessment process to an effective governance tool for sustainability. In making these recommendations, we have reflected on what the contributors to Part II of this book have explored and on our own assessment in the previous chapter of how the *IAA* stacks up against the fourteen components of next-generation impact assessment. We have organized our recommendations according to the main phases in the federal assessment process first identified in Chapter 3, starting with triggering and then considering planning and scoping, process options and design, decision making, follow-up, strategic and regional assessments, and the assessment of projects on federal lands and outside Canada.

We use the terms *law reform* and *legislative reform* to refer to changes that could be reflected in the statute or in regulations. When we refer to the *IAA*, we refer to the statute, not the regulations. Where we think it is important, we specify whether the reform should happen in the statute or regulations, but our focus is generally on ensuring that the reforms are enshrined in law. We also at times refer to guidance and policy for

---

1    SC 2019, c 28, s 1.

matters that require more flexibility to adjust as experience warrants or are too detailed to be enshrined in regulations. Finally, we cannot hope to fully reflect the rich analysis in Part II; rather, our aim here is to highlight improvements needed in the implementation of the *IAA*, key regulations that are missing, and opportunities to further strengthen the Act through law reform when the opportunity arises.

## B. APPLICATION AND TRIGGERING FOR DESIGNATED PROJECT ASSESSMENTS

As discussed in Chapter 7, the *Canadian Environmental Assessment Act, 2012 (CEAA 2012)*[2] represented a significant departure from the triggering process under the *Canadian Environmental Assessment Act (CEAA 1995)*,[3] which the *IAA* does not reverse. Leaving aside the debate about which basic approach as captured in these Acts is better, the *IAA*'s approach to triggering the project-level assessment process is inadequate in a number of ways. The current list of projects in the designated project regulations does not capture all projects that warrant a federal assessment. There are no clear, detailed criteria to justify the current list or to guide decisions respecting whether a given project should be subject to a federal assessment. Once these criteria are established, preferably as part of the designated projects regulations, they should guide the expansion of the current project list[4] and its regular updating. The same criteria should also be used to guide ministerial determinations as to whether to designate proposed projects that are not on the project list under section 9 of the *IAA*.

We suggest that the overall basis for developing the criteria should be whether a proposed project is "likely to adversely impact matters of federal interest that are consequential for present and/or future generations."[5] Areas of federal interest are those listed in the *IAA*, subject to considering additions, including Canada's key international obligations

---

2    SC 2012, c 19, s 52.

3    SC 1992, c 37. The entry into force of the Act was delayed until 1995 to allow for key regulations to be developed and passed.

4    *Physical Activities Regulations*, SOR/2019-285.

5    The wording is adapted from similar wording proposed by the Expert Panel; see Expert Panel for the Review of Environmental Assessment Processes, *Building Common Ground: A New Vision for Impact Assessment in Canada* (Ottawa: Canadian Environmental Assessment Agency, 2017) s 3.2.1, online (pdf): *Government of Canada*

on issues such as climate change and biodiversity. Consideration should be given to adding to the list of issues of federal interest through Schedule 3 of the *IAA* once the jurisdictional issues are clarified through the constitutional challenge initiated by the Province of Alberta.[6]

Once appropriate criteria for consequential impacts on matters of federal interest are set out in regulations, the list of designed projects should be expanded to include all projects that are sufficiently likely to meet this threshold. Similarly, the Act should require the minister, when considering whether to designate proposed projects that are not on the list, to take into account the same criteria to determine the projects' likelihood of having consequential impacts on matters of federal interest. That should be the ultimate test for the application of the *IAA*. The discretion to designate or not designate projects should be limited to the proper application of these criteria, thus reducing the risk of a politicized triggering process.

As discussed in detail in Chapter 7, a key issue in the design of the criteria will be the threshold for what is considered "consequential for present or future generations." It will be important for the selection of types of projects that warrant a federal assessment as well as thresholds in terms of the size of the projects or their impacts for triggering an assessment. The criteria that are to be applied to select project types and thresholds will need to be set out in some detail in the designated projects regulations. To ensure consistency in the application of these criteria, we suggest that the *IAA* provide an opportunity to appeal designation decisions to an independent appeal body.[7] In addition, an appeal body would avoid the risk of lengthy delays that could result from judicial review applications of designation decisions. Such a body could serve a similar function where other process decisions are made through a combination of legislative criteria and discretion. The value of an appeal body would be to encourage good faith and

---

www.canada.ca/content/dam/themes/environment/conservation/environmental-reviews/building-common-ground/building-common-ground.pdf.

6   See *IAA*, s 2, definition of effects within federal jurisdiction. In September 2019, Alberta's Lieutenant Governor in Council referred two constitutional questions to the Alberta Court of Appeal respecting the constitutional validity of the *IAA* and the *Physical Activities Regulations* (above note 4). At the time of writing, this case was still before the court.

7   For a detailed discussion of the important role that an appeal body could play in improving the accountability, consistency, and quality of decision making in the *IAA*, see Chapter 19.

consistent application of legislative criteria and accountability without undue delay.

A challenge with the implementation of an effective triggering process will be how to establish criteria and make appropriate determinations about the potential consequence of a proposed project before decision makers have had the benefit of an impact assessment. Critical to this will be to develop a meaningful legal test that can be applied based on information readily available at the early planning stages of a proposed project. To illustrate, the role of cumulative effects in making the triggering determination needs to be clear, particularly for determinations about projects not on the initial list. Are the consequences of a proposed project considered in isolation of other activities and impacts, or will there be some consideration of cumulative effects in determining whether a proposed project's impact is consequential for present and future generations? Does it matter whether a project would foreclose future development in the region because it uses up the remaining carrying capacity of the receiving environment, making further development regionally unsustainable? Ultimately, given the challenge of a lack of information at the triggering stage, what might be needed are criteria that consider whether a project is proposed in a context where cumulative effects are likely to be a critical issue rather than detailed knowledge of the state of the receiving environment.

Another issue in need of attention in the implementation and reform of the *IAA* is early triggering. The need for earlier triggering has long been recognized. Unfortunately, there is no significant progress on this issue in the *IAA*. The current information requirements for proponents to commence an assessment actually work against early triggering, as do the firm timelines in the planning phase and the complete reliance on proponents to decide when to trigger the process. Part of the solution might be to return to the idea of requiring an initial project description with minimal information requirements well before the start of the planning phase, to be updated as part of the impact statement at the start of the assessment phase. This would reduce a barrier to early triggering by making it clear that proponents should trigger the assessment before they have completed a detailed project design. Prescribing a pause between filing the initial project description and the start of the planning phase would provide additional incentive for proponents to trigger the process early and give everyone potentially affected more time to prepare for the planning and assessment phases of the process. As discussed in the next section, early triggering has to work in combination with an expanded planning phase.

## C.  THE PLANNING PROCESS

The planning process is one of the key innovations of the *IAA*. However, it is in need of reform if it is to serve its intended function.[8] The issue of early triggering discussed in Section B is, of course, critical for an effective planning phase. It is only through the early involvement of all potentially affected interests—well before the start of the current 180-day planning process—that effective and collaborative planning with other jurisdictions, affected Indigenous communities, and other potentially affected parties can be achieved. Among the key issues to consider in reforming the planning process are the following:

- *The need for more flexible timelines that are appropriate for the specific project rather than the current approach of standard timelines for all projects, regardless of the size of the project or the complexity of the assessment.* The flexibility should start with the time allocated to the planning phase but extend to the assessment phase as well. To address proponents' concerns about certainty, a firm timeline for the assessment phase should be one of the outcomes of the planning phase, with the current timelines in the *IAA* serving as defaults rather than as set timelines. These changes can only be implemented through statutory reform as the current approach to timelines is enshrined in the Act itself.

- *The need for more legislative clarity on how to implement the planning process in a manner that is consistent with the commitment to implement the* United Nations Declaration on the Rights of Indigenous Peoples (UNDRIP), *as explored in Chapter 6.* This includes co-governance with affected Indigenous communities where appropriate and an assurance that Indigenous knowledge is a central component of the assessment process. What legislative reforms are needed to implement an *UNDRIP*-compliant planning process, including the commitment to free prior informed consent,

---

8    Different aspects of the planning process are addressed in various chapters in Part II. See, for example, Chapter 8, chapters 9 to 13 on scope, and Chapter 15.

will ultimately depend on the outcome of discussions that need to take place between the federal government and the Indigenous peoples of Canada.

- *The need to ensure that all affected interests have the opportunity to be appropriately involved in a consensus-based planning process is key to designing a cooperative assessment process that is fit for purpose.* This would include selecting appropriate methods of public engagement from a comprehensive range of engagement methods and ensuring the active engagement of all affected jurisdictions. To achieve this, timeline changes recommended above and regulations on the effective implementation of the planning phase are needed.

- *The need to establish a formal planning committee for each assessment that serves as the main vehicle for implementing a cooperative assessment approach during the planning phase is an important part of making the planning phase work.* There is a need for legislative clarity on the role and mandate of the planning committee. Key among the issues to be clarified is the representation of interests on the committee beyond affected jurisdictions. The committee should have responsibility to advise the Impact Assessment Agency of Canada (the Agency) on all aspects of the planning phase, including scope, terms of reference for the impact statement, process options and timelines for the assessment phase, and the design of an appropriate public engagement program. This change should be implemented through a planning phase regulation.

- *The need to ensure that cooperation agreements with other jurisdictions under section 114 of the IAA do not undermine the flexibility of the planning committee to design an appropriate cooperative assessment through the planning process.* The power to enter into cooperation agreements should focus on establishing broad principles that can be used to focus individual assessment agreements but should not predetermine or limit the ability of the planning process to design a cooperative approach suitable to each individual assessment. This can be clarified through a planning phase regulation or through an amendment to section 114 of the *IAA*.

- *The need to ensure that panels are appointed as early as possible and are provided with the opportunity to participate in the planning process, including regarding modes of public engagement, information needs, and scope determinations.* This means that either the planning phase has to be extended to allow for panels to be appointed and have input or the outcome of the planning phase should not be finalized until reviewed and approved by the panel once it is appointed. A planning phase regulation can help clarify some of these issues; however, changes to the Act are ultimately needed.

- *The need to develop a planning phase regulations to provide detailed criteria to guide decisions as to whether assessments proceed under the Agency-led process or by panel review.* Under previous Acts, panel reviews have tended to be more comprehensive, rigorous, and participative and have been more clearly independent from government decision makers. The criteria for the process decision under the *IAA* need to be carefully designed to ensure that the decisions are informed by the design needs of the circumstances, such as the desired forms of public engagement, panel independence, and multi-jurisdictional collaboration. In short, in developing criteria, careful thought will have to be given to the relative strengths and limitations of Agency-led assessments and panel reviews under the *IAA.*

- *The need for clarity on the information to be provided for the assessment by participants other than the proponent, including by federal departments and agencies, regulators, other jurisdictions involved in the assessment, and non-state actors, as appropriate.* This clarity could be provided through the planning phase regulations.

- *The need for broader consideration of alternatives in the planning phase and clarity on the role of alternatives in making the various section 63 determinations and the ultimate public interest determination.* A combination of broadening of the scope of alternatives in section 22 and addressing the role of alternatives in the planning phase regulation is warranted to ensure an appropriate role for alternatives. In short, the use of alternatives in the project decision needs to be both broadened and planned.

- *The need for more clarity on the scope and information-gathering implications of the requirement in the IAA to consider the impact of the proposed project on Canada's environmental obligations.* In particular, Canada has taken on a number of obligations regarding the protection of biodiversity. Clear guidance on what those obligations are and how they are to be addressed is needed.

## D. ASSESSMENT PROCESS OPTIONS AND DESIGN

The *IAA*'s two process options, along with options for joint assessments, are generally suitable, particularly given the flexibility of the Agency-led process to adjust depending on the size or complexity of the project and its assessment. In this section, we focus on three areas in which the assessment process under the Act should be reformed. First, we consider reforms to realize the promise of meaningful public participation in both Agency-led assessments and those led by panels. Next, we consider the need for flexibility in the scope of the assessment and information needs to ensure that decisions made during the planning phase do not undermine the ability of the assessment phase to be able to make sound recommendations on each of the decision-making elements identified in section 63. Finally, we consider reforms to ensure that panels have the powers and responsibilities to implement effective assessment processes.

### 1) Meaningful Public Participation

The following changes are needed to provide a proper legislative framework for meaningful public participation.[9]

Section 2 should be amended to include an appropriate definition of meaningful public participation. We recommend the following:

> Meaningful public participation requires the design of a process that is informed by a thorough understanding of the needs, values, and concerns of the public; that provides a genuine opportunity to influence decisions; and that uses multiple and customized methods of engagement that promote and sustain fair and open two-way dialogue in a manner that is sensitive to those potentially affected.

Decades of experience have shown that no amount of voluntary guidance on its own is going to ensure that meaningful participation is achieved. Clear direction on meaningful public participation should be set out in regulations. To facilitate this, the regulation-making power

---

9    For a detailed discussion of public participation, see Chapter 15. Different aspects of public participation are also discussed in other chapters in Part II, such as chapters 16 and 19.

in section 112 should be amended as required to provide for regulations dealing with the following subject matters:

- details on how to ensure meaningful public participation in each of the key phases of the impact assessment process, including the planning phase, the assessment and review phase, the decision-making phase, and the follow up phase
- the key purposes of participation in the assessment planning phase (e.g., participation in the development of the final project plan to be submitted, the development of guidelines, and the establishment of a public participation plan)
- meaningful public participation that is culturally appropriate and appropriate to the circumstances and that allows for deliberative processes that promote learning about the values, priorities, and aspirations of affected communities
- protecting fundamental procedural rights in hearings, such as the right to cross-examine expert witnesses while avoiding what participants often find to be undue intimidation during questioning of witnesses and allowing for deliberative processes that promote learning about the values, priorities, and aspirations of affected communities
- the role of the public in the development of a plan for participation in the follow-up phase
- the design and implementation of the participant funding program, including requirements for funding that covers participants' time and costs and sufficient funding for participants to retain experts and legal assistance where required for effective engagement
- the manner in which information relevant to the assessment, and all follow-up data and information, will be made permanently and publicly accessible

## 2) Flexibility to Adjust Scoping and Information Gathering

Striking an appropriate balance between certainty and predictability for participants in the assessment process on the one hand and the flexibility needed to ensure an effective and fair assessment process that offers a sound basis for decision making on the other hand is a critical element of an effective assessment process, regardless of whether the assessment is led by the Agency or a panel. In this section, we identify some key issues in need of reform in this regard.

With respect to the scope of the assessment, it is our view that in the absence of flexibility to adjust the scope during the assessment phase of a project, the long-standing tradition of broad scoping without attention to focusing on what really matters will continue. Only if there is an ability to make adjustments during the course of the assessment phase will parties be willing to compromise during the planning phase to focus on the most important lines of inquiry apparent at that early stage. The more difficult it is to adjust the scope as participants learn more about the process, and the predicted effects of the proposed project and alternatives during the assessment phase, the less willingness there will be to focus on what matters. The *IAA* therefore should be reformed to grant power to the Agency or the panel in charge of a given project assessment to adjust the scope in appropriate circumstances.

It is important to recognize how much the scope of assessments has changed. This is explored in some detail in Part II of the book. Among the new areas of focus are the contribution to sustainability, climate commitments and environmental obligations, gender implications, social and health impacts and benefits, and corporate social responsibility and human rights.[10] Appropriate guidance will be a critical first step in effectively integrating these issues into the assessment process. However, this broader scope is also a clear signal that a business-as-usual approach to scoping is not an option. This is another reason why we advocate for flexibility to adjust the scope throughout the assessment process.

With respect to information gathering, there is a need for clarity on sources of information beyond the direction to proponents in the form of the Tailored Impact Statement Guidelines. Clarity on what information will be provided by other participants in the process will be critically important. It will also be important to design each assessment process to enable those in charge of the assessment to fill unanticipated information gaps during the course of the assessment as much as possible. Access to competent analysis with respect to the broad range of subject matters covered in sections 22 and 63, the means to retain outside

---

10    For more detail on some of these issues, see Chapter 9 on sustainability, Chapter 12 on gender, Chapter 13 on climate change, and Chapter 20 on human rights and the role of proponents and consultants.

experts as needed, and the ability to request additional information from participants are all critical powers that need to be granted to the Agency teams and panels responsible for conducting project assessments. The required powers need to be set out in the *IAA*. The responsibility to use these powers to ensure that information gathering is properly planned should be set out in the planning phase regulations.[11]

The Agency team or panel in charge of the assessment of a particular project needs to have direct budgetary control over hiring experts and for pursuing alternative dispute resolution (ADR) options in appropriate circumstances. Experience has shown that delays in federal decision making during panel processes (such as ministerial or Agency approval) hamper the ability of those in charge of the assessment to retain experts and to pursue mediation or other forms of ADR to resolve disputes that arise during the course of an assessment. This problem is exacerbated under the *IAA* due to its rigid legislated timelines. An important part of the solution to this problem is to give those in charge of the assessment the authority to directly retain experts and mediators or facilitators and to ensure that they have the power to select and hire these experts.[12]

## 3)  Adjustments to the Panel Review Process

The gradual erosion of the panel's role in the assessment process is a concerning trend in the federal assessment process that started two decades ago and has continued under the *IAA*. In line with our recommendations with respect to the planning phase, we recommend reforms to ensure that panels are involved in key planning aspects of the assessment process, including the identification of information needs and scope determinations. In this section, we highlight the key reforms needed to protect and restore the critical role panel reviews have played in assessments in Canada.

Panels should be appointed as early as possible during the planning phase. Appropriate timelines for review panels should be determined

---

11  Existing provisions, such as s 26 of the *IAA*, although helpful, apply too late in the process to ensure that those responsible for providing information are identified during the planning phase of the assessment process.

12  For a more detailed discussion of mediation and ADR in environmental assessment, see Meinhard Doelle & A John Sinclair, "Mediation in Environmental Assessments in Canada: Unfulfilled Promise?" (2010) 33:1 *Dalhousie Law Journal* 117.

at the conclusion of the planning phase in consultation with the panel. The 600-day period should serve as a default, not as a rigid legislative timeline. Panels, not the minister, should have discretion to suspend time while the proponent is responding to the panels' information requests. Panels should have the power to request information from proponents and other participants as appropriate to ensure that they have the information needed to reach sound conclusions and recommendations with respect to each decision-making element identified in section 63 of the Act. These recommendations should be implemented through panel procedure regulations along with the planning phase regulations recommended above.[13]

## E.  PROJECT DECISION MAKING

There has been much debate over the years about the best way to make project decisions at the end of the project assessment process.[14] Some, such as the Expert Panel for the Review of Environmental Assessment Processes, have recommended that project decisions be taken out of the hands of elected officials and instead be made by panels or an independent commission.[15] It is not our intention here to weigh in on this debate over administrative versus political decision making. Rather, we offer suggestions on how to improve the political decision-making process as prescribed in the *IAA*, and, in particular, how to take advantage of the unique contribution panels and Agency assessment teams can make to good project decisions by the minister or Cabinet. Although we focus our comments on panel reviews, much of what we say has equal application to Agency-led assessments, keeping in mind, of course, that there are important differences between these two processes.[16]

Our basic proposition is that panels and Agency assessment teams will be more immersed with the assessment of the full range of predicted impacts and benefits, and with the risks and uncertainties, associated

---

13   Existing provisions, such as ss 52 and 53 of the *IAA*, although helpful, come too late in the process to ensure that the allocation of responsibility to gather information is properly allocated during the planning phase of the assessment process.

14   Meinhard Doelle, *The Federal Environmental Assessment Process: A Guide and Critique* (Markham, ON: LexisNexis Canada, 2008). See also Chapter 14.

15   See the discussion in Chapter 4.

16   The substance of the decision-making test that should be applied is discussed in detail in Chapter 14.

with proposed projects than the ultimate decision maker. With our reforms, panels and Agency teams will have carefully considered alternatives and alternative means of carrying out the project. No one else will be involved in the process who will have the unique combination of having carried out a detailed analysis of the proposed project's impacts and benefits and the big picture perspective on its contribution to the public interest. The minister or Cabinet will certainly not have this detailed knowledge. This is particularly true now that the scope has been broadened to include all benefits and impacts of a proposed project. In light of this, it is a missed opportunity not to require the panel (section 51) and the Agency assessment teams (section 28) to apply the criteria in section 63. Panels and the Agency should make recommendations to the minister and Cabinet about each of the criteria in section 63 (in accordance with guidance to be set out in regulations). With that advice in hand, the minister or Cabinet is then still free to reach their own conclusion on whether and under what conditions the project is likely to meet each of the section 63 criteria and is in the public interest.

The minister or Cabinet can, of course, reach a different conclusion, either because they disagree with the analysis of the panel or the Agency team or because Nation-to-Nation negotiations carried on outside the assessment process with affected Indigenous communities warrant a different conclusion. In that case, we recommend a new provision in the *IAA* that would require the minister to give written reasons for deciding not to follow a recommendation of the panel or Agency, creating transparency and accountability for the final project decision. This would still leave ultimate accountability in the hands of elected officials and allow the results of Nation-to-Nation negotiations to feed into the final project decision. There was a similar provision in section 38(2) of the original version of *CEAA 1995*:

> A responsible authority referred to in (1) shall, in accordance with any regulations made for that purpose, advise the public of:
>
> ...
>
> (c)    the extent to which the recommendations set out in any report submitted by a mediator or a review panel have been adopted and the reasons for not having adopted any of those recommendations.[17]

---

17    This provision was part of the original CEAA as passed in 1992, but repealed before the entry into force of the Act in 1995.

Ultimately, without a clear role in process design, scoping, information gathering, and making recommendations to decision makers on how to apply the section 63 criteria to reach a "public interest" conclusion, review panels are increasingly at risk of becoming little more than facilitators of public hearings and note takers on the views expressed by participants.

To enable panels to offer advice that is ultimately helpful to decision makers, regulations under the *IAA* are needed to offer clear criteria on how to make each of the section 63 determinations. In particular, regulatory criteria should be provided for the determination on the project's contribution to sustainability, the project's impact on climate commitments and environmental obligations such as the protection of biodiversity, and the project's impact on Indigenous communities and rights. The regulatory criteria should be founded on an understanding of how Western science and Indigenous knowledge contribute to the understanding of a project's impacts and benefits. The criteria need to recognize and deal with the uncertainties associated with the predictions made during the course of an assessment. Finally, the criteria need to be designed with the commitment to implement the *IAA* in a manner consistent with *UNDRIP*.

## F.  POST-IMPACT ASSESSMENT (FOLLOW-UP) PROCESS

As explored in detail in Chapter 16, the key for an effective follow-up program is the tracking of whether predictions made during the assessment turn out to have been accurate, whether mitigation measures are as effective as predicted, and whether terms and conditions are complied with and prove to be adequate. Effective follow-up requires the results of this analysis to feed into adaptive regulatory approaches for approved projects and learning processes for future assessments.

Key among the missing legislative provisions on follow-up is that there needs to be a clear responsibility (not just a power) to amend terms of approval in the event that predictions about impacts or mitigation turn out to be wrong. The *IAA* should provide for specific criteria to be set out in regulations for when and how the power to amend the terms and conditions for approval is to be exercised. Decades of experience show that in the absence of clear responsibility and criteria, the mere power to act on the results of follow-up will not be enough.

Although there is an obligation to publish the results of follow-up in some form, there is not enough clarity in the *IAA* that all data collected on the actual impacts of an approved project will be publicly accessible. The Act should clarify that all data collected are public and that all data and all documents prepared will be permanently and publicly available.

There is also no clarity on how interjurisdictional cooperation will be achieved in a way that will ensure clear accountability for implementing the follow-up program, sharing the results, and ensuring appropriate action in response. The *IAA* should include requirements for the minister or the Agency to negotiate implementation agreements with any jurisdiction that takes on follow-up responsibilities, with the goal of ensuring full transparency and accountability. These could be set in specific follow-up regulations.

The *IAA* should be amended to provide that federal authorities have a legislated responsibility to carry out their regulatory or other duty, power, or function with respect to approved projects in such a manner as to ensure the effective implementation of the follow-up programs, full transparency of the results through a central federal registry, and appropriate action in response.

There should be clear legislative provisions that require the Agency to enable and facilitate the active engagement of affected Indigenous and local communities in the implementation of follow-up programs, including monitoring programs for any impacts of particular concern to an affected community, regardless of which authority oversees the implementation of the follow-up program, and provide sufficient funding for that engagement.

As explored in Chapter 16, there should also be a clear legislated responsibility for the Agency to track compliance with monitoring and reporting obligations regardless of the lead authority. The Agency should also report annually on resulting conclusions about compliance, the lessons learned about predictions made during the assessment, and the resulting actions in terms of adaptive management of the approved project.

There should be a clear legislative accountability for the Agency to ensure that any lessons learned about the accuracy of predictions made and the effectiveness of mitigation measures are reflected in any future assessment where those lessons may be relevant. Reviewing and comparing the analysis carried out during the assessment against actual impacts tracked during the follow-up stage and sharing the results of this analysis with the public and in future assessments will be a critical part of this responsibility.

Finally, there should be a clear and effective process for the continuing improvement of assessments. The legislative review called for in the *IAA* is an important part of this, but it is not sufficient. Other elements include a regular review of regulations and a quality assurance program that collects information about the effectiveness of the implementation of the project, the federal project, strategic assessment, or regional assessment and assesses them against clear and measurable objectives. These additional elements can initially be implemented through policy development but should eventually be enshrined in law.

## G.  REGIONAL AND STRATEGIC ASSESSMENTS

Definitions for regional and strategic assessments need to be added to the *IAA* through legislative change to clearly separate one from the other. A regional assessment should be defined as an assessment whose primary defining features are its regional scope and its focus on understanding the interactions between all past, present, and potential future human activities and the natural world within a given study area. Another defining feature should be its recommendations for an appropriate mix of human activities in the region to ensure its sustainability and the resilience of its ecosystems. A primary aim of a regional assessment should be to inform future project assessments on how to ensure that proposed projects in the region make a net positive contribution and are preferable to alternatives. A strategic assessment should be defined as dealing with a more narrow range of issues than a regional assessment, such as a given policy, plan, or program or a specific issue or type of human activity.[18] Section 95 should be amended to eliminate the restriction of strategic assessments to issues relevant to project impact assessment. This would open the door to bringing the assessment of policies, plans, and programs currently carried out through the Cabinet directive under the *IAA*.

---

18    For a detailed discussion of regional and strategic assessments under the *IAA*, see chapters 11 and 17.

The Act also needs to include better incentives for provinces and other affected jurisdictions (such as municipalities and Indigenous communities) to carry out cooperative regional and strategic assessments jointly with the federal government. Funding, a commitment to collaborating in creating a common sustainability-based foundation for future project decision making, and a commitment to proceed with a federal assessment if it is a federal priority even in the absence of interest from other jurisdictions appear to be obvious motivations for other jurisdictions to get involved. These recommendations could all be implemented through regulations on regional and strategic assessments under the *IAA*.

The process to be followed for regional and strategic assessments (including a planning phase and an assessment phase similar to project assessments), the decisions to be made at the conclusion of them, and how the results of these assessments are to be used at the project level should be more clearly set out in legislation. A regional study that does not have a clear strategic focus and recommendations for the preferred combination of activities in light of issues such as cumulative effects, resilience of ecosystems, and long-term sustainability of the region should not qualify as a regional assessment. Regulations should be developed to ensure that these issues are properly addressed in regional assessments.

A roster of regional and strategic assessments to be carried out would also be helpful, as would a commitment to initiate a minimum number of regional and strategic assessments in any given year. The list of possible regions and issues is long, so a commitment to certain priorities and level of effort will be critical. The process for triggering a regional or strategic assessment should be formalized in the Act, with clear criteria for making such decisions set out in regulation. Triggers for both should include recommendations from the project assessment tier, petitions from the public, and initiation at the initiative of the minister.

The proposed approach to strategic assessments could also be significantly enhanced as the current approach misses the opportunity to ensure that strategic assessments are used effectively to make project assessments more efficient, effective, and fair by resolving high-level policy issues before specific projects are proposed and assessed (or in parallel with project assessments where necessary). As explored in more detail below, the planning phase for project assessments in particular provides opportunities for sequential or parallel project and strategic assessments. The responsibility to consider the need for a strategic assessment to fill policy gaps should be included in the planning phase regulations recommended earlier in this chapter.

The *IAA*'s new planning phase at the project level offers an ideal opportunity to identify policy issues that warrant resolution to ensure good project decisions. The proponent has up to three years following the conclusion of the planning phase to complete its impact statement. This provides a unique opportunity to explore policy issues identified during the course of the planning phase and to initiate a strategic assessment process to resolve them before the project assessment is concluded.

In short, there will be issues that arise at the project assessment level that cannot be resolved between the proponent and interested members of the public because their implications go beyond the scope of a particular project assessment. This will be particularly relevant in cases of emerging or transitioning industries and with any significant shift in our understanding of the sustainability implications of established industries. Ideally, this need will be recognized long before individual projects are proposed. In some cases, however, the need is not identified until a proponent proposes a specific project. In such a case, the proponent, governments, and interested members of the public should be able to initiate a parallel process under the *IAA* for a strategic assessment to address such broader issues in an equally open forum with similar objectives of resolving the issues in such a way as to maximize net contributions to sustainability. Of course, in areas with significant development pressures, where time permits, the better process for addressing these issues would be a regional assessment.

If policy issues are raised during the planning phase of a project assessment, the proponent and public should have a formal opportunity to alert the Agency or minister, who would then be responsible for deciding whether to initiate a parallel strategic assessment process to move forward on the policy issues raised. Providing this direction would include the following steps in a process set up through a combination of regulations and guidance:

1) The identification of potential policy gaps in the planning process for all project assessments, open to public comment

2) A public determination of whether a policy review through a strategic assessment is warranted for any identified policy gap

3) Recommendation by the Agency to the minister that a significant policy gap needs to be filled by way of an open, consultative, public strategic impact assessment (sometimes referred to as the "policy off-ramp")

4) Clear direction that work on the proposed project assessment would, in most cases, be able to continue with the scoping and information-gathering phases, but the project assessment would not be completed until the policy gap was filled and policy direction provided through the strategic assessment

5) A requirement that no final project decision be made until the policy gaps are filled. Under the *IAA*, the minister could be allowed to decide otherwise in a transparent manner, where the minister concludes that a precautionary approach to the project decision would still enable the project assessment to be completed and a project decision to be made without having to wait for the completion of the strategic assessment

It is important to note that the assessment of federal policies, plans, and programs is not brought in under the Act. Chapter 17 explored the unsatisfactory history of the implementation of the Cabinet directive on strategic environmental assessment. The *IAA* should therefore include requirements for the assessment of federal policies, plans, and programs that would replace the Cabinet directive and address its main deficiencies of a lack of transparency, accountability, and public participation and the absence of meaningful substantive principles or goals.

Finally, experience with regional and strategic assessments has shown that independent administration is critical for the effectiveness and credibility of the process and its results. The *IAA* should be amended to ensure that the assessment process is not in the hands of anyone who may have a vested interest in the outcome. Placing assessments in the hands of independent panels should be the default option, with Agency-led assessments or assessments led by committees involving a full range of interests as alternatives to be considered in appropriate circumstances. The composition of committees set up to oversee regional and strategic assessments needs to be clarified in regulations. They should be set up as independent bodies to operate in a transparent manner, with Indigenous representation, representation from the affected jurisdiction, and members representing key public interests.

## H. FEDERAL PROJECTS

Projects on federal lands and projects outside Canada have become the poor cousin of the federal assessment process. This is surprising given that there is clear constitutional jurisdiction for the assessment of these projects. There is every opportunity for these federal projects to serve as the testing ground for innovation rather than to lag behind the assessment process for designated projects. We recommend that the assessment of federal projects be brought more in line with the process for designated projects under the *IAA*, including a broadening of the scope of assessments.[19]

It is important to recognize that the transition from *CEAA 1995* to *CEAA 2012* resulted in the disappearance of the funding trigger for initiating an assessment, and this has not changed under the *IAA*. In the past, federal funding for projects resulted in a federal assessment, including for those outside Canada. Federal funding is not a trigger under the *IAA*, and this gap was not addressed through appropriate funding triggers on the designated projects list. A further opportunity to seek to fill this gap through triggers for federal funding decisions at the strategic level was also missed. More generally, there is a need to provide better links in the *IAA* between the federal projects process and strategic assessments, such as by requiring strategic assessments of official development assistance plans, trade and investment policy, and infrastructure support programs.

There is a need for more transparency and process clarity for assessments carried out under the federal projects process. Clear opportunities for public participation are a key part of a suitable process for federal projects. Finally, there should be a formal bump-up option for projects assessed under the federal projects process that warrant a full assessment by the Agency or a panel. These changes will require a combination of amendments to sections 81 to 91 of the Act and the development of appropriate implementing regulations and guidance.

---

19   The process for projects on federal lands and outside Canada is considered in detail in Chapter 18.

## I. CONCLUSION

The *IAA* has the potential to be a significant step forward in the evolution of the federal assessment process. However, in its current form, its effectiveness is far from guaranteed through clear legal obligations on government officials and proponents. Rather, and as was the case with its predecessors, its effectiveness depends on the proper exercise of significant discretion and on the development of effective regulations, policy, and guidance. In some areas, such as triggering, planning, and decision making, further law reform will undoubtedly be necessary for the Act to realize on its promise. This should not come as a surprise. As many of us have yet again experienced in the development of the *IAA*, law making is not a perfect process, and ensuring that impact assessment processes are effective will be a continuing effort. A commitment to continuous improvement in the end may be the most important goal of any assessment process. We hope that this book will make a modest contribution to both the effective implementation of the *IAA* as it was passed in 2019 and to its continuous improvement through further policies and guidance, regulations, and law reform.

# Contributors

**Hugh Benevides** has degrees in geography (Carleton) and law (Dalhousie) and is called to the bars of Ontario and Nova Scotia. He has worked as legislative assistant in the House of Commons, as counsel to the Canadian Environmental Law Association and East Coast Environmental Law, and as Canadian legal officer at the Secretariat of the North American Commission for Environmental Cooperation. He was strategic advisor to leading public interest groups in their federal law reform efforts from 2017 to 2020 and was an alternate delegate, and later, a delegate to the Multi-Interest Advisory Committee from 2016 to 2019. His main research interests concern Canada's political economy and its implications for environmental law and policy.

**Jill Blakley** is an associate professor in the Department of Geography and Planning, University of Saskatchewan. Jill specializes in cumulative effects assessment and strategic environmental assessment, particularly related to regional-scale natural resource development programs. She serves as a member of the Parks Canada Strategic Environmental Assessment Continuous Improvement Program Committee and is lead editor of the forthcoming volume *Handbook of Cumulative Impact Assessment* (Northampton, MA: Edward Elgar Publishing Inc, 2021). Her work to establish principles and a process for regional strategic environmental assessment is endorsed by the Canadian Council of Ministers of the Environment, and has been applied by Transport Canada, the Wildlife

Conservation Society (Canada), Alberta Environment and Parks, and Fisheries and Oceans Canada, among others. Jill is currently synthesizing lessons from more than fifty cases of regional assessment across Canada to foster best practices in cumulative effects assessment.

**Alan P Diduck** is a professor and department chair in the Department of Environmental Studies and Sciences, University of Winnipeg. Before joining the university, Alan was a lawyer for and the executive director of the Community Legal Education Association, a social profit organization providing public legal education and information services. His research deals with community involvement in environmental governance, particularly environmental assessment. An important focus of his work is the learning implications of involvement and the consequences for social aspects of sustainability, such as adaptive capacity and environmental justice. Alan served as an expert witness on monitoring and adaptive management during the environmental assessment hearings for the Bipole III Transmission Line and Keeyask Generating Station in Manitoba.

**Meinhard Doelle** is a professor of law at the Schulich School of Law, Dalhousie University, where he serves as Associate Dean, Graduate Studies. He was the Canadian Chair at the World Maritime University from 2019 to 2021. Meinhard served as a policy advisor to the federal government during the development of the *Canadian Environmental Assessment Act* and as a member of the Regulatory Advisory Committee, advisory to the Canadian Environmental Assessment Agency and then minister of the environment. He co-chaired the Tidal Energy Strategic Environmental Assessment in 2007, served on the Lower Churchill Joint Federal–Provincial Review Panel from 2009 to 2011, and co-chaired the Nova Scotia panel on aquaculture from 2013 to 2014. He currently serves on the Technical Advisory Committee for the new federal *Impact Assessment Act* in Canada. Meinhard has written on a variety of environmental law topics, including climate change, energy, invasive species, environmental assessments, and public participation in environmental decision making.

**Patricia Fitzpatrick** (she/her/hers), PhD, is a professor in the Department of Geography and an instructor in the Master's in Development Practice — Indigenous Focus program at the University of Winnipeg.

Trish is a settler in the territory of Anishinaabeg, Cree, Oji-Cree, Dakota, and Dene Peoples and the homeland of the Métis Peoples, located in Treaty One. Her research program focuses on different aspects of environmental governance surrounding major- and mega-project development in Canada. Her academic and professional experience spans the areas of impact assessment, public participation and engagement, environmental governance, follow-up, monitoring and adaptive management (including independent oversight), and corporate social responsibility. Over the past twenty years, Trish has been involved in fourteen Canadian assessment and regulatory hearings for mining and energy projects, focusing predominantly on the provincial and territorial north.

**Robert B Gibson** is a professor in the School of Environment, Resources and Sustainability at the University of Waterloo. He has worked on improving assessment law and application since the mid-1970s, including in federal jurisdiction, most provinces, and all three territories and with several Indigenous authorities. His assessment-related efforts for the past few decades have focused mostly on integration of serious commitment to sustainability in next-generation assessment law and practice and in individual assessments at the project and strategic levels. His most recent book is *Sustainability Assessment: Applications and Opportunities* (Routledge, 2017).

**Stephen Hazell** is emeritus general counsel with Nature Canada, and president of Ecovision, a consultancy. Stephen served as Nature Canada's director of policy and general counsel, among other capacities, from 2012 to 2019. He was executive director of Sierra Club Canada (2006–2009) and of Canadian Parks and Wilderness Society (2000–2003). He served as director of legislative and regulatory affairs at the Canadian Environmental Assessment Agency, developing the regulations for the implementation of the *Canadian Environmental Assessment Act*. He has also served as adjunct professor in environmental law at the University of Ottawa Faculty of Law. Stephen holds a master of science degree in plant ecology from the University of Toronto and a law degree from Queen's University. He has written numerous scholarly articles, as well as *Canada v. The Environment*, his 1999 book on federal environmental assessment law and policy.

**Anna Johnston** is a staff lawyer at West Coast Environmental Law, where she works on environmental impact assessment, cumulative effects, and climate law. She co-chairs the Environmental Planning and Assessment Caucus of the Réseau-Canadian Environmental Network, and in 2020 was appointed to the federal Minister's Advisory Council on impact assessment. From 2016 to 2019, she was a delegate to the Multi-Interest Advisory Committee appointed to assist the Minister of Environment and Climate Change in reviewing and revising Canada's federal environmental impact assessment processes. Anna holds a Master of Laws from Dalhousie University, and an LLB and BA from the University of Victoria.

**Jamie Kneen** co-founded MiningWatch Canada in 1999. As communications and outreach coordinator, he leads the organization's social media and public engagement as well as strategic research and communications. His specific focus includes MiningWatch's Africa program (and previously Latin America), in addition to uranium mining and environmental assessment policy and practice in Canada, and he has been involved in the environmental assessment of many projects. Jamie is co-chair of the Environmental Planning and Assessment Caucus of the Canadian Environmental Network and has served on the federal environment and climate change minister's Multi-Interest Advisory Committee on Environmental Assessment and previously on the minister's Regulatory Advisory Committee on the *Canadian Environmental Assessment Act*. He also coordinated a participatory research, training, and capacity-building program on community-based land use planning and environmental assessment for the Commission for Defence of Indigenous Rights in Talamanca, Costa Rica, as a Cuso cooperant.

**Arlene Kwasniak** is professor emerita of law in the Faculty of Law and a senior research fellow with the Canadian Institute of Resources Law at the University of Calgary. Her interests include environmental assessment law and policy, public resources law and policy (e.g., water, public lands, wildlife, and habitat), municipal law, and interjurisdictional and economic approaches to attain sustainability goals. Arlene has published and presented extensively in these areas. She received the Canadian Bar Association/Law Society of Alberta Distinguished Service Award for Legal Scholarship in 2013 and has served on numerous governmental and non-governmental committees, including the North American Instream Flow Council, the Alberta Water Council, the Wetlands Team, the federal Regulatory Advisory Committee on environmental assessment, and the Alberta Water Management Review

Committee. For decades, Arlene has volunteered with the Canadian Environmental Network Environmental Planning and Assessment Caucus, and she has worked on environmental law reform matters with government, the public, and non-governmental organizations.

**Jason MacLean** is an assistant professor in the Faculty of Law, University of New Brunswick, and an adjunct professor in the School of the Environment and Sustainability, University of Saskatchewan. Jason's research and teaching focus on developing transdisciplinary approaches to climate change and sustainability policy-making across multiple sites and scales of governance.

**Sara Mainville** has been called to the Ontario bar since 2005. She has a management degree (Lethbridge) and an LLB (Queen's) and earned an LLM (Toronto), which has engaged her in a lifetime study of Indigenous jurisdiction's important role in legally reconciling Indigenous sovereignty in Canada. She has practised law as a solo practitioner and taught jurisprudence to undergraduate students after being an associate in a well-known Anishinaabe-led law firm in Ontario. In 2014, Sara was elected chief of Couchiching First Nation. She returned to law in 2016 by joining Olthuis Kleer Townshend. Sara is very proud of her participation in the negotiations that led to the creation of the First Nations Sovereign Wealth LP, a partnership of 129 First Nations in Ontario that involved 14 million Hydro One shares and $29 million in seed capital. She is greatly interested in First Nations' inherent regulatory authority and advocating for their legitimate place in Canada.

**Adebayo Majekolagbe** is a doctoral candidate at the Marine and Environmental Law Institute, Schulich School of Law, Dalhousie University, and a Vanier and Killam scholar. In his research, he explores the intersections between impact assessment, climate change, and just transition, particularly in the context of fossil fuel-dependent economies.

**Sharon Mascher** is a professor in the Faculty of Law at the University of Calgary, an affiliated faculty member of the Canadian Institute of Resources Law, and an honorary fellow in the law school at the University of Western Australia. Beyond her academic roles, Sharon has served in various advisory roles to government and for several years was a member of the Environmental Defenders Office (Western Australia) Management Committee. Her main research interest focuses on governance and regulation at the intersection of energy, environment, and climate law.

**Bram Noble**, PhD, is a professor in the Department of Geography and Planning at the University of Saskatchewan. He specializes in environmental assessment with a focus on cumulative effects and strategic assessment. He has served as an advisor on environmental assessment to industry, Indigenous governments, and numerous national and international panels and agencies and has worked as a consultant on both project impact assessments and regional cumulative effects initiatives.

**Martin Olszynski** is an associate professor in the University of Calgary's Faculty of Law. His primary research interests are in environmental, natural resources, and water law and policy. He holds BSc and LLB degrees from the University of Saskatchewan, an LLM from the University of California at Berkeley, and is currently pursuing a PhD in resource management at the University of British Columbia's Institute for Resources, Environment and Sustainability. He was a member of the Council of Canadian Academies' expert panel on integrated natural resources management (2016–19) and is currently a member of the Minister of Environment and Climate Change Canada's advisory committee on impact assessment.

**Renée Pelletier** is the managing partner at Olthuis Kleer Townshend. Her practice includes work on Aboriginal and treaty rights litigation and specific claims. She has litigated judicial review applications and appeared before various levels of courts on motions, trials, and appeals. Renée was cited by the Supreme Court of Canada in the high-profile case *R v Ipeelee*, 2012 SCC 13. She regularly advises and represents Indigenous clients on consultation matters, regulatory and environmental matters, reserve land management, and impacts and benefits agreements. Renée is especially passionate about assisting her Indigenous clients in achieving greater self-determination. She also strives to incorporate the legal traditions of her Indigenous clients into the work she does on their behalf. Renée has also served as a member of the Federal Environmental Assessment Expert Review Panel, which engaged Canadians and Indigenous peoples and provided recommendations to the Government of Canada on reforms to federal environmental assessment processes. Renée is a member of the New Brunswick and Ontario bars. She is French Acadian, her first language is French, and she is fluently bilingual in both French and English. Renée is also a member of the Indigenous Bar Association and a frequent guest lecturer on Aboriginal and environmental law. She is recognized as one of the best lawyers in the field of Aboriginal law by *Best Lawyers* magazine and is listed as a "consistently recommended" lawyer in the *Canadian Lexpert Directory*.

**Justina Ray** has been president and senior scientist of Wildlife Conservation Society Canada since its incorporation in 2004. In addition to overseeing the operations of this non-governmental organization, Justina is involved in research and policy activities associated with conservation-based planning, environmental assessment, and biodiversity conservation, with a particular focus on wildlife in northern boreal landscapes. Over the years, Justina has been appointed to numerous government advisory panels related to species at risk and land use planning in Ontario and Canada and was co-chair of the Terrestrial Mammals Subcommittee of the Committee on the Status of Endangered Wildlife in Canada between 2009 and 2017. She is an adjunct professor at the University of Toronto (Department of Ecology and Evolution, Graduate Department of Forestry) and Trent University (Environmental & Life Sciences Graduate Program).

**Maureen G Reed** is a distinguished professor in, and assistant director, academic, of the School of Environment and Sustainability at the University of Saskatchewan. She also holds a UNESCO chair in biocultural diversity, sustainability, reconciliation, and renewal with Dr Jim Robson. Her research focuses on models of governance that can help communities become resilient and environmentally and socially sustainable. She has conducted research and supported government agencies to address gender (in)equity in forestry, intersectional analyses of the impacts of climate change, and the structural and procedural inequalities embedded within planning and assessment processes.

**Sara L Seck** is an associate professor and associate dean, research at the Schulich School of Law, Dalhousie University, and a member of the Marine & Environmental Law Institute. She has published widely on business and human rights, international law, and environmental and climate justice, often with a focus on extractive industries. Sara is co-editor of *Global Environmental Change and Innovation in International Law* (Cambridge University Press, 2017), co-editor of a 2019 special issue of the *Canadian Journal of Women and the Law* on resource extraction and the human rights of women and girls, and co-editor of the *Cambridge Handbook on Environmental Justice and Sustainable Development* (Cambridge University Press, 2020). Current research projects include assisting the United Nations Environment Programme's Environmental Rights Initiative to clarify the responsibility of businesses to respect and support environmental rights and a SSHRC Knowledge Synthesis Grant on responsible business conduct and impact assessment law.

**Penelope Simons** is an associate professor in the Faculty of Law (Common Law Section) at the University of Ottawa. Her research focuses on business and human rights and in particular on the human rights implications of domestic and transnational extractive sector activity; state responsibility for corporate complicity in human rights violations; the regulation of transnational corporations; gender and resource extraction; and the intersections between transnational corporate activity, human rights, and international economic law. She is the co-author with Audrey Macklin of the University of Toronto of *The Governance Gap: Extractive Industries, Human Rights, and the Home State Advantage* (Routledge, 2014). She also co-authored *Integrating Sustainable Development into International Investment Agreements: A Guide for Developing Country Negotiators* (Commonwealth Secretariat, 2013) with Tony VanDuzer and Graham Mayeda. Penelope is a member of the Human Rights Research and Education Centre, the Interdisciplinary Research Group on the Territories of Extractivism, and the Centre for Environmental Law and Global Sustainability, all at the University of Ottawa, as well as the SSHRC-funded Canadian Partnership on Strengthening Justice for International Crimes. In 2018, Penelope was awarded the Walter S Tarnopolsky Award, recognizing her as "an individual who has made a significant contribution to human rights."

**A John Sinclair** is a professor and the director of the Natural Resources Institute, University of Manitoba. His main research interest focuses on governance and learning as they relate to resource and environmental decision making. He has been very active over the last twenty-five years in relation to environmental assessment law and policy. Through current research grants, he is considering the role of learning in meaningful participation, best approaches for incorporating climate change considerations in assessment, and the elements of next-generation assessment. John has been a member of the Canadian Environmental Network's Environmental Planning and Assessment Caucus for many years and was also a member of the Canadian Environmental Assessment Agency's Regulatory Advisory Committee, advisory to the Canadian Environmental Assessment Agency and then minister of environment and the recent Multi-Interest Advisory Committee, on federal assessment process reform and advisory to the minister of environment and climate change.

**Jason Unger** is the executive director of and general counsel at the Environmental Law Centre (Alberta). Jason has focused on research and advocacy in environmental law and policy over the past eighteen years, including in relation to environmental assessment in Alberta. He has advised clients before joint panels under the *Canadian Environmental Assessment Act* and on provincial assessments. His research has focused on regulatory and policy reform to ensure accountability and certainty for environmental outcomes. In addition to environmental assessments, his research interests span water law, administrative law, species at risk, and liability for environmental harms.

**Heidi Walker** is a PhD candidate in the School of Environment and Sustainability at the University of Saskatchewan. Her research focuses on the gendered, intersectional, and social dimensions of climate hazards and resource development. She has previously published in the area of public participation in environmental assessment. Heidi is also the program manager for community-engaged research at The King's University.

# Table of Cases

# Index

563

F after a page number indicates a figure.
T after a page number indicates a table.